William Vickrey is one of the truly important figures in contemporary economics. Over the past fifty-five years he has published several books and some 140 papers scattered over many journals. This book offers a thoughtful selection from these papers, organized so as to bring out the scope and yet the unity of the work. Vickrey has the unique distinction of having contributed, often seminally and always operationally, to all major branches of public economics. The papers collected here cover Social Choice and Allocation Mechanisms, Taxation, Pricing in Public Utilities and in Urban Transportation, Urban Economics and Macroeconomic Policies. Each topic is introduced by one of the four editors, and the book is completed with a full annotated bibliography of Vickrey's work. For the first time, we have convenient access to a set of important, creative and stimulating contributions, which have helped shape the modern field of public economics. This is a fascinating overview of the field and of the life-time work of a great economist.

Public Economics

Public Economics

SELECTED PAPERS BY WILLIAM VICKREY

edited by

RICHARD ARNOTT, KENNETH ARROW,
ANTHONY ATKINSON
AND
JACQUES DRÈZE

CAMBRIDGE
UNIVERSITY PRESS

Published by the Press Syndicate of the University of Cambridge
The Pitt Building, Trumpington Street, Cambridge CB2 1RP
40 West 20th Street, New York, NY 10011-4211, USA
10 Stamford Road, Oakleigh, Victoria 3166, Australia

© Cambridge University Press 1994

First published 1994
Reprinted and first published in paperback 1996

Printed in Great Britain at the University Press, Cambridge

A catalogue record for this book is available from the British Library

Library of Congress cataloguing in publication data applied for

ISBN 0 521 45439 5

Contents

Foreword

This volume is meant as a tribute to William Vickrey on his eightieth birthday. We are pleased to express in this way our admiration and gratitude to an outstanding economist and to a marvelous human being.

Two of us had the benefit of being Vickrey's students at Columbia, and of writing dissertations under his friendly, inspiring supervision. We all share a deep appreciation for his work. The fact that it took four editors to select and introduce the papers collected here is indicative of Vickrey's breadth of interests.

The most difficult step in our project was choosing between one and several volumes. Our final option for a single volume, in spite of the wealth of available material, rests on the hope that specialist readers will discover contributions in related areas.

In order to facilitate the use of this volume, the papers are grouped under six main headings, plus a few "miscellany." Each part opens with a brief introduction by one of the editors. We have not attempted to coordinate the style or content of these introductions, which also reflect different contacts with the work and personality of William Vickrey. The minor element of repetition and cross-referencing in these introductions reflects the complementarities of the different parts.

A special bonus to users of this volume is the annotated bibliography, which came right out of Vickrey's computer and is reprinted (with his kind permission) with minimal editing, thus with unadulterated spontaneity.

Richard Arnott undertook the painstaking task of assembling the papers listed in the bibliography and making them available to the other editors. He will gladly make copies of these papers available to interested readers, upon requests addressed to him at Boston College (Economics), Chestnut Hill, Mass. 02167, USA.

Ms. Kelly Chaston shared with Richard Arnott responsibility for proofreading. She deserves the gratitude of the editors and readers for her dedicated attention to that demanding task.

We thank Cambridge University Press, and in particular economics editor Patrick McCartan, for their enthusiastic endorsement of our project. Material support from the Economics Department at Boston College and from the Center for Operations Research and Econometrics (CORE) at Université Catholique de Louvain is also gratefully acknowledged.

Happy birthday to you, Bill, and many happy years ahead. It was a rewarding pleasure to reread or discover your extensive work. You are never dull, whether in writing or in person. We have learned a lot from you, and we arc glad to provide the economics profession with a new opportunity of becoming acquainted with your innovative ideas.

The Editors
Boston College, Stanford University
Cambridge University, Université Catholique de Louvain.

Acknowledgments

The author would like to thank the publishers of the following articles for their kind permission to reprint them in this book.

Chapter 1 "Measuring Marginal Utility by Reactions to Risk," *Econometrica*, 13 (1945, Econometric Society)

Chapter 2 "Utility, Strategy, and Social Decision Rules," *Quarterly Journal of Economics*, 74 (1960, MIT Press)

Chapter 3 "Counterspeculation, Auctions, and Competitive Sealed Tenders," *Journal of Finance*, 16 (1961, American Finance Association)

Chapter 4 "Auctions and Bidding Games," *Recent Advances in Game Theory* (1962, Princeton University Press)

Chapter 5 "Averaging of Income for Income Tax Purposes," *Journal of Political Economy*, 47 (1939, University of Chicago Press)

Chapter 6 "Cumulative Averaging after Thirty Years," *Modern Fiscal Issues: Essays in Honor of Carl S. Shoup*, Richard M. Bird and John G. Head, Eds. (1972, University of Toronto Press)

Chapter 7 "An Integrated Successions Tax," *Taxes*, 23 (1945, University of Toronto Press)

Chapter 8 "Expenditure, Capital Gains, and the Basis of Progressive Taxation," *The Manchester School*, 25 (1957, Blackwell Publishers)

Chapter 9 "The Problem of Progression," *University of Florida Law Review*, (1968, University of Florida, College of Law)

Chapter 10 "Marginal- and Average-Cost Pricing," *The New Palgrave*, vol. III, Eatwell *et al.* Eds. (1987, Macmillan)

Chapter 11 "Some Objections to Marginal-Cost Pricing," *Journal of Political Economy*, 56 (1948, University of Chicago Press)

Chapter 12 "Responsive Pricing of Public Utility Services," *Economics of the Regulated Communications Industry in the Age of Innovation* (1970 Seminar, New England Telephone, mimeo)

Chapter 13 "Airline Overbooking: Some Further Solutions," *Journal of Transport Economics and Policy*, 6(3) (1972, University of Bath)

Chapter 14 "A Proposal for Revising New York's Subway Fare Structure," *Journal of the Operations Research Society of America*, 3 (1955)

Chapter 15 "Pricing in Urban and Suburban Transport," *American Economic Review*, 52(2) (1963, American Economic Association)

Chapter 16 "Congestion Theory and Transport Investment," *American Economic Review*, 59 (1969, American Economic Association)

Chapter 17 "The City as a Firm," *The Economics of Public Services*, Martin S. Feldstein and Robert F. Inman, Eds., Proceedings of a conference held by the International Economic Association at Turin (1977, London, Macmillan, New York, Wiley)

Chapter 18 "General and Specific Financing of Urban Services," *Public Expenditure Decisions in the Urban Community*, Howard G. Schaller, Ed. (1963, Resources for the Future)

Chapter 19 "The Impact on Land Values of Taxing Buildings," *Proceedings of the 62nd National Tax Conference*, Boston (1969, Tax Institute of America)

Chapter 20 "The Optimum Trend of Prices," *Southern Economic Journal*, 25 (1959, Southern Economic Association)

Chapter 21 "Design of a Market Anti-Inflation Program," *Incentives-Based Incomes Policies*, David C. Colander, Ed. (1986, Ballinger Publishing)

Chapter 23 "Today's Task for Economists," Presidential Address to the American Economic Association, 6 January, 1993 (revised 3 February, 1993). Original version published in *American Economic Review* (March 1993, American Economic Association)

Chapter 24 "Resource Distribution Patterns and the Classification of Families," *Studies in Income and Wealth*, 10 (1949, National Bureau of Economic Research)

Chapter 25 "On the Prevention of Gerrymandering," *Political Science Quarterly*, 76 (1961, Academy of Political Science)

Chapter 26 "One Economist's View of Philanthropy," *Philanthropy and Public Policy*, F.G. Dickinson, Ed. (1962, Columbia University Press)

William Vickrey

May be Bill Vickrey could be described as a theorists' theorist, and some of his achievements, like an article on auction markets singled out in the full text of the 1978 AEA citation, do require experts to appreciate them fully. But pure theory was never Bill's main objective. He is an economists' theorist, certainly an applied economists' theorist, as well as a theorists' applied economist. He seems always to have believed that the principles and analytical tools of economics can be put to work in the social interest. His mind is always on potential applications – in policy-making, legislation, administration, and institutional architecture. The AEA citation rightly describes his work as "persistently operational."

James Tobin at the presentation of
the 1992 Frank E. Seidman Distinguished Award
in Political Economy.

The selected papers by William Vickrey reprinted in this volume speak for themselves. There is no need for an introduction, and no claim on our part that a brief overall presentation adds to the contents of the book. Still, we wish to invite prospective readers to avail themselves fully of the opportunity provided by the convenient availability, in a single volume, of a set of papers written over a span of more than fifty years and covering a broad range of topics.

The motivation for this project came from our conviction that easy access to a representative set of Vickrey's published papers would be valued by economists, not only today, but for many years to come. There is of course the additional motivation of paying tribute to William Vickrey, as he approaches his eightieth birthday. But the essence of the tribute lies in our conviction of the lasting value of the papers, as originally written. The element of personal gratitude, for all we have learned from our friend and could not at the time have learned from anyone else, is genuine but ancillary. The conviction that this book will be of lasting service to the profession is in itself the main tribute.

All the papers in this book are resolutely modern. Whether written in 1939, in the forties, fifties, or later, they are part of the contemporary development of our discipline. With remarkable intuition, Vickrey sensed very early how new ideas or tools – ranging from decision theory to electronics technology – could contribute new solutions to old problems; and he sensed how new problems – associated with the scale economies of modern technology or with urban congestion and pollution – required appropriate solutions inspired by well-established principles. We wish to invite users of this volume to reflect on the continued challenge of discovering the potential applications of new concepts, while identifying the conceptual issues raised by evolving economic realities.

Surveying the lifetime work of a creative economist provides an opportunity to search for that person's implicit answers to a set of questions permanently confronting all of us: What problems are worthy of attention? How should these problems be approached? What constitutes a significant result? Where are the open challenges? Answers to these questions remain in part subjective, as they reflect not only a person's interests and values but also his skills, background, and environment. There is much to be learned from the revealed preferences of others. Vickrey chose for his Presidential Address to the American Economic Association in January 1993 the title "Today's Task for Economists." That address is reprinted below as chapter 23 – with the preceding twenty-two chapters revealing the main tasks that economist Vickrey had taken up over the previous fifty-five years. We wish to invite users of this volume to reflect on what we do, or should do, as economists, and how to do it better.

The title, and organization, of the book recognize the recent emergence of "Public Economics" as a well-defined field, with its place in graduate curricula, its specialist journals and textbooks, its meetings and societies. The work of William Vickrey is intimately associated with that development, for which in several important respects he provided seminal inspiration. In comparison with the more traditional, more institutional, and narrower field of "public finance," the new field encompasses all aspects of the "economics of the public sector"[1] and of "government's effect on the economy."[2] The *Editorial* of the *Journal of Public Economics* (1, 1972) lists such areas as "taxation, fiscal policy, planning and control of public expenditure (including specific areas such as health, education and transport), redistributive effects of the government's budget, management of public enterprises, regulation of public utilities, social security, metropolitan and local finance, tax harmonization, etc. . . ." For each of these areas, modern public economics covers issues ranging from the logical *foundations* rooted in social choice theory, through the theoretical and empirical *analysis* of problems specific to the area, to the development of *implementable guidelines*.

It is remarkable that a single person's contributions could provide landmarks for such a broad and diversified field, both along the "horizontal" dimension corresponding to the *substantive scope* of the field, and along the "vertical" dimension corresponding to its *methodological depth*. And it is even more remarkable that these contributions could combine the merits of precursory *anticipation, originality,* and *classicism.*

The *substantive scope* of the field is charted by Musgrave (1959) under three headings, corresponding to the distributive, allocative, and stabilization functions of the state. In the organization of the present volume, the distributive function

---

[1] Atkinson and Stiglitz (1980) p. 3, Boadway and Waldasin (1984).
[2] Auerbach and Feldstein (1987).

corresponds to part II, devoted to taxation; the allocative function corresponds to parts III and IV, dealing with pricing policies in public utilities and transportation; and the stabilization function corresponds to part VI devoted to macroeconomic policy. In addition, the logical foundations, in terms of social choice theory and strategic behavior, are the subject matter of part I; and the integration of the diverse functions at the municipal level is treated in part V. Nearly all significant areas of modern public economics are thus covered by Vickrey's work.

The *methodological depth* of the field is exceptionally well covered also, because Vickrey spans the full range from the logical foundations through the analysis of area-specific problems to the detailed discussion of implementable procedures. On this score, Vickrey occupies a rather unique place among contemporary economists. As early as 1945, he sketched the basis of modern utilitarianism, later developed by Harsanyi (1953, 1955), and he introduced the concept of the "original position" (behind the "veil of ignorance") which is central to the construction of a *Theory of Justice* (Rawls, 1971). When Vickrey treats allocative problems of public utilities and transportation, in the late forties and early fifties, the need for public intervention is not simply assumed or taken for granted; rather, it is founded on specific features leading to market failure: increasing returns, externalities (congestion), or uncertainty. Vickrey's original recommendations (about subway fares, road pricing, or airline overbooking) are developed in response to these specific features. And the recommendations bear the unique Vickrey trademark of being developed all the way to the stage of practical implementation. Thus, in the area of taxation, cumulative averaging ("a master stroke of simplification and tax neutralization") provides the practical answer to achieving "neutrality with respect to the time of realization or reporting of all forms of income" (Vickrey, 1972, p. 117). Forty years later, Atkinson and Stiglitz (1980, p. 64), reviewing *Intertemporal Decisions and Taxation*, note: "The fundamental difficulty is the translation from economic concepts to tax legislation." Vickrey in 1939 had not stopped short of overcoming concretely that fundamental difficulty. In the area of public transportation, the subway fare structure he proposed in 1951–2 for New York City on the basis of a precursory second-best welfare analysis is supported by a detailed description of the new electronic turnstiles required to implement the variable fares (geared to time-of-day and to origin–destination). Similarly, the "Statement on the Pricing of Urban Street Use" to a Congressional Hearing in 1959 was supplemented by an actual on-the-spot demonstration of "Electronic Vehicle Identification" equipment. A similar attention to practical implementation underlies another innovation, namely the "Second Price Auction" better known today as the "Vickrey Auction."

No other economist exemplifies to the same degree the ability of treating a relevant problem all the way from the conceptual clarification, through the careful efficiency analysis, down to the development of a practically implementable solution. In that respect, William Vickrey stands in a class by himself. That he could do this in such diverse areas as taxation, public and private transportation, and demand revelation is at first sight amazing. On second thoughts, it is perhaps natural, because the same methodological orientation, and the same imaginative creativity, are at work in the different areas. And the insistence on operationality is inherent to public economics, where we cannot rely on profit motives or survival of the fittest to bring about the innovations required to achieve efficiency (in the face of increasing returns, externalities, or incomplete markets). There is no substitute here for intellectual creativity, guided by sound economic reasoning and mobilized toward social efficiency.

The examples mentioned above, and the concluding emphasis on creativity, validate our earlier assertion that Vickrey's work "combines the merits of anticipation, originality and classicism." The merit of *anticipation* is evident. In the forties and fifties, Vickrey was using such concepts as incentive compatibility or constrained (second-best) optimality, which did not become standard tools until much later; and he was drawing attention to a set of problems like peak loads, congestion, or pollution, the importance of which was recognized much later. Many economists – including the authors of the citation presenting Vickrey as a Distinguished Fellow of the American Economic Association in 1978* – wonder why several important contributions by Vickrey were recognized and

---

*The citation is worth quoting in full.

Many of us have had the experience of thinking we were the first to show the neutrality of a particular tax scheme, to prove the incentive characteristics of a particular bidding institution, to deduce the redistributive implications of the expected utility hypothesis, to invent a demand revealing process, and so on, only to find that William S. Vickrey had done it earlier – sometimes much earlier – and whereas our "original contribution" may have contained minor or even a substantive error, Vickrey had done it correctly. Some great scholars receive recognition from the beginning, but, inscrutably, with others it takes a little longer. His numerous works, appearing in all the leading journals in economic, law, operations research, finance, and taxation, contain many seminal contributions, and many more that would have been seminal but for the fact that the profession was not yet ready for his ideas. Thus, his "Counterspeculation, Auctions and Competitive Sealed Tenders", *Journal of Finance*, 1961, (1) invents a class of demand revealing processes for private goods, (2) develops with clarity the important concept of incentive compatibility, and (3) operationalizes these theoretical insights in the form of realizable auctioning institutions. Only later after the profession had discovered solutions to the "free-rider" problem was it possible to adequately appreciate Vickrey's astonishing precursory insights.

appreciated only ten years later, or even more. In other words, they simply wonder why he was repeatedly ahead of his time – better to praise him than to blame the rest of us!

Originality is a combination of independence and creativity. Independence is needed to wander off the established paths, into uncharted territory where creativity expresses itself. Offhand, originality is the least transferable intellectual quality. Still, we have found it instructive to speculate on what makes our friend Bill so original a thinker. One element is uncompromising logic, pushed to the limit, even if that limit lies outside traditional borders.[3] There are other elements and we invite readers to search for them. Vickrey's originality comes here hand-in-hand with *classicism* – an unusual combination. Classicism is a matter of elegance and enduring excellence; more often than not, it results from a laborious quest for perfection, with interaction between attention to detail and purification of the overall architecture. Originality, on the other hand, requires initial neglect of detail, and search for new forms of architecture. It is not through style, formalism, or polished presentation that Vickrey achieves classicism. It is rather through unity of perspective and simplicity of basic reasoning, progressively purified by repeated use. Across fields of application, spanning the range of public economics, one easily traces the same unrelenting quest for economic efficiency. The role of prices in guiding decentralized decisions receives privileged attention. Yet Vickrey is not a prisoner of the competitive paradigm. He recognizes the limitations of the market, and the need to translate "Short-Run Marginal Social Costs" into (responsive) prices susceptible to guiding individual decisions toward the achievement of overall efficiency. Here again, "the fundamental difficulty is the translation from economic concepts to operational pricing schemes," if we may borrow a felicitous formulation.

Today, when the virtues and limitations of the market mechanism are in need of deeper understanding, Vickrey's often precursory and original quest for efficiency is at the same time modern (i.e., relevant to the issues of the day) and classic (i.e., endowed with the enduring elegance of unity and simplicity). We invite readers to search throughout the volume for these basic ingredients and to find inspiration for extending Vickrey's quest further.

---

[3] Jacques Drèze comments and illustrates: Of this propensity I became aware the very first time that I ever saw him. I had come to Columbia as a graduate student in September 1951 and was walking from International House toward campus on the first day of classes, when I was overtaken by a tall grey-haired man rollerskating at good speed with a bulging briefcase under one arm and under the other a three-sided cardboard box spun with coloured threads. I had seen William Vickrey and his home-made teaching aid, a three-dimensional indifference surface. A few weeks later, over the Thanksgiving pumpkin pie at his home, I dared ask why he was rollerskating to work. The answer was sheer deductive logic applied to the joint choice of residence and means of commuting – train plus rollerskates – for a Columbia Professor not enamored with "America's rubbershod sacred cow." Actually, he wondered why none of his colleagues had come to the same conclusion . . .

* * *

It may help the thoughtful reader to be generally acquainted with our friend's career. Here too, facts speak for themselves and tell a transparent story.

William Vickrey was born in 1914 in Victoria, British Columbia (Canada). He attended Yale, obtaining a Science B.S. in 1935, then went to Columbia University for graduate work in economics, obtaining an M.A. in 1937. The Ph.D. degree was awarded there in 1947, after completion of the *Agenda for Progressive Taxation*. The intervening ten years, including World War II, had been spent in various research or advisory positions related to taxation.

Vickrey joined the faculty of Columbia University in 1946 and never left, except for a few sabbatical leaves. His working life was devoted mostly to teaching and research, but also included a significant amount of advisory or consulting services on behalf of public institutions or utilities, and a fair amount of nonspecialist writing and lecturing.

The advisory and consulting missions encompass the major areas of Vickrey's applied research – taxation, public utilities, transportation, urban problems. His association with Carl Shoup as a graduate student and research assistant led to "cumulative averaging" in 1939, as a result of concern with the tax treatment of capital gains. In 1949, Shoup and Vickrey laid the foundations for the postwar tax structure of Japan. This was followed by a number of tax missions, notably to Puerto Rico, Venezuela, and Liberia. Vickrey also spent a year as an adviser on fiscal matters for the United Nations, working in Singapore, Malaysia, Iran, Zambia, Ivory Coast, Lybia, and Surinam.

The work on public utilities started with the Electric Power Industry in 1939, and gained momentum with the famous study of subway fares, on behalf of the "Mayor's Committee for Management Survey of the City of New York" in 1951. In 1959 he studied traffic congestion in Washington. Further studies on urban planning and transportation took him to India,[4] Argentina, and Venezuela. Over the years, he developed ideas for efficient pricing of electricity, telephone services, urban transportation, street and road use, municipal services, airlines, etc.. He also kept up with every conceivable technological development in these areas, visiting experimental designs on site and attending specialized conferences.

---

[4] One of us once heard from an Indian economist that, of all foreign economic advisers, Vickrey had been the most directly helpful, because he had produced new railway schedules that permitted substantial energy saving and improved service. Sure enough, while collecting material for this survey, we came across two unpublished memoranda dealing respectively with "The Economising of Electric Power" (Calcutta, 1962) and "The Use of Power by Suburban Trains" (Calcutta, 1963) – the latter of which develops principles of railway scheduling and applies them to detailed scheduling of a particular line. The principle of "skip-stop scheduling" used there also appears in his recommendations for New York.

The quest for efficiency of public services made him a crusader, advocating innovations through lectures for the National Tax Association, the NBER, Public Utility Conferences, or Transportation Symposia – but also through testimony at hearings or letters to the New York Times. Often, there is an expression of impatience at the slow acceptance of new ideas by regulatory or operating agencies[5] – but the crusade goes on . . . In recent years, this impatience with blatant inefficiencies has been focused on the macroeconomic field. Irrational budget accounting, excessive concern with inflation, insufficient attention to wasteful unemployment have become favorite themes, as illustrated in part VI.

The interaction between academic research and concern for practical affairs has thus worked to mutual benefit. Vickrey's success at developing implementable innovations rests in part on the familarity with real situations, enhanced by the consulting and advisory missions. Familiarity with real-world situations may sound like an easy path to originality. It is – but only for those whose interest in life is matched by power of abstraction, intellectual independence, and uncompromising logic.

Response to practical challenges is only one facet of our friend's intellectual curiosity. His interest in ethics and philosophy has led to several papers, one of which is reprinted in part VII. Interdisciplinary contacts always appealed to him, in particular through seminars. Bill Vickrey's fearsome participation in seminars is part of his legend, and in particular earned him the "Rip van Winkle" award from the Center for Advanced Study in the Behavioral Sciences "for deep and uninterrupted concentration while attending seminars."[6] At Columbia, he shows up at seminars in many fields, and invariably attends the inter-disciplinary ones. Exposure to ideas from other fields is another path to originality – but only for those who are perceptive enough to grasp deep ideas, and constructive enough to transfer them across fields. There is no easy path to originality.

It is thus with conviction that we invite users of this volume to absorb its substance, but also to reflect on "Today's Task for Economists," and to search for the attributes of originality in economic research. So long as some readers do this, our tribute to William Vickrey will remain alive.

---

[5] Vickrey's Presidential Address to the Atlantic Economic Association in October 1992, entitled "My Innovative Failures in Economics" begins as follows: "You are looking at an economist who has repeatedly failed in achieving his objective, even though achieving considerable esteem among his fellows."

[6] We have often heard a younger colleague report: "I went to give a talk at Columbia. There sat that tall white-haired man, asleep with his head against the wall. All of a sudden, without raising an eyelid, he mumbled the most penetrating question – and I wondered for a while whether I still had a paper . . ."

References

Atkinson, A.B. and Stiglitz, J.E., *Lectures on Public Economics* (New York: McGraw-Hill, 1980).

Auerbach, A.J. and Feldstein, M., *Handbook of Public Economics* (Amsterdam: North-Holland, 1987).

Boadway, R.W. and Wildasin, D.E., *Public Sector Economics* (Boston: Little Brown and Co, 1984).

Harsanyi, J., "Cardinal Utility in Welfare Economics and in the Theory of Risk-Taking," *Journal of Political Economy*, 61 (1953), pp. 434–5.

"Cardinal Welfare, Individualistic Ethics and Interpersonal Comparisons of Utility," *Journal of Political Economy*, 63 (1955), pp. 309–21.

Musgrave, R.A., *The Theory of Public Finance* (New York: McGraw-Hill, 1959).

Rawls, J.R., *A Theory of Justice* (Cambridge, Mass.: Harvard University Press, 1971).

Vickrey, W.S., "Cumulative Averaging after Thirty Years," in *Modern Fiscal Issues: Essays in Honour of Carl S. Shoup*, R.M. Bird and J.G. Head, Eds. (Toronto: University of Toronto Press, 1972), pp. 117–33.

PART I

Social Choice and Allocation Mechanisms

If utility is defined as that quantity the mathematical expectation of which is maximized by an individual making choices involving risk, then to maximize the aggregate of such utility over the population is equivalent to choosing that distribution of income which such an individual would select were he asked which of various variants of the economy he would like to become a member of, assuming that once he selects a given economy with a given distribution of income he has an equal chance of landing in the shoes of each member of it. Unreal as this hypothetical choice may be, it at least shows that there exists a reasonable conceptual relation between the methods used to determine utility and the uses proposed to be made of it.

Econometrica, 13 (1945), p. 329.

Bill Vickrey's overriding theme of economics in the service of the public sector is developed in many different keys, from the specifics of pricing of urban transport to the broad principles underlying the allocation of social resources and the means by which they can be effectuated. At each stage in the development of his thought, Vickrey has been in touch with the most important developments of other scholars, to which he has always added his own innovations which, in turn, have had profound repercussions.

There is a certain characteristic style of understatement and specificity of application in Vickrey's work which has in some ways helped, in perhaps more ways hindered the full understanding of his originality. It is especially illustrated by the first paper reprinted in this Part, "Measuring Marginal Utility by Reactions to Risk," which appeared in 1945. I remember reading it with interest; it was one of the first papers to refer to von Neumann and Morgenstern's *Theory of Games and Economic Behavior* and especially to their statement of the representation of choices among risky alternatives by comparison of expected utilities. Vickrey gives a low-key discursive account of methods of measuring marginal utility of income by assuming some commodity independent in utility of all others, as suggested by Irving Fisher and then Ragnar Frisch, and prefers the measurement of utility by risks, an idea which he attributes to F. Zeuthen as well as to von Neumann and Morgenstern. He instances a number of practical difficulties in the actual measurement. In the middle of the discussion, he introduces the deep idea that risk-measured utility is the appropriate concept for determining optimal income distribution, by postulating that an individual evaluates any one income distribution by considering that he or she might with equal probability occupy any place in that distribution. This is presented in one paragraph, occupying half a page, with no formulas. Although I had read it, it made little impression on me, and I had forgotten it completely when I took up the problem of social choice. John Harsanyi did develop the idea independently nine years later, with appropriate axiomatization. Here Vickrey has not merely the germ but the whole idea, that John Rawls later called the "veil of ignorance," under which judgments of justice are to be made, though Rawls drew a maximin rather than a utilitarian implication.

Vickrey then moves quickly to the conflict between equality and incentives and formulates explicitly the optimization problem when, as we would say today, the productivities of individuals are private information. He even derives an appropriate Euler equation but goes no further, leaving it to James Mirrlees some twenty years later to give an explicit characterization. Thus in effect two major papers appear as remarks by the way in an examination of the usefulness of risk reactions for measuring marginal utility.

Vickrey's paper, "Utility, Strategy, and Social Decision Rules," goes over the ground of social welfare functions, with a discussion of strategic elements in social decision-making (what might today be called "implementation theory"). He insightfully reformulates my conditions for an ordinally based social welfare function, in particular correcting an error in my requirements on the range of preference profiles (this error had also been found by Julian Blau). He explores the consequences of imposing more severe constraints on the range of preference profiles, a field that was also explored by Kenichi Inada and Amartya K. Sen. He raises the question whether misrepresentation of preferences can be profitable and comes close to stating the impossibility results found later by Allen Gibbard and Mark Satterthwaite. He then turns to social welfare functions defined by cardinal utility and restates, somewhat more emphatically, his earlier emphasis on deriving utilitarianism from the expected-utility theorem, as well as raising a number of other important questions.

In "Counterspeculation, Auctions, and Competitive Sealed Tenders," he starts the game theory of auctions when individual valuations are private information. In simple language and almost as if the matter were self evident, he introduces what is very much the Clarke–Groves mechanism and then specializes it to the second-price auction. This is extraordinarily original and has, as far as I know, no precedent, even in raising the question. The whole field of implementation is brought out in a remarkably simple way, though Vickrey again turns to practical questions and special cases immediately. The results are further developed and many special cases studied in a subsequent paper, "Auctions and Bidding Games," where, for instance, it is shown that different bidding methods lead to the same revenue for the seller.

This summary will, I hope, reveal both the originality and the modesty of Bill Vickrey's work. Small paragraphs have great thoughts concealed in them.

I

·

Measuring Marginal Utility by Reactions to Risk

Many attempts have been made to measure marginal utility. Some of the methods used have been plausible, others less so, but none of them has been very successful. To some extent the difficulty has been with the inadequacy of the data, but the basic difficulty with most of the actual attempts has been with the nature of the fundamental assumptions required by the methods used. Indeed, it has been maintained that, aside from purely introspective appraisal, marginal utility cannot be measured at all. It may well be that the attempt to derive a utility function from conventional data on consumer budgets, demand curves, prices, or choices is a wild-goose chase after a function that would have a doubtful meaning even if it could be determined. On the other hand, by considering individual reactions to choices involving risks, a more meaningful result may be obtainable.

Utility and Choices between Assured Alternatives

To clarify the issue, let us review briefly the notion of utility and its relation to indifference maps and consumer choice. Studies of consumer choices between definite and certain alternatives tell us only the rank of the various situations in the preference of the individual or group being studied. This will be true whether the data are sought by asking questions of individuals as to their choice between hypothetical alternatives, or whether the data consist of the observed choices of individuals confronted with actual income and price situations. If it be assumed that these choices are consistent, all of this information can be contained in an indifference map. If the marginal utility can be inferred unequivocally from such

Econometrica, 13 (1945), pp. 215–36.

studies it can also be inferred from the corresponding indifference map, for the choices themselves can be inferred from the map. Conversely a utility function that cannot be inferred from such a map must be dependent upon some additional data or on some unsubstantiated assumption.

An indifference map can be described by a function $U(x, y, z \ldots w)$, each value of U giving an indifference contour passing through all those combinations of quantities (strictly, rates of consumption) of the several commodities $x, y, z, \ldots, w$, which are deemed equally desirable by the individual concerned. Combinations giving larger values for U will be those deemed more desirable, those giving smaller values for U less desirable. But any other function $V = V(U)$ will also give the same indifference map, and will therefore describe the behavior of the individual just as effectively as U, provided only that the function is monotone increasing, that is, that $V'(U)$ is everywhere positive. We can for example put $V = U^2$, $V = \log U$; in terms of the map itself there is in general no meaningful criterion for determining which of the many admissible functions $V(U)$ is *the* utility function or which function V_x'/P_x should be taken to represent the "marginal utility of money."

In some cases, however, we may be able to find a function V that has certain unique properties. If among the various functions that are capable of describing a given indifference map there exists one for which V_x' is independent of the quantities of all commodities other than x, then to be sure this V is unique. For if there is some other function W that describes the given indifference map and has a first derivative W_y' that is independent of the quantities of all commodities other than y, the W is necessarily but a linear function of V and can be considered identical with V. To show this we put $V'(X) = f(x)$, and upon integrating get $V = F(x) + G(y, z, \ldots, w)$. If then we have some other function $W(V)$ for which $W_y' = h(y)$, then $h(y) = W_y' = W'(V)V_y' = W'(V)G_y'$ and $W'(V) = G_y'(y, z, \ldots, w)/h(y)$; thus $W'(V)$ is independent of x. But since V depends on x, $W'(V)$ must not depend on V; i.e., $W'(V)$ must be a constant and W a linear function of V. V and its linear transformations are therefore the only functions that possess such a property.

Most attempts to determine marginal utility hitherto have been based on the assumptions first that some utility function can be found that will thus make the marginal utility of some commodity independent of the quantities of all other commodities and second that this function when found has some special validity for the purposes at hand. The methods suggested by Irving Fisher,[1] and the isoquant, quantity-variation, and translation methods of Ragnar Frisch[2] all

---

[1] Irving Fisher, "A Statistical Method for Measuring Marginal Utility," in *Economic Essays in Honor of J. B. Clark* (New York, 1927), pp. 157–93.

[2] Ragnar Frisch, *New Methods of Measuring Marginal Utility*, Beiträge zur Oekonomische Theorie (Tübingen, 1932), 142 pp.

involve such assumptions. If the assumptions were well founded and the data adequate, all of these methods would tend to produce the same result. They differ chiefly in the data used, in the population covered, and in the additional assumptions made as a partial substitute for more complete data.

On the other hand to say that the marginal utility of one commodity x is independent only of the quantity of some other commodity y but not necessarily of all the remaining commodities $z, \ldots, w$ is insufficient to establish a unique utility function, for there exist utility functions that can be transformed by a nonlinear transformation in such a way that this criterion is satisfied with respect to other commodities. For example if we consider the function $U = (x^a + y^a)(z^a + w^a)^b$, then on this utility scale $U_x' = ax^{a-1} (z^a + w^a)^b$ is independent of y but not of z or w, and similarly the marginal utility of y is independent of x. If now we consider another utility scale $V = \log U = \log (x^a + y^a) + b \log (z^a + w^a)$, then on this scale $V_x' = ax^{a-1}/(x^a + y^a)$, so that the marginal utility of x is now independent of z and w but not of y, and similarly for z and w. Or we could put $W^b = U$, and on this third scale the marginal utility of z, W_z', will be independent of w, and that of w independent of z, while both will depend on x and y. Thus if all that is stipulated is that the marginal utility of some one commodity shall be independent of the quantity of some other, we could conceivably find as many significantly different utility functions satisfying this condition as there are commodities in excess of one.

It is more than likely that the widely varying results obtained with different commodity combinations indicate that at most the independence criterion is satisfied only as between pairs of commodities or groups of commodities. If so, the use of different pairs of commodities would result in different utility functions even with complete and accurate information. Thus the widely divergent results obtained may not be entirely the result of the inadequacy of the data, but may be inherent in the method used.[3]

Assuming that there exists a utility function for which the marginal utility of some commodity x is independent of the quantity of all the others, we must be able to express the price of x in terms of any other commodity y in the form

$$P_{x/y} = \frac{f(x)}{g(y, z, \ldots, w)}$$

and similarly for $P_{x/s} \ldots, P_{x/w}$. However, it is sufficient to show for some one other commodity, say y, that

$$\frac{P_{x/y}(x, y, z, \ldots, w)}{P_{x/y}(x, y_0, z_0, \ldots, w_0)} = \frac{P_{x/y}(x_0, y, z, \ldots, w)}{P_{x/y}(x_0, y_0, z_0, \ldots, w_0)}$$

---

[3] Cf. the results obtained by James N. Morgan in "Can We Measure Marginal Utility?" *Econometrica*, 13 (April, 1945), pp. 129–52, especially the chart on p. 133.

for some initial sets of values x_0, y_0, z_0, . . ., w_0, and for all other values of x, y, z, . . ., w. It may well be doubted whether it will ever be possible to find a commodity x which will satisfy these rather rigorous conditions. Even if an "equivalent commodity" made up of some group or combination of commodities is used, together with some price index for the group, the likelihood of finding these conditions fulfilled over the entire range of incomes and over substantially the whole range of consumption patterns is remote.

The possibility of finding such a "commodity" is somewhat improved if we are content to find these conditions satisfied only over a given range of utility. If we can find one commodity or combination whose marginal utility can be made independent of quantities of other commodities by a suitable choice of utility function between the utility contours A and B, and another "commodity" for which the marginal utility can be made independent between B and C by using some other utility function, we might proceed to splice together several utility functions and thus cover the whole range of utility.

But even assuming that we could in this way find a utility function that would be unique in satisfying this independence criterion, there is still grave doubt as to what significance is to be attached to it. For example, we might well come across an indifference map describable by the function $U = ye^x$; obviously this U is not an acceptable measure of utility, for U_{xx}'' is positive. There is however a transformation $V = \log U = x + \log y$ which satisfies the independence criterion, but here too V is hardly acceptable as a measure of utility, for V_x' is a constant, whereas we normally expect a declining marginal utility. $W = \log V$ or $Z = V^{1/2}$ would be more acceptable as measures of satisfaction, but neither of them satisfy an independence criterion.

Of course, if the utility function is to be used only in ways that are related to this independence property or its corollaries, there can be no objection. But constructors of such utility functions usually do not stop there: they almost always infer that this function (or at least the function that they are sure they could get if only the data were more tractable) rather than any other is the most suitable measure of the satisfactions represented by the different contours of the indifference map and hence of the "sacrifice" involved in descending from one contour to a lower one. Usually in the background there is the objective of translating the "equal sacrifice" or "proportional sacrifice" criteria into actual schedules for income tax progression. This step, however, cannot be inferred from the independence property alone, but rests on a separate and unsupported assumption.

There are in other words two separate fundamental assumptions involved in measuring marginal utility by any of the independence methods: The first is the factual assumption that the indifference map of the individual or group being studied is such that it can be described by a function of the form $F(x, y, z, . . .,$

$w) = X(x) + G(y, z, \ldots, w)$. This assumption could be proved or disproved in any given case if sufficient data were available. The second assumption is that this particular function rather than any other such as F^2 or log F is the proper measure of utility or sacrifice. This assumption neither can be verified in terms of the usual data on consumer choice, nor does it appear to be supported by any compelling a priori reasoning. An "independence utility function" may exist and may even be discovered by statistical investigations without necessarily bearing any relation to subjective pleasure or utility. As a method of predicting consumer behavior in response to price changes, one utility function has no advantage over any other, as long as we are dealing with a riskless static equilibrium. As a basis for determining the proper progression of the tax structure, an independence utility function has no demonstrable competence. The jump from certain rather obscure properties of the behavior of individuals in response to price changes to conclusions as to the desirable distribution of income is a rather drastic one, and requires more justification than a mere casual identification of a function that satisfies an independence criterion with one that is to be summed over all individuals and maximized.

Other approaches to the problem of measuring marginal utility have been suggested, but no attempt has as yet been made to translate them into numerical results. In general such methods rely on data not contained in the ordinary indifference map.

Pareto has suggested that the rapidity with which consumers adjust to new conditions may be an indication of the absolute magnitude of the change in their utility that is brought about by their adaptation to the change.[4] But it is doubtful whether any uniquely valid scheme for relating such rates of change to utility can be set up, and in any case the statistical problem of discovering the quantitative relation, assuming that it exists, would be almost insurmountable. Pareto also supposes that in addition to finding an independence utility function in the case where choices are consistent, utility might be defined uniquely in the cases where the integrability conditions are not satisfied and "utility" depends not only on the consumption pattern achieved, but on the path by which it was reached.[5] As it is difficult either to determine such a function or to define its significance for social policy if it could be determined, this possibility also offers little hope.

Paul A. Samuelson has suggested that a clue to the shape of the utility function may be obtained by observing the choices of individuals concerning the distribu-

---

[4] "Pour traiter un problème de dynamique, il faudrait connaître non seulement le sens dans lequel l'individu se meut, mais encore l'intensité du mouvement correspondant à une certaine valeur de l'accroissement de la fonction-indice." Vilfredo Pareto, "Economie Mathematique," in *Encyclopédie des Sciences Pures et Appliquées*, Tome 1, Vol. 4, Fascicule 4, p. 598.

[5] *Ibid.*, p. 614.

tion of consumption through time.[6] However, this method rests on assumptions that the utility at one point of time is independent of consumption at other points of time, that the utility function is not subject to change through time, and that some schedule of subjective discounts of future utilities can be postulated a priori. These assumptions are by no means easy to justify, and when in addition one is in practice confronted with consumers who have only a very limited freedom to adjust their consumption through time, who are uncertain about the future, and who face constantly changing consumption possibilities, prospects for such a method are almost nil.

F. Zeuthen has also made a similar suggestion: "Such a choice [between *changes* in utility positions] may appear . . . where the same will control several non-simultaneous consumptions . . ."[7] Apparently he intends to refer primarily to distributions of consumption through time, but the quotation also suggests situations where the head of a family for example controls the consumption of the various members. However, it would be necessary to know on what principle the individual controlled the consumption of the various members; the only workable assumptions are either that the marginal utility of the various members be made equal or that the total utilities of the members are adjusted according to some norm. Even so, the results give us only a comparison of the marginal or total efficiency of the various members of the family as "utility machines" as judged by the head of the family; we get little or no information on the shape of the utility function of any one individual. Indeed, on the usual postulate of equal utility functions for all individuals, an equal distribution of outlays among members of the family would have to result unless the head of the family were to some degree "selfish" and arrogated to himself a larger share in the family resources.

Utility and Choices between Risky Alternatives

A more promising approach involves using the reactions of individuals to choices involving risk. As long as an individual is confronted only with situations involving merely the substitution of one commodity for another in ratios governed by prices, the question is merely one of preferences as between one certain situation and another certain situation, and utility is defined only as to rank and not as to magnitude. But if the choices available to individuals involve elements of risk, the behavior of individuals can be made to define uniquely a utility function that can

---

[6] Paul A. Samuelson, "A Note on Measurement of Utility," *Review of Economic Studies*, 4 (February, 1937), pp. 155–61.

[7] F. Zeuthen, "On the Determinateness of the Utility Function," *Review of Economic Studies*, 4 (June, 1937), pp. 236–9, esp. p. 237.

be interpreted directly in terms of sacrifice. Such an approach has been suggested by von Neumann and Morgenstern[8] and by F. Zeuthen.[9] It promises to give more concrete meaning to utility and marginal-utility functions, and appears to be more directly related to problems of social policy such as the distribution of income.

Consider an individual who is faced with a choice between two alternative courses of action, one of which will land him on utility contour B, while the other course has equal chances of landing him on either contour A or contour C. We may consider that a rational choice between these two alternatives would involve the maximizing of the mathematical expectation of some utility function. That is, we may define rational behavior as a behavior capable of being described by the maximization of the mathematical expectation of some function, and we may define utility as the function whose mathematical expectation is thus maximized. If then we can discover situations in which individuals choose "rationally" among alternatives involving risks, and can observe these reactions in sufficient detail, we should be able to discover the "utility" function so defined, at least to within linear transformations. In the above case if the individual is on the margin of indifference as to whether he will choose the certainty of B or the equal chance of A or C, then the difference between $U(A)$ and $U(B)$ is the same as the difference between $U(B)$ and $U(C)$. Similarly, if an individual is on the margin of indifference between the certainty of B and a situation in which the probability of landing on contour X is k and that of landing on A is $1 - k$, then $U(B) = kU(X) + (1 - k)U(A)$ or $U(X) = U(A) + [U(B) - U(A)]/k$. The utility function is thus determined except for the arbitrary assignment of values to two initial contours of the map; this is equivalent to the selection of a zero point and a unit of measurement.

Samuelson has raised the objection that the ranking of changes from one indifference curve to another is not of itself sufficient to determine the utility function to within linear transformations.[10] The mere ranking of the differences $D(a, b)$ between the various indifference surfaces does not necessarily imply that D must be a cardinal quantity. However, any system of ordering of changes that does not admit of such cardinal expression involves a type of behavior that can be characterized as either irrational or as containing dynamic elements that are not covered by the utility function of a given person at a given time. Rational individual behavior can be considered to require that the ranking of a given change be unaffected by the number of steps in which that change is made. If this postulate be granted, then if changes can be ranked they can also be measured,

[8] John von Neumann and Oskar Morgenstern, *Theory of Games and Economic Behavior* (Princeton, 1944), 625 pp., esp. pp. 15–20.
[9] Zeuthen, "On the Determinateness," pp. 236–9, esp. p. 237.
[10] Paul A. Samuelson, "The Numerical Representation of Ordered Classifications and the Concept of Utility," *Review of Economic Studies*, 6 (October, 1938), pp. 65–70.

and accordingly utility can be measured. For then any change $D(a, c)$ can be subdivided into a number of subchanges $D(a, b_1)$, $D(b_1, b_2)$, $D(b_2, b_3)$, . . ., $D(b_{n-1}, c)$ such that each subchange is of the same rank as the unit change $D(a, b_1)$. The change $D(a, c)$ can then be assigned a magnitude corresponding to the number of such unit changes.

This method of course fails if the desirability of a given change depends on the number of steps. This might be the case, for example where there is a utility or disutility attached to changes per se. But where we are considering not changes representing actual successive situations in time but merely differences between alternative hypothetical states to be enjoyed at the same future point of time, such a utility or disutility of change is irrelevant. But even so, the utility function obtained might depend on the starting point from which the various alternatives are to be reached. To state this possibility in another way, the utility associated with a given situation may depend not only on the situation attained but upon the path and the rate at which it was reached. This is essentially Pareto's case of nonintegrability, and involves again either dynamical considerations or irrational behavior on the part of individuals. For practical purposes, we may consider the additional postulate required for the conversion of a ranking of changes into a cardinal utility function sufficiently well satisfied.

When we look at the possibilities of applying this theoretical analysis to actual data, however, and so deriving an actual utility function, the prospects are not encouraging. In the field of business ventures, it is not possible to ascertain with any great definiteness what the a priori probabilities of various degrees of success or failure are. Indeed for the purpose of this analysis it is not so much the objectively appraised chances of success or failure that are needed but rather the investor's own estimate of these chances. These subjective estimates are still less capable of being observed, although they might possibly be elicited by questionnaire.

Possibly we can come closer to finding the required data in the field of insurance. We can consider most forms of insurance as methods of exchanging risky positions for less risky ones. The mathematical expectation of the money income in the less risky insured position will be less than the mathematical expectation of the money income in the uninsured position by the amount absorbed by the insurance company in overhead and profits. But here again, although we are in a better position to gauge the objective probabilities of loss, it is by no means certain that the average purchaser of insurance has any accurate notion of these probabilities. Indeed, most purchasers of insurance would probably be quite surprised if they were told how large a fraction of their premiums is required to pay overhead expenses and profits as compared with the fraction returned to policyholders as dividends and indemnities.

Even assuming that this subjective bias can be dealt with, we still have the problem of deciding over how long a period a given loss is to be spread. For example, if a $10,000 house burns down, are we to consider this as equivalent to decreasing the owner's income from $6,000 to $1,000 over a period of two years, or as equivalent to a decrease from $6,000 to $4,000 over a period of five years? Possibly some answer could be obtained to this question from a study of the relations between fluctuations in income and fluctuations in the expenditures of individuals; as yet, however, the data needed for such a study are not available in suitable form.

Assuming that policyholders are informed and rational, and that we can form some judgment of the period over which uninsured losses should be spread, we might be in a position to derive some conclusions about a utility function from a study of the degree to which persons at different economic levels carry the practice of insurance against casualties, as compared with the net overhead cost of such insurance. One would expect to find that the wealthier classes would tend to insure only relatively large risks, since small casualties could produce only a small differential in the marginal utility. At the other end of the scale, the poorer classes would have more occasion for insurance, since their economic position is relatively insecure. But since insurance in small amounts is comparatively costly, such persons might still be found to insure only against the more important calamities. Also since insurance depends to a large extent on sales effort, and information about the various types of insurance available is not too widespread, the lower income classes may fail to take full advantage of insurance, particularly as agents tend to concentrate their sales efforts on prospects promising larger commissions. Moreover, in such comparisons account would have to be taken of the fact that the income tax discriminates in favor of life insurance and against most forms of casualty insurance.[11] But as the degree to which this is generally appreciated by taxpayers is uncertain, appraisal of this factor is difficult.

Furthermore, there is abundant evidence that individual decisions in situations involving risk are not always made in ways that are compatible with the assumption that the decisions are made rationally with a view to maximizing the mathematical expectation of a utility function. The purchase of tickets in lotteries, sweepstakes, and "numbers" pools would imply, on such a basis, that the marginal utility of money is an increasing rather than a decreasing function of income. Such a conclusion is obviously unacceptable as a guide to social policy. A small fraction of such gambling can be attributed to the presence of an eleemosynary element. But for the bulk of such gambling the explanation must be sought elsewhere. One explanation that is consistent with maintaining the assumption of rationality in other dealings would be that the purchase of lottery

---

[11] William Vickrey, "Insurance under the Federal Income Tax," *Yale Law Journal*, 52 (June, 1943), pp. 554–85, esp. pp. 555–6, 563–4.

tickets represents the purchase of a right to hope, however forlornly, in a situation otherwise intolerably barren of this psychological necessity. Other forms of gambling can perhaps be ascribed to the persistence of an egoistic delusion that one's own skill or judgment is better than the opponent's, or to utilities derived in the process rather than from the end result.

Even with insurance, considerations other than the maximization of the mathematical expectation of utility enter the picture. Insurance may be taken out because it is the "sound" thing to do, without much thought as to the net cost. Or insurance may be purchased to avoid the responsibility for taking precautions against the casualty involved. Jewelry, for example, is often insured against theft or loss not so much because the loss would seriously affect the economic status of the owner, but rather to avoid the worry which the possibility of loss would otherwise cause. Indeed, it is probably true to say that if the jewelry is so valuable in relation to the income of the owner that insurance would be justified on grounds of maximizing the expectation of utility alone, then the ownership of the jewelry is in itself an unwise extravagance.

In practice, the outlook for actually determining marginal utility by this method is thus not bright. If the determination can be made at all from data on observed behavior, data relating to insurance probably offer the best field for the attempt. But even this may fail, and it may be necessary to resort to the uncertain procedure of asking hypothetical questions, with all the attendant possibilities for misunderstanding and for bias arising from differences between what people think they would do and what they actually would do under the hypothetical circumstances.

Utility and the Optimum Distribution of Income

From a theoretical point of view, however, the "risky choice" approach to the measurement of marginal utility does offer the advantage that it ties in rather directly with questions of distribution of income and the proper graduation of progressive taxation, particularly insofar as these questions are conceived of in terms of maximizing the aggregate utility. If utility is defined as that quantity the mathematical expectation of which is maximized by an individual making choices involving risk, then to maximize the aggregate of such utility over the population is equivalent to choosing that distribution of income which such an individual would select were he asked which of various variants of the economy he would like to become a member of, assuming that once he selects a given economy with a given distribution of income he has an equal chance of landing in the shoes of each member of it. Unreal as this hypothetical choice may be, it at least shows that there exists a reasonable conceptual relation between the methods used to determine utility and the uses proposed to be made of it. With the independence method of determining a utility function, there is no obvious connection between the operational definition of the function and the uses to which it is to be put.

Assuming that the marginal utility of money declines with increasing income, maximizing the total utility derived by a population from a given fixed aggregate income implies that this income be distributed equally, due allowance being made for varying needs. On such a basis, the exact shape of the utility function is irrelevant to a determination of the proper distribution. But the aggregate amount of income to be distributed cannot in practice be considered independent of the way in which it is distributed. It is generally considered that if individual incomes were made substantially independent of individual effort, production would suffer and there would be less to divide among the population. Accordingly, some degree of inequality is needed in order to provide the required incentives and stimuli to efficient cooperation of individuals in the production process. As soon as the need for such inequality is admitted, the shape of the utility curve becomes a factor in determining the optimum income distribution.

With these practical effects to consider, the question of the ideal distribution of income, and hence of the proper progression of the tax system, becomes a matter of compromise between equality and incentives. If the total income to be distributed can be taken as a function of the degree of inequality, we can still express the solution in terms of maximizing the aggregate utility. The conditions will naturally be more involved than the mere partition of a fixed total. The appropriate solution would lie somewhere between the extremes of complete equality of income on the one hand and that degree of inequality needed to maximize total income on the other.

What is involved in such a problem may perhaps be made clearer by formulating it in mathematical terms. By means of taxation (or in some cases a subsidy), we are to establish a relation $r = r(z)$ between the output z_n of the nth individual and his income, r. The output itself will be a function of the individual's income, r, the incentives offered, dr/dz, and the characteristics of the individual himself

$$z_n = f_n\left(r, \frac{dr}{dz}\right).$$

We wish to choose the function $r(z)$ in such a way as to maximize ΣU, where $U = U(r)$ is the utility arising from an income of r. Normally it is necessary to assume that U is the same function for all individuals. We have also to satisfy the condition that the net revenue equals a given required amount: $\Sigma(z - r) = R$. In form, this is a problem in the calculus of variations.

Unfortunately, in arriving at a solution to this problem, we are even more in the dark about the effect of incentives on individual output and of inequality of income distribution on the total output of the community than we are about the utility function. A wide variety of opinions have been expressed on the subject, ranging from communalists and egalitarians declaring that pride of workmanship and social approval are all that is necessary to elicit the full cooperation of individuals in production, to doctrinaire advocates of *laisser faire* maintaining that each individual must be allowed to retain as nearly as possible the full marginal product of his labor if maximum output is to be maintained. The prospects for resolving these conflicting opinions and obtaining a convincing quantitative estimate of the relation between the distribution of income and the national output are probably not much better than that for the determination of the utility function itself. The reactions of individuals to different scales of remuneration and different degrees of tax progression are so involved with other factors that the best available statistical techniques applied to the most detailed and extensive data will have a hard time isolating the relation between reward and effort.

Some of the difficulty may be side-stepped by reformulating the problem by means of some simplifying assumptions. If the utility function is made to depend not only on income r but also on productive effort w (thus in effect including the utility of leisure in the problem), we may suppose that the effort put forth by the nth individual will be such as to maximize $U(r, w)$. Suppose the work w required of the nth individual to produce an output z is given by $w = w(z, n)$. Again we wish to maximize ΣU by varying $r(z)$ subject to the condition $\Sigma(z - r) = R$.

If we substitute $w(z, n)$ in $U(r, w)$, we can get a function $V(r, z, n) = U(r, w)$. The nth individual in adjusting his effort for maximum V will put $V_z' + V_r'p = 0$, where $p = r'(z)$ and $q = r''(z)$. This defines a relation between z and n; if we put $G(z, n) = V_z' + pV_r' = 0$ where the variable r has been eliminated by substituting $r(z)$, we can then put $G_z'dz = -G_n'dn$. Using a Lagrange multiplier, we can take care of the revenue condition by maximizing

$$\int [U + \lambda(z - r)]dn = -\int [V + \lambda(z - r)]\frac{G_z'}{G_n'}\,dz$$

where for convenience we shift to a continuous integral instead of a sum of discrete elements. If we now put

$$J(z, r, p, q) = [V + \lambda(z - r)]\frac{G_z'}{G_n'},$$

the Euler equation is

$$J_r' - \frac{d}{dz}J_p' + \frac{d^2}{dz^2}J_q' = 0.$$

This reduces to

$$(V_r' + \lambda)G_z' + G_n' \frac{d}{dz} \left[\frac{\lambda V_r'(1 - p)}{G_n'} \right] - \lambda(1 - p)[V_{rr}''p + V_{rz}''] = 0.$$

Expanding this expression in terms of *U, w, r,* and their derivatives produces a completely unwieldly expression. Thus even in this simplified form the problem resists any facile solution.

These formulations are in effect a refinement of the "minimum sacrifice" criterion as suggested by Edgeworth[12] and others. This criterion is by no means universally accepted, however. Simons rejects the whole notion of sacrifice as a criterion for tax progression,[13] while others have argued for "proportional sacrifice" or "equal sacrifice." "Proportional sacrifice" is meaningless unless some arbitrary zero is chosen for the utility function. Nor does choosing the point of minimum subsistence solve the problem, as marginal utility may not be integrable to this point.[14] Fisher, without giving the matter much thought, stated as though it were a matter of course that the proper criterion is equal sacrifice, recognizing explicitly that whether this results in regressive or progressive taxation depends on the elasticity of the marginal-utility function.[15] He may of course have merely selected the only criterion according to which the utility function by itself would give an unequivocal and acceptable answer to the progression problem.

Even though the assumption that choices in situations involving risk are based on maximizing the expectation of a utility function may not hold true, a utility function derived by the use of this assumption may still be a reasonable guide to the optimum distribution of income. If individuals prefer to have the spice of adventure that comes from taking a sporting chance once in a while, this behavior will tend to produce a less sharply declining marginal-utility curve. Relating this marginal-utility curve to a given production–distribution relationship will result in a more unequal distribution of income being indicated as the optimum adjustment. If we assume that individual preferences for taking chances individually are indicative of a corresponding preference for a wider range of possible variation in income, this more unequal distribution of income may be considered an allowance for this preference.

We cannot be certain that this indicated shift in the distribution of income is of the proper amount, however. For example, if the speculative propensity were

---

[12] Francis Y. Edgeworth, "The Pure Theory of Taxation, III," *Economic Journal,* 7 (December, 1897), pp. 550–71; also reprinted in Edgeworth, *Papers Relating to Political Economy* (London, 1925), Vol. II, pp. 63–125.

[13] Henry C. Simons, *Personal Income Taxation* (Chicago, 1938), 238 pp., esp. pp. 5–27.

[14] See Robert L. Bishop, "Consumer's Surplus and Cardinal Utility," *Quarterly Journal of Economics,* 57 (May, 1943), pp. 421–49.

[15] Fisher, "A Statistical Method," p. 185.

strong enough so that the "marginal utility" curve derived from observed risky choices increases with income over some range, then the indicated distribution of income might become bimodal; such a result is almost certainly overshooting the mark.

Unlike the "risk utility" function, there is no obvious relation between the method used in obtaining the "independence utility" function and its use as a criterion for evaluating distributions of income. In fact there is no obvious reason to suppose that there will be any relation between a "risk utility" function and an "independence utility" function, even if the latter is found to exist. We have then in the risk method of determining utility not merely a new method of arriving at a utility function, but an entirely new function with new properties. These properties may be similar to those erroneously ascribed to the independence utility function, but this of itself does not establish any relationship.

Determining a utility function by reference to choices involving risk, while simple in theory, is not easy in practice. Such a procedure does not entirely avoid the making of assumptions that may be seriously remote from reality. A risk utility function is also likely to be considerably more difficult to determine from the available data than an independence utility function. Yet if and when it is determined, it will be considerably more definite in concept and more logically applicable to problems at hand.

2

*Utility, Strategy, and Social Decision Rules**

A social welfare function can be thought of as an operator which, when fed data relating to the preferences of the individuals in a society, will produce a social choice. Much if not all of welfare economics can be considered to be essentially a search for such social welfare functions having acceptable properties. Arrow's justly famous but often misunderstood impossibility theorem is in effect a signpost warning that certain approaches to the search for social welfare functions lead to a dead end. As a first step in considering the current state of welfare economics, it is important to be clear as to just what roads are in fact impassable: exploration of the possibilities for circumventing the impasse will then be more effective.

Arrow's Theorem

From the time of Bentham until fairly recently, the underlying basis of much of welfare economics could be expressed in terms of a social welfare function consisting of the summation of individual utilities over all members of society, and ranking social states according to the magnitude (or perhaps the pcr capita average) of this sum. Difficulties with cardinal measurement of utility, and particularly with interpersonal comparisons, have led to attempts to avoid the use of cardinal utility in the construction of social welfare functions. The notion of a

* *Quarterly Journal of Economics*, 74 (1960) pp. 507–35; reprinted in part in *Readings in Welfare Economics*, K. Arrow and T. Scitovsky, Eds. (Irwin, 1969) pp. 456–61.

* The author wishes to express his appreciation of the very helpful comments by Abram Bergson and Robert Dorfman which have helped him clarify a number of points; this, of course, does not necessarily impute agreement to them.

Pareto optimum is, of course, an early manifestation of this tendency. Arrow's theorem is in effect an attempt to examine just how far one can get in constructing social welfare functions that will consider only ordinal preferences.[1]

Arrow's theorem states that if the arguments of a social welfare function are restricted to the rankings of the alternative social states in the preferences of the various individual members of society, then no social welfare function is possible that satisfies certain seemingly reasonable postulates. A set of such postulates, slightly weaker than the set used (or at least than the set actually required) by Arrow in his original presentation, is as follows:

1 *Unanimity. If an individual preference is unopposed by any contrary preference of any other individual, this preference shall be preserved in the resulting social ordering.* (This is, of course, the principle of Pareto optimality.)

2 *Nondictatorship. No individual shall enjoy a position such that whenever he expresses a preference between any two alternatives and all other individuals express the opposite preference, his preference is always preserved in the social ordering.* (This does not of itself preclude an individual's being granted a paramount interest in a limited number of choices, such that his preferences in this limited area are always respected.)

3 *Transitivity. The social ranking given by the social welfare function is in each case a consistent ordering of all the feasible alternatives.* Ties in the social ranking need not be excluded, though in any actual decision-making process some tie-breaking device would have to be resorted to, and the effect of such tie-breaking might better be included in the social welfare function so as to make it yield strict orderings only. If ties are admitted between two or more alternatives, the relation between these alternatives must be one of equivalence with respect to ranking among the alternatives, not of uncertainty, so that if xPy and yIz, then xPz.[2] We reject a function which tells us that x is better than y, but cannot indicate a choice between z and x nor between z and y; if x is better than y, then necessarily z is either better than y or worse than x (or both).

4 *Range. There is some "universal" alternative u such that for every pair of other alternatives x and y, and for every individual, each of the six possible strict orderings of u, x, and y is contained in some ranking of all of the alternatives which is admissible for the individual.* By an admissible ranking is meant one with which the social welfare function is required to

---

[1] Kenneth J. Arrow, "A Difficulty in the Concept of Social Welfare." *Journal of Political Economy*, (August, 1950), pp. 328–46. *Idem, Social Choice and Individual Values* (New York: Wiley, 1951).

[2] xPy means x is preferred to y; xIy means x and y are indifferent alternatives.

be capable of dealing, in combination with other admissible rankings selected on a particular occasion by other individuals. Certain rankings might be excluded, for example because they appear inherently inconsistent by some test, or perhaps because they are deemed contrary to the patent interests of the individual concerned. This form of the range postulate restricts such exclusions fairly severely: for example, it precludes any restriction on the voting of an individual which would prohibit his ever expressing a preference for a specified x over a specified y, though it does permit the exclusion of certain triplets of the form $xPyPz$. It will be seen later that it is possible to obtain the basic result with range postulates less demanding than this, but more complicated.

5 *Independence.   The social choice between any two alternatives shall not be affected by the removal or addition of other alternatives to the field of feasible alternatives under consideration.*

Proof of the Arrow Impossibility Theorem

A proper appreciation of the scope of the theorem is facilitated by going over a brief proof of the theorem. Such a proof in terms of the above postulates is made possible by introducing the concept of the "decisive set." A set of individuals D is here defined to be decisive for alternative x against alternative y in the context of a given social welfare function, if the function is such that whenever all individuals in D express a preference for x over y and all other individuals express the contrary preference, then the social welfare function yields a social preference for x over y. It can then be shown that by virtue of the transitivity and independence postulates a set that is decisive for any one choice must be decisive for all choices among alternatives covered by the range postulate. A one-person decisive set thus contains a dictator, which is not permitted. But it can be shown that if a decisive set is split into two subsets, one of these subsets must itself be decisive; since the set of all individuals must be decisive by virtue of the unanimity postulate, repeated splitting must eventually lead to a one-person decisive set, violating the nondictatorship postulate.

In detail, the proof is as follows. Suppose D to be a set of individuals which is decisive for x against y. Then by virtue of the range postulate, for each individual in the society there must be some admissible ranking of all of the feasible alternatives within which the alternatives x, y, and u are ranked $xPyPu$, and likewise another admissible ranking in which $yPuPx$. The social welfare function is therefore required to be defined for the case where all members of D have a preference $xPyPu$, while all others have $yPuPx$. But these preferences satisfy the conditions under which the decisiveness of D for x against y is effective, so that application of the social welfare function to this case must yield a social ranking in which x is preferred to y. By the unanimity postulate, y must in this case be socially preferred to u, so that by the transitivity postulate x is socially preferred to u. But in this case only members of D prefer x to u as individuals, while all others prefer u to x; since in this case the preference of the members of D for x over u prevails in the social choice against the opposition of all of the individuals not in D, and since by the independence postulate this preference must prevail regardless of changes in the individual rankings of y or any of the other alternatives, the set D is also decisive for x against u. Iteration of exactly similar arguments with the members of D voting $zPxPu$ and all others voting $uPzPu$ shows that D must be decisive for any fourth alternative z against the universal alternative u, and a further iteration with members of D all voting $zPuPw$ and others $uPwPz$ shows that D must be decisive for any given alternative z against any other alternative w. Thus a set that is decisive for any one decision must be decisive for all decisions covered by the range postulate.

Again, let D be a decisive set containing two or more persons, let A be a proper subset of D, let $B = D - A$, and let C be the set of persons not in D, if any. Some decisive set D must exist, since at least the set of all persons in the society is a decisive set by virtue of the unanimity postulate. Consider the case where the members of A have the preferences $xPyPu$, the members of B have $yPuPx$, and members of C have $uPxPy$. Since the members of A and B agree in preferring y to u and together form a decisive set, while the members of C have the opposite preference, the resulting social ranking for this case must put y above u. If in addition the social welfare function is made to put x below y, in this case, the members of B will then be the only ones having a corresponding preference, so that B would be decisive for y against x. On the other hand if the social welfare function does not in this case put x below y, it must by transitivity place x above u, making A decisive for x against u. In either case, one of the proper subsets of D is itself decisive, and a repetition of the argument eventually leads to requiring a one-person set to be decisive, i.e., to contain a dictator.

The Variations from Arrow's Treatment

While the above treatment follows the general approach pioneered by Arrow, there are significant differences. For example the transitivity postulate is included by Arrow in his definition of a social welfare function, whereas here it is displayed as an explicit postulate subject to questioning in its turn. On the other hand Arrow added another explicit postulate, not directly represented among the above five, which can be termed the "nonperversity" postulate. Stated somewhat loosely, this postulate is as follows:

6 *Nonperversity. A change in the preference expressed by an individual between two alternatives shall never operate to change the social preference in the opposite direction, other individual preferences remaining unchanged.*

The function of this postulate is taken over, in the above proof, by using the unanimity and the nondictatorship postulates in slightly stronger forms than the corresponding postulates used by Arrow. Arrow in effect omitted the italicized words in the nondictatorship postulate, restricting the concept of dictatorship to cases where the dictator is absolutely independent of the choices of others, whereas the postulate in the above form would term a person a dictator even if his expressed preferences could be perversely frustrated, in some cases, by his finding too many individuals agreeing with them. Given the nonperversity postulate, however, the two forms of the nondictatorship postulate are equivalent, so that the two postulates of Arrow, taken together, are stronger than the non-dictatorship postulate used here.

Similarly, Arrow's "Nonimposition" postulate merely requires that for any two given alternatives, one is not always to be preferred to the other in the social ranking, regardless of individual preferences; this by itself is a weaker requirement than the unanimity postulate used here. But since the unanimity condition can be derived by applying the nonperversity postulate to the nonimposition postulate, the present set of postulates taken as a whole is weaker at this point also.

On the other hand, Arrow's range postulate as given by him appears to be weaker than that used here: he merely requires that there exist some set of three alternatives such that there exist, among the admissible rankings of all alternatives for each individual, rankings which rank the three selected alternatives in all possible transitive orders. Unfortunately this is not adequate: Arrow errs in assuming that he can restrict his universe of discourse at a crucial point to three such alternatives without loss of generality.[3] For his definition of dictatorship is in terms of choices among all possible alternatives; his proof that a (one-person) set decisive for one choice is decisive for all choices actually holds only for choices within the selected triplet of alternatives, and can be extended to other choices only if the range postulate is correspondingly broadened, as it has been here. This can perhaps be best understood in terms of the following counterexample to Arrow's theorem as presented: consider three persons choosing among alternatives $w, x, y,$ and $z,$ subject to the constraint on the individual orderings that w must be put either at the top or at the bottom of the scale; let the social welfare function place w at either the top or bottom of the social preference scale

---

[3] Arrow, *Social Choice*, p. 51.

according to majority rule, and rank $x, y,$ and z according to the preferences of a designated individual from among the three; this individual might be termed a "semidictator." This social welfare function satisfies all of Arrow's postulates as literally given; it fails to satisfy the stronger range postulate presented here.

Relaxing the Postulates

The significance of Arrow's theorem is most readily brought into sharp relief if the various postulates are relaxed one at a time and the possibilities that are thus opened up for the construction of a social welfare function examined. This procedure also serves to show that each of the postulates given is at least in some degree necessary to the proof of the theorem.

Thus waiving the unanimity requirement admits the use of an imposed social welfare function which always gives the same arbitrary predetermined social ranking regardless of individual preferences. Waiving the nondictatorship requirement admits the use of a social welfare function that always makes the social ranking agree with that of some designated individual, who is thus the dictator. In either case the remaining four postulates are satisfied; on the whole, however, functions that violate either the unanimity or the nondictatorship postulates are of relatively little interest: they hardly deserve the name of social welfare functions at all.

Intransitive Social Orderings

Waiving transitivity admits, for example, of the use of pairwise weighted majority voting, the weights being such as to make ties impossible while not giving any one person a majority of the weight. This, of course, permits the occurrence of the Condorcet effect, or "paradox of voting," but otherwise the postulates are satisfied. Another possibility under this head is the "Pareto" social welfare function which admits that x is socially preferable to y if and only if some individual prefers x to y while none prefers y to x; in all other cases the social welfare function produces a symmetric relation xJy which can be called "uncertainty" or "indecision" and which lacks the transitivity property of the "indifference" relation. That is, xJy and yJz do not necessarily imply xJz, as contrasted with the indifference relation xIy which is an equivalence relation.

Another possibility is that while in a given case intransitivity occurs, it occurs only among alternatives that are all necessarily inferior to some dominating alternative, so that if the dominating alternative is required to be actually available by some constraint on the nature of the set of feasible alternatives, intransitivity will always be irrelevant to the decision actually to be made. It is not easy, however, to construct instances of this.

Restrictions on Individual Choice

Rather more interesting are the various ways in which the range requirement can be relaxed so as to permit a social welfare function to be constructed. Here the case most discussed in the literature is that of "single-peaked preferences," where the admissible individual rankings are such that the alternatives can be ordered along a one-dimensional continuum in such a way that starting with the alternative ranked at the top in any given admissible individual ranking, the alternatives will rank successively lower as we proceed in either direction along the continuum. In other words, in any admissible ranking of the alternatives, no alternative can rank higher than any of the alternatives lying along the continuum between this first alternative and the top-ranking alternative. This criterion is likely to be satisfied, for example, when the alternatives represent different amounts to be spent on some program, or when political parties or candidates can be ranged in order from radical to conservative. In such single-peaked cases, weighted majority rule, with suitable restrictions on the weights to prevent ties or dictatorship, provides a class of acceptable social welfare functions meeting the remaining four requirements; the result is the selection of the median alternative.

Less well known is the case of the "single-troughed preferences," which is obtained by simply reversing all rank orders in the preceding case. It also admits the construction of a social welfare function satisfying the four nonrange postulates, but in this case the result is fairly trivial, since the top ranking social choice must be one of the two extreme alternatives at either end of the continuum, which end being determined, for example, by weighted majority rule.

Single-peaked and single-troughed patterns do not exhaust the possibilities, however. Where there are just three alternatives, proscription of any one of the six strict rankings of the three alternatives permits a social welfare function to be constructed as follows: establish as a "standard" ranking one of the circular permutations of the proscribed ranking, e.g., if the proscribed ranking is $zPyPx$, the standard ranking may be either $yPxPz$ or $xPzPy$. Then pairwise weighted majority rule in which the standard ranking is added in to the voting with a weight of just under half of the total weight produces a transitive social ordering satisfying the unanimity, non-dictatorship, and independence postulates. This can be described as the case where "one plus God is a majority."

With four alternatives we can have cases where we have neither a cyclical triplet (e.g., $xPyPz$, $yPzPx$, and $zPxPy$) nor single-peaked nor single-troughed patterns. With the following set of admissible orderings: $wPxPyPz$, $wPxPzPy$, $wPzPxPy$, *wPyPxPz, xPyPzPw, xPzPyPw, yPxPzPw*, and *zPxPyPw*, majority rule with weights that preclude ties or dictatorship yields a transitive social welfare function. Since *w* appears at the bottom of some of the rankings, *w* must be located, in the single-peaked case, at one end of the sequence along the underlying continuum, but if this were so, then only one ranking with *w* at the top would be possible; since there are four such rankings, all distinct, representation as single-peaked preferences is not possible for this set of orderings. A symmetrical argument disposes of the single-troughed possibility. Since *w* never appears between two other alternatives in the admissible orderings, *w* cannot enter into a cyclical triplet, and since *x* never appears as the third alternative among *x, y,* and *z*, a cyclical triplet over *x, y,* and *z* is not to be found among these orderings.

Thus fairly wide possibilities exist for defining ranges of admissible rankings sufficiently narrower than that specified by postulate 4 to permit one or more social welfare functions to be constructed satisfying the remaining postulates, yet broad enough to cover an interesting range of cases. On the other hand postulate 4 is itself somewhat stronger than is absolutely necessary to support the theorem. Actually, what is required is that the set of admissible rankings be rich enough so that a set that is decisive for one choice, say for *x* over *y*, can be shown by a sequence of steps to be decisive for a range of choices wide enough so that if any single individual had the power to enforce any choice of his within this range against universal opposition, this would be considered an intolerably dictatorial position. Now if all six strict orderings among any given set of alternatives *x, y,* and *z* are admissible, then decisiveness for any one of them over any other, say for *x* against *y*, implies complete decisiveness for any choice within the field of these three alternatives. Accordingly, if we can start from some such triplet of alternatives and proceed to extend the field of alternatives by a "triangulation" process in which one new alternative at a time is successively added to the field of alternatives already triangulated, in such a manner that as each new alternative is added it is possible to find two alternatives already in the triangulated set such that for each individual there exist admissible rankings containing each of the six strong rankings of these three alternatives, one new and two old, then the unanimity, transitivity, and independence postulates together imply that some individual must be a dictator over the field of alternatives thus triangulated. In the range postulate as given, the universal alternative *u* served as a pivot around which all other pairs of alternatives could be triangulated, but there are many other less stringent forms of triangulation.

If the set of admissible rankings is to be the same for all individuals (i.e., they are all given identical ballots to mark), then it seems a likely conjecture that the possibility of such triangulation may be a necessary as well as a sufficient condition for the impossibility theorem to hold. On the other hand the admissible ways of ranking the alternatives may well vary from individual to individual. For example some individuals may be considered a priori to have no valid reason for expressing a preference between two alternatives that are indistinguishable in terms of their direct effect on them; or one alternative may be considered to be so obviously or inherently more advantageous to them than the other as to warrant their being precluded from voting contrarily, whether from ignorance or for strategic reasons. If such restrictions are allowed, triangulation seems to be a sufficient but not a necessary condition for the Arrow social welfare function to be an impossibility, and the impossibility theorem may hold in terms of even less demanding requirements on the range of patterns of preference over which the function is to be defined.

Indeed, it may be possible to find cases where rather reasonable constraints on individual preferences make possible the construction of a social welfare function satisfying the other requirements, as generalizations of the single-peaked and single-troughed cases, or otherwise. But the problem of just what specifications of the range will make possible the construction of satisfactory social welfare functions promises to be a difficult one, particularly as varying degrees of partial dictatorship that fall somewhat short of that stipulated in the nondictatorship postulate may also be considered fatally objectionable.

Relaxing the Independence Postulate

A more promising line of inquiry seems to be the consideration of various modifications of the independence postulate. This is indeed the postulate which, together with the restriction of the argument of the function to mere rankings, rules out the more usual Benthamesque welfare functions that are obtained by summing individual utilities. Indeed, it does seem rather prodigal to throw away, in deciding between two alternatives, whatever indication regarding the intensity of individual preferences for one over the other is furnished by the relative rankings of other alternatives, even though these other alternatives may not be actually available, either at the moment, or , indeed, ever.

Once we decide to relax the independence postulate, there are many ways in which a social welfare function can be constructed, many of which adequately fulfill the remaining postulates. For example, the sum of the ranks assigned to each alternative by the various individuals may be taken as indicating the social ranking, as is frequently done in preferential balloting; more generally, some set of values could be assigned to the ranks which might be considered to be more representative of the degree of distance to be expected between the ranks than the mere rank numbers. One attractive way of assigning such numbers would be by doing this in such a way that the resulting distribution of values would approximate a normal distribution with unit variance. Or some kind of sequential elimination procedure could be specified, as in various schemes of proportional representation.

All such schemes will, of course, be open to the objection that the social choice may be affected by changes in the range of alternatives presented to the individuals, even when the selected alternatives are not themselves excluded or included by the change. But this will be true in considerably varying degrees. Where the number of alternatives is small, omission or inclusion of one or two alternatives may be crucial; where the number of alternatives is large, however, omission or inclusion even of a number of alternatives constituting the same proportion of the total number may be much less likely to affect the result. Appropriate selection of the values assigned to the various ranks in the procedure indicated in the preceding paragraph may help to minimize the influence of changes in the range of alternatives offered, and the particular set of values which produces a normal or near-normal distribution may indeed under some conditions be the one that does minimize these effects. To examine this hypothesis in detail, however, would take us too far afield.

Strategic Misrepresentations of Preferences

There is another objection to such welfare functions, however, which is that they are vulnerable to strategy. By this is meant that individuals may be able to gain by reporting a preference differing from that which they actually hold. For example, if there are two groups roughly equal in numbers, with group A ranking the four alternatives in the order $xyzw$, while group B has the preference order $zxwy$, then if both report correctly and the social decision is derived by summing ranks, x becomes the social choice, whereas if the B's, instead of reporting their genuine preferences, report instead the ranking $zwyx$, then z becomes the social choice, and the B's have succeeded in shifting the social choice in the direction of their own preferences by a strategic misrepresentation. In general, whenever intensity of preference is given effect in the social welfare function, whether directly as such or through considering the number of intervening ranks, it will be to the advantage of an individual or group, whenever it can be discerned in advance which alternatives are likely to be close rivals for selection as the social choice and which alternatives are almost certain to be defeated, to exaggerate preferences among the close rivals, at the expense, if necessary, of understating the relative intensity of preferences for or against the less promising ("irrelevant") alternatives, whether this lack of promise is due to technical difficulty or impossibility or simply to lack of general appeal. Such a strategy could, of course, lead to counterstrategy, and the process of arriving at a social decision could readily turn into a "game" in the technical sense. It is thus not for nothing that we often hear references to "the game of politics."

It is clear that social welfare functions that satisfy the nonperversity and the independence postulates and are limited to rankings as arguments, are also immune to strategy. For if some individual prefers x to y, and as a result of his reporting this and other preferences correctly the social choice is nevertheless y, there is nothing this individual can do to improve matters for himself by misrepresenting his genuine preferences, even if joined by others who also prefer x to y, since changing of expressed preferences concerning other alternatives can, by the independence postulate, have no effect on the social choice as between x and y, nor, by the nonperversity postulate, can a change in the expressed preference of this group for x over y, say by some or all of the members claiming to prefer y to x, improve the chances of obtaining x. It can be plausibly conjectured that the converse is also true, that is, that if a function is to be immune to strategy and be defined over a comprehensive range of admissible rankings, it must satisfy the independence criterion, though it is not quite so easy to provide a formal proof for this. Immunity to strategy and independence are thus at least closely similar requirements, if not actually logically equivalent.

Of course, susceptibility to strategy is an objection of varying degrees of seriousness according to the circumstances of the case. Where the number of individuals is large and the social welfare function assigns no outstanding role to any one individual, and where the individuals are unorganized and without systematic knowledge of each other's preferences or advance information as to which alternatives are the more likely candidates for the social choice, no individual may have the knowledge required or the time and sophistication to work out a strategy that will have a significant edge over that of reporting his preferences honestly. But where individuals are few or well organized or well informed, and the number of likely alternatives is limited, the situation may pass from one analogous to perfect competition to one analogous to oligopoly where the process of arriving at a social choice may become a game of strategy with all the uncertainties regarding the outcome that this entails. An analysis of the ways in which a social welfare function might be set up so as to minimize the probable influence of strategy might be interesting, but appears from this vantage point to present formidable difficulties. While in what follows we will be evaluating social welfare functions in part in terms of their susceptibility to strategy, this criterion will play a subordinate role.

Social Welfare Functions Based on Cardinal Utility

Once we decide to accept some susceptibility of social welfare functions to strategy, there seems to be no reason to limit the argument of the function to rankings, and we naturally turn to the Benthamite social welfare function consisting of a summation of individual utilities. If each individual is to report his own utility evaluations for each of the alternative social states, however, it is necessary to specify a little more closely just how these evaluations are to be made, whether because it may not be clear a priori what the standards of measurement are, or because in the absence of any constraint a strategy of exaggeration might be so obviously and generally attractive as to result in the complete demoralization of the process. Moreover, while Bentham and his followers often seemed to assume as a matter of course that eventually some methods of assigning quantitative values to pleasures and pains would be developed that would be interpersonally valid, more modern writers have been increasingly skeptical of this possibility.

Calibration by Threshold of Discrimination

Indeed, the only method thus far suggested for actually measuring cardinal utility that gives rise naturally to a unique basis for interpersonal comparisons is that of Armstrong, who uses just noticeable differences of satisfaction as a unit.[4] But there seem to be many serious objections to the acceptance of such a unit. The ability of an individual to distinguish levels of satisfaction may vary rather systematically with the temperament, training, and occupation of the individual: does one really want to weight more heavily the preferences of an introvert than an extrovert, of a sybarite than an anchorite, of a professor of economics or psychology than a professor of chemistry or German literature? An affirmative answer might be maintained in some of these cases, but surely not in all.

Moreover, the difficulties involved in actually performing such a measurement appear more and more formidable as one seeks to make the definition more nearly operational. In the psychophysical experiment to which this proposed determination of utility is analogous, the conditions of the experiment must be carefully specified and the objects to be ranked must differ, so far as possible, only in the quality to be ranked and not in other irrelevant dimensions, if consistent results are to be obtained. For example, in comparing weights, different results are to be expected if the two weights are close together and can be hefted several times in alternate sequence, than if they are placed at opposite ends of the campus; of it the objects to be compared as to weight are all, say, books, the

---

[4] W. E. Armstrong, "Utility and the Theory of Welfare," *Oxford Economic Papers*, 3 (October, 1951), pp. 259–71. J. Rothenberg, "Marginal Preference and the Theory of Welfare," *Oxford Economic Papers*, 5 (October, 1953), pp. 248–63, with "Reply" by Armstrong. J. Rothenberg, "Reconsideration of a Group Welfare Index," *Oxford Economic Papers*, 6 (June, 1954), pp. 164–80.

results may be expected to be different from those where the objects are books, pillows, lampshades, and lead ingots. Moreover, the experiment must usually be repeated a sufficient number of times to reduce to a reasonable level the effects of differences in the degree to which subjects would be willing to guess where they are not sure.

In the measurement of utility, however, the circumstances under which the comparison is to take place are so far removed from those of the psychophysical experiment as to lead to doubt as to whether the analogy has any validity at all. The experiment consisting of having the subject actually experience the various social states to be evaluated is certainly out of the question as a practical matter, and may not even be conceivable, in any fully consistent sense, as a *gedankenexperiment*, since a social state includes a complete set of anticipations regarding the future. The alternative social states must therefore be presented to the subject, not through direct experience but by description. Now if the descriptions of the states being compared differ in more than one parameter, we will have the difficulty that the accuracy with which the difference in utility is perceived will depend on the degree of qualitative difference in directions roughly orthogonal to utility. For example, even though a subject would probably assert with considerable certainty that he would prefer a trip to Paris plus 1,000 francs spending money to the same trip with only 950 francs to spend, he might at the same time find it quite difficult to decide between, say a trip to Honolulu plus x dollars of spending money and either Paris plus 1,000 francs, on the one hand, or Paris plus 800 francs, on the other.[5] Or more generally, a subject might be quite willing to assert that he would be better off with an income of $5,001 than with an income of $5,000, prices being the same; but if we consider another set of prices p_2 and ask how much money income must be obtained to make a person definitely and perceptibly better off than with $5,000 at prices p_1, and on the other hand, (and independently) how much money income could be obtained at prices p_2 and still leave the individual definitely and perceptibly worse off than with $5,000 at prices p_1, the difference between the two p_2 incomes thus determined, which should be equivalent to two "*jnd*'s" will in general be much larger than twice the $1 difference in incomes that was perceptible when prices were held the same at p_1. Moreover, this difference will in general depend on the degree of divergence between the prices p_1 and the prices p_2. Thus there seems to be no suitably unique and uniform measure of utility to be obtained by this method.

It might be thought that something could be salvaged by sharpening the question that is being asked of the subjects. Thus it may be felt that when a respondent states that at constant prices a $5,001 income is better than $5,000, he is saying, in effect, not that he could actually "feel" the difference, but that he can

[5] This illustration is adapted from one given by Howard Raiffa.

tell in which direction the change for the better lies, so that if a sequence of differences of the same kind were combined he would be able to tell the difference, just as an assertion that a weight of 1,000 grams is heavier than one of 999 grams is not the same thing as stating that if asked to select the heavier of two such weights he could do it infallibly, under specified conditions. Thus the respondent must be asked to report, not whether he is able to tell reliably that one state is preferable to another, but rather that if allowed to experience the two states (in "sequence"?) he would "feel" significantly different, and moreover, he must be required to suppress any temptation he might have for strategic reasons to shade his reports in the direction of distinguishing smaller differences than would "really" be significant.

Even if these difficulties could be overcome, there would be undoubtedly a considerable bias introduced in such a measure of utility arising from the fact that for most respondents differences in the neighborhood of their current level of income would appear to be relatively more vivid and significant than differences between incomes both of which are remote from their current state. Thus one might expect a person with a small income to minimize the importance of differences between high incomes, and vice versa, and this natural bias would reinforce any tendency there might be to give consciously biased reports for strategic reasons. Thus for a number of widely differing reasons, measuring utility by minimum sensible increments seems to offer little promise for purposes of constructing social welfare functions.

Independence of Marginal Utilities as a Criterion of Cardinality

Another approach to the measurement of utility is the Fisher–Frisch construction[6] based on the assumption that classes of commodities can be defined in such a way that the marginal utility derived from a given increment in one class of commodities consumed will be independent of the amount of consumption in the other class.[7] If this assumption can be accepted, a utility function is defined up to a linear transformation, and can be determined from observations on the choices of an individual under a suitable variety of circumstances. This still leaves no basis for interpersonal comparisons; Fisher and Frisch hurdled this barrier by in effect assuming that the average behavior of consumers within each income stratum could be taken as the behavior of a "typical" consumer in the various income and

---

[6] Irving Fisher, "A Statistical Method for Measuring Marginal Utility," in *Economic Essays in Honor of J. B. Clark* (New York: Macmillan, 1927), pp. 157–93. Ragnar Frisch, *New Methods of Measuring Marginal Utility* (Tubingen: J. C. B. Mohr, 1932).

[7] This is not quite the same thing as saying that the total utility must be expressible as the sum of separate utilities produced by the two commodity classes considered in isolation, since a third class of commodities may enter the picture, as in the utility function $U = \log(x + z) + \log(y + z^2)$.

price situations, and that all deviations of individuals in either behavior or utility from that of this typical or average individual could be neglected insofar as the construction of a social welfare function that considers only the distribution of incomes is concerned. This was done in the first instance in order to permit the construction of a utility function from consumer studies by income classes, but this assumption also has the effect of hurdling the interpersonal chasm.

Given the assumption that independence exists as between two commodity classes, a utility function could be determined, to within linear transformations, for each individual separately, in principle at least. This would leave the interpersonal chasm unbridged, but would require less heroic assumptions. But the assumption that independence exists is in itself no mean hurdle to take. It involves first that the behavior of the individual be compatible with this assumption: as a counterexample, the utility function $U = \log (x^2 + xy)$ satisfies all of the usual requirements, but there is no monotonic transformation of this U that will make x and y independent. It also involves the assumption that if behavior is capable of being so explained, the utility function so determined will be relevant to the construction of a social welfare function. This is by no means assured, and indeed it is possible to exhibit cases where absurd results would be obtained. For example, $U = \log [\log(x + 3) + 2y + y^2]$ is a utility function that produces indifference curves convex to the origin throughout, with declining marginal utility for an adequately wide range of values, which range can be extended at will by suitable transformations of the function. If we decide to select for welfare purposes that transformation that produces independence, we have as the selected function $V = \log(x + 3) + 2y + y^2$, and the marginal utility of y is everywhere an increasing function of y, which in many cases would be completely unacceptable. Considering the many points at which doubts are raised, it does not appear that a utility determined by reference to independence has any special virtue as a basis for a social welfare function.

Risk, Utility, and Income Distribution

There seems to be much more promise, for social welfare function purposes, in the Bernoullian utility function, which has been given such a modern vogue by Von Neumann and Morgenstern.[8] This function rests on the hypothesis, of course, that human behavior in the face of risk can be explained in terms of maximizing the mathematical expectation of a utility function; if the facts do

---

[8] Daniel Bernoulli, "Exposition of a New Theory on the Measurement of Risk" (1738), trans. Louise Sommer, *Econometrica*, 22 (January, 1954), pp. 23–36. J. Von Neumann and O. Morgenstern, *Theory of Games and Economic Behavior* (2nd edn., Princeton University Press, 1947). W. Vickrey, "Measuring Marginal Utility by Reactions to Risk," *Econometrica*, 13 (October, 1945), pp. 319–33.

conform to such a hypothesis, then the relevant utility function is determined uniquely to within linear transformations. Thus like the independence utility function, the Bernoullian utility function provides no immediate basis for interpersonal comparisons.

There is a sense, however, in which the Bernoullian utility function appears to have a logical connection with the selection of a social state that is somewhat closer than any possessed by the utility functions discussed previously. For example, if for the moment we make the heroic assumption that, abstracting from differences in age, sex, or family status, each individual has preference patterns exactly similar to those of every other individual, then we can take any two income–price situations as calibrating points for the setting up of a utility function, and interpersonal comparisons will be independent of the choice of calibrating points. The analogy in thermometry is the selection of two temperatures as calibrating points for gas thermometers using different gases as the thermometric medium: if we assume that all gases are "perfect" in that they follow the same law of expansion, it makes no essential difference what temperatures we select for calibration. Let us now further imagine a series of communities, each with the same resources, with individuals all having the same tastes, but differing within each community as to talents (but each community enjoying the same distribution of talents). Unequal degrees of talent among individuals would tend to produce corresponding differences in individual incomes; we can imagine that each of the communities adopts some form of redistributive policy, which, however, can be pushed beyond a certain point only at the expense of reducing total output through the effects on incentives. Suppose that different policies are adopted in the different communities, and then consider the choice of a potential immigrant who is making up his mind as to which of the various communities to migrate to. If he knows his own talents exactly and is able therefore to predict the net income he will enjoy in each of the communities, he can, of course, make his choice accordingly on the basis of these net incomes without recourse to the imputation of utility. If on the other hand he is quite uncertain as to the role that his talents will enable him to fill in the various communities, he may, if his tastes are the same as those of everyone else, make his decision on the basis of maximizing his expected utility, the alternative utilities in question being those of the various members of a given community, and the probabilities attached to each being the immigrant's appraisal of the probability of his being able to attain a comparable role if he chooses in favor of that community. If we identify the social welfare with the attractiveness of the various communities to this prospective immigrant, we see that the social welfare function takes the form of a weighted summation of individual utilities. If the immigrant is completely ignorant as to what role he will fill in the new community and weights the roles of all individuals equally, we get the Benthamite summation of individual utilities with the utilities being Bernoullian.

Interpersonal Comparisons and Differences in Tastes

It is possible to relax somewhat the rather drastic assumptions as to similarity of tastes and still retain some interesting properties. Assume for example, that tastes vary only in such a way that for each individual the ratio of the income necessary to achieve a given level of satisfaction at one set of prices to the income necessary at another set of prices is independent of the level of satisfaction specified (i.e., that the "true" index of the cost of living between two price situations is independent of the level of income); this will be true in particular when there is "expenditure proportionality," i.e., when for any given set of prices expenditure on any given commodity varies in direct proportion to income. A change in prices will then change the scale, but not the shape, of the relation between utility and money income. If in addition we assume that the utility function is such that for some set of prices utility is proportional to the logarithm of income, then any given change in prices changes the utility of all incomes by a constant amount, and leaves the marginal utility of money unaffected. There is then no inconsistency in postulating that the marginal utility of money at a given level of money income is the same for all individuals, whereas under more general assumptions, making interpersonal comparisons on the basis of equating the marginal utility of money at given income levels at one set of prices would give results that would in general differ from those obtained if the same procedure were adopted using another set of prices as a basis. Thus differences in taste do not make consistent interpersonal comparisons impossible, but the differences must be confined to very special kinds of difference. The fact that the logarithmic function turns out to have such special properties in this connection may perhaps be scored as a minor triumph for Bernoulli's intuition, for this was the function that he picked out to use in resolving the Petersburg paradox. His intuition may have been somewhat stronger than his logic at this point, however, for while this function resolves the particular paradox that was presented to him, it does not resolve all paradoxes of this type. Indeed, only if a utility function has an upper bound is it impossible to construct a gamble of the Petersburg type that will yield an infinite expectation of utility. However, the fact that a Petersburg-type paradox can be constructed giving an infinite expectation of utility for the logarithmic utility function is probably not a serious objection to its use, especially if we note that the infinite sequence of tosses of coins or the equivalent required for such a paradox could never be carried out in a finite period of time with the aid of a finite amount of equipment.

Utility Calibration in Terms of a Field of Alternatives

However, just as few thermometric substances behave as perfect gases, we can hardly expect individual preferences to follow such conveniently regular patterns, and if the problem of interpersonal comparisons is to be resolved, it must be by means of some more or less arbitrary rule. From the fact that we cannot expect to satisfy Arrow's independence postulate we can derive the suggestion that the resolution will have to depend in some way upon the choice of the field of alternatives to be considered. Let us suppose, then, that we can, by some standards, select a set of alternatives that are to be considered in the construction of the social welfare function. What standards are to be appropriate for this selection, and indeed what is meant by an alternative will be discussed more incisively after we have discussed the methods to be used in the construction of the function.

Given a set of alternatives, we may suppose that each individual is able to place each of the alternatives on his own utility scale, using whatever aribtrary unit and zero point appeals to him, thus obtaining a utility $U_i(x)$ for each individual i and each alternative x. We will not be concerned here with the selection of the zero point, since in any comparison of social states with the same population, changes in these zero points will cancel out in any comparison of two states. The problem before us is one of reducing differences in utility on these various individual scales to a common unit, by determining for each individual a calibration factor by which his own arbitrarily selected utility units are to be multiplied in order to convert them to the common units which are to be aggregated in evaluating the social welfare. It is worth noting that the mathematical procedure is exactly the same whether we interpret it as a reduction of variously selected utility units to a common basis, or whether we regard it as the application of weights to individual utilities in accordance with their respective social "importance," as in the more general "Bergsonian"[9] social welfare function.

Several alternative methods of performing this standardization or calibration can readily be devised; they will all, of course, involve some degree of arbitrariness. By analogy to thermometry, we can arbitrarily select two social states, A and B, and then adjust each individual utility scale by first subtracting $U_i(A)$ and then multiplying by a factor $\dfrac{100}{U_i(B) - U_i(A)}$, so that selected state A is always given a value of 0 and state B is always given a value of 100. To avoid anomalous results, states A and B must be so selected that B is universally preferred to A.[10] This is not too difficult, particularly if we do not limit ourselves to states that are actually realizable. In this type of social welfare function, the preferences of individuals who happen to have a special liking for B or a particularly strong aversion to A will be given relatively little weight compared with those to whom

[9] A. Bergson (Burk), "A Reformulation of Certain Aspects of Welfare Economics," *Quarterly Journal of Economics*, 52 (February 1938), pp. 310–34.
[10] C. Hildreth, "Alternative Conditions for Social Orderings," *Econometrica*, 21 (January, 1953), pp. 81–94.

there is very little difference between *A* and *B*. The resulting social choice may thus be affected fairly substantially by the choice of the calibrating points *A* and *B*.

One possible choice of *A* and *B* which may seem to get away from this arbitrariness to a considerable extent is their specification for each individual separately as the best and worst imaginable states, respectively, or perhaps as "perfect misery" and "perfect happiness." But this seems to be making too much depend on the powers of imagination of the individual, and in any case would be placing the reference points relatively far from the range of ordinary experience so that the difficulty for individuals of ranging the available states on a scale so specified would be substantially increased. A slight modification of this method would be to take as the calibration points for each individual the best and the worst of the set of alternatives presented for evaluation, i.e., to specify that the unit of utility be such that the utility range of the set of alternatives being considered is, say, 100. While this seems better than any of the preceding calibrations, it still makes the social choice susceptible to substantial erratic shifts produced by the inclusion or exclusion of alternatives that are outstandingly liked or disliked by particular individuals. In order to avoid this it would seem preferable to use as the basis for calibration some less sensitive measure of the dispersion of the utilities of the social states, such as the standard deviation, the interquartile range, or the mean difference. While the social choice would then still depend on the way the set of alternatives to be considered is chosen, this dependence would be fairly regular rather than erratic.

Different Concepts of a Field of Alternatives

There is still a fairly wide range within which the social choice can vary depending on how the set of alternatives to be presented is constructed. Not only can the field of alternatives be wider or narrower, but the alternatives themselves may be defined so as to include or exclude a variety of aspects of the situation. At one extreme the alternatives can be presented atomistically, and perhaps uniformly for all individuals, for example by defining the alternatives for each individual as income–price situations. Alternatives so defined would abstract almost completely from social or political aspects of the situation, although it would be possible to add, without altering the essential nature of the evaluation, such individualistically perceived neighborhood effects as whether the highways are crowded or relatively free of congestion, or whether the neighbors play loud music late at night. At the other extreme each alternative to be presented could be defined as a complete state of society, so that each individual in appraising the state of society will be able to appraise it not only in terms of his own role within that society, but also, if he is so inclined, in terms of the roles that that society assigns to others.

If the alternatives are to be in some sense realizable, as in some degree they must be if the individuals concerned are to take the evaluation at all seriously, then there is an essential difference between the two types of alternatives, even when the social states are evaluated on a completely individualistic basis. In the former case the range of alternatives offered the individual can be the same for all individuals, whereas in the latter the requirement that the role offered the individual must be capable of being imbedded in a feasible social state is much more restrictive. With the former type of alternative a common laborer can be asked to assign utilities to alternatives ranging from starvation to great luxury, whereas a state where all common laborers live in great luxury is not a feasible one, and even though it might be possible to introduce some system of lotteries whereby such a state might be achieved by a few of them, for any one individual a state where he has won a substantial lottery prize will play a small part in any reasonably defined field of alternatives. Accordingly, in contrast with the definition of an alternative as a role, definition of an alternative as a complete social state will tend to mean that for the common laborer the field of alternatives consists of social states that provide for him preponderantly low incomes, with a relatively small variation in this income over the field of alternatives, while for, say, a talented writer the range of incomes he could be specified to enjoy in various feasible social states would be much wider.

If the alternatives to be evaluated are to consist of complete feasible social states, and the individual utility functions are to be standardized on some dispersion measure over the field of alternatives, a rather serious difficulty arises in that the weight attached to the preferences of an individual will be inversely related to the dispersion of the possibilities for him among the feasible states, and thus greatest weight is given to the preferences of the undistinguished and least weight to the preferences of those who in one way or another are outstandingly different and capable of being selected for more or less unique roles in the community. This bias may be an essentially democratic one, but I think that there are many who would seriously question any social welfare function that had a strong bias of this character as being a step toward the apotheosis of mediocrity.

Unfortunately, there are also problems involved in avoiding this difficulty by returning to the atomistic approach, once strategic elements are admitted. For strategic considerations will strongly indicate to each individual that his influence on the actual social outcome will be enhanced by his minimizing the contribution of his evaluations of unlikely or nonfeasible alternatives to the variance of his evaluations, thus increasing the variance, after standardization, of their evaluations among the likely alternatives. Even though the number of independent members of the society be large and the number of likely alternatives also large, so as to reduce to a negligible level the prospect of strategic biasing of the evaluations of the likely alternatives, it may be extremely difficult to imagine a situation in which this virtual elimination of the nonfeasible alternatives from the set according to which utilities are to be standardized produces a satisfactory weighting of individual utilities. One saving consideration may be that the mass of the undistinguished might be less likely to possess the perspicacity necessary for this application of strategic considerations; it is not unlikely, however, that demagogues would be found to teach them. Moreover, though the differentiated individuals would be more likely to appreciate the strategic possibilities open to them, the degree to which such strategy would be effective would in general be less, since for them fewer of the alternatives would be nonfeasible.

Economic Choice and Socio-political Choice

The valuations in the above procedures were made, so to speak, by economic man; it is, of course, also possible to consider alternatives in the valuation of which political man and ethical man are to have a voice. To a very large extent the attributes of social states that are of interest to political, ethical, and social man are indivisible or at least interdependent, to an extent that is at least less true of the mere economic wants. One man's desire for freedom to propagate ideas may run directly counter to another's desire for protection against the intrusion of unwelcome thoughts in a manner that is quite a different matter from the competition for the allocation of resources between satisfying the material wants of two or more individuals. In the latter case it is at least conceivable that the two sets of wants might be satisfied simultaneously, either at the expense of third parties, or by postulating an enlargement of the resources available. But in the case of political, social, and moral wants, the conflict is inherent in the nature of the wants themselves, rather than in any limitation of the available resources; the wants are inherently for social states as such, and not merely for the results that may be deemed to flow from a social state for a particular individual. By the same token, the range of realizable states, viewed as complete states, will be the same for all, so that insofar as political, social and moral wants are concerned, there will be much less of a tendency to bias in the calibration of the utility scales than in the case of economic wants. In any actual appraisal, however, political, moral, and social wants as well as economic wants will be involved, so that the problem of calibration bias will remain.

Evaluation and Role Identification

There is another dimension to the nature of the valuation of social states or alternatives by individuals, and that is the degree of egotism on the one hand or of objectivity on the other with which the evaluation is made. At the egotistical extreme, the role which the evaluator is to play in each of the alternative social states is explicitly defined, and the evaluation is of the desirability of this role in the context of the social state. Or the identification of the role of the evaluator may be less precise, i.e., he may consider social states in terms of the role accorded to members of his profession, his class, or to individuals having the same degree of intelligence or skill. On the other hand, he may be able to achieve a more or less complete objectivity and appraise the social state independently of any identification of himself with a role or class in the social state. In this case the evaluator is in effect constructing a social welfare function of a sort. Viewed as a social welfare function this is indeed a dictatorial one in that preferences of others, other than the evaluator, do not enter directly, but only to the extent that the evaluator imputes preferences to the remainder of the population and evaluates the strength of these preferences himself. Since changes in actual or expressed preferences do not enter as arguments into the social welfare function, they do not affect the social choice. Such a function is a dictatorial one whether it is a case of "Big Brother knows best" or a case of "l'état, c'est moi." In fact, any welfare function for which the arguments consist solely of objective data consisting of prices, incomes, institutions, and the like, thus abstracting from the declared preferences of individuals, is ultimately dictatorial in this sense.

A Hierarchy of Social Evaluations

However, the more usual concept of a social welfare function is one in which individual preferences enter as arguments. But if each individual arrogates to himself the privilege of taking the evaluations of others and combining them in his own way into a higher-order evaluation (and why not?) the result is as many social welfare functions as there are individuals. These functions are, however, not dictatorial in the strict sense, or at least need not be, for each individual may well use a method of combination which if consistently applied would require him to overrule his own preferences in certain cases. If these derived welfare functions are clearly distinguished from the original "utility" functions, there is no need to conclude, as Little[11] seems to, that social welfare functions are all ultimately dictatorial.

[11] I. M. D. Little, "Social Choice and Individual Values," *Journal of Political Economy*, 60 (October, 1952), pp. 422–32.

Actually there is no need to stop with one round of such a procedure, which indeed might leave us with so many different social welfare functions that we would not be very much closer to our goal of a unique social welfare function. The initial set of evaluations, into which only objective data and not preferences enter as arguments, may be termed a "zero-level" evaluation, or set of utility functions. In these terms the usual social welfare function would be a "first-level" evaluation into which the "zero-level" evaluations would enter as arguments. If, however, we admit that each individual is to be free to make this first-level evaluation in any reasonable way he chooses, this leaves us with the possibility of as many first-level evaluations as there are individuals willing to undertake the task. These first-level evaluations could then in principle be used as arguments in a second-level evaluation, and so on in a potentially infinite series. Such a series may coverge, in either a finite or an infinite number of stages, to a limit in which the evaluations are all identical: i.e., sooner or later a stage is reached where all evaluations of order higher than n differ at most to an inconsequential extent. If this occurs, we may term this limit the "consensus" and consider it to be "the" social welfare function of the group. If no such limit exists, then it might be said that there is no unique social welfare function for the group.

Such a schema may be considered to be a somewhat elaborate model of what may actually take place, in a sense, in groups such as Quaker meetings, which arrive at decisions only where a consensus or "sense of the meeting" can be arrived at on the basis of discussion and exchange of opinions and ideas. Since, however, inaction is also a decision, and the process of arriving at a consensus necessarily takes time, the procedure has a conservative bias which may be completely frustrating unless the individuals in the group have an underlying respect for the desires and opinions of others. The process is not as interminable as the theoretical possibility of convergence of an infinite sequence might suggest, however: when a stage is reached at which the limit to which the series converges becomes apparent, if not exactly, at least to within an acceptably small margin of error, the remainder of the process can be short-circuited and the result arrived at immediately.

It may be possible to avoid this sequence of evaluations by a kind of simultaneous equations approach in which the same evaluations are simultaneously the results of and also part of the inputs to the evaluation process. That such a construction is probably not logically impossible might be indicated by Von Neumann's assertion of the logical possibility of constructing a machine capable of reproducing itself. As a model to be followed operationally, however, this does not seem to have much promise.

Possible Extremes of Egalitarianism and Anti-egalitarianism

Conceivably, a social welfare function determined along these lines might turn out to be some kind of weighted sum of individual utilities, individual utilities being determined by reference to preferences among risks or by some other criterion. But this is by no means necessary or even likely. Consider again our potential immigrant, and suppose that he has a very strong liking for equality as such. If in one economy everyone has an income of $4,000, and in another 90 percent have an income of $4,500 while the remainder enjoy an income of $10,000, the immigrant might well choose the first community, whereas none of the usual social welfare functions would normally reproduce this result. Such a result can be rationalized in several ways: at one level the "envy effect" of the existence of the $10,000 roles on the utility perceived in the $4,500 roles may reduce the utility of the $4,500 role below that of the $4,000 role in the egalitarian economy, and if the immigrant considers himself excluded, by reason of social origin or capacity, from the $10,000 role this may be sufficient to produce the indicated choice. Or the envy effect may be strong enough to outweigh even the superiority of the $10,000 role over the $4,000 role weighted by the one-tenth of the population that are to enjoy it, and this attitude may persist in spite of all the smacking over the head that Sir Dennis' Archbishop can manage.[12] Such a result could not be rationalized in terms of a utility held to be an increasing function of income independently of the social context, whether with increasing or decreasing marginal utility.

In the opposite direction, it is far from certain that such a potential immigrant would prefer an economy *C* with a uniform income of $5,500 to economy *B*, given complete uncertainty as to role, as would be postulated not only by egalitarians but also by utilitarians who presume a declining marginal utility of money. A desire for variety, excitement, or tangible rewards for achievement may play a part in this. There may also be vicarious satisfaction derived from watching or reading about the ceremonials and antics of an elite, particularly if the nature of these activities is inherently such that they could not be engaged in generally. At this point, of course, the tycoon who passionately guards his privacy would be cheating the public of part of the consideration by which his retention of a disproportionate share of wealth and income is justified. It is even conceivable, though perhaps of negligible likelihood, that *B* would be preferred to an economy *D* in which everyone has an income of $11,000, by reason of the greater variety of relationships and more stimulating atmosphere of *B*. However, at least as long as the question is formulated in purely static terms, many are likely to feel that the more extreme manifestations of such egalitarian or anti-egalitarian attitudes

---

[12] D. H. Robertson, "Utility and All What?" *Economic Journal*, 64 (December, 1954), pp. 665–78.

represent aberrations that can be heavily discounted, if not disregarded entirely, in the formation of social policy.

Social Choice in a Dynamic World

If dynamic considerations are admitted, the social preference will ordinarily be considered to shift substantially in the direction of a greater dispersion of incomes, while at the same time the difficulties of social decision increase. Where direct government intervention in the processes of capital formation is relatively undeveloped, and the cultural milieu is such that the marginal propensity to save rises with increased individual income, concentration of incomes may, up to a point, lead to an increase in aggregate savings and in capital formation. And even where fiscal and monetary policy is developed to the point of being capable of offsetting, by appropriate shifts, any reduction in aggregate savings brought about by equalization of incomes, dispersion of incomes may be considered to contribute to the rate and richness of cultural and technological development by providing an advance market for the new and for the unique.

But as soon as the rate of progress becomes an important criterion, the problem arises of allowing, in a social welfare function, for the impact of alternative social states on the opportunities that will be opened up to generations yet unborn. In any event, the decision will have to be made by the present generation without the benefit of any direct expression of views by the remoter future generations. Unless, indeed, the assertion is made that the infinite future transcends the finite present and that therefore maximum progress at any present cost is to be the goal, the issue transcends economics. But while such an attitude, though never stated in such an extreme form, appears to have been a tacit postulate of much neoclassical economics, for example with Irving Fisher,[13] in more recent times this attitude seems to be much more characteristic of Communist countries than of the West.

The Role of Economics

Thus in many social decision situations it can be seen that even where the question as it originally appears is expressed in economic terms, economics may be unable to proceed very far toward an answer without heavy recourse to ethics, political science, sociology, or even psychology. But this must not be taken as a denial that there are important areas where economics can and should be given substantially

---

[13] Irving and Herbert Fisher, *Constructive Income Taxation* (New York: Harper, 1942).

the last word, as where conflicts of interest either do not arise or can be compensated or otherwise resolved. Even where actual compensation is impossible and the Pareto condition cannot be satisfied, cases do arise where it can be stated with confidence that the gains outweigh the losses on almost any reasonable basis of interpersonal comparison. It simply will not do for the economist to abdicate every time an interpersonal comparison looms on the horizon: if the economist declines to make the comparison, there will be no dearth of others, often with less claim to expertise in the matter, to offer to do so. At the very least, economics must be prepared to collaborate with ethics, political science, sociology, and psychology in a comprehensive approach to social decisions wherever such an approach seems called for. Problems of social choice will not vanish merely because the tools available to handle them are declared to be imperfect. The normative logic of social choice, though it yields by itself no final answers, does provide guidance as to the lines along which answers may fruitfully be sought.

3

·

Counterspeculation, Auctions, and Competitive Sealed Tenders

In his *Economics of Control*, A. P. Lerner threw out an interesting suggestion that where markets are imperfectly competitive, a state agency, through "counter-speculation," might be able to create the conditions whereby the marginal conditions for efficient resource allocation could be maintained. Unfortunately, it was not made clear just how this counterspeculation was to be carried out, and to many this term denotes just one more of the empty boxes that rattle around in the economist's cupboard of ideas. And there appears to have been, in the years since *Economics of Control* first appeared, no attempt to examine critically just what this intriguingly labeled box might in fact contain.

In section 1 this counterspeculation box will be further examined; it turns out that most of the devices that most immediately suggest themselves under this heading prove to be inordinately expensive in terms of their demands on the fiscal resources of the state relative to the net benefits to be realized, at least where the commodity in question is finely divisible. The other extreme case, where there is only a single indivisible item to be allocated, is examined in section 2; in this case the possibilities for reaching an optimum solution in a market with a limited number of participants become considerably brighter: the common or progressive type of auction can be shown to provide better chances for optimal allocation than the regressive or "Dutch" auction. The implications of these findings for the more significant cases where contracts are let or sales made by competitive bids or tenders are examined in section 3; the analysis reveals a likelihood that certain modifications of current practices in these areas, more specifically by making the award price equal to the second highest (or lowest) bid price rather than the highest bid price, might prove generally beneficial in improving the allocation of

Journal of Finance, 16 (1961), pp. 8–37.

resources without being as prejudicial to the interests of sellers (or buyers) as might at first seem to be the case. Section 4 deals with the somewhat more complicated and general class of cases where there are several identical items to be auctioned, and section 5 deals with the application of the concepts derived in section 4 to the sale of a number of identical units under sealed-bid conditions; it turns out that here, too, significant gains can be expected from certain departures from currently prevalent practices.

1   The Exclusive Public Marketing Agency

To simplify the problem, let us consider the simple case of a standardized commodity in which the only imperfection in the market consists of the fact that either buyers or sellers or both are too few in number to ignore the repercussions of their actions on the market price but are either too numerous, too naïve, or too isolated from each other to engage in any overtly or tacitly concerted action. We will also assume that the individual marginal-cost and marginal-value curves of the sellers and buyers are well defined and have moderate positive and negative slopes, respectively. The normal result in such a case is that less than the optimal quantity will be produced and sold, and this will be true even though a "countervailing power" type of balance between buyers and sellers maintains the price at the same level as would result under strictly competitive conditions.

Let us now assume that there is established an exclusive public marketing agency to which all sales of this commodity must be made and from which all supplies of the commodity must be bought. A simple solution to the problem would be available if the public marketing agency could determine with confidence what the equilibrium competitive price would be and could then establish this price for its purchases and sales in such a way that neither buyers nor sellers could expect to have any influence over it. This price would then be a fixed datum to buyers and sellers, and competitive behavior could be expected. This is, indeed, the type of solution that comes most readily to mind on first meeting up with the concept of "counterspeculation."

The trouble with this as a workable solution is that much of the information that the marketing agency would need in determining the competitive equilibrium price would have to come from reports and actions of buyers and sellers, who would have an incentive to understate prospective demands and supplies or to curtail their actual sales and purchases in the hope of inducing the marketing agency to change the price in their favor. In a static situation, a marketing agency might conceivably manage not to be misled by such misinformation and to withstand the blackmail of curtailments in purchases or sales. But in a dynamic situation, where the equilibrium price is continually changing, it would be much more difficult to ascertain the equilibrium price, keep the price at this level, and simultaneously persuade buyers and sellers that future changes in the published price will not be influenced by any tactical deviations on their part. Moreover, if the marketing agency should, under the guise of "stablization" or otherwise, attempt to keep the price fixed over any extended period of time, even slight disequilibria at this price are likely to induce speculation against the pegged price, which, even if it does not succeed in inducing a change in the pegged price, will, unlike speculation over a market-determined price, necessarily of itself involve some misallocation of resources.

What the marketing agency needs, in order to determine the optimum pattern of transactions in its commodity, is an unbiased report of the marginal-cost (= competitive supply) curves of the sellers and of the marginal-value (= competitive demand) curves of the purchasers, or at least of the portions of these curves covering a range of prices that will be sure to contain the equilibrium price. The problem is then for the marketing agency to behave in such a way as to motivate the buyers and sellers to furnish such unbiased reports. One method, though an expensive one, is to arrange to purchase the commodity from suppliers and to sell it to purchasers on terms that are dependent on the reported supply and demand curves in such a way that the suppliers and purchasers will maximize their profits, individually at least, by reporting correctly, so that any misrepresentation will subject them to risk of loss (or at least offer no prospect of gain).

For example, the marketing agency might ask for the reporting of the individual demand and supply curves on the understanding that the subsequent transactions are to be determined as follows: The agency would first aggregate the reported supply and demand curves to determine the equilibrium marginal value, and apply this value to the individual demand and supply curves to determine the amounts to be supplied and purchased by the various individual buyers and sellers. The amount to be paid seller S_i would, however, somewhat exceed the amount calculated by applying this marginal value to his amount supplied; in effect for the rth unit supplied, S_i would be paid an amount equal to the equilibrium price that would have resulted if S_i had restricted his supply to r units, all other purchasers and sellers behaving competitively. In terms of figure 3.1, D_n is the aggregate demand curve, S_n is the total supply curve, and the intersection at E indicates the equilibrium marginal value; S_{n-i} is the aggregate supply curve of the sellers other than S_i, and its intersection with the horizontal line PE at G indicates the amount GE to be supplied by i; the amount to be paid to i for this supply is indicated by the area $EFGMQ$, between the total demand curve D_n, the supply curve of the competitors S_{n-i}, and the quantity axis. Payments to other suppliers would be determined similarly, each supplier being considered in turn as the "last" supplier, giving rise to a total payment to suppliers that can be represented by the area $0QEFGF'G'F''G'' \ldots P0$.

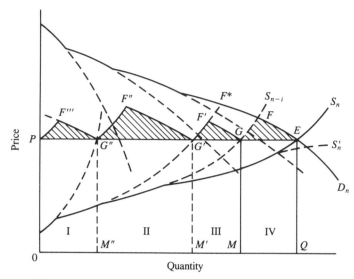

Figure 3.1 Counterspeculative Payments to Suppliers

Given this method of determining payment, no individual supplier would have any direct incentive to misrepresent his supply schedule. If he misrepresents his true supply curve in a way that makes the total supply curve go through the correct point E, this will cause no change in the amount he is called upon to supply or to his own receipts, though it is likely to affect the receipts of (but not the demands on) other suppliers. On the other hand, if a misrepresentation is made that causes the aggregate supply curve to miss the point E – say, by falling below it as in the curve S'_n – this will entail his being called upon to supply additional units for which the marginal revenue received by this supplier will be less than the marginal cost to him of producing this increment of output, so that, on balance, he will be worse off. Conversely, for errors that would push the supply curve above the correct equilibrium point E, the amount that will be ordered from him will be reduced, but the amount paid for his supply will be cut by more than the marginal-cost savings to him, and again he would be worse off, on balance.

An exactly symmetrical method could simultaneously be adopted for dealing with the demand side of the market: purchasers would receive the indicated equilibrium amounts of the commodity but would pay a price represented by the area $EKLNQ$ in figure 3.2, determined by the aggregate supply curve S_n and the demand curve D_{n-j} of the purchasers other than j. Again the individual purchasers would have no direct incentive for misrepresenting their demand schedule and would have a positive incentive for insuring that at the equilibrium value their demand would be correctly reported.

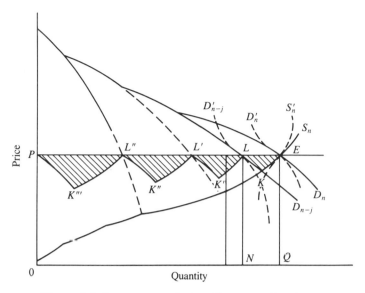

Figure 3.2 Counterspeculative Charges to Purchasers

Since, in advance of filing their supply or demand schedules, suppliers and purchasers will in general be somewhat uncertain of the exact level of the eventual equilibrium price, incentives to report correctly at the equilibrium price actually cover a considerable range about this equilibrium price. On the other hand, if traders have a fairly confidently held expectation that the equilibrium price will fall within a certain narrow range, there may be an indirect community of interest in shading the reported demand and supply curves outside this range in the direction of greater inelasticity, as indicated by the dotted curves S'_{n-i}, S'_n, D'_{n-j}, D'_n. Such shading for prices above the equilibrium value would result in higher payments to other suppliers, and below the equilibrium value would result in lower charges to other purchasers; no supplier or purchaser would benefit directly from his own misrepresentation, however, and optimum allocation would still be preserved.

The basic drawback to this scheme is, of course, that the marketing agency will be required to make payments to suppliers in an amount that exceeds, in the aggregate, the receipts from purchasers by the sum of the shaded areas in the two diagrams. The average price paid to suppliers will exceed the competitive equilibrium price OP, and the average price received from purchasers will be less than OP. This solution would indeed permit optimum allocation of resources to be achieved if there were a source of public funds that was without adverse influence on resource allocation in other directions. Even if such an ideal revenue source existed, such a scheme would still be open to criticism as discriminating in favor of larger units, since they would be obtaining a higher average price as producers and a lower average price as purchasers than would their smaller competitors. In figure 3.1, for example, supplier *II* gets the amount $M''G''F''G'M'$ for his supply of $M''M'$, whereas supplier *III* gets $M'G'F'GM$ for a supply of $M'M$. Moreover, there remains under the scheme a positive incentive for firms to merge into larger units for the sake of obtaining more favorable treatment. Thus in figure 3.1, if suppliers *III* and *IV* were to merge, they would automatically become entitled to an additional payment indicated by the quadrilateral area $F'F^*FG$. Considering the fact that public funds are obtainable only at a significant cost in terms of overhead expenses of collection as well as of misallocation of resources at other points, it is highly doubtful whether the carrying out of such a scheme in full could ever be justified.

It is tempting to try to modify this scheme in various ways that would reduce or eliminate this cost of operation while still preserving the tendency to optimum allocation of resources. However, it seems that all modifications that do diminish the cost of the scheme either imply the use of some external information as to the true equilibrium price or reintroduce a direct incentive for misrepresentation of the marginal-cost or marginal-value curves. To be sure, in some cases the impairment of optimum allocation would be small relative to the reduction in cost, but, unfortunately, the analysis of such variations is extremely difficult; considering the slight likelihood that any such scheme would be put into practice, further analysis will here be concentrated on situations more closely realized in practice.

2   Simple Auctions

Where the resource to be allocated comes in a small number of discrete indivisible units rather than consisting of a fungible commodity, the chances of insuring an optimum allocation of resources are considerably improved, since here there will be in general a certain range of prices, all leading to the same optimal allocation of the resources being traded, though, of course, to somewhat different distributions of income among the parties to the trade. The simplest case is one in which there is a *single unique indivisible object* to be sold to one of a number of potential purchasers. The purchaser and the price may be determined by any of a number of auctioning or bidding procedures, and the results will in general be significantly different according to the procedure adopted.

The simplest procedure to analyze is that of the ordinary or progressive auction, in which bids are freely made and announced until no purchaser wishes to make any further higher bid. The normal result (among rational bidders!) is that the bidding will stop at a level approximately equal to the second highest value among the values that the purchasers place on the item, since at that point there will be only one interested bidder left; the object will then be purchased at that price by the bidder to whom it has the highest value. (For simplicity, we shall assume that price can vary continuously and that there is no minimum increment between bids.) This result is obviously Pareto-optimal.

It is interesting to contrast this with the so-called "Dutch auction," in which the auctioneer announces prices in descending sequence, the first and only bid being the one that concludes the transaction. A mechanized form of this procedure is actually used in wholesale flower marketing in the Netherlands and has proved very economical of time and effort. In the analysis of this form of auction, however, we find that we are faced with what is essentially a "game" in the technical sense. Each bidder, in attempting to determine at what point he should be prepared to make a bid so as to obtain the greatest expectation of gain, will need to take into account whatever information he has concerning the probable bids that might be made by others, and the bids made by others will in turn depend on their expectations concerning the behavior of the first bidder. To put in a bid as soon as the price has come down to the full value of the object to the bidder maximizes the probability of obtaining the object, but guarantees that the gain from securing it will be zero; as the announced price is progressively lowered, the possibility of a gain emerges, but as the gain thus sought increases with the lowering of the point at which a bid is to be made, the probability of securing this gain diminishes. Each bidder must thus attempt to balance these two factors in terms of whatever knowledge he has concerning the probable bids of the others.

The Dutch auction game   To make this problem tractable, we shall suppose that the knowledge that each bidder has about the motives and probable behavior of the others can be derived from a set of probability distributions from which the value of the object to each of the bidders is conceived to be drawn. For simplicity, we shall assume that all bidders have the same conception of the probability distribution from which any given player is deemed to derive the value he places on the object; the given player, of course, knows the actual value he places on the object but is assumed also to know the distribution from which others consider his value to be drawn. These distributions need not be the same for all bidders, i.e., some may be considered to be more likely to place a high value on the object than others.

The situation can be considered analogous to a formal parlor game in which each player actually does draw a value at random from his own individual probability distribution of values (e.g., by drawing a card at random from a deck having a composition known to all the players), and then, knowing that value, but without directly revealing it to others, and knowing the probability distributions from which the other players are respectively drawing their values, but not knowing any of the values actually drawn, each player makes a bid without knowing the bids made by any of the other players; after all bids have been made, they are compared, and the player with the highest bid wins an amount equal to the excess of his value over his bid, the remaining players winning nothing. In the case of tie bids we can assume the tie to be broken by a random drawing giving each tied player the same probability of winning. Given a specific set of underlying probability distributions, the problem is then to determine how each bidder should determine his bid in order to maximize his gains. Unfortunately, the general theory of games gives an embarrassingly rich set of answers.

However, if we rule out such elements as collusion among bidders, side payments, communication, or signaling, the solution most appropriate to the situation being studied seems to be the noncooperative equilibrium point analyzed by Nash.[1] This equilibrium point is defined in this case as a set of functions $x_i(v_i)$, one such function for each player, relating the bid x_i to be made to the value v_i that he draws from his list, such that if any one player is able to determine (e.g., from observation over a sufficiently large number of plays of the game, or repetitions of analogous situations, or a study of an analysis such as this one!) just what functions are being used by the other players, or at least the resulting probability distribution of bids for each of the other players, which is all that concerns him directly, and considers these distributions to be fixed, at least for the time being, he can nevertheless find no way of changing his own function $x_i(v_i)$ in such a way as to increase his expected gain.

Unfortunately, while it can be shown that at least one such equilibrium point exists in each case and that we are not hunting a will-o'-the-wisp, the analytical determination of such equilibrium points involves extremely difficult mathematics in all but the simplest cases. However, some instructive hints can be derived from the examination of the more tractable cases.

The homogeneous rectangular case   One simple case is that in which all of the individual values are drawn from the same rectangular distribution, which, by suitable choice of scale and origin, we can make the interval (0, 1). Also we shall assume a linear utility function over the range of gains involved, so that we can speak in terms of maximizing expected money gains rather than having to allow for any "risk aversion" or "risk preference" that might be represented by a nonlinear utility function. In this case the unique equilibrium strategy is for each player to determine his bid according to the relation

$$b_i = \frac{N-1}{N} v_i ,$$

---

[1] See, e.g., Luce and Raiffa, *Games and Decisions* (New York: Wiley, 1957), pp. 170–3.

where N is the number of bidders. It is fairly easy to see that if all players behave in this way, no one player can gain by deviating from this pattern. It will be shown later, as part of the solution of a more general case, that this equilibrium point is indeed unique. If players conform to this norm, the highest bid will always be made by the player drawing the highest value for the object, so that the result will be Pareto-optimal (the seller being included, of course, among those to be preserved against loss in any proposed reallocation that would contradict this optimality).

It can also be shown (see appendix I), that the two methods of auctioning produce, in this case, the same average expected price and hence the same average expected gains to the buyers and sellers, respectively. However, the variance of the price is greater under the common or progressive type of auction than with the Dutch auction by a factor of $2N/(N - 1)$ while the variance of the gain to the buyer is greater by a factor of N^2. If we introduce an element of risk aversion for purposes of evaluating these results (but not for deriving the results!), the Dutch auction thus proves slightly superior by reason of the smaller dispersion of the gains to each of the parties.

Nonhomogeneous cases   If the assumption of homogeneity among the bidders be abandoned, the mathematics of a complete treatment become intractable. It is fairly easy to show, however, that while the progressive auction still produces the Pareto-optimal allocation of the object, the Dutch auction will not, in general. Consider, for example, the case where there are two bidders, one drawing from a distribution rectangular between 0 and 1, the other drawing from a rectangular distribution ranging from a to b (see appendix II). If $a \neq 0$, the essential asymmetry of the positions of the two players prevents their reacting similarly to similar value drawings, and the object may go to the bidder for whom it has the lower value.

An attempt at a complete solution for the above case runs into difficulties. In order to have at least one complete analysis of a nonhomogeneous case, we can further simplify by supposing that the value to be drawn by the second bidder is fixed at a, rather than varying over a range from a to b. In this case we must allow the second bidder to use a mixed or randomized strategy, so as to distribute his bids over a range, even though he has only a fixed value, since if he were always to bid the same amount c, then bidder 1 would tend to just outbid him whenever v_1 is greater than c, giving bidder 2 in turn an incentive to change his fixed bid, and no equilibrium would be possible. On the other hand for a bidder such as 1, whose values are drawn from a continuous distribution of positive range, there is no need for any randomization, and the bids can be determined as a single-valued function of the value drawn.

The analysis of this case is taken up in detail in appendix III. The equilibrium strategies are illustrated in figure 3.3, which gives the results for $a = 0.8$. The

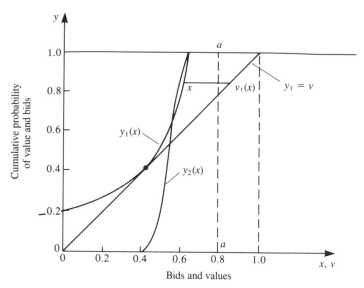

Figure 3.3 Equilibrium Strategies for the Asymmetrical Case with $a = 0.8$

bidder with the fixed value a will have to distribute his bids over the range from $a/2$ to $a - \frac{1}{4}a^2$ according to the cumulative frequency distribution $y_2(x)$, y_2 being the probability of a bid of less than x by player 2, where

$$y_2\,(x) \;=\; \frac{a\,(2-a)}{2\,(2x-a)}\; e^{[2/(2-a)-a/(2x-a)]}\,.$$

The bidder with the variable value makes a bid x depending on the value v_1 that he draws given by

$$x \;=\; a\left(1 - \frac{a}{4v}\right)$$

the curve $y_1(x)$ in figure 3.3 shows the cumulative probability of the various bids x, and the value corresponding to any given bid is obtained by looking for the point on the line $y_1 = v$ where the cumulative probability of the value corresponds to the cumulative probability of the given bid. If a value is drawn of less than $\frac{1}{2}a$, there is no possibility of gain for bidder 1, since bidder 2 always bids at least this amount; in this event bidder 1 may make bids falling anywhere within the shaded area without upsetting the equilibrium.

The difference between the mean results for the Dutch auction and the common progressive auction procedure in situations of this type varies according to where the second bidder's fixed value a lies in relation to the range of values

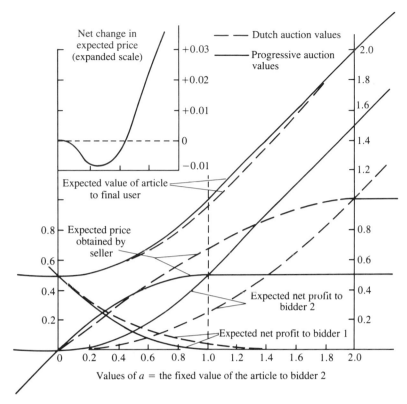

Figure 3.4 Comparison of Average Expected Results of the Dutch Auction
with those of the Progressive Auction in an Asymmetrical Case

over which the randomly assigned value of the first bidder may vary. In the
common auction, for values of v_1 greater than a, bidder 1 gets the article at a price
of a, while for a v_1 less than a, bidder 2 gets the article at a price of v_1. The average
price is thus $a - \tfrac{1}{2}a^2$. With the Dutch auction the average realized price turns out
to be greater than this for a greater than about 0.43, and less for values below
about 0.43. Figure 3.4 gives a general picture of how the average expected values
for the price, the net gain to the two bidders, and the total gain differ for the two
methods of various values of a.

To extrapolate rather boldly from these instances, one can perhaps hazard the
guess that where the bidders are fairly homogeneous and sophisticated, the Dutch
auction may produce results that are reasonably close to the Pareto-optimal, but
where there is much variation in the state of information or the generally expected
intensity of desire of the various players for the object, or where the bidders are
insufficiently sophisticated to discern the equilibrium point strategy or for some
other reason fail to use this strategy, then the Dutch auction is likely to prove

relatively inefficient from the point of view of securing an optimum allocation. In the symmetrical case, the Dutch auction produces the same average price and the same average gain, but with a smaller dispersion of the gains to the bidders and of the realized price.

3 Sale or Purchase of a Single Lot by Sealed Bids

A considerably greater degree of importance attaches, not to auctions as such, but to cases in which a contract is to be let on the basis of competitive sealed tenders. This may be a construction contract or the sale of a parcel of property or the underwriting of a security issue. Actually, the usual practice of calling for the tender of bids on the understanding that the highest or lowest bid, as the case may be, will be accepted and executed in accordance with its own terms is isomorphic with the Dutch auction just discussed. The motivations, strategies, and results of such a procedure can be analyzed in exactly the same way as was done above with the Dutch auction.

Since it has been shown that the Dutch auction has certain characteristics in some circumstances that may be considered disadvantageous as compared with the more certainly Pareto-optimal results of the progressive auction, it is of interest to inquire whether there is not some sealed-bid procedure that would be logically isomorphic to the progressive auction. It is easily shown that the required procedure is to ask for bids on the understanding that the award will be made to the highest bidder, but on the basis of the price set by the second-highest bidder. If this procedure is carried out, then the optimal strategy for each bidder (assuming, as is indeed necessary in the analysis of the progressive auction itself, the absence of collusion among bidders) will obviously be to make this bid equal to the full value of the article or contract to himself, i.e., to the highest amount he could afford to pay without incurring a net loss or to that price at which he would be on the margin of indifference as to whether he obtains the article or not. Bidding less than this full value could then only diminish his chances of winning at what would have been a profitable, or at least not unprofitable price and could not, collusion aside, affect the price he would actually pay if he were the successful bidder. Bidding more than the full value, on the other hand, would increase his chances of winning, but only under circumstances that would involve him in an unprofitable transaction, the price to be paid being greater than his value.

Judging from the preceding analysis of the Dutch auction paradigm, there would in many, if not most, cases be a considerable advantage to all concerned in shifting to this "second-price" method of handling sealed bids. In cases in which, by reason of asymmetry among the bidders, errors in evaluation, or mistakes in strategy, the result with the "top-price" method is nonoptimal, a change to the "second-price" method will yield an increase in the aggregate profits to be shared among seller and buyers. The fact that in the symmetrical case when the correct equilibrium strategy is employed there is no change in the average realized price would tend to indicate that when there is a gain through a change from a nonoptimal to an optimal one, the gain would, on the average, be shared between buyers and sellers. On the other hand, the study of the asymmetrical case indicates that there are some extremes where the Pareto-optimal progressive auction or second-price methods result in a lower average expected price to the seller than the nonoptimal Dutch auction or top-price method, and other extremes where they result in a lower average expected gain to the buyers. On the whole, however, in a reasonably active market it seems likely that it would be quite rare for the asymmetry among the buyers to be so substantial and so apparent that one could say a priori that one party or the other would tend to lose from the shift. In the large majority of cases one could be fairly sure of at least some overall gain from the shift (one can be certain of no overall loss), with a fairly strong expectation that this overall gain would be shared by both buyers and sellers in the long run.

In addition to the gain from the improved allocation of resources, there is another possible gain that is not covered in the above analysis, which abstracts from the costs involved in the negotiations. In the top-price method of negotiation, as in the Dutch auction, bidders, in order to maximize their expectation of profit, must concern themselves not only with their own appraisal of the article but also with their estimate of the value that others will place on it and their expectation of the bidding strategy that others will follow. This involves a considerable amount of appraisal of the market situation as a whole, in addition to an appraisal of what the article is worth to the particular bidder himself. Where the bidders are wholesalers who are purchasing the article or lot for retailing in a retail market shared by all the bidders, there may be no great difference between appraising the article for one's self and estimating what others will value the article at. But especially where the various bidders want the article for different purposes or where the article will be retailed in different areas or by different methods by different bidders, the general appraisal of the market does involve substantial additional information-gathering activity. Moreover, failure to perform this general appraisal with reasonable uniformity is likely to increase the chances that the optimum allocation will not be achieved. It is one of the salient advantages of the second-price method that it makes any such general market appraisal entirely superfluous, whether considered from the standpoint of individual gain or from that of the overall allocation of resources. Each bidder can confine his efforts and attention to an appraisal of the value the article would have in his own hands, at a considerable saving in mental strain and possibly in out-of-pocket expense. In the first instance this saving might redound largely to the benefit of the bidders; as a corollary, however, more bidders might be induced to put in bids, resulting in a better allocation of resources and a higher price for the seller.

The second-price method may not be automatically self-policing to quite the same extent as the top-price method, but there should be no real difficulty. It would be necessary to show the second-best bid to the successful top bidder so that he would be able to assure himself that the price he is being asked to pay is based upon a bona fide bid. To prevent the use of a "shill" to jack the price up by putting in a late bid just under the top bid, it would probably be desirable to have all bids delivered to and certified by a trustworthy holder, who would then deliver all bids simultaneously to the seller. Under these circumstances, the seller would have no incentive to do other than sell to the top bidder, showing him as his price the second-best bid. Where the seller is a governmental body or a large corporation, so that the agent handling the sale might not be adequately motivated to serve the interests of his principal, it would be desirable to publish the final terms of sale; if this is done, any bidder whose bid has been improperly overlooked would at least be on notice of this, though, unless he was actually the top bidder, he would have only an indirect interest in lodging a protest. If he were uncertain as to the amount of the bid put in by the successful bidder, his protest would be motivated by a hope of being top bidder, so that there would be some advantage at this point of not announcing the top bid, but only the effective price. Even this would not prevent the top bidder and the agent from showing the top bid to the second bidder, together with a quieting douceur, so as to be able to set the price at the third highest bid. If corruption of this order cannot be prevented, then this would constitute a serious disadvantage of the second-price method.

If selling at the second bid price is better than selling at the top price, one is tempted to ask, as a matter of completeness, would not selling at the third bid price be even better? The answer is no, as might be expected from the fact that the second-price method is Pareto-optimal, and there is no further gain to be had from improvement in the allocation of resources. In the game paradigm, the equilibrium strategy for the third bid price game will be to make a bid somewhat higher than the value drawn, since the danger of a Pyrrhic victory in which the price to be paid exceeds the value is offset by the increased probability of gains in cases where the second bid exceeds this value but the third bid falls below it. The optimum strategy depends on the strategy of others, and the need for more information and the possibility of nonoptimal allocation are reintroduced.

On the other hand the Dutch auction scheme is capable of being modified with advantage to a second bid price basis, making it logically equivalent to the second price sealed-bid procedure suggested above on page 66. As presently practiced, speed is achieved by having a motor-driven pointer or register started downward from a prohibitively high price by the auctioneer; each bidder may at any time press a button which will, if no other button has been pushed before, stop the register, thus indicating the price, flash a signal indicating the identity of the successful bidder, and disconnect all other buttons, preventing any further signals from being activated. There would be no particular difficulty in modifying the apparatus so that the first button pushed would merely preselect the signal to be flashed, but there would be no overt indication until the second button is pushed, whereupon the register would stop, indicating the price, and the signal would flash, indicating the purchaser. This would involve some increased difficulty in learning to control the timing of the button-pushing so as to indicate a desired bid, particularly if, in order to save time, the price register or indicator is made to move fairly rapidly. An even more rapid procedure could be developed, with relatively little increase in the apparatus required, if each bidder were provided with a set of dials or switches which could be set to any desired bid, with the electronic or relay apparatus arranged to search out the two top bids and indicate the person making the top bid and the amount of the second bid.

4 Multiple Auctions

Another intersting case occurs where there is more than one identical object to be sold, but each bidder has use for at most one. Here there are two variations on the progressive type of auction: simultaneous and successive. In simultaneous auctioning the m items can be put up simultaneously, and each bidder permitted to raise his bid even when this does not make his bid the highest. When a point is reached such that no bidder wishes to raise his bid further, the items are awarded to the m highest bidders. If we assume the bid increment to be negligibly small, the results will be that the bidding will stop at a price equal to the $(m + 1)$st highest value among those placed on the articles by the bidders, this being the bid of each of the bidders placing a higher value on the item – assuming that the $(m + 1)$st bidder doesn't bother to make a profitless bid. Bidders with the top m values thus secure the article at a uniform price equal to the $(m + 1)$st value; the result is again Pareto-optimal.

This method is applicable, however, only if the items are actually identical so that there is no problem of deciding who gets first choice and no variation in the value imputed to the various items by a given bidder. In part because of the possibility that there may be minor variations in quality among the items, the more frequent procedure in such cases is for the items to be auctioned off successively, one at a time. With this procedure, an element of speculation or strategy is present during the auctioning of all but the last item, as each bidder must consider whether he should push the bidding up higher on the current item or sign off in the hope that a subsequent item will become available at a lower price. This situation has characteristics similar to that of the Dutch auction.

Consider the game paradigm of the case where there are two items to be auctioned off among N similar bidders, their similarity being represented by each bidder drawing the respective value that any of the items is to have for him, if he secures one, from a distribution that is common to all the bidders. To exclude the complicating element of information that might be inferred from the way the bidding in the auction of the first item develops, it will be assumed that the first auction at least is by sealed bids, price being determined by the second highest bid. The problem is for each bidder i to determine the bid b_i to be made for this first item, as a function of the value v_i that he has drawn. By virtue of the symmetry among bidders, we can assume that this function $b_i(v_i) = x(v)$ is the same for all bidders.

Suppose this function $x(v)$ to have been established and that a bidder, having drawn a value v, is contemplating a deviation from this normal rule by raising his bid from $x(v)$ to $x(v) + dx$. Such a change will affect the outcome only in those cases where this causes the bidder in question to obtain the first item, whereas he would have failed to do so in the absence of this deviation; that is, the deviation will be consequential only where the highest of the other bids lies between $x(v)$ and $x(v) + dx$. The consequence, if any, will be that the increased bid secures the first item at a price between $x(v)$ and $x(v) + dx$, instead of the bidder being almost certain to be the top bidder for the second item auctioned, given that the values v_i will rank in the same order as the normal bids $x(v_i)$ made for the first item, and disregarding the vanishingly small relative probability that two other bids would fall in the range from $x(v)$ to $x(v) + dx$.

The price that would have been paid for the second item is the highest of the $N - 2$ values drawn at random from the common distribution by the $N - 2$ unsuccessful bidders in the second auction; for the case of a rectangular distribution over the interval from 0 to 1, this price has an expected value of $[(N - 2)/(N - 1)]v$ since, if the increment of bid dx being considered causes any change in the outcome at all, none of these unsuccessful bidders can have drawn a value greater than the value v drawn by the deliberating bidder. The bid for the first item must then be at least equal to $[(N - 2)/(N - 1)]v$, or there would be an expected gain from increasing the bid; a similar argument shows that it cannot be greater without creating an incentive to lower the bid.

The equilibrium situation then is that each bidder puts in a bid of

$$b_i = \frac{N - 2}{N - 1} v_i$$

for the first article, or alternatively, in the more usual form of bidding, competes in the bidding up to this level but no further. The second highest value among the

N values drawn will average $(N - 1)/(N + 1)$, and the second highest bid, which determines the price of the first item, will then have an average expectation of $(N - 2)/(N + 1)$. This is also the average expected price for the second item, which is, indeed, the average expected price when the two items are auctioned simultaneously as described above. But, as with the Dutch auction of a single item, there is in the successive auction a slightly different dispersion of the prices. There is, also, a tendency in nonsymmetrical cases for the results to be other than Pareto-optimal. Unfortunately, even the simplest of the nonsymmetrical successive auction cases would involve at least three bidders, and the complications of a complete analysis appear too formidable to go into here.

5 Multiple Sales by Sealed Bids

A type of transaction that is of considerable practical interest is that of the sale of a number of identical items, say an issue of bonds, on the basis of sealed bids. The more usual practice is to accept a certain number of bids starting from those offering the highest price, the effective price for each transaction being the price of the individual bid. An alternative method is to set the effective price at the level of the last bid accepted and permit all successful bidders to benefit from this same uniform price. The usual rationale for this procedure is one of avoiding discrimination in the final price among the various buyers, even though the differential would be based on the bid submitted. The present analysis indicates that this method has the more material advantage of reducing the probability that a bidder's own bid will affect the price he receives, thus inducing bids closer to the full value to the bidder, improving the chances of obtaining or approaching the optimum allocation of resources, and reducing effort and expense devoted to socially superfluous investigation of the general market situation.

To obtain these advantages in full, however, it is necessary to go one step further than is usually done and make the uniform price to be charged to the successful bidders equal to the first bid rejected rather than the last bid accepted; only in this way is it possible to insure that each bidder will be motivated to put in a bid at the full value of the article to himself, thus assuring an optimum allocation of resources, at least for the case where the number of items to be offered is absolutely fixed, and avoiding any incentive for wasteful individual expenditure on general market research. Again it appears that, in spite of what appears to be at first glance the establishment of a needlessly low price, this "first rejected bid" pricing can be expected in the long run to yield just as high an average price as the "greedier" method.

It is important to realize, however, that this result applies only to cases where each bidder is interested in at most a single unit, and there is no collusion among the bidders. As soon as we consider the more general case where an individual bidder may be interested in securing two or more of the units, while the number of bidders is still too few to produce a fully competitive market, the possibility of so arranging things that the Pareto-optimal result is achieved without impairing the expectations of the seller disappears. It is not possible to consider a buyer wanting up to two units as merely an aggregation of two single-unit buyers: combining the two buyers into one introduces a built-in collusion and community of interest, and the bid offered for the second-unit will be influenced by the possible effect of this bid on the price to be paid for the first, even under the first rejected bid method. Where individual bidders may buy more than one indivisible unit, we are, in effect, back in a variant of the exclusive marketing-agency case, where the interests of the marketing agency are merged with those of a single monopolistic seller. In such a case, while the marketing agency need have no concern for the amounts above the competitive equilibrium price which the Pareto-optimal marketing scheme of pages 57–9 would require to be paid to itself as seller, it would be concerned for the amounts by which the revenues from the purchasers would fall short of the competitive equilibrium price, or at least the amount by which these receipts fall short of the possibly somewhat smaller revenues which could in fact be secured on the basis of any other method of approximating the efficient allocation under imperfectly competitive conditions. Nor could optimal results be obtained merely by restricting all bids to an offer to take up to a given quantity at any price below a specified price, the final terms being a price equal to the price bid by the first unsuccessful bidder, each bidder bidding more than this being allotted the amount which he specified. Under such a scheme, for any quantity that a bidder might decide to specify, it would be advantageous for him to specify as his bid price the full *average* value of this quantity to him, since he would prefer this quantity to be allotted at any price lower than this bid rather than be excluded altogether, and a change in his bid price within the range in which he would be successful would not affect the contract price. If a particular bidder is sure that changing the *quantity* he specifies will not affect the contract price, as would be the case if the change is small enough so as not to change the identity of the first unsuccessful bidder and, if his demand curve is linear over the relevant range, his quantity specifications would tend to equal the quantity he would demand at the mean of the prices that he expects to result. To the extent that he is mistaken as to the ultimate price, misallocation will result. Even more serious, the resulting bids do not provide in themselves the information necessary to enable the marketing agency to determine the Pareto-optimal result.

6 Summary

The problem of securing Pareto-optimal results in imperfect markets is thus a moderately difficult one. In the special class of cases where it is known that each purchaser will want a specified quantity or none at all (in particular, where the entire lot or contract must be taken up by a single bidder or where each bidder wants either one unit or none at all) and the total amount to be sold is fixed in advance, it is possible, by establishing in advance that the price is to be determined by the first rejected bid, to achieve the Pareto-optimal result. Moreover, in spite of this method appearing to accord a lower price than necessary after the bids are in, the higher level of bids induced by this method results, on balance, in a price averaging-out at the same level as would be obtained under Dutch auction, individual bid pricing, or last accepted bid pricing methods, at least for cases where the bidders are symmetrical with respect to the a priori information which each one has about the probability distribution of the values or bids of the others. In such cases there is a rather strong presumption that a switch from other methods of negotiation to a first rejected bid pricing method would be to the long-run advantage of all concerned, the gain being derived from the greater certainty of obtaining a Pareto-optimal result and from the reduction in nonproductive expenditure devoted to the sizing-up of the market by the bidders. To be sure, these conclusions are based on a model in which a high degree of rationality and sophistication is imputed to the bidders; nevertheless, in many markets the frequency of the dealings and the professional characteristics of the dealers are such as to make such an assumption not too far from reality; moreover, the change to the first rejected price method would substantially diminish the amount of sophistication required to achieve the optimum result.

Where there is a significant asymmetry in the a priori positions of the bidders, this conclusion must be somewhat modified: the one complete analysis of an asymmetrical case shows that in some cases the change to the first rejected bid method may be to the advantage of the seller but that in other cases it may be substantially to his disadvantage. To extrapolate rather rashly from a single example, one may hazard the generalization that, in the change to the first rejected bid or progressive method, bidders who have relatively greater knowledge of the probable behavior of other bidders, either through greater astuteness, more intensive research, or simply through their own position being inherently less patent than that of other bidders – as is exemplified in the example given by bidder 1 having a value drawn from a distribution over the interval $(0,1)$, and knowing the fixed value the article has for bidder 2, whereas bidder 2 is in relative ignorance concerning the value drawn by bidder 1 – will tend to lose the advantage which their superior information gives them in the less determinate situation, whereas the less informed bidders tend to gain, sometimes rather substantially, as their lack of information becomes irrelevant to their behavior in the situation where all they are called upon to do is to make a bid equal to their full value. In situations where the relatively uninformed bidders are the ones more likely to be the successful bidders, the seller can expect to lose, whereas if the informed bidders are the ones more likely to become purchasers, the seller stands to gain from the change. The total gain from the change will always be positive, however.

When it comes to markets where the amounts which each trader might buy or sell are not predetermined but are to be determined by the negotiating procedure along with the amount to be paid, the prospects for achieving an optimum allocation of resources become much dimmer. A theoretical method exists, to be sure, which involves essentially paying each seller for his supply an amount equal to what he could extract as a perfectly discriminating monopolist faced with a demand curve constructed by subtracting the total supply of his competing suppliers from the total demand, and symmetrically for purchasers. But whether this method is thought of in terms of an exclusive state marketing agency operating as an intermediary between suppliers and sellers or in terms of sales or purchases by a government agency on its own account, the method is far too expensive in terms of the inflow of public funds that would be required, in a context where perfectly efficient sources of additional public revenues do not exist. Indeed, if speculation in the usual sense is trading motivated by the prospect of profit, it would hardly be expected that "counterspeculation," motivated by substantially contrary objectives, could be anything but a losing proposition. It may be that further analysis might reveal methods of dealing with imperfect markets that would produce a substantial improvement in the allocation of resources without incurring prohibitive costs, but the analysis of the relatively simple cases discussed here has already shown itself fairly intricate, so that the matter must be left here for the time being.

APPENDIX I: Analysis of the Homogeneous Rectangular Single-prize Bidding Game

Given N players, designated by $i = 1,2,3, \ldots, N$, each drawing a value v_i from a rectangular distribution ranging from 0 to 1, and bidding for a single prize, the probability that the first $N - 1$ players all draw values between 0 and v while the Nth player draws a value between v and $v + dv$ is $v^{N-1}dv$; allowing for the possibility that any of the N players might have the top value, the probability that the highest value drawn lies between v and $v + dv$ is then given by the expression $dP_1(v) = N v^{N-1} dv$. In this event the price, assuming that each player puts in a bid $b_i = [(N - 1)/N] v_i$, will be $p_d = [(N - 1)/N] v$, and thus the expected price is

$$\bar{p}_d = \int p \, dP_1 (v) = \int_0^1 \left(\frac{N - 1}{N}\right) v \, N \, v^{N-1} d \, v = \frac{N - 1}{N + 1},$$

corresponding to an expected highest value drawn of $N/(N + 1)$. This result can be compared with the results under progressive or "common" auctioning, where the price is equal to the second highest value drawn. The probability that this second highest value lies between v and $v + dv$ is then given by the expression $dP_2(v) = N(N - 1) v^{N-2}(1 - v) \, dv$, so that the average price is

$$\bar{p}_c = \int v \, dP_2 (v) = \int_0^1 N \, (N - 1) \, (v^{N-1} - v^N) \, d \, v$$

$$= (N - 1) - \frac{N \, (N - 1)}{N + 1} = \frac{N - 1}{N + 1},$$

which is the same as for the Dutch auction. The bidders' surplus again has the expected value of $1/(N + 1)$, and the expected value of the object in the hands of the successful bidder is again the same, $N/(N + 1)$. Thus in terms of average expected outcomes, the two methods of auctioning are equivalent.

The probability distributions of the gains realized by the buyers and sellers, however, are quite different under the two methods of auctioning. The variance of the price under the Dutch auctioning method is

$$\sigma_{pd}^2 = \int (p_d - \bar{p}_d)^2 dP_1 (v)$$

$$= \int_0^1 \left(\frac{N - 1}{N} v - \frac{N - 1}{N + 1}\right)^2 N \, v^{N-1} d \, v = \frac{(N - 1)^2}{N \, (N + 1)^2 \, (N + 2)}.$$

Under the progressive auction method the variance is

$$\sigma_{pc}^2 = \int (p_c - \bar{p}_c)^2 dP_2 (v)$$

$$= \int_0^1 \left(v - \frac{N - 1}{N + 1}\right)^2 N \, (N - 1) \, (v^{N-2} - v^{N-1}) \, d \, v = \frac{2 \, (N - 1)}{(N + 2) \, (N + 1)^2}.$$

The difference in variance for the gain to the buyers is even wider: in the Dutch auction the buyer's gain is $v - p = v - [(N - 1)/N] v = v/N$, v being the highest value drawn; the range of possible gains is from 0 to $1/N$, whereas with the progressive auction the gain can vary all the way from 0 to 1. Since with the Dutch auction the gain is always proportional to the price

$$g_d = \frac{1}{N - 1} p_d,$$

we have for the variance of the gain

$$\sigma_{gd}^2 = \frac{1}{(N-1)^2} \; \sigma_{pd}^2 = \frac{1}{N(N+1)^2(N+2)} \; .$$

With the progressive auction, for a given bidder to obtain a gain of g or more after drawing a value of v requires that all other bidders draw values less than $v - g$; the total probability of some bidder obtaining a gain of more than g thus is

$$P_c(g) = N \int_{v=g}^1 (v-g)^{N-1} \, dv = (1-g)^N \; .$$

The variance of the gain, then, is

$$\sigma_{gc}^2 = \int (g - \bar{g})^2 dP_c(g) = \int_{g=1}^0 \left(g - \frac{1}{N+1} \right)^2 d(1-g)^N$$

$$= \frac{N}{(N+1)^2(N+2)} \; .$$

This is N^2 times as great as for the Dutch auction.

APPENDIX II: Analysis of Asymmetrical Rectangular Two-person Bidding Games

Bidder 1 draws his value v_1 from a rectangular distribution ranging from 0 to 1, while bidder 2 draws his value v_2 from a rectangular distribution ranging from a to $b \leqslant 1$. Let $y_1(x)$ and $y_2(x)$ be the respective probabilities of a bid of less than x by bidders 1 and 2, respectively, and $v_1(x)$ and $v_2(x)$ the value drawings by the two players that are to lead them to make a bid of x. Then the expected gain $E(g_1)$ to bidder 1, if he draws a value v_1 and makes a bid of x, will be the amount of gain if he is successful, $(v_1 - x)$, times the probability of success, which is, of course, the probability $y_2(x)$ that bidder 2 bids less than x.

A necessary condition for an equilibrium point such that neither bidder can gain by bidding other than according to the relation $v_i(x)$, then, is that $E(g_1) = y_2(x)$ $(v_1 - x)$ shall be a maximum with respect to x, which requires, for all values of x for which $y_2(x)$ is continuous

$$\frac{\partial E(g_1)}{\partial x} = -y_2(x) + (v_1 - x)\frac{dy_2}{dx} = 0 \; , \tag{1}$$

and similarly

$$\frac{\partial E(g_2)}{\partial X} = -y_1(x) + (v_2 - x)\frac{dy_1}{dx} = 0 \; . \tag{2}$$

From the way v_1 and v_2 are drawn, we can put

$$y_1 (x) = v_1 (x) \tag{3}$$

and

$$y_2 (x) = \frac{1}{b - a} [v_2 (x) - a] \tag{4}$$

(e.g., if the probability of a bid of less than x by bidder 2 is 0.3, then the value drawing that induces a bid of x must be $v_2(x) = a + 0.3[b - a]$).

If the solution is to be Pareto-optimal, we must have $v_1(x) = v_2(x) (= v(x))$ for all values of x for which both v_1 and v_2 lie within the range of possible drawings; otherwise there would be the possibility that the person drawing the lower value would obtain the object, leading to misallocation of resources. But if we make the indicated substitutions, this requires simultaneously that

$$- v + (v - x) \frac{dv}{dx} = 0, \tag{5}$$

and

$$- \frac{1}{b - a} (v - a) + (v - x) \frac{1}{b - a} \frac{dv}{dx} = 0, \tag{6}$$

which is possible only if $a = 0$. If we restrict the model to the case $a = 0$, equation (5) can be written $v \, dv = v \, dx + x \, dv = d(xv)$, which can be integrated directly to give $\frac{1}{2}v^2 = xv + c$, or $x = (v/2) - (c/v)$. If we assume some lower bound for bids as v approaches zero (having normalized the v_1 values to the range 0 to 1, we cannot rule out negative bids per se), this implies that $c = 0$, and we get, for the bidding rule, simply $x = v/2$ for $0 \leqslant v \leqslant b$.

However, not even this provides an equilibrium, since if player 2 follows this pattern, then for $v_1 > b$, bidder 1 will increase his gain without diminishing his chances of success by reducing his bids from $\frac{1}{2}v_1$ to $\frac{1}{2}b$; if he does this, however, there will then be a temptation for player 2 to bid more than $\frac{1}{2}b$ on some occasions, since by doing so his chances of winning are substantially increased. Hence Pareto-optimality is incompatible with Nash equilibrium in this case also.

If we abandon the requirement of Pareto-optimality and look for a general Nash equilibrium point without this stipulation, the solution runs into considerable mathematical difficulty. For purposes of simplification we can put

$$z_1 = \frac{y_1}{y_1'} \quad \text{and} \quad z_2 = \frac{y_2}{y_2'}, \quad \left(y_1' = \frac{dy_1}{dx}, \text{ etc.} \right), \tag{7}$$

so that equations (1) and (2) become

$$v_1 - x = z_2 \tag{8}$$

$$v_2 - x = z_1; \tag{9}$$

while substituting equations (3) and (4) in equation (7) we get

$$z_1 = \frac{v_1}{v_1'} \tag{10}$$

and

$$z_2 = \frac{v_2 - a}{v_2' - a} . \tag{11}$$

Using equation (8) to eliminate v_1 from equation (10) and using equation (9) to eliminate v_2 from equation (11), and clearing fractions, we have

$$z_1 z_2' + z_1 = z_2 + x \tag{12}$$

and

$$z_2 z_1' + z_2 = z_1 + x - a . \tag{13}$$

Adding equations (12) and (13), we get

$$z_1 z_2' + z_2 z_1' = 2x - a . \tag{14}$$

Since the left-hand side of equation (14) is an exact differential, we can now integrate

$$z_1 z_2 = x^2 - ax + k . \tag{15}$$

Solving equation (15) for z_1 and putting the results in equation (12), we have

$$(x^2 - ax + k)(z_2' + 1) = z_2(z_2 + x). \tag{16}$$

While equation (16) is now a relatively simple differential equation involving only $z_2(x)$, $z_2'(x)$, and x, it resists solution by analytical methods (even for $a = 0$) while if an approximate numerical quadrature is to be made, it is not immediately obvious what the required boundary conditions are to be that will determine k and the second constant of integration.

APPENDIX III: A Simplified Asymmetrical Bidding Game

In this game bidder 1 draws his value v_1 from a rectangular distribution of range 0 to 1, while bidder 2 has the fixed value $v_2 = a$.

If we allow bidder 2 to determine his bid x by a random drawing from a distribution selected by him, we can now let $y_2(x)$ be the probability that his bid will be less than x, this function now being determined directly by bidder 2. The equilibrium conditions then become

$$- y_2(x) + (v_1 - x)\, y_2'(x) = 0 \tag{17}$$

$$- y_1(x) + (a - x)\, y_1'(x) = 0 , \tag{18}$$

where for bidder 1 we again have

$$y_1(x) = v_1(x) . \tag{19}$$

Equation (18) can ge integrated directly, after dividing through by $y_1(x)\,(a - x)$ to separate the variables, giving $\log (a - x) + \log y_1(x) = x_1 \log k$, or $(a - x)\, y_1(x) = k$, which by the use of equation (19) gives

$$x = a - \frac{k}{v} \tag{20}$$

as the rule by which bidder 1 is to determine his bid, at least for any range of x where $y_2'(x)$ is continuous.

To determine an appropriate value for the constant of integration k, some general propositions concerning the necessary nature of the various probability distributions can be invoked. Obviously, the probability $p_i(x)$ that a bid of x by bidder i will be a winning bid for i, is a nondecreasing function of x for any given behavior pattern of the remaining bidders. Also $v_i(x)$ must be a nondecreasing function for each bidder i, for suppose v^* to be a value drawing greater than v, and x^* and x the corresponding bids, with $x^* < x$; then, if $p(x^*) = p(x)$, it would become profitable to make a bid of x^* rather than x in response to a drawing of v; if $p(x^*) < p(x)$, it would become profitable to interchange the bids and bid x for a value of v^* and x^* for a value of v, the gain being

$$[(v^* - x)\, p + (v - x^*)\, p^*] - [(v - x)\, p + (v^* - x^*)\, p^*]$$

$$= (v^* - v)\,(p - p^*) > 0.$$

If the value drawings of the different players are uncorrelated, this interchange will have no repercussions on the other players.

Let x_m be the greatest lower bound of the possible winning bids under equilibrium conditions. It can be shown that if $y_i(x)$ has a discontinuity at x_d, implying that the probability p_d that bidder i makes a bid of exactly x_d is positive, then $x_d \leqslant x_m$. This can be seen as follows: suppose $x_m < x_d$; let B be the least upper bound of all bids $b \leqslant x_d$ by bidders other than i, and let V be the least upper bound of all values corresponding to such bids by bidders whose possible bids individually have the least upper bound B. If $B < x_d$, bidder i could increase his expected gains by reducing all his bids of x_d to $B + \varepsilon$, since there are no competing bids in the interval. Hence $B = x_d$. If $V > x_d$, then, for any $\varepsilon > 0$, there exists a value v_ε capable of being drawn by some bidder $j(\neq i)$ with a corresponding bid b_ε, such that $x_d - \varepsilon < b_\varepsilon \leqslant x_d$ and $V - \varepsilon < v \leqslant V$; raising this bid from b_ε to $x_d + \varepsilon$ will increase the probability of winning by at least $p_d p_i(x_d)$, and this will be sufficient, for sufficiently small ε, to outweigh the reduction in the amount of profit in case of a win by something less than 2ε, so that this cannot be an equilibrium situation, and for equilibrium we must have $V \leqslant x_d$. If $V < x_d = B$, then all bids b^- such that $V < b^- < B = x_d$ have $v^- < b^-$ resulting in a loss if they are the winning bid; if no such bids win, we have $x_d \leqslant x_m$, Q.E.D. Any such bid that might win can be profitably reduced to a bid equal to v. If, finally, $V = x_d$, and there is some bid $b^* < x_d$ with $p_j(b^*) > 0$, then for any $\varepsilon > 0$, there will exist a value v^+ capable of being drawn by some bidder j $(\neq i)$, with a corresponding bid b^+, such that $x_d - \varepsilon < v^+ \leqslant x_d$ and $x_d - \varepsilon < b^+ \leqslant x_d$, implying $v^+ - b^+ < \varepsilon$; so that, for sufficiently small ε, $p_j(b^+) (v^+ - b^+) < \varepsilon < p_j(b^*) (v^+ - b^*)$, implying that in this case it would be profitable to reduce the bid from b^+ to b^*. Hence $p_j(b^*) = 0$ for all $b^* < x_d$, and $x_d \leqslant x_m$.

Any bids with lumped probabilities can thus occur, if at all, only at the bottom of the range of possibly successful bids, implying that for bids above the minimal winning bid and for value distributions that are dense, the function $v(x)$ must be continuous, while $x = v$ can occur only for $x = x_m$.

In the case at hand, equation (20) must hold at all points where $x \neq v_1$ and $y_2 \neq 0$; k must obviously be positive, otherwise the relationship would be perverse. In this two-bidder case, the maximum bid must be the same for the two bidders, since any bid by one higher than the maximum bid of the other could be reduced with profit. Suppose $k < a^2/4$, so that the condition $x = v_1$ is realizable at the two roots r_1 and r_2 of the quadratic equation $x^2 - ax + k = 0$; if r_2 is the larger root, $x_m = r_2$ and $y_2(r_2) = 0$. Putting this in equation (17), we obtain

$$\frac{y_2'}{y_2} = \frac{a - x}{(x - r_1)(x - r_2)}, \quad \text{or} \quad (r_2 - r_1)\frac{y_2'}{y_2} = \frac{r_1}{x - r_2} - \frac{r_2}{x - r_1}. \quad (21)$$

This can be integrated to yield

$$(r_2 - r_1) \log y_2 = r_1 \log (x - r_2) - r_2 \log (x - r_1) + \log A, \quad (22)$$

or

$$y_2^{r_2 - r_1} = A (x - r_2)^{r_1} (x - r_1)^{r_2} . \tag{23}$$

This function runs from $y_2(r_2) = 0$ to $y_2(a - k) = 1$, by suitable choice of the constant of integration A, so that $a - k$ is the maximum bid for player 2 as it is for player 1, as indicated by putting $v_1 = 1$ in equation (20).

This equilibrium has only a precarious stability, however, for its stability depends, on the one hand, on player 1 actually bidding according to equation (20) for all drawings of v from 0 to 1, even though this means making potentially dangerous bids of more than v for drawings of v between r_1 and r_2; any reduction in such bids would create an inducement for player 2 to put in some bids of less than r_2, and the equilibrium breaks down. Even if player 1 persists in following equation (20) to the letter, there is no positive short-run disadvantage to player 2 if he puts in bids of less than r_2; indeed, while neither player gains immediately by lowering his bid, he does not lose, and the resulting breakdown of the equilibrium tends to shift the equilibrium in the direction of a higher value of k, which is ultimately to the advantage of both bidders, so that one can hardly call the solutions reached for these values of k really stable.

On the other hand if $k > a^2/4$, the function $v_1 = k/(a - x)$ lies entirely above the line $v_1 = x$, so that $v_1 - x > 1/h$, say, for some fixed positive h for all x; equation (17) now implies

$$y_2' = \frac{1}{v_1 - x} y_2 < h y_2 ,$$

so that the curve $y_2(x)$ is always flatter than curves of the form $y = A e^{hx}$ and thus can never reach the x-axis, no matter how far out on the negative x-axis we go. Nevertheless, in practice there will always be some lower bound on the bids that will be accepted. If the bidding distributions are terminated by a lumped probability at this lower bound, however, it immediately becomes profitable to shade the minimum bids upward, and no equilibrium is established.

There remains the case of $k = a^2/4$; now $v_1(x)$ is tangent to $v = x$ at $x = a/2$. Equation (20) now becomes

$$v_1 = \frac{a^2}{4 (a - x)} ,$$

and putting this in equation (17) gives

$$y_2 = \frac{1}{4 (a - x)} (a^2 - 4 ax + 4 x^2) y_2' , \quad \text{or} \quad \frac{y_2'}{y_2} = \frac{4 (a - x)}{(2x - a)^2} , \tag{24}$$

which can be integrated to give

$$\log y_2 = - \log (2x - a) - \frac{a}{2x - a} + C . \tag{25}$$

For all values of C we have $y_2 = 0$ for $x = a/2$. Bidder 2's minimum bid is thus $a/2$, and all bids of less than this by bidder 1 are nonwinning. In order for the maximum bids to be the same, since we have, for $v_1 = 1$

$$x = a - \tfrac{1}{4} a^2 ,$$

for $y_2 = 1$ we must have

$$\log y_2 = 0 = - \log (a - \tfrac{1}{2} a^2) - \frac{2}{2 - a} + C , \tag{26}$$

so that

$$C = \log \frac{a (2 - a)}{2} + \frac{2}{2 - a} ,$$

and equation (25) becomes

$$\log y_2 = \log \frac{a (2 - a)}{2 (2x - a)} + \frac{2}{2 - a} - \frac{a}{2x - a} . \tag{27}$$

This solution for the case $a = 0.8$ is illustrated in figure 3.3. The pro forma bids put in by player 1 when he draws a value of less than $a/2$ can take any form between the limits $x = v_1$ and $x = a - (1/4v_1)a^2$, without leading to any immediate breakdown of the equilibrium. Other bids would not be immediately disastrous, but, of course, a bid of greater than v would risk loss if the bid were successful, while consistent bids of less than $a - (1/4v_1)a^2$ would tempt bidder 2 to change his strategy.

The expected payment by bidder 1 would be

$$\int_{v_1=(1/2)a}^{1} y_2 (x) \, x \, d \, v_1 (x) ,$$

and similarly for bidder 2 it would be

$$\int_{v_2=0}^{1} v_1 (x) \, x \, d \, y_2 (x) .$$

Integrating this latter expression by parts, we have

$$\int_{y_2=0}^{1} v_1 x \, d \, y_2 = v_1 x y_2 \Big|_{y_2=0}^{y_2=1} - \int_{y_2=0}^{1} y_2 \, d \, (v_1 x)$$

$$= v_1 x \Big|_{y_2=0}^{y_2=1} - \int_{y_2=0}^{1} y_2 \, v_1 \, dx + y_2 x \, d \, v_1 . \tag{28}$$

Table 3.1

Average expectation of	Progressive auction			Dutch auction	
	$a \leq 0$	$0 \leq a \leq 1$	$a \geq 1$	$0 \leq a \leq 2$	$a \geq 2$
1 Payment by 1......	a	$a-a^2$	0	$(1-[a/2])^2(a/2)(2-[a/2])$ $-F(a)$	0
2 Payment by 2......	0	$\frac{1}{2}a^2$	$\frac{1}{2}$	$1/4a^2(3-a)$	1
3 Receipts of seller (1+2)	a	$a(1-a/2)$	$\frac{1}{2}$	$a/2(2-a+[a^2/2]-[a^3/8])$ $-F(a)$	1
4 Net gain of 1.......	$(1-2a)/2$	$\frac{1}{2}(1-a)^2$	0	$\frac{1}{2}(1-[a/2])^4+\frac{1}{2}F(a)$	0
5 Net gain of 2.......	0	$\frac{1}{2}a^2$	$a-\frac{1}{2}$	$\frac{1}{4}a^2$	$a-1$
6 Total value (3+4+5)	$\frac{1}{2}$	$\frac{1}{2}(1+a^2)$	a	$\frac{1}{2}+\frac{1}{2}a^2-\frac{1}{32}a^4-\frac{1}{2}F(a)$	a

where $F(a) = \frac{1}{4}a^2(1-\frac{1}{2}a)e^{2/(2-a)} \int_0^{1-a/2} [u/(1-u)]e^{-1/u}du$

Since the limits of integration are equivalent, the integral of the last term is equal to the expected payment of bidder 1, so that the total expected payment received by the seller is

$$a - \frac{a^4}{4} - \int_{x=a/2}^{a[1-(1/4)a]} \frac{a\,(2-a)}{2\,(2x-a)} e^{[2/(2-a)-a/(2x-a)]} \frac{a^2}{4\,(a-x)} \, dx \qquad (29)$$

$$= 1 - b^2 - b\,(1-b)^2\,e^{1/b} \int_0^b \frac{1}{(1-u)\,u} e^{-1/u} \, du \; ,$$

where

$$u = \frac{2x-a}{a} \quad \text{and} \quad b = \frac{2-a}{2}. \qquad (30)$$

The integral in equations (29) cannot be evaluated in terms of standard functions, but it can readily be evaluated for specific values of a and b, for example, by Simpson's rule. The interesting comparison is with the progressive auction in which, for v_1 greater than a, bidder 1 gets the article at a price a, while for a v_1 less than a, bidder 2 gets the article at a price of v_1. The average price thus is $a - \frac{1}{2}a^2$. With the Dutch auction the average realized price turns out to be greater than this for a greater than about 0.43, and less for values below 0.43.

The expected consumer's surplus, for the optimal allocation achieved with progressive auctioning is $\frac{1}{2}(1 - a)^2$ for bidder 1 and $\frac{1}{2}a^2$ for bidder 2, yielding a total expected value of $\frac{1}{2}(1 + a^2)$. Under the Dutch auction the expected

Social Choice and Allocation Mechanisms

consumer's surplus for the first bidder is $\int y_2(v_1 - x)dv_1$ for the first bidder and $\int v_1(a - x)dy_2$ for the second. These integrals again must be evaluated by approximate numerical methods; it is possible, however, to express the various quantities in terms of a common integral function as is shown in summary table 3.1.

Figure 3.4 gives a general picture of how these various quantities behave as *a* changes.

4

·

Auctions and Bidding Games

The analysis of auction and bidding situations that are of considerable practical importance can be facilitated, at an abstract level at least, by the introduction of a variable-sum paradigm, in which the successful bidder is deemed to gain an amount equal to the difference between the value of the object or contract to him and the price that he is required to pay for it in accordance with the rules of the particular type of auction, the unsuccessful bidders having a gain of zero. In many forms of auction, each bidder's strategy will depend on what information he may possess concerning the value of the object to the other bidders; in many cases of interest, this information will be subject to a considerable margin of uncertainty. In the game paradigm of the situation, this incomplete information is represented by considering that the value of the object to each player has been obtained by a drawing from a distribution of values, the distribution from which each player draws being known in advance to all the players, though the value drawn in a particular play of the game will in general be known only to the drawing player himself.

The game paradigms then proceed as follows: each player first draws a value from his own distribution, after which the bidding procedure being studied is carried out, the price and the successful bidder determined, and the indicated gain paid to the winning player. Questions of interest to economists concern the effect of alternative auctioning methods on the average gain and the variance of the gain to the various buyers and sellers, and on the likelihood that an efficient or "Pareto-optimal" outcome is achieved, which means in this case that no bidder will be found to have drawn a higher value than that of the successful bidder. Among the types of auctions that are of interest are the simple progressive auction

Recent Advances in Game Theory (Princeton University Press, 1962), pp. 15–29.

in which the auction is concluded only when no one wishes to put in a higher bid, the item then being sold to the highest bidder, and the Dutch auction in which prices are announced in a downward sequence by the auctioneer, the auction terminating as soon as some buyer accepts the announced price. Some sealed-bid procedures are substantially isomorphic with one or the other of these, although this does not exhaust the possibilities that merit consideration.

In a previous publication[1] the analysis was carried out for the case where there is a single item to be sold, bids can be varied continuously, and all bidders draw their values from the same continuous rectangular distribution; it was shown that in this case both the progressive auction and the Dutch auction are efficient, and both produce the same expectation of gains for the various players; the variance of the gain is greater, however, for both buyers and sellers, under the progressive than under the Dutch auction procedure. Difficulties were encountered with asymmetrical cases: the analysis was carried through only for a two-person case where one bidder drew his value from a rectangular distribution, the value to the second bidder being fixed. In this case the Dutch auction is not in general Pareto-optimal, and the mean expectation of the parties is not the same under the two methods, the Dutch auction being in general slightly to the advantage of the variable-value bidder, considerably to the disadvantage of the fixed-value bidder, to the considerable advantage of the seller when the fixed value is relatively high and slightly to his disadvantage when the fixed value is relatively low. The present paper will add two further cases to the analysis: (I) the case of N players drawing values symmetrically from the same continuous distribution, but competing for m identical objects, bids being continuous and no bidder having a use for more than one subject, and (II) a discrete case with N bidders drawing values from differing distributions, but with only two discrete values available to be drawn and two discrete bids allowed, there being a single object to be sold.

Symmetrical Bidding Games with Replicated Prizes

Let there be N bidders, and m identical prizes, with $m < N$. The symmetry of the situation is expressed by having each of the N bidders draw independently a value v_i from the common distribution of values given by $y(v)$, y being the probability that a value of less than v is drawn. We assume that collusion between the players is not allowed, so that the appropriate analysis is that of the Nash equilibrium point:[2] an equilibrium is a set of strategies relating the bids to be made to the

---

[1] William Vickrey: "Counterspeculation, Auctions, and Competitive Sealed Tenders," *The Journal of Finance*, 16 (March, 1961), pp. 8–37.

[2] Cf. R. Duncan Luce and Howard Raiffa, *Games and Decisions* (Wiley, 1957), pp. 170 ff.

values drawn such that for each player and for each value drawn, no other bid will increase the expectation of gain, assuming that all other players follow equilibrium strategies similarly defined. It is easy to see that the bids must bear a nonnegatively monotonic relation to the values drawn; otherwise a rectifying transposition of the bids would increase the expected gain of the player concerned, without repercussions on the rational motivations of the other bidders.

Since each bidder is in the same overall position as every other, they can be assumed to behave similarly given similar value drawings, and we can describe the behavior of all bidders by a common bidding function $x_i = x(v_i)$, v_i being the particular value drawn by the ith bidder and x_i being the resulting bid. We will write $dP(m, N, v, dv)$ for the probability that the mth highest of the values drawn by the N bidders lies between v and $v + dv$; this probability is the product of the probability.

$$N \, y'(v) \, dv = N \frac{dy}{dv} \, dv = N \, dy \qquad (1)$$

that one of the N bidders draws a value in this interval, and the probability

$$\frac{(N-1)!}{(m-1)! \, (N-m)!} \, (1-y)^{m-1} \, y^{N-m} \qquad (2)$$

that among the remaining $N - 1$ bidders, $m - 1$ of them draw values above v (y in the above expression being the probability of a drawing of less than v), while the remaining $N - m$ bidders draw values below v; thus

$$dP(m, N, v, dv) = \frac{N!}{(m-1)! \, (N-m)!} \, [1 - y(v)]^{m-1} \, [y(v)]^{N-m} \, y'(v) \, dv. \qquad (3)$$

The Highest Rejected Bid System

Consider first a bidding system in which the m objects are awarded to the m highest bidders at a price equal to the $m + 1^{\text{st}}$ bid. Under this system the optimal strategy for each bidder is obviously for him to put in a bid equal to the value drawn, since lowering the bid below this point can only reduce the probability of being a successful bidder, without increasing the amount of gain in case one would have been successful at a lower bid; raising the bid above this point can only improve the chances of success in those cases where success would involve paying more than the object is worth. The price will thus be equal to the $m + 1^{\text{st}}$ highest value drawn; the probability that this value falls between v and $v + dv$ is then $dP(m + 1, N, v, dv)$, and the average price is

$$\int_{v=-\infty}^{\infty} v \, dP(m + 1, N, v, dv)$$

$$= \int_{y=0}^{1} v(y) \frac{N!}{(m)! \, (N - m - 1)!} (1 - y)^m \, y^{N-m-1} \, dy. \qquad (4)$$

The Individual Bid Pricing System

Considering next the system where each successful bidder must pay the amount of his bid, the determination of the equilibrium strategy is slightly more difficult. An individual, having drawn a given v, may consider changing his bid from the normal $x(v)$ to a deviant $x(v) + dx$; the probability that he would thereby gain the amount $v - x$ by moving from the unsuccessful into the successful class of bidders is the probability that the mth of the remaining $N - 1$ bids was in the interval $(x, x + dx)$, which is the same as the probability that the corresponding value is in the interval $(v(x), v(x + dx))$, which is $dP(m, N - 1, v, dv)$. On the other hand the probability that the bidder in question was already in the successful class of bidders and hence stands to lose the amount dx by thus raising his bid is the probability that the mth among the other bids was below x, i.e., that the mth among the other values was below v, which is

$$\int_{u=-\infty}^{v} dP(m, N - 1, u, du) = P(m, N - 1, v) . \qquad (5)$$

If no bidder is to have any incentive for deviating from the normal bidding relation $x(v)$ in either direction, the expected gains and losses from deviation must be in balance, so that

$$(v - x) \, dP(m, N - 1, v, dv) = P(m, N - 1, v) \, dx, \text{ or} \qquad (6)$$

$$u \, dP(m, N - 1, u, du) = x \, dP(m, N - 1, u, du) + P(m, N - 1, u) \, dx . \qquad (7)$$

Integrating

$$\int_{u=-\infty}^{v} u \, dP(m, N - 1, u, du) = x \, P(m, N - 1, u) \Big|_{u=-\infty}^{v} = x \, P(m, N - 1, v) , \qquad (8)$$

whence

$$x(v) = \frac{1}{P(m, N - 1, v)} \int_{u=-\infty}^{v} u \, dP(m, N - 1, u, du); \qquad (9)$$

(9) and (5) together then give the equilibrium bidding function, provided that the indicated integrations can be carried out for the specified distribution function $y(v)$.

To obtain the average outcome, we note that given a bid of x, the probability that it will be successful is again $P(m, N - 1, v)$, and the average expected payment by a given bidder is

$$\bar{c} = \int_{v=-\infty}^{+\infty} x(v) \, P(m, N - 1, v) \, y'(v) \, dv \, . \tag{10}$$

Substituting from (9), this becomes

$$\bar{c} = \int_{v=-\infty}^{+\infty} \int_{u=-\infty}^{v} u \, dP(m, N - 1, u, \, du) \, y'(v) \, dv \, . \tag{11}$$

By use of the general relation

$$\int_{r=a}^{b} \int_{s=a}^{r} F(r, s) \, ds \, dr = \int_{s=a}^{b} \int_{r=s}^{b} F(r, s) \, dr \, ds \, , \tag{12}$$

we obtain

$$\bar{c} = \int_{u=-\infty}^{+\infty} [\int_{v=u}^{+\infty} y'(v) \, dv] \, u \, dP(m, N - 1, u, \, du) \tag{13}$$

$$= \int_{u=-\infty}^{+\infty} [1 - y(u)] \, u \, dP(m, N - 1, u, \, du). \tag{14}$$

Since we have N bidders and m articles, the average price per article is

$$\bar{p} = \frac{N}{m} \bar{c} = \int_{u=-\infty}^{+\infty} u \, \frac{N}{m}[1 - y(u)] \, dP(m, N - 1, u, \, du) \tag{15}$$

$$= \int_{y=0}^{1} u(y) \frac{N}{m} (1 - y) \frac{(N - 1)!}{(m - 1)! \, (N - m - 1)!} (1 - y)^{m-1} y^{N-m-1} dy \tag{16}$$

$$= \int_{y=0}^{1} u(y) \frac{N!}{m! \, (N - 1 - m)!} (1 - y)^m y^{N-m-1} dy \, , \tag{17}$$

which is identical with (4), showing that the expected price realized on the average by the seller will be the same with individual bid pricing as with first rejected bid pricing.

The Last Accepted Bid System

Finally, we examine the case where the price is set by the lowest bid accepted. In this case, a bidder will gain or lose nothing by changing his bid from x to $x - dx$

unless exactly $m - 1$ bids out of the remaining $N - 1$ are above x; if there are more than $m - 1$ such bids, the bid of x is already insufficient, and lowering it to $x - dx$ will have no effect; if there are fewer than $m - 1$ such bids, the change does not affect the price he must pay, except in the vanishingly small number of cases where two of the other bids fall within the interval $(x - dx, x)$ If there are exactly $m - 1$ other bids greater than x, then if one or more of the other bids falls in this interval, the result is a loss of the potential profit, $v - x$; otherwise the result is to lower the price and increase the profit by dx. The relative probabilities of these two alternatives, given exactly $m - 1$ bids greater than x, are

$$1 - [1 - \frac{dy}{dx} \frac{1}{y(x)} dx]^{N-m} \quad \text{and} \quad [1 - \frac{dy}{dx} \frac{1}{y(x)} dx]^{N-m} \,,$$

respectively, so that if the expected gain is to balance the expected loss, we have, neglecting higher-order terms

$$(v - x)(N - m) \frac{1}{y(x)} y'(x) \, dx = dx. \tag{18}$$

Multiplying by an integrating factor y^{N-m} and rearranging, we have

$$v(y) \, (N - m) \, y^{N-m-1} \, dy = y^{N-m} \, dx + x(N - m) \, y^{N-m-1} \, dy \,, \tag{19}$$

which integrates to

$$\int_{z=0}^{y(v)} v(z) \, (N-m) \, z^{N-m-1} \, dz = x \, y^{N-m} \,, \tag{20}$$

whence the bidding function $x(v)$ is given by

$$x(v) = [y(v)]^{-(N-m)} \int_{z=0}^{y(v)} v(z) \, (N - m) \, z^{N-m-1} \, dz \,. \tag{21}$$

To obtain the average expected price, we note that the probability that the ruling price will lie between x and $x + dx$ is the probability that the mth bid lies in this interval, i.e., that the mth value drawn lies in the interval $(v, v + dv) = (v(x), v(x) + v'(x)dx)$; this probability is $dP(m, N, v, dv)$. The average expected price is then given by

$$\bar{p} = \int_{v=-\infty}^{+\infty} x(v) \, dP \, (m, N, v, dv) \tag{22}$$

$$= \int_{y=0}^{1} y^{-(N-m)} \int_{z=0}^{y} v(z) \, (N - m) \, z^{N-m-1} \, dz \frac{N!}{(m - 1)! \, (N - m)!} \, (1 - y)^{m-1} y^{N-m} \, dy \,.$$

$$\tag{23}$$

Making use of (12), this can be written

$$\bar{p} = \int_{z=0}^{1} \int_{y=z}^{1} \frac{N!}{(m-1)!\,(N-m-1)!}\,(1-y)^{m-1}\,dy\,v\,(z)\,z^{N-m-1}\,dz \qquad (24)$$

$$= \int_{z=0}^{1} \frac{N!}{m!\,(N-m-1)!}\,(1-z)^{m}z^{N-m-1}\,v(z)\,dz\ , \qquad (25)$$

which is again identical with (4) and (17), showing that for the symmetrical case in which the value distributions of the bidders are uniform, the expected price is the same for all three methods of handling the bidding. The variance of the price, however, differs substantially for the different bidding methods, so that on this score there may be reason to prefer one method rather than another.

Probably a more important basis for choice, however, is the fact that method *a*, the highest rejected bid system, achieves Pareto-optimality without requiring sophisticated analysis on the part of the bidders, since the bidding function is simply $x = v$, which is independent of the distribution $y(v)$. With the other bidding methods, errors by the bidders either in analysis of the problem or in estimating $y(v)$ will, unless they are identical errors, lead in general to variations in the bidding function used by different bidders, giving rise to the likelihood of nonefficient results.

Discrete Bids and Values

While in most cases bids and values can vary by increments which for most practical purposes are negligibly small, nevertheless this is not quite the same thing as a mathematical continuum; moreover cases do arise in which the available bids or values vary by significantly large steps. As an extreme case of discreteness of bids and values, and one which is also reasonably simple, we consider the situation where the single article to be bid for can have, for each of the N bidders, one of only two distinct values, to be designated v and w, respectively, with $v < w$, and where only two bidding levels, g and h, respectively, are permitted, with $g < h$. The value u_i that the article has in the hands of the ith bidder is put equal to v or w as the case may be, by each player drawing from his own distribution, a_i being the probability of the ith player drawing the low value v, the probability of his drawing the value w being then $1 - a_i$.

In the Dutch auction, or highest bid price, version of the game, after drawing his value each player makes a bid of g or h; if all players bid g, then one of the N players is selected at random with probability $1/N$ to receive $u_i - g$, the others getting nothing. If one or more players bids h, then one of these n players is selected at random with probability $1/n$ to receive $u_i - h$. The second bid price version is the same except that if only one bidder bids h, he obtains $u_i - g$, rather than $u_i - h$. Under the open or progressive auction procedure, a tentative winner is first selected at random, after which the other bidders are given an opportunity to bid. If none of the players bids h, then the tentative winner wins $u_i - g$. If one or more of the players bids h, the tentative winner is then given the opportunity to bid h if he wishes, and the final winner is then drawn at random from among those who have bid h, the amount thus won being $u_i - h$.

We wish to find the equilibrium points of these games and evaluate the expected outcomes under various circumstances, in terms of efficiency and expected price. Also, we may suppose that the bids g and h are under the control of the seller, within limits, though the values v and w are exogenously fixed, and ask what procedure and what values of g and h will yield the highest price. We may realistically suppose that g is not permitted to be set higher than v, reflecting the idea that bidding is voluntary.

With the second bid price procedure, as long as $v < h < w$, bidders will be motivated to make a bid of h if and only if they draw a value of w, and the results will be Pareto-optimal. The price will be g if the number of players drawing w is either 0 or 1, otherwise it will be h, so that the expected price will be

$$\bar{p}_2 = [\prod_{i=1}^{N} a_i + \sum_{i=1}^{N} \frac{1 - a_i}{a_i} \prod_{j=1}^{N} a_j] (g - h) + h \qquad (26)$$

$$= \prod_{i=1}^{N} a_i [1 - n + \sum_{i=1}^{N} \frac{1}{a_i}] (g - h) + h \qquad (27)$$

where the first term in the brackets in (26) represents the probability that all of the players draw v, the second term being the probability that just one of the players draws w. If we put, for brevity

$$R = \prod_{i=1}^{N} a_i \quad \text{and} \quad S = \sum_{i=1}^{N} \frac{1}{a_i} \qquad (28)$$

then (27) can be written

$$\bar{p}_2 = R (1 - N + S) (g - h) + h . \qquad (29)$$

With the open auction procedure, with $v < h < w$, bidders will raise their bid to h if and only if they draw a value of w, except that if a bidder is selected as the tentative winner, he will raise his bid on drawing a value of w only if one or more other bidders raise their bids. Thus in this case the price will be g whenever all bidders draw v, and will also be g on those occasions when only one bidder draws w and he is also selected at random as the tentative winner. Thus we have

$$\bar{p}_0 = [\prod_{i=1}^{N} a_i + \frac{1}{N} \sum_{i=1}^{N} \frac{1 - a_i}{a_i} \prod_{j=1}^{N} a_j] (g - h) + h \qquad (30)$$

$$= \frac{1}{N} R S (g - h) + h . \tag{31}$$

This result is also Pareto-optimal.

With the highest bid price, single sealed-bid procedure, a much more elaborate analysis is required, and indeed equilibrium points meeting the Nash conditions exist in such great profusion that it is only by appealing to certain second-order dominance considerations that the stable outcomes can be reduced to a manageable set. We note again that good strategies must involve a nonnegative monotonic relation between bids and values, since otherwise a rectifying transposition of the bids would increase the expected gain of the player concerned without changing the situation from the point of view of the other bidders. Accordingly, good strategies can be completely described by specifying the proportion of low bids made. This proportion for player i can be designated x_i; $x_i < a_i$ means, for example, that low bids are made only on a drawing of v, a drawing of w always entails a bid of h, and that bids of h on a drawing of v occur with a frequency of $a_i - x_i$.

The probability of player i winning on a bid of g is then

$$p_{gi} = \frac{1}{N} \frac{1}{x_i} \prod_{j=1}^{N} x_j . \tag{32}$$

Evaluating the probability of winning with a bid of h is more complicated. From the symmetry among the players with respect to the bidding process, we can write

$$p_{hi} = \sum_{r=0}^{N-1} \frac{1}{r+1} \sum_{\substack{|S|=r \\ i \notin S}} = r \prod_{j \in S} (1 - x_j) \prod_{\substack{k \notin S \\ k \neq i}} x_k = \sum_{r=0}^{N-1} b_r \sum_{\substack{|S|=r \\ i \notin S}} = r \prod_{j \in S} x_j , \tag{33}$$

where r represents the number of other bidders bidding h, and the coefficients b_r are to be determined. This can be done, to show that they are all positive, by noting that if $x_1 = x_2 = \ldots x_N = x$, we have, for the probability that some player will win

$$1 = \sum_{i=1}^{N} x_i \, p_{gi} + \sum_{i=1}^{N} (1 - x_i) \, p_{hi}$$

$$= x^N + N (1 - x) \sum_{r=0}^{N-1} b_{rN} C_r \, x^r \tag{34}$$

whence

$$b_r = \frac{1}{N} \frac{1}{_N C_r} = \frac{r! \, (N - r)!}{N \, N!} > 0. \tag{35}$$

Given the strategy of the other players, if player i draws a value u_i the expected gain with a bid of g is $p_{gi}(u_i - g)$ and the gain with a bid of h is similarly

$P_{hi}(u_i - h)$. Accordingly, $0 < x_i < a_i$ can represent a good strategy for i (mixing bids on a drawing of v) only if the expected gain for the two bids is the same, or

$$p_{hi} (v - h) = p_{gi} (v - g); \tag{36}$$

$$v = h + (h - g) q_i \text{, where } q_i = \frac{p_{gi}}{p_{hi} - p_{gi}} \tag{37}$$

But while under these circumstances the strategy x_i may be an equilibrium one, it will have only a very limited stability, since in the first instance player i can increase x_i to $x_i = a_i$ without changing his expected gain on the assumption that this provokes no reaction from other players. On a second level of analysis, moreover, it can be seen that any reaction of other players must be in the direction of increasing x_j, which will increase p_{hi} and p_{gi}, increasing the expected gain of player i. This is shown as follows: q_j can be written

$$q_j = \frac{A x_i}{B x_i + C} = \frac{A}{B + \dfrac{C}{x_i}} \tag{38}$$

where A, B, and C are nonnegative polynomials in the x_k which do not involve either x_i or x_j. Thus we have

$$\frac{\delta q_j}{\delta x_i} \geq 0 . \tag{39}$$

If player j was formerly in equilibrium with a bid of g this would mean

$$p_{hj} (u_j - h) \leq p_{gj} (u_j - g), \qquad \text{or} \tag{40}$$

$$u_j \leq h + (h - g) q_j \tag{41}$$

and increasing x_i must if anything increase q_j and thus reinforce player j in his choice of the bid of g; if player j was formerly in equilibrium with a bid of h, the only possible effect would be a reduction in his bid to g, which would involve, if anything, an increase in x_j, and hence, from (32), (33), and (35), an increase in p_{gi} and p_{hi}. Accordingly, if initially we had $0 < x_i < a_i$, player i could never lose and might gain by increasing x_i to $x_i = a_i$. Similarly, if initially we had $a_i < x_i < 1$, there would be nothing to lose and the possibility of a gain by increasing x_i to $x_i = 1$. Thus all equilibrium points with $x_i \neq 0$, a_i, or 1 are dominated by equilibrium points in which the x_i are restricted to these three values, and we can confine our attention to these points.

We thus have the following possibilities to consider

$x_i = a_i = 0$ is in stable equilibrium only if $h + (h - g)q_i < w$; (42:I)

$x_i = 0 < a_i$ is in stable equilibrium only if $h + (h - g)q_i < v$; (42:II)

$0 < x_i = a_i <= 1$ is in stable equilibrium only if $v \leq h + (h - g)q_i < w$;

$$\text{(42:III)}$$

$a_i < x_i = 1$ is in stable equilibrium only if $w \leq h + (h - g)q_i$; $\qquad$ (42:IV)

$a_i = x_i = 1$ is in stable equilibrium only if $v \leq h + (h - g)q_i$. $\qquad$ (42:V)

The possibilities presented by allowing equality as well as the strict inequality specified on the right-hand side of (42:I), (42:II), and (42:III) are also equilibrium possibilities, but of precarious stability in that under these conditions there is also no immediate disadvantage and a possible ultimate advantage to player i in increasing x_i.

Now if there is any player j with $x_j = 0$ (i.e., j always bids h), this requires condition (42:I) or condition (42:II) to be fulfilled; since $(h - g)q_i$ is positive, this means $h < w$. Moreover, $x_j = 0$ implies $q_i = 0$, from (32) and (37), so that condition (42:IV) would require $w \leq h$, which is contradicted, so that

$$x_j = 0 \rightarrow [x_i \neq 1 \quad \text{or} \quad x_i = a_i = 1] . \qquad (43)$$

Thus if any $x_j = 0$, we can limit all other strategies to $x_i = a_i$ or $x_i = 0$. Moreover if $x_j = 0 \neq a_j$, this implies $h < v$, from (42:II), and $q_i = 0$, from (32) and (37), hence conditions (42:III), (42:IV), and (42:V) cannot be met, so that

$$x_j = 0 \neq a_j \rightarrow x_i = 0 \text{ for all } i. \qquad (44)$$

Thus if there is any player who always bids h, then either all players always bid h, or all players bid g or h according as they draw v or w.

If no player has $x_j = 0$, we can further eliminate the possibility that one player has $x_i = a_i < 1$, while another has $a_j < x_j = 1$, since this requires, from (42:III) and (42:IV)

$$h + (h - g) q_i < w \leq h + (h - g) q_j \qquad (45)$$

whence

$$q_i < q_j . \qquad (46)$$

But from (38), we have

$$q_j = \frac{A}{B + \dfrac{C}{x_i}} \quad \text{and} \quad q_i = \frac{A}{B + \dfrac{C}{x_j}} \qquad (47)$$

where A, B, and C are independent of x_i and x_j and are nonnegative, so that

$$q_i < q_j \longleftrightarrow x_j < x_i \qquad (48)$$

contradicting the assumption that $x_i < 1 = x_j$.

Accordingly, in a stable equilibrium either all players have $x_i = a_i$, i.e., $\vec{x} = \vec{a}$, or all players have $x_i = 1$, or all players have $x_i = 0$. If all players always bid g ($x_i = 1$), then $p_{hi} = 1$, $p_{gi} = \dfrac{1}{N}$, and $q_i = \dfrac{1}{N - 1}$, so that this will be an equilibrium point if and only if h satisfies (42:IV), or

$$\frac{g}{N} + (1 - \frac{1}{N}) \, w \leq h \; . \tag{49}$$

On the other hand if $x = a$ is to be an equilibrium point, (42:III) must be satisfied for all q_i , and in particular

$$h < \frac{w + g \, q_j \, (a)}{1 + q_j \, (a)} \; , \text{where } j \text{ is such that } a_j \; = \; \min_k a_k \; . \tag{50}$$

There is thus an overlapping region where both $\vec{x} = \vec{a}$ and $x_i = 1$ for all i are stable equilibria, where h satisfies both (49) and (50). Within this range, however, the point $\vec{x} = \vec{a}$ has only a precarious stability, for while it is to the immediate disadvantage of any one player to shift from $x_i = a_i$ to $x_i = 1$, as long as the other players make no change in response, such a player, particularly near the upper end of the range for h, can have considerable hope of thereby starting a stampede of all of the players to $x_j = 1$, and if successful in this he would stand to gain. We will assume, therefore, that if the seller controls h, he must set it to preclude $x_i = 1$ from being a stable equilibrium point if he is to maximize his expected price, so we must have

$$h < \frac{1}{N} \, [g + (N - 1) \, w] \; . \tag{51}$$

The expected price will be

$$\bar{p}_1 \; = \; [\prod_{i=1}^{N} x_i] \, g + (1 - \prod_{i=1}^{N} x_i) \, h \; = \; R \, g + (1 - R) \, h \; . \tag{52}$$

If we associate each of the three procedures with the respective bounds on g and h, we obtain the following expressions for the upper bounds on the expected price

$$\bar{p}_2 < \bar{p}_2^* \; = \; R(1 - N + S)(v - w) + w, \text{ from putting } h \; < \; w \text{ and } g \; = \; v \text{ in (29)}, \tag{53}$$

$$\bar{p}_0 < \bar{p}_0^* \; = \; \frac{1}{N} \, RS(v - w) + w, \text{ again with } h \; < \; w \text{ and } g \; = \; v \text{ in (31)}, \tag{54}$$

$$\bar{p}_1 < \bar{p}_1^* \; = \; \frac{1}{N} \, [R(N - 1) \, (v - w) + (v - w)] + w, \tag{55}$$

this time putting (51) in (52) with $g \; = \; v$. The question to be answered is which of the three procedures, under various circumstances, gives the highest expected price.

We have immediately that

$$\bar{p}_2^* - \bar{p}_0^* = \frac{(v - w)}{N} R(N - N^2 + NS - S) = \frac{R}{N}(w - v)(N - 1)(N - S) < 0,$$

$$(56)$$

since $N < S$ (excluding the trivial case where all the $a_i = 1$). Accordingly we can consider the open auction procedure, where available, to be definitely better for the seller than the second bid price procedure.

Comparing the open auction and the first bid price procedure, we have

$$\bar{p}_0^* < \bar{p}_1^* \longleftrightarrow \frac{RS}{N}(v - w) + w < \frac{1}{N} (RN - R + 1)(v - w) + w \tag{57}$$

$$\longleftrightarrow \quad RN + 1 - R < RS \tag{58}$$

$$\longleftrightarrow \quad \frac{1}{R} < S + 1 - N . \tag{59}$$

If we put $\frac{1}{a_i} = 1 + c_i$, then we have

$$\frac{1}{R} = \Pi(1 + c_i) \tag{60}$$

and

$$S = \Sigma(1 + c_i) = N + \Sigma c_i \tag{61}$$

$$S + 1 - N = 1 + \Sigma c_i < \Pi (1 + c_i) = \frac{1}{R} \tag{62}$$

which implies $\bar{p}_1^* < \bar{p}_0^*$, so that the open auction procedure is also better for the seller than the first bid price procedure.

If the open auction procedure is not available, however, we need to compare the first and second bid price procedure as follows:

$$\bar{p}_1^* < \bar{p}_2^* \longleftrightarrow \frac{1}{N} (RN - R + 1)(v - w) + w < R(1 - N + S)(v - w) + w ,$$

$$(63)$$

$$\longleftrightarrow \quad NR(1 - N + S) < RN - R + 1 \tag{64}$$

$$\longleftrightarrow \quad 1 - N^2 + NS < \frac{1}{R} \tag{65}$$

$$\longleftrightarrow \quad 1 + N \Sigma c_i < \Pi (1 + c_i) . \tag{66}$$

Here the results are no longer uniform: the first bid-price system is to the seller's advantage when the c_i are relatively small, corresponding to a_i close to 1, implying that drawings of h are comparatively rare. When drawings of h are generally more frequent, with low values of the a_i and high values of the c_i, the second price system is to the seller's advantage. Since all three methods give Pareto-optimal results if the bid levels are properly set, what is to the advantage of the seller is to the disadvantage of the buyers.

None of the three methods requires the seller to know the a_i in setting the bidding levels to produce the most advantageous results for himself, though the first bid price procedure does require him to know the number of bidders, or more precisely, the number of bidders that the bidders themselves expect to make bids. The values of the a_i are thus of interest to the seller only in selecting the procedure, and not in adjusting the bid parameters within that procedure.

PART II

Taxation

It is always gratifying to an author when a demand arises for reprinting a book of his that has gone out of print. In this case, however, the gratification is considerably attenuated by the thought that after 23 years the extent to which the problems have been resolved has been insufficient to generate a degree of obsolescence for the book that would have made its reprinting of historical interest only ... All told ... it is a sobering thought that were the book to be entirely rewritten in terms of the current situation, there is remarkably little that would require changing

Agenda for Progressive Taxation,
"Reprints of Economic Classics"
(Edition, 1972), p. 5 and p. 7.

Bill Vickrey occupies a unique position among public finance economists. His contributions to taxation, simultaneously analytical and policy-relevant, are characterized by an inventiveness which is unrivaled. They derive from a powerful, yet essentially simple, view of the logic of taxation, a logic which has guided his writing over more than half a century. His deep understanding of the underlying principles goes together with a grasp of the fine texture of tax legislation, giving him a rare breadth of perspective.

The best known of Vickrey's writings on taxation is his *Agenda for Progressive Taxation*, published in 1947. This was his – 496 page – doctoral dissertation. But it was no usual doctoral thesis. As the title indicates, it was an agenda for reform, concluding with twenty-one recommendations, divided into

> vital immediate changes,
> bargain counter: simple but effective adjustments,
> fundamental reforms involving basic changes,
> further refinements.

Vickrey's aim was the "perfection of the tax base," an objective which he regarded as a prime prerequisite of steeply progressive taxation.

In planning his agenda, Vickrey drew on his experience in the Tax Research Division of the Treasury, but the distinctive feature is that he was able to distill from the everyday policy issues of the Treasury the central analytical ingredients. These ingredients in turn he was able to generalize, so that out of a series of practical problems grew an organizing framework for overall reform.

A prime example is his invention of *cumulative averaging*, described by one reviewer as "a silver thread" running through the chapters as "the solution for many hard problems" (Blough, 1947, p. 671). The basic idea was set out in the

Journal of Political Economy article in 1939, reprinted here as chapter 5, and its origins are described in the first paragraph of chapter 6, in which Vickrey returned to the subject after thirty years. Discussion with Carl Shoup of the problem of taxing capital gains brought him to the principle that the tax should be neutral with respect to the date at which the gain is realized, removing the incentive for taxpayers to vary the timing of transactions simply for tax purposes. Vickrey's insight led him moreover to conclude that this principle then generalizes naturally to all classes of income. Neutrality over time is achieved by treating all tax payments as credits to an interest-bearing account in the taxpayer's name with the treasury. The current tax due is then found by comparing the accrued amount with that due on the cumulated total income, where the latter includes the interest credited on the tax account.

This sounds complicated, but there are, as Vickrey emphasizes, compensating savings in complexity in other areas, allowing the removal of provisions in the tax code concerned with the time allocation of income. In chapter 6 he estimates that the adoption of cumulative averaging would allow the income tax code to be cut by a half. Moreover, some areas of complication, such as those arising from changes in marital status, are now less important in countries which have moved to independent taxation of husbands and wives.

The same logic of neutrality led to a second major Vickrey invention: the *bequeathing power succession tax*. As is described in chapter 7, the United States capital transfer taxes operated in such a way that minor changes in the form of transmission of property could lead to large changes in the tax liability. In an article entitled "The Rationalization of Succession Taxation," published in *Econometrica* in 1944, Vickrey carried out a mathematical analysis of this issue. Chapter 7 contains a less technical discussion. The key concept is that of "potential wealth" ("bequeathing power" in the *Agenda*), which is based on the present value of inherited wealth and taxes paid. According to Vickrey, a person "who keeps an estate intact in this sense and then passes it on to others is then neither better or worse off as a result of having thus held the estate" (1947, p. 225). This position can be debated, as may the mathematical formula proposed to calculate the potential wealth, but there is no doubting the great originality of Vickrey's approach to the problem.

In the league table of tax inventors, Vickrey's nearest rival, at least in the Anglo-Saxon world, is probably Nicholas Kaldor. This gives particular interest to Vickrey's review article of the latter's book on *An Expenditure Tax*, reprinted as chapter 8. Vickrey had written earlier (1943) on the expenditure tax, arguing that consideration should be given to improving the income tax. He comments particularly on the proposal of Irving Fisher for a spendings tax, to which Fisher gives the following rejoinder:

Some of the faults and injustices in the present income tax could be mitigated by Vickrey's ingenious plan for "averaging", but this sort of mending is, after all, like putting a patch on ragged clothing when what is needed is a new suit (Fisher, 1943, p. 170).

But, as an experienced writer on tax reform, Vickrey is well aware of the lack of symmetry between the actual tax code and a new system, not yet put into practical effect and exposed to the realities of vested interests. As he says in chapter 8,

Even-handed comparison of two taxes in terms of imperfect practice is difficult . . . not only because imperfection is always more complex than perfection, but because the nature of the imperfections to be encountered in practice are difficult to predict.

The last article reprinted – on "The Problem of Progression" – is a good demonstration of the breadth of Vickrey's perspective. He describes the social welfare basis for choosing between tax systems in terms of the veil of ignorance:

Suppose that, lined up on the docks of Plymouth, there are a number of ships about to sail for various equivalently endowed regions of the New World, offering participation in communities in which varying degrees of redistributive taxation are to be employed.

The choice depends on the balance of insurance with incentives. That Vickrey should have given the clearest account of the optimal income tax problem prior to Mirrlees (1971) is not perhaps remarkable if one remembers that in 1945 he had himself formulated the problem, complete with Euler equation, in the section on "Utility and the Optimum Distribution of Income" in his *Econometrica* article on "Measuring Marginal Utility by Reactions to Risk." But chapter 9 is not just concerned with pure theory. Vickrey examines the difference between nominal and effective progression, and the political economy of tax reform. He understands quite clearly the political obstacles to tax reform. One suspects that he is not surprised, even if he is saddened, by the way political forces in the United States and in Britain have combined to dismantle the progressive rate structure rather than pursue the objective of a truly progressive income tax.

The contributions of Vickrey to the understanding of taxation go far beyond those described here. There are, for example, his ideas on corporate taxation, on tax-exempt government bonds, and on land value taxation. There is his work on the tax treatment of charitable contributions (1962), which has been described as "the first fundamental study of the economics of charity" (Feldstein, 1976, p. 91). Even if – as indicated in the extract from the preface to the 1972 reprinting of the *Agenda* – Vickrey's ideas have not enjoyed wide practical success, he has had enormous influence on our thinking about taxation. He may have been a man ahead of his time, but his contemporary influence has been remarkable.

References

Blough, R., "Review of Agenda for Progressive Taxation," *Amercian Economic Review* 37 (1947) pp. 670–3.

Feldstein, M.S., "Charitable Bequests, Estate Taxation, and Intergenerational Wealth Transfers" in *Public and Urban Economics*, R.E. Grieson, Ed. (Lexington: Lexington Books, 1976), pp. 91–109.

Fisher, I., "Destructive Taxation: A Rejoinder," *Columbia Law Review*, 43 (1943), pp. 170–5.

Kaldor, N., *An Expenditure Tax* (London: Allen and Unwin, 1955).

Mirrlees, J.A., "An Exploration in the Theory of Optimum Income Taxation," *Review of Economic Studies*, 38 (1971), pp. 175–208.

Vickrey, W.S., "The Spending Tax in Peace and War," *Columbia Law Review*, 43 (1943), pp. 165–70.

Agenda for Progressive Taxation (New York: Ronald Press, 1947).

"One Economist's View of Philanthropy" in *Philanthropy and Public Policy*, F. Dickinson, Ed. (New York: Columbia University Press, 1962), pp. 31–56.

5

·

Averaging of Income for Income Tax Purposes

It has long been considered one of the principal defects of the graduated individual income tax that fluctuating incomes are, on the whole, subjected to much heavier tax burdens than incomes of comparable average magnitude which are relatively steady from year to year. That changes in the allocation of income, which often have no relation either to physical realities or the real financial status of the taxpayer, should substantially affect his income-tax burden is obviously not in accordance with the principle of taxation according to ability to pay.

Two notable attempts have been made to remedy this situation by the introduction of an averaging process. In the state of Wisconsin from 1928 to 1932 the state income tax was assessed on the basis of the average income for the last three years, with certain adjustments at the transition years. However, legal difficulties arose in the collection of the tax from individuals who left the jurisdiction of the state and in the case of corporations dissolving; moreover, as incomes fell drastically with the onset of the depression, there was widespread objection to paying taxes during lean years based in part on the large incomes of the more prosperous years. This experiment had therefore to be abandoned after only five years of operation.[1]

The Commonwealth of Australia in 1921 enacted a provision that the rate of tax to be applied to the income of the current year was to be determined by reference to an average of the income for the last five years. New South Wales had had a

Journal of Political Economy 47 (1939), pp. 379–97; reprinted in *Readings in the Economics of Taxation*, Carl S. Shoup and Richard A. Musgrave, Eds. (Irvin, 1959), pp. 77–92.

---

[1] For the details of the Wisconsin averaging method see Wisconsin Tax Commision, *Rules and Regulations of the Wisconsin Tax Commission under the Income Tax Act of 1931* (Madison, 1932), pp. 215–19.

similar provision applying only to income from "primary production" (pastoral, agricultural, and mining) since 1912. This type of provision seems to avoid the difficulty encountered by the Wisconsin scheme of requiring heavy tax payments in years of reduced income. The application of this provision has again been restricted to income from primary production beginning with 1938 by the 1936 revision of the Commonwealth law.[2]

From 1812 to 1926 England also assessed portions of its income tax on the basis of averages. This, however, was not done for the purpose of avoiding excessive taxes on fluctuating incomes but appears, rather, to have originated as an attempt to estimate current income from the income of past years in cases where collection by withholding at the source proved impracticable. As this averaging applied directly only to the flat-rate normal tax, the effect in equalizing tax burdens was negligible.[3]

In the United States the special provisions concerning capital gains are founded in part on the theory that such gains frequently cause large fluctuations in the income of the taxpayer and so subject him to higher rates; they also, however, constitute, in part at least, a concession to those who maintain that capital gains should not be taxed as income at all. Unfortunately, the relief thus granted is capricious in its incidence, probably excessive in most cases, and opens considerable loopholes for tax avoidance.

Inequality of burden as between taxpayers of fluctuating and of steady incomes is not the only difficulty that is introduced by arbitrarily cutting up the income of the taxpayer according to time periods and assessing the tax for each period independently. In theory the determination of the accrued income between two points of time requires that valuations of all assets be made both at the beginning and at the end of the time period – an almost impossible task when the period is short, and an especially difficult one when there is no regular market for the assets in question. Supreme Court decisions and administrative exigencies have made it necessary to use so-called "realized income" as a base; one result of the use of this base has been that opportunities for manipulations designed to reduce the tax burden by shifting income from one year to another have been multiplied. Such manipulations have in turn evoked a complex system of rules and penalties designed to prevent such tax avoidance, such as the undistributed-profit tax, the

---

[2] For the details of the Australian averaging method see Norman Bede Rydge and J. B. Collier, *Commonwealth Income Tax Acts 1922–1929* (Sydney, 1929), pp. 82–113; also J. B. Collier and Norman Bede Rydge, *New South Wales Income Tax Acts* (Sydney, 1930), pp. 30–35.

[3] For a discussion of the British averaging provisions see H. B. Spaulding, *Income Tax in Great Britain and the United States* (London, 1927), pp. 211–28. A summary of the history of these provisions is given in: Great Britain: Royal Commission on the Income Tax (The "Colwyn Commission"), *Report* (London, 1920), App. 7(*m*). Testimony on the averaging provisions is indexed under "Assessment, average basis of."

regulations concerning allowances for depreciation and obsolescence, the penalty taxes on personal holding companies, and the disallowance of wash sales, sales among members of one family, and the deduction of large net capital losses from other income. These provisions, on the whole, have not only failed effectively to stop the avoidance but have also in many cases dealt excessively harshly with individuals who happened to be caught by the legal provisions without having had any intention of avoiding taxes.

Now a method of taxation which considers as a whole the income of the taxpayer over a long period of assessing the tax should, if properly designed, leave the total burden of tax unaffected by such shifts of income between the various years within the period, and should also result in a much closer approach to equality in the burdens of taxpayers with steady and fluctuating incomes than is possible under the crude averaging devices cited above. It is an obvious extension of the principle of taxation according to ability to pay that no taxpayer should bear a heavier or lighter burden merely because certain items of his income happen to be earned or realized in one year or another, regardless of whether this be by chance or by design of the taxpayer and regardless of any fluctuations in the needs of the government for revenue or the rates of tax in effect at various times. If a practicable system of taxation which satisfies this criterion can be put into effect, then many of the arbitrary, unpopular, and complicated provisions designed chiefly to prevent the manipulation by the taxpayer of his income in his own favor will no longer be necessary and may be discarded.

To be practicable, a method of assessment must meet certain requirements. The most important of these, for present purposes, may be summarized as follows:

1 The discounted value of the series of tax payments made by any taxpayer should be independent of the way in which his income is allocated to the various income years.

2 The revenue for any given year should be capable of being raised or lowered by suitable modifications of the rates without too long notice.

3 If the taxpayer leaves the jurisdiction at any time, there should be no accumulations of untaxed income left behind and no tax due except possibly the regular tax for the last year. (This was one difficulty with the Wisconsin method.)

4 Any given tax payment should not be too large in relation to the income of the period immediately preceding.

5 Transition to and from other methods of assessing income tax should be simple.

6 The method of computing the tax should not be beyond the ordinary taxpayer's capacity.

7 The administrative burden should not be excessive.

There are two steps in devising a method of assessment which will meet these criteria. The first is to determine a method of computing the final closing payment at the end of the averaging period (for example, at the death of the taxpayer) which will satisfy criterion 1; the second is to provide for the payment of suitable instalments during the averaging period which will satisfy criteria 2, 3 and 4.

Consider first two taxpayers, A and B, both of whom start with the same capital, obtain the same rate of return, and have identical earnings and expenditures during the period, the only difference being that A pays taxes on his income during the period, whereas B manages, by one method or another, to postpone the payment of the taxes until the end of the period. B's total income for the period will then exceed A's total income by the compound interest on the amounts which A paid as instalments on his income tax but which B avoided paying and so was able to invest. If, then, to A's total income is added the compound interest on the taxes which A has paid from the time they were paid to the end of the period, an amount which will be called the 'adjusted total income' is obtained which is the income A would have had if he had paid no taxes during the period. It may readily be seen that this adjusted total income will remain the same for any given taxpayer, regardless of any changes that may occur in the allocation of the realization of his income to the various years within the averaging period. If the final payment is determined in such a way that the aggregate present value of the taxes paid with respect to the income period is dependent only on this adjusted total income, then criterion 1 will be satisfied. A standard for the graduation of the tax that immediately suggests itself is that the taxpayer with a steady income throughout the averaging period shall be unaffected by the change in method of assessment, so that the taxes paid by a given individual A with a fluctuating income shall have the same present value as the taxes that would have been paid on an annual basis of assessment by a taxpayer C with a steady income of such magnitude that C's adjusted total income is equal to that of A. This standard satisfies criterion 2, at least with respect to the total payments of any one taxpayer.

In providing for the payment of annual instalments previous to the end of the income period, criterion 2 suggests that each year be treated as if it were the end of an averaging period, except that, instead of requiring a final and conclusive valuation of the capital assets of the taxpayer, any reasonable valuation tendered by the taxpayer may be accepted for the purpose of computing the accrued capital gain or loss. Any errors in valuation at this point will make no difference whatever in the total burden ultimately imposed upon the taxpayer but will merely alter somewhat the time of payment. This treatment will avoid any questions of unpaid and uncollectible taxes, will keep the tax payments fairly well in step with the income of the taxpayer, and will cause revenues to respond promptly to increases or decreases in the rates.

The principles involved in the computation of the tax for each year will then be as follows: First, the adjusted total income of the taxpayer for the period from the beginning of his averaging period to the present will be calculated by adding to his total income for the period the compound interest on the taxes which he has paid with respect to this income. The size of the constant income which would have yielded the same adjusted total income over this period is then calculated. The next step is to calculate the present value of the taxes that would have been payable on such a constant income according to the present methods of assessment and the rates for the various years of the income period. The present accumulated value of the taxes already paid by the original taxpayer is then deducted from this sum, and the remainder is the tax currently due.

At first sight this method of determining the annual payments to be made by the taxpayer may seem hopelessly complex; it is possible, however, by constructing special tables and carrying figures forward from previous returns, so to arrange the computation that the actual work required of the taxpayer will be considerably less than that at present required of taxpayers having capital gains and losses. The special tables would be prepared by the Treasury, would be comparable in every respect to the surtax tables now in use, and would give the total tax payable on given amounts of adjusted total income, with marginal rates to be applied to income between the bracket limits given in the table. There would be one such table prepared for each number of years for which individual taxpayers will have been subject to this averaging method of assessment.[4] Then from a previous

---

[4] The following is a sample of such a table for taxpayers averaging over two years. The rates taken are the surtax rates of the revenue act of 1936 for both years, with interest at 5 percent.

Adjusted total income (dollars)	Total present value of tax (dollars)	Rate of tax on excess within next bracket (percent)
0	0	0.0000
8,000	0	4.0959
12,004	164	5.1186
16,009	369	6.1408
20,015	615	7.1625
24,022	902	8.1836
28,030	1,230	9.2043
32,039	1,599	11.2441
36,050	2,050	13.2818
40,063	2,583	15.3176

This table is precisely similar to present surtax tables except for the fact that the figures are not rounded and that the amounts in the first two columns are a little over twice the corresponding

return or certified transcript the taxpayer would copy the total adjusted income and the total value of tax payments as of last year. The total value of taxes previously paid is then multiplied by the rate of interest fixed by the Treasury to obtain the interest accrued during the past year upon taxes previously paid. This interest is then added to the value of taxes paid as of last year to get the present value of taxes paid, and is added together with the adjusted total income from the previous return and the income reported for the past year to get the new adjusted total income. From the appropriate surtax table the taxpayer then obtains the total present value of tax corresponding to this adjusted total income by exactly the same procedure as is used at present in computing the surtax corresponding to a given surtax net income; from this total value of tax the taxpayer then deducts the total present value of past taxes paid, and the remainder is the payment due for the current year.[5] These computations are fairly simple compared with many

amounts in present tables. These amounts would be a little more than three times as large for a table for taxpayers averaging for three years, and so on.

The figures given in the table are computed as follows: A taxpayer with a steady annual income (after exemptions) of $12,000 pays a surtax each year, under the present law, of $440. Interest on the first year's tax at 5 percent is $22. This $22, added to the total income for the two-year period of $24,000, gives the adjusted total income of $24,022 given in the first column. The total present value of the tax is $440 + $440 + $22 = $902. The next higher level of income in the present tables is $14,000, giving similarly an adjusted total income of $28,030 and a total present value of tax of $1,230; thus, the size of the total adjusted income bracket is $4,008, and the tax on this bracket is $1,230 − $902, or $328. The rate of tax on this bracket is therefore $328 ÷ $4,008, or 8.1836 percent.

[5] The required computations might be set out as follows on the income-tax return.

1 Net income this year (after exemptions)	$18,500.00
2 Adjusted total income as of previous year (copied from item 5 of previous year's return)	9,200.00
3 Total value of income taxes paid as of previous year (copied from item 6 of previous year's return)	252.00
4 Interest of past year on taxes paid (5 percent of item 3)	12.60
(The rate of interest may be varied from year to year by the Treasury in accordance with current economic conditions. The rate of interest must, of course, be the same as that used in the computation of the surtax tables.)	
5 Adjusted total income (sum of items 1, 2, and 4)	27,712.60
6 Present value of tax on item 5 (computed from surtax table)	1,204.60
7 Present value of past income taxes paid (sum of items 3 and 4)	264.60
8 Tax due (item 6 minus item 7)	939.42

The figures given are for the 1938 return of a taxpayer who is averaging over the two years 1937–8, having a net income, after exemption, of $9,200 in 1937 and $18,500 in 1938. For the first year, items 2, 3, and 4 are zero, so that item 5 for the first year is simply the income of that year, and so appears unaltered in item 2 above.

Item 6 is calculated as follows: The largest amount in the first column of the surtax table not greater than item 5 is $24,022.00, the excess being $3,690.60. The tax on the first $24,022.00 is given in the second column, $902.00; the tax on the excess at the rate given in the third column, 8.1836 percent, is $302.02, a total of $1,204.02. Except for the unrounded figures, this computation is precisely the same as that now required in computing surtax.

less equitable proposals for averaging and with the present computations required in the case of capital gains.

The chief drawback seems to be that a separate table is needed for each number of years for which taxpayers are permitted to average their income. Thus, after fifteen years of operation, fifteen separate tables would need to be drawn up; and while the individual taxpayer would need to consult only one, either the burden of selecting the proper table will have to be placed upon the taxpayer or the Treasury will have to undertake to mail each taxpayer the proper table on the basis of the records of previous returns. Whichever method is chosen, this should not prove an insuperable obstacle. Criteria 6 and 7 are thus fairly well satisfied.

Failure of the current tax liability to keep pace with the ability to pay of the taxpayer in accordance with criterion 4 has been a serious obstacle to the adoption of other forms of averaging, and actually was a contributing cause in the repeal of the Wisconsin averaging provision. It is possible to show, however, that under the foregoing method of computation the amounts of tax successively due will, under very general conditions, not bear too high a relation to the income of the preceding year. Under the Wisconsin method, a man with a sharply reduced income found that he still had to pay a tax based on the relatively high income obtained by averaging the income of the last three years. Here, on the other hand, a reduction in current income below the average of past years will cause the average, including the current year, to fall below the average on which the tax for previous years was based, and therefore will reduce the tax which should be payable with respect to those years. The excess of tax actually paid over the tax assessable in view of the reduced average is, in effect, credited to the taxpayer and applied in reducing the tax for the current year. In fact, it can be shown mathematically that, if the rate remains unchanged and the income for the current year is less than the average income, the tax payable for the current year will be less than, or at most equal to, the tax that would have been payable for that year on a straight annual basis of assessment. Actually, the only case where the payment due in any given year can bear an unreasonable relationship to the income of the year immediately preceding is the case of a drastic rise in the scale of basic surtax rates accompanied by a sharp decrease in the income of the individual taxpayer.[6] Thus, no provision for the relief of hard cases need be made

---

[6] If for the sake of simplicity it is assumed that income accrues and tax is assessed continuously, the equivalent constant income $\bar{r}$ of taxpayer C is determined by the following relation expressing the equality between the adjusted total incomes of A and C (see pp. 107–8)

$$\int_0^t \{r(\tau) + s(\tau) [e^{i(t-\tau)} - 1]\}d\tau = \int_0^t \{\bar{r}(t) + z(\bar{r}, \tau) [e^{i(t-\tau)} - 1]\}d\tau,$$

where $r(\tau)$ is the income of A at time τ, $s(\tau)$ is the tax payable, i is the rate of interest, e is the base of natural logarithms, $\tau = t$ is the time at which the current computations are being made, except in the years immediately following a sharp increase in rates. Even in the years when such relief is necessary, the form of the relief may be made fairly simple without opening any very serious loopholes, since the number of taxpayers who will be eligible for relief will be relatively small. The relief might take the form of a provision that the tax payable in any one year shall not exceed an amount determined by applying a supplementary rate schedule, somewhat higher than the regular basic one, to the income of the taxpayer for the previous year. The reduced tax payment may be carried over as a basis for calculating subsequent payments, so that in most cases the government will not, in the long run, lose any revenue through the granting of this relief except in the most extreme cases.

Unlike such moving-average plans as the Wisconsin plan discussed on page 105, no particular problems arise at the time of inauguration or abandonment of an averaging plan such as that outlined in the preceding four paragraphs. At the start, the basis that is already calculated for property in the hands of the taxpayer is all that is necessary to obtain an initial value for the capital assets of the taxpayer. If at any future time it is desired to abandon this method of assessment,

$\tau = $ zero is the beginning of the current averaging period, and $z(\bar{r}, \tau)$ is the tax payable on a nonaveraging basis on an income r according to the schedule in effect at time τ; $\bar{r}$ may be called the "average income" of A.

The total present value of the taxes on the incomes of A and C are to be equal; therefore

$$\int_0^t s(\tau)\, e^{i(t-\tau)} d\tau \;=\; \int_0^t z(\bar{r},\, \tau)\, e^{i(t-\tau)} d\tau.$$

Differentiating these two expressions with respect to t and solving for $s(t)$

$$s(t) \;=\; z(\bar{r},\, t) + [r(t) - \bar{r}(t)]\, \bar{m},$$

where $\bar{m}$ is the "mean effective marginal tax rate" given by the equations

$$\frac{1}{\bar{m}} = 1 + \frac{\displaystyle\int_0^t [1 - m(\tau)]d\tau}{\displaystyle\int_0^t m(\tau) e^{i(t-\tau)} d\tau}, \qquad m(\tau) = \frac{\partial z(\bar{r},\, \tau)}{\partial r}.$$

m thus corresponds to the rate of tax on the top bracket of income.

If the rates are progressive, it follows that

$$\frac{\delta^2 z}{\delta r^2} > 0.$$

Then, if $r < \bar{r}$ and if $m < \bar{m}$, which in particular will be the case when rate schedules are kept unchanged or lowered (and even if rates are raised slightly), then the basis may again be taken as that last declared by the taxpayer or as corrected by whatever restrictions it is deemed necessary to reimpose. These problems of allocation of income occur in any case with even greater frequency under a straight annual basis of assessment.

It is apparent that such an averaging device can prevent the avoidance of tax by the shifting of income only with respect to shifts of income between years within the averaging period. If it is permitted to shift income between years included in an averaging period and previous or subsequent years, whether or not they are included in other averaging periods, the possibility of avoidance will re-emerge. It will therefore be necessary to reintroduce at the close and commencement of each averaging period such safeguards as may be available to prevent such shifting of income between one averaging period and another.

The simplest method of preventing such shifting of income is to require that an inventory of the assets of the taxpayer be made at the end of each averaging period and that the capital gains and accruals so revealed be included in the income of the last year of the preceding averaging period. While this procedure might involve a prohibitive amount of administrative work if valuation each year

$$s \; < \; s(\bar{r}, t) + (r - \bar{r}) \, m + \tfrac{1}{2} (r - \bar{r})^2 \, \frac{\delta^2 z(p, \, t)}{\delta r_2} \; = \; z(r, \, t)$$

where $r \leq p \leq \bar{r}$. Thus, the tax is less than it would be without averaging.

If, on the other hand, $r > \bar{r}$, then, since $\bar{m} < 1$

$$r - s \; = \; (r - \bar{r}) \, (1 - \bar{m}) - z(\bar{r}) + \bar{r} > \bar{r} - z(\bar{r}) \; ;$$

that is, the residue after the tax is greater than the residue from an income equal to the average income.

If $z(\bar{r})/\bar{r} < \bar{m}$ (which will permit the current rate to be considerably higher than past rates), then

$$s \; = \; z(\bar{r}) - \bar{m}\bar{r} + \bar{m}r < \bar{m}r \; ,$$

that is, the overall rate of tax will be less than $\bar{m}$.

Finally, if $r > \bar{r}$ and $z(\bar{r})/\bar{r} > \bar{m}$(which implies that current rates are considerably higher than past rates), then

$$\frac{s}{r} \; = \; \frac{1}{r} (r - \bar{r}) \left(\bar{m} - \frac{z(\bar{r})}{\bar{r}} \right) + \frac{z(\bar{r})}{\bar{r}} < \frac{z(\bar{r})}{r} \; ;$$

that is, the overall rate of tax will be less than that on the average income.

The only case left out of the foregoing limitations on the tax is the case where $r < \bar{r}$ and current rates are so much higher than previous rates that $z(\bar{r})/\bar{r} > \bar{m}$. This is the only case in which there is a possibility of relief provisions being required.

The conclusions arrived at on the assumption of continuous payments are *a fortiori* true in the case where the payments are made annually, since similar relations can be obtained from those above by integrating the continuous payments over successive yearly intervals.

were required, as is the case when assessment on a strict accrual basis is proposed, only a small fraction of this work would be required here, since the valuation would be made only at relatively long intervals.

There are many reasons why the averaging period should be made as long as possible. Obviously, the longer the averaging period, the smaller will be the administrative task of valuation and checking valuations. If the averaging periods are arranged so that their ends are staggered, then the effect of the valuation date upon the markets may be reduced by lengthening the averaging period, since then the amount to be valued at any one time will be smaller. The incentive for the taxpayer to attempt to shift his income from one period to another will be smaller the longer the averaging period, since it will be more difficult for him to forecast for the longer period what the size of his income will be and to what rates he will be subject; moreoever, the actual variations in average income and average rates as between one period and another are likely to be smaller. However, the saving in interest to the taxpayer who transfers income from the last year of one period to the first year of the next will be substantially greater, since the interval between the average date of payment of the tax will be not one year but an entire averaging period. In general, the increase in equity afforded by the averaging method of assessment will become greater as the period is made longer.

The logical limit would seem to be to extend the averaging period from the majority of the taxpayer until his death. (Although it would be possible to start the averaging period at birth, the difficulties involved seem to outweigh any possible advantages, especially as such a procedure would tend to favor those who had taxable income during their minority.) If this plan is adopted, then only two valuations throughout the life of each taxpayer become necessary: one at the majority of the taxpayer and one at his death. The valuation at death is in most cases already required for estate-tax purposes, while the valuation at the time of the taxpayer's attainment of majority would usually involve only a very small amount of property and would be relatively easy to enforce, since in general it would be to the taxpayer's advantage to report as completely as possible.

This plan involves the imposition of a tax upon the capital gains accrued upon the taxpayer's property at the time of his death. That such gains should be taken into account in the return for the year in which the taxpayer dies has already been proposed as an independent reform designed to plug an important loophole. Doubts have been expressed, however, as to the constitutionality of such an assessment. If the direct imposition of such a tax does prove unconstitutional, indirect methods of accomplishing the same end will probably not be difficult to fund. There is the possible device of offering the averaging plan, coupled with the voluntary acceptance of such an assessment by the taxpayer, as an alternative to being taxed on an annual basis as at present; since in most cases the averaging method would, under identical rate schedules, result in a reduction of the tax burden, most taxpayers would probably elect the averaging plan. The rates applicable to those electing the annual basis of assessment might even be made somewhat higher, in order to offset any advantage that this election might have in affording loopholes for avoidance. Another method of inducing the taxpayer to accept such an assessment voluntarily might be to impose a special estate tax upon the transfer of assets containing such unrealized gains. The tax on the unrealized gains might even avoid the constitutional issue by being formulated as such an estate tax graduated according to the average income of the taxpayer.

Extending the averaging period from the majority of the taxpayer to his death automatically provides for a staggering of the ends of the averaging periods of different taxpayers so as to reduce to a minimum the influence on markets of the necessary valuations. The problem immediately arises, however, of how to treat taxpayers whose family status changes. One solution would be to cut the averaging period arbitrarily at the time of marriage, divorce, or death of spouse. Such a procedure, however, imposes a fairly heavy tax burden upon marriage, since the individual who marries will not be able to average his previous low incomes with his subsequent presumably higher incomes (or, in less frequent cases, vice versa) and will therefore have to pay heavier taxes than the man who remains single and is able to average over the longer period. This factor may altogether outweigh the concessions given the family man in increased exemptions; and, if it does so, will run directly counter to most accepted notions of ability to pay. Another method of dealing with the problem would require separate returns to be filed and the tax computed and paid separately by each member of the family.

A more radical but probably more satisfactory method in the long run would be to go one step farther than the community-property states and consolidate the entire family income in one return, apportion this family income among the various members of the family according to propotions fixed by statute, and compute a tax separately for each member of the family, using for each person the appropriate previous total adjusted income. This method has the advantage that it is likely to prevent to a very large extent the avoidance of tax by various methods of redistributing income between members of the family. Moreover, it would elmininate the arbitrary and unjustified advantage now enjoyed by residents of the community-property states. On the whole, this seems a more equitable method of taxation than that at present in effect, even if not used in conjunction with any averaging basis of assessment. In order that this change should not be thought of merely as a method of increasing the relief given the wealthy on account of their families, it should be accompanied by a decrease of about 50 percent in the income levels at which various rates of tax become effective, so that the actual change in the tax burden of the married will be relatively slight, with a substantial increase in the burdens of those individuals of large incomes who have no family with which they share this income.

Another important question is how far the averaging device should be extended to individuals with the lower incomes. A rigorously thoroughgoing application of the first criterion would result in requiring every adult to file a return no matter how small his income, and in permitting individuals to accumulate, as a deficit to be offset against any future income, any excess of exemptions and allowable deductions over gross income. This procedure is open to two very serious objections. The administrative job of auditing this vast number of returns would be staggering, especially as it would be necessary to check even those returns that were obviously not taxable, since if the taxpayer later has a large income, the amount of deficit reported in previous returns will affect his tax in such a year. The statistics might be interesting but would probably be rather expensive! The other serious drawback is that Congress might at some later time find that, having previously been somewhat more generous with exemptions and deductions than it would want to be at that time, the taxpayers would have accumulated such a backlog of deficits against which to offset any current income that no matter how far exemptions were then reduced, very little income from the lower brackets could then be made subject to tax. Thus, the result could conceivably be considered financial embarrassment on the part of the government, or alternatively a breach of faith with the taxpayer through the abrogation of the right to set off these accumulated deficits against current income.

A simple method of getting around these difficulties is to permit personal exemptions to be deducted only to the extent of net income. This would restrict the carrying-forward of negative income to cases where business losses, capital losses, and other deductions exceed net income; in such cases a slight penalty would attach in that the benefit of the exemption for that year would be lost. Under such limitations there would be no incentive in the bulk of cases for the filing of nontaxable returns in the expectation of future increased income.

In connection with a flat-rate tax at a fairly low rate, such as the present normal tax, the application of the averaging method of assessment under the foregoing restrictions would make a slight but on the whole insignificant difference, provided only that full carry-over of losses is permitted. It may therefore be quite sufficient, at least at first, to apply the averaging method to the computation of surtax only, continuing to calculate the normal tax on an annual basis as heretofore. This plan would cut the initial administrative load down very sharply; and after experience has been gained with these returns, the plan might be extended to cover the normal tax of those paying surtax, or all taxpayers, as seems desirable on the basis of such experience.

In the case of corporations the opportunities for avoiding taxation by shifting income from year to year are more limited than in the case of individuals, since the corporation income-tax rates are but slightly graduated and since the rates themselves seem to have been, at least in the past, rather more stable from year to year than the rates of the individual income tax. Nevertheless, the application of this averaging method, or some modification of it, may be of advantage even here, since the Treasury would thereby be freed from the necessity of checking inventory, depreciation, obsolescence, and the like, except at times of reorganization and to make sure of the absence of double counting. The question is not as important as with the individual income tax, however, since the need for the undistributed-profits tax and the special capital-gains provisions would not be affected, these being largely devices to patch up the unsatisfactory operation of the individual income tax.

Any averaging device will, of course, require a certain amount of record-keeping. The current records required under the present proposal consist of only four items: the year in which the taxpayer commenced to average, the adjusted total income, the total present value of past taxes, and the total value of the capital assets of the taxpayer as declared in his latest return. Further information may be filed but is not normally necessary for the checking of future assessments. It is probable that the decrease in other administrative work which is made possible by the employment of this method of assessment, such as the checking of capital-gains computations and checking deductions for depreciation and the like, will more than make up for the keeping of more complete records.

The averaging method of assessing income tax is not without its drawbacks. The keeping of records, the slightly more complicated method of computing the tax, the required final valuation at death (and perhaps at times of change of marital status), the existence of several surtax tables among which the correct one must be selected, the occasional need for the payment of refunds (in addition to refunds of overpayments resulting from error), and the more detailed treatment of family returns are the chief points at which objections may be raised. Special groups will also require particular attention: some approximate methods of dealing with part-year returns must be devised, unless the number of surtax tables to be used is to be multiplied to an extent that may be considered intolerable; aliens who draw their income from foreign sources in some years may obtain unfair advantages under the normal operation of such an averaging device and may require special provisions; changes of residence status may present difficult problems in the case of states employing such an averaging device, as may the taxation of nonresidents. These difficulties and the many possible methods of dealing with them cannot, however, be discussed at length here.

Against these minor drawbacks are to be set substantial gains in equity as between taxpayers with steady and those with fluctuating incomes, taxpayers with fixed and those with readily manipulated incomes, taxpayers with capital gains and those with other forms of income, and single and family taxpayers. The fact that similarly circumstanced taxpayers are treated similarly produces, in turn, still further desirable results, such as a substantial decrease in the worry, expense, and economic waste which now result when taxpayers seek to minimize their tax burden, a reduction in the amount of litigation, and a decrease in the influence of the income tax upon business transactions and the economic life of the community. For example, the securities market should be freer from the extraneous influence of the arbitrary rules concerning capital gains and losses, while the influence of the income tax in reducing the amount of capital for risky enterprises should be diminished, as abnormal profits in one or two years will no longer subject the taxpayer to such high rates.

The undistributed-profits tax, as well as the surtaxes on personal holding companies and corporations improperly accumulating surplus, could be repealed completely without fear of reopening loopholes for tax avoidance. The special provisions for the taxation of capital gains could also be repealed, as such gains could be included in net income without imposing any special hardships upon the recipients of such gains, while the limitations on the deduction of capital losses could be removed without thereby opening any loopholes.[7] The removal of the incentive to shift income from depression years, when rates are high, to prosperous years, when rates are low, should increase the cyclical stability of yield and in turn reduce the pressure to limit the deductibility of losses in times of depression, as was done in 1932. It is possible that this factor may also have some influence in reducing the severity of the business cycle.

The method of assessment outlined in this article has been developed on the assumption that the base to be adopted for income taxation is "accrued income" as opposed to the "paid-income" or "accrued-income-less-net-savings" base advocated by Irving Fisher.[8] It is possible to adapt this method of assessment, with

---

[7] Many of the complicated, controversial, and often arbitrary regulations for determining when gains are realized may be discarded; or, if this is not done, at least there will no longer be any incentive for contention on either side. The only necessary requirement is that any amounts received from property be either reported as income or applied to reduce the basis of the property. Indeed, separate accounting for individual assets is no longer necessary; a simple declaration by the taxpayer of the estimated total value of his capital assets as of the end of the year is all that is necessary, and accuracy need not be insisted upon. Similarly, regulations for the allowance of depreciation and obsolescence may be discarded and the allowance made as the taxpayer sees fit. The problem becomes chiefly one of avoiding double counting and seeing to it that taxpayers do not postpone realization of income to the point where there is danger of loss of tax through insolvency, or realize prematurely in the hope of being able to gain through the application of relief when in later years the taxpayers report lower incomes. This latter danger is already taken care of through the provisions in existing law for jeopardy assessments; further protection could be added by stiffening the qualifications for the application of the relief provisions. It may be desirable to provide a slight incentive to taxpayers to report income and pay taxes as early as possible by setting the interest rate used in the computation of the tax slightly above the market rate.

[8] The expenditure tax advocated by Irving Fisher is expounded in greatest detail in "Income in Theory and Income Taxation in Practice." *Econometrica*, 5 (1) (January, 1937), also less technically in "A Practical Schedule for an Income Tax." *Tax Magazine* (July, 1937).

a few slight changes (changes which, on the whole, make its operation even simpler), to operate on the latter base; in the case of a "paid-income" tax, however, the advantages of the averaging method are much less striking than is the case with the accrued-income tax. The paid-income tax is said to be inherently less difficult of administration than the various forms of accrued-income tax; if so, there would be less room for improvement in that direction; in any case, the administrative difficulties, if they exist, are not of the variety that would be reduced to any large extent by an averaging method. On the other hand the paid-income tax assessed on a straight annual basis may have a much more severe effect in accentuating the business cycle through encouraging spending in times of prosperity, when taxes are low, and discouraging it in times of depression and fiscal need, when taxes are high, than is the case with the accrued-income tax. Also a rather severe transitory effect upon sales may be expected at times of sharp increase or decrease in rates. The application of an averaging device would substantially eliminate both of these untoward effects. The possibility of the simplification of administration in the one case, and of the equalization of burden in both cases by means of such an average basis of assessment should make it easier to discuss the relative merit of these two bases for taxation on the basis of their long-run economic and social effects without having the issue confused by considerations of cyclical effects, relative ease of administration, and degree of discrimination against fluctuating incomes.

6

·

*Cumulative Averaging
after Thirty Years*

It is perhaps peculiarly fitting that an article on cumulative averaging should be included in this volume, since it was largely as a result of discussions between Carl Shoup and myself, back in the summer of 1938, over possible methods of taxing capital gains, that the concept of cumulative averaging developed. As we devised and rejected one scheme after another, either on grounds of what then seemed to be intolerable administrative complexity or on grounds that under some circumstances capricious results would occur that would have unacceptable incentive effects, the idea emerged that ideally, at least, the method of taxation should be such that the tax should be completely neutral with respect to the time at which a gain is realized, i.e., that the taxpayer should have no incentive in the long run for preferring to realize at one time rather than another on account of the tax. From this it was a short step to requiring neutrality with respect to the time of realization or reporting of all forms of income. It then remained only to work out the implications of this requirement for the formulation of the tax, and to devise procedures for the assessment of the tax that would be administratively feasible.

The scheme that was developed as a result of these stipulations[1] involved considering all payments of income tax, with respect to income reported since some base starting date, as interest-bearing deposits in a taxpayer's account with the treasury. The accumulated balance in this account would then be available as a credit against whatever tax is found to be due for the entire period to date, on the basis of the total income thus far reported for the period, according to a tax

Modern Fiscal Issues: Essays in Honor of Carl S. Shoup, Richard M. Bird and John G. Head, Eds. (University of Toronto Press, 1972), pp. 117–33.

[1] The basic concept of cumulative averaging was first published in [4]. The scheme was developed further and described more fully in [3], pp. 172–95, 285–7, and 417–27.

schedule appropriate to the period covered. The tax payment currently due would then be the excess, if any, of the cumulative tax so computed over the amount in the taxpayer's account. Eventually, when the averaging period is closed, as by the death of the taxpayer or in accordance with some other appropriate criterion, all unrealized gains or losses and accruals of income not previously reported are brought to account through a valuation of the assets of the taxpayer at that time (such as would in any case be required for estate tax purposes), and the corresponding final tax payment or refund made.

It is readily seen that if this procedure is followed the present value of the tax payments, computed as of any given date using the rates of interest credited on the taxpayer's account as the discounting factor, will remain unaffected by any shifts in the reporting of income within the averaging period. All that is required for the neutrality of the tax, with respect to the timing of realization, to be assured, is that the shifting of the reporting of income between the given averaging period as a whole, and previous or subsequent periods, should be effectively blocked.

It is immediately apparent that if the method of assessment is such as to make it a matter of relative indifference to the taxpayer and to the Treasury whether a gross income item or a deduction is reported in one year or another, many of the intricate rules governing the timing of the reporting of such items become essentially redundant and can be dropped, with great consequent simplification of the tax law. We will return to this presently. There remains, of course, the matter of preventing double counting of items or complete omissions, as well as the preventing of the shifting of income from one taxpayer to another, but that is another matter outside the province of averaging.

Although many of those who have discussed averaging schemes have dismissed cumulative averaging out of hand as being too complicated [2, vol.3, pp. 257], it actually turns out that the procedures required for the calculation of the tax under this scheme are not at all complicated, and that the administration is quite simple. For any given year, indeed, the calculations required in computing an individual's tax under cumulative averaging turn out to be substantially simpler than those for any other form of averaging in common use. The procedure is as follows: the current cumulated income is obtained by adding to the corresponding cumulated income, as reported in the previous year's return, the net income (after personal exemptions) for the current year, inclusive of the interest credited on the tax deposit account (which is, in effect, to be treated no differently from interest earned on any other type of deposit). On this new cumulated income the taxpayer computes, by means of an appropriate tax table, the total tax due for the entire averaging period to date. This computation of the tax from the table is in every way similar to the computation now required for the tax for a single year, the only difference being that the taxpayer must use a table appropriate to the number of years in his averaging period: if this is the seventh year of his averaging period, the corresponding seven-year table will contain income and tax figures roughly seven times what they would be for a one-year table, the percentage tax rates being roughly the same. From this total tax due can then be deducted the amount, including accrued interest, in the taxpayer's tax deposit account, and the balance will be the tax currently due.

The only additional operations that are required, over and above those required for a simple annual return, consist of the carrying forward from the previous return of the three items of cumulative income, cumulative tax balance, and the year with which averaging began: a multiplication by a rate of interest, three additions, and one subtraction. By way of contrast, the fairly straightforward averaging scheme included in the 1969 Canadian proposals for tax reform [1] would require carrying forward four income items, possibly from four separate returns, four additions (one of them of five items), two subtractions, two tax table computations (rather than one), three one-digit divisions, and one multiplication by five. The computations required for the current United States averaging provisions can be even more complex. While in the simplest possible case the computations are comparable to those of the Canadian proposal, the supplementary form provided for applying the averaging provisions contains space for no less than fifty-two entries. Of course, it is contemplated that the US averaging provisions will be resorted to only in a relatively small number of cases involving relatively severe fluctuations of income, but this in turn means that only the more extreme inequities due to fluctuating incomes will be rectified, and then only partially.

If abatement of inequities due to fluctuating incomes were the only issue, one might perhaps be willing to accept an averaging method which, while complex, would be applied relatively infrequently, rather than one which, while simpler, would by its nature have to be applied in a routine fashion each year by whole classes of taxpayers, even if at first only the taxpayers with incomes in the upper brackets would be involved. But while the objective of most averaging devices is limited to reducing excess burdens on fluctuating incomes, it has become increasingly clear, since cumulative averaging was first devised, that in addition to dealing with the fluctuating income problem, cumulative averaging has an even more important function to perform in serving as a key element in a far-reaching simplification of the entire structure of the personal income tax.

Indeed, the original motivation for the development of the idea arose, as noted above, from a desire to eliminate the complexities involved in the separate treatment of capital gains and to do away with the consequent need for elaborate and often arbitrary criteria for the Sisyphean task of distinguishing such gains from ordinary income. But the simplification possibilities extend beyond capital gains to all forms of time-allocation of income, including such matters as depreciation rates, expensing versus capitalization of outlays, accruals of pre-mium and discount, bad debt and contingent liability reserves, and distributed versus undistributed profits. Cumulative averaging would enable drastic simplifi-cations to be made in the tax law covering all of these areas, amounting in many cases to the complete deletion of entire sections. A recent check indicated that if full advantage were taken of the various opportunities for simplification, adoption of cumulative averaging would enable the currently applicable text of the internal revenue code to be cut in half, and the regulations probably by an even greater proportion [5]. Another indication is that of the 161 pages of the 1970 edition of *Your Federal Income Tax*, the taxpayers' guide put out by the Internal Revenue Service to aid the general taxpayer, seventy-five pages of the material consisted of matter that could be greatly abbreviated, and in most cases eliminated entirely, if cumulative averaging were in effect.

If cumulative averaging has so much to offer for so little, one may well ask why, in the thirty years that have elapsed since the proposal was first put forward, it has been first ignored and then passed over in favor of less thorough and more complicated averaging methods? It seems possible to point to a number of factors that have contributed to this result, the understanding of which may place the future of cumulative averaging in a different light.

Perhaps the most important factor has been the fact that cumulative averaging has had the reputation of being excessively complicated. In the original presenta-tion, indeed, the principle was presented that the present value of the tax paid on the cumulative basis should be so calculated as to be the same as that paid on the annual basis by a taxpayer with an equivalent constant income over the period. To those not persevering to a discussion of the practical application methods, this formulation seemed to promise formidable complexity. On later examination, however, this standard turned out to be not a necessary nor even a particularly desirable one. But though all that this standard implies was a particular rule by which the various tax tables for the various averaging periods might be con-structed from the tables in effect on an annual basis for the individual component years, the definition of the tax in these terms cast an aura of complexity over the entire procedure. Even though the taxpayer need know nothing about the method of constructing the tables in order to use them (any more than he has to understand the legislative history behind the present tables), it would presumably be necessary to explain the method of constructing the tables to maintain a consistent pattern among them to the congressmen called upon to enact the legislation. In addition it may have been felt that taxpayers would be disturbed at being asked to use tables derived in a way they did not fully understand, even if the mode of use were quite simple. Moreover, in the initial presentation it was felt necessary to demonstrate that the cumulative averaging method would never result in a current tax payment that would be unduly large relative to the income reported for the immediately preceding year (a failing that had led to the abandonment of some previous averaging schemes), and the mathematics that were used for this demonstration were moderately involved. All of this apparently created an impression of complexity that has not yet been dissipated.

Subsequent analysis has made it clear that there is no real advantage in using a constant income as a standard, but that on the contrary there is good reason for departing somewhat from it. The tax tables for the various averaging periods can in fact be determined quite independently of one another without breaching the neutrality of the tax with respect to shifts of income within any given averaging period. The consideration governing the desired relation between the tax tables is chiefly one of achieving equity between taxpayers with differing averaging periods. If a constant income is used as standard, then in general taxpayers whose averaging periods are cut short for one reason or another, whether by death, change of residence, citizenship, marital status, or otherwise, will bear higher burdens, if their average incomes vary from one averaging period to another, than those averaging over the combined periods or over longer periods. While this differential is a far less serious matter than those arising from income fluctuation in the absence of averaging, it is a differential which it would be desirable to minimize. Such differentials can indeed be significantly reduced without any added administrative or compliance burden simply by computing the tax tables for the various periods on the basis of generating a total present value of tax that would be the same as that which would be paid on an annual basis on an equivalent income that had some standard pattern of fluctuation impressed on it. For example, a tax on the income of a taxpayer covering the years from age twenty to age sixty could be computed so as to be comparable to the tax that would have resulted on an annual basis if his cumulated income had been generated by an annual income that started at a relatively low level and had increased steadily at, say, 5 percent per year. Or more elaborate patterns of fluctuations could be used as a basis. The result of this procedure would be that the taxpayer with an average degree of fluctuation in his income over the years would find that he would bear the same ultimate tax, whether he was able to continue his averaging period uninterruptedly over a long period, or whether the total period were split up into two or more separate averaging periods. Taxpayers with unusually fluctuating incomes, especially in terms of long period variation, would generally find a slight advantage in having longer averaging periods, while persons with unusually stable incomes might find a slight advantage in having their income experience broken up into a number of shorter averaging periods for tax purposes. But since such differences would usually be relatively small and their direction often hard to predict, and since in any case the closing of an averaging period would normally be tied to an important event such as marriage, death, divorce, or change of residence or citizenship that is not likely to be avoided, postponed, or advanced for the sake of minor and problematical tax advantages, any remaining nonneutrality of the tax at this point is unlikely to have serious consequences.

Such a modified standard for the setting up of tax tables does, indeed, reduce greatly the seriousness of the problem of dealing with changes in the status of the taxpayer, which was a problem often thought of as presenting formidable difficulties with cumulative averaging. For a country such as Canada, the problem might be considered most serious with respect to international migration of taxpayers, though in the United States it would be primarily change of marital status that would be of concern. Conceptually the simplest method of dealing with change of status is simply to break the averaging period at each such change, requiring a valuation of assets to be made at such times, with a bringing to account of all unrealized accruals revealed by such a valuation, so as to block the artificial shifting of reported income from one averaging period to another. Use of an appropriate standard pattern of income fluctuation in setting up the tables will then reduce the impact of the change of status on the overall tax burden to a minimum. A slightly more elaborate method, which would reduce the impact of marital change still further, would be to split the income of a married couple in two and require the inclusion of each half of the income in a separate cumulative average income for each spouse, continuing the averaging period for each spouse right on through changes in marital status, and computing a separate tax for each spouse based on his own history prior to marriage. There would still have to be an inventory of assets at the time of change of marital status in order to block transfers of income from one spouse to the other with respect to income for periods during which they were not married, but the degree to which the overall tax burden would be dependent on such a valuation would be considerably reduced, in many cases being uncertain in direction at the time the valuation is made, so that there would be less difficulty than otherwise with the valuation process. The problem of change of marital status of course occurs with other averaging schemes as well: in the current US scheme a very elaborate set of rules is required to deal with it. In any case, the problem of dealing with change of status does not seem to be an insuperable one.

Aside from practical considerations, cumulative averaging is sometimes objected to on grounds that as a matter of general philosophy a lifetime of income is too much to consider as a unit for tax assessment.[2] The objection seems to be to long-term averaging in general rather than to cumulative averaging specifically, though the objection has particular application to cumulative averaging in that cumulative averaging loses much of its appeal if the averaging periods are made

---

[2] "We could see no justification for using a lifetime, or the lengthy periods described above, as the interval over which income should be averaged" [2, vol. 3, p. 257].

too short and relatively frequent asset valuations are required. The objection is often articulated rather loosely, so that it is difficult to discern the precise nature of the objection, but there appear to be three somewhat distinct aspects to this category of opposition.

One aspect appears to consist of a feeling that in embarking on cumulative averaging one is undertaking a very long-term commitment to a rather specific pattern, and since, in the nature of the case, there can be no absolute guarantee that the future steps required to carry out the program will actually be implemented as promised, some of the beneficial effects of the promised neutrality of the tax may not in fact be forthcoming. It is not merely a matter of an administration being confident that the program will actually be carried out by its successors, but also one of persuading the taxpayer that this will occur as planned. If the taxpayer has doubts on this score he may well take a 'bird in the hand is worth two in the bush' attitude, and continue to act to minimize his current tax liabilities, discounting his increased future tax liabilities not only for futurity, but, in addition, to reflect an unquenchable hope that in the event he may be able to wriggle out of these liabilities in some fashion or other. If controls on depreciation and other means of deferring the realization of income are relaxed, such a taxpayer might be able to do more in this direction than previously. It may be possible to counter this tendency to some extent by offering relatively high rates of interest to be applied in accumulating the taxpayer's cumulative tax account, but at best it is likely to be some time before the taxpayer comes to feel the same degree of security in this nontransferable balance as he does in a transferable government bond, and offering a higher rate of interest may actually inhibit the development of such a sense of security.

A second, slightly related consideration is that in some sense the cumulation of income and tax over long periods conflicts with the notion of a statute of limitations. But the statute of limitations has always been a somewhat difficult concept to apply in the field of income taxation where what is income now cannot in practice be entirely freed from dependence on accounting entries made many years previously.

A third, and possibly more deeply felt, element in this philosophical opposition is the notion that in some sense, after the lapse of a sufficient number of years, an individual's personality changes to such an extent that his current tax liability should not be made to depend on what his income was a long time ago. A man in his fifties is considered in some sense a different person from the same man in his twenties, and the fact that the earlier personality had a low income is considered to be no reason for reducing the tax on the later personality, and an earlier high income no reason for either a higher tax in later years of low income, as with moving average methods, nor a higher earlier tax a reason for a lower tax payment in the later years of low incomes, as with cumulative or loss carry-back methods. Such an attitude may be related to the fact that in a number of cases variations in income over time will entail variations in expenditure over time, either because the individual does not foresee the changes in income with sufficient certainty to make the adjustment, or because he is simply unable to borrow against his future prospects. In such a case there is a real difference between the impact of a given tax on an individual with an uneven income and that of an equivalent tax on an individual with an equivalent steady income (in terms of present value). It is not clear, however, whether consideration of the dependence of the pattern of expenditure on the pattern of income would argue for less or more concession to the varying income than is afforded by long-term averaging, cumulative or other.

There are actually two almost diametrically opposed positions which can be taken with respect to such situations. One is that the tax should be levied in such a way as to produce minimum aggregate sacrifice in terms of some utility concept. Under this theory, if A has an income of $10,000 for an early twenty-year period, compensated by a $50,000 income in a later twenty-year period, whereas B has a steady $30,000 income for the entire forty years, and if the patterns of consumption are constrained by an inability or unwillingness on A's part to borrow against uncertain future prospects, it can well be held that a progressive tax assessed without averaging, by impinging more heavily on the spending out of the $50,000 income, would impose a smaller total sacrifice than an averaged tax that would attempt to adjust A's tax payments in the later period so as to equalize the tax between A and B over the entire forty years. Much as one might want to compensate A for his early relative impoverishment and low standard of living by tax adjustment in the later period, this can be done only by a transfer of income to the current A, to whom each dollar transferred will have a very low marginal utility, at an inordinately high cost in utility to other taxpayers such as B. Even in the most extreme case, however, such an argument would hardly justify a total absence of long-term averaging, which would imply that A would have to pay a tax during the later period equivalent to that paid by C who has had a $50,000 income all along. Both because C is likely to have a larger stock of accumulated consumer durables, and because A, in the process of adapting his lifestyle to his improved status, is likely to have had to make additional purchases and take a loss from the obsolescence of earlier purchases relative to current needs and standards, there is reason to judge that the marginal utility of income to A is higher than the marginal utility of income to C, so that for minimum aggregate sacrifice the marginal rate on A should be lower than that on C, even if it were admitted that A's rate should be higher than B's.

The contrary view is, of course, that A has suffered sufficiently relative to B if, whether from inability to forecast or inability to borrow, A has been unable to allocate his resources to consumption over time in the manner that would have turned out to be most satisfactory for him, and that to impose a higher tax burden on *A* in addition to this inherent handicap is to compound the disadvantage. Thus it can be argued that, even though in such cases long-term averaging does not produce the ideally desired result, it would still remain true that long-term averaging would be a step in the direction of such a goal relative to annual assessment, or to averaging limited to shorter periods. If one makes the normal assumption that the social welfare function has a smooth dome-like shape near the maximum, rather than a sharp peak (and given the uncertainties surrounding the function it would be difficult to claim otherwise, at least in terms of an *ex ante* consensus concept), then this consideration provides an added argument in favor of long-term averaging rather than against it, since abating an inequity in a region somewhat removed from the optimum would then be more important than a corresponding abatement in its immediate neighborhood, where the welfare function is not too steep.

To highlight the point with an admittedly extreme case, suppose a childless old prospector *P* with a life expectancy of only five years, after grubbing around for fifty years eking out a bare subsistence, suddenly strikes a bonanza worth $1,000,000. Even total tax exemption would hardly enable him to make up for the grubby years sufficiently to leave him well enough off to make most of us willing to choose his lifetime lot rather than that of a salaried man *S* who had enjoyed a steady income throughout the fifty years of $20,000, subject to a $5,000 tax. A concept of equity that attempts to equalize the lots of *P* and *S* would thus call for going much further than lifetime averaging. On the other hand, even taxing him on a five-year averaging basis, so as to produce a tax at the same rate as would be paid by an individual who has had $200,000 a year most of his life, say 55 percent, leaving him with the capability of spending say $100,000 a year over the remainder of his life, would appeal to some as being over generous, given the windfall nature of his income and his presumed lack of experience in the fine art of large-scale spending, and to others as being too rigorous, given the prospector's need to make up for lost time and the additional costs involved in establishing himself in his new prosperity. But to go all the way to lifetime averaging and reduce the tax to only 25 percent, leaving the prospector with an extra $50,000 a year that he will hardly know what to do with, at the cost of getting the corresponding sum elsewhere, will seem to many to be too high a price to pay in an attempt to approach an unattainable equity goal that may itself appear questionable.

While such an extreme case may serve to dramatize an issue, it is obviously not typical, and it would be wrong to determine policy by focusing attention on such cases. To the extent that the individuals concerned in fact do adjust their consumption patterns in relation to their overall resources, rather than keeping the time pattern of their consumption approximately in line with that of their income, neither of the mutually offsetting arguments presented above holds. Such adjustment of expenditure is particularly likely to happen in cases where a high income in the earlier years of a taxpayer is of such a nature as to cast doubts on its extended duration, as with athletic or entertainment stars, or where the income is in the nature of a windfall. Yet it is precisely in cases such as these that existing averaging methods fall down. A professional athlete, for example, who starts at age twenty with an income of $3,600 which increases steadily to reach $100,000 per year at age forty, after which he retires from active participation in athletics on an income of $25,000, will obtain no benefit whatever from the current US averaging provisions if, as could well happen, current income never exceeds four-thirds of the previous four-year average by more than the required $3,000. He would, in any case, derive relatively little benefit from any averaging scheme limited to a five-year period, as seems to be the general length of averaging periods being considered currently. In such cases it is difficult to find any cogent reason for saying that long-term averaging is inappropriate.

Setting forth a clear-cut case of a high-income period followed by a low-income period, in which there is no saving for the rainy day, is somewhat more difficult than for the reverse sequence. But while such cases can perhaps be discounted as being too infrequent to be a dominant concern in the consideration of averaging, for the sake of analytical symmetry we may consider the case, for example, of *D*, who expected to continue until his retirement in a $50,000 executive job, but in mid career finds the company dissolving and his specialized skills unmarketable elsewhere, so that he is down to an income of $10,000 with accumulated savings far below what he would have set aside had the event been foreseen. On the basis of a clean break with the past and no "carryover of personality" one might accept the idea that the current tax on *D* should be the same as that on *E* with a steady $10,000 income, as occurs with no averaging, or with averaging schemes, such as the current US scheme, that apply only where current income is above the average rather than below. It would require a hypothesis that whatever carryover from the past there is causes on balance a reduction in the marginal utility of income at a specified current income level to justify, on the basis of the minimum sacrifice criterion, a higher current tax on *D* than on *E*. This is, indeed, what would result from a moving-average type of averaging that has a sufficiently long period to span the two income periods, and what happens, to a lesser extent, with the Australian type of averaging which applies to the current income a rate of tax determined by reference to an average of current and past incomes. Moving average schemes seem, however, to have been largely abandoned, in part because they produced this effect, possibly to an excessive degree, and this may also have been a factor in the demise of the Australian type of averaging.

Cumulative averaging, however, produces the opposite result in such cases, in line with what happens with loss-carrybacks for more extreme cases and briefer periods. The effective marginal rate on the last dollar of *D*'s $10,000 income is roughly equal to that on B's \$30,000 income, but the total tax payable on the \$10,000 income is lower than that payable on E's similar current income, by reason of the credit resulting from reassigning, in effect, income, originally falling in the upper brackets and originally paying taxes at the higher rate applicable to these brackets, to lower brackets taxable at lower rates. Looked at from a strictly current cash flow standpoint, this would, indeed, again run counter to a principle of maximizing total utility or minimizing sacrifice in the short run. However, in this particular context cumulative averaging operates in a manner that can be considered to be closely parallel to the way in which social security and unemployment insurance programs operate. In both of these programs, benefit payments in periods of unemployment or retirement are increasing functions of income earned in previous periods. The effect is quite analogous to making tax payments vary inversely with previous income, and it is difficult to see how one can logically object to the operation of cumulative averaging in such circumstances as these without implicitly condemning the corresponding features of the social security system.

Even on minimum sacrifice grounds, these aspects of the social security system and of cumulative averaging can in principle be rationalized, by the notion that previous experience at a high income level increases, rather than decreases, the marginal utility of income at a given lower level of current income. The intensity of an effect of this sort, that would be required to justify either cumulative averaging or the social security provisions on a minimum sacrifice basis without carryover of identity, seems likely to be greater than most observers would feel exists in fact, though as this is essentially a subjective matter there is little that can be said here with assurance. Accordingly, it seems difficult to justify the pattern of the social security system without assuming some carryover of identity even over fairly long periods, and difficult to allow such considerations as justifications for the social security system without also allowing them on behalf of cumulative averaging.

Indeed, the main rationale for social security systems is that of the purchase by tax payments of benefits to accrue in later periods of low income. To be sure, the actuarial equivalence is often remote, and in some cases higher benefits are based on higher previous incomes even in the absence of a higher previous tax. But it is not too far-fetched to view cumulative averaging as a supplement to the social security system, in which payment of tax on a high income creates a right to a contingent future benefit in the form of a tax abatement, or refund, in the event of a low future income.

Accordingly, to justify objections to cumulative averaging on the basis of the excessive length of the averaging period for cases of declining income, it would be necessary to find some excuse for not applying these same objections to the social security system, a seemingly difficult task. Indeed, the effect of the many existing provisions in the tax law, which are designed, somewhat tortuously and with significant discriminatory lock-in effects, to enable individuals to defer taxation of a portion of their earnings, can be distinguished from that of cumulative averaging only in that they require specific action on the part of the taxpayer, often at considerable cost in terms of accounting expenses and loss of freedom of action. It is difficult to see why a pattern of taxation is desirable if achieved by the taxpayer deliberately and at a cost, but undesirable if achieved automatically and without overheads.

The corresponding objection to the application of cumulative averaging over long periods in cases of increasing income has a slightly better case, but still depends for its validity on the absence of any anticipation on the part of the taxpayer of his future higher income, plus a denial of the notion that equity would require the taxpayer to be allowed to make up for lost time, plus the acceptance of something akin to minimum sacrifice as a criterion for taxation. When examined in this way, the objections to long-term averaging seem weak indeed, compared to the outstanding advantages in terms of simplicity and equity in other directions. The continued presentation of such objections seems to be based more on a reflex reaction to something new than on a well thought out position.

A more potent objection, though one not often explicitly articulated, is that a large part of the advantages associated with cumulative averaging are obtainable only in conjunction with major tax reform in other directions, involving, as a minimum, full inclusion of capital gains and losses in income on the same basis as other income. The thought of proposing not only the averaging scheme itself, but also a sharp departure from an elaborate scheme of capital gains taxation built up over decades, is enough to give even the most enthusiastic reformer pause. At the very least, one can anticipate a rather significant transition problem: unless the change is made with substantial retroactive effect, one can expect a flood of capital transactions designated to realize gains under the old, more favorable conditions, rather than allow them to be carried forward into the new regime, and even of transactions at fictitiously high prices designed to buy a future fully deductible loss (or reduction of fully taxable gain) with a partial tax on an immediate gain. Given the months of open debate which the enactment of such far-reaching legislation would require in the United States, it would be difficult to secure acceptance of a sufficient degree of retroactivity to obviate this result. The problem would be less severe in parliamentary regimes, but it would still pose a serious problem.

To avoid the waste involved in the spate of transactions that might be thus stimulated, it might be felt desirable to offer taxpayers the alternative of voluntarily writing up their assets to current market value, paying an immediate tax on the corresponding capital gain under the old rates. This would involve a formidable task of checking to insure that the valuations thus tendered by the taxpayers were not excessive, particularly as this would be a concentrated, nonrecurring task coinciding with the introduction of a new system with its shake-down problems. One could expect that taxpayers would by and large write up their gains, but save the high basis of assets that had accrued losses. It would do little good to require that any taxpayer taking advantage of this write-up provision must do this for all assets, reporting losses as well as gains: those for whom this would be disadvantageous would simply go back to selective market transactions unless, indeed, revaluation were made mandatory for all taxpayers in specified classes, e.g., all those who had reported incomes of $50,000 or over in any of the preceding five years. One way or another the transition could be handled, but it would be a strain.

But while reform of capital gains taxation would be essential to achieving any major part of the simplification obtainable through cumulative averaging, this does not mean that cumulative averaging would not be practical and advantageous, even in the absence of such reform. Absence of capital gains reform would of course give rise to a temptation to be stingy about the scope of averaging: since the capital gains provisions are in part rationalized on the ground that they offer an offset to the greater irregularity of such income, it could be considered making a double allowance if income from capital gains were not only partially exempted from tax, but made subject to averaging on the taxable portion as well. However, in view of the very slight degree to which the capital gains treatment can in practice be justified as being in lieu of averaging, and the signficant discrimination that still remains between taxpayers whose capital gains are in fact highly erratic and small relative to other income, and those whose capital gains are more nearly regular and constitute a large fraction of their income, this seems an altogether inadequate justification for the substantial added complexity that this imposes on the averaging process. For example, the form used in the current US averaging provision has thirty-six out of fifty-two entries that are concerned with excluding capital gains and other special forms of income from the scope of averaging. Since the scope of averaging is already severely restricted by the requirement that current income exceed four-thirds of the average income of the previous four years by more than $3,000, there would seem to be no need for the further restrictions and their added complexity as a means of limiting the number of cases in which averaging would be used, and little or nothing to be gained by them in terms of equity. The whole thing, when examined in detail, begins to look like a green whiskers project.[3]

---

[3] "For he had hit upon a plan
To dye his whiskers green,
And then to use so large a fan
That they could not be seen."

In Canada, the fact that the proposed new averaging provisions may be introduced, along with a treatment of capital gains that approximates full taxation, may save the scheme from the growth of such excrescences. Thus, while the complexities in the existing law can spread their contagion into an averaging plan to make it more complicated than it would normally be, this need not happen if it is determined that complications will not be introduced merely to restrict the scope of averaging to cases where it is conceptually appropriate, but will be eschewed unless the realistic consequences of omitting the complexity are sufficient to justify it. Cumulative averaging can be kept simple, and, even if initially introduced on an optional basis, or restricted to certain classes of taxpayers, say those with incomes over $10,000 or even $30,000, would be far simpler than existing averaging provisions. More important, it would lay the groundwork for possible further simplification in other aspects of the tax law.

Another aspect of the objection to the cumulative averaging, based on its entailing widespread reform of other aspects of the tax law, is resistance to reform as such. Even if, initially, it is proposed to apply cumulative averaging only to an income tax unchanged in other respects, it nevertheless poses an inherent threat to powerfully entrenched forces. To the many groups of taxpayers that benefit from one special provision or another, cumulative averaging may be felt to expose more clearly the illogical or discriminatory nature of the special privileges, and thus constitute a threat to those who benefit from them. Even were one to offer a substantial reduction in the top bracket rates as an offset to the elimination of the loopholes, and even if this could be done in such a way that few, if any, individuals would be worse off as a result of the bargain, many of those affected might well prefer the known evil of high top rates, applied only to the unwary and the financially immobile, to the possibility that having traded away their special positions a subsequent congress, not considering itself bound by what in any case would have to be a somewhat vague bargain, might again raise the rates against taxpayers now deprived of their shelters.

Cumulative averaging, with its potential for simplification, may be an even more direct threat to lawyers and accountants whose knowledge of the intricacies of the present tax law is a valuable asset which they might be loath to see become largely obsolete. For the same reason, it may also be a threat to those legislators who value the power to trade and manipulate that an intricate law provides. While such individuals are not numerous, they are strategically placed to influence the development of the tax law, and their opposition, even though covertly and even subconsciously motivated, may be important.

Nevertheless, it is reasonable to hope that if the typical businessman can be made to realize that cumulative averaging offers the prospect of his being able to keep his accounts in any consistent way he sees fit, and to organize and formulate his transactions to suit his own purposes without fear of unfavorable tax consequences to himself, or of special tax advantages that might be elicited by his competitors, or of tax-motivated takeovers and mergers, sufficiently powerful support for cumulative averaging and associated reforms may be generated to overcome the inertia and resistance of the entrenched forces. Without cumulative averaging as a focus for a consistent reform program, experience with the 1969 tax legislation seems to indicate that piecemeal attempts to reform are likely to generate new complexities and inequities as fast as the old ones are cleaned up. And without general reform, the personal income tax threatens to deteriorate into such an unsatisfactory instrument that it may gradually lose its primacy as a revenue source and be forced to yield place to arbitrary or regressive forms of taxation, such as the various forms of corporation tax and the value added tax. Far from being a particularly elegant, but comparatively minor refinement, of the income tax, cumulative averaging may well be the essential key to retaining for the personal income tax its proper role in an adequately progressive revenue system. More than ever, it merits first place on any "Agenda for Progressive Taxation" [5].

References

(1) Hon. E.J. Benson, Minister of Finance, *Proposals for Tax Reform* (Ottawa, 1969).
(2) *Report of the Royal Commission on Taxation*, 6 vols. (Ottawa, 1969).
(3) W. Vickrey, *Agenda for Progressive Taxation* (New York, 1947).
(4) W. Vickrey, "Averaging of Income for Income Tax Purposes," *Journal of Political Economy,* 47 (June, 1939).
(5) W. Vickrey, "Simplification Through Cumulative Averaging," *Law and Contemporary Problems* (Summer, 1970).

7

An Integrated Successions Tax

The present gift, inheritance, and estate tax structure has many defects, among the most important of which are the many ways in which minor changes in the form of transmission of property, and especially in the channels through which it is transmitted, produce substantial differences in the tax burden, even though the ultimate beneficiaries be the same. Not only are these differences often capricious and inequitable, but they frequently depend on fine points of law so that litigation is encouraged and taxpayers are confused and irritated. To take advantage of these differences testators often alter the disposition of their property in directions which are likely to be less rather than more desirable from the point of view of the community at large.

A major root of the difficulty is that succession taxes are ordinarily computed on each transfer separately with very little if any reference to the relation of that transfer to past transfers or to the likelihood that the same property will be subjected to further succession taxation at a subsequent transfer. Minor exceptions to this rule are the exemption frequently found of property previously taxed within a specified period, and the lower rates sometimes found on the inheritance of a widow, which may be a partial compensation for the fact that such property is more likely to be taxed again relatively sooner than property bequeathed to children. Because the tax is thus assessed largely without regard to frequency of transfer, the taxpayer is under strong pressure to provide for the transfer of his property to ultimate beneficiaries with as few intervening taxable transfers as possible. Property is therefore bequeathed directly to grandchildren and where possible to great-grandchildren in preference to the more normal procedure of transferring the property to the widow, children, and grandchildren in turn.

Taxes, 23 (1945), pp. 122–7.

Where the heirs thus selected for tax reasons are minors or are otherwise considered less responsible, the possible dangers of such immediate succession are sometimes hedged about with trust provisions, and trusts may even be set up for the benefit of unborn individuals. Even under the new restrictions contained in the Revenue Act of 1942, the use of limited powers of appointment can operate to remove the corpus of an estate from federal estate taxation for an extended period. There seems to be nothing to prevent one or more states from providing still larger havens for tax avoidance through liberalizing their restrictions or mortmain, perhaps even realizing a little revenue thereby at the expense of the federal Treasury.

The forms of property tenure thus promoted have serious effects on the economic life of the community. The overhead of fiduciary administration and institutional investment is wastefully multiplied, while the supply of capital available for investment in equities and risky and pioneering investments is curtailed. The resulting testamentary provisions are frequently not as suited to the execution of the wishes of the testator as those that might be chosen were the minimizing of taxes not a consideration.

An Approximate Solution

In order to produce a more equitable distribution of the succession tax burden and reduce the influence of the tax on the forms which testamentary dispositions take (or at least bring these influences to operate in socially desirable directions) the tax should be so assessed that approximately the same burden will be imposed on the transfer of a given sum from one generation to another regardless of the number of steps in which this is done. This implies that bequests among contemporaries and between spouses should be taxed lightly if at all: they will be taxed again soon enough, on the average, and in any case will be taxed again before the property reaches the succeeding generation. On the other hand, bequests spanning several generations should be made to bear a commensurately heavy tax.

Distinctions of this kind of course form no part of a pure estate tax which takes no account of the relationship of the testator to the legatee. Such distinctions are quite analogous, however, to those now made in many inheritance taxes. It would be only a small step from such inheritance taxes to proposing that all succession taxes take the form of an inheritance tax having the rates graduated according to the number of generations between decedent and legatee: transfers to grand-children would be taxed approximately twice as heavily as transfers to children, and so on. Actual inheritance taxes in most cases graduate the tax on the basis of consanguinity rather than number of generations, and appear to reflect a concept akin to *legitim* rather than an attempt to equalize the tax burden. Even in the case of the inheritance of a widow, the tax appears to be lighter primarily because of presumed greater need rather than from any consideration of frequency of transfer.

However, it is likely to prove difficult to define in all cases the number of generations between two persons, particularly if the blood relationship is either involved, remote, or insignificant. A graduation based on such a distinction would probably prove difficult to apply and provocative of litigation; it might also be difficult if not impossible to arrive at a definition that was completely consistent with itself. A much simpler and more universal method of graduation would be according to the difference in age between testator and legatee. Thus for legatees older than the decedent the tax rates might be made very moderate, if indeed there is occasion for any tax; an older spouse in particular could properly be completely exempt. For legatees younger than the decedent the rates would be increasingly steep as the difference in age becomes greater. For example the rate applicable to a legacy where the age difference is forty years would be such as to produce a tax burden equal to the tax at the twenty year rate plus the present value (allowing for interest and income taxes) of a second tax levied twenty years hence at the twenty year rate on the balance.

The progression of such a tax could be based on either the size of the estate or the size of the legacy. While the progression on the estate basis would involve less change from present federal practice, this would involve some arbitrary ordering of the various legacies comprising the estate, and would seem on the whole to be less logical than a graduation according to the size of the inheritance. Progression based on size of inheritance would encourage wider distribution of legacies and would more nearly relate the tax burden to the ability to pay of the legatee who is more likely to be the bearer of the actual burden than the testator.

If progression is to be on the legacy basis, however, it is necessary to guard against evasion through multiple gifts or legacies. This may be done by making the tax cumulative in a manner similar to that now employed on the federal gift tax; that is, the legacy or gift received by a given individual would be added to the sum of all previous gifts and legacies received by him from all sources, and the net tax would be the difference between the tax computed on this total and the tax computed on the previous total, both taxes being computed on the basis of the age difference involved in the current transfer.

The table below shows one form in which the tables for the computation of the tax might be prepared. The method of computing the tax may be illustrated by the following example: A testator born in 1890 leaves $1,000,000 to an heir born in 1915 who has received previous gifts and bequests totalling $9,500,000. The total age difference is thus twenty-five years. For the first fifteen years of this difference, the tax on $10,500,000 is $3,496,440 plus 43.9 percent of $500,000, or

Table 7.1 Sample Portion of Table for the Computation of Inheritance Tax Graduated by Age Differences

Accumulated Total amount of inheritances and gifts received	Schedule I For use where legatee is older or less than fifteen years younger than testator or donor				Schedule II For use where legatee is at least fifteen but less than thirty years younger than the testator or donor				Schedule III For use where legatee is 30 but not 45 years younger
	Schedule I-a Tax where legatee is older than testator or donor		Schedule I-b Additional tax for each year by which legatee is younger than the testator		Schedule II-a Tax where legatee is 15 years younger than testator		Schedule II-b Additional tax for each year in excess of fifteen by which legatee is younger than testator		Etc,
	Total tax on amount in col. 1	Rate of tax on excess	Total tax on amount in col. 1	Rate of tax on excess	Total tax on amount in col. 1	Rate of tax on excess	Total tax on amount	Rate on excess	
(1)	(2)	(3)	(4)	(5)	(6)	(7)	(8)	(9)	
$ 0	$ 0	1%	$ 0	0.07%	$ 0	2.05%	$ 0	0.13%	—
5,000	50	2%	3.50	0.15%	102.50	4.25%	6.50	0.25%	—
10,000	150	3%	11	0.21%	315	6.15%	19	0.39%	—
20,000	450	4%	32	0.30%	930	8.5%	58	0.50%	—
—	—	—	—	—	—	—	—	—	—
—	—	—	—	—	—	—	—	—	—
—	—	—	—	—	—	—	—	—	—
9,000,000	629,350	9.5%	162,006	2.28%	3,059,440	43.7 %	122,504	1.42%	—
10,000,000	724,350	9.7%	184,806	2.28%	3,496,440	43.9 %	136,704	1.54%	—
20,000,000	1,694,350	9.9%	412,806	2.30%	7,886,440	44.4 %	290,704	1.64%	—
50,000,000	4,664,350	10.0%	1,102,806	2.36%	21,206,440	45.4 %	782,704	1.64%	—

$3,715,940, while the tax on the previously acquired $9,500,000 is $3,059,440 plus 43.7 percent of $500,000, or $3,277,940, so that the net tax on the current transfer for the first fifteen years of age difference is $438,000. Similarly, for each additional year of age difference, the tax on the $10,500,000 is $136,704 plus 1.54 percent of $500,000 or $144,404, while the tax on the $9,500,500 is $122,504 plus 1.42 percent of $500,000, or $129,604, making the net additional tax for each additional year $14,800. For the ten years in excess of fifteen the additional tax is $148,000 and the total tax $586,000. Alternatively, the computation required of the taxpayer might be shortened, at the expense of presenting him with a somewhat more elaborate array of figures, by setting up a separate table for each year of age difference. However, if the tables are to be printed on the instruction sheet, the arrangement here presented would seem about as extensive as permissible.

Thus without a great departure from present methods of assessment we can get a considerable improvement in the distribution of the tax burden and greatly diminish undesirable effects of succession taxes on the forms of devolution of property. Nevertheless there will remain many minor forms of capriciousness in the tax, and possibilities for avoidance will not be eliminated entirely, so that there will still be substantial pressures tending to complicate settlements and wills, with the resultant confusion and irritation of the taxpayer. The following is an extreme and perhaps unlikely but nonetheless pertinent example of the possibilities for avoidance: a testator wishing to pass his entire estate on to his son, instead of bequeathing it directly, could split it up among a number of his son's contemporaries, where the tax would be small because of the small amounts involved in each person's total inheritance, with the understanding, possibly enforced in some indirect manner, that these would in turn deed the split-up estate to the son, on which occasion the tax would be small because of the small age difference. The use of multiple trusts in this fashion could be inhibited by considering any trust as having the same age as the grantor, so that all distributions by the trust would be taxed approximately the same as direct distributions by the grantor. Even so, a number of factors, such as income tax, interest on the postponed taxes, the possibility of a change in rate schedule between one transfer and another, and the fact that the inclusion of interest on the corpus of the estate will push it into a higher bracket all would be factors to be considered and weighed by the testator in deciding upon the form of devolution to be selected.

A More Precise Solution

To eliminate these inequities and repercussions, prevent resort to artificial devices, and relieve the testator of the burden of considering the effect of alternative forms of devolution on the taxes he and his heirs will have to pay, it would be desirable to set up the succession tax structure in such a way that the tax burden would be exactly the same on the transfer of a given sum from one individual to another regardless of the number of steps or the channels through which this transfer is effected, and as nearly as may be regardless of the time at which it takes place. Needless to say, to establish a progressive tax which accomplishes this aim, collects an appropriate instalment of the tax at each successive stage, and yet takes into account all the various factors involved, will require a fairly radical departure from our present methods of assessing such taxes. Yet it appears possible to devise a tax which very closely achieves this result, and to reduce it to a form in which the computations required of the taxpayer should not prove unduly burdensome, even though the rationale of the computations and the derivation of the tables upon which these computations are based may be fairly abstruse.

"Potential Wealth"

If the total tax paid depends only on the ultimate distribution of inherited wealth, we can consider as corresponding at a given time to a given amount of inherited wealth in the hands of an individual born in a given year an amount of taxes considered to have been paid on previous transfers of this inherited wealth and on the interest on this wealth as it accumulated in the hands of the various holders. We want this amount of taxes to be independent of the form of previous transfers and to depend only on factors related to the current situation, such as the date, the amount of inherited wealth held, and the date of birth of the current holder. Inherited wealth can conveniently be defined as the sum of all gifts and bequests previously received, increased each year by the interest on the sum at a statutory but not necessarily constant rate, and decreased each year by the income tax attributable to this income computed at the top rates applicable to an income bearing a suitable assumed relation to the amount of inherited wealth owned at the time, and decreased similarly by gifts or bequests made, and by any succession taxes paid. If we add to this inherited wealth the present value of the taxes corresponding thereto, we have the "potential wealth" which the individual would have had had there been no taxes on the transfer of this wealth or on the income derived therefrom. If we discount this potential wealth to some arbitrarily chosen base date, we have a discounted potential wealth which we will call P. The P for a given individual will now not change as long as he is involved in no transfers and as long as his income bears the assumed relation to the amount of inherited wealth. Moreover, if a transfer takes place between two persons, the combined P of the two persons remains unchanged, since what is subtracted from their combined inherited wealth is added to their combined imputed taxes.

We can now construct tables which will enable the taxpayer to compute P readily if he knows his inherited wealth w, the date of his birth b, and the current date t, and also conversely to compute w if he knows P, b and t. The computation of the tax on a given transfer would then proceed as follows: Donor and recipient would both carry forward from a previous return their respective P's as of before the transaction (if there were no previous return P would be zero). From the tables they would both compute the corresponding initial w's. If the donor is giving a certain gross amount, he would then deduct this from his old w to get his new w as of after the transaction, and by again using the tables, we get a new P corresponding to this new w. The amount by which this new P is less than the old is then the amount to be added to the recipient's old P to get his new P, and from this new P the tables would give the recipient's new w. The excess of this new w over the recipient's old w would be the net amount he is entitled to receive, free of tax, and the difference between this and the gross amount given by the donor would be the tax to be paid.

In the case where it is desired to make a transfer of a given net amount free of tax, the computation is merely done in the reverse order. Adding the net gift to the recipient's old w we get his new w, from which the tables give his new P, from which together with the two old P's obtained in the same way as previously the new P of the donor can be calculated. The tables will then give the donor's new w which determines the gross cost of the gift and thus the amount of the tax. It should be noted that the w's, unlike the P's, do not stay constant from one transaction to the next, and thus cannot be carried forward from a previous return but are most conveniently computed anew from the P's.

The new taxpayer need not of course be concerned with the manner in which the tables themselves are computed. Moreover at any one time taxpayers will be concerned with only one value of t, so that during any one year the only tables with which it is necessary to confront the taxpayer will be a table giving P in terms of w and b and a table giving w in terms of P and b for the current value of t. Such tables would be very similar to the one of which a portion is shown above. However, as this form of tax can be made to equalize tax burdens fairly accurately, the degree of approximation introduced by using the same additional tax per year (or in this case P or w) over a considerable range of years may detract substantially from this equalization and it may be desirable for the sake of the more accurate results obtainable as well as the simplification of the computations required of the taxpayer to give a separate schedule for each annual value of b. Or if this number of tables is considered too great, taxpayers may be grouped into five- or ten-year age groups, the only drawback being the introduction of some discrimination (but no loophole for avoidance) between persons at the top of one age group and those at the bottom of the next.

Mathematical Formula Desirable

Actually the setting up of a set of tables, which will give a reasonable pattern to the tax, involved more than mere cut and try. There are a number of ways in which anomalies can arise which should if possible be avoided. It is essential, for example, to set up the tables in such a way that the P corresponding to a given w in one year will be the same as the P corresponding to the w a few years later that results from the accumulation of interest less income taxes on this w, assuming no intervening transfers and some arbitrary reasonable relationship between w and taxable income. An exemption must be provided for with a reasonably continuous behaviour of the tax near the exemption level. The exemption will necessarily increase in terms of current dollars over the lifetime of any one individual, but in general it seems undesirable that it should increase in successive years for persons attaining a given age in such years. The tax should be progressive throughout, both with respect to wealth and to age differences. To insure that insofar as possible desirable properties are incorporated in the tax, it seems wise to derive the table from some mathematical formula which can be readily analyzed rather than attempting to set it up by cut and try methods.

An extensive analysis of the various possible functions would be out of place here; it is hoped that such an analysis will be made available to those interested by publication elsewhere. Suffice it here to say that if we take m as the sum which would amount to w if accumulated from the date of birth of a given individual (or from some other fixed age) with interest less the income tax on this interest at the then current rates on an assumed corresponding total income to the current date, then the function P must be such as to be expressible in terms of b and m only. In particular, one function that appears to possess desirable properties and produces a reasonable distribution of the tax burden is:

$$P = \frac{m \, e^{e^{ab}} \, (\log m/E)^k}{A \, (b)}$$

or in a different form,

$$\operatorname{loglog}(PA(b)/m) = ab + k \operatorname{loglog}(m/E).$$

In this expression, $m = E$ determines the exemption level, $A(b)$ is the amount of \$1 accumulated from a base date to the time b (the time when the given individual attains a specified fixed age) at compound interest, and a and k are arbitrary constants that determine the steepness of the graduation of the tax. Below the exemption level, P is defined as $P = m/A(b)$ for purposes of transfers between persons below and above the exemption level; for transfers between persons both of whom are below the exemption level this function automatically gives a zero tax.

At the exemption level P has the same value whichever function is used, so that there is no discontinuity. a may be any positive number, but k must be greater than 1 and for maximum smoothness of graduation in the neighborhood of the exemption should be greater than 2. This function has the property that the exemption at a given attained age is constant regardless of the date of birth, although this exemption necessarily increases as the attained age increases. A further property of this form of function is that if the division of an estate of a given size among a number of heirs a given number of years younger results in no tax, this same result will hold for a similar distribution involving persons all a given number of years younger. Thus the rate at which estates must be split up in order to avoid the payment of succession taxes will remain the same from one generation to the next, depending only on the size of the estate.

Where there is net savings out of personally earned income over the lifetime of an individual, some gifts or bequests will utlimately be made from this personally earned savings, and in such a case subtracting the total of all gifts and bequests from inherited wealth will produce a negative w. For such negative values of w we can conveniently define P as being a negative quantity of the same magnitude as the P for a positive w of the same magnitude: $P(-w) = -P(w)$. This not only has the convenience of putting the tables to a double use, but serves to minimize the possibilities for avoidance of indirect transfers effected through the shifting of the burden of such items as household expenses. For example, if a husband and wife are of the same age and the wife has an inheritance, she may either save it intact and transfer it to the children, or may use it to defray household expenses while her husband saves a corresponding additional amount out of his earnings and makes a bequest to the children out of personally saved income rather than inherited wealth: with the above definition of P for cases where transfers are made from personally saved wealth, the tax is the same in either case or in any intermediate case. In cases where the age of the husband and wife are not the same, it will probably be extremely difficult to bring into exact account such indirect transfers between the members of one household; however, in the typical case in which the gainfully employed member of the family is the older and is also the one which normally takes care of the family expenses, the normal state of affairs is the one which also minimizes taxes and the tax would introduce no pressure for change.

In the absence of any reliable and uniformly inclusive records of gifts and bequests received in the past by present property holders, and in view of the fact that it would in general be to the advantage of most taxpayers to conceal any such past receipts and to claim that their bequest and gifts are derived entirely from personally saved income, it will probably be necessary to assume arbitrarily that all wealth held at the inauguration of the new method of taxation is derived from personally earned income and set the initial P at zero for everyone. This will avoid the necessity for any initial valuations or archaeological investigations such as plague excess profits taxes.

Special Problems

In any system of taxation that makes the tax burden independent of the channel of transmission, there will be transfers on which a refund of taxes will be payable. For example if a transfer from *A* to *B* bears a lower tax than from *A* to *C*, then if a transfer from *A* to *B* via *C* is to bear the same tax burden as a transfer direct from *A* to *B*, the transfer from *C* to *B* must call for a refund equal to the difference between the tax on the transfer from *A* to *C* and the tax on the transfer from *A* to *B*. While strict adherence to theory would require that such refunds be paid automatically and without restriction, in practice it may be desirable to place limits on such refunds, particularly since in some cases they may not be actual refunds of amounts previously paid. In the case of wealth held at the inauguration of the tax and wealth accumulated out of personal savings, for example, a refund would be indicated on all transfers to persons below the exemption level, although no tax has previously been paid. The amount of this indicated refund would become larger as the date of birth of the donor advanced, and would eventually result in a quite substantial state subvention of gifts from persons who have accumulated large savings from their earnings to persons who are exempt. To avoid this it seems proper to limit the payment of refunds to cases where taxes were actually previously paid on a previous transfer, and perhaps even to the amount paid on the occasion of a transfer to the present donor. Refunds thus disallowed might also be allowed as a credit against taxes payable on the subsequent transfer of wealth by the present recipient. This would involve some departure from the principle that the tax burden should be independent of the channel of transmission, and there would be reintroduced some pressure for the taxpayer to avoid those modes of transmission that would involve such a disallowed refund. Such cases would probably not be sufficiently numerous to cause much trouble, particularly if a disallowed refund is permitted to be used as a tax credit.

Transfers to philanthropic organizations will present much the same problem in an intensified form. Such organizations cannot be treated as individuals; indeed to do so would subject gifts to them to prohibitively high taxation. Nor is it practicable to treat such contributions as a form of personal expenditure and thus exclude them from the operation of the tax entirely, for to do so would merely create an incentive for such contributions to be made through some intermediary such that the transfer to the intermediary would call for a refund. It is thus necessary to treat such organizations as in effect exempt individuals, and to permit refunds to be made in the case of such transfers to exactly the same extent as on distributions to individuals below the level of exemption.

Trusts and Fiduciaries

For transfers involving trusts, fiduciaries, and powers of appointment, there is no serious problem, as such entities are mere intermediaries and cannot consume the estate themselves. The only question is how much of the tax shall be paid on the transfer of the estate to the trust or other entity and how much of it shall be left to be paid on the distribution to the ultimate beneficiaries. In order to provide a practical rule for determining how much of the total tax is to be paid immediately, it might be stipulated that a trust is to be considered an individual younger by a fixed number of years than its grantor, or having a fixed age at the time of its creation, or an age related to that of the ascertainable beneficiaries. What rule should be used would depend on the degree to which it is desired to keep the property in the trust down to the amount eventually to be distributed, and on the degree to which it is desired to limit the number of cases in which the government would act in effect as co-trustee through the collection of a high tax at the inception of a trust with a refund of a portion thereof at its liquidation, as might happen if too stringent an assumption were made. As for powers of appointment, the line between the power of appointment so general as to constitute ownership and one so specific as to constitute trusteeship would again be a matter of relative indifference, as the total tax burden would be the same whatever line is adopted; the matter at stake would be merely whether the tax should be collected immediately or an equivalent amount later.

Gifts to corporations present a more difficult problem. In principle such a gift is a gift to the stockholders in proportion to their interest, but to compute a tax on this basis would be almost impossible except in the most closely held corporations. In view of the infrequency with which such transfers would fill a genuine need, particularly in the case of widely held corporations, it will not be too necessary to insure that such transfers are not discriminated against. Where a large share in the equity of the corporation can be traced to a few individual owners, the gift may be apportioned among them and the tax assessed accordingly, while the gift apportionable to unidentifiable or scattered holders might be subject to a fairly stiff flat tax. In any case this remains an awkward type of transfer to deal with. Fortunately it does not appear to be very frequent. Of course, gifts by all stockholders in proportion to their holdings would be more in the nature of an assessment and would not constitute a transfer of wealth which would be taxable under a succession tax.

Interjurisdictional transfers are also difficult to deal with. For transfers from donors outside the jurisdiction of the taxing authority to recipients within, it will be necessary to restrict the P of such donors to $P = m/A(b)$ for negative values of m, and in the case of property traceable to within the jurisdiction to values of P resulting from original transfer outwards from the jurisdiction, and to use also values of b belonging to the original recipient of such outward transfer. Since of course no tax can be levied on a transfer between parties both of whom are outside the jurisdiction, to do otherwise would open the door to avoidance through arranging transfers from A to X to Y to B, where X and Y are outside the jurisdiction.

For transfers from donors inside to recipients outside the jurisdiction, it will be necessary to ignore in most cases any inherited wealth of the recipient from sources outside the jurisdiction unless some degree of cooperation can be obtained from the outside jurisdiction which would also have to have a similar tax law in effect. Even if similar laws are in effect in two jurisdictions, any difference in rate schedules would probably make any integration of the tax over the combined jurisdiction exceedingly difficult. Because of the difficulty of maintaining the principle of invariance in the case of interjurisdictional transfers, if there is to be reasonable assurance that no types of such transfers are more favorably treated than intrajurisdictional transfers, thus affording a loophole for avoidance, some types of such transfers will probably be more heavily taxed and even fairly heavily penalized. For this reason, this form of taxation seems unsuited for adoption by the several states. The states and other small jurisdictions had accordingly best content themselves with the cumulative inheritance tax graduated by age difference.

Interference of the Income Tax with a Complete Solution

As long as we retain an income tax, however, there remains in any case a bias in favor of transfer through intermediate holders that have no other source of income than the earnings of the estates held, and a bias in favor of postponing transfers where the income of the donor is smaller than the income assumed from his wealth in computing the tables and vice versa. In particular there is still a general bias in favor of trusts as intermediaries. As the bias in favor of such institutional investment was one of the chief defects which motivated the search for a new form of succession taxation, as long as this bias remains the proposed method of assessment can be considered only partially successful. Complete success in removing this bias can come only with the elimination of the income tax in favor of the spending tax. In theory, it would be possible to treat each tax as a separate case and go back over the income tax returns to see what would have been the effect of the shift of the income from the inherited wealth on the income taxes of donor and recipient and make allowance for these taxes in computing the successions tax. But such computations could not be reduced to manageable tables and would have to be made at great labor in each case individually. The sheer amount of work involved removes any such treatment from practical consideration. Moreover the end result would be merely an offsetting of the tax on the unspent interest against the succession taxes, a result which could be much more simply achieved by replacing the income tax with a spendings tax.

Nor would it do merely to eliminate from the income tax base the income presumed to come from inherited wealth, possibly imposing a separately graduated tax on such income which could then be allowed for exactly in the succession tax tables. There would still be an incentive for individuals to dispose of their personal savings by gift as soon as possible and thus obtain immediately for the interest on the sum transferred the more favorable status of income from inherited wealth subject to separately graduated rates. Only a shift to a spendings tax can permit complete invariance of the tax burden with respect to varying channels of transfer.

Spendings Tax

Indeed, continued retention of the income tax rather than a shift to the spendings tax can be justified only upon one of two grounds: either that the succession taxes are inadequate, a ground which would be removed by the adoption of some such scheme as that here proposed, or on the ground that concentration of economic control, as distinct and separate from concentration of current or potential purchasing power, is a proper subject for inhibitive taxation. If this be the case, and if the income tax is considered the most appropriate available method of inhibiting such concentration of control, then perhaps a tax structure which favors fiduciaries and persons of small earned income as channels of transmission and also favors multiple rather than single channels may have a reasonable relationship to acceptable social goals. If the income tax is considered to have the weight and steepness of graduation appropriate to bring the desired influence to bear on the concentration of economic power, then perhaps it is superfluous to make any allowance for income taxes in computing succession taxes, inasmuch as any such allowance would reduce this influence. However, it would seem at least possible that methods of taxation more closely related to the concentration of economic control than the income tax could be devised. Concentration of economic control hardly attains serious proportions until levels of income considerably above the present exemption levels are reached, and probably a combination of a spendings tax with an income tax having relatively high exemptions (say $10,000 or even higher) would constitute a tax system more appropriate for this purpose than an income tax alone.

Moreover income from personal services and from bonds or fixed indebtedness carries with it relatively little economic control and could appropriately be excluded from the base of an income tax designed for this purpose only. Even though income from equities and other participating interests may be but an inaccurate index of the degree of economic control exercised by the individual, inasmuch as great variations occur both in capital structures and in distribution of stock ownership which produce great variations in the leverage of a given investment, a special graduated tax on such income with a high exemption might be a suitable supplement to a spendings tax. If such a tax were adopted, its rationale would be inconsistent with any offsetting allowance in the succession tax. Such a tax could be graduated quite steeply, and could even have rates of over 100 percent at extremely high levels, provided that such rates were reached gradually over a period of time: any person not willing to meet part of this tax from other income would always be able to shift his investments to the nonparticipating kind, thus avoiding the tax and distributing economic control more widely. The exemption could well be put at such a level that an ordinary controlling interest in a small or medium-sized business would be exempt from tax or at least taxed only at moderate rates, and that only large concentrations of control would be reached. This however is only a collateral issue to the assessment of succession taxes.

Rate Changes

Any tax which like succession taxes is levied at irregular intervals can be reasonably equitable in its incidence only if the rates of tax remain reasonably stable from year to year. From this point of view past changes in estate tax rates have been somewhat too frequent. Even the scheme here proposed will not work satisfactorily if changes in the schedules are made too frequently. This does not mean, however, that schedules once set up may never be changed, or that an underlying form of function once determined upon must be adhered to ad infinitum. In particular, schedules and portions of schedules that have not yet been used to determine a tax, either directly or through their counterparts applicable in previous years, can be changed without raising any special problems, while portions of schedules that have been but little used can be changed without causing serious difficulty. Such changes will come to affect substantial numbers of returns only over several years, however, and the effect of such changes on total revenues will be slow. Where a more rapid change in revenues is desired, it will be necessary to modify schedules that have already been used. Even here it is possible to devise satisfactory methods for shifting gradually, as transfers are made, from the old P to the new without giving up the principle of invariance on the one hand or imposing intolerable tax burdens on the other, albeit with considerable increase in the complexity of the computations during the transition. Succession taxes should not be relied upon for any dominant part of total revenues, however, and if at all possible, changes in the schedules should be made far enough in advance so that once a portion of the schedules has been used to compute a tax, it and the corresponding portions of schedules for use at different times should stay in effect until they become obsolete through the death of all the persons to whom they might be applicable.

Summary and Appraisal

The cumulative inheritance tax graduated by age differences would go far toward alleviating the inequities and pressures arising under the present type of estate taxation. However, it would seem that the additional advantages of going all the way to a tax which as nearly as may be is independent of the channels of transmission (or at least, if the income tax or a variant thereof is retained, depends on channels of transfer in a consistent and socially desirable direction) would far outweigh any additional complexities involved. The additional computations involved are three or four additional additions and subtractions, and four instead of two references to the tables; the type of table being substantially the same in both cases; the additional datum required amounts to only the initial P of the donor, the initial P of the recipient being equivalent to the accumulated total of previous inheritances and gifts required for the cumulative inheritance tax. It would be necessary to file duplicate returns on each transfer, one for the file of the donor and one for the file of the recipient (these might be reduced to mere excerpts for this purpose) and presumably to disclose to the payer of the tax the P of the other party, if not vice versa as well. As the P would not necessarily bear any definite relationship to the total wealth of an individual, although it might give some indication of it, this disclosure would probably not meet with serious objections on the part of taxpayers.

On the other side of the ledger, it would no longer be necessary for a testator to consider in great detail the tax effects of a contemplated disposition of his estate; he could concentrate his attention on the desired ultimate distribution of his estate and on the most appropriate channels for putting his desires into effect. No longer would he have to speculate on whether a proposed beneficiary might survive and cause a contemplated gift to produce a tax saving or whether a premature death might turn the anticipated tax saving into an additional tax burden. No longer would trusts be set up primarily for tax avoidance purposes, with the result that institutional overheads would be reduced and the supply of equity and risk-bearing capital increased. Probate and fiduciary counsel would spend less of their time in advising their clients on how to avoid the clutches of the tax collector and more of their time in more productive endeavors. Moot questions of law as to the precise occasion on which a taxable transfer takes place will become unimportant, as the tax burden in most cases will be the same whichever way the line is drawn. Finally greater equity in the distribution of the burden and the absence of capricious variations in the tax should produce more willing cooperation on the part of the taxpayer in the assessment of the tax.

8

·

Expenditure, Capital Gains, and the Basis of Progressive Taxation

Although the idea of a progressively graduated tax based on aggregate personal expenditure is by no means new, the lack of practical experience with any such tax is a perennial excuse for speculation about what such a tax would involve in practice, and the appearance of Nicholas Kaldor's recent book[1] advocating such a tax as a substitute for the surtax on personal incomes, following close on a series of far-ranging Royal Commission reports[2] is a further occasion for a re-examination of this tax in the light of present day income tax practices.

Income and Expenditure Taxes Compared in Ideal Terms

In this area, more than in most, there is a sharp distinction to be drawn between considerations that would apply to the comparison of theoretically perfect taxes of the various types and those that would apply to the taxes as actually administered. Kaldor's treatment suffers considerably from a tendency to compare an idealized expenditure tax with the income tax as it exists, which is inappropriate unless indeed the tacit assumption is made that by turning over a new leaf a degree of perfection can be attained that has become difficult or impossible in the older form of taxation by reason of the accumulation of special vested interests and

The Manchester School, 25 (1957), pp. 1–25; excerpted in *Public Finance*, R.W. Houghton, Ed., Penguin Modern Economics Reading (1970), pp. 117–28; reprinted as 'Ausgaben, Kapitalgewinne und die Grundlage Progressive Besteurerung' in *Finanztheorie*, Horst Claus Recktenwald, Herausgeber, (Cologne: Kiepenhauer und Witech 1969), pp. 425–33.

[1] Nicholas Kaldor, *An Expenditure Tax* (London, Allen and Unwin, 1955), pp. 249.
[2] Royal Commission on the Taxation of Profits and Income: *First Report* (13 February, 1953), Cmd. 8761; *Second Report* (9 April, 1954), Cmd. 9105; *Final Report* (20 May, 1955), Cmd. 9474.

commitments to untenable positions. Kaldor's lack of success in getting the majority of the recent Royal Commission to accept a proposal for fuller taxation of capital gains[3] might indeed thus partly justify his approach. On the other side, even less tolerable is the reverse error of ignoring the difficulties of the present system, merely because they are somehow being lived with, while making the most of all of the difficulties, real or imagined, associated with the new.

Even-handed comparison of two taxes in terms of imperfect practice is difficult, however, not only because imperfection is always more complex than perfection, but because the nature of the imperfections to be encountered in practice are difficult to predict, particularly with respect to the new law. As a first approximation, therefore, it is helpful to compare a reasonably perfected income tax with an equally idealized expenditure tax; when this has been done it will be easier to assess what changing to a new basis of taxation may have to offer as compared to reform of the existing tax.

If we begin accordingly by considering on the one hand a comprehensive income tax that insures that all forms of income, whether as dividends, interest, or capital gains sooner or later pay income tax on the same footing, and in which irregularities in the receipt or realization of income are adequately dealt with by some system of averaging, and on the other a correspondingly perfected spendings tax, we find that at least some of the differences between the two forms of taxation disappear.

Eliminating Bias against Risk

For example, it is quite true that income tax laws as actually applied in nearly all countries have a considerable bias against risky investment.[4] This arises in some cases because with annual assessment and inadequate averaging under progressive rates the realization of a large profit will push incomes up into the higher surtax brackets, whereas a corresponding loss, even if fully deductible, will cause tax abatement at a lower marginal rate. In other cases, particularly the development of new products or processes by firms established for this purpose, profits, if the venture is successful, often present themselves most naturally in the form of dividends at a relatively high level, taxable at the full rates as income, whereas if the venture is a failure, so that much or all of the investment is lost, this will ordinarily rate as a capital loss, deductible, if at all, only subject to various restrictions and resulting in a relatively low level of tax abatement. A somewhat similar phenomenon arises even more specifically if the investment is in bonds

---

[3] See Cmd. 9474, pars, 80–117, pp. 25–40; pars. 34–84, pp. 365–82.
[4] See, for example, Kaldor, *Expenditure Tax*, chapter III, pp. 102–29.

subject to risk of default of principal, in which case again the higher rate of interest obtained in consideration of the risk is fully taxed, but the loss in the event of default gets inadequate tax consideration.

But neither of these effects is inherent in the concept of an income tax. With full consideration of all gains and losses in the tax base, averaging of income over a sufficiently long period would greatly reduce the difference between the rate at which a gain would increase tax and the rate at which a loss would diminish it, since the marginal rate would depend not on the income for a single year but on the income of an extended period taken as a whole, in relation to which the gain or loss would be much smaller and thus cause much less variation in the point on the scale of progression at which the taxpayer would find himself. Moreover, to the extent that this bias against risky investment persists even with adequate averaging, it may be considered to reflect a consistent social policy. For if the progression of the tax schedule is deemed a reflection of the extent to which the public policy looks with disfavor on inequality in the distribution of income, then it will be equally in accord with public policy to discourage individuals to place such large parts of their capital in such hazardous ventures as would carry an unduly heavy risk of greatly enriching or impoverishing them. Such a degree of bias against risky investment is inherent in any progressive tax system, including an expenditure tax, since the eventual spending of the proceeds of a successful venture would be subject to higher rates of tax than would the expenditure foregone in case of loss.

Consistent treatment under almost any concept of income would seem to require the avoidance of situations where the revenue plays "heads I win, tails you lose" with the taxpayer, and the allowance of full deduction of losses in all cases where the profits, if realized, even if in a somewhat different nominal form, would have been taxed. But it is extremely difficult to do this consistently unless substantially all gains and losses are brought into consideration in the determination of net income (with the possible exception of certain losses not of an investment nature, such as gambling losses, or casualties related to consumption such as a mishap to a personal automobile). Losses from ventures whose successful outcome will normally result in taxable profits appear in a wide variety of ways, so that it is difficult to deny deductibility to any wide category of loss from investment without introducing an anti-risk bias. And it is hardly to be expected that deductibility should be allowed for any given type of loss without correspondingly taxing the gains in what appear to be analogous cases. Thus a full taxation of capital gains would seem to be a prerequisite for avoiding this anti-risk bias in the income tax.

Curiously enough, it is as a means of mitigating this bias that partial or complete exemption of capital gains is often advocated. But it is doubtful whether any kind of capital gains exemption can do anything but substitute one kind of bias for another, namely bias in favour of investments that are likely to reap their return in capital gain form over those more likely to reap returns in forms taxable in full; this distinction does not necessarily involve any significant element of risk, witness the case of the gilt-edged short-term bond selling at a discount because its coupon rate has been fixed below the market rate, possibly with tax advantages in mind. Insofar as the elimination of bias against risk is concerned, averaging plus inclusion of capital gains and losses in the income tax base can be considered an alternative to shifting to an expenditure tax. Kaldor would appear to be in error in his repeated assertion that a tax on accrued income would discriminate against risk more severely than the existing income tax.[5]

Offsetting Pressures for Retention of Corporate Earnings

Another point where existing income taxes offend is in their impact on corporate finance and more particularly on the disposition of corporate profits. Especially where corporations are owned predominantly by shareholders in the upper surtax brackets, the tax results in considerable pressure for companies to avoid the distribution of taxable dividends, and instead to retain large fractions of their net earnings, either for expansion of the company's own business, retirement of debt, or investment in securities of third parties. There is considerable difference of opinion as to whether this is on balance desirable, and the balance of considerations may shift from one side to the other over time; but whatever position is taken in general, the specific form in which the tax pressure is exerted seems to bear no relation to any public purpose. From one point of view such retention is undesirable in that it subjects the investment process to biases in the direction of pandering to the already suspect desire of corporation executives to add to their economic imperium in possible disregard of productivity considerations; in that it reduces the supply of investment funds available to rapidly growing smaller corporations through the flotation of new securities (as a supplement to what they could secure through the retention of their own earnings where this is justified by prospective returns); and in that it tends to encourage the growth of established companies with consequent tendencies for monopoly and the dominance of the economy by the very large companies. In the United States, concerns of this nature have been reflected in such phenomena as the short-lived surtax on undistributed profits of 1936–9, the notorious section 102 surtax on corporations having improper accumulations of surplus, and the special penalty taxes on personal holding companies that accumulate undistributed profits.

---

[5] *Ibid.*, pp. 117, 121.

In Britain, the quite properly greater concern for anti-inflationary considerations and the greater tolerance toward monopoly have resulted in what is to the American observer the amazing spectacle of a profits tax which discriminates against distributed profits, adding its pressures to those of the surtax. Yet it is highly doubtful whether such a provision has had any important direct anti-inflationary effects (particularly as the individuals whose dividends were thereby kept low probably had low propensities to consume and were in many cases in a position to finance consumption expenditures in other ways), even though such measures may have filled a need in making restrictive policies in other directions more palatable politically. Granting everything that may be said in favor of internal financing as being economical in avoiding the expenses connected with the flotation of securities, and as directing funds more or less automatically in the directions that have been proved most profitable in the past, nevertheless it seems hardly appropriate to further reinforce these factors, which are quite adequately under consideration by company directors, by artificial and irrelevantly modulated tax pressures. Moreover the consequence for the present seems to be that such a provision, once enacted, is difficult to eliminate without causing a windfall to shareholders in the form of increased share prices, which in turn could only be tolerated on equity grounds if there were adequate provision for the taxing of the resulting capital gains.

It is entirely possible to design an income tax structure that is reasonably free from such irrelevant and unintended influences on company policy. Indeed, under an income tax with full inclusion of gains and losses and cumulative averaging in which the interest factor is taken into account,[6] the deferment of the realization of the income by the shareholder that results from the retention of earnings by the company would not affect the ultimate burden of the shareholder, and such a tax would therefore be reasonably neutral on this point. Even if a less pretentious form of averaging is used that does not take into account the interest factor, it would be possible to keep the tax system as a whole reasonably neutral by applying to the accumulated undistributed earnings of companies an annual tax at say 1 percent or 2 percent, this being deemed to be equal to an interest charge of say 5 percent on the surtax which is being postponed by reason of the nondistribution of the earnings.[7] Problems of discrimination against risk and pressures on dividend policy are thus both capable of being taken care of within the framework of the income tax concept, and it is accordingly only to a limited extent that an expenditure tax can be considered necessary to achieve these ends.

---

[6] Cf. the writer's *Agenda for Progressive Taxation* (New York: Ronald, 1947), chapter V, esp. pp. 122 ff.

[7] Cf. the writer's "A Reasonable Undistributed Profits Tax," *Taxes* (February, 1945), pp. 122–7.

Comparative Effects on Saving: the Net Rate of Return

A third major claim for the expenditure tax is that it will encourage saving. How weighty this consideration is will depend on the context of general economic conditions, anticipations regarding the future of the tax, the motives that influence the saving of individuals, and possible criteria as to the socially desirable amount of saving. If the tax is thought of as a permanent and long-established tax, then as Kaldor and others before him have shown,[8] the effect of changing to an expenditure tax is to permit the individual to adjust the time pattern of his consumption, through corresponding adjustments in his savings program, so that it will bear a correct relation to the relative social costs of providing goods and services at different times as this relative cost is reflected in the market rate of interest, whereas the income tax distorts this relationship, making present rather than future consumption unduly attractive to the individual in spite of its higher drain on the resources of the community. This is the traditional analytic argument for preferring the expenditure tax to the income tax, and there is certainly no denying its validity, nor any possibility of amending the income tax so as to avoid this defect without in effect converting it into an expenditure tax. Opinions will differ, however, as to how important the changes that would occur on this basis would be. It is at least arguable that the increase in the savings of an individual in a 16/- in the pound tax bracket that results from increasing the net rate of return on his savings, after tax, from say 1 percent to 5 percent by shifting from an income tax to an expenditures tax, and similarly for other taxpayers, is not of paramount importance to the economy as a whole.

Savings in an Emergency

There is a case of a different order to be made, not discussed by Kaldor, for a temporary expenditures tax to be applied at a time of great general shortage of consumer goods, as during a war or other emergency period.[9] In this case the tax is specifically not expected to continue after the emergency is over, or at least only at much lower rates, so that deferment of expenditure not only defers the tax, but reduces the applicable rate, and the incentive for individuals to save, at least temporarily, is greatly enhanced. In such contexts the argument for the expenditure tax is much stronger than it is for a permanent tax; indeed it can be considered as a form of graduated generalized rationing. One could even argue

---

[8] Kaldor, *Expenditure Tax*, chapter II, pp. 79–101.
[9] Cf. the writer's "The Spendings Tax in Peace and War," *Columbia Law Review*, 43 (1943), pp. 165–70.

that the possibility of such emergency use would be a reason for using the tax in normal times in order to have the administrative machinery ready for the emergency.

Effects on the Concentration of Economic Power

A much more controversial issue that arises in considering an expenditure tax as a permanent tax is the effect of such a change on the concentration of the ownership of wealth and of economic power. Kaldor claims that "by making the expenditure tax sufficiently progressive it would always be possible to prevent the rich from saving too much,"[10] but this is patently erroneous, since spendings tax rates, however progressive, could have no effect on a man who persisted in living on a frugal scale in spite of his great wealth, even leaving out of account the easing of this frugality by the nontaxable perquisites that almost invariably accompany the possession of great wealth. Possibly there may be some who would view such accumulations of wealth in private hands with equanimity and even approval so long as the spending tax rates were such as to induce their possessors to treat them as funds held in trust rather than for personal gratification through consumption of the income. It can be hazarded, however, that the weight of opinion would regard with some misgiving even that accumulation that might be made by a man such as Henry Ford within his own lifetime, let alone an accumulation continued unchecked over several generations. If a spendings tax is to be substituted for an income tax, some complementary form of progressive taxation seems called for to check the more extreme accumulations.

Corresponding Adjustment of Death Duties

The usual recourse at this point is to invoke heavy death duties as the remedy. Even without balking at the very substantial possibilities that would still remain for the accumulation of wealth within a single lifetime, one can point to the very serious difficulties, often overlooked, that stand in the way of setting up an effective, sharply progressive succession tax that is reasonably free from untoward consequences. Present-day death duties are subject to major avoidance through gifts *inter vivos*, through skipping generations by the setting up of trusts or otherwise, and in many other ways; if these avenues of avoidance were effectively blocked, another very troublesome one of international transfers and migrations would arise that could be blocked only at the expense of seriously interfering with

[10] Kaldor, *Expenditure Tax*, p. 97.

legitimate and desirable international movements of capital; the present international convention to the effect that only the jurisdiction of situs may tax real property would have to give way. Kaldor suggests that an appropriate succession duty should vary the rate of tax according to the net wealth of the recipient,[11] possibly also the difference in age between transferor and transferee would need to be taken into consideration[12] so as to avoid the incentives that would otherwise develop if the rates were at all steep to skip over as many generations as the rules against perpetuities will allow, with consequent undesirable tying up of property in various kinds of trusts to the detriment of the supply of venture capital and of flexibility in the use of property.

Thus at least one of the liabilities of the expenditures tax is that its substitution for an income tax renders more crucial the solution of the far from easy problem of developing an adequate succession duty. To make a fair comparison between the two taxes thus requires considering not merely the change to the expenditure tax itself, but also the appropriate changes in succession taxation that would be called for. This necessarily greatly complicates the comparison. However, a not too difficult comparison becomes available if in lieu of imposing a specific succession tax we merely on the one hand apply the expenditures tax to all gifts and bequests, considering them to be a form of personal consumption of the donor, while under the income tax on the other hand we consider gifts and bequests to be taxable income to the recipient. Such an arrangement would not be satisfactory in practice, because of the avoidance possibilities mentioned above, so that caution must be used in interpreting the comparison. Assume a stable price level, and suppose further that in both the income tax and the expenditure tax, to avoid the effects of fluctuations from year to year in the tax base, which with the inclusion of gifts and bequests would be particularly severe, the tax is assessed on a cumulative basis, comparable to the method used for PAYE, the final tax liability being assessed on the basis of an aggregate of the income or expenditure over the entire period, prior tax payments being considered a deposit against the ultimate liability, compound interest being credited at an appropriate rate on this deposit. The aggregate amount brought to account for tax purposes for any individual will be the same in both cases, the difference between the impact of the two taxes being entirely due on the one hand to the relative weights given the quantities reported for the various years in aggregating them, and on the other hand to the timing of the interim payments on account.

[11] *Ibid.*, p. 101.
[12] Vickrey, *Agenda for Progressive Taxation*, pp. 216 ff.

Weighting Effects

As to weighting, in the case of an income tax it would be appropriate to make each year's income count the same as any other, to avoid any arbitrary effects on the tax burden due to shifts in the time of realization of income; for the spendings tax it would be more appropriate to use a present value of the expenditures of various dates at compound interest so as properly to express the slighter burden imposed on society by the later consumptions. The weighting is then such as still to preserve the difference between the two taxes in the net rate of return offered in terms of future consumption or ability to make bequests in return for present abstinence: under the expenditure tax this remains equal to the market rate of interest, in the income tax it is reduced by the marginal rate of tax, and thus the increased incentive to save produced by the spending tax can be represented by this change in interest rate.

Timing Effects

As to the difference in the timing of payments for the two taxes, this depends on the way in which income is realized for tax purposes. At one extreme, if income is realized for tax purposes only as needed to provide funds to finance personal expenditure, then the timing of the payments of the two taxes becomes quite similar. This is indeed the ultimate extreme of the policy of allowing accelerated depreciation, or granting initial capital allowances, in that in effect all investments are written off to zero as soon as made, with the implication that all subsequent amounts realized from such assets, of whatever character, would then be treated as income and not return of capital. The writing down process would presumably be limited in the case where the taxpayer had indebtedness, so as not to produce a negative nominal net worth. The effect of shifting from such a tax to an expenditure tax would then be limited to the incentive effect produced by the fact that future expenditure would be taxed relatively more lightly than present expenditure, and there would not be any element of leaving the more frugal taxpayer with greater resources at his command under the expenditures tax than under such an income tax.

Another way of looking at the matter is to consider that allowing the taxpayer to postpone the realization of income is in effect to allow him to postpone the payment of the corresponding tax, which can be considered equivalent to a loan of the corresponding funds from the government to the taxpayer. If, as under an income tax, this postponement will often depend on purely nominal differences in financial arrangements that are more or less under the control of the taxpayer, it becomes necessary, in the interests of equity between taxpayers differing in the flexibility of their finances and of avoiding the distortion of normal financial arrangements in response to tax pressures, to charge an appropriate rate of interest for these deferments or loans. This is not in present practice done, at least not in any systematic way, but it can readily be done in conjunction with cumulative averaging. On the other hand if the deferment of tax is coordinated with a deferment of consumption, as under an expenditures tax, then one can without inequity omit the charging of interest on the tax deferred, thus producing the appropriate incentive for saving. One can readily afford to provide such incentives for saving when the saving is net aggregate saving, but can generally ill afford to provide even more moderate incentives for particular forms of saving when these may be offset by dissaving in other forms so that the incentives would operate more to divert savings from its natural channels than to increase the total flow of savings.

Thus even within the income concept it would be possible to provide a procedure whereby tax on reinvested income would be deferred, thus avoiding the tendency of heavy income taxation to impinge on the funds that might be used by frugal and skillful entrepreneurs to expand the scale of their operations. What is inherently and necessarily different in the expenditure tax approach is merely that there is appropriate differentiation between the present values of the tax attracted by increments of present consumption as compared with increments of future consumption.

Comparison in Practical Terms

Inadequate Succession Tax Adjustment

If on the theoretical level the difference between the two principles of taxation comes down to this relatively minor basic element of weighting through time, what of the differences that arise on a more practical level? To begin with, it must be admitted that a shift from an income tax to an expenditure tax is unlikely in practice to be coupled with a corresponding shift in the succession taxes of the exact nature assumed in the above comparisons. Such a shift would indeed involve new problems of administration and avoidance practices, and on the whole any shift in succession taxes is likely to be smaller than that called for to achieve the theoretical balance relative to the *status quo ante*, so that the expenditure tax alternative is likely to involve rather more of a problem of increased concentration of economic power than the idealized version might indicate; on the other hand the stimulus to savings may at the same time be correspondingly greater.

Effects of Lack of Averaging

Secondly, while there seem to be no insuperable difficulties to the adoption of some form of long-term averaging, either for income tax or expenditure tax purposes, there is little relevant experience to go on, and such averaging might fail of adoption. In the absence of such averaging the incentive effects of the two taxes become rather more uncertain, as they come to depend considerably on the anticipations held concerning future rates of tax as compared to present rates. Again, without averaging, accelerated writing off under an income tax is likely to produce serious inequities if carried beyond a very restricted range, unless indeed it is so generalized as to become tantamount to a shift to an expenditures tax.

Introduction of an expenditure tax might have rather unfortunate effects if there is no averaging to smooth the impact, particularly if it is introduced either gradually over a period of years, or with considerable advance discussion rather than as a full-scale *fait accompli* (which would be difficult enough under British legislative procedures; it would be virtually impossible in the United States). Taxpayers would be on fairly definite notice, possibly for a number of years, that with high probability spendings tax rates would be on the increase, so that there would be considerable tax advantage in advancing expenditures from the later to the earlier years of lower rates, or possibly to periods before the effective date of the tax. The "buy now before Budget" appeal would no longer be limited to a narrow range of goods or to the offer of better hire-purchase terms, but be universalized in terms of net expenditure, so that for a period the effect of the new tax on savings might actually be adverse. Kaldor seems to feel that this difficulty would be minimized by natural limits to the short-run supply of consumer durables[13] but if the number of taxpayers to be brought under the tax at any particular stage is small, this limit would seem not very restrictive, particularly since if rates are at all steep, other forms of expenditure such as travel may well be capable of being pushed ahead. Short of springing the tax as a surprise on a full scale, which seems politically unlikely, such effects could be avoided only by advancing the effective date of the new tax sufficiently so that taxpayers by and large would have had little advance warning, and using a cumulative method of assessment from that date. Even this might be difficult if, as seems otherwise desirable, the gradualness of the introduction consists in part of starting with the top of the income distribution and gradually lowering exemptions so as to bring more and more taxpayers within the scope of the tax.

Even aside from this transition problem, averaging seems likely to play a more crucial role in a spendings tax than in an income tax. While it may well be that the degree of variation from year to year in the conceptual expenditure tax base of a

[13] Kaldor, *Expenditure Tax*, p. 220.

given taxpayer would vary less from one taxpayer to another than that of the income tax base, the nature of the graduation that might be thought appropriate for an expenditures tax might well make these more important. And while in principle the expenditure reckoned with respect to consumer durables may well be smoothed out in time by considering only notional interest and amortization figures spread over several years rather than the initial outlay in a lump sum in the year of purchase, this would involve serious administrative difficulties were it extended to more than a very few items, such as housing and perhaps automobiles. Many types of 'lumpy' expenditure, such as for travel, fail to lend themselves easily to the consumer durables treatment, and even where the consumer durables concept applies, as for example to many of the outlays involved in setting up a new home, the items are too numerous to make anything but some kind of aggregate treatment feasible. On the whole it would seem that if the expenditure tax is to achieve its objects it is highly desirable that it should be accompanied by some kind of averaging. Once we admit this, however, we must also admit that a similar application of averaging to the income tax and surtax would go far toward achieving many of the ends for which the shift to the expenditure tax is advocated, such as the mitigation of bias against risky investment.

Separate Taxation of Small Incomes

But even more important than the quesiton of averaging is the matter of how far can or should the practical application of the tax go in attempting to make the actual tax base conform to a theoretically consistent concept. Here it is high time that we gave much more extensive and explicit recognition to the fact that income taxes, which in their initial stages were taxes imposed on a relatively small number of taxpayers at rates such that exact niceties in the determination of the base were not essential, have now become taxes which extend on the one hand to large masses of taxpayers where more than a very limited effort per taxpayer expended in the determination of the base would be wasteful of resources, and on the other to top marginal rates where defects in the base result in serious inequities and unwholesome influence on economic behavior. This is of course recognized everywhere to the extent that administration is concentrated on the larger returns and there is thus a tendency to overtook minor items and errors in the smaller returns. In the United States this is further recognized in the simplified tables, the short form of return, and the optional standard allowance for deductions; in France this finds expression in the practice of allowing small taxpayers to compute their tax on the basis of more or less arbitrary schedules or "*forfaits*"; and in the United Kingdom of course, there is the separation of the assessment of the surtax from that of the income tax, though the practical effect of this separation is minimized by the assessment of both taxes on substantially the same base.

The requirements of these two segments of progressive taxation differ so greatly, indeed, as to raise the question of whether it is not in order to complete the separation and define the tax bases separately for the two in terms appropriate to each, rather than continue what can at best be an unsatisfactory compromise. The mass tax would thus be defined in terms facilitating collection at source, simple procedures and returns, and a minimum of details or minor adjustments. The progressive frosting would be defined independently in a manner such as to minimize opportunities for avoidance, untoward economic influences and arbitrary discriminations, and with ease of administration considered in relation to the number of taxpayers involved and the types of problems that are prevalent in dealing with such taxpayers.

Kaldor's proposal for an expenditure tax as a substitute for the surtax is indeed one way of effecting such a separation. But such a separation is also possible within the income tax area. One might, for example, consider at this point that the recommendation of Kaldor and others in the dissenting minority of the Royal Commission that capital gains be subject to income tax but not to surtax[14] might well be inverted and turned into a recommendation that such gains and losses should be ignored for normal tax purposes but made subject to surtax, after grossing up or the equivalent. Such a treatment would be more in accord with a general principle of confining complications to that part of the tax applicable to the top bracket taxpayers, and at the same time would go much further than the minority suggestion in maintaining the progression of the tax and minimizing uneconomic influences flowing from the tax. Indeed, such a treatment could well be considered correct in theory insofar as capital gains in securities are a reflection of undistributed company earnings, since in such cases they will already have borne tax at the normal rate, and can be considered as equivalent to a net dividend.

Coordination of Mass Tax and Surtax

As a minor technical matter, it should be observed at this point that if the base for a surtax differs from that for a normal tax, then in order to minimize the effect among taxpayers at the top of the scale of imperfections in the base of the normal tax, it is essential to adjust the base for the surtax appropriately. This can be done either by grossing up all income subject to surtax by including a notional normal tax even though some items of income are not subject to an explicit normal tax, or

---

[14] Cmd. 9474, par. 62, p. 374.

by using as a base for the surtax the income net of normal tax in all cases, with suitable adjustment in the surtax rates to be applied. For example, if the taxable income is the same for both taxes, it makes little difference whether we have a normal tax of 9/- in the £ and a surtax of 10/- on the grossed up income, or the same normal tax with a surtax at a rate of 10/11ths on the income net of normal tax. If however for reasons of administrative convenience or otherwise some items of income escape normal tax, then if these items are not grossed up but the surtax is nevertheless on a gross basis, these items will be taxed only at 50 percent instead of at 95 percent, whereas if they are grossed up, or if the surtax is assessed at the higher nominal rate on a net basis, they will bear tax at approximately 91 percent, as compared with the full combined rate of 95 percent. As the grossing up of items to include a notional normal tax where no such tax has actually been paid will be a little mysterious to most taxpayers, probably the preferable procedure is to assess the surtax at the higher rate on a base net of normal tax. This device might also serve to facilitate, psychologically, a partial retreat from excessively high top bracket rates.

The minority suggestion of taxing capital gains only under the normal tax does have the advantage of avoiding the need for averaging, since such gains would be taxed almost entirely at a flat rate, relatively few taxpayers to whom capital gains are significant being in the reduced rate income levels. But as averaging in any case seems quite an appropriate element of a surtax conceived of as a refined levy applied to relatively few taxpayers, this argument loses weight. Averaging, indeed, can serve as a means whereby the scope of the surtax might be acceptably narrowed: for example the surtax might be started with a rate of 3/- in the £ on income above £2,500, instead of at 2/- in the £ on income above £2,000, thus reducing the number of persons subject to surtax by about 25 percent[15]; without averaging this sharp jump in the rate would tend to increase too severely the inequities resulting from fluctuating incomes, whereas with averaging this obstacle vanishes. On the incentive side, too, averaging moderates the jump, since at the time of deciding whether to work harder or not the taxpayer will ordinarily be somewhat uncertain as to whether his cumulated income will ultimately average out below or above the margin where the extra 3/- applies.

Choice of Base for a Mass Tax

If we look first at the mass tax, it seems that the use of an expenditure concept here as the main basis of the tax would encounter considerably difficulty. To be

---

[15] If rates above £3,000 remain unchanged, ranging from 3/6 to 10/– in the £, the loss in revenue would be about £10 million, out of a total income tax and surtax of about £2,000 million.

sure, the existing normal tax is in effect something of a hybrid, containing several elements related to expenditure mingled with the income items, such as the allowances in respect of certain types of saving, to wit life insurance and building and loan societies, and on the other hand the inclusion in the tax base of certain periodic receipts which are in part a return of capital, such as some types of annuities. We have then not so much a question of proceeding from an existing income tax to a new expenditures tax, but of finding that approximation or compromise most suitably balancing economic and administrative considerations. One could, indeed, go a long way toward broadening the range of investments that qualify for allowances and extending the categories of realizations that attract tax. But it does not seem that one can do this to the extent that would approach a spendings tax concept without requiring the taxpayer to file a moderately detailed return, which for this level of taxation would seem to be something to be avoided if possible.

In the other direction, a somewhat closer approach to a consistent income concept would seem to be both desirable and attainable without serious added administrative burden. The allowance for life insurance, for example, so long as it is not generalized to a wide area of savings, would seem to be an unwarranted concession to a particular form of saving and might well be eliminated, at least as to new policies; on the other hand allowance might well be made for the return of capital element in annuity payments[16] as also for the income element in lump sum benefit payments. On the other hand, as suggested above, all capital gains on transactions in domestic securities might be ignored regardless of the frequency of the transactions or their relation to the main business of the taxpayer, on the ground that the tax has already been borne at the source.

Information Requirements for Capital Gains and for Expenditure Taxation

When it comes to considering what form of tax on incomes will be appropriate at the upper end, it is clear that no reasonably close approach to a consistent income concept can be obtained without taking capital gains and losses fully into account. A strict accounting for such gains and losses, however, requires the eventual production of data on the cost of nearly all investments and on the proceeds of nearly all disinvestments, the only exceptions being those where cost and proceeds are identical, such as bank deposits. But this information comes very close to being sufficient to determine the base for an expenditure tax as well, since this is to be computed, not by adding up expenditure items, but rather by taking

---

[16] Cf. Committee on the Taxation of Trading Profits (the "Tucker Committee"). *Second Report*, Cmd. 9063, pars. 477–505.

total receipts, deducting outlays for other than personal expenditure, and adjusting for changes in cash balances and bank deposits. Income items and the proceeds of disinvestments would constitute the great bulk of the receipts, the main other items being gifts, bequests, prizes, and the like which would not be too much trouble to keep track of; the principal deductible outlays would be investments, the figures for which would be the same as those on the cost side of capital gain calculations. For persons in the higher income ranges, among whom capital transactions are likely to be of some importance, there is thus very little difference between the administrative burden involved in the assessment of a refined income tax that covers capital gains and that for an expenditures tax. This is particularly true if outlays for consumer durables are assessed on a cash outlay basis, hire-purchase payments, for example, being used as a base rather than the nominal cash price, with averaging being relied on to avoid inequities.

The administrative difficulties involved in an expenditures tax confined to upper bracket taxpayers are thus of somewhat the same order of magnitude as those involved in the taxation of capital gains and losses. One should not, however, take the difficulties encountered in the United States as an index of these difficulties, for there a major part of the difficulty arises precisely because capital gains are taxed on a different basis from other forms of income, and it becomes necessary not only to compute the various gains but to determine whether they are capital gains or ordinary income, a matter which has over the years absorbed vast quantities of legal talent. If such gains were treated on exactly the same footing as other profits, the determination of these niceties, frequently of a hair-splitting nature, would be unnecessary. The administrative burden would be eased at other points as well: determination of whether a given item should be treated as a current expense or a capital outlay, for example, would be less crucial, since in the long run any reduction in present profits brought to account will show up as an increased capital gain. In conjunction with cumulative assessment, indeed, such changes in accounting practice, and others involving depreciation, and accruals of all kinds, will leave the ultimate total tax burden unaffected, so that issues of this kind can safely be left to the discretion of the taxpayer's own accountants, and the revenue can be relieved of the burden of inquiring into such matters. For schedule D taxpayers, indeed, the result might be a net simplification.

There is, however, one important source of difficulty in the assessment of capital gains that is absent under the expenditure tax: for a newly established tax regime, especially, the assessment of capital gains sooner or later requires either a valuation of all assets of taxable persons as of an inaugural date, if gains accrued under the prior regime are to be exempted, of if they are not to be so exempted, a determination of costs of acquisition of such assets, often long after the event with the consequent difficulty of obtaining adequate information. Even with a long established assessment of capital gains, the need for the determination of the costs involved in a particular acquisition may not become evident immediately, for example if the taxpayer is not yet favored with an income of surtax magnitude, so that when the determination does take place, often only at the time of assessment for the year covering the date of sale, it may partake of some of the difficulties of archeological research. For the expenditure tax, on the other hand, the costs that are relevant are always those incurred during the expenditure year, so that they are thus much more readily ascertainable.

If it be admitted then that at the upper end of the progressive scale a refined tax base of some kind is essential, and that for an income tax this implies inclusion of capital gains and losses in the base, then there would seem to be little to choose between income and expenditure on administrative grounds, at least for those classes of taxpayers where property incomes and dealings in capital assets are of importance. In this area, accordingly, once can make the choice on the basis of economic effects, political appeal, or other grounds.

The Advantages of a Fresh Start

One consideration of a tactical nature that may in practice be of some importance is that the shift to a new principle of taxation gives an opportunity for a fresh start on the detailed provisions, with less need for tender treatment of old commitments and vested interests. In the United States, for example, one of the advantages sometimes cited for an expenditure tax is that it would side-step the issue of exempt government securities (and also, formerly, of exempt government salaries). In Britain the matters of annuities, income covenants, and the like are examples. Another element of this kind is that the change might facilitate a fresh look at the reasonableness of the top rates, since the basis of graduation would be quite different. As Kaldor points out,[17] the natural and from many points of view preferable method of assessing the tax is to exclude the tax itself from the base; thus a tax on an inclusive base of 60 percent, for example, becomes a tax of 150 percent on the exclusive base; the rate corresponding to the top income tax rate of 19/- in the £ would be 1,900 percent, or £19 of tax on each £1 of expenditure.

But granting that among the highly refined tax bases needed at the top of the progressive scale, the expenditure tax might be as easy to administer as the income tax, are there not other alternatives that are acceptable and less difficult? The line of least resistance, indeed, is to follow the majority of the Royal Commission and carry on with the existing system with minor revisions. But surely, in the light of what has been said above, and as the minority of the Royal Commission insists, continuation of the present tax situation is not a satisfactory

---

[17] Kaldor, *Expenditure Tax*, pp. 232–8.

solution. When one considers the manifold opportunities for avoidance that exist under the present law, together with the degree to which incentives for avoidance are increased by pushing rates up to 90 percent and even 95 percent[18] together with the relatively small amount of revenue produced by these last increments in the rates even if the tax base could be assumed to be unaffected,[19] it seems highly likely that these rates have entered the area of negative returns and that the last increments neither yield any net revenue in the long run nor contribute materially to the real progression of the tax, while they do drastically magnify the inequities between taxpayers who differ in the degree to which the loopholes are readily available to them. If nothing can be done to improve the tax base, retention of these top rates can only be considered a form of economic sadism, by which the wealthy are penalized without any consequent benefit to the rest of the community. The *status quo*, or anything approaching it, is not an acceptable alternative.

An Annual Surtax based on Net Worth

There is, however, another alternative meriting consideration, and that is the imposition of an annual tax at progressive rates on net fortunes, at rates ranging up to say 3 percent to 6 percent. At first glance it might seem that such a tax would be unacceptable because its administration on a reasonably refined basis appears more difficult than a correspondingly refined expenditure or income tax covering approximately the same number of taxpayers at the top of the distribution; not only would some sort of balance sheet have to be established for each such taxpayer, but if serious pressures for the postponement of realization of gains are to be avoided, some kind of fairly frequent valuation of assets will be required. But this is offset to a considerable extent by the fact that at given high levels of progression the pressures and opportunities for avoidance and the consequent

[18] For example, raising the rate from an aggregate of 18/- to 19/- increases the revenue obtainable from the income affected by less than 6%, but it doubles the amount of fully taxable income that the taxpayer would be willing to sacrifice in order to obtain a receipt in non-taxable form or in a form taxable at a given lower rate.

[19] Figures for 1953–4, the latest available at the time of writing, indicate that out of a total income tax and surtax revenue of £2,008 million, of which £134 million was surtax, only £36 million would have been lost by levelling off the surtax rates at a maximum of 5/- in the £, or 70 percent combined income tax and surtax, even assuming no abatement of avoidance practices as a result of the reduction in rates. For a levelling off at 7/-, or an 80 percent combined rate, only £10 million would have been lost, while the last increment from 90 percent to 95 percent, which again doubles the incentives to avoidance felt by taxpayers with over £100 million of income altogether, produced only £2.4 million gross. Figures are derived from the 98th Report of the Commissioners of Her Majesty's Inland Revenue for the year ended 31 March, 1955, Cmd. 9667, pp. 14, 78.

need for accuracy in the determination of the tax base seem less than with an income tax. This can be shown most vividly by a somewhat exaggerated example as follows: suppose that the group with net fortunes of 10 million pounds or over have incomes equal to 7 percent of their wealth: an annual tax on net wealth at a marginal rate of 8 percent would correspond in progressivity of burden to a marginal income tax rate of 114 percent, but would have nowhere near the disastrous incentive effects that such an income tax would have: the income tax would make it to the taxpayer's advantage actually to suppress his income[20] whereas the net worth tax would merely tend to discourage saving and encourage dissaving or dissipation of capital in gifts and personal expenditure; it would still be to the advantage of the taxpayer to derive as much income as he could in any particular period from such capital as he then had. Thus even though the base of the net fortunes tax would be inherently more difficult to define and determine than that of an income or spendings tax, greater imperfections in definition and determination could be tolerated at high levels of progression than for the other taxes. The net administrative difficulty of achieving a satisfactory standard might thus be smaller.

Nevertheless, to throw on a net fortune tax the entire task of providing progression at the top end of the scale is probably not an acceptable solution, as the relief that would thus result for those whose incomes are "earned" or derived from noncapitalized sources would probably be considered excessive. At most one could regard the introduction of the net fortunes tax as making it possible to reduce the top rates of the income tax to levels where the inequities and distortions produced by the present form of tax would be more nearly tolerable. And while a net fortunes tax might be regarded as in some measure redressing inequalities resulting from the greater availability of various forms of avoidance to property incomes than to earned incomes, this correction would be an overall matter and would still leave substantial individual inequities: the availability of loopholes would still vary greatly from one form of property to another. Indeed in

---

[20] Marginal combined rates exceeding 100 percent do occur in practice, particularly in the case of new businesses, though since the impact may be spread over several years the combined effect is often not fully appreciated. If for example a new business is started 1 Sept., 1953, and makes up its books to 30 June of each year, then the assessment for the year 1953–4 will be the income allocable to the period to 5 April, or 43/60 of the income for the ten months to 30 June, 1954; at a 9/-standard rate, this is equivalent to about 6/5 in the £. The entire income for this first accounting period will again be included in the assessment for 1954–5 and also for 1955–6, at 9/- in the £ each time, or a total of £1/4/5 in the £. As long as the proprietors have enough income to be taxable at the full standard rate, any expenditure, however wasteful, that qualifies as a deduction in computing net income for this initial period, will be a profitable investment in terms of income tax reduction over these three assessment years. If the proprietors are in addition subject to surtax, the situation is of course even more extreme. (See *Report of the Committee on the Taxation of Trading Profits* (April, 1951), Cmd. 8189, pars. 19, 24, 27.)

some cases even salaries can be converted into capital gains, as has been done on a considerable scale in the American movie industry through film stars obtaining compensation in the form of a share in the film produced; a somewhat similar phenomenon in Britain was dealt with by the Royal Commission under the heading "Post-cessation receipts."[11] Considerable improvement may thus be obtained with the aid of a net fortunes tax, but it does not in itself provide a complete answer to the problem of progression.

There is, indeed, no royal road to effective, equitable, and reasonably distortion-free progression of the degree represented by the nominal rates standing on the statute books of most industrialized countries. The major alternatives, aside from continuing to tolerate the absurdities and inequities of the *status quo* with only minor revisions are: (1) to retreat from the attempt to apply steep progression at the top of the scale, to whatever degree is necessary to reduce the inequities and distortions arising from the present tax base to tolerable levels, (2) to substitute a net fortunes tax for some of the graduation of the income tax, partly as an offset to some of the inequities, (3) to reform the income tax, at least as applied to upper bracket taxpayers, so as to provide full inclusion of capital gains and losses and some form of averaging, and (4) to adopt a spendings tax for upper bracket taxpayers. Of these only the last two offer a fundamentally satisfactory and sound solution; both involve a considerable additional administrative burden of about the same order of magnitude, the balance between them probably depending on the details of the way each tax would be applied. The economic advantages of the expenditure tax are not negligible, though as compared with a reformed income tax they are considerably less striking than might at first be thought. If ever enough resolution is mustered to deal with the problems of progressive taxation in a thoroughgoing manner, the expenditure tax will merit serious consideration, and Mr. Kaldor's book will have provided a valuable challenge.

[21] Cmd. 9474, chapter 12, pp. 80–3.

9

The Problem of Progression

In a literal and formal sense, progressive taxation is taxation that imposes a rate that varies more than in proportion to the tax base. In a less precise but more fundamental sense, progressive taxation is taxation that conforms to a concept of ability to pay, which in turn is deemed to increase more than in proportion to various cardinally measurable indicia of the individual's economic status. Since income is one of the most readily available indicators of ability to pay, the income tax furnishes the great bulk of the progressive element in most modern tax systems. Thus, progression generally tends to be measured in terms of how the tax burden varies with income, regardless of the fact that income is in many circumstances an imperfect and even misleading measure of ability to pay.

This is particularly so in cases where income is subject to fluctuation. A pensioner aged eighty, living on an annuity of 10,000 dollars a year bought with savings out of high income from past years, may be comfortably well off and able to pay a substantial tax without hardship. His accruing income, however, by any definition sufficiently rigorous and uniformly applicable to serve as a satisfactory tax base, would be only a fraction of the 10,000 dollars since much of the annuity must be considered a return of capital. By contrast, a man of fifty living on a salary of 8,000 dollars a year might be considered to have a much greater income, but a tax payment equal to the pensioner's would impose a much greater hardship on the wage earner because of the higher living expenses connected with his work and because of his need to save for his own retirement. A general sales tax, possibly with food exempted, might conform more accurately to the relative ability to pay of the two; but if the progressivity of the tax is measured in terms of the relation between tax and income, the sales tax would be termed regressive.

University of Florida Law Review (1968), pp. 437–50.

Over any broad range of economic status, however, the sales tax by itself fails rather seriously to measure up to what most people feel is an appropriate degree of progressiveness. This failure can be remedied by assessing a tax in a graduated manner on the total consumption expenditure of individuals and families. The ability to pay of individuals under such a tax would be related to their level of expenditure or standard of living, the assumption being that the more lavish the scale of expenditure the less the sacrifice in giving up part of it. Indeed, a long line of economists starting with John Stuart Mill and including Irving Fisher and Secretary of the Treasury Ogden Mills, have held that the proper base for the principal progressive tax should be consumption expenditure, not income.[1] Earlier advocates were ready to accept the income tax on the ground that it would be simpler to administer, but more recent developments seem to indicate that at levels where itemization of deduction is common, the differences might well be more in favor of the expenditure tax than against it. At the very least, one should not regard income as the only available base for progressive taxation.

Even if agreement can be reached as to the base against which progression is to be measured, measuring the degree of progression in a given tax structure, or deciding upon a particular pattern of tax progression remains a problem. One common way of measuring the progression of a tax or a tax system is by comparing the degree of economic inequality in the distribution of the selected economic base as it is after the tax burden has been deducted with what it would be before this deduction. The degree of inequality may be defined for this purpose in terms of such measures as the Gini ratio[2] or its equivalent, the area between the Lorenz curve[3] and the diagonal line representing complete equality. This comparison may prove unreliable because the progression of a given tax schedule, so measured, depends on the income distribution to which it is applied and, at least for more extreme changes, the measure produces results at variance with what seem to be normal evaluations in the relative desirability of alternative income distributions. Suppose, for example, that we are to distribute 1,100,000 dollars of net income after tax among 100 persons, and that one tax schedule results in ten after-tax incomes of 1,100 dollars and 90 of 12,100 dollars while another tax schedule results in one income of 110,000 dollars and 99 of 10,000 dollars. Most

---

[1] I. Fisher and H. Fisher, *Constructive Income Taxation* (1942) (contains an extensive bibliography on the subject); A. Marshall, *Office Papers* (1926), p. 338; J.S. Mill, *Principles of Political Economy*, book. IV, Ch. 11, no. 4 (1927), pp. 813–1180 (Ashley variorum ed. 1936); A. Pigou, *A Study in Public Finance* (1928), pp. 135–44; Mills, "The Spending Tax," *Bulletin of the National Tax Association*, 7 (1921), pp. 18–20.

[2] The Gini ratio may be defined as the ratio of (a) the mean of the absolute differences in income between all pairs of income recipients, to (b) the mean income. See note 4 below.

[3] The Lorenz curve is a curve through all points such that the abscissa measures the percent of total population having a specified economic state or worse, while the ordinate measures the percentage of the total distribuend – income, expenditure, wealth – accruing to this group. See note 4 below.

persons, I think, would express a significant preference for the latter result; indeed in the former case there would be a strong likelihood that some relief, either via public welfare, tax revision, or private charity would be proposed for the ten individuals with incomes insufficient to maintain decency and health, whereas the probability of action to redistribute part of the 110,000 dollar income would seem much less likely. Yet the Gini ratio is 0.18 in both cases.[4]

For those who are uncertain whether any sufficiently objective meaning can be attached to an expression of preference for one income distribution rather than another, let me suggest the following *gedanken-experiment*:[5] Suppose that, lined up on the docks of Plymouth, there are a number of ships about to sail for various equivalently endowed regions of the New World, offering participation in communities in which varying degrees of redistributive taxation are to be employed, but which are in other respects similar. Given at least some uncertainty concerning how productively your own particular talents will fare in the new environment, so that a corresponding uncertainty exists as to what place you will eventually occupy on the prospective income distribution, what type of redistribution would you tend to prefer in making your choice among the various colonies? How would this preference be altered by taking into consideration the types of individuals that the various plans would attract? How would the decision be made where there is no advance information at all as to which particular individuals are more or less likely to succeed in the new environment? While many of those who have some degree of confidence in their superior capabilities, even as against a group selected in terms of their being attracted to such a venture, may find it difficult to give full weight in any such evaluation to the possibility of their eventually filling a menial role, even hypothetically, in such a situation, the concept may be an aid in developing some degree of objectivity in the appraisal of income distribution.

The classical utilitarian view implies that some degree of redistribution will be preferred, and that individuals will accept a somewhat lower average expectation

---

[4] There are $100 \times 100 = 10,000$ income differences (including the comparison of each individual with himself) of which, in the first case $10^2 + 90^2 = 8200$ are zero and $10 \times 90 \times 2 = 1800$ are $11,000, a mean difference of $(8200 \times 0 + 1800 \times \$11,000)/10,000 = \$1,980$; dividing by the mean income of $11,000 gives 0.18 as the Gini ratio. Similarly in the second case the ratio is also 0.18. $\{[(1^2 + 99^2) \times 0 + (2 \times 99) \,(\$110,000 - \$10,000)]/10,000\} \,/ \,(\$1,100,000/100) = 0.18$.

The Lorenz curve in the first case consists of two straight lines connecting the corners $(0,0)$ and $(1,1)$ of the unit square with the intermediate point $(10/100, (10 \times \$1,100)/\$1,100,000) = (0.1, 0.01)$ representing the fact that the lowest 10 percent of the population get 1 percent of the income. The area of the triangle between this Lorenz curve and the diagonal is $\frac{1}{2} \,(0.1 - 0.01) = .045$; this is exactly $\frac{1}{4}$ of the value of the Gini ratio, which is, indeed, a relationship that holds generally. The Lorenz curve for the second case has as its intermediate point $(0.99, 0.90)$; the area is obviously the same.

[5] A hypothetical procedure the results of which, for practical reasons such as cost or morality, cannot be determined by actually carrying it out, but can only be imagined.

of income in return for a smaller degree of dispersion of incomes or risk. This is, indeed, the reaction found every day in the securities market. But one cannot preclude the presence of gamblers' and adventurers' predilections, so that even if a completely egalitarian community could offer a standard of living superior to any attainable in a more competitive community, the zest of the struggle would make a community where some have incomes of 6,000 dollars and some of 9,000 dollars preferable to one where all have 10,000 dollars. Nor, at the other extreme, can one exclude the case where the Jones's superiority is so painful that a community where income is uniformly 6,000 dollars is preferred to one where most have 7,000 dollars and a few have 10,000 dollars. However, in the former case one is tempted to suggest that the otherwise egalitarian community should consider setting up a gambling casino, if it can reconcile this with its moral philosophy, with appropriate controls to prevent any of the gamblers from proceeding to a point where their plight begins to prey on the sympathies of their neighbors. Or the egalitarian community might be able to find some means of permitting the adventurers to opt out of part or all of the redistributive system, though how to do this without permitting adverse selection to operate may be an insoluble problem. In the latter case we may, along with Sir Dennis Robertson, call upon the Archbishop of Canterbury to do what he can to exorcise the green-eyed monster.[6]

More relevantly, it seems fairly certain that the degree of inequality incidental to providing the incentives for maximum net productivity is currently more than adequate to satisfy the predilections of the venturesome. Therefore, once subjective bias based on the current status of the individual is removed, there should be wide agreement that a substantial degree of progression is appropriate. But exactly what degree must for the moment be left to the vagaries of the political process, until someone manages to distill from observations of the behavior of investors in risky markets, individuals in other risky situations, and estimates of the impact of impairment of incentives on net productivity, some more objective standard for tax progression, striking a balance between the maximization of the distribuend and the maximization of the satisfaction derivable from a given distribuend. Until this is done, and probably even afterwards, decisions as to income distribution remain, in blunt terms, the resultant of a power struggle between the few who have exceptional confidence in their own ability, or good fortune, and all the others.

In the absence of such an analysis based on observation of individual behavior in circumstances involving risk, there seems to be no generally applicable measure that will yield acceptable comparisons between widely differing scales of progression; yet one can seek to measure the degree of progression existing at a given

---

[6] Robertson, "Utility and All What?," *Economic Journal*, 64 (1954), pp. 665–78.

point along the scale. A measure that immediately suggests itself to economists is the elasticity of ex-tax income with respect to pre-tax income, or the percentage increases in post-tax income associated with a 1 percent increase in pre-tax income. If one adopts the principle that the rate of progression so defined should be uniform over the whole range of incomes, one is equipped with a rule that permits an entire tax schedule to be determined, once the level of the exemption is decided upon and either the initial marginal rate or the aggregate revenue to be obtained is given.[7] Too much should perhaps not be claimed for this standard of progression, but it is among the simpler, if not the simplest of the formulas that can be applied over an unlimited range of incomes and used to provide almost any degree of total tax burden required. It also has the property that if the second tax is applied by such a formula to income remaining after a first such tax, the combined tax burden still conforms to the formula. A further interesting, though perhaps not highly important, property is that if the income before tax is distributed according to the Pareto law (which may be expressed by saying that every time income is increased by a given percentage, the number of individuals having that income or higher diminishes by another constant percentage) then income after tax is also distributed according to the Pareto law; though little theoretical significance has been given to this particular law, it has been found to describe the upper end of income distributions in various times and places remarkably well.

The constant elasticity progression rule can even be extended quite naturally to a negative income tax: the exemption level is then merely the income level at which the tax switches from negative to positive. Adoption of such a principle of progression, at least as a starting point, might serve to moderate the somewhat arbitrary tinkering with rate schedules that often takes place under existing circumstances.

Income Tax Progression, Loopholes, and Economic Waste

A practical difficulty with any such pattern of progression is that if strictly adhered to it implies marginal rates at the top of the scale that lead, under existing definitions of the tax base, to severe inequities and distorting incentives. Some of these distortions are almost unavoidable under any administrable definition of the tax base, but many if not most of them are the result of defective definitions of the tax base and are in principle remediable, though in some instances it is difficult to

---

[7] Examples of the application of such a graduation are given in W. Vickrey, *Agenda for Progressive Taxation* (1947), p. 464. See also Edgeworth, "Methods of Graduating Taxes on Income and Capital," *Economic Journal*, 29 (1919), pp. 133, 144. See Appendix, table 9.1, for comparison of some of the formula-derived rates with the marginal rates of 1965.

complete the remedy in any brief time period without discriminatory infringment on vested interests acquired in reliance on the continuation of existing provisions. These defects seem to have been accumulating steadily since the 1920s as the result of piecemeal tinkering and the application of *ad hoc* remedies, sometimes to genuine inequities but often to spurious but equally persuasively argued ones, until the final result is far beyond what was already described in 1938 by Henry Simons as a process of "dipping deeply into great incomes with a sieve."[8]

The game of "loopholes" is indeed played today with such assiduity that in the upper ranges, at least, the income tax has become regressive rather than progressive. With nominal rates going up to 70 percent for the year 1965, the last for which I have the complete *Statistics of Income data*, the maximum average effective rate of the federal income tax was 36.43 percent on the 100,000–500,000 dollar bracket, and above that level the effective rate of tax actually declines to 30.81 percent on incomes exceeding 1,000,000 dollars.[9] Even this is only in terms of that part of total net income actually reported on tax returns; in addition there are large amounts of income that go unreported and untaxed. Some of the larger clear-cut omissions fall under the headings of tax-exempt interest, interest accrued on life insurance, and accrued capital gains on which income tax will never be paid (the assets being held or exchanged tax-free until the death of the taxpayer, or donated to tax-exempt foundations or institutions). If these types of income were included in the computation of the average effective rate, the failure of the income tax to retain any semblance of effective progression at the top of the scale would be even more striking.

It is not merely that the loophole game defeats the intent expressed in the progressive rate schedule, nor even that inequities result between those more or less able to take advantage of the loopholes, nor that vast quantities of high-priced talent are squandered on the unproductive intricacies of the game; the most serious aspect of the loophole game is the distortion and waste that it engenders in the manner in which the economy of the country is run. Insurance policies are taken out where the insurable interest in itself would not warrant incurring the inevitable overhead costs; capital best adapted to riskbearing and equity investment is diverted to government bonds; unfair and often wasteful competition from manufacturers using facilities financed with tax-exempt bonds develops; development and exploitation of limited natural resources is wastefully accelerated; government projects are made to appear more productive relative to private projects than would be the case without tax distortion; internal financing is encouraged beyond the point at which it conforms to economic needs, with consequent growth of protean corporate empires and reduction in the vigor of

---

. [8] H. Simons, *Personal Income Taxation* (1938), p. 219.
[9] See Appendix, Table 9.2.

competition; investors are locked in and capital is restrained from seeking the most productive forms and applications. It is not too much to say that in the process of aborting tax progression, loopholes have as a byproduct reshaped the entire pattern of our economy, in most cases for the worse.

The Unpromising Politics of Income Tax Reform

It is not difficult, in principle, to devise a progressive income tax that would be free from the distorting effects on economic activity that inhere in these various loopholes and indeed that would, through assessment on a cumulative basis over the years, largely eliminate the artificial incentives now existing for having transactions recorded in one income year rather than another, or for postponing the realization of income for tax purposes by one device or another.[10] Such a tax could, indeed, almost completely eliminate the distorting influence of the tax on many phases of business activity. There would remain, to be sure, the almost inescapable tendency of the tax to favor nonmarket as contrasted with market activity, and the stimulus to the "expense-account" economy resulting from the practical impossibility of dealing equitably with the wide variety of perquisites and expense account items that muddy the line between deductible business expenses and personal consumption. But income tax consequences would no longer be of direct concern in decisions concerning the buying and selling of securities, depreciation accounting, retirement of equipment, or the selection of investments. Many of the intricacies of the law could, indeed, be eliminated entirely and the sheer bulk of the internal revenue code cut in half.

To be sure, such a general closing of loopholes would, if existing rates were maintained, produce a degree of progression that would appear unduly severe to many of those concerned, though not, perhaps, to most of the majority that approved the existing rate scale. To a naïve observer, the obvious resolution would be to reform the tax base and reduce the progression of the rates

---

[10] Briefly, the principle is to consider all payments with respect to an individual's income tax payments as deposits in an interest-bearing tax account and to compute, at the end of each year, a cumulative tax on the cumulative total of all income realized since a base starting date, at rates graduated appropriately to the time interval included. The current payment is then simply the difference between the tax thus computed and the balance in the tax account. The only additional information required to be carried forward from year to year consists of the basic starting date, the cumulated income, and the cumulated tax balance; the tax computation is otherwise the same as at present once the taxpayer has been supplied with the set of rates appropriate to his base date. The computations would be much simpler than those required for existing averaging and income spreading computations, which would be eliminated. Postponement of realization of an item of income still postpones tax payment, but since interest then fails to accrue in the tax account the result is simply equivalent to a loan at the stipulated interest rate. *See* W. Vickrey, *Agenda*, pp. 172–94.

simultaneously so that the net result would be an overall degree of progression unchanged or only slightly increased, a much more equitable distribution of the burden within income classes, and a greatly reduced interference of the tax with the efficiency of the economy. Yet such a resolution seems hardly to get to the stage of serious discussion, let alone enactment into law.

Strong forces, indeed, are arrayed against any such reform. First and most obviously, there are the special interests that draw advantage from particular loopholes that could hardly be fully compensated by any general reduction in rates. These include, for instance, the life insurance industry with respect to interest earnings included in benefits, the oil interests with respect to depletion, and state and local governments with respect to exempt interest. Even where, as with the case of tax-exempt interest, possibilities exist for compensating the interested governments for the loss of the privilege, the change is resisted vigorously. Perpetuation of an irrational, discriminatory, and inefficient privilege of long standing, which appears to be capable of indefinite retention, is preferred to the promise of a more explicit subvention for which the risk of discontinuance would be considered greater, if only because the arbitrariness and inequity of the compensation payment, though no greater than that of the exemption, would be more obvious and less firmly rooted in past practice.

Second, there is the perhaps only subconscious feeling on the part of the loophole players that it is far easier to hold the line on the maintenance of a loophole than on the level of progression of the rates. Indeed, given the inherent limitations on the degree to which future governments can be committed in advance to the continuation of any given policy, there is no way of assuring that the rate concession granted in exchange for the abolition of the loopholes would actually be maintained over any future period. And to those to whom the whole notion of progression of tax rates is anathema because of the manner in which the existence of such tools enables the majority to despoil the wealthy minority, loopholes constitute a last bulwark of the defense against such exploitation, so that any loophole, no matter how offensive to equity or prejudicial to economic efficiency, may become a cherished element in these defenses.

Third, it is at least possible that the large vested interest of tax lawyers and tax accountants in their knowledge of the intricacies of the existing code, and the threat to their livelihood posed by any drastic simplification of the tax law, lead subconsciously at least to a preference for dealing with tax problems by introducing new complications and intricacies that will enable the tax expert to enhance his importance as a guide through the maze, rather than by basic reform going to the heart of the matter and bringing principle and practice closer together rather than farther apart. To be sure, few if any practitioners would consciously advocate complication for its own sake, but there is a certain satisfaction to be had from working out intricate solutions, defending them against other proposals, and perhaps ultimately working out an even more intricate compromise. This satisfaction may help to explain the ever mounting weight of the tax law.

More important, however, is the fact that it is difficult, if not impossible, to carry out a fundamental reform of the tax law over any brief period without generating windfall gains and losses on a wide scale and in a capricious and inequitable pattern. Not all of those suffering windfall losses will be those who have in the past enjoyed undue benefits, nor will windfall gains accrue to individuals relatively overtaxed in the past. Two wrongs do not make a right, even when the second wrong results from trying to right the first one. Take as an example the relatively simple case of the tax exempt security: immediate abolition of the exemption on all such securities would of course subject the recent purchaser of such securities to an unconscionable capital loss, while on the other hand the elimination of the exemption for future issues only would probably result in a substantial, though smaller, windfall gain, by reason of the prospective greater scarcity of such instruments. Methods of gradually increasing the proportion of taxable interest on outstanding government bonds could in principle be worked out to maintain the relative market values of such securities approximately unchanged. But this would be a rather difficult process to carry out in practice, because of the problem of predicting the market's attitude toward the future and because of the difficulty of committing future Congresses to implementing such a policy. In the field of depletion the problem would be complicated even more by the far more intricate contractual relationships existing and the accounting chaos that has developed as a result of nearly fifty years of special tax privileges.

The difficulty often encountered in attempting to undo a piece of economic folly is seen in one of its most acute manifestations if one considers the establishment of a proper progression of the individual income tax to include the reintegration of the corporation tax in the individual income tax structure as a method of collecting individual income tax at the source, as was the case (very roughly) prior to 1936.[11] Because of the special relation of the corporate income tax to investment, any announcement of a prospective reduction in this tax is likely to have a stimulative impact on investment over and above any consequence via the budgetary balance, so that during the period of adjustment, the avoidance of inflation on the one hand and severe monetary stringency on the other would require other tax revenues to be increased by more than the reduction in the corporation income tax. This need for a heavier nominal tax burden during the period of transition is indeed a severe political difficulty, particularly as the burden of the alternative taxes will be more apparent than that of the corporate income tax.

---

[11] Before 1936, dividends were exempt from normal tax in the hands of individuals, the corporation income tax being considered to be a rough collection at source of this part of the individual tax.

The main difficulty, however, is that of avoiding inequitable and unproductive windfall gains to stockholders. While a great deal has been written on the long-run incidence of the corporate income tax, it is clear that regardless of what the long-run incidence may be considered to be, in the short run any sudden reduction in the corporate income tax rate will result in windfall gains to shareholders. Such windfall gains can largely be avoided if the reduction in the corporation income tax is carried out over a long enough period of time, probably ten years or more, and if this reduction is known in advance so that additional investment can be planned and carried out at a rate sufficient to maintain a reasonably close approach to equilibrium. But this is a large order. It requires first that a program of corporate income tax reduction be determined that will do the trick, then that a Congress undertake to carry out this program, including the necessary increases in other taxes, that subsequent Congresses honor this commitment, and finally and most difficult of all to insure, that those responsible for making investment decisions actually have confidence that the commitment will be carried out and make their investment decisions accordingly. In addition, during the transition period the increased incentives for taxpayers to attempt to shift taxable corporate income to later years by one device or another so as to enjoy the reduced rates will generate severe pressures on the tax administration. Given the popularity of the corporate income tax as the tax nobody pays (and indeed it can be argued that the tax is not, in fact, paid by any of the current generation, but by future generations of wage earners whose productivity will be lowered by absence of the equipment with which to work that is not installed currently because of the tax), the prospects for any such rectification of the tax structure seem dim indeed.

Alternatives

The income tax is sick, and the prognosis is unfavorable. But there are other progressive taxes to be considered besides the income tax. A possible alternative approach would be to discard entirely the upper portions of the progressive income tax scale and replace it with other forms of progressive taxation. The obvious candidate for this replacement would be a graduated expenditure tax. While the complete replacement of the income tax by an expenditure tax would pose formidable administrative and compliance problems, partial replacement may be a fairly attractive proposition. If the expenditure tax exemption levels were set to correspond roughly with the income tax exemption levels of the 1920s, the taxpayers involved would be largely taxpayers itemizing deductions and having moderately involved problems with their current income tax; for such taxpayers the problem of providing the additional data needed to compute the expenditure tax would be a relatively minor one. It is perhaps not too much to hope that an expenditure tax could be kept relatively free of the type of special-interest provisions with which the income tax has been encrusted; not only can a fresh start be made, but hopefully the temptation to grant special treatment to this or that type of expenditure are fewer and less likely to engender economic waste than the temptations to give special treatment to specific forms of income. Outside the always vexing area of expenditures on the borderline between business and personal expense, the concept of personal expenditure seems to be easier to grasp than that of income.

An expenditure tax, however, leaves relatively untouched the really large aggregations of wealth and income that far outstrip any urge to spend on personal consumption and represent to a large extent the sheer accumulation of economic power. While some may be content to leave these accumulations to fructify in the hands of the accumulators, others will feel that more of a contribution to the public purse can properly be exacted than will come from an expenditure tax and a base-rate income tax, either simply in terms of some concept of ability to pay, or in terms of attempting to curb the development of concentration of economic power that might prove inimical to the functioning of a democratic society.

At first glance it might appear that the succession taxes[12] already perform this function. On examination, however, it becomes evident that the loopholes in the income tax are nothing compared with those of the succession taxes. Indeed, it is hardly an exaggeration to say that the bulk of the revenue derived from the upper reaches of the estate tax constitutes a quasi-voluntary contribution from decedents too short-sighted or indifferent to take the requisite steps to avoid the tax. Nor do the prospects for plugging these loopholes on any wide scale seem bright. While it is possible to devise a form of succession duty that will make the burden reasonably independent of artifical or accidental variations in the manner in which wealth is passed from one generation to another, the method by which this can be done is fairly involved, and represents a sharp departure from existing practice;[13] moreover no method has yet been devised for dealing in a satisfactory and nondiscriminatory way with transfers to or from persons outside the taxing jurisdiction. Reinforcing the succession taxes to take over the progressive function of the upper reaches of the income tax thus seems an unlikely prospect.

A better instrument for this purpose would be an annual tax based on the net worth of the taxpayer, at graduated rates. The problem of administering this tax

---

[12] The term "succession taxes" is here meant to include all forms of estate, inheritance, and gift tax.

[13] This involves converting accumulations during a decedent's lifetime into a quantity termed "bequeathing power" and conceptually allowing this bequeathing power to be passed from hand to hand unchanged, but collecting as a tax the difference between the amount of wealth a given amount of bequeathing power is deemed to represent in the hands of the older testator or donor and the wealth it is deemed to represent in the hands of the younger recipient, according to appropriate formulas and tables.

on a large scale would of course be formidable, but if it is regarded primarily as a substitute for the top rates of the income tax, it can be applied on the basis of a fairly large exemption, say 200,000 dollars (roughly the current equivalent of the federal estate tax exemption of the 1920s) and the number of taxpayers kept to a level that makes fairly sophisticated procedures acceptable. The advantage of the net worth tax is not only that it would start out free from accumulated impairments, but that when carried to a corresponding level of progression, it is inherently less likely to cause efficiency-reducing repercussions than is the corresponding income tax. This can be seen most clearly by reference to examples in which the tax is carried to levels considerably beyond what would be likely to happen in practice, as follows.

Suppose an individual is earning 8 percent on the last $1 million of his assets, or 80,000 dollars. If this were subject to a marginal income tax rate of 80 percent, the tax payable would be 64,000 dollars, and the incentive to sacrifice some or all of this income in favor of nontaxable returns or satisfaction would be considerable. If on the other hand the income tax is limited to a maximum rate of, say, 40 percent and a net worth tax at a marginal rate of 3.2 percent is imposed instead, the total tax burden is the same, but the incentives for distortion of activity into wasteful or inefficient channels are greatly reduced. To consider an even more extreme case, if the net worth tax were raised to 5 percent, at the margin, the total tax would be 82,000 dollars, equivalent to an income tax of 102.5 percent. An income tax at this level would be obviously absurd, since the result would be simply to lead the taxpayer to abandon or sabotage all income above the point where the rate reached 100 percent. With the net worth tax, unless local government bonds are made exempt from this tax as well as the income tax, there is much less opportunity for avoidance.

These extremes are presented not to advocate that any such rates be applied in practice but to illustrate more forcefully the advantages of making use of a net worth tax. To some, of course, this superiority in terms of lack of adverse impact on the efficiency of the economy may be precisely the greatest disadvantage involved in such an innovation: as long as the adverse effects of progression are severe, this fact protects the wealthy taxpayer from progression being carried beyond a given point; abate the deleterious repercussions and he is less well protected.

Aside from the economics of such a tax, there is the rather serious legal question whether such a tax could be levied at the federal level without another constitutional amendment, since it might well be held to fall under the constitutional proscription against direct taxes. One possible way out would be to levy the tax nominally on the net income deemed to be derived from the net worth, there being a rebuttable presumption that the income, for this purpose, amounted to a standard percentage of the net worth. The taxpayer attempting such a rebuttal would be required to use a very inclusive definition of net income, including accruals of unrealized capital gains, imputed income from equity in durable consumer goods, and the like. Stating the tax in this way, though conceptually a bit awkward, would have the considerable advantage, from some points of view, of protecting the wealthy minority somewhat against excesses of progression, since it would be relatively easy to block the enactment of rates applicable to the pseudo-net income derived from net worth, which when added to the rates applicable to actual net income would combine to rates over 100 percent. Since the standard presumed rate of return would tend to be set considerably lower than rates of return generally realized, in order to minimize cases of successful rebuttal of the presumption, the net effect would be to limit the progression to a maximum level considerably short of the "window-dressing" levels reached by the nominal bracket rates of income taxes in the past. The baneful effects of the rates at the top end of the progression would be substantially less than those produced by a comparable degree of effective progression derived from the income tax alone.

States, to be sure, are for the most part constitutionally empowered to levy an explicit net worth tax. There is not much to be looked for in this direction, however, for states generally derive relatively much less revenue from the upper end of their progressive income tax rate scales than does the federal government, and given the mobility of wealthy individuals among states, there is little likelihood of any great change in this situation.

Summary

The complex of political forces impinging on the formulation of our progressive tax system has, indeed, produced a monstrosity that can hardly be given high marks either as to effective progression and equity on the one hand or as a maintenance of economic efficiency on the other. While the situation could in principle be remedied quite adequately within the general rubric of the income tax, political prospects for doing this are not bright. It is perhaps an appropriate time to give serious consideration to the introduction of expenditure and net worth taxes as components of the progressive tax structure that might enable the deadlock to be broken so that the drag of the tax system on the efficiency of the nation's economy can be reduced.

Appendix

Table 9.1 *Progression by Constant-Elasticity Formula*

Income levels		Alternative constant-elasticity progression scales							1965 rates	
As multiple of personal exemption	On basis of 4-person family exemption	Marginal rates (%)							Nominal	Adjusted for capital gains[b]
1.0	$ 2,600[a]	8.0	10.0	12.0	14.0[c]	16.0	18.0	20.0	14.0	
1.2	3,120	9.3	11.6	13.9	16.2[c]	18.4	20.6	22.9	14.0	
1.5	3,900	10.9	13.6	16.2[c]	18.7	21.3	23.8	26.2	15.0	
2.0	5,200	13.0	16.0[c]	19.0	22.0	24.8	27.6	30.4	16.0	
4.0	10,400	17.7	21.6[c]	25.3	29.2	32.7	36.1	39.4	19.0	
10.0	26,000	23.5	28.5	33.2[c,d]	37.7	41.9	45.8	49.5	32.0	33.0
25.0	65,000	28.9	34.8	40.2[d]	45.2	49.8	54.1[c]	58.0	53.0	39.0
100.0	260,000	36.4[d]	43.2	49.4	54.9	59.8	64.2	68.2[c]	70.0	34.5
500.0	1,300,000	44.0[d]	51.7	58.3	64.0	68.9	73.2[c]	76.9	70.0	30.0
5,000.0	13,000,000	53.5	61.6	68.3	73.9[c]	78.5	82.3	85.4	70.0	

Notes: [a] Giving effect to a minimum standard reduction of $200.
[b] Estimated by interpolation from data in table 9.2.
[c] Relative position of nominal 1965 rates.
[d] Relative position of adjusted 1965 rates.

Table 9.2 *Actual and Nominal Income Tax Progression*

Income class (Thousands of dollars)	Adjusted gross income	Excess of net long-term gain over short-term loss	Reported net loss	Allowable net loss	Itemized deductions	Net income reported	Tax	Effective rate	Range of marginal rates
				Millions of dollars				Percent	
(1)	(2)	(3)	(4)	(5)	(6)	(7)	(8)	(9)	(10)
10–15	91,768	1,984	684	162	11,729	80,509	10,712	13.31	19–36
15–20	29,935	1,447	377	78	4,029	26,331	4,189	15.91	22–42
20–50	39,648	3,942	731	122	5,382	35,628	7,440	20.88	25–58
50–100	12,440	2,497	181	23	1,801	11,729	3,654	31.15	50–69
100–500	7,164	3,501	61	4	1,303	7,554	2,752	36.43	60–70
500–1,000	946	952	2	–	185	12,440	408	32.80	70–70
Over 1,000	1,434	1,656	2	–	334	1,957	603	30.81	70–70

Source: US Treasury Dept', Internal Revenue Service, Statistics of Income 1965, Individual Income Tax Returns

(2) Table 3, page 10, col. (2).

(3) Table 12, page 29, col. (48) plus col. (60).

(4) Table 12, page 27, col. (4).

(5) Table 12, page 27, col. (3).

(6) Table 3, page 11, col. (47). The standard deduction is not deducted, since this would tend to understate income relatively more at the lower income levels and thus exaggerate the regressivity of the tax. The omission results in understating the regressive tendency.

(7) Col. (2) + (0.5) col. (3) – (col. (4) – col. (5)) – col. (6).

(8) Table 4, page 14, col. (59).

(9) Col. (8) ÷ col. (7).

(10) Page 169 (reference is primarily to Schedule II, Joint Retuns, as this is the schedule applicable to over 90% of the Adjusted Gross Income in the range shown).

PART III

Marginal-cost Pricing

In the case of electric power ... there should be at least two or three emergency rates for dealing with situations where there is either a major unanticipated surge in demand or a substantial breakdown on the supply side ... If such a system were in effect, then by ... applying the emergency rates, customers could be more effectively induced to curtail non-essential usage than in the case now where one must resort partly to exhortation, partly to substandard voltages, and in extreme cases to cutting off power supply entirely to select areas at various times, in order to curtail demand in emergencies ... If something like this had been available a few years ago in New York, the rather nasty power failure that took place when cables overheated under Central Park could have been averted.

The Bell Journal of Economics and Management Science, 2 (1971), p. 344.

Over a span of forty years (1948–87), William Vickrey wrote some forty papers bearing on marginal-cost pricing (MCP). A few address general issues, such as the relevance of short-run versus long-run concepts. Most deal with applications, ranging over public utilities (electricity, telephone), public and private transportation (subways, bridges, congested streets) curb parking, urban services (water, fire protection) and air travel. In the process, Vickrey has dealt with a large number of conceptual and practical issues; he has also made a number of creative suggestions for efficient pricing schemes. In line with Vickrey's idiosyncratic style, many subtle theoretical points are made almost casually, as part of the discussion of specific applied problems.

Giving a proper account of that varied work would have been difficult, were it not for the comprehensive entry on "Marginal and Average Cost Pricing" which Vickrey wrote for *The New Palgrave Dictionary of Economics*. That entry, divided into fifteen sections, covers concisely most of the MCP issues on which Vickrey has written.

We reprint that *Palgrave* entry as chapter 10 and recommend it strongly to all users of this volume. Generally speaking, a main reference for the contents of the first five sections of the *Palgrave* survey is the paper on "Some Objections to Marginal Cost Pricing," published in 1948 in the *Journal of Political Economy*, reprinted here as chapter 11. That paper also contains an early formulation of Vickrey's approach to what later become known as "airline overbooking" – a subject dealt with in the seventh and eighth sections of the *Palgrave* survey and treated at length in chapter 13 below. Next, the 1970 paper on "Responsive Pricing of Public Utility Services," reprinted as chapter 12, corresponds to the tenth, eleventh, and twelfth sections of the survey. The next sections there are covered under parts IV and V of this volume.

The nature of Vickrey's interest in this area is unambiguous, and perfectly summarized in the opening sentence of chapter 13: "As you know, I'm kind of hipped on the idea of marginal-cost pricing: the use of pricing as a device for improving the efficiency with which we use various facilities." Historically, that *normative* concern had been pursued with precursory brilliance by the French engineer Dupuit (1933),[1] then by Hotelling (1938), with special reference to public utilities. The renewed attention it received after World War II represented a shift of emphasis, from the *positive* concern with pricing policies of business firms, which had been in the foreground of the "marginal-cost controversy" spurred by the pre-war investigation of Hall and Hitch (1939) at Oxford.

While Vickrey was interacting with Hotelling at Columbia University, the French tradition was revived with much "energy" at Electricité de France (EDF), by a group of engineers concerned with the management of nationalized public utilities; see Drèze (1964) or Nelson (1964) for survey presentations. It is appropriate to bring out the parallelism and respective originalities of the two developments, which were essentially simultaneous.[2]

The original themes addressed by both Vickrey and the French engineers are identical: (i) the proper conceptual definition of marginal cost; (ii) the relationship of short-run to long-run marginal costs, and investment criteria; (iii) fluctuations of marginal costs over time; and (iv) the implications of a budget constraint. The convergence of concerns is noteworthy, given that the two developments were independent and were proceeding in altogether different institutional environments.

The French engineers were directly involved in the management of EDF, and assumed operating responsibility for tariffs and investments. Their research was directly linked to practical needs. It had the benefit of being specifically focused,[3] and tailored to realities with which they were directly familiar. They also had the great advantage of team work. One remarkable feature of this applied research by "company staff" at EDF is its formal elegance and its firm rooting in abstract theory. Yet, it was being translated into operating tariffs (the so-called "green tariff") and actual investment programs.

In contrast, William Vickrey was working by himself, as an independent academic at Columbia University. True, he had the benefit of serving as a research assistant for a study on the Electric Power Industry in 1939–40, and as a consultant on the New York subway fare structure in 1950–1. But his 1948 paper (chapter 11) is a piece of academic research, starting off from the academic

---

[1] The 1993 volume reprints a set of articles published in the nineteenth century, starting in 1844. See Vickrey (1968a) for a suggestive biographical notice on Dupuit.

[2] Vickrey's early contributions appeared in 1948 and 1952; the more significant early contributions at EDF were those of Boiteux (1949), Dessus (1949) and Gaspard and Massé (1952).

[3] In particular, on a nonstorable commodity.

literature, and addressing general issues. When he mentions applications, they range over electricity, bus transportation and airlines, without the benefit of a predetermined focus. Yet the identification of relevant issues and priorities is the same! And the conclusions reached stand in general agreement.

Vickrey's 1948 article starts with a defense of the principle and applicability of marginal-cost pricing in the presence of increasing returns (decreasing costs). Interestingly, the first objection addressed there is the lack of simple tests for project evaluation when sales revenues are allowed to fall short of total costs (when prices are set below average costs). Vickrey convincingly argues that project evaluation requires a full *cost–benefit analysis*, irrespective of what pricing policy is adopted.[4] But the assessment of costs and benefits depends upon the use of the project facilities, hence upon the pricing policy. Later on,[5] Vickrey spelled out the optimal squencing of decisions, as stated in the fourth section of the *Palgrave* entry: first define a pricing policy, then invest, and finally set actual prices in view of actual developments (and in conformity with the policy, of course).

The same ideas can be found in the early papers of Dessus (1949) and Boiteux (1949). Moreover, one point is stressed repeatedly there, which receives only passing recognition in Vickrey's article: the equality of short-run and long-run marginal costs, *when capacity is optimal for realized output* (the "envelope theorem"). Boiteux goes on to argue that, when capacity adjustments are called for, prices should be geared to the hypothetical marginal costs associated with optimally adjusted capacity, rather than to current costs. That viewpoint possibly accounts for the repeated reference of the French engineers to long-run marginal costs as the proper basis for efficient pricing[6] – a viewpoint emphatically rejected by Vickrey.[7] The French view is related to the concern about covering fixed costs, that of Vickrey to the concern about using existing facilities efficiently.

The key concept, repeatedly emphasized by Vickrey, is "Short-Run Marginal Social Cost" (SRMSC). Much of his attention is devoted to the proper identification and measurement of that concept. Two important ideas are introduced already in 1948: (i) the cost of an item sold today is not its past recorded cost, but what it will cost in the future to replace the item; (ii) if the item is available in limited supply, or is perishable, then the SRMSC is given by the value of the item to the marginal alternative buyer.

The first idea, reviewed in the third section of the *Palgrave* survey and developed further in 1970,[8] also has implications for the imputation of depreciation

---

[4] Cost–benefit analysis was an essentially informal tool in 1948. See Prest and Turvey (1965).
[5] See Vickrey (1969, 1985).
[6] See, e.g., Massé (1987).
[7] See, e.g., Vickrey (1985).
[8] See Vickrey (1970a).

allowances, and for the efficient use of heterogeneous equipment, when output fluctuates. These implications are reviewed in the ninth section of the Palgrave entry.[9]

The second idea is central of a number of suggestions, both practical and theoretical, made by Vickrey over the years. The best known of these is of course the "Second-Price Auction," whereby the winner is charged precisely the SRMSC, as defined by the value of the item to the second bidder, who is also the "marginal alternative buyer."

The distinction between "private" and "social" marginal cost often hinges on externalities. Congestion costs are a prime example, encountered first on the subways in the form of discomfort to other passengers, later at tollbridges in the form of queue length (see part IV). Other examples come from automobile accidents or pollution, two topics on which again Vickrey was a precursor.[10]

As an interesting sideline, note in the sixth section of the *Palgrave* survey how the "marginal cost of heterogeneous sets of uses" is to be computed by weighting these uses "in proportion to responsiveness of each usage category to the change in price."

Turning to fluctuations of marginal costs over time, by far the most significant – though definitely not the only – origin of these comes from fluctuations in the demand for nonstorable services produced by equipment with imperfectly flexible capacity.[11] It is useful to distinguish three cases: (i) fluctuations of a repetitive, periodic nature, which can be handled by a pre-announcd time-varying tariff; this is the subject matter of "peak-load pricing"; (ii) fluctuations of a totally erratic, unpredictable nature, which can at best be handled by *ex post* corrective actions; this is the subject matter of "responsive pricing"; (iii) fluctuations which cannot be predicted by the seller, but well by some buyers; when the "unit of service" is substantial enough to justify elaborate arrangements, these could be handled through "speculators' markets."

Peak-load pricing was in the foreground of the French preoccupations, and the elegant theoretical contribution of Boiteux (1949) is an acclaimed classic; Vickrey dealt systematically with that issue at an applied level in his "Proposal for Revising New York's Subway Fare Structure" (chapter 14 below). Erratic fluctuations entered the French preoccupations through "interruptible contracts"; otherwise, unexpected tariff adjustments are discarded, to avoid imposing additional uncertainty on consumers. Vickrey, on the other hand, has been attracted by the potential efficiency gains of using the price mechanism to ration

---

[9] See Vickrey (1971a) for further discussion of depreciation charges, especially under inflation.

[10] See Vickrey (1968b, 1970b).

[11] Supply-side fluctuations originating from plant failures, rainfall accumulation in reservoirs, investment discontinuities are not ignored; see for instance the pricing of water in chapters 12 or 18 below.

demand in the face of congestion. He has advocated repeatedly the use of "responsive prices," which vary with the actual load of the system *as it evolves over time*, without following a preannounced path independent of future, imperfectly predicted developments.

The practical application of responsive pricing requires a suitable information technology, which is readily available in some cases (telephones), easily described in other cases (electricity), but unavailable in still others (water supply). Vickrey had developed these ideas in the fifties, starting with a first approach (later to be superseded and abandoned) to responsive pricing of curb parking,[12] followed by the testimony on congestion pricing in Washington in 1959 (see also chapter 15 below). The term "responsive pricing" itself, and the detailed discussion of applications to telephone or electricity, came later; chapter 12 gives a formulation that may be regarded as definitive.[13]

The same paper contains an important innovation regarding regulation. The idea of responsive prices, adapted continuously to conditions of supply and demand, is hard to reconcile with the practice of regulation, under which price changes are subject to approval by a regulatory commission. The solution proposed by Vickrey consists in using an *escrow fund*, into which a utility transfers any excess of sales revenues at responsive prices over what they would have been at regulatory prices, or from which it draws to make up the difference when responsive prices fall below regulatory prices. It does not seem that such a scheme has ever been used; yet it seems well suited to the problem posed.

The third case was introduced for the first time by Vickrey in 1948, with reference to the problem of reservations for long-haul air travel, which is singled out for attention because the "unit of service" is substantial enough to justify elaborate arrangements. If a speculators' market were organized for seats on a particular flight at a future date, the price on that market would evolve in the same way as on any other futures market, and in particular would reflect the value of a seat to the marginal passenger. Vickrey explains how the airlines can mimic such a market, in an attempt to increase seat occupancy while improving customer service and overall efficiency. We have included as chapter 13 a further elaboration twenty-five years later, to show the contribution of further ideas developed in the meantime, such as the second-price auction and escrow funds. This application is described in the seventh and eight sections of the *Palgrave* entry.

Having understood the distinctions between the three cases, one is left to wonder how to decide which one fits best a particular empirical situation. For

---

[12] See Vickrey (1954); the basic idea is described at the end of chapter 13.

[13] As late as 1968, Vickrey still uses the term "reactive pricing" – which no longer appears after 1970. Chapter 12 is a reprint of the mimeographed release by New England Telephone of a seminar presentation in 1970. It has the appealing informality of a "talk." A revised version has appeared in *The Bell Journal of Economics and Management Science* 2 (1971), pp. 337–46.

instance, at what stage of system overload should the standard peak-load tariff give way to responsive surcharges? Beyond what distance does an airplane trip qualify for organization of a speculators' market? Theoretical analysis of these questions calls for balancing the welfare costs to consumers of the added price uncertainty against the cost of quantity constraints (associated, say, with fully engaged telephone exchanges or fully booked planes). The analogy with second-best wages rigidities[14] suggests that the answer is not obvious, so that further theoretical analysis remains needed.

Finally, regarding the implications of a budget constraint, it is interesting to contrast two stages in the thinking of both the French engineers and Vickrey. In 1949, Boiteux concludes that EDF receipts at MCP fall slightly short (by a 7 percent margin) of covering average costs, and suggests raising prices across the board by the same margin. Some years later, his theoretical work on second-best pricing under a budget constraint (Boiteux, 1956) leads him to rediscover the Ramsey "inverse elasticity rule."

As for Vickrey, he realizes in the early fifties that MCP would lead to a substantial aggravation of the New York subway deficit, to be covered by the city budget presumably through higher taxes. He realizes that such taxes are bound to cause distortions, and proceeds to "guesstimate" the welfare cost of these distortions – summarized in a "marginal cost of public funds" (MCPF), which he evaluates at 130 cents to the dollar. He then proceeds to seek an efficient balance between the distortions caused by raising subway fares above marginal costs, and the MCPF. To that end, he compares alternative fare structures, evaluates the welfare losses (on the basis of "courageous" elasticity assumptions), and stops where these exceed 30 cents to the dollar of additional revenue. In that process, *he seeks precisely to implement* (operationally) *the Ramsey conditons* – but not against a fixed budget constraint: against a fixed MCPF, which is in principle a superior criterion (since it amounts to choosing optimally the level of the constraint).[15]

The last comparison is revealing of Vickrey's talent for applying highly sophisticated reasoning to the discussion of specific applications. In a sense, it is unfortunate that he seldom felt motivated to bring out *formally* the generality of his analysis. It is left for the readers to understand that generality and transpose the reasoning to other areas. On the other hand, it is difficult to regret that Vickrey devoted much of his own attention to consider applications of MCP in the diverse areas covered in the following chapters and again in parts IV and V.

[14] See Drèze and Gollier (1993).

[15] In later publications, Vickrey (1971b) refers explicitly to the Ramsey rule, and also develops an alternative, more operational, formulation (see also section XIII of the *Palgrave* survey).

References

Boiteux, M., "La tarification des demandes en pointe," *Revue Générale de l'Electricité*, 58 (1949), pp. 321–40; translated as "Peak-load pricing," *Journal of Business*, 33(2) (1960), pp. 157–79.

Boiteux, M., "Sur la gestion des monopoles publics astreints à l'équilibre budgétaire," *Econometrica*, 24 (I) (1956), pp. 22–40.

Dessus, G., *Les principes généraux de la tarification dans les services publics* (Paris: Union Internationale des Producteurs et Distributeurs d'Energie Electrique, 1949).

Drèze, J.H., "Some Postwar Contributions of French Economists to Theory and Public Policy," *American Economic Review*, 54 (1964), 4–2, pp. 1–64.

Drèze, J.H. and Gollier, C., "Risk-Sharing on the Labour Market and Second Best Wages Rigidities," *European Economic Review* (1993).

Gaspard, R. and Massé, P., "Le choix des investissements energétiques et la production d'electricité en France," *Revue Française de l'Energie*, 4 (1952), pp. 5–15.

Hall, R.L. and Hitch, J.C., "Price Theory and Business Behaviour," *Oxford Economic Papers*, 2 (1939).

Hotelling, H., "The General Welfare in Relation to Problems of Taxation and of Railway and Utility Rates," *Econometrica*, 6 (1938), pp. 242–69.

Massé, P., "Public Utility Pricing," *The New Palgrave: A Dictionary of Economics*, J. Eatwell, M. Milgate and P. Newman, Eds. (London: Macmillan, 1987), pp. 1069–72.

Nelson, J.R., *Marginal Cost Pricing in Practice* (Englewood Cliffs: Prentice-Hall, 1964).

Prest, A.R. and Turvey, R., "Cost-Benefit Analysis: A Survey," *Economic Journal*, 75 (1965), pp. 683–735.

Vickrey, W., "The Economizing of Curb Parking Space," *Traffic Engineering* (1954).

"Dupuit, Jules," *Encyclopedia of the Social Sciences*, 4 (1968a), pp. 308–10.

"Automobile Accidents, Tort Law, Externalities, and Insurance: an Economist's Critique," *Safety: Law and Contemporary Problems*, 33(3) (1968b), pp. 464–87.

"Current Issues in Transportation," in *Contemporary Economic Issues*, Neil Chamberlain, Ed. (Irwin, 1969), pp. 185–240.

"Time's Arrow and Marginal-Cost Pricing: Comment," in *New Dimensions in Public Utility Pricing*, Harry M. Trebing, Ed. (East Lansing: Michigan State University, 1970a).

"The Possibilities of Air Pollution Control through Various Forms of Effluent Charge," *Study of the Social and Economic Effects of Changes in Air Quality* (Corvallis: Oregon State University, Mimeo, 1970b), pp. 56–70.

"Interrelations between Interest Rates and Depreciation Rates," in *Utility Regulation during Inflation*, J.E. Haring and J.F. Humphrey, Eds. (Glendale, Calif.: Occidental College, 1971a), pp. 56–69.

"Maximum Output or Maximum Welfare: More on the Off-Peak Pricing Problem," *Kyklos*, 24 (2) (1971b), pp. 305–29.

"The Fallacy of Using Long-Run Cost for Peak-Load Pricing," *Quarterly Journal of Economics* (1985), pp. 1331–4.

10

Marginal- and Average-Cost Pricing

In a pure and simple static world of perfect competition, where production units purchase or rent all their inputs in competitive markets and each sells a single homogeneous product competitively, production takes place at a point of constant returns to scale where the marginal cost and average cost of the product are equal to each other and to its price. If in addition there are no neighborhood effects of externalities operating outside the market, the result will be Pareto-efficient, meaning that there is no feasible alternative arrangement that would be better for someone and no worse for anyone.

Difficulties with the Concept of Average Cost

As soon as production takes place with durable capital facilities that must be adapted to the needs of an individual firm there may no longer be an effective market for these facilities and a cost of their use during any particular period must be determined by other means. In the rather extreme case of the "one-horse-shay" asset that in a static environment yields a stream of identical services over a known lifetime, a constant periodic rental cost can be derived by the use of a "sinking fund" method of depreciation in which the rent is the sum of an increasing depreciation charge and a decreasing interest charge on the net value. But where the value of the service varies over time, whether because of physical deterioration, an increasing cost of maintenance needed to keep the item in "as new" condition, or shifts in demand, this would in principle cause depreciation charges to vary; in practice this is done in one of a number of arbitrary ways by

The New Palgrave, Eatwell *et al.*, Eds., Vol. III (Macmillan, 1987), pp. 311–18.

using "straight-line" or various forms of "accelerated" depreciation. If these charges are used as a basis for pricing, where competition is imperfect enough to give some leeway, the results can be correspondingly arbitrary.

More serious problems arise in the increasingly widespread cases of joint production of several distinguishable products or services. Where competitive markets exist, the market conditions dictate the allocation of joint costs among the various products, as when a meat-packing establishment produces steaks, hides, glue, and offals. There is no way in which one can determine a meaningful average cost of hides by considering only the production process. Where the products, though economically widely different, are physically similar, it is tempting to cut the Gordian knot and average over the entire output, often at the cost of serious impairment of economic efficiency. Even when elaborate rationales are concocted by cost accountants, unless demand conditions as well as production conditions are taken into account the results are essentially arbitrary.

One can do a little better with marginal cost, at least if one is seeking a short-run marginal social cost (hereafter SRMSC), which is the concept that would be relevant for efficiency-promoting pricing decisions. Unless a consumer is presented with a price that correctly represents the marginal social cost associated with the various alternatives open to him, he is likely to make inefficient decisions.

The Importance of Emphasizing the Short Run

One often finds in the literature proposals to use a "long-run marginal cost" as a basis for setting rates. The trouble is that in an operation producing a multitude of products with interrelated costs it is not possible even to define in any precise way what could be meant by a "long-run marginal cost," any more than one could define a relevant long-run marginal cost for the hides and steak that are derived from the same carcass in the face of fluctuations over time in relative demand.

The attempt to use a long-run concept seems to be motivated in part by the notion that in some sense the long-run concept is more inclusive in that it allows for variation in capital investment and would include a return on such investment, whereas short-run marginal costs would fail to cover the costs of capital investment. In the single-product steady-state case, however, which is the only case for which the long-run marginal cost can be clearly defined, if the investment in plant is at the optimal level, i.e., the level which will result in the given output being produced at the lowest total cost, short- and long-run average-cost curves will be tangent to each other at the given output, and short- and long-term marginal costs will be equal. Short-run marginal-cost prices will therefore cover just as much of the total cost as will prices based on "long-run marginal cost." If short-run marginal cost is below the long-run marginal cost, this would indicate that the installed plant is larger than optimum, and conversely if plant is below optimum size, short-run marginal cost will be above long-run marginal cost.

Flexible Versus Stable Prices

A long-run approach is sometimes advocated on the ground that it results in more stable prices. Price rigidity, however, exacts a high toll in terms of reduced efficiency. It is sometimes argued that stable prices are required for intelligent planning for installations that commit the investor to the use of a given volume of service. There is nothing in a SRMSC pricing policy, however, that precludes providing the consumer with estimates of the probable course of prices in the longer term, or even entering into long-term contracts to purchase specified quantities of service. If they are not to interfere with efficiency, however, such contracts should allow for the possibility of purchasing additional amounts at the eventual going rates, or of selling back some of the contracted-for output if this should prove profitable for the consumer.

Lack of flexibility in pricing has, indeed, been a major source of inefficiency in the use of utility services, whether arising as a result of the cumbersomeness of the regulatory procedures in privately owned utilities, or of bureaucratic inertia in publicly owned ones. At times it has even appeared that it takes longer to carry out the bureaucratic procedures involved in altering a price than to install additional capacity, whereas in terms of the underlying capabilities prices can and should be altered on shorter notice than the time taken to adjust fixed capital installations.

Optimal Decision-making Sequence

The efficient pattern of decision making consists of first establishing a pricing policy to be followed in the future (as distinct from the application of that policy to produce a specific set of prices), then planning adjustments to fixed capital installations according to a cost–benefit analysis based on predicted demand patterns and predicted application of the pricing policy, subject to whatever financial constraints may be applicable, and then eventually determining prices on a day-to-day or month-to-month basis in terms of conditions as they actually develop.

Too often a rigid adherence to inappropriate financial constraints results in a pattern of pricing over time that leads to gross inefficiency in the utilization of facilities that are added in large increments. In the setting of tolls on bridges, for example, a high fixed toll is often imposed from the start in an attempt to minimize early shortfalls of revenues below interest and amortization charges. When the indebtedness incurred to finance the facility is finally paid off, tolls are often eliminated, sometimes just at the time that they should be increased in order to check the growth of traffic and congestion and defer the necessity for the construction of additional facilities

The Forward-Looking Character of Marginal Cost

Since changes in present usage cannot affect costs incurred or irrevocably committed to in the past, it is only present and future costs that are of concern in the determination of marginal cost. Past recorded costs are relevant only as predictors of what current and future costs will turn out to be. The marginal cost of ten gallons of gasoline pumped into a car is not determined by what the service station paid for that gasoline, but by the cost expected to be incurred to replace that gasoline at the next delivery. The substantial time-lag that often exists between a change in price at the raw material level and its reflection at the retail level is one of the pervasive failings that contributes to the inefficiency of the economic system.

Another more important case in which future impacts are of vital importance in the calculation of marginal cost is where congestion accumulates a backlog of demand that has to be worked off over a period of time. A particularly striking case of this occurs when traffic regularly accumulates in a queue during rush hours at a bottleneck such as a toll bridge. The consequence of adding a car to the traffic stream is that there will be one more car waiting in the queue from the time the car joins the queue until the queue is eventually worked off, assuming that the flow through the bottleneck will be unaffected by the lengthening of the queue.

The marginal cost of a vehicle trip will be measured in terms of a number of vehicle hours of delay equal to the interval from the time the car would have arrived at the choke point if there had been no delay, to the time the queue is finally worked off. This is not measured by the length of the queue at the moment, but will be determined by the subsequent arrival of traffic over an extended period. A car arriving at the queue after it began to accumulate at 7:30 may get through the bottleneck at 8:00, after being delayed by only fifteen minutes, but if the bottleneck will not be worked off until 10:00 the marginal cost will be 2¼ vehicle hours of which only ¼ hour is borne by the added car itself. The remaining two hours, if evaluated at $5 per vehicle hour, would indicate that under these conditions the toll that would represent this externality would be $10. Marginal cost cannot be determined exclusively from conditions at the moment, but may well depend, often to an important extent, on predictions as to what the impact of current consumption will be on conditions some distance into the future.

Marginal Cost of Heterogeneous Sets of Uses

It will often happen, for various reasons, that the same price will have to be applied to a nonhomogeneous set of uses. To set such a price properly, the marginal costs of the various uses within the set covered must be combined in some way to get a marginal cost relevant to this decision. It would be wrong, however, merely to average the marginal costs of all the uses for which this price is to be charged. Rather, the decision as to whether a decrease in a given price is desirable must consider the cost of the increments or decrements in the various outputs that will be bought as a result of the price change. In averaging the marginal costs of the various usage categories, the weighting will have to be in proportion to the responsiveness of each usage category to the change in price.

For example, if a price is to be set for electricity consumption on summer weekday afternoons, in a system where air-conditioning is an important load, consumption and marginal cost may be higher on hot days than on warm days, but it may be considered too difficult to differentiate in price between the two categories of days. An increase in the price for this entire set of periods may induce some customers to adjust the thermostat setting. But during hot days the equipment may work full tilt without reducing the temperature to the thermostat setting, whereas on warm days there will be a reduction in power consumption. The marginal cost relevant to the setting of the common price would then be determined predominantly by the lower marginal cost of the warm-day consumption, and relatively little, if at all, by the higher marginal cost hot-day consumption.

Anticipatory Marginal Cost

In many cases a customer will make his effective decision to consume an item some time in advance, and it will be the expected price as perceived by him at that time that determines his decision. If, as in services subject to reservation, a firm price must be quoted the time the reservation is made, it is the expected marginal cost as of that moment that should govern the price charged. In the case of a service where the demand is highly variable and to a considerable extent unpredictable, such an expected marginal cost would be an average of marginal costs that might arise under alternative possible developments, possibly ranging from a very low value, if there turns out to be unused capacity, to the possibly quite high value if another latecomer must be turned away. The respective probabilities of these outcomes, as estimated at a given time, will vary with the proportion of the total supply already sold, the time remaining to the delivery of the service, and the pricing policy to be followed in the interim.

At one extreme, for long-haul airline reservations where the unit of sale is large, one might find it worth while to have a fairly elaborate pricing scheme in which the price quoted would vary according to the proportion of seats on a given flight already sold and the time remaining to departure, in simulation of what an ideal speculators' market might produce, the price at any time being an estimate of the price which, if maintained thereafter, would result in all the remaining seats being just sold out at departure time. This would correspond to marginal cost in that the sale of a seat at any given time would slightly raise the price during the remaining period to decrease demand by one unit, at a price that would be expected to be on the average equal to the price at which the seat was sold, indicating that the price was equal to the value of the seat to the alternative passenger.

Quality–Volume Interrelationships

In principle, in the absence of barriers to entry, competition would induce the supply of just sufficient seats on the various routes to cause revenues produced by such pricing to just cover costs. Even this, however, would be optimal only on those routes where traffic is so heavy that even with planes of a size producing the lowest cost per seat, further increases in service frequency would be of negligible value. On most routes there will remain economies of scale in that either providing more seats at the same frequency of service with larger planes would reduce costs per seat, or providing more seats with the same size of planes would provide an increased frequency of service that would be of value to others than the additional riders. In the latter case the marginal cost of providing for the additional passengers would be calculated by deducting the increase in the value of the service by reason of increased frequency from the cost of providing the added seats.

If it were possible to adjust plane size and frequency in a continuous fashion, then if the situation is optimal the two marginal costs would be equal. In practice both plane size and service frequency can be varied only in discrete jumps, so that this relation would be only approximate. Optimal price would be above a downward marginal cost calculated on the basis of a reduction in service, and below an upward marginal cost calculated on the basis of an increase in service. The decreases and increases might involve a combination of frequency and plane size changes. To preserve the formulation that price should equal marginal cost it may be useful to define marginal cost in such cases as consisting of the range between these upward and downward values rather than as a single point.

In practice, between the existence of economies of scale and the imperfect cross-elasticity of demand between flights at various times and with different amenities, removal of regulation tends to result in an emphasis on nonprice competition, attempts to subdivide the market by various devices and restrictions to permit discriminatory pricing, and a bunching of service schedules at salient times and places that provides a lower overall level of convenience than would be possible were the given number of seat miles distributed more efficiently.

Where the unit of sale is small it may not be worth while to incur the transaction costs of varying price in strict conformity with SRMSC. One could, in theory, apply the same principle to the sale of newspapers at a given outlet. The price of a newspaper would vary according to the number of unsold papers remaining and the time of day. This would result in less disappointment of customers having an urgent desire for a paper late in the day and encountering a sold-out condition, and fewer unsold papers returned. But unless some ingenious device can be found for executing such a program at low transaction costs, it probably would not be considered worth while, even by the most sanguine advocate of marginal cost pricing.

Wear and Tear, Depreciation, and Marginal Cost

Even in the absence of lumpiness or technological change, existing methods of charging for capital use often fail to give a proper evaluation of marginal cost. This is especially true where the useful life of a unit of equipment is determined more by amount of use than by lapse of time. In the extreme case of equipment that must be retired at the end of a given number of miles or hours of active service, or after the production of so many kwh of energy, and which, in one-horse-shay fashion, gives a uniform quality of service over its lifetime without requiring increasing levels of maintenance, the marginal cost of use at a given time will be the consequent advancing of the time of retirement of the equipment. The marginal cost of using the newest units will be the lowest, and will advance over time at a rate equal to the rate of interest as the equipment ages and the advancement of replacement consequent upon use becomes less and less remote.

In a service subject to daily and weekly peaks, the newest equipment will be allocated to the heaviest service, operating during both peak and off-peak hours. Equipment will be relegated to less and less intense service as it ages. The marginal cost of service at a particular moment will be that for the oldest unit that has to be pressed into service at that instant. The rental charge for the use of the unit will vary gradually over the entire range of demands, rather than dropping off to zero whenever the full complement of equipment is not required. At the other end, in this extreme case, the service provided would not necessarily be held constant by price variation over an extended peak period: under the conditions postulated it would be possible to provide for needle peaks by planning for the stretching out over time of the final service units of the oldest equipment. In this way the required peak capacity can be provided at a cost much lower than that which would be calculated by loading all the capital charges for the added equipment on this brief period of use.

Another way of looking at the matter is to appeal to the proposition that perfect competition under conditions of perfect foresight will produce optimal results. To this end one can suppose a situation in which vehicles are rented by the hour from a large number of lessors operating in a competitive market. For simplicity, initially, one can assume all vehicles to be of the one-horse-shay variety, being equivalent to bundles of hours of active service, with the quality of service being independent of age up to a final "bubble-burst" collapse. Also, for simplicity, assume a steady state in which vehicles are scrapped and replaced at a constant rate over time, so that at any given moment vehicles are evenly distributed by age.

A common market rental price for all vehicles at any given time of the week will emerge, being higher as the number of vehicles in service at the time is greater. During any given week, each renter will have a reservation price for his vehicle, such that he will rent his vehicle during those hours for which the market rental is above this reservation price and never when the market rate is lower. This reservation price will increase over time for any given vehicle at the market rate of interest, since a renter will rent his vehicle if and only if the net present value of the rental discounted back to the time of purchase exceeds some fixed amount. The owner would not want to rent his vehicle for a net present value less than he could have got by selling one of this stock of service units at some other time at or just below his reservation price. New buses will have the lowest reservation price and will be assigned to the schedules calling for the most hours of service per week, while old buses will be held idle during slack hours and used only for peak service. As each bus ages it will be assigned to less and less heavy service along the load-duration curve.

This pattern of usage can be regarded as resulting from a desire to recover the capital tied up in the usage units of each bus as rapidly as possible. It is related to the practice in electric utilities of using the newest units for peak service, in that case motivated in part by the tendency for the newer units to be more efficient in thermal terms. To be sure, occasionally new units are designed specifically for peaking service, with a correspondingly low capital cost, though this is a relatively recent phenomenon related to a slowing-down of secular increases in potential thermal efficiency.

In any case, where wear-and-tear is a factor, one cannot properly allocate depreciation charges primarily to peak service, however defined, nor should they be spread evenly over all service, much less spread evenly over hours of the week so that vehicle hours in off-peak periods would get higher charges than during the peak. Rather the depreciation charge per vehicle hour will vary gradually and in a positive direction with the intensity of use of the equipment at any given hour.

The analysis becomes a little complicated when equipment life is dependent on mileage or loading or intensity of use as well as hours of active service, so that different rentals would properly be chargeable according to the nature of the service for which the unit is being rented. Also further analysis is required if equipment is laid up between runs at isolated terminals rather than at a central depot where a market could be postulated, or if the fleet contains vehicles varying in size or other characteristics. It would even be theoretically appropriate to charge different fares for the same trip at the same time if made on vehicles with different origins or destinations. (In Hong Kong, indeed, the practice is to charge a flat fare on each route, but to differentiate the fare fairly elaborately as among routes. On segments where routes converge, this has the unfortunate result of unduly concentrating riding on buses with the lower fares, even where the higher fare buses have empty seats and are making stops in any case for other passengers.)

Costs of major overhauls that are performed at relatively long intervals would also complicate the picture. There are also problems associated with gradual or sudden changes in overall demand levels, or special events that can be anticipated sufficiently to present an opportunity for reacting in terms of a change in price. The picture can be further complicated if, as was discussed above, there are changes in available technologies or other changes in quality or cost. But the same method of analysis in terms of a hypothetical competitive market can be used to obtain appropriate results.

For the sake of simplicity the above analysis has been couched mainly in terms of a bus service, but the analysis is applicable wherever the useful life of equipment is in part a function of the intensity with which it is used.

Responsive Pricing

In some cases, notably in telephone and electric power services, the technical possibility exists for conveying information as to the current price to customers at the instant of consumption, and for customers to respond to such information in a worthwhile manner at modest cost. In the case of telephone service the information as to the level of charges for local calls can be substituted for the dial tone, with information on rates for long distance calls provided to users who wait for it before dialing the final digits. If the charge exceeds what the customer is willing to pay the call can be aborted with little occupancy of equipment or inconvenience to the user. Prices can be varied from moment to moment in accordance with marginal cost, as estimated from the degree of busyness of the relevant sets of equipment.

In the case of electric power, the costs of providing for a variation of the price according to the conditions of the moment would be somewhat greater. But if the facilities take the form of remote meter reading, either by carrier current over the power lines or by a separate communications channel, much of the cost would be covered by the avoidance of costs involved in manual meter reading. A signal of rate changes can then be provided to the customer as a byproduct of the signal required to initiate a new rate period. The customer can then respond either manually or by installing automatic equipment which will adjust the operation of such items as air-conditioning and refrigeration compressors, water heaters and the like, according to the level of rates in a manner determined by the customer himself. Retrofitting of existing meters by attaching a pulse-generating device such as a mirror and photo-electric cell to the rotor shaft of the existing meter and feeding the pulses to electronic counters and registers should be possible at relatively low cost.

Such responsive pricing would be especially valuable in dealing with emergencies, providing greater assurance of the maintenance of essential services than is possible with existing techniques, and making it possible to reduce substantially the cost of providing reserve capacity. In the case of floods, conflagrations, breakdowns in transit, or other emergencies that under present conditions tend to result in the overloading of telephone facilities and difficulties in completing calls of a vital nature, rates can be charged that are high enough to inhibit a sufficient number of less important calls so that the ability of the system to handle vital calls promptly is preserved. This is difficult to do with present techniques, for while it is relatively easy to give priority to calls originating at such points as police stations, hospitals, and the like, most emergency calls are calls to rather than for these points and it is much more difficult to distinguish such calls close to the point of origin. And there are always a certain number of vital calls not distinguishable in terms of either origin or destination.

Again, in the case of unscheduled power cuts, it would be possible to cause an almost instantaneous shedding of substantial water-heating and refrigeration loads, followed, in the case of an extended cut, by partial shedding of elevator, transit and batch process loads for which it is more inconvenient to respond quite so promptly, after which a sufficient refrigeration load can be picked up as needed to avoid food spoilage. Many of the serious consequences of major power blackouts could have been avoided had such a system been in place at the time. Reserve capacity might well be cut back to provision for scheduled maintenance, leaving the load-shedding capability of responsive pricing to function as a reserve. In many cases the speed of response possible with responsive pricing would be faster than the reaction time within which reserve capacity can pick up load, leading to better voltage regulation and a higher quality of service to customers remaining on the line. And if, in spite of everything, areas must be cut off completely, responsive pricing would also be of considerable help in facilitating a smooth recovery from an outage: instead of having a whole army of motors trying to start up at once upon the restoration of power, with consequent load surges, voltage fluctuations, and malfunction of equipment, load could be picked up smoothly and gradually as the price is lowered from the inhibiting level.

Preserving Incentives with Escrow Funds

With privately owned utilities the regulatory process is too slow to permit prices established directly by regulation to be constantly adjusted to changing current conditions, unless indeed the regulators were to assume a large part of what are normally the responsibilities of management. The problem thus arises of how to allow the prices to be paid by customers to be varied by the utility management without giving rise to incentives for behavior contrary to the public interest. Even if a formula could be devised that would require the utility to adjust prices to track short-run marginal cost, if the utility were allowed to keep the revenues thus generated without restriction, this would set up undesirable incentives for the utility to skimp on the provision of capacity in order to drive up the marginal cost, price, revenues, and profits.

A resolution of this dilemma can be achieved by separating the revenue to be retained by the utility from the amounts to be paid by customers. We can have the "responsive" prices paid by customers vary according to short-run marginal social cost, while the revenues to be retained by the utility are determined by a "standard" price schedule fixed by regulation in the normal manner, the difference being paid into or out of an escrow fund. Failure of the utility to expand capacity adequately would drive marginal cost up, and with it the responsive price, causing revenues to flow into the escrow fund, but the only way the utility could draw on these funds would be to expand capacity sufficiently to drive marginal cost down, causing the responsive rate to fall below the standard rate on the average, entitling the utility to make up the difference from the escrow fund as long as it lasts. Excessive expansion would result in the escrow fund being exhausted, with a corresponding constraint on the revenues obtainable by the utility from the unaugmented low responsive rates.

The setting of the responsive rates would have to be to a large extent at the discretion of the operating utility, though the regulatory commission could monitor the process and even attempt to establish guidelines according to which the responsive price should be set. The utility would normally have no incentive to set the responsive rate below marginal cost, since this would merely increase sales and hence costs by more than any possible long-run increase in revenues to the utility. To be sure, in the short run it might be able to draw on the escrow fund to the extent of the excess, if any, of the standard rate over the responsive rate, but since from a long-run perspective there will normally be other more advantageous ways of drawing on this fund this will not be attractive.

When marginal cost is below the standard price, which would tend to be the usual situation, the utility would in general have an incentive to set the price between the marginal cost and the standard price, since each additional sale produced by the lower price will yield an immediate net revenue equal to the difference between marginal cost and the standard price, offset only by the drawing down of the escrow fund by the difference between the responsive and the standard price. When marginal cost is above the standard price, which with a properly designed standard rate schedule with time-of-day variation should happen relatively rarely, the utility would have an incentive to set the price at least at the marginal-cost level, since to set it lower would tend to increase output at a cost in excess of anything the utility could ever recover. How much higher than marginal cost the price might be set would in theory be limited by the condition that the price could not be high enough to curtail demand sufficiently to drive marginal cost below the standard price. If the standard price has an adequate time-of-day variation, this constraint, loose as it may seem, may be sufficient. Additional guidelines could of course be imposed by the regulatory commission for those rare occasions where this constraint might seem insufficient to keep prices within bounds.

Actual Steps Toward Responsive Pricing

Some actual practices of utility companies are steps in the direction of responsive pricing. Contracts for "interruptible" power provide for load shedding at the discretion of the utility subject to some overall limits. As these are fairly long-term contracts that usually require *ad hoc* communication between the utility and the customer, their applicability is limited and there is no assurance that the necessary shedding will be done in the most economical manner. Many customers are reluctant to submit to load shedding that is not under their control at least to some extent, and that might be imposed under awkward circumstances. Where reserves are ample and interruption is highly unlikely, such contracts have been challenged as being a form of concealed discriminatory concession. On the other hand customers entering into such contracts in the expectation of not being interrupted may feel aggrieved if interruption actually takes place.

Another experimental provision applied by a company with a heavy summer air-conditioning load is for a special surcharge to be applied to the usage of larger customers on days when the temperature at some standard location exceeds a critical level. And another company bases its demand charge on the individual customer's demand recorded at the time that turns out to have been the monthly system peak load, supplying the customers with information as to moment-to-moment variations in the system load. This leads to interesting game-playing on the part of customers as they attempt to keep their own consumption down at times that look as though they might become the monthly peak, with the result that this action may itself shift the peak to another time.

Economies of Scale, Subsidy and Second-Best Pricing

Where there are economies of scale, prices set at marginal cost will fail to cover total costs, thus requiring a subsidy. One reason for wanting to avoid such a subsidy is that if an agency is considered eligible for a subsidy much of the pressure on management to operate efficiently will be lost and management effort will be diverted from controlling costs to pleading for an enhancement of the subsidy. This effect can be minimized by establishing the base for the subsidy in a manner as little susceptible as possible to untoward pressure from management. But it is unlikely that this can be as effective in preserving incentives for cost containment as a requirement that the operation be financially self-sustaining. To achieve this, prices must be raised above marginal cost, and in a multi-product operation the question arises as to how these margins should vary from one price to another within the agency.

Another objection to subsidy is that it raises hard questions of who should bear the burden of the subsidy. More fundamentally the taxes imposed to provide the subsidy will often have distorting effects of their own, and minimizing the overall distortion would again require prices to be raised above marginal cost. One can, indeed, regard these excesses of price over marginal cost as excise taxes comparable to other excise taxes that might be levied to raise a specified amount of revenue.

The answer given to the problem of how to allocate excise taxes and other margins of price above marginal cost so as to minimize the overall loss of economic efficiency given by Frank Ramsey in 1927 can be expressed for the case of independent demands as the inverse elasticity rule, which says that the margin of price over marginal cost as a percentage of the price shall be inversely proportional to the elasticity of demand. A more general formulation is one that states that prices shall be such that consumption of the various services would be decreased by a uniform percentage from that which would have been consumed if price had been set at marginal cost and demand had been a linear extrapolation from the neighborhood of the "second-best" point.

A more transparent formulation, devised by Bernard Sobin in work for the US Postal Service, is the requirement of a uniform "leakage ratio," leakage being the difference between the net revenue actually derivable from a small increment in a particular price and the hypothetical revenue that would have been obtained had there been no change in consumption as a result of this increment. Leakage is the algebraic sum of the products of the changes in consumption of the various related products induced by the small change in a given price, and the respective margins between their prices and marginal costs. Leakage is a measure of the loss of efficiency resulting from the change in the particular price, and the leakage ratio is the ratio of this loss of efficiency to the hypothetical gain in gross revenue if there had been no change in consumption. If one leakage ratio should be greater than another, the same net revenue could be obtained at greater economic efficiency by getting more revenue from the price with the smaller leakage ratio and less from the other. The second-best solution accordingly requires that all leakage ratios be equal.

This analysis can be extended to the case where the agency is being subsidized by taxes which involve an adverse impact on the economy, in terms of marginal distorting effects, compliance costs, and collection costs, which can be expressed as the "marginal cost of public funds" (MCPF). For a net decrease in the subsidy derived by increasing a price, which can be considered to be equivalent to imposing a tax equal to the difference between the marginal cost and the price, $MCPF = LR/(1 - LR)$, where LR is the leakage ratio. A second-best optimum is then one where the MCPF's are equalized over both external and internal taxes.

Special Sources of Subsidy: Land Rents and Congestion Charges

In the case of goods and services with economies of scale that are provided primarily to consumers within a particular urbanized area, methods of financing may be available that involve no marginal cost of public funds or even result in an enhancement of efficiency. The existence of large cities, indeed, is to a predominant extent due to the availability in the city of goods and services produced under conditions of economies of scale: if there were no economies of scale, activity could be scattered about the landscape in hamlets, with great reduction in the high transportation costs involved in movement about a large city. If prices of these services are reduced to marginal cost, the increased attractiveness of the city as a consequence would tend to drive up land rents within the city, and it appears quite appropriate that a levy on such rents should be used to finance the required subsidies. And while there are practical and conceptual difficulties in defining exactly how land rents or land values should be specified for purposes of levying a tax, it is generally considered that a tax on land values, properly defined, has negligible adverse impacts on the efficient allocation of resources.

Indeed, there is a theorem of spatial economics which states that in a system of perfect competition among cities, the availability in the city of services and products subject to economies of scale, priced at their respective marginal social costs, will generate land rents just sufficient to supply the subsidies required to permit prices to be lowered to marginal cost. Among the more important of these services are utility services such as electric power, telephone, cable communications, water supply, mail collection and delivery, sewers and waste disposal, and local transit. It is not clear just how broad the conditions are under which this theorem would hold, and there are difficulties in capturing all land rents for subsidy purposes, but steps in this direction are clearly desirable.

On a more intuitive level, one can note that a person who occupies or uses land that is provided with services such as the availability of transit, electricity, telephone, mail delivery, and the like will be requiring that these services be carried past his property to serve others whether or not he himself uses them. The user of tennis courts located conveniently in a built-up area should no more be excused from contributing to the costs of carrying these services past the courts, even though no direct use is made of electric power, telephone, mail, or other services, than he should expect his auto dealer to cut the price of an automobile by the cost of the headlights and windshield wipers merely because he asserts that he will never drive at night or in bad weather. Tennis players will indeed pay a rent enhanced by the presence of these services and the consequent greater demand for the land for other purposes, but the rent will go to the landlord, not to the purveyor of the services, and the price of the services to those who use them will be too high for efficiency, unless indeed they are subsidized by other taxes that have their own distorting effects.

It is a corollary of this theorem that it would be to the advantage of the landlords in the area, *faute de mieux*, to agree collectively to pay a tax based on their land values, in order to subsidize the various utility services to enable the prices to be set closer to marginal social cost. They could expect in the long run that this action would increase their rents by as much or more than the taxes. To be sure, they might do better by getting someone else to pull their chestnuts out of the fire, but they can do this only at considerable damage to the overall efficiency of the economy of the city, to say nothing of the inequity of such a parasitic relationship.

In addition to land rents in the conventional sense, there is the land used for city streets for the use of which no adequate rental is generally charged. Charging on the basis of SRMSC for the use of congested city streets would in most cases yield a revenue far in excess of the cost of maintaining such facilities, which could appropriately be used for the subsidy of other urban facilities. Properly adjusted, such charges would increase efficiency by bringing home to the users the costs that their use directly imposes on others.

Formerly it would have been considered impractical to attempt to charge for the use of city streets according to the amount of congestion caused: the collection of tolls by manual methods at a multitude of points within the city might well create more congestion than it averted. Advances in technology have, however, made it possible to do this at minimal interference with traffic flow and at modest cost. One method, proposed as long ago as 1959 and recently carried to the point, is to require all vehicles using the congested facilities to be equipped with electronic response units which will permit individual vehicles to be identified as they pass scanning stations suitably distributed within and around the congested areas so that the records thus generated can be processed by computer and appropriate bills sent to the registered owners at convenient intervals. If properly done, this would greatly improve traffic conditions so that the net cost of the revenue to the road users would be far less than the amount collected as revenue. A pilot installation has recently been tested in Hong Kong with satisfactory results, but full implementation appears to have been deferred, because of the political situation associated with the impending transfer of sovereignty.

Indeed, one can define "hypercongestion" as a condition where so many cars are attempting to move in a given area that fewer vehicle miles of travel are being accomplished than could be if fewer vehicles were in the area but could move more rapidly; for example if 1,000 vehicles in an area move at 8 mph and produce 8,000 vehicle miles of travel per hour, reducing the number of cars in the area at a given time to 800 might raise speed to 11 mph producing 8,800 vehicle miles of travel per hour. By restricting the flow of traffic in the period leading up to the hypercongestion period, road pricing could prevent hypercongestion from occurring, except possibly sporadically, and in any case so improve conditions that more movement would be accomplished during the peak period at faster speeds. The improvement during peak periods might even be such that total movement throughout the day would be increased, and where conditions are now severe users could find that they are better off than before, even inclusive of the payment of the congestion charge.

If there are bridges, tunnels, or other special facilities for which a toll is already being charged, and which regularly back up a queue during the morning rush hour, substantial revenues can be obtained at no overall net cost to the users by adding a surcharge to the toll during the period where queueing regularly threatens, rising gradually from zero to a maximum and down again in such a way that by gradual adjustment regular queueing is substantially eliminated. The toll surcharge will then be taking the place of the queue in influencing decisions as to when to travel, and in general those who plan their trips in terms of time of arrival at their destination will be able to leave as many minutes later as they formerly wasted in the queue, pass the bottleneck at the same time as before, and arrive at their destinations at the same time as before. The extra toll will be roughly the equivalent of the value of the extra time enjoyed at the origin point, and the revenue will in effect be obtained at no net burden on the users. In practice the results may be even better than this as a result of the added encouragement to car-pooling, the reduction of obstruction to cross-traffic, and the expediting of emergency or other trips where the delay had been a particularly serious matter.

Gains in the evening may be not quite so dramatic. The situation is not symmetrical, as typically the timing of the trip will be determined in terms of time of departure, which is separated by the queue from the time at the bottleneck. On the other hand the risk of conditions approaching gridlock is greater, since the accumulation of queues inside circumferential bottlenecks is more likely to create congestion, and there is less of a physical barrier to the simultaneous emergence of large quantities of traffic from parking lots into the downtown streets than there is in the morning to the convergence on the congested area of traffic arriving from the outside.

Congestion charges should be imposed, at least notionally, without exception on all forms of traffic. Such charges would be a necessary element in the cost–benefit analysis by which decisions are made as to the level and pattern of bus service to be provided, even though they would not be directly relevant to the determination of the price structure to be applied to that service.

Paradoxes in the Behavior of Marginal Social Cost

A strict calculation of marginal social cost in particular circumstances may produce what may appear to be quite paradoxical results. For example, in many circumstances it will be optimal, and even essential, to maintain at least a minimum frequency of service in off-peak hours with buses of a standard size, resulting in there being practically always a large number of empty seats in each bus. Under these circumstances the cost of carrying additional passengers is predominantly the cost of boarding and alighting, including the time of the driver and the other passengers on the bus who are delayed in the process. This cost will be relatively higher if the bus is half full than if it is nearly empty. The result is likely to be that the cost of a trip from a point near one end of the run to a point near the other end, at both of which points the bus is likely to be lightly loaded, may be smaller than for a shorter trip between points near the middle of the run where the bus is likely to be more heavily loaded. This is not a trivial matter: if it were there would be no sense to the refusal of express buses with empty seats to pick up local passengers. It is highly unlikely, however, that fares based on such a seemingly perverse behavior of cost would meet with popular approval. Indeed, the original US interstate commerce legislation contained prohibitions against higher rates being charged shorter hauls than for any longer hauls within which they might be included.

Another paradoxical example can occur in mixed hydro-thermal electric power systems: an increase in fuel prices could result in the marginal cost of power at particular times being reduced rather than increased. If hydro-dams are spilling water at certain seasons of the year, increased fuel costs may make it economical to increase the installed generating capacity to make use of the spilling water, even for a briefer period of time over the year than was previously worth while. If during the wet season installed hydro-generating capacity is more than sufficient to meet trough demand, marginal cost during such periods will be substantially zero, or at most limited to a small element of wear and tear on equipment pressed into service. Installing more turbo-generators would expand the period during which this low marginal cost is effective, so that while increased fuel costs cause marginal cost to rise during the peak, the result could also be to lower marginal cost in these intervals into which the period of exclusive hydro-supply expands.

In the case of long-distance telephone service, the drastic reductions in the cost of bulk line-haul transmission have created a situation where distance, especially beyond the range where separate wire transmission is economical, is relatively unimportant as a cost factor, and where satellite transmission is involved, ground distance is indeed irrelevant. What remains important is the number of successive circuits, with their associated termination and switching equipment, involved in the making of a call. Thus a call between two small communities over a moderate distance, for which the volume of calling is insufficient to warrant the provision of a separate circuit, will generally cost substantially more than a call between important centres over a much longer distance, since the latter will involve only a single long-haul circuit, while the former will require patching through two or more long-haul circuits.

Another anomaly occurs when an innovation promising substantial reductions in costs appears on the horizon, such as has happened repeatedly in telecommunications. Any further installation of the old technology in the interim before the new technology is actually available will involve an investment which will have its capital value diminished over a brief period to that determined by its competition with the new technology. High depreciation or obsolescence charges are in order, and the prospect of the new lower costs results in higher current prices which would serve to hold back current demand and lessen the amount of old technology required to be installed.

Marginal-cost pricing is thus not a matter of merely lowering the general level of prices with the aid of a subsidy; with or without subsidy it calls for drastic restructuring of pricing practices, with opportunities for very substantial improvements in efficiency at critical points.

References

Beckwith, B.P., *Marginal Cost Price-Output Control* (New York: Columbia University Press, 1955).

Mitchell, M., Manning, G., and Acton, J.P., *Peak-Load Pricing* (Cambridge, Mass.: Ballinger, 1978).

Nelson, J.R. (Ed.) *Marginal Cost Pricing in Practice* (Englewood Cliffs: Prentice-Hall, 1964).

Ramsey, F., "A Contribution to the Theory of Taxation," *Economic Journal*, 37 (March, 1927), pp. 47–61.

Vickrey, W., "Optimization of Traffic and Facilities," *Journal of Transport Economics and Policy*, 1(2) (May, 1967), pp. 1–14.

"Congestion Theory and Transport Investment," *American Economic Review*, 59(2) (May, 1969), pp. 251–60.

"The City as a Firm," in *The Economics of Public Services*, M.S. Feldstein and R.F. Inman, Eds., Proceedings of a conference held by the International Economic Association, Turin, Italy (London: Macmillan; New York: Wiley) pp. 334–43.

"Responsive Pricing of Public Utility Services," *Bell Journal of Economics and Management Science* 2(1) (Spring, 1971), pp. 337–46.

11

·

Some Objections to Marginal-Cost Pricing

Ever since Alfred Marshall suggested that the allocation of resources might be improved by subsidizing decreasing-cost industries,[1] the idea has been treated with some skepticism, not only by the public at large (few of whom, indeed, have been confronted with the idea) but even by economists presumably able to understand the principles involved. Even now that the notion has been given greater precision by the work of Pigou,[2] Hotelling,[3] Lange,[4] Lerner,[5] and others – so that we can speak of a "rule" that, to produce an optimum allocation of resources, the prices of all goods and services actually being produced must be set uniformly equal to their respective marginal costs (even though, in the case of decreasing-cost industries, this may involve a subsidy) – objections to the application of this principle continue to be raised on various grounds. It is the purpose of this article to examine in some detail just how much weight should be given to these objections.

Journal of Political Economy, 56 (1948), pp. 218–38.

[1] *Principles of Political Economy* (8th edn; London: Macmillan, 1920), Book V, Chapter xiii, 5–7, pp. 472–5.
[2] A. C. Pigou, *Economics of Welfare* (4th edn; London: Macmillan, 1946), Chapter xi, 10–12, pp. 222–5; see also 1st edn, p. 194.
[3] Harold Hotelling, "The General Welfare in Relation to Problems of Taxation and of Railway and Utility Rates," *Econometrica*, 6 (July, 1938), p. 242.
[4] O, Lange, "On the Economic Theory of Socialism," in Benjamin E. Lippincott Ed., *The Economic Theory of Socialism* (Minneapolis: University of Minnesota Press, 1938).
[5] A. P. Lerner, *Economics of Control* (New York: Macmillan, 1944), esp. pp. 174–227.

Difficulties in the Selection of Projects

One of the leading objections to the marginal-cost pricing policy for decreasing-cost industries is that the admitted necessity for a subsidy leaves no simple and obvious test of whether or not the project is worth while as a whole. Under competitive conditions, where decreasing-cost conditions are absent or insignificant, the amount of profit or loss furnishes not only a prima facie test of the relative efficiency of the management but a guide as to whether or not the industry or activity should be expanded, contracted, or ultimately abandoned. In a dynamic world, continuous information of this sort is vitally necessary, and to have it furnished in such a straightforward and unequivocal manner is a considerable advantage. It must be admitted that, with decreasing-cost industries, a policy of marginal-cost pricing precludes the development of any comparably simple answer to questions as to which projects should be undertaken and which abandoned.

But the difficulty is not with marginal-cost pricing as such but with the technological character of the decreasing-cost industries. When prices in such industries are above marginal cost, existence of a profit (or "breaking even") may indeed show that the project has been worth while; but a level of output at which all costs are covered is normally not the best output, nor is the absence of any possibility of profit (or even of covering costs), any indication that a project would not be well worth while. Thus we must choose between subsidized operation at the best level of output – with some uncertainty as to whether it would not be better to shut down completely – and self-supporting operation in which we know not only that the project is, on the whole, worth while operating but also that we are not operating the project at the best level.

It is sometimes thought that discriminatory pricing offers a way out of this dilemma. Indeed, the defense of discriminatory rate-making is a familiar part of railroad and public utility literature: that discrimination can at times yield a better allocation of resources than can flat rates that must cover total costs appears to be a well-accepted doctrine. But it is something else again to show that discriminatory pricing can yield revenues covering all costs while producing as good an allocation of resources as a policy of uniform prices at marginal cost.

In certain special circumstances it may, to be sure, be possible to develop methods of discriminatory pricing which will enable costs to be recovered from revenues without substantial departure from the optimum allocation of resources produced with marginal-cost prices. R. H. Coase, for example, has recently suggested that this result may be achieved by "multi-part pricing," in which the total amount charged each customer is the sum of a flat "customer charge" for each consumer regardless of the quantity of the service taken (provided it be greater than zero), and a charge per unit of service taken, set at the marginal-cost level.[6] But this device can achieve the desired result in but a limited number of cases, and, in many of these cases, success in achieving the optimum allocation of resources may require information of the same order as that required to determine whether or not the project as a whole is worth while under a policy of uniform marginal-cost prices.

One case in which multi-part pricing can give the required result is where the "economies of scale" are internal to each consumer. Such a case is Mr. Coase's example of a ring of consumers supplied from a central source by independent radial transportation services. However, in this case there are no economies of scale (in the sense here relevant) of the kind that give rise to the problem treated by Hotelling and Lerner, since the average cost per person supplied is not affected by the number of persons supplied. In effect, there are two items being supplied: the commodity itself and an individualized facility for delivery of the commodity at a given point; under the conditions assumed, neither, considered separately, involves decreasing costs.

The situation is quite different if the consumers are supplied not by a radial service individual to each consumer but by a unified or coordinated delivery service, making a circuit of the consumers and only one radial round trip to the source of supply. Under these circumstances, considerable difficulty may be found in obtaining optimum consumption by any feasible set of charges that will cover the total costs, particularly if individual demand curves vary widely.

Indeed, in any discussion of marginal-cost pricing, it is necessary to distinguish carefully between multi-part schedules designed to extract a larger-fraction of the value of the service from the consumer and multi-part schedules designed to reflect more accurately the marginal cost of a service having several parameters. In the provision of electricity, for example, there is a legitimate place, on cost principles, for a charge to the customer based on the marginal cost of connecting him to the distribution system and of maintaining the necessary accounts; for charges for maximum demand, based on the marginal cost of increasing the capacity of the meter, service connection, distribution transformer, and other facilities in the immediate neighborhood; for heavier charges for peak than for off-peak current, based either on the marginal cost of increasing central-station capacity or on variations in the marginal cost of generation at various outputs as generating units of varying efficiency are put into service; for other variations in charges with fluctuations in seasonal demand or in the supply of hydro-electric power. Thus it should not be thought that marginal-cost pricing would necessarily be uniform, or even more uniform than present systems of rates. The issue is not one of relative complexity of rate schedules but of the purpose that these complexities are designed to serve.

[6] R. H. Coase, "The Marginal-Cost Controversy," *Economica*, 13 (new series; August, 1946), p. 169.

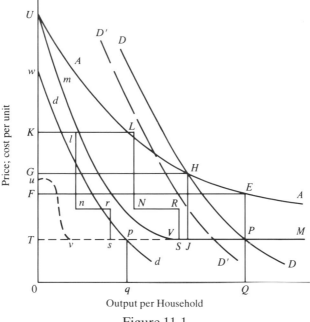

Figure 11.1

If charges for all these various elements of the service, based on their respective marginal costs, provide revenues sufficient to cover total cost, then there is, of course, no problem. Indeed, it is difficult to see how such cases really belong in the decreasing-cost category at all; the question of multi-part pricing in such cases seems hardly relevant to the main issue of how to economize the potentialities of decreasing-cost industries.

Another case in which the Coase solution can succeed is that in which the demand is homogeneous and the commodity nontransferable. For example, consider an electric utility supplying only domestic service to a community in which the consuming households are all of the same size, income, and tastes. In figure 11.1, suppose that D is the demand curve of each household, and M and A the (long-run) marginal- and average-cost curves, respectively, of the utility, with the abscissa representing output per household. (The area under the extreme left-hand portion of the marginal-cost curve, near the axis, includes the fractional share of the household in the fixed costs; i.e., the marginal cost of the first unit includes all the fixed costs. For simplicity, the marginal cost is assumed constant over the range of actual operations.) In general, if it is worth while to operate the utility at all, it will best be operated at the output Q, determined by the intersection of M and D. It will be desirable to operate the utility if, in the diagram, the area under the demand curve exceeds the area under the marginal-cost curve between the axes and the ordinate at the proposed output (assuming, as we do throughout this article, that income effects are negligible). The argument is the same if the abscissas are regarded as representing the total, rather than the average, ouput and consumption.

In these very special circumstances it is generally possible, whenever the operation of the utility is worth while, to find a multi-part rate schedule that will cover the costs of operation (including all costs of a new venture, but possibly not covering all the irrecoverable "sunk" costs of a project already in operation) and still insure that all consumers will consume the optimum amount, Q. In fact, in this particular case, it would suffice for the utility to offer the optimum amount of current Q for a lump sum QEF, sufficient to cover costs, on an all-or-nothing, take-it-or-leave-it basis. Of course, this would require the utility to know what the optimum consumption Q is. Or, more realistically, if there is a considerable margin between total costs and the area under the demand curve at the optimum consumption, it will generally be possible to work out some type of block rate, such as $GHJPM$ or $KLNRSM$, that will accomplish the same result and which may even allow for some variation of demand among households – between, say, D' and D – without causing any one household to stint itself uneconomically.

In this particular case it is always theoretically possible to find such a schedule for a desirable project; but, since it is not known in advance whether the project is desirable or not, it will not be known whether it is possible to find such a schedule in a specific instance. And, where the margin of benefit from a project is at best small (where the area under D exceeds the area under M by only a small margin at the optimum point), then, even though such schedules exist, it may be difficult to find them. In the interesting cases in which the decision as to whether or not to operate the utility is a close one, a self-liquidating management seeking a profitable but nonrestrictive block-type schedule would probably face difficulties of the same order as those that would confront subsidized managers, operating on the Lerner–Hotelling plan, trying to determine whether or not the service should be supplied.

But the real difficulty arises from the fact that demand is not uniform, as is assumed in the above example. Suppose, for example, that, in addition to the original households, there is an equal number of lower-income households having individual demand curves represented by d. The cost of providing for these additional consumers will fall on the horizontal part of the marginal-cost curve so that, for these consumers, the relevant part of the marginal-cost curve may be represented by the line TM or possibly by the line uvM, where the area Tuv represents the additional cost of extending the distribution system and connecting each of the new customers. This area will often be very much less than the corresponding area TUV for the original customers, since adding additional customers to a distribution system will usually involve a much smaller cost per customer than the cost of setting up the original system divided by the original customers. Optimum use of resources obviously requires that these new custo-mers consume an amount $0q$ (determined by the intersection of marginal-cost and demand curves at p) as long as the area under the demand curve exceeds that under the marginal-cost curve as adjusted to include connection costs.

Now, if a multi-part schedule is to induce these new consumers to take this optimum amount of service, it cannot impose a charge for this service greater than the area $0qpw$ under the demand curve and must therefore lie below (say) the schedule *KlnrsM*. But this schedule, if applied to all consumers, would not provide sufficient revenues to cover costs. If the same multi-part rate is to apply to both sets of customers, we are likely to have a situation in which a schedule which will avoid causing the small consumers to stint will obtain insufficient revenue from the large consumers. Thus one is forced either to a subsidy or to some departure from the optimum consumption.

Some mitigation of this situation may be obtained by discriminating between the two classes of consumers on the basis of some index of the intensity of their demand, such as the size of the house or apartment. Indeed, electricity schedules have been used in which the number of kilowatt-hours in the various rate brackets has been made to depend on the size of the premises of the consumer. For example, in figure 11.1, the schedule *KLNRSM* would be applied to households with large premises and schedule *KlnrsM* to those in smaller houses. (A similar effect is produced when the rate brackets depend on the connected load of the consumer, particularly where the consumer's peak-hour demand bears no close relation to this connected load, so that the differentiation is, in fact, a method of discriminating between customers with different demand schedules rather than between those whose use patterns have different marginal costs.) If such a system of schedules is successful in obtaining optimum use, then the last unit consumed for each customer will fall within the bracket in which the rate is equal to the marginal cost. Each customer will then pay a total charge equal to the marginal cost of his consumption plus an amount depending on the size of his premises, a result not unlike what would happen if the rate were set at marginal cost throughout and the deficit financed through increased property taxes or local rates.

In general, however, not all variations in the demand curves of individual households will be so closely related to objective facts upon which a discrimin-ation can be based. Thus, it will usually not be possible to find a system of schedules under which each consumer's last units of consumption are paid for at the marginal-cost rate. No matter how ingenious the rate schedule, there will nearly always be a significant number of customers whose marginal consumption is charged at rates above the marginal cost and who therefore stint themselves and consume less than the optimum amount. Some methods of discrimination are expensive to administer and are thus wasteful on this account, even if successful in achieving the optimum allocation of the service in question. Moreover, many forms of discrimination result in a discrepancy between the price and the marginal cost of other goods or services and are thus not admissible. A differential based on the size of premises raises the effective marginal cost to the occupant of enlarged housing and results in an uneconomical stinting in the direction of enlarged housing facilities. (This is not to say that a charge based on the size of the lot may not be justified on the ground that the length of main or distribution line required to serve a given number of customers will be greater if lots are large than if they are small. Such a charge would properly be assessed against every owner past whose property mains must be run, whether he takes the service or not. Nor does it exclude a customer charge based on the marginal cost of making the connection, reading meters, and billing. These are merely methods of reflecting marginal cost more accurately, not of discriminatory pricing.) In effect, even the ingenious "objective rate plan"[7] was but an *ex post facto* surcharge based upon the consumption of the base period; and, if its operation had been foreseen by the customers, a very serious repression of base-period consumption would have resulted.

The problem of discriminating so as to cover total costs without causing undue curtailment of consumption is even more intractable when we consider cases in which the customers are at large and not permanently attached to the system. Some approach to a multi-part schedule can be achieved in transportation service, for example, through such devices as multi-trip tickets and weekly, monthly, or season passes; but, even assuming that the cost of these added complexities can be neglected, the travel of passengers who travel only at the higher fares is unduly restricted, assuming uniformity of costs and some elasticity of demand. In actual practice, at least in the United States, use of these special fares usually results in higher fares being charged when marginal costs are lower, and vice versa. Commuters, charged the lowest fares on a weekly or monthly basis (on a short-run basis, the marginal price of additional trips to the commuter whose ticket covers more trips than he can use is often zero), usually ride in rush hours when facilities are taxed and marginal costs are high; irregular riders, who are charged either the full regular fare or an intermediate multi-trip fare, are more evenly distributed throughout the day, and the marginal costs of taking care of them are much less.

---

[7] The objective rate plan was a means of enabling lower rates to be offered for future consumption without lowering revenues from present consumption. Two rate schedules – the old and the new (lower) one – were in effect simultaneously. A customer was charged at the old rates for a consumption equal to his consumption in the base period, and at the new rates for the balance of his consumption. After a shorter or longer transition period, the old rate was usually dropped and the new rate used for all consumption. The method is a sort of base-period excess-profits tax in reverse and is obviously inapplicable as a permanent measure.

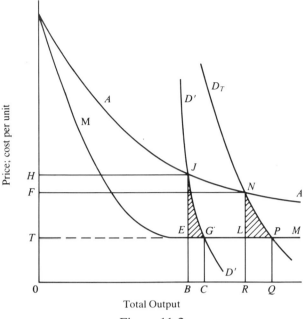

Figure 11.2

A multi-part schedule becomes completely impossible in the case of books, where each customer will want but one copy. Discrimination is here possible through book clubs, through special editions and bindings, through reprints, and through progressive reduction in price over a period of time. But all these methods involve increases in cost of production and distribution, and none can cover total costs without uneconomically stinting distribution in some respect.

It thus appears that, with certain very limited exceptions, discrimination in price will lead to some misallocation of resources, though the misallocation may be less than under a flat average-cost price. If there are two prices charged for the same service, at least one will be greater than the marginal cost, and the application of the lower price must be restricted in some way. Unless the restriction meets the almost impossible condition that all uses not qualifying for the lower rate either can bear the higher price or will not bear the marginal-cost price, then some uses that could pay the marginal-cost price but not the higher price will be excluded, and this exclusion will represent a misallocation of resources. There may be some instances of multi-part schedules that meet this criterion, but they are few, and the problem of what to do in other cases remains.

For example, suppose that D_T in figure 11.2 represents the total demand for a commodity and D' the demand that is not eligible for the lowest rate, which is assumed to be equal to the marginal cost M (the marginal cost is again, for simplicity, assumed to be constant over the relevant range of outputs). If a higher rate H is charged for that consumption D', an amount BC will fail to be taken, inasmuch as it is neither eligible for the lower rate nor able to bear the higher rate H; the total value to the consumers of this consumption would have been the trapezoidal area $BCGJ$, and the additional cost of producing it would have been $BCGE$, so that the net social loss occasioned as compared with a flat marginal-cost price would be the triangular area JEG. Obviously, the more inelastic the ineligible demand D' the smaller will be the loss; and, if D' is sufficiently less elastic than D_T, the net loss JEG may be less than the net loss NLP resulting if a flat price F equal to average cost had been charged for an ouptut R. While ingenuity in defining the restrictions on the use of the lower rate T can help some in this direction, at best there will always be some elasticity left in the demand curve D'.

The previous discussion, of course, assumes that the amount charged for one use has no effect on the demand for other uses. Where there are such interactions, the complete analysis becomes more complicated, but our conclusions remain substantially unchanged. In cases like the usual domestic electric-rate schedule – where the different rates are in the form of a step rate-schedule, so that the consumption of a certain minimum amount at one rate is made a prerequisite to the enjoyment of the other – some improvement in the situation results through the interaction of the two types of demand. In figure 11.3, suppose that the consumer's demand curve is D and the rate schedule $KLNM$. Then, if area NHP exceeds pLH, the consumer will consume TP rather than Kp; but, if not, then he will consume at p (neglecting income effects). In effect, this amounts to a "tie-in" sale, in which the consumer may purchase the amount NP at the lower price T only on condition that he also buys pL at the price K. Thus, if the higher rate were reduced from k to K, this consumer might increase consumption from kp' to TP rather than only from kp' to Kp. On the other hand, for the consumer whose demand curve is D', a reduction in this rate would reduce revenue by $klLK$ without any increase in consumption. Thus, even though the existence of the lower rate for higher levels of consumption may lure some consumers to use more at the higher rate in order to get to the lower rate, the variations among customers make it very difficult to take any substantial advantage of this fact.

It does not therefore appear that multi-part pricing succeeds in exorcizing the dilemma. Either we accept marginal-cost pricing, with attendant subsidies and the necessity for making the overall decision as to whether to undertake a given service, without any positive check (even retrospectively) on whether the decision was right or wrong; or we accept a more or less substantial misallocation of resources. It is one thing to insist, with Dupuit, that willingness to pay is the touchstone by which the value of a service is to be tested and measured ("Il n'y a pas d'utilité qu'on ne veut pas payer") and another to insist on actually collecting an amount sufficient to cover costs; there is a vast difference between ascertaining

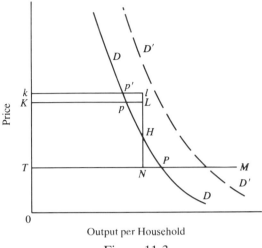

Figure 11.3

(by experiment, if necessary) what various consumers are individually willing to pay for various quantities of a given good or service and getting these various consumers actually to pay, simultaneously and continuously, these various different prices for the same commodity.

Of the two horns of the dilemma, it seems to this writer that Mr. Lerner's is by far the more comfortable. A "Coase-plan" manager who is instructed to collect, if he can, his entire costs from revenue, will, if he succeeds – at least insofar as the matter is judged solely from comparing costs with consumers' appraisal of their own benefits – be able to tell us positively that the project was worth while. But if he fails, and the project is abandoned as a result, the decision is very likely to be an error. Moreover, as we shall see, even if the project, when operated in an attempt to make it self-liquidating, not only fails to produce revenues that cover costs but is socially not worth while, it would still be possible that, if the project were operated with rates at marginal cost, it could become worth while. And in any case there will be the loss from failure to operate the project at its most economical output.

Managers operating under Lerner's "rule," to be sure, will be able to furnish no objective proof of the correctness of their judgment in operating or declining to operate the project. But it is precisely in those cases in which the issue judged by Lerner's "rule" is so close that there is room for difference of opinion that, if the decision is left to managers operating on a self-liquidating basis, they are most likely to come up with a wrong answer.

As to whether the service should be continued or abandoned, the answer may depend on the type of pricing policy to be followed, in addition to the relation between the demand and cost curves. Three pricing policies may be distinguished:

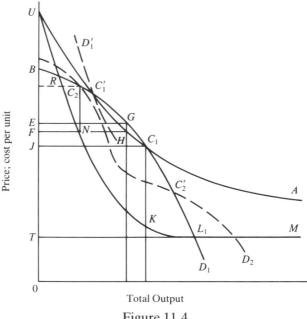

Figure 11.4

(1) that which maximizes profits or net revenues (or minimizes losses); (2) that which maximizes welfare subject to making revenues equal costs; or (3) that which maximizes welfare unconditionally, i.e., sets prices at marginal costs. Of course, if policy 1 produces a loss or 3 produces a profit, 2 is eliminated as a separate alternative. Policy 3 is the only one that can be aimed at by successive approximations, based on estimates of cost curves alone, with any assurance of achieving a close approximation of the goal. Policies 2 and 1 involve estimating demand curves as well as cost curves and are, therefore, unlikely to be closely approached in practice. Hence, for policies 1 and 2 it is necessary to distinguish between the theoretical maximum result and the probable actual result, given imperfect knowledge of the various demand curves involved. Such a distinction is less necessary for policy 3, since marginal cost can be ascertained relatively easily and small errors in estimating marginal cost are in this case less important.

Ordinarily, if the balance of considerations indicates that operation of a facility is preferable to its abandonment under any given rate policy, operation will be all the more preferable under a marginal-cost rate policy. In the absence of external repercussions not reflected in prices, operation is desirable whenever there exists a rate policy that would cover costs. But the absence of any rate schedule that will cover costs does not necessarily imply that the operation is undesirable, nor does the failure of a given rate schedule to cover costs necessarily indicate that no such cost-covering schedule exists. Indeed, there is no algorithm for discovering cost-covering rate schedules in the absence of a fairly complete knowledge of the demand curves. Furthermore, many, if not most, of the operations characterized by decreasing costs involve fairly heavy fixed commitments; and it is by no means certain that it is any easier to predict in advance whether such a project will be able to become self-liquidating than it is to predict whether it will prove to have produced benefits greater than its costs under marginal-cost pricing. Criticism of the Lerner scheme, on the ground that it requires estimating demand curves, thus becomes much less significant when it is realized that, in a dynamic economy, many, if not most, of the large-scale decisions involve estimates of future demand rather than mere reaction to current demand.

To avoid the difficulties involved in the analysis of situations requiring estimates of demand for long periods in the future, let us first examine the situation arising when increasing returns occur without any large irrecoverable commitment of fixed capital. Consider, for example, the establishment of a bus line. Here the "sunk costs" – which will consist merely of the cost of setting up the organization, getting into operation, acquainting the customers with the service, and determining the size of the demand – can for present purposes be ignored. If the line is abandoned, the equipment itself can be diverted to other services with relatively little loss, particularly if the same organization operates several lines.[8] The decision as to whether to continue the operation of the line or not can then be based largely on current experience and such slight allowance as must be made for

---

[8] Lest it be argued that a bus line does not exhibit decreasing costs, it may be pointed out that, (a) where increased demand is met by increasing the size of the buses without changing the frequency of service, there will be economies directly reflected in costs, inasmuch as a thirty-passenger bus will cost less than twice as much to operate as a fifteen-passenger bus; (b) as traffic increases, the load factor is likely to increase; (c) where increased demand is met by increasing the frequency of the schedule, costs may rise in proportion to the bus-miles run, but the increased frequency is an improvement in service which is of some value to customers and hence must be counted as "increasing return," even if not, strictly speaking, a "decreasing cost" (that is, if demand increases from sixty passengers per hour to eighty passengers per hour, with the result that service is increased from a twenty-minute to a fifteen-minute interval – assuming the load factor to be constant at twenty passengers per bus – then the addition of the extra hourly schedule does two things: [1] the original sixty passengers have an improvement in service and [2] an additional twenty passengers are provided for; accordingly, in computing the marginal cost upon which the fare should be based, the value of the improvement in service to the original sixty passengers should first be deducted from the cost of running the additional bus each hour, and only the balance divided by the twenty additional passengers to get the net marginal cost); (d) where returns from increased frequency of service fall off, additional patronage may often permit the offering of alternate routes or express service. In general, increasing returns will be eliminated only when the service becomes so intensive that traffic congestion is created. The foregoing types of increasing returns are in addition to any increasing returns that there may be in the greater utilization of the roadway; it may be assumed for present purposes that this factor is taken into account by adjusting vehicular taxes to represent the marginal costs of providing and maintaining the roadways as occasioned by added traffic.

changes expected in the immediate future can be disregarded for purposes of analysis. We will assume that the cost curves of the project are fully known but that only the single point on the demand curve at which operations are currently taking place is known with certainty. Six types of situation can arise, depending on the general relations between demand and costs.

First, let us suppose that the demand is such that the "Self-Liquidating Authority" (S.L.A.) succeeds by some rate schedule in making the line pay. If the "Marginal-Cost Authority" (M.C.A.) were to operate the line under these conditions, it would operate nearer to the optimum, and the margin by which the service is justified would be greater.

This is illustrated by the demand curve D_1 in figure 11.4 (For simplicity, the diagram is restricted to the case in which only a single rate is charged, but the conclusions are valid with only minor qualifications for the case in which more complicated schedules are used.) The S.L.A. can make ends meet at a price J and an output JC_1; the margin by which the operation would be justified would be the triangle JBC_1. This margin of social benefit is, incidentally, much greater than the maximum profit $FEGH$ that could be made at a price E and an output EG, with an average cost F. On the other hand the margin of justification for the project under the M.C.A. – the price being T and the output TL_1 – would be the sum of the areas JBC_1 and C_1KL_1. But the S.L.A. might equally well break even at C'_1; since the demand curve is unknown outside this point, the S.L.A. may well remain there indefinitely under the impression that the demand curve is D'_1 rather than D_1. Or if the S.L.A. does experiment with larger outputs, the margin of profit GH may be small and the progress toward C_1 agonizingly slow, even though the advantage for the entire economy of C_1 over C'_1 is likely to be substantial. The history of electricity rates is a case in point.

The second possibility is that the S.L.A. does not succeed in making ends meet, although there exist one or more sets of rates, unknown to the S.L.A., by which they would be able to make ends meet. As in figure 11.4, the S.L.A., as we have seen, could make ends meet at point C_1. But if the S.L.A. knows its demand curve with certainty only at the point at which it is currently operating, it might well experiment only with operations at point C_2 or C'_2, under the mistaken impression that the demand curve was of the form D_2 and that these points represented loss-minimizing points, thus never finding out that it would be possible to operate profitably at point C_1. While, with a single price, it might be considered possible to explore the entire gamut of possible prices experimentally, with multi-part rate schedules the possible combinations are too numerous ever to be investigated fully. Obviously, if the line were operated at the hypothetical profitable set of rates its existence would be justified and, a fortiori, would be justified if operated at marginal-cost rates by M.C.A.; however, there is no way of knowing with absolute certainty whether operation at the rates actually charged

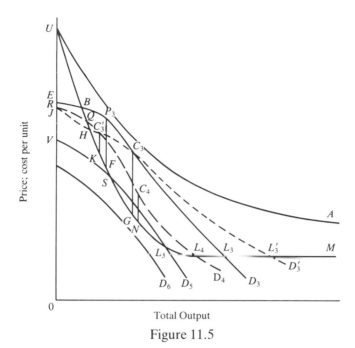

Figure 11.5

by the S.L.A. is preferable to abandonment, though there is strong probability in this direction. Thus, operation at C'_2 is definitely superior to abandonment of the project, as must be true of any point between C_1 and L_1; operation at point C_2 may or may not be preferable to abandonment, and, as the curve D_1 is drawn, it actually would be better to shut down than to operate at point C_2, since the area, C_2NR is less than RBU.

The third possibility is that, although no set of rates exists at which the S.L.A. can make ends meet, the operation of the service is still preferable to its abandonment – even at the rates which the S.L.A. set in the hope of minimizing their financial loss, though possibly not at the rates which would actually minimize their loss. Or the reverse may be true: the operation might be beneficial at the rates which would actually minimize the loss but not at the rates more or less blindly set by the S.L.A. In either case the operation would definitely be desirable if undertaken by the M.C.A. with rates at marginal cost.

For example, in figure 11.5, if D_3 is the actual demand curve, then P_3 is the point which would maximize profit or minimize loss, whereas the S.L.A. might very well operate at C_3 under the impression that the demand curve was D'_3 rather than D_3. In this case it would be better to abandon the project than to operate at P_3, since area P_3FB is less than EBU; desirable to operate at C_3 rather than abandon the project, since area C_3GB exceeds EBU; and, of course, still more desirable to operate at L_3.

On the other hand if D'_3 is the actual demand curve and if the loss-minimizing operation at C_3 is desirable (area C_3GH exceeds HJU), it is still possible for the S.L.A. to operate at C'_3 under the mistaken impression that the demand curve was D_4 and that this point was the one that would minimize their loss. Here, operation at C'_3 is less desirable than shutting down, as area C'_3KH is less than HJU, though operation at either C_3 or L'_3 would be preferable to shutting down.

Fourth, it may be possible that operation would be definitely undesirable at any set of rates which the S.L.A. would be likely to set in the hope of minimizing the loss, as well as at the rates which actually minimize the loss, but that operation by the M.C.A. would be definitely advantageous. Thus in figure 11.5, if D_4 is the actual demand curve, it would require a lower price and larger output than C_4 to make the operation justifiable (area C_4NQ equals area QRU), but no company attempting to cover its costs would set a price this low. Operation at L_4 would be definitely worth while.

Fifth, if operation by the M.C.A. is uneconomical – as would be the case in figure 11.5 if the demand curve is D_5, where area SL_5GNS is less than area SVU – then there is no method of operation that would be advantageous, and the project should be liquidated. In this fifth case, there is no automatic indication to the M.C.A. that it should shut down the project, and the decision will have to be based on the estimated area under the demand cuve. But a sixth type of case may arise (illustrated by D_6 in figure 11.5), in which at all outputs the price obtainable is less than the marginal cost. In this case, whatever the initial situation, contraction of output to the demand at the current price will raise marginal costs, calling for a further increase in price, a further reduction in demand, a further increase in marginal cost, etc., until the project is liquidated. Thus there are some automatic checks to extreme overexpansion of increasing-return projects even under a Lerner regime.

Hence, whenever any substantial subsidy is involved, the M.C.A. could introduce a substantial bias in its decisions to undertake new projects, undertaking only those that showed a substantial estimated surplus of benefit over costs, and still find itself undertaking practically all the projects that the S.L.A. could undertake, with little or no risk of undertaking projects that are not worth while. Requiring each project to pay its own way may be the only way of making absolutely sure that the community does not persist in investing in uneconomical projects; but to adopt a policy that results in a substantial bias against undertaking increasing-return projects seems a rather costly method of insuring that errors in the other direction are avoided.

Difficulties in the Computation of Marginal Cost

Another objection to the policy of setting price at marginal cost is based on the fact that reality does not conform to the regular and perfectly defined curves of the theorist, so that, in practice, marginal cost may be not only quite difficult to determine with any approach to accuracy but also subject to extreme and erratic fluctuation, depending on the precise circumstances of the moment.[9]

As to the uncertainty of marginal cost, it would seem that much of this argument is based on a misapprehension of the issue. With respect to the disposal of an accumulated stock, the relevant marginal cost is not that due to any change in production in the past, for that cannot be changed. Rather it is the cost of replacing an item of the stock if it is sold and if it is felt desirable to replace it; or, if it is not to be replaced, the marginal cost to society of delivering a unit to any one consumer is the unavailability of that unit to someone else: in other words, the (very short-run) marginal social cost of a unit of a perishable commodity already produced is nothing else but the maximum price that will sell the entire supply.

When it comes to planning for future production, the question is one of estimating what costs will be incurred in the future. What the accountant measures is not the estimated (*ex ante*) average cost of future output (even assuming that the costs associated with the product of a given period can be segregated) but is either the historical cost of past output (often involving some completely arbitrary allocations as between products or between periods of production) or the average cost of the future output, determined (*ex post*) after it has been produced, which knowledge, of course, comes too late to be of any use, except as a check on the degree of error in the original estimates. A rational decision concerning future production must be based on estimates of future costs; and it is just as easy, if not more so, to estimate the difference between the costs of two alternative future outputs, and hence the marginal cost, as it is to estimate the total cost, and hence average cost. Indeed, it may often not be possible to estimate future average costs at all without some wholly arbitrary allocations of cost. For the T.V.A., for example, it would have been at any time meaningful to ask what the probable cost of delivering additional kilowatt-hours to any specified point on the system at any specified time in the future would be; assuming complete technical information, an answer could be given within reasonable limits; different answers could at least be traced to definite differences in expectations concerning prices of materials, costs of construction, the feasibility of various methods and techniques, and the state of demand; moreover, the range

---

[9] Cf. Harry Norris, "State Enterprise and Output Policy and the Problem of Cost Imputation," *Economica*, 14 (new series; February, 1947), p. 54.

of answers would tend to narrow considerably as the specified future time of delivery is made less and less remote. On the other hand it would not be possible to compute an average cost per kilowatt-hour, even at the wholesale delivery points, without first making some allocation of the costs for flood control and navigation. There is no principle known to economic theory or any rule universally agreed to in practice which will specify how this allocation should be made.

Nor is the difficulty confined to multiple-purpose projects, such as the T.V.A. Even when only one uniform product is being produced, there is always the question of how much of the cost of the capital employed should be charged to past production and how much to future. In cases of constant or increasing costs, to be sure, it is theoretically possible to determine uniquely the "correct" distribution of the depreciation charges over the years, as the theoretically correct distribution is simply that which will make the costs, including the depreciation, equal the price at each point of time, the price being determined in a competitive market. But when there are decreasing costs, the allocation through time of that part of the depreciation allowance that forms part of the intra-marginal residue is completely arbitrary. To that extent, therefore, the behavior of average cost through time will also be arbitrary, because although the general level of average cost may be determined for the entire life of the capital assets, there is no objective criterion as to whether the costs should be considered as increasing, decreasing, or constant through time. As a corollary, there will be no objective criterion which would enable one to decide whether to make a relatively low allocation of depreciation charges to the early years and thus expand the industry rapidly from the very beginning or to write off the capital rapidly, raise the price in the early years, and thus expand somewhat more slowly, at least at first. Average-cost pricing (or multi-part pricing intended to cover all costs) not only does not give the right answers but does not even give single-valued answers, either as to price structure or as to allocation of resources. It has been said of the concept of "net national product" that it can be defined but cannot be measured, whereas "gross national product" can be measured but cannot be defined (except by the application of arbitrarily selected criteria). Similarly, in a decreasing-cost industry, "marginal cost" is a definite concept, though it may be difficult to measure, while "average cost" for a specific type or date of output may be completely arbitrary, though accountants may be able to compute it with great accuracy in accordance with their more or less arbitrary rules.

Fluctuations in Marginal Cost

A third objection to marginal-cost pricing is that marginal cost is subject to extreme and erratic fluctuations, at least on a short-run "fine-structure" basis. To illustrate, if we consider transatlantic plane service in fifty-passenger planes once a day, the addition of a fifty-first passenger on any given occasion may involve an extremely high marginal cost, while the addition of another passenger riding in an otherwise empty seat may involve an extremely low marginal cost. But it is at least doubtful whether any advocate of marginal-cost pricing has ever seriously proposed that prices should slavishly follow marginal cost in every detail, without making some allowance for administrative costs involved in such detailed rate structures and for the fact that, beyond a certain point, the consumer may become so confused that the more intricate rate schedule would cease to function effectively as a guide to consumer choice, thus losing its *raison d'être*.

In transatlantic plane service, however, the unit of service is so substantial that it would be worth while going to considerable expense in administration to achieve better allocation and utilization of space, while passengers would be willing to give considerable attention to a more complicated fare structure. It is interesting to examine just what fare structure would be theoretically appropriate under the extreme assumptions of a perfect and frictionless market.

For simplicity, let us assume that the schedules and the amount of service to be offered must be determined, say, sixty days in advance (we ignore cancellations due to weather, etc.) and that costs resulting from filling empty seats are negligible. In our hypothetical perfect market, the airline may then sell out the planned number of seats to a number of competing speculators at that price which will just dispose of the entire supply. The speculators, in turn, will sell the tickets to the passengers at prices which they vary from time to time. Let us further assume that there is complete information at all times as to the number of tickets remaining unsold (and that the distinction between speculators and potential passengers is complete); that only one price prevails at any one moment of time for tickets for any one future schedule; that each speculator behaves in a perfectly competitive manner (that is, as though his own current action would have no effect on future prices); that, on the average, speculators make neither profit nor loss; that interest can be neglected; and that the whole process is without cost.

One may then suppose that there is an average or normal time-pattern of sales and that, if sales follow this pattern, the price of seats will remain constant through time at a level which will just sell the last seat at the time of departure. This level will then be the price offered by the speculators to the airline. If, at any time, more seats have been sold than this normal pattern would call for, the price will rise, in the expectation that demand for seats in the remaining period at the normal price will exceed the remaining supply (because the remaining supply is reduced and possibly also because the higher demand already shown may be taken as evidence of higher demand in the remaining period), while, if seats sell unusually slowly, prices will fall. A few seats will in any case be held to nearly the last moment in the hope of selling to "emergency" passengers but, if no such passengers turn up, will be sold at the last minute for whatever they can bring. Also a sharp increase in price for any given departure may induce some passengers to take their profit on their ticket and thus for the time being act as speculators, perhaps simultaneously buying a ticket for another date at a lower price (although, unlike the speculator, this may be supposed to involve the passenger in some expense due to change of plans).

Leaving aside for the moment the problem of determining the amount of service to be offered, this plan would result in about as close an approach to the optimum allocation of resources as is possible. A prospective passenger would be offered passages at varying future dates at different rates, depending on the apparent demand. Passengers for whom the date of departure is flexible would have an incentive to adjust their plans so as to produce a fuller utilization of the service and leave a wider choice for latecomers. At the same time, open space would always be available for last-minute essential trips. Unsold space would be at a minimum consistent with keeping some space for last-minute travelers, and space would be used as nearly by those to whom it is worth most as would be consistent with the need of some passengers to make plans ahead of time and the constant fluctuation in plans of others.

In practice, of course, the operation of such a market of speculators would be neither costless nor perfectly competitive, and these factors would tend to offset any advantage such a system would have over a flat charge. But, for airlines that so desired, it would be possible to achieve substantially the same effect as the free speculative market just described by setting up a schedule of prices at which tickets would be sold, depending on the relation between the number of tickets remaining unsold and the time remaining until departure. Also the initial price would have to vary with such seasonal and other fluctuations in demand as are predictable long in advance. Thus, when the size of the unit of sale is such as to warrant some increase in the cost of sales to secure better utilization, the erratic fluctuation of marginal cost is not so much an objection to pricing based on marginal cost as it is an indictment of orthodox practices that reflect sluggish competition combined with a not inconsiderable remnant of the medieval idea of the *justum pretium*.

To be sure, such a flexible pricing policy would run into very substantial difficulties if applied to any but the largest units. The cost of holding an auction sale just before the departure from New York of each train for Philadelphia would probably exceed any waste of unused space obtaining under a reasonably well-adjusted predetermined rate, to say nothing of the difficulty of providing for passengers at intermediate stations. This is not to say that the consideration of marginal-cost behavior would not indicate substantial possibilities for improvement even here, however. Unfortunately, space does not permit discussing further cases in detail.

In the transatlantic airline case, if we turn to the problem of deciding how many schedules to operate, it is apparent that the decision should be based on a comparison of the marginal cost of the additional schedule and the expected value of the area under that portion of the demand curve to be satisfied by the additional schedule, as estimated either by the perfectly competitive speculators or by the airline itself (plus any value assigned to the increased frequency of service). Then, should the expected demand be just not quite large enough to warrant an additional schedule, this initial price charged (or the expected revenue from sales) would have to be somewhat higher than the incremental cost per seat of the additional schedule, while, if demand were just sufficient to justify the regular number of flights rather than one less, the price would be somewhat lower than the incremental cost. If one were to assume that costs varied exactly in proportion to the number of schedules flown (and that the value of the service was unaffected by frequency), then, if the fluctuations in demand were reasonably random and symmetrical, marginal-cost pricing of this sort would, on the average and in the long run, produce revenues sufficient to cover total costs; in fact, this is another case in which there are no increasing returns to scale in the relevant sense. On these special assumptions, then, it would be possible to operate with prices at marginal cost without subsidy.

Of course, most operations of this type are subject to increasing returns of one sort or another (in terms of improvement of quality of service, if nothing else), so that operation at marginal cost would involve a subsidy. But, even so, the economies of scale are usually moderate compared with the substantial fluctuations in demand; accordingly, a much closer approach to marginal-cost pricing than now generally prevails should be possible even without a subsidy. That utilities and other similar enterprises do not actually achieve such a result is traceable to the imperfect competition necessarily associated with decreasing costs; the administrative inertia of large-scale operations; inflexibilities associated with the practical necessities of regulation of private concerns by public bodies; the presence of discrimination (not necessarily undesirable if the enterprise is required to be self-sustaining) based on supposed differences in the elasticity of various demands; and the persistence of the just-price notion.

Socio-political Considerations

The foregoing discussion relates to the more formal side of the economics of the subject. But, even when the broader economic aspects of the problem are considered, the case for marginal-cost pricing is by no means weakened, particularly in those cases in which the commodity in question is a fairly standardized provision for one or more of the basic material wants of the public and there is no widespread moral, philosophical, or political difference of opinion over the type of product that should be offered. In the more important of such cases involving any substantial degree of increasing returns, the provision of the good by a *de facto* monopoly is usually accepted without question, whether the monopoly be operated by a private company or by a governmental body; and to argue with reference to a competitive system operating in a free market is to advocate an alternative which, in practice, does not exist, even approximately; in such cases the question of whether or not there shall be a monopoly is not at issue.

On the contrary, whether the monopoly be private or public, subsidized operation at marginal cost is likely to diminish greatly the problems of control, as compared with operation aimed at covering total cost. Whether the operation is in private or in public hands, if rates are set above marginal cost in an attempt to cover the entire costs of the operation, the solution of the problem of how to fix rates so as to achieve this end with the least possible misallocation of resources calls, at best, for the exercise of very refined judgment, even in a milieu free from contending interests. In practice, moreover, contention by interested parties makes the achievement of a close approach to the best solution even more difficult. For example, where there are different classes of consumers, decisions as to which classes shall bear charges to cover the intra-marginal residue of costs (often loosely called "overhead costs") will often provoke heated argument. Again, when a question is raised as to whether a given demand is sufficiently elastic to permit a rate reduction without loss of net revenue, the decision is at best difficult; but when consumers and stockholders (or taxpayers) get into the argument, a cool-headed decision is unlikely, and often the dangers of action under pressure induce a recourse to a stubborn adherence to the *status quo* and so inhibit the experimentation without which no definite information can be obtained. Making these decisions so as to maximize welfare is extremely difficult, and the correctness of the decisions is impossible to demonstrate, even *ex post*. This uncertainty often produces a situation in which it becomes very easy for the decisions to be made primarily on the grounds of political expediency. Disputes over the distribution of the national income can be handled much more reasonably if they are brought into the open in discussions of rates of income tax and other deliberately income-redistributing measures. Such considerations can be excluded from rate-fixing problems only by setting rates at marginal cost. A case in point is the invidious comparison often made between the Ontario Hydro-electric Power Commission and the Niagara Hudson Power Company in New York: the former is alleged to have improperly distributed its intra-marginal costs so as to favor the residential consumer, while the latter is charged with having favored the industrial user at the expense of the residential consumer.

Again, subsidized operation at marginal cost will usually eliminate the need that is often felt for surrounding such *de facto* public monopolies with legal prohibitions against competition. As long as it is necessary to cover costs from revenues, it is often deemed necessary to prohibit private competitors from operating in the same field, in order to prevent "skimming the cream" and impairment of revenues or uneconomical duplication of services. The Post Office, in the United States and elsewhere, is protected against competition by legal prohibitions against the carrying of letter matter by private persons. And it is reported that the nationalization of transport in England involves a similar prohibition of private truck competition in that field. Even privately operated utilities are often protected in this way by an exclusive franchise. While necessary from some points of view, such prohibitions – in addition to being a somewhat arbitrary restriction on individual freedom – often hamper the development by private initiative of interstitial services at points where the public agency lacks the initiative, the flexibility, or the information and foresight to provide it and may hamper the dovetailing of the competing service with other activities outside the competence of the public agency with considerable loss of economies; in addition, these restrictions also remove a valuable outside check on the efficiency with which the public agency operates.

With rates at marginal cost, however, no such prohibitions would be necessary, and, indeed, they would be undesirable. Any competing concern that can do a profitable business in the face of the subsidized marginal-cost rates of the public agency will then be either filling a need by providing a service not supplied by the agency or demonstrating a more efficient method of providing the service and should be encouraged rather than otherwise. It will not be necessary, for the sake of a general standardization and integration, to repress private initiative in the interstitial field and thus lose many of the economies that come from joint production of various commodities and services and the superior flexibility of private and small-scale arrangements.

On the other hand, there are fields where the political and sociological implications of subsidized operation are too important to set aside. For example, when it comes to the purveying of literature, information, news, entertainment, opinions, and the like, one may well hesitate before proposing that the state should subsidize all or even any large part of such enterprises to the extent necessary to permit pricing at marginal cost. It would be impossible and intolerably wasteful to subsidize the writing, editing, and typesetting of everything that would sell a few hundred copies at prices to cover only printing, binding, and distribution; and, if only some items are to be subsidized, some more or less official agency must make the selection. To provide a supercensorship board of this kind is at least a substantial departure from the best traditions of freedom of press, opinion, and artistic expression; and although it would not be necessary to prohibit publication absolutely where the needed funds could be obtained from private supporters or from the sales of the product, even here the works unable to secure the official approval would have a hard time in competition with the publicly subsidized product. Even more hesitation will be felt toward financing news-gathering services out of public funds or toward producing motion pictures at public expense to be shown without royalty or rental.

Of course, when compared with the actual selection performed by commercial publishers and motion-picture producers, one may be tempted to say that a properly constituted and open-minded public body might well do a much better job. But at this point the economist must admit that he is out of his field and should preferably defer judgment until after searching consultation with his colleagues in the fields of sociology, political science, literature, and the arts.

Summary

Our conclusions may be summarized as follows:

1 In nearly all cases involving decreasing costs, even the best scheme of multi-part pricing will be unable to cover costs and, at the same time, achieve optimum consumption (though, in a substantial number of cases, it may be able to approach the optimum closely enough so that the difference appears insufficient to warrant going over to a subsidy).

2 There is no algorithm for arriving at that one of the many possible multi-part schedules that produces the closest approach to the optimum while simultaneously covering total costs. The amount of information needed to determine this optimum schedule is far greater (it involves substantially a knowledge of each individual demand curve) than the information needed to determine whether a project is worth while (which involves only a knowledge that the area under a segment of the aggregate demand curve exceeds costs). In practice, therefore, given the projects to be undertaken, even the inferior possibilities of multi-part pricing are likely to be less fully realized than the possibilities under marginal-cost pricing.

3 In determining which projects to undertake, even where the change is fully reversible and there are no sunk costs, a substantial class of potentially worth while projects will necessarily be turned down under the multi-part pricing policy, even if complete knowledge of demand curves were available, so that the optimum multi-part schedule could be achieved in all cases. Failure to achieve the best multi-part schedule will enlarge this class of erroneously rejected projects. Under marginal-cost pricing, all errors in the selection of projects will be due to errors in estimating the higher-price segments of the demand curve. Improved market-research techniques will reduce these errors.

4 Where projects involve heavy irrecoverable outlays, as is true with most increasing-return projects, errors of forecasting of both costs and demand will be superimposed upon both schemes. It appears that the errors of this sort are more serious in their effects under a self-liquidating program than under a marginal-cost program, in that marginal-cost pricing is well adapted to salvaging mistakes with a minimum loss, whereas the attempt to cover costs in a project having a disappointing development will often seriously increase the aggregate cost of the error. Moreover, the fact that action must, in any case, be based on estimates diminishes the supposed advantages of the multi-price program in avoiding estimates of the shape of demand curves beyond the area of immediate experience.

5 The comments on multi-part pricing apply, *mutatis mutandis*, to most, if not all, schemes of discriminatory pricing not based on differentials in marginal cost.

6 The aura of definiteness surrounding average cost as a basis for setting future prices is spurious: the allocation of the intra-marginal residue among products or over time is completely arbitrary, while past average costs give little better estimates of future average costs than they do of future marginal costs. The difficulties of estimating marginal cost are solely technical, not conceptual.

7 Even though marginal cost may fluctuate erratically, this indicates not that marginal cost should be discarded as a basis for prices but that, where the administrative costs would not be prohibitive, prices should likewise fluctuate fairly drastically. Existing price policies in many fields appear much too uniform for optimum utilization of resources, even if the condition is retained that projects must be self supporting.

8 In some instances the application of marginal-cost pricing involves serious political and sociological consequences which must be investigated. But there are substantial fields in which these factors are entirely absent, in which the only issues are economic, and in which there need be no hesitation in carrying out policies determined upon economic grounds alone.

12

·

Responsive Pricing of Public Utility Services

As you know, I am kind of hipped on the idea of marginal-cost pricing: the use of pricing as a device for improving the efficiency with which we use various facilities. Basically, we do observe, when we have perishable commodities sold in markets, that prices fluctuate, sometimes drastically, sometimes in ways that cannot be predicted long in advance. If this is a good thing for produce which is a slightly perishable commodity, why isn't it also a good thing for utility services which are almost instantaneously perishable? Well, we do, of course, observe to a very limited extent and, in my judgment, a much too limited extent, fluctuations in prices on a basis that is scheduled in advance; that is, we have reduced rates for night and evening telephone service, we have reduced off season rates in hotels, and we have, to some extent, off-peak rates for electric power, and so on. But what can be achieved in this way toward efficient use of resources is limited by the fact that scheduled price variations cannot take account of those fluctuations in demand and supply that are basically unpredictable or, at least, unpredictable long enough in advance for administrative machinery to roll. Moreover, in many cases even though we can predict, for example, that there will be traffic jams in the neighborhood of the stadium on the day of the World Series, or we can pretty well predict that on certain holidays certain facilities will be overcrowded, nevertheless, in a good many cases where we could in principle do this predicting job, the complexity and cost of setting up the schedules to allow for all of these fluctuations in demand and supply strictly limits the amount of rate variation that we can manage. So what I am really going to discuss is the possibility of having rates that would fluctuate directly in response to shifts in demand and supply,

Economics of the Regulated Communications Industry in the Age of Innovation, (1970 Seminar, New England Telephone, mimeo), pp. 61–78.

whether or not these are predictable, but mainly in relation to those that are not completely predictable.

Of course, price fluctuation is not just good for its own sake, it is good only in relation to some kind of decision. That is, the person who is going to make an effective decision as to whether he is going to use a given service or not, has got to know the relevant prices at the time he makes the decision, or the price is not serving any useful function. Pricing is no use at all in the case where I decide I am going to take a trip to Chicago on the basis of an expectation that the fare will be $20.00, and I arrive at the airport with all my baggage and I find that it is $30.00; that has served no purpose because now I am thoroughly committed to the trip; and in spite of the fact that, if I had known this in advance, I would have made other arrangements, nevertheless now that I *am* committed, I am not going to go back home and consider all that time wasted. So we do have a problem here; we can't just go ahead and vary the price. We have to do this in ways related to what we want to accomplish, namely the guidance of decisions as to how the service is to be used.

Suppose we are going to have a price which varies according to demand and supply. What is the principle on which we base this price? Here, of course, we come straight back to the idea of marginal cost. What is the marginal cost of a particular service at a particular time? If I go out to the telephone and dial my home number with the idea of talking to my wife, what is the marginal cost of that service? Under present conditions, strictly short-run marginal cost is pretty much zero on the basis that there is unlikely to be any real shortage of equipment. The only immediate result of my making the call would be a totally negligible increase in power consumption, a probably favorable effect on the switching equipment through exercising it and, for all practical purposes, an overall cost that turns out to be zero. Do we then want to set a price *at* zero? Well, obviously setting a price at zero would tend to increase the amount of calls made and create a condition in which there *would* be a marginal cost, though not a marginal cost in the usual sense. The marginal cost of making a call at a given time and place, in the sense that is relevant here, is a social cost consisting mainly of the deterioration in the quality of service that results to other potential users. In the case of a telephone call, it consists of the increased probability resulting from my occupying the lines that someone else (attempting to make a call during the course of my call) will encounter a no-circuit condition, is thus frustrated in his attempt to make a call, and has to either abandon the call or make it at another time. So the marginal cost in this case is not any outlay by the telephone company but consists of a deterioration in the quality of service available to fellow users.

It is tempting to say that the marginal cost is a potential loss of revenue to the Telephone Company; that is, if I make a call and prevent somebody else from making a call, that other person would have paid something for that call, which means the Telephone Company lost some revenue. But to think of *that* loss as, in some sense, marginal cost to the Telephone Company, is not really relevant for our purpose here, because, for one thing, it is quite possible that the person who was frustrated in making his call has a completely inelastic demand in the sense that, if he doesn't make the call now, he will make it later on. We still have a marginal cost to the extent he is inconvenienced (he would rather make the call now than later on). So that if one sets rates according to marginal cost, the rates have accordingly to be set in terms of the probability of another customer's being frustrated multiplied by some measure of the degree to which he is frustrated. Now obviously, this varies rather sharply. As long as you have a reasonable number of unused circuits, there is no other frustrated customer and the marginal cost is effectively zero. But as you get closer and closer to the saturation point, the probability of another customer being frustrated rises sharply, so one will have sharp fluctuations in marginal cost on this basis.

To come back to the notion that the customer must have knowledge of the price at the time he makes an effective decision, telephone service is peculiarly attractive in this situation because, being a communications system, the facilities are already there in place, so to speak, for communicating the price set-up to the customer. Moreover, unlike the fellow who packs for an airplane trip and goes down to the airport, the degree to which the user makes an outlay of time and effort as a precommitment to the use of service at a particular time, is relatively slight. If I pick up the telephone and I learn by some means that the rate for the call I intended to make is higher than I really want to pay at that moment, I have not gone to any great amount of trouble. There has not been any waste of time and effort in simply learning, in terms of the price at that time, that I do not really want to make the call right away.

Perhaps I ought to stress the way the system I have in mind would work. The way it would appear to a customer for long distance service, at any rate, is simply this: a customer picks up the phone, gets the ordinary dial tone, dials the area code, dials the office code, and then he has the option of waiting a few seconds, and, if he does, he will hear recorded announcements something like "the charge for this call is 15c a minute" or "the charge for this call is 20c a minute" or "50c a minute" or "$1.00 a minute" or whatever the case may be. At this point, he can complete the call, or he can hang up, in effect saying, "at this price I'm not interested, but I hope to make the call later on when the price is lower." If he does in fact dial the remaining four digits and wait for the call to go through, the charge will be at the rate which was indicated. I would assume that the time at which the call starts would establish the rate for the duration of the call – well, within limits. You should certainly guarantee that rate for a call of ten or fifteen minutes; for a person who starts a call at a low-rate time and continues talking two hours you might say that, if he talks that long, he would have to risk the possibility while talking that the rate may go up. Basically, that is the way the setup ought to appear to the customer.

The technology, I think, is within reach – in fact, has been in reach for as long as we've had tape recordings. The way the system would work technologically would be that, at a representative number of toll centers, you would have apparatus to periodically measure the relative degree of occupancy of the circuits along various corridors and the value of, say fifty or sixty parameters thus determined would then be broadcast from each center in turn on a round-robin circuit to each local toll center which would indicate the relative degree of occupancy of the circuits on a suitable number of corridors plus, perhaps, indications of local congestion in particular areas, such as in the Catskills on Yom Kippur. This information then would be available at each local toll center and could be converted into a set of announcements that would be fed back the moment that you dial the area code for the more distant call, or the area code plus the office exchange for the immediate area (and perhaps the adjacent one). There is also the possibility of course, of using this set-up for local service. In that case, instead of the rather meaningless dial tone you hear when you pick up the phone, you could get a repeated recording "1c," "2c," "5c," or whatever the charge per unit would be for local service at that particular time. Probably you could expect a certain amount of extra overheads in that there would be an increased number of cases in which subscribers would pick up the phone and either decide they didn't want to make a local call immediately on the dial tone, or decide they didn't want to make the long-distance call after they had dialed into the local toll center. There would be some additional occupancy of a certain amount of equipment, but, in most cases, it would be fairly brief. The equipment occupied would not be terribly expensive, I think, if this were properly programmed. I do not think that the increased cost on that score is a problem and, as I will indicate later, the economies in other directions of equipment would be extremely important.

Well, this would be fine for a publicly owned telephone system such as exists in most countries outside the United States. A problem comes up as soon as one has a privately owned, regulated company. If you have a schedule which, in effect, is a relation between the degree to which the system is busy and the rate to be charged, and it says the more congested the system, the higher the rate, then basically you have a built-in incentive to a private company to keep the equipment down to the minimum possible amount and have the rates shoot up sky-high. This cannot be tolerated, of course. However, I think there is a way around this, and this is through the use of a dual rate structure and a kind of escrow fund. The customer need not know anything about this, but for regulatory purposes, you would have to have two rate schedules: one is the rate schedule established according to current practice that determines the amount of revenue that the Company is entitled to retain out of what the customer pays; and a second schedule that depends upon the occupancy of the system, which determines what the customer actually pays. If the customer pays more than the established regulatory rate, the balance is put into an escrow fund; if the customer pays less than the established regulatory rate, then the Telephone Company would be entitled to draw the difference from the escrow fund, so the only effect of failure to expand the system to meet the demand would be basically that the volume of service would be less, and hence the revenue the Telephone Company would be entitled to keep would be less; and in the meantime, if there was a shortage of service, the revenues in the escrow fund would continue to pile up but would be unavailable to the Company until such time as the Company expands and increases the service thereby driving customer reactive rates below the retention rates.

This is perhaps the most novel notion that is being expressed here. I think it works. I am perhaps a little bit less certain as to how well an escrow fund of this kind can be made to work than I am of the value of the responsive price in and of itself.

The responsive price has more than just the everyday value of increasing the efficiency with which the services are used. It decreases very substantially, I think, the average cost per call to the customer, because what we are really doing is saying, "well, except in the wee small hours of the morning, when there simply is not sufficient demand at *any* price to fully occupy the system, the system is going to have a 90–5 percent load factor throughout those periods of the day when there is any demand at all for service." In addition to this, there are certain things that one can do with this kind of pricing that one simply cannot do in any other way. One of these is the meeting of emergencies. If you have a flood or a tornado, or any kind of emergency or disaster which either destroys vast amounts of equipment so that the amount of service that can be rendered is limited or causes a vast increase in calling rate, there simply is no good way at present to preserve adequate service for emergency purposes. It is true you can disable a certain number of telephones and say that, since available service is limited, you will disable all but doctors, police, ambulance services, and so on from originating calls. The trouble is that this operates in many cases at the wrong end; the person who wants the ambulance cannot be identified. It is a fairly expensive proposition to attempt to somehow distinguish calls to emergency numbers, and I am not really sure whether it would be within the bounds of technical feasibility or not. At any rate, I do not think, as far as I know, it is done to any extent except manually. This means, of course, that precisely at the time when manual operators are in great shortage, you are imposing an additional burden in that, if anybody wants an emergency call to go through he has got to get the operator to put it through, because the automatic switching has been disabled in order to preserve the system from overload and breakdown. However, if you have my kind of responsive pricing, you can, in addition to some of the regular rates, put some really stiff rates on for emergency situations such as this. This would, if not completely, at least to a large extent discourage all but the most essential calls, which means you could get something that you cannot get now *at any price*, namely, the ability to get through if you really have to in an emergency.

There's another byproduct to this system which is that it would generate some information which, if not directly, at least indirectly would bear on the question of what is the optimum of service quality. I think that up to a couple of years ago, I would have been of the opinion that simply because managers of Telephone Companies are more immediately associated with high-priced executives than with people to whom the primary concern is the cost of their calls, they have tended to provide something I call a "nickel-plated service." Some of you are familiar with the story of how the New York–Chicago–St. Louis Railway got its name – somebody wanted to buy it and a price was quoted that evoked the response, "'What's your damn' railroad made of, 'nickel-plate?'" I think, in some sense it is quite possible that Telephone service is "too good" in that it is consequently too expensive. At least some users might prefer a slightly less expensive service, with a possibility they might not be able to get a dial tone at all times. Well, the overall service quality would be of less importance with reactive pricing since those who really want service could have it. The present situation is: if you dial a number and get a response in one way or another that says "no circuits," there's really not much you can do about it. Responsive pricing, if it really works the way I think it would, would create a condition in which the "no circuit" problem would be almost unknown. You may get a response when you dial that the price is very high, but you would almost never get a response saying that your call cannot get through because there simply are no circuits. I think this is perhaps one aspect which should be extremely attractive to those people who want some availability of high-quality service: to be able to provide the high quality without having to make the large investment in equipment that would be necessary in order to have this quality of service uniformly available under the present conditions.

It is rather interesting to explore the same idea in other areas. In the case of airline reservations to which I have already referred, we really don't want to have an auction at LaGuardia Airport every time a flight leaves. We do not want, in effect, to have a person go down to the airport and find the price is higher than he really wanted to pay, and he either has to regret his decision to fly or he has to say, "I'll have to write off my trip to the airport and count that as a dead loss." What we really need here is something approximating a speculator's market in reservations. We used to have a speculator's market in theatre tickets in New York, and at various times and places where travel reservations have been really short, there's been a certain amount of black market dealing in reservations. By and large, this has been considered somehow a "nasty" business. It has been regulated out of theatre tickets, and we no longer have a speculator's market, at least operating above-board. Ticket agencies now charge a flat fee for service, and there is no real variation in the price according to supply and demand for various facilities. One can imagine that the airlines could simply sell off blocks of reservations to a bunch of speculators who could deal on their own. The trouble with this is that it is quite expensive, and the speculators, for reasons of their own, tend not to be very cooperative in furnishing information about the state of the market. A speculator's market in theatre tickets or plane reservations is not like the New York Stock Exchange. The New York Stock Exchange is not a very appropriate apparatus for dealing with units-of-sale of, say, 10 to 100 dollars or maybe even for trans-Atlantic flights, 300 or 500 dollars. They are accustomed to much larger units of sale and all that apparatus is really too expensive for this. But it *is* possible to imagine that the airlines themselves, or perhaps a cooperative agency set up by the airlines could, in effect, simulate the action of the speculator's market. The way that it might be done would be this. Flights would be classified in terms of the degree to which individuals normally make reservations in advance. People make reservations longer in advance for trans-Atlantic flights, let us say, than they make reservations for flights from LaGuardia to National or from LaGuardia to O'Hare. They tend to make reservations further ahead of time if they are going to Keokuk, where there are only two flights a day, than if they are going to O'Hare where there's a flight every half hour. Now for any particular flight, you can suppose that there is some price which will, on the average, be expected to sell out the plane exactly. If everything goes according to expectations, the sales curve (seats filled versus time remaining until departure) goes up and at the time the plane departs it is nicely full. Everything has gone according to schedule. The trouble is things never do go according to plan, and the actual sales may deviate substantially from the expected sales curve on a given flight. Well, my proposal is simply this: in addition to a standard starting price for this flight (which should fill it under normal expectations), there would be a series of prices which would guarantee close to 100 percent capacity utilization even when incoming reservations deviate from the expected pattern under the "normal" price. These prices could represent 80 percent of normal fare, 60 percent of fare, 40 percent of fare, 20 percent of fare, and markups of 120 percent, 150 percent, etc. Let us say you phone in for a reservation at some point in time and the plane just happens to be abnormally slow in booking, then you might be quoted a price of 60 percent or 70 percent of the basic price. According to a schedule for that particular class of flights giving the appropriate discount as a function of the time remaining until departure, and the proportion of available seats already sold. If the plane is unusually heavily booked, you'd be quoted a premium price. And once anyone has bought a ticket, he has bought a firm reservation which commits him to pay that price. It is in a sense a final sale subject to some form of refund procedure whereby, if you buy a ticket at the standard price and you decide not to go, you may or may not get a refund for the full amount that you paid. You get the refund at the going price minus a service charge. If you had been lucky and you purchased a ticket on a plane subsequently more heavily booked, you could make a profit on your ticket. But, the expectation would be a mild penalty on the average for booking a reservation and then not using it.

In what sense does all this represent marginal-cost pricing? Well, at any particular time if the price being quoted according to the best information available at that time is the price to be maintained until the departure of the plane, then, say, all but the last four or five seats will be sold when the plane leaves. If a passenger attempts to make a reservation at this time, it will raise the price, and may force someone else off the plane. In this case the marginal cost is the cost of denying to some other passenger the privilege of flying at that particular time. The cost is not a cost to the airlines but the cost in terms of opportunity to someone else. Well, here we have the possibility of a scheme whereby instead of 45 percent load factors, we could be running 95 percent. This immediately implies that the average fare on a plane would go down about 50 percent. Moreover, it would mean that the individual who was willing to adapt his plans at the last minute to the relative demand and supply situation would be able to pick up trips for probably 40 percent of this half fare, or, in other words, 20 percent of the existing rate. This would be available not merely to students and military personnel but to everybody. At the other end of the scheme, the businessman, who at 4:00 in the afternoon says that he has just got to catch that 7:00 plane to Rome tonight, will be fairly sure of being able to get a seat even during the peak season – which he cannot always do now. Although one can sometimes get emergency seats now by calling friends at the airlines or through other under-the-counter ways, this is always difficult and sometimes impossible. Under the proposed schemes, we would, in effect, be saying that anybody who really needs to have a seat on a particular flight, even at the last minute, is going to be pretty sure of being able to get it by standard procedures. The people who make their plans long in advance would be given a choice. They would go to a travel agent and say, "I want to go to Seattle on the 17th so what have you got?" He would quote a morning flight at this price, an afternoon flight at that price, and so on. In effect you do get a much more efficient utilization of the system this way.

This is something that could not have been done readily before the advent of computerized reservations systems, but with the computerized reservation system I really don't think there is any basic difficulty. There is to be sure the problem of communication. A person who walks up to the ticket counter and wants to take account of various price possibilities will perhaps spend more time discussing the various schedules and prices than he would under the present system where he simply looks at the schedules, then decides on a particular schedule and, in most cases, makes a reservation then and there. Of course, even under the present scheme, you can have quite a long colloquy on whether to use a particular schedule at family fare, or youth fare, or this, that and the other, but there's relatively little of this. My proposal would make it almost universal. One exception, of course, would be the executive who wants a set schedule regardless of the price, and, in the case of the airlines, there's a fair amount of that kind of travel: people who are not paying for their own tickets and make the choice regardless of the fare. This, in turn, means that since the portion of the traveling public that would respond to the fares is small, the fare fluctuations would be rather extreme. Thus the person who is paying for his own ticket could probably pick up some very big bargains in the schedule.

There are some other interesting possibilities for responsive pricing. I will mention two or three of them briefly. One is for water supply. The usual notion about water supply is that people ought to have a specified supply of water regardless of cost, and the water system is designed to provide this supply; if there is then a shortage, the name of the water engineer is mud. If a price is charged, it is usually justified as the lowest rate of charge that will finance all or an appropriate part of the cost of the system, and is seldom thought of as a means of controlling use. Nevertheless, if we want to avoid wasting resources on needlessly large water supply systems, and at the same time avoid needless stinting in the use of what supply is available, control of use through pricing related to marginal cost is essential.

In this particular case there are some rather interesting special rules that can be applied in determining the short-run marginal cost of water. These rules say, in effect, that as long as there is water going over the spillway in excess of the amount that is necessary to maintain the required minimum flow of the river down stream (if that is a concern) the marginal cost of water use is zero. This is assuming that the aqueducts and mains are adequate (the distribution mains usually must provide water for fire-fighting purposes so that the capacity is seldom approached by normal domestic use). If you have the reservoir full and can accurately predict future demand and supply conditions, the rate of increase in price has to be greater than or equal to the interest rate. If the price were declining or rising less rapidly than the interest rate, this would mean, in effect, that you could take some water out of the reservoir and sell it now at a higher price representing a higher present value, rather than keeping it and selling it later at a price representing a lower present value. If the reservoir is neither full nor empty, the price should be rising at exactly the relevant rate of interest. If the reservoir is empty, what you are doing is limiting your use to the current flow into the reservoir and during this period the price trend has to be less than or equal to the interest rate, because if the price were rising more rapidly, then instead of keeping the reservoir empty, you ought to save some of that water that you are selling at the low price, put it in the reservoir, and sell it later at a higher present value.

Well, these are at least some of the constraints that would be imposed on us by this situation. There is one difficulty here with respect to metering. Meters are not read with sufficient frequency to allow a scheme like this to work fully. Nevertheless, if they are read quarterly, and the cycle of surplus and drought is fairly lengthy, a great deal can still be done. These rules would, of course, have to be modified somewhat to allow for uncertainty about the future, but the general pattern would still stand.

One factor that looms large in a case like water supply is that new supplies come in very big lumps. What marginal-cost pricing would require in such cases is the reverse of what very often happens. When you have a new supply you find that this increases the water supply budget and therefore, the rates are raised in order to pay for the new supply. What ought to be done, however, if demand grows gradually, is to increase the rate just before the new supply comes in, thus postponing somewhat the date at which the investment in the new supply must be made, then drop the rate down to zero until the new supply is being fully utilized and finally raise the rate again to contain the demand to the new supply level.

In the case of electricity, Électricité de France has gone a long way further than any other electric utility in the direction of marginal-cost pricing for power, or at least toward peak and off-peak pricing. They have a fifty-cycle system and have developed a device which consists of a small 133-cycle generator in the power plant which can give a short pulse of high intensity. Because of the short duration, it is a little like radar because you can get very big short pulses without heating the thing up to the point of damage. They send out pulses over the whole system with 133 cycle current. They have little relays attached to meters that are sensitive to the 133 cycles so that at any particular time they can send out this pulse to change the rating of the meter. They operate this on a fixed schedule which applies three different set rates.

This could be expanded. In addition to the three rates, there ought to be at least two or possibly three emergency rates for dealing with situations in which there is either a breakdown or some excess demand. If we had such a system in effect, then by sending out the appropriate pulses, we could apply these emergency rates and customers would have switches that would respond to the emergency rates by turning off certain types of equipment that don't have to run continuously, like refrigerators or air-conditioners. A few years ago if we had something like this in effect in New York, we might have been able to avoid that rather nasty "brown-out" that took place when the cables blew up in Central Park. Then it was a matter of being a very hot day when everybody had their air-conditioners turned on. This summer, by the way, in order to control the situation they may have to engage in selective load shedding by cutting various neighborhoods off one after another or by allowing the voltage to sag. But, that is an inefficient way of doing it. What we want to do is turn off the air-conditioners, refrigerators, and a few other similar types of apparatus like that and *still* keep the elevators running, subways running, and traffic lights working without suffering the loss of efficiency that results from low voltage or voltage regulators for equipment sensitive to voltage drop. Having to provide a separate emergency power plant for the elevators, street lights, and so on is an expensive proposition. So we have a rather interesting application in the case of electric power.

Let me just mention briefly two other areas, one of which is probably an exercise in misguided ingenuity. When it comes to parking, there is a feeling abroad that the parking meters should not be used as a method of pricing, but that they should only be used as a method of rationing. In other words, you do not control parking by charging a high price so that those who use it are the ones who are willing to pay the highest price. Rather, you say, this area is for people who want to park twenty minutes, this other area is for people who want to park forty minutes, and if someone wants to park for an hour in a twenty minute area, he cannot. This may seem an appealing proposition, but to an economist a very misguided one. There are people who have a toothache and need to go to the dentist. They see a twenty minute parking space in front of the dentist's office, but they know they are going to be in the dentist chair at least half an hour. What are they going to do? Well, they have to park way down the street according to the rules. Yet it is essentially more urgent for these people to park close by. In another case they may be on an errand that involves a lot of packages and want to be near the car. They do not want to have to carry the packages way down the block, and they don't want to double park while they shift the packages in. The efficient way to do it is to allow them to occupy this close-in parking space for a longer period as long as they are willing to pay a higher price for the longer period.

But, we still have to consider the fact that the supply of parking spaces is rigid whereas, the demand constantly fluctuates. The ordinary parking meter suffers not only from the defect of being designed as a rationing device, but also from the mechanical defect of not being able to vary the rate. You have either one rate or no rate at all, by and large. Sometime ago I began to think about this and came up with a rule which says that the rate for parking ought to vary in accordance with the number of spots occupied, so ideally you connect twenty or thirty parking spaces into some sort of a system. If there are, say, four spaces vacant out of twenty, charge 10c an hour; if three spaces, you charge 30c an hour and so on until if they are all full you charge $1.00 an hour. The price you charge for parking then will respond to the intensity of the demand. In this case I should say, however, a responsive pricing system is probably too expensive to apply. You would have to interconnect the meters here and arrange for them to run at different rates. Then there is the problem of payment. One could have some sort of payment by subscriber card rather than dropping coins in the meter. That is probably better than the very elaborate method I once worked out which supplied each person who wanted to park in a given area with a parker's key. When he wanted to park, he would put his parker's key in the meter and turn it, releasing a meter key, which he would take with him and at the same time his parker's key would be locked in the meter. Then when he came back, he would put the meter key back in the meter; at that point he could not recover his own key until he had fed the meter with the amount that had accumulated. The device compels the person to pay after he comes back, because obviously, if you have a reactive pricing system, there is no way for the parker to know at the time he parks how much it's going to be.

This raises another question: to what extent is it desirable to have the rate fluctuate *ex post* in terms of what the experience has been? In this case of the parker, it is virtually impossible to administratively fix a set of rates in advance that will take care of all the fluctuations in the demand for parking that occur in the course of a day, a week, etc. If that then is the case, what about the person who comes in, parks his car and leaves it for four hours but has no guarantee as to what the rate is going to be? He will be just taking his chances, so what good is the fluctuation of the rate? The answer I would make to this is: in the case of parking, which is a repetitive exercise for most people (people park, if not in the same place, or in the same neighborhood, under similar circumstances repeatedly), they more or less get to know what the pattern is in the neighborhood and behave accordingly.

13

·

Airline Overbooking:
Some Further Solutions

In earlier issues of this Journal there has been discussion of a method of dealing with airline overbooking [1], [2], [3]. Under this method, in the event of more passengers with confirmed reservations showing up than can be accommodated on the plane, they would be asked to submit sealed bids indicating the minimum amount of money they would be willing to accept as compensation for changing their plans at that moment to the next best alternative, the passengers submitting the lowest bids being then bumped and compensated accordingly. Professor Simon correctly claims that this method would be clearly superior, at least on the average and for any given level of overbooking, to methods based on random selection, selection in terms of position in some queue, or indeed other methods not mentioned such as selection on the basis of ultimate destination and connections, or the offer of arbitrarily fixed compensation to those quickest to respond to the offer. There remain, however, imperfections that lead one to ask whether one cannot do better than this.

As Professor Falkson points out, paying the bumped passenger on the basis of his bid gives him an incentive to overstate his price, and the degree of this overstatement by passengers may vary, so that the person with the lowest bid who is therefore bumped may not in fact be the person who would have accepted the lowest compensation. Simon does not indicate whether, in the case where n passengers must be bumped, each will be paid his own bid or all will be paid the same amount equal to the nth lowest bid; but the incentive to overbid is present in either case, though far weaker where all will be paid the same. It is even possible that in isolated cases the arbitrary method would produce a result closer to Pareto-optimal than the bidding procedure. This defect can be remedied fairly

Journal of Transport Economics and Policy, 6(3) (1972), pp. 257–70.

simply, however, by asking passengers to bid on the understanding that if there are n passengers to be bumped the payment will be a uniform one equal to the $(n + 1)$th lowest bid. In this case the individual passenger will find that his best strategy is to bid the actual lowest amount he would be willing to accept. To bid lower would introduce a probability that he might be bumped on unfavorable terms. To bid higher would merely reduce his chances of being bumped on favorable terms, while not affecting the amount he will receive if he is in fact bumped. The position of the airline will not be impaired: under fairly reasonable assumptions, the level of the bids will tend to be decreased just enough to ensure that the $(n + 1)$th bid under this revised proposal would average no higher than the nth lowest bid under the original proposal ([4], [5], and later work summarized in [6], [7]). The procedure would be strategically equivalent to the clumsier open-auction procedure in which passengers bid *viva voce*, making successively lower bids until no passenger is willing to make a lower one.

If we ask whether the airline would actually gain by introducing any such auction procedure, the answer is not so clear. Much depends on its susceptibility to the ill-will engendered by uncompensated bumping. If an airline is in a strong monopoly position on a given route, or has relatively little repeat traffic and can contrive to avoid having its record become generally known to prospective passengers, it may consider that it is maximizing its net revenues by a policy of relatively heavy overbooking and frequent bumping. It might find that inaugurating a policy of paying for the bumps that it is now imposing on the public without payment would cost it money, and that maximizing net revenue under these circumstances would require less overbooking rather than more. A different answer might be given if a policy of compensating for bumps enabled the airline to charge a higher fare, which would affect its place in various tariff and cartel arrangements.

Even where competition is such that the airline has reason to be jealous of its image in the mind of the traveling public, compensation for bumping would have to be considered in conjunction with such matters as compensation for lost baggage, overnight arrangements for passengers missing connections, and other types of compensation for service below standard. The institution of compensation on the basis of bids for bumping might be expected to be at least as cheap a form of enhancing the airline's image as any other, but this cannot be guaranteed from the analysis.

A Simulated Speculator's Market

Falkson [2] suggests that what is really wanted is some form of advance auction that would avoid the waste of effort involved in the bumped passengers having to make the trip to the airport and possibly missing opportunities to make the best of alternative arrangements. He also suggests somewhat vaguely a system of flight priority insurance, without working out in detail how this could be put into practice. If, however, one follows this line of thought and uses as a model a free speculator's market in future reservations, the following scheme emerges as probably as good as any that can be devised.

Airlines would sell reservations on future flights at prices that reflect fairly closely what the outcome of a competitive futures market in those reservations would produce at any given moment. The price for a reservation on a given future flight would vary from time to time according to the relationship between the number of seats already sold for that particular flight and the number that would normally be expected to have been sold at that time before the flight. The price at any given time for a further reservation on that flight would be such as to generate an expectation that, if the price were kept constant at this level, the remaining seats would just be sold at flight time. The price would in fact fluctuate either up or down as further reservations were made at a faster or slower rate than that anticipated; but there would at any given time be no expectation that the price in the future would on average be either higher or lower by any substantial amount, though possibly a slightly rising price expectation might be maintained to encourage early reservations, especially as departure time drew near. Reservations would be regarded as final sales, not normally subject to recontract, but passengers changing their plans would be entitled to turn in their reservations at the price ruling at the time of turn-in, less an appropriate handling charge to cover the associated costs and to discourage speculation by people with no intention of traveling.

One would, of course, not expect to have a separate pricing schedule or algorithm for each flight independently. Flights or flight legs would be grouped in five or ten classes according to how far ahead passengers normally make reservations for them, using such criteria as national or international, short or long-haul, and the overall schedule frequency. Thus London–Glasgow would probably fall in the shortest lead category, London–Paris would fall in a somewhat longer lead category, London–New York longer still, and Lisbon–San Juan the longest. For each class of flights a table would be prepared showing, for each number of days or number of hours before departure time, the proportion of seats normally sold by that time on occasions when the price is equal to the standard price for that flight and traffic demand is such that the plane is just comfortably full by departure time. When sales for any flight were running ahead of this normal pattern, the tables would give premium percentages to be applied to the normal fare according to the proportions of sold and unsold seats and the time remaining to departure; and conversely, where sales for a flight were slower than the normal pattern, the table would give discounts to be applied. Thus, when an enquirer asks whether space is available, the reservations computer returns an answer giving the applicable fare for the requested flight as well as, possibly, the differing fares for some of the more likely alternatives. Obviously, such a scheme would have been difficult to implement before the advent of computerized reservation systems, but with them the difficulties, while considerable, seem surmountable.

It is an essential part of the scheme that the making of a firm reservation should be considered a final sale subject to resale if plans change, rather than the securing of an option; and it is this feature that is effective in dealing with the problems of the no-show and overbooking. In principle, no-shows would be entitled only to a return of the amount at which their ticket could be sold at the time of departure, though the severity of this sanction might be mitigated by putting a floor under the refund, either as a percentage of the amount paid or as a percentage of the standard fare, or possibly both. A floor would also have to be used as a limit to the discount at which reservations would be sold; otherwise a passenger, having originally booked at a higher fare, would be able to gain by turning in his original reservation for a refund and rebooking at the current lower fare. Marginal-cost pricing principles would allow the fare to fall to very low levels when vacant seats remain on a given flight, the low fare representing then merely the cost of added fuel, meals, service, wear and tear, and reduction of amenity to passengers resulting from the occupancy of another seat; but a floor substantially above this level may be desirable in practice to preserve at least some revenue for the airline. This is particularly necessary for airlines whose service includes some low-density routes, where economies of scale are significant and the maintenance of a high schedule frequency is of substantial value to passengers.

The advantages of the scheme go far beyond merely dealing with the problem of overbooking; indeed, if that were all that would be accomplished it would hardly be interesting. The scheme should make it possible to achieve load factors of 0.85 up to 0.95 and possibly higher, while at the same time almost eliminating instances where a passenger urgently wanting to travel on a given flight finds that it is sold out. With this increase in load factor, average fares could be cut nearly in half. Passengers able to adjust their plans would be given an incentive to select the less heavily booked flights, leaving more space for others on the more heavily booked flights. Those able to shift their plans on fairly short notice would be able to pick up bargains at a quarter or even less of the present fares. Those having urgent last-minute changes in their plans would be assured of having space available at some price almost always; under present practices space is frequently not available at any price, short of *sub-rosa* inside dealings with the airline personnel.

Even with computerized reservation service in full operation, the system is not without its disadvantages, which may outweigh the advantages where the unit of sale is small or little inconvenience is caused to marginal potential customers if they are turned away at the last minute. This will apply to long-distance telephone calls or short-haul flights on routes with frequent service. But where the unit of sale is large, and customers incur trouble and expense in preparing to use the service, as in long-distance flights or flights on low-frequency routes, the benefits of the scheme should greatly outweigh the costs and disadvantages. At least for the fairly large class of passengers who travel nonstop from origin to destination on single-hop flights and who make their reservations at the point of origin, either one-way or round-trip, there is not much of a problem. The businessman who is insensitive to price can merely, as now, call up and ask for a reservation on the schedule of his choice. He will rarely need to concern himself about confirmation or about the price, since he can be very confident of being able to get the reservation and moderately confident that the impact of more flexible passengers on the reservations market will keep price differentials to a range within which they would not be likely to affect his decision. The price-sensitive shoppers and the bargain hunters can convey to the agent serving them the general nature of their preferences, upon which the agent can ascertain from the reservations centres of the various airlines concerned the current quotations for the more likely schedules and report them to the customer, who can then make his choice among the various schedules and rates. This is, indeed, a substantial increase in complexity over present practice in this relatively simple case, but the improved results would seem to make it well worth while.

Group Sales

An interesting question is what the practice should be when a reservation is requested for more than one seat at a time, as with groups traveling together. One is tempted to provide that the price quoted for the first passenger in the group should be extended to all passengers in the group, even though if the reservations were made separately but in rapid succession the price for the successive reservations would tend to rise, and to rise especially sharply if the reservations were being made close to departure time. However, in spite of the fact that this would be fairly closely analogous to the present practice of granting special low rates to groups of various kinds, it seems preferable for a number of reasons to price a group reservation as though it were a sequence of single reservations. This in general will mean that if a group wishes to travel together in the same plane, and is not large enough to warrant the use of a charter flight or to cause the airline to run an extra flight in part for the group, it will tend to pay more than if its members spread themselves over two or more flights. This result, while it may seem surprising at first blush, is entirely in accordance with the costs implicit in the situation. A large group making reservations on a single flight is substantially increasing the likelihood that individuals subsequently attempting to make reservations on that flight will find the price prohibitive and will thereby be diverted to flights which to them are less desirable. The larger the group, the greater the number of persons that will have to be diverted and the greater the average reduction for each person in the desirability of the service finally used. Similarly, the later the group reservations are made the smaller will be the number of potential subsequent reservations-makers from among whom the diverted passengers must be selected and the greater the loss in service desirability. The pricing of group reservations as if made singly thus produces prices that conform to costs, and produces appropriate incentives for distributing the group over a number of flights if this is feasible, or for making the group reservations at the earliest possible date so as to allow the necessary displacement of other passengers to take place at minimum cost to them.

Pricing on a one-by-one basis also obviates the need for measures to prevent the speculation which might occur if speculators were able to make spurious reservations for a large group based on the price of the first reservation, and then resell them at prices enhanced by the spurious demand thus created. While this could be obviated by placing special restrictions on resale of group tickets, there would remain a considerable incentive to overbook for groups.

Should Quotations be Firm Offers?

A closely related problem concerns the degree to which the prices quoted for the purpose of enabling the customer to make a selection are to be considered firm offers, even within a specified time limit. From the standpoint of good customer relations, it would seem desirable to hold these prices fixed for some reasonable time during which the customer could collect the various quotations and make up his mind. On the other hand there would be the added administrative chore of keeping track of all these quotations, the persons to whom they were made, and the time limits applicable to them. Further, if the time period for which the quotation is to constitute a firm offer is at all substantial, this opens the possibility that an agent for a group, or a speculator, might ask for such quotations in a large number of different names simultaneously and independently, thus getting the same low price quotation for all, and then make the several purchases at these low prices, thus acquiring a substantial block of reservations at a price considerably lower than would have obtained if they had been purchased in a more normal way. This problem could be dealt with by treating each outstanding firm offer as a sale for the purpose of computing further price quotations during the period of its validity. Even this procedure would be vulnerable to manipulation, albeit one fairly costly to carry out, by maintaining a constant flurry of enquiries regarding a given flight that would maintain its price at a spuriously high level over a period of time, during which potential passengers would be diverted by the high price to other flights, and then allowing the outstanding quotations to expire and picking up the manipulator's own reservations at a price depressed by reason of the diversion of passengers which he had engineered. The costs of carrying out such a manipulation, however, would probably be so high relative to the possible gains that in most cases the danger could be disregarded.

Even so, the cost of maintaining even a fairly short list of firm quotations would be considerable. The simpler procedure would be to treat quotations as made for information and guidance only and not as firm offers; when the passenger had made his choice on the basis of this tentative set of prices he would then make a firm request for a specific reservation, possibly specifying the maximum price he was willing to pay (either the price just quoted or one somewhat higher), above which he would prefer some other flight for which he had been quoted a price. Usually, of course, the quoted price would hold. In some instances, however, as when in the interim a large block of reservations had been made, the effective price at the time of the passenger's firm request would be substantially higher than the previous quotation. If this price were higher than the maximum indicated by the passenger the reservation would not be made, and he would be asked to make another selection. Ordinarily reductions in price below the quotation would amount to only a single step, resulting from the lapse of time during which no reservations were made; in rare instances large reductions could occur in the event of a large block of cancellations. Even so, it is possible that these price variations would generate sufficient unfavorable passenger reaction to require the more costly procedure of holding quotations as firm offers for an appropriate time interval, much as at present reservations are held subject to the subsequent purchase of a ticket within a reasonable time.

Through Bookings

A more difficult problem is that of passengers wishing to make arrangements for trips involving connecting flights and complicated itineraries. For single-flight trips involving more than one hop in the same plane, it would seem easy and appropriate to adopt the straightforward procedure of deriving a through fare by adding up the currently applicable fares for the separate legs and subtracting an amount representing the saving from reduced costs of passenger handling at the intermediate stop. Connecting flights, however, especially where different airlines are involved, are more troublesome.

There is no particular difficulty, even here, if the problem is merely one of quoting a fare for an itinerary already specified: simply adding the fares for the separate flights, possibly with an arbitrary concession representing check-in and ticketing costs, would again be satisfactory (though here the costs involved in interline accounting may cancel most of the savings in check-in costs over caring for entirely separate passengers for the different legs of the trip). The problem is to provide the prospective traveller with an appropriate selection of itineraries from which to choose. Under present circumstances, with no variations in fares, it is already often difficult and time-consuming, even with the aid of quick-reference time-tables, for a travel agent to find the itinerary best suited to the needs of his client. Most travel agents, indeed, will stop considerably short of a complete search unless prodded to the point of harassment by the client.[1] If each potential itinerary has a different price attached, and if even these prices are not available in a tariff but must be obtained by enquiry, the complexity is multiplied. Where times of departure and of arrival are the only matters of concern, it is possible to eliminate a large number of itineraries that are "dominated" by one of those selected for consideration,[2] i.e., that depart earlier and arrive later than the dominating itinerary. Where price is a consideration, however, domination *strictu sensu* would require in addition that the price of the dominated itinerary be as high or higher.

Perhaps when the next generation of computers comes along it will become possible to key in the potential passenger's needs in fairly general terms, including a schedule of the value placed by the passenger on free time at the origin and free time at the destination, and possibly even of time at various alternative stopover points, and to have the computer respond with an appropriate selection of itineraries that are close to optimal in terms of these specifications. For the present, however, the best that can be hoped for is for a travel agent to formulate, with the aid of such intuitions, experience, and reference materials as he can dispose of, a number of alternative itineraries which he hopes will include one best meeting his client's needs, submit these itineraries to the reservations system to obtain quotations, and report the results to his client for selection.

---

[1] The writer's own experience includes finding, after considerable search, that, rather than any of the connections listed in the *Official Airline Guide*, the best after-business connection from Washington to San Francisco is via an on-line connection at Atlanta; that to have dinner in Denver and meet a class the following morning in New York is not impossible after all, but requires going via Dallas; and that the best overnight connection from Boston to Tokyo is made at Chicago, not at New York or on the West Coast.

[2] Procedures have been developed by the writer for generating, within reasonable limits of computer time, a complete listing of undominated itineraries between the more important origin–destination pairs, and for providing data that would facilitate an exhaustive search by an agent in the case of the more exotic trips, provided that timing is the dominant consideration. To allow for possible fare differentials, especially if these fluctuate from day to day, makes the problem vastly more complex. (The routings cited in the previous footnote, incidentally, proved to be available at no extra fare.)

Where agents are located at a distance from the nearest centre where current reservation information is maintained, and especially where more than one airline is involved, this is a fairly expensive procedure both in agents' time and in communications charges. To be sure, the present system is not without its drawbacks, many of which would be eliminated under the proposed scheme: for instance, the multitude of rates based on arbitrary criteria as to routes, length of stay, number and composition of the group, and the like. But, even with allowance for the elimination of such complexities in current tariffs, the added complexity and cost is substantial.

One possible solution would be to provide for interline tickets to be sold at fixed fares according to simplified versions of the present tariffs, or possibly to apply the responsive pricing scheme only to the originating airline portion of the trip, and to make bookings for the subsequent connections at fixed fares. It would not be possible, in general, to close off the passenger's option to proceed one leg at a time, taking his chances on the price fluctuations for the successive legs of the itinerary, but being virtually assured of not being stranded by being unable to obtain space on the continued flight. Disparities would then occur between those booking through and those booking one leg at a time. These would be particularly awkward where a trip can be made with either on-line or interline connections, or with either a single flight or connecting flights. But the disparities would not be any greater, on the whole, than those that arise now in the application of various reduced-rate tariffs.[3]

Potential Gains from Efficient Pricing

Whatever solution is adopted for these ancillary problems, an efficient pricing technique for the bulk of the airline traffic would yield substantial returns, far outweighing any possible costs of the procedure. Indeed, rough calculations based on assumptions that seem not too far from the facts indicate that this potential gain might be of the order of 55 percent of gross revenues earned in those operations to which the scheme would be applicable.[4] Even if the assumptions on which this estimate is based are considered grossly wide of the mark, the benefits

---

[3] Existing tariffs are indeed already so complex that in planning any trip involving several flights it is often worth while to obtain independent quotations through several channels. Thus on a recent trip the writer was assured when purchasing the ticket that a certain possible alteration in the itinerary would remain available at no extra charge, but when booking the change he was required to pay an additional fare. When on returning home he asked about a possible refund of this overcharge, the eventual advice was that the fare ought to have been even higher than what had been paid, and that the traveler had better leave well enough alone!

[4] See Appendix.

on any reasonable appraisal of the system amply justify at least experiments in the more favorable segments of the airline travel market.

To be sure, this potential 55 percent gain is to be compared, not with the rather unsatisfactory *status quo*, but with what might be attained with a comparable degree of astuteness applied to attacking the problem of unsold seats along more conventional lines, involving discriminatory promotional fares of various kinds designed to attract off-peak traffic, combined with reduction in excess capacity where this can be accomplished without undue reduction in effective frequency. Here, however, there are fairly severe limits on what is practicable. Given complete freedom to adjust fares on a flight-by-flight and leg-by-leg basis, the airlines could in principle come fairly close to full utilization of capacity with fares fixed for each schedule on the basis of projections made, say, three to six months in advance. This might well increase substantially the frequency with which potential passengers would be unable to find space at any price on the schedule that suited their needs; almost certainly there would be little or no improvement in this respect over present conditions. In practice the exigencies of tariff specification within a manageable scope of words usually result in substantial compromise, and it is often difficult to frame a promotional tariff in terms comprehensible to the customers which will fill otherwise empty seats without adding to peak loads or unduly impairing revenues from peak traffic. Opinion within the industry seems to be that load factors of 60 to 65 percent would represent a highly satisfactory and possibly ideal level of achievement under present practices, and that load factors could not be pushed much if any above 70 percent without serious deterioration in the availability of service. While such an improvement would involve a potential gain of 10 percent or perhaps 20 percent on current gross revenues in terms of social efficiency, the balance of gain attainable from going all the way to a "responsive" pricing system would seem to be well worth the effort, since the gain over the best that would otherwise be available could well amount to the equivalent of 25 percent of gross revenues.

Efficient Pricing and Competition

Indeed, the main real obstacle to such a scheme may be, not doubts about its impact on efficiency, but fears of its consequences on the competitive relations between airlines. At present the industry operates largely as a form of cartel, with rates kept at a uniform level by agreement, leaving only various forms of "nonprice" competition. Attempts have occasionally been made to limit even some of the aspects of the nonprice competition, as in the case of the famous "sandwich war." The present proposal would tend to bring the industry much closer to the competitive ideal. Even if an agreement were reached over the way in which the price would be made to depend on the state of reservations at a given time, it would be much more difficult to ensure that the various airlines adhered to such a convention, whether formally subscribed to or merely established as the conventional norm. Even if there were no deviation from the established rate function, competition in the introduction of new schedules would tend to drive rates and profits down to levels where only normal profits were earned; since introducing a new schedule would almost automatically fill it, albeit at somewhat reduced rates, less risk would be involved than when a new schedule can attract traffic only in terms of nonprice parameters. Cartel action would then, to be effective, have to turn to regulating frequencies and possibly timings of flights. It may be hoped, however, that the effect would be to turn competition toward efficiency and reduce excessive competition in frills, unneeded schedule frequency, and the like.

Regulation of Private Monopoly and the Use of Escrow Funds

Routes served exclusively by nationalized airlines would cause no special difficulty, assuming that the management was reasonably well motivated to act in the public interest, or at least to maximize the level of service (within whatever financial restraints were imposed) rather than to maximize an accounting profit or surplus. Regulated private airlines with a route monopoly, however, are a different matter, since, even if the regulatory authority were to keep control over the rate formula, the airline by cutting back service would push up the average level of effective rates. This difficulty can be handled by establishing, in addition to the reactive rate charged to the customer according to the level of demand, a retention rate which would determine the amount that the airline would be entitled to retain for each revenue passenger carried. Any excess of the reactive rate over the retention rate would be paid into an escrow fund, and whenever the reactive rate was below the retention rate the airline would be entitled to withdraw the difference from the escrow fund. Failure of the airline to expand its operations to the point justified by demand would merely lead to an accumulation in the escrow fund, which the airline company could realize only by expanding operations so as to drive the reactive rates below the retention rate.

Impacts on Unregulated Monopoly

The problem of curbing the monopoly power of private companies is thus not insuperable. Even so, it is probably not entirely academic to ask what would be the effect of permitting an unconstrained monopolist to use such a pricing scheme rather than limiting him to the use of a uniform, nondiscriminatory rate. Unfortunately not much can be said on this in general terms. One can, of course, assert with confidence that opening up a new option to the monopolist can hardly hurt him, and is likely to work substantially to his advantage. But whether the monopolist's reaction would be such as to impose an additional burden on consumers greater or less than the gain to the monopolist, or even to confer a benefit on consumers, would depend on circumstances.

At one extreme, consider a case where the off-peak demand has a sharp downward kink, and where its duration relative to that of the peak is sufficient to make the location of this kink decisive for the price the monopolist will find most profitable if prices are uniform. Suppose too that the peak demand is nevertheless large enough relative to the cost of expanding capacity to induce the single-price monopolist to expand his capacity sufficiently to take care of the peak demand at the price determined by the kink in the off-peak demand. If the monopolist is allowed to discriminate in these circumstances he will keep the off-peak price the same, and, if the peak demand is not too elastic, raise the peak price and cut back on capacity – a reaction that will raise rates to peak users by more than the resulting gain to the monopolist, and thus constitute a move away from Pareto-optimality. At the other extreme, if we consider the same case except that peak demand is sufficiently elastic for marginal revenue from expanding peak sales to exceed the cost of expanding capacity, the monopolist will find it to his advantage to reduce the peak price below the off-peak price and to expand his capacity. In this somewhat paradoxical case both the peak users and the monopolist benefit, while the situation of the off-peak users remains unchanged. Other examples can doubtless be constructed, not involving such blatantly paradoxical results, in which all parties benefit by the greater freedom of action according to the monopolist. And there are also possibilities that the monopolist may gain substantially at the cost of a relatively minor loss to the customers.

On the whole, however, the likelihood of cases arising in which the gain to the monopolist is obtained only at the cost of excessively high burdens to the customers seems sufficient to indicate great caution in allowing reactive pricing to be used by unregulated monopolists. Where there is public ownership, however, or where regulation or competition can be effective in keeping prices down to levels yielding only normal profits, reactive prices provide an opportunity for substantial improvement of the efficiency of utilization of the service offered by the airlines. This is especially true of the longer flights on routes with a volume of traffic sufficient to support a high frequency of service.

Low Frequency Routes

Routes where frequency is low present another problem. It is possible that the level of service that could be financed by reactive prices at levels that would bring about full utilization of the service would involve either an unsatisfactory frequency of schedules or the use of low-capacity aircraft with a relatively high cost per seat-mile. Since this is essentially a case where there are substantial economies of scale, with overall marginal cost substantially below overall average cost, one appropriate remedy would be to subsidize the operation, either from general revenues or from excess revenues earned on routes of heavier density where the economies of scale are substantially smaller. If subvention is not possible, a second-best solution will be to arrange the rates so that traffic in each time period is some uniform fraction of what it would have been if a subsidy had been available sufficient to defray the intra-marginal residue of cost and permit prices to be set equal to marginal cost [8]. A practical rule-of-thumb approximation to this would be to establish a level of service that appears to be optimal, given the constraints, and then place a floor under the rates, sufficiently above the marginal cost of having a passenger occupy an otherwise empty seat to permit the revenue constraint to be met. It is of course possible, though unlikely, that following this prescription would result in so slight a variation of rates as to make the whole procedure hardly worth while. In any case the establishment of the optimum level of service would involve the exercise of considerable judgment in appraising the relevant elasticities and cross-elasticities of demand, and complete accuracy is not to be hoped for. But in appropriately selected situations reactive pricing can yield very high dividends.

Appendix

Estimating the Gain from Responsive Pricing

Let

Q_0 = total current available seat miles,

Q_1 = total available seat miles under responsive pricing,

s = incremental cost of accommodating passengers in existing space,

c = cost per seat mile, exclusive of incremental passenger costs s,

P_0 = current revenue per passenger mile,

i = index of flight leg classes, classified according to load factor,

f_i = average load factor of flight legs in the ith class, currently,

w_i = proportion of total available seat miles in the ith class,

P_i = responsive price to be charged for the flight legs in the ith class,

$x_i(p)$ = demand for travel on flight legs in the ith class at price p,

e = elasticity of demand, assumed uniform for all classes of flight legs,

$F = \Sigma f_i w_i$ = overall average load factor.

Now if current revenues are just sufficient to cover current costs, we have

$$\Sigma P_0 w_i f_i Q_0 = cQ_0 + s\Sigma w_i f_i Q_0 , \qquad \text{or} \qquad (1)$$
$$(P_0 - s)\Sigma w_i f_i = c. \qquad (1a)$$

The constant elasticity demand curve for the ith class can be written

$$x_i(p) = w_i f_i Q_0 \left[\frac{P_0}{p}\right]^e , \qquad (2)$$

and the new price P_i which will result in filling the available space in the ith class of flight legs will be given by

$$x_i(P_i) = w_i Q_1 = w_i f_i Q_0 \left[\frac{P_0}{P_i}\right]^e , \qquad (3)$$

it being assumed that the space offered in all classes of flight legs is reduced uniformly by the ratio Q_1/Q_0. Solving (3) for P_i we get

$$P_i = P_0 \left[\frac{Q_0 f_i}{Q_1}\right]^{\frac{1}{e}} \qquad (4)$$

If revenues are to be sufficient to cover the cost under the new regime, the (uniform) contraction in the volume of space offered must be such as to satisfy

$$\Sigma P_i w_i Q_1 = cQ_1 + sQ_1 , \qquad \text{or} \qquad (5)$$

$$\Sigma P_0 \left[\frac{Q_0 f_i}{Q_1}\right]^{\frac{1}{e}} w_i = c + s . \qquad (5a)$$

Solving for Q_1, we get

$$Q_1 = Q_0 \left[\frac{P_0}{c+s}\right]^e [\Sigma f_i^{\frac{1}{e}} w_i]^e . \qquad (6)$$

The gain in consumers' surplus resulting from lowering prices from the uniform P_0 to the various levels P_i can be expressed as

$$\Delta S = \Sigma \int_{P_i}^{P_0} x_i(p) \, dp = \Sigma \int_{P_i}^{P_0} w_i f_i Q_0 \left[\frac{P_0}{p}\right]^e dp = Q_0 P_0^e \Sigma w_i f_i \int_{P_i}^{P_0} p^{-e} \, dp \quad (7)$$

$$= \frac{1}{1-e} Q_0 P_0^e \Sigma w_i f_i (P_0^{1-e} - P_i^{1-e}). \qquad (7a)$$

If we put $F = \Sigma w_i f_i$ for the overall average current load factor, and $R = Q_0 P_0 F$ for total current revenues, we have, using (4)

$$\Delta S = \frac{1}{(1 - e)} Q_0 \Sigma w_i f_i P_0 \left[1 - \left(\frac{P_i}{P_0} \right)^{1-e} \right] \tag{8}$$

$$= \frac{1}{1 - e} Q_0 P_0 \Sigma w_i f_i \left\{ 1 - \left[\frac{Q_0 f_i}{Q_1} \right]^{\frac{1-e}{e}} \right\} \tag{8a}$$

$$= \frac{1}{1 - e} Q_0 P_0 \left[F - \frac{Q_1}{Q_0} \Sigma w_i f_i^{1/e} \left(\frac{Q_0}{Q_i} \right)^{1/e} \right] \tag{8b}$$

and using (5a) and (6), this becomes

$$\Delta S = R \left(\frac{1}{1 - e} \right) \left[1 - \left(\frac{c + s}{P_0} \right)^{1-e} (\Sigma f_i^{1/e} w_i)^e \left(\frac{1}{F} \right) \right] \tag{9}$$

For the case where $e = 1$, the above expression is indeterminate, and the corresponding solution is

$$\Delta S = R \left[\log \frac{P_0}{c + s} + \frac{1}{F} (F \log F - \Sigma w_i f_i \log f_i) \right], \tag{10}$$

where the logarithms are natural.

Evaluation of the above formula, using data supposedly representative of recent experience on the domestic routes of a US carrier, suggests $\Delta S = 0.55R$. This figure was obtained on the basis of assuming $e = \frac{2}{3}$, a figure somewhere near the lower end of the range of estimates produced by industry sources, and probably a very conservative figure. The average load factor for given flight numbers over a two-week period in October 1970 was distributed as follows: 1.4 percent of the flight numbers averaged under 0.10 load factor, 7.1 percent between 0.10 and 0.20, and for subsequent load factor classes, frequencies of 0.166, 0.226, 0.190, 0.144, 0.106, 0.051, 0.031, and finally 0.001 for the flights averaging over 0.90 load factor for the fourteen-day period. This yields an average load factor of $F = 0.43$, and a value of 0.45 for the expression $(\Sigma f_i^{1/e} w_i)^e$, which is fairly insensitive to moderate changes in the dispersion of load factors about a given mean. Thus, even though data by individual flights would presumably have given a somewhat wider dispersion of load factors, this would not greatly affect the value of ΔS. Ticketing and passenger service expenditures are estimated at 18 percent of the total; but, since much of this expense is determined in terms of peak traffic conditions, only about 10 percent out of this 18 percent is estimated to constitute net incremental cost of carrying passengers in available seats, so we can put $s/P_0 = 0.10$, and $c/P_0 = 0.9F = 0.387$, and thus obtain the above result.

If on the other hand all planes were loaded uniformly to 43 per cent of capacity, the two rightmost parentheses cancel, and we have $\Delta S = 0.63R$. At the other extreme, if we start from a situation in which the 0.43 load factor results from 43 percent of all flights being full and the rest empty, we get $\Delta S = -0.135R$. This result reflects the fact that if the empty flights are filled by charging a zero price the value of the service obtained will be less than the cost of the extra service provided, while meeting these costs would entail raising fares on the full flights and cutting back on the number of flights provided.

A load factor of 0.43 may be considered unusually low, and is well below what would be aimed at even without responsive pricing. If we start from a load factor of 0.70 (perhaps the highest level that one could maintain with satisfactory service without responsive pricing) and assume that that 0.70 is the result of a distribution of load factors uniform over the range from 0.40 to 1.00 (which might be fairly representative of what could be expected under these conditions), we obtain $\Delta S = 0.25R$.

From this benefit something might, to be sure, be subtracted on the ground that increased loading and reduced frequency may somewhat impair the value of the service, though this would seem to be adequately taken care of by assuming a low value of elasticity. Possibly one might on this account want to use a value for s/P_0 greater than 0.10. On the other hand no allowance is made in these estimates for cross-elasticity: the elasticity values are in terms of a uniform change in all prices, which presumably involves shifts between traveling and not traveling by air at all. In addition to these shifts there would be shifts of travel time from peak to off-peak times. This shifting will generate substantial additional benefits over and above those that are in principle included in the above formulas; but there is no easy way of evaluating these additional benefits, particularly as in the absence of experience with responsive pricing there is little data available by which the appropriate cross-elasticities could be estimated. Thus the estimates of $\Delta S = 0.25R$ can be considered a rock-bottom figure, and the actual gain from shifting to responsive pricing would almost certainly be substantially greater than this.

References

(1) Simon, J.L., "An Almost Practical Solution to Airline Overbooking," *Journal of Transport Economics and Policy*, 2(2) (May, 1968), pp. 201–2.
(2) Falkson, L.M., "Airline Overbooking: Some Comments," *Journal of Transport Economics and Policy*, 3(3) (September, 1969), pp. 352–4.
(3) Simon, J.L., "Airline Overbooking: A Rejoinder," *Journal of Transport Economics and Policy*, 4(2) (May, 1970), pp. 212–13.
(4) Vickrey, W., "Counterspeculation, Auctions, and Competitive Sealed Tenders," *Journal of Finance*, 16 (May, 1961), pp. 8–37.

(5) "Auctions and Bidding Games," *Recent Advances in Game Theory*, The Princeton University Conference (1962), pp. 15–29.

(6) Reichert, A.O., *Models for Competitive Bidding Under Uncertainty*, Department of Operations Research and Department of Statistics, Stanford University, 2 January 1968, mimeo, 268 pp.

(7) Griesmer, J.H., Levitan, R.E., and Shubik, M., "Toward a Study of Bidding Processes," *Naval Research Logistics Quarterly*, 10 (1963), pp. 11–21, 151–73, 193–217; (1968), pp. 415–33.

(8) Vickrey, W., "Maximum Output or Maximum Welfare? More on the Off-peak Pricing Problem," *Kyklos*, 24 (1971), pp. 305–30.

PART IV

———————— • ————————

Pricing Urban Transportation

I will begin with the proposition that in no other major area are pricing practices so irrational, so out of date, and so conducive to waste as in urban transportation . . .

However, with a little ingenuity, it is possible to devise methods of charging for the use of the city street that are relatively inexpensive, produce no interference with the free flow of traffic, and are capable of adjusting the charge in close conformity with variations in costs and traffic conditions. My own fairly elaborate scheme involves equipping all cars with an electronic identifier which hopefully can be produced on a large-scale basis for about $20 each. These blocks would be scanned by roadside equipment at a fairly dense network of cordon points, making a record of the identity of the car; these records would then be taken to a central processing plant once a month and the records assembled on electronic digital computers and bills sent out.

American Economic Review, 53
(1963), p.452 and pp.457–8.

That traffic congestion is an externality which can be dealt with efficiently via pricing was recognized by Pigou and Knight. Vickrey, however, was the pioneer in the practical application of this insight. From his study of New York subway pricing up to the present day, he has devoted a major portion of his professional life to the advocacy of congestion pricing in urban transportation. He has also written a string of influential academic papers on urban transport economic theory, one of which is arguably the most important contribution to the subject in the last quarter-century. He deserves the reputation as the father of urban transport economics.

Vickrey's interest in urban transportation came about by accident. In the early 1950s Carl Shoup and Robert Haig directed a study of New York City's finances. Vickrey was assigned the task of proposing a transit fare structure for New York City. His study, presented in article form in chapter 14, is altogether remarkable because of the quality of its economic reasoning, its originality, and its anticipation of many subsequent developments not only in urban transport economics but also in the economic theory of public policy/optimal taxation. It was the first modern work in urban transport economic policy analysis.

In the article, Vickrey started off with a general statement of the efficiency of marginal-cost pricing, and then went on to derive the marginal cost of trips according to origin–destination and time of day. His cost analysis is noteworthy in its detailed treatment of the technology and costs of passenger congestion. Having derived what would now be termed the first-best fare schedule, he went on to discuss second-best adjustments to the fare schedule. His discussion anticipated much of the optimal tax literature of the 1970s. He recognized that there are several margins of scale economies in subway travel, including frequency of service, train length, and network density. He also recognized that the deficit resulting from marginal-cost pricing with scale economies would have to be financed using distortionary taxation, and estimated the marginal cost of public funds to be 30 cents on the dollar. He then discussed the efficiency loss due to deviations from marginal-cost pricing: "the product of one-half the deviation in fare (from marginal cost) and the difference in volume of traffic." He went on to discuss additional considerations which might justify deviations from marginal-cost pricing – equity, popular acceptance, inefficient pricing of car travel, and the effects on spatial structure. Throughout his discussion he is sensitive to practical detail. Another noteworthy feature of his study is its attention to the mechanics of fare collection. Vickrey advocated that a traveler should pay a quarter (the maximum fare) upon entering the system. The traveler would receive a magnetically encoded token indicating time and point of entry. Placing this token in the exit turnstile, he would then receive a refund equal to the difference between a quarter and the fare. All Vickrey's subsequent work on urban transportation as well has addressed the technology of implementing congestion pricing.

With the benefit of hindsight, it is interesting to see what Vickrey did *not* do that would be done in a good modern study. He did not derive the second-best transit fare structure; *viz.*, he did not achieve an analytical formulation of the second-best problem. Nor did he estimate the degree of returns to scale in subway travel. He also seriously underestimated the importance of the underpricing of urban auto travel in the determination of the optimal subway fare structure. These oversights notwithstanding, the New York subway fare study was path-breaking, and much of the subsequent work in urban transport economics entails elaboration and formalization of its insights and conceptual framework.

Vickrey's next major work in transportation, in the late 1950s, was a study of Washington, DC's urban transportation problems. Like the New York study, it considered public transportation – in this case the bus system. But its signal contributions were to the pricing of urban auto travel. By this time Vickrey had clearly come to recognize the quantitative importance of the underpricing of rush-hour auto travel. He proposed electronic toll assessment to deal with the problem, and devoted several pages of the study to the engineering detail and costing of such a system. Other noteworthy features of the study are its breadth and subtlety of conceptualization, an independent derivation of Ramsey pricing, and the first appearance of "responsive congestion pricing" – dealing with stochastic demand by basing the congestion toll on realized usage – here applied to parking. In its stress on congestion pricing of urban auto travel, it anticipates the celebrated 1964 UK Smeed Report.

"Pricing in Urban and Suburban Transport" (chapter 15), published in 1963, is the best-known of a large number of papers he has written for a more general audience which advocate congestion pricing. As with his other papers written in a similar vein, its style is both distinctive and curious. In an attempt to make the argument more broadly accessible, Vickrey replaced mathematical analysis with verbal argumentation. But the economic argument was so sophisticated and dense that only those economists who were well-trained and analytically fluent could fully appreciate it. As a result, his popular writings have not in fact been very "popular." At the same time, because of the nonanalytical style of their presentation, many of his important insights have been overlooked by economists or recognized only later after being independently discovered by someone else. Thus, Vickrey's work would probably have had more impact on the profession, and the quality and originality of his work would probably have been more widely and sooner recognized, had he published analytical papers in the top journals and let others do the popularizing.

"Pricing in Urban and Suburban Transportation" starts with a beautifully written (Vickrey is certainly one of the most distinguished stylists in the profession) and well-argued statement of the social costs of mispricing in urban transport, continues by investigating alternative methods of automatic toll assessment, and concludes with a discussion of how marginal-cost pricing in urban transport would impact route and mode choice and land use. The problem posed at the end of the paper – the effect of mispricing urban transportation on urban spatial structure – was an active research topic in urban economics during the 1970s.

Economists' pleas for congestion pricing in urban transport seem to have fallen on deaf ears. Why has the profession been so unsuccessful? Part of the reason is that most of us have been lazy. We have been content to assert the wisdom of congestion pricing, without devoting much effort to popular persuasion or much attention to practical implementation. Vickrey has been the most notable exception, but even his proposals, however, have typically been met with indulgent amusement. But, at least as important, we have underestimated the psychological costs associated with fine congestion pricing; having to do a detailed cost–benefit calculation for the timing and route choice of each trip would contribute considerably to the stress of urban life. Nevertheless, since congestion in many cities outside North America is so severe that something sensible will have to be done soon, the widespread implementation of some form of coarse congestion tolling of urban auto transport must be only a few years away. Congestion pricing is being widely discussed in European policy circles and the notion is slowly gaining popular acceptance – a recent poll in London found the majority to favor congestion pricing if the revenues generated are used to finance improvements in the transport system. Thus, a generation from now Vickrey may well be regarded as a prophet, ahead of his time.

"Congestion Theory and Transport Investment" (chapter 16), published in 1969, is a seminal paper of deceptive simplicity. As the title suggests, it examines the modeling of traffic congestion and implications for the determination of optimal transport capacity. At the time the paper was written, urban economists modeled traffic congestion as a simple type of flow congestion – average travel speed over the period of analysis depends on the average flow of traffic and the width or capacity of the road. This treatment of congestion is deficient in two important respects. First, it fails to deal with the fact that a given level of flow is consistent with more than one velocity; for example, zero flow may correspond to free flow or gridlock. In assuming that flow and velocity are negatively related, it ignores traffic jam (hypercongestion) situations. Second, in assuming that average speed depends only on average flow, it treats congestion as essentially static. Transport engineers had been working for many years with dynamic models of flow congestion that accounted for hypercongestion and the dependence of congestion on the past evolution of flow, but such models were analytically unmanageable. Vickrey captured the essence of the transport engineers' treatment, while dramatically simplifying it, by modeling congestion as a queue behind a bottleneck. Remarkably, this bottleneck model of congestion has received strong empirical support from recent, very detailed traffic flow studies.

But Vickrey's paper went much further. He recognized that the bottleneck model of congestion permits analysis of the *dynamic* equilibrium of rush hour auto congestion. The point can be simply illustrated. There is a group of commuters, all with the same work start time, who travel along a single road from a common origin to a common workplace in the morning rush hour. Along the road is a single bottleneck of fixed capacity. If the arrival rate at the bottleneck exceeds capacity, a queue develops. Commuters decide when to depart from home. In doing so, they trade off travel time (queuing) costs against the costs of arriving at work early or late. Equilibrium then requires that the trip price be independent of departure time; for example, with no toll the time-early cost of the first commuter to depart should equal the cost of queuing behind the bottleneck for the commuter who arrives on time. Application of this equilibrium condition permits solution, under alternative tolling regimes, of the evolution of the queue length over the rush hour, as well as the equilibrium departure pattern.

Because of its simplicity, the model permits the analysis of all the standard topics in urban transport economics but now accounts for the dynamics of rush-hour congestion. This paper by Vickrey is almost certainly the most important in urban transport economics over the last quarter-century. Not only has it spawned a large literature, but it has also changed the way urban economists and traffic engineers perceive rush-hour congestion. For instance, we now take it as obvious that worsening congestion will lead to a lengthening of the rush hour, though previously this was rarely even mentioned.

It is of interest to note that the importance of this paper, like so many others by Vickrey, was not recognized until long after publication. The bottleneck model was independently discovered by traffic engineers in the early 1980s. Only then did urban economists return to Vickrey's model and begin exploring its implications.

> Full many a gem of purest ray serene,
> Th' unfathom'd caves of Vickrey's papers bear.

One of the frustrating features of Vickrey's work is that so many gems of insight are presented in such a casual and offhand manner, without emphasis or elaboration, that it is easy to overlook them. At the same time, for this reason his papers bear rereading and rereading.

The reader will have noticed how little has been said about the intellectual antecedents to Vickrey's contributions to urban transport economics. His work draws heavily on welfare economics and is informed by the literature on traffic engineering. But it appears that his thinking on urban transport economics evolved almost completely independently of other work in the field. It is hard, however, to conceive of any urban transport economist today whose work does not bear a substantial intellectual debt to Vickrey's contributions.

14

--- · ---

A Proposal for Revising New York's Subway Fare Structure

As a part of the study of the finances of the City of New York directed by Carl Shoup and the late Robert M. Haig, under the auspices of the Mayor's Committee on Management Survey, the writer was assigned the problem of what could be done about the transit fare structure. Initially, at least, the problem was formally presented in terms of the possibilities for reducing the drain of the transit deficit on the city's finances. However, other aspects of the problem had to be considered if a basis for a balanced judgment was to be provided. Indeed, as the study was finally presented, emphasis was placed on the influence of the fare upon the utilization of the transit system by the riding public, this being the aspect that most closely conditioned the recommendations and at the same time the aspect that appeared to be least familiar to those to whom the report was addressed.

Aspects of the Problem

The transit fare problem can be thought of in terms of six fairly distinct but interrelated aspects. The starting point of the study was the revenue or fiscal aspect: fare changes will generally change the revenues or deficit of the transit system and thus affect the tax rates that the city will have to levy to meet its overall financial requirements. A second aspect is the purely mechanical problem of how fare structures of different types can be collected cheaply and effectively. Third is the distributional problem of how the fare structure or the alternative

Journal of the Operations Research Society of America, 3 (1955), pp. 38–69; reprinted as "Revising New York's Subway Fare Structure", in *Operations Research for Management*, Joseph F. McCloskey and John Coppinger, Eds. (Johns Hopkins University Press, 1956), vol. II, pp. 101–33.

sources of revenue will affect the distribution of income among the population of the city. Fourth is the political problem of the degree to which the fare structure is acceptable to riders and taxpayers as reasonable and equitable, by whatever standards are popularly applied. Fifth are the ecological, geographical, and social aspects, consisting of the effects of a fare structure on the geographical pattern of the city's development, the concentration or decentralization of business and industry, on hours of work, and on patterns of living of the public generally. Sixth is the utilization aspect, which is the one on which this study is concentrated: this concerns the effect of the fare structure on the efficiency with which the facilities and services available are utilized by the traveling public. Any actual fare structure will reflect a compromise among revenue, mechanical, political, distributional, ecological, and utilization considerations.

The Meaning of Efficient Utilization

The utilization aspect is one that is very seldom given much consideration by non-economists, and is often completely ignored, even by economists. As it is perhaps the least familiar aspect, it will bear explication. To achieve optimum utilization in the economist's sense, it is necessary to insure that the value of the benefits produced by all of the services provided by a utility shall exceed the costs of rendering that service by as large a margin as possible. Such excesses are, indeed, a measure of the essential social gain from any economic activity, and the competitive system finds its chief justification in the fact that under idealized conditions perfect competition will indeed achieve such a maximum of this excess. The conditions of perfect competition are not and cannot be achieved in such an industry as transit, which is subject to substantial economies of scale, so that if this goal of optimum utilization is to be achieved it must be pursued consciously rather than allowed to emerge as the result of an automatic process.

If we are to be assured that this excess, or social gain, is as great as possible, service must be provided and used to such a degree that no further possible service remains that would carry a benefit to the users greater than the increment of costs occasioned by the increment of service. Conversely, no service should be rendered where the costs occasioned exceed the value of the service. For example, if there is a train operating between two points at a given time on which it can be reliably predicted that there will be a substantial number of vacant seats, so that additional passengers could be carried at almost negligible cost, and if there are potential passengers who would ride this train between the two points if the fare were reduced, then the existing fare fails, to this extent, to produce an economically efficient utilization of transit facilities. Conversely, where congestion occurs, the fare may fail to reflect the relatively high cost either of providing additional service at such times, or of the added discomfort to existing passengers occasioned by the crowding in of additional passengers. In such cases, if there are passengers who would cease to ride or who would reduce their riding if the fare were raised to a level commensurate with such costs – indicating that for these passengers the value of the service to them is less than the cost to the rest of the community – there is a wasteful overutilization of the facilities. Only as the fare fully reflects at all times and between all points the cost of carrying additional passengers will the fare structure achieve an efficient utilization of the facilities.

Of course, there are limits to the degree to which a price or rate can be made to follow sudden and possibly erratic fluctuations in cost, even aside from mechanical considerations. The fare structure will be effective in promoting efficient utilization only to the extent that its relevant elements are known to the prospective passenger at the time he makes a decision to make a particular trip. If the fare that will be charged is unknown to him, it will fail to function as a guide in his decision as to whether or not a particular trip is worth while in view of the cost that will be occasioned. A fare structure must therefore not be so erratic that passengers would be unable to adjust to it. Nor is it in general useful to adjust a fare according to unpredictable emergency or other conditions that may arise after the time at which the passenger has made his effective decision to make or not to make a particular trip. But regular or frequent riders in particular, who make up a large part of subway traffic, can be expected to learn fairly quickly the parts of the fare structure that concern them, even though in its entirety the fare structure might be fairly complex. Regular and predictable variations in the costs of providing particular types of additional transit service, according to time of day, direction of travel, and the points between which passengers travel are quite extreme; even if followed very roughly, such variations lead to rate structures dramatically different from those in common use. Under conditions in New York, for example, many trains must be run empty for substantial distances to get them to and from the points where they can carry passengers, and over these sections additional passengers can be carried at no perceptible increase in costs. Additional service during nonrush hours can often be provided merely by adding cars to existing trains, the costs being merely added power and added maintenance, on the order of 3 or 4 cents per seat per trip. Additional rush-hour service, however, requires the purchase of additional equipment with added capital charges, additional personnel, and increased demand charges as well as energy charges for power, so that even on the assumption that adequate track capacity exists for such service, costs of rush-hour service amount to a minimum of 20 cents per trip for moderately long trips in the direction of the rush, even after allowing for the larger proportion of standees. Where track capacity is limited, additional rush-hour traffic can often be accommodated only by creating very serious crowding conditions, with consequent deterioration of the service to existing passengers, or by the construction of new lines at very great expense, in addition to the additional expenses referred to above, all of which may push the cost of the longer rush-hour trips up as high as 40 or 50 cents per passenger.

The Structure of Subway Costs

To develop figures that would give some idea of how costs do vary with changes in the volume and character of the traffic, six parameters were selected as representing those aspects of the traffic handled and the service supplied that would substantially determine the necessary costs of operations. These are:

T = Train miles operated per year
C = Car miles operated per year
M = Peak number of cars in service
N = Number of passengers carried (per year)
P = Peak number of passengers carried per hour
S = System layout, being some rather vaguely specified composite measure of the territory served, route miles, number of stations, and the like. The system layout parameter, to be sure, is somewhat vaguely defined, and does, indeed, function as a residual catch-all into which influences not expressed by the other parameters can be tossed. However, as for most of the analysis this parameter will be considered to remain constant, this does not matter too much. (It is not quite the same thing as track capacity.)

Operating costs were then allocated to these various parameters according to the degree to which such costs were assumed to be influenced by such a parameter. For example, the wages of motormen are clearly a train-mile cost. Although operation of rush-hour trains may in some instances lead to a relatively higher cost for motormen's wages than at other times – owing to difficulties of scheduling tracks to meet minimum day and maximum swing limitations – this effect was difficult to evaluate, and was not allowed for. Energy charges for traction power are a car-mile cost, while demand charges for traction power are a peak-car cost (M). Energy and demand charges for station and tunnel lighting, etc., are a system-layout cost. Wages of conductors were apportioned somewhat arbitrarily between car-mile and train-mile costs: Most trains have a single conductor, but when trains are lengthened to more than eight cars or the equivalent, a second conductor is usually assigned. Track maintenance was assigned partly to car-miles, but also partly to train-miles – on the theory that frequent train service diminishes the efficiency of track gangs; part-of-way and structure maintenance, including most of the cost-tunnel drainage, ventilation, and maintenance, was assigned to system layout. Proceeding somewhat arbitrarily in this way, and in many cases having to rely on subjective judgment and consultation with operating personnel, all operating expenses were assigned. By expressing all service parameters in terms of indexes with the value for 1949–50 as a base, and applying to these indexes the percentage distribution of costs, the following formula was arrived at. This was taken to represent the operating cost function for the neighborhood of the 1949–50 pattern of operations

$$X = 0.18\ T + 0.32\ C + 0.29\ S + 0.09\ M + 0.07\ N + 0.04\ P + 0.01$$

This procedure tacitly assumes that constant returns to scale would prevail for a proportionate expansion, in every dimension, including "system layout." Probably this would not be strictly true for any method of measuring "system layout" that would be relevant here. This might ordinarily lead to an overstatement of marginal costs at margins involving expansion of system layout, but the special methods used to estimate costs on this margin probably have largely avoided this bias, which in any case would be almost completely lost in the very large margins of uncertainty that remain in this area. The constant term 0.01 in the above formula actually represents an error of rounding, but is left in as a symbolic reminder of the probable but unascertained economies of scale.

Rush-hour versus Nonrush-hour Traffic

This allocation enables some rough computations to be made of the cost of increasing various types of traffic. For example, if we wish to provide for an increase in traffic during the nonrush hours when trains are of less than maximum length, and wish to do this without changing the quality of service, i.e., without changing the frequency of trains, this will be possible merely by adding cars to existing trains, so that the only parameters affected will be C and P. If the increase amounts to 10 percent of the total number of passengers, P will go from 1.00 to 1.10; on the other hand, since the number of passengers per car mile is considerably lower for nonrush hours than for the average – by reason of less crowding not entirely offset by a slightly shorter average trip – C may have to go from 1.00 to, say, 1.15 to preserve the same quality of service. Accordingly, the above formula would give a value for X of 1.0487 times its base value. In other words, the marginal operating cost of nonrush hour traffic is slightly less than half the average operating cost per passenger (0.0487/0.10).

On the other hand an increase in traffic during the rush hour will call for an increase in all of these parameters, with the possible exception of S in those cases where the track capacity is not fully utilized. A 10 percent increase in the total number of passengers, concentrated in the rush hour, would require perhaps a 7 percent increase in C, since passengers per car-mile average higher in rush hours than for all traffic combined. In cases where trains are already of maximum length, train miles would have to be increased, but not by as much as car-miles, since rush-hour trains are longer than average, and some trains could be lengthened: the increase may perhaps be 5 percent. On the other hand the number of cars in use and the peak number of passengers would go up 30 percent; peak-hour passengers being one third of the total, roughly, would go up 10 percent. The combined effect of all these parameter changes would be to cause total operating expense to rise by 8.34 percent, assuming that track capacity is available without changes in the system layout. Thus under these circumstances the operating cost of carrying rush-hour passengers is some 73 percent higher than that of nonrush passengers, though it is still some 17 percent below the average operating cost per passenger.

This however does not include capital charges. Capital charges are virtually unaffected by changes in nonrush-hour traffic; neither additional equipment nor additional facilities will be needed to accommodate an increase in such traffic. Increases in rush-hour traffic will at the very least require the purchase of additional equipment, and may require substantial outlays for additional trackage, lines, or station facilities; and with those outlays, the associated maintenance expenses will increase. The capital charges contained in the accounts, however, bear no close relationship to any real alternatives available currently, so that these purely arbitrary sums cannot be used for purposes of estimating marginal cost. The capital charge elements of marginal cost had therefore to be estimated on a somewhat different basis than the operating-cost elements.

Indeed, the above cost figures were for rush-hour and for nonrush hour traffic as a whole, whereas it seems worth while to go into considerably more detail in distinguishing the costs of various types of traffic.

Nonrush-hour Trips

If we start with a simple case, that of a line with relatively light traffic, so that trains are of less than maximum length during the nonrush hours, we can readily compute the cost of increasing the volume of service, i.e., car miles, while keeping the quality of service constant by keeping the train frequency and number of passengers per car the same. This increase works out at 12.2 cents per car mile at 1950 price levels, or $3.34 per car per round trip for the average round trip of 27.3 miles. At an average of fifty seats per car, this will be 0.24 per seat mile or 6.7 cents per seat round trip. It remains to translate this to a cost to be assessed against particular passengers.

The problem is a simple one if it is mandatory to provide seats for all passengers, if all passengers ride past some intermediate point on the run, if trains must all be operated from one end of the line to the other, and if traffic is balanced in both directions. Then, the fare can be a flat fare regardless of distance traveled, made up of 3.35 cents car-mile costs per one-way seat trip, plus 0.4 cents passenger costs, plus perhaps a margin to allow for the vacant seats that must be left to allow for unpredictable fluctuations and the fact that fractions of a car cannot be operated – perhaps 4 cents in all. If there are, in addition, passengers who want to ride exclusively on one side or the other of the peak load point, they may be carried free or at a nominal charge of 1 cent to cover passenger costs. If traffic is not balanced, the total of approximately 8 cents per passenger round trip would either be so divided between the traffic in the two directions as to bring the traffic into balance – if the traffic is sufficiently responsive to fare changes – or, if traffic cannot be balanced by adjusting the fare, the 8 cents would be charged entirely to the traffic in the heavy direction, the light direction traffic being charged a nominal 1 cent – if anything.

If there is not a definite single peak on the run, passengers getting on and off in more or less irregular fashion, the total cost for a seat round trip can be apportioned among the various segments of the trip in such a way that the fare is zero for any segment where traffic is substantially less than the peak, and that over each of the other segments the fare is just high enough to limit traffic to a uniform maximum level. The fare for any trip would then be the sum of the fares for its various component segments, plus a small charge per passenger to cover marginal "passenger" costs associated with getting on and off the train and collecting fares.

Where standees are permitted, the apportionment of the cost among the passengers becomes somewhat more complicated, though perhaps the variations in the rate of fare per mile smooth out somewhat. If we make the assumption that at no point does the crowding become such as to cause any discomfort, the cost of carrying additional standees will be zero. Occupancy of a seat, likewise, has no cost wherever there are a substantial number of vacant seats. Occupancy of a seat when all seats are filled has a cost that can be measured in terms of the fact that some other passenger is deprived of that seat and thus has to stand. The sacrifice thus imposed on the more or less randomly determined passenger who must stand because a given passenger has a seat can be considered roughly independent of all factors other than the distance, or – perhaps better – the time during which the seat is occupied. To be sure, where standees are few, the chances are that anyone who strongly desires a seat can get one in a relatively short time as passengers get on and off. Therefore, the unknown person who is forced to stand because a particular passenger takes a seat is probably less anxious for a seat on the average than might be the case where standees are more numerous. Also, occupancy of a seat when vacant seats are few may mean that the passenger who might otherwise have occupied the seat may have to walk some distance to find a seat, and some reduction of elbow room may result. These factors argue for not making too sharp a distinction between times when there are standees and times when there are none.

As long as we do not attempt to collect different fares from sitting than from standing passengers, the cost of a particular trip will have to be based on the probability or frequency with which passengers of a given type are likely to occupy seats over portions of the trip when all seats are taken. Indeed, given some estimate of the average value placed by passengers on sitting rather than standing, per mile or per minute of travel, the marginal cost of a given trip may be calculated by multiplying the number of minutes or miles that a given passenger on the average will be expected to occupy a seat within the standee-carrying portion of the run by this estimated value of a seat.

This may sound at first as though marginal cost had become completely divorced from the actual outlays involved in furnishing the service. However, if we examine how the volume of service should be adjusted so as to maximize the excess of value over cost, we find that a sufficient number of cars should be run so that the standee-carrying portion of the round trip is just long enough so that valuing the provision of additional seats for this length of trip at the estimated value to the passenger will just equal the cost of providing additional seat trips. Thus, if the value of a seat is appraised at an average of 0.4 cents per mile, and the cost per seat round trip of 23.7 miles is 6.7 cents, then the volume of service offered on such a run should be so adjusted that there are, on the average, standees for 16.75 miles of this total round trip. If service is adjusted in this way, a marginal cost computed in terms of the value of the seat to a passenger will turn out to correspond to a value derived by appropriately allocating the costs of providing additional seats. In evaluating the probability that a given passenger will get a seat, it might be appropriate to take into consideration the fact that passengers getting on at terminals, or before the train has filled up, will probably get a seat that they may retain to their destination, whereas passengers boarding the train when all seats are ordinarily taken may have a rather slim chance. On the other hand it is probably not feasible to charge a lower fare to gentlemen of the old school who cannot bear to sit in the presence of a standing lady, nor to charge a specially high fare to nice old ladies, pretty blondes, or pregnant women who might be thought more likely to provoke a resurgence of gallantry.

Rush-hour Trips

During the rush hours, or at other times when the number of standees becomes so large as to cause discomfort, the cost picture again becomes more complex. If an increment in traffic is packed into the existing car-miles of service, the out-of-pocket costs to the transit authority may be fairly slight, consisting chiefly of additional platform guards, and possibly additional station agents and overtime payments to crews of delayed trains. The main costs of accommodating the additional passengers will be borne by the existing passengers, who will suffer the increased crowding, and, of course, will also have a smaller chance of obtaining a seat. If the costs of such crowding are computed on a marginal basis, which is the basis that is relevant for this purpose – rather than in terms of the average degree of discomfort – the cost can mount up extremely rapidly as crowding increases. For example, 200 persons may get into a car without serious discomfort, but let another twenty passengers be added and conditions may become so bad that the original 200 passengers would be willing to pay on the average 3 cents each to have the former conditions restored, or altogether $6.00. The addition of twenty passengers has thus imposed costs of $6.00, or 30 cents each, though the average discomfort is valued only at 3 cents. The discomfort that an individual himself experiences is thus a completely inadequate representation of the total increment of discomfort that his decision to ride adds.

The burdens thrown on fellow passengers by increased rush-hour riding are not confined to the actual discomfort of the increased crowding, but extend also to such matters as the longer running times that result because of the longer station stops and the possibility of having to allow one or two trains to go by before one can squeeze aboard. And if station stops get much longer at key stations, the situation may become aggravated by a reduction in the number of trains that can be operated in a given period of time. For example, at 60,000 passengers per hour it may be possible to run thirty ten-car trains per hour with 200 passengers per car; but at 63,000 passengers per hour, service may be slowed to twenty-nine trains per hour, so that a 5 percent increase in total traffic requires an increase in loading to about 218 passengers per car, a 9 percent increase. If each passenger values this deterioration at only 2 cents in this case, the marginal cost attributable to the 5 percent increase in total passengers will be 40 cents per passenger.

It might be thought that to evaluate marginal cost on the basis of such a subjective appraisal of the money value of the discomforts of crowding is extremely approximate and rough, and indeed it is. It is even less feasible as a direct measurment than would be the ascertaining of a value of sitting rather than standing, per mile. A survey inquiry of passengers as to what they would be willing to pay to sit rather than to stand would at least be a clear and definite question to which one might with care get sensible answers. To inquire concerning the value attached to the avoidance of varying degrees of crowding would be extremely difficult, as it would be hard to determine the conditions that the respondent had in mind when giving his evaluation. Nevertheless some evaluation of this general character is implicit in any decision to increase or decrease service during the rush hour. If the cost of added service is less than the value of the reduction in crowding that would thereby be obtained, the service should be added, and otherwise not; on the other hand if the savings from a reduction in service are greater than the value of the increased crowding resulting, the reduction should be made, and otherwise not. Of course, this decision must be modified where frequency of service is a consideration. In most cases rush-hour service is already so frequent that increases or decreases in frequency mean relatively little to the passengers.

Thus if we assume, rashly, that the Transit Authority has succeeded in properly adjusting service in this manner, and has not been deterred from such a policy by political or financial pressure, we could take the upward and downward incremental costs of service as the upper and lower limits for the marginal cost in terms of injury to fellow passengers. These upper and lower limits may coincide, but often there will be some difference between the costs of making some substantial increase in the volume of service and what can be saved through a reduction in service – as, for example, when track capacity is being fully utilized and increases in service would require additional trackage, but a reduction in service might not make possible any reduction in the trackage requirement.

In any case it is important to estimate directly the cost of increasing service during rush hours. We have as a minimum the car-mile costs of 12.2 cents per car-mile; in addition there are the costs allocable to the number of cars in use, amounting to $2,330 per car per year. At the peak of the rush hour, additional service requires the addition of equipment that is not needed except for that particular run; indeed on many lines there are runs made with equipment that is put in service at the beginning of the run and taken out at the end. Thus this $2,330 per year is to be divided among two trips per day, morning and evening, 250 weekdays a year, or $4.66 per trip. But in addition to the operating costs associated with increases in the rolling stock on hand, there are the capital charges for interest and amortization. If these together are figured at 5 per cent on the cost per car of some $80,000, we have another $4,000 per car per year, or $8 per car per trip. Thus under the most favorable conditions, where there is still room to increase the length of trains, a car round trip costs $3.34 + $4.66 + $8.00 = $16; dividing this among 200 passengers per car (while the average "capacity" of subway cars is around 240, there is always considerable unevenness of loading both because of irregularities in timing of the trains and because of distribution of passengers along the train, so that overcrowding begins somewhat below nominal "capacity") gives 8 cents per passenger, adding 0.7 cents per passenger for "passenger" costs and another 2.5 cents for "peak passenger" costs. This gives a total of 11.2 cents as an estimate of the marginal cost for an average long-haul rush-hour rider under these circumstances.

As operations push against capacity, rush-hour marginal costs mount further. The first thing likely to happen is that trains will reach maximum length, whereupon, in order to operate more service, more trains must be operated.

Train-mile costs at 48 cents per train mile for the average 23.7 mile round trip amount to $11.50 per train trip, or $1.15 per car per trip. While some credit may be taken against this for the value of the increase in the frequency of service, at the frequencies likely to occur in rush-hour service this element is likely to be small. As a result, the typical marginal cost is pushed up to nearly 12 cents.

When track capacity is reached, however, rather drastic increases in costs take place. It is difficult to make any very definite calculations of such costs. The historical cost of construction of the present system layout, which might be in some cases taken as a guide, is difficult to disentangle from the complicated financial record. To do this, would require all kinds of very difficult adjustments in terms of price levels, changes in construction standards and conditions, allowances for obsolescence, and the like. Moreover it is desirable to allow at least to some extent for the fact that the system layout is at least in part a function of making service available to given areas rather than of increasing the quantity of a given quality of service.

The Second-Avenue Proposal

One opportunity for gaining some insight into this element of the marginal cost in the longest-run sense is provided by the proposed Second Avenue trunk line. This construction program lies predominantly within Manhattan, and proposes to make use to a large extent of existing outlying lines to feed traffic to it, and, at the same time, by means of connections to lines to Brooklyn, to enable these lines to be used more fully. This line, with six tracks, would provide additional capacity on each track for thirty-four ten-car trains per hour, and thus would represent an additional capacity for 1,020 cars per hour into and out of downtown Manhattan. Present capacity is for the equivalent of about 4,812 cars per hour, if the smaller cars are counted as two-thirds of the larger; with this capacity, it is estimated that about 337 million passengers per year are carried past the peak-load points during the three rush hours, in the direction of the rush. If the same degree of utilization could be attained, it could be expected that the new facilities could provide for an additional 71 million rush passengers per year.

The cost of this new facility, exclusive of rolling stock, was put at $436 million; accepting this at face value and allowing interest and amortization at only 4 percent per year, this cost would produce an annual charge of $17,440,000 per year; if this were divided among the 71 million rush passengers, it would produce a cost of 24 cents per passenger. This added to other costs would result in a total marginal cost of providing for increased rush-hour traffic, where additional track capacity is needed, of 36 cents.

Of course, it may not be considered proper to charge the entire cost of the improvement to the rush-hour passenger: other benefits are obtained which to some extent can be credited against the cost. Both rush and nonrush passengers will obtain an improvement in service to the extent that the stations on the new line are more convenient for them than those on the old. For the nonrush-hour rider, however, this benefit is not free of disadvantage: division of service between two routes will usually mean less frequent service. Moreover, in this particular case, one of the objectives is the demolition of the last elevated line remaining on Manhattan, with consequent benefits to property values; however it should be noted that if this demolition is carried out, the net addition to capacity is only 800 cars per hour rather than 1,020.

In any event, the addition to the system layout represents an increase of about 9.6 percent in the number of track miles, and so can be expected to entail a corresponding increase in the operating expenses attributable to system layout, which for the existing system amounted to $47 million a year. The expected increase would then be $4.5 million, which distributed over the 71 million rush passengers adds another 6.3 cents to the cost per passenger, bringing the total to 42 cents.

What this means is not necessarily that marginal cost on present lines under actual conditions *is* 42 cents in terms of the costs of added crowding, but rather that the construction of the Second Avenue line, considered primarily as a means of easing congestion on existing lines, cannot be justified until conditions on the parallel Lexington Avenue line would, in the absence of the new line, result in congestion of a degree felt to entail a marginal cost of 42 cents per passenger. Even this 42 cent figure may be too low, for it was based on an assumption that the new facility could be fairly fully utilized; whereas, in the actual situation, the increase in capacity represented by the new line is so large that there is serious doubt, in view of the downward trends in rapid transit traffic recently, that it would ever become as fully utilized as the present system. Indeed, even in purely mechanical terms, there is doubt as to whether the connections included in the immediate plan are physically capable of delivering to the trunk line a capacity volume of traffic, unless, at least, substantial diminution of service on existing lines is assumed.

The pattern of marginal cost that thus emerges is somewhat as follows, with the level of cost assignable to rush-hour traffic subject to a somewhat wide margin of error. There is a cost of 1 cent or less for traffic going against the rush and riding essentially as a superfluous byproduct of the rush-hour traffic, and also for short-haul traffic in the outlying sections of the routes; a cost of 4–6 cents for nonrush-hour traffic covering the entire standee-carrying portion of the run, and correspondingly less for trips covering a shorter distance within the peak traffic zone – the cost depending also to some extent on whether conditions are such that additional trains are required for the additional traffic, and the degree to which the train mile cost can be chargeable to improved frequency of service rather than to increased volume. During near-rush periods, when traffic is predominantly in one direction, but still short of taxing the supply of rolling stock, a cost of 8 to 10 cents is indicated for the longer trips. For rush-hour trips on lines with adequate track capacity, there is a cost of around 12 cents for the longer trips; while where track capacity is fully used, the marginal cost can range from 20 cents up to 40 cents for trips that span the entire zone in which discomfort exists, and up to 50 cents for the longest trips under the most severe congestion.

But while one can justify a 50 cent cost figure under very extreme conditions, and even perhaps under conditions actually existing in some instances (e.g. in the Lexington Avenue express service) further analysis was limited to a top figure of 25 cents. One reason for this figure was the convenience of using a 25 cent coin in payment of fare; another was a general feeling that fares above this level would prove extremely difficult to sell politically. This limitation could also be rationalized to some extent by considering that the easing of congestion that might well result from some of the fare proposals being considered might in many cases bring marginal costs down to somewhere not too far from this figure as a maximum. Also, since it would probably not be possible to distinguish between congested and uncongested parallel routes in most instances, averaging of such costs would tend to hide the more extreme cost figures.

The Mechanics of a Marginal Cost Fare

The aim of efficient utilization can be closely approached only if it is possible to provide reasonably cheaply for the actual collection of a fare that corresponds fairly closely with marginal cost. Fortunately it was possible to devise a method of collecting such a fare that meets these requirements. Briefly, it was proposed to require each passenger to deposit a quarter in an entrance turnstile, which would deliver to each passenger a metal check that the passenger would be required to carry with him to his destination. The check would bear notches or perhaps magnetic patterns coded to represent the station or zone of entry and perhaps also the date; the passenger would insert this check into an exit turnstile as he left the subway; the exit turnstile would be able to determine from the check the origin of the passenger, and then, according to this origin and the time of exit, would determine the proper refund and deliver it to the passenger. While no working model of such a turnstile has been produced, fairly detailed specifications have been drawn up, and there seems to be no serious technical difficulty involved. The costs of installing such turnstiles over the entire system would of course be considerable, but very rough estimates appeared to indicate that this cost would not be large enough to require any modification of the recommendations. Such a fare scheme could not be put into effect until the turnstile installation is substantially complete, of course, and the design, manufacture, and installation of the turnstiles would involve a considerable lapse of time.

With such a method of fare collection, it becomes possible to vary the fare in almost any manner desired, except for allowing special multiple ride rates, a form of fare variation that bears no direct relation to marginal cost. Special fares for school children would likewise require special arrangements, as would transfers to and from other lines. Fortunately, the New York subway system has been almost entirely a separate and distinct unit, without transfer arrangements with other lines except for a brief period beginning in 1948 when a combination surface-subway rate was available. Even then, the number of such combination fares collected was relatively small.

When fares are being based on marginal cost, of course, there is no occasion for special combined fares or transfer privileges; a passenger using two different lines in succession occasions just as much cost as when the two portions of the trip are made by two different persons. It is only when fares are for some reason to be allowed to differ from marginal cost that such transfer arrangements become appropriate.

Partly because marginal cost is in any case an approximation subject to considerable error, and partly to avoid having to handle large numbers of pennies, fares may well be rounded to the nearest 5 cents; if this is done, the pattern of fares given in the "M" columns of table 14.1 emerges.

Accommodation to Competing Objectives

But in a practical problem it is seldom desirable to adhere to one criterion to the exclusion of others, and this is no exception. Fares set at a marginal-cost level will, because of the economies of scale of transit service, produce substantially less revenue than is necessary to cover the full costs of the operation, and thus will constitute a drain on the city budget that must be met by increasing other taxes correspondingly. If tax administration and compliance costs were independent of the level of tax collections, and if the level of tax rates had no significant deleterious effects on the efficiency with which the private sector of the economy functions, one could consider that it would be appropriate to set the fares strictly according to marginal cost. But in general tax revenues cannot be increased without imposing some social costs over and above the net revenue secured, so that if the transit deficit can be decreased by raising fares above marginal cost without causing too serious a loss due to less efficient utilization of the transit system, the loss in transit underutilization may be made up to some extent by reductions in losses attributable to high tax rates.

It may be mentioned in passing that while an excess of cost over revenues from marginal-cost rates is likely to be particularly great in rapid transit service where there is a large element of cost for the exclusive right of way, it is by no means a minor matter for other transit media. Even for bus service, as traffic increases as a result of fare reductions – considering area served, population, and traffic conditions to be otherwise constant – economies of scale result from the appropriate increases in size of buses, and from higher average loads where the service can be more closely accommodated to the volume of traffic, wholly aside from whatever minor economies of scale there may be in the larger organization. More important, where increased traffic brings either an increased frequency of service, or increased variety of service – taking passengers closer to their destination, or reducing travel time – the value of this improvement in service to the existing passengers can be credited against the additional cost, leaving the costs allocable to the increase in service of the same quality at a level much lower than the average cost per unit of service. Thus even for bus service, a fare structure set at a marginal cost that reflected all these factors would produce a revenue falling far short of total cost.

Another factor to be considered is that fare collection is costly, and different schemes of fare collection involve different costs. For the New York subways, it was estimated that costs of fare collection amounted to some $12 million a year, out of total revenues of $160 million. A zone-time fare would require considerable additional equipment and some additional personnel adding perhaps $3 million or more to the annual cost. One may inquire whether there may not be some other methods of fare collection that might achieve a result reasonably close to that of the marginal-cost fare, but with lower collection cost.

To evaluate these possibilities, it is necessary to determine to what extent the efficiency with which the transit system is used will be affected if fares are varied in various ways from the marginal-cost level, and also what the effect on revenues will be. This requires a knowledge of the patterns of traffic and the responsiveness of traffic to fare changes.

Patterns of Traffic and Their Elasticity

Estimating the pattern of traffic in a form suitable for the present purposes required the combining of a wide variety of data with a considerable amount of casual observation, a priori hunch, guesswork, and arbitrary allocation. The basic data consists of the hourly readings on the turnstiles at each station. At some stations, particularly on the older lines, the controls for the two directions of

Table 14.1 Volume of Traffic Responsiveness to Fare Changes and Marginal Cost by Length of Trip, Time of Day, and Relation to Downtown Area

Length of trip, miles	Traffic in the direction of the rush															Non-rush-hour traffic			Traffic against the rush		
	Peak hour			Before or after the peak hour by																	
				0 to 30 minutes			30 to 60 minutes			60 to 90 minutes											
	Q^a	V^a	M^a	Q	V	M	Q	V	M	Q	V	M				Q	V	M	Q	V	M

1 Traffic to, from, or through Manhattan below 65th Street

Length of trip, miles	Q^a	V^a	M^a	Q	V	M	Q	V	M	Q	V	M	Q	V	M	Q	V	M
0 to 1	6	1	5	4	1	5	2	—	0	2	—	0	17	4	0	4	1	0
1 to 2	13	1	5	8	1	5	4	1	5	3	—	0	43	10	0	10	2	0
2 to 3	21	2	10	11	1	5	6	1	5	4	1	5	59	12	0	4	1	0
3 to 4	20	2	10	10	1	5	6	—	5	4	—	5	55	11	5	5	1	0
4 to 5	19	1	15	11	—	10	6	1	5	4	1	5	49	6	5	6	1	0
5 to 6	20	1	15	11	1	10	6	1	5	4	1	5	39	5	5	7	1	0
6 to 8	52	4	20	31	2	10	18	2	10	14	1	5	100	13	5	16	3	0
8 to 10	72	5	25	44	3	15	26	2	10	18	1	10	135	17	5	21	3	0
10 to 15	68	4	25	39	2	15	24	2	10	17	1	10	108	15	5	16	2	0
Over 15	4	—	25	3	—	15	2	1	10	2	—	10	10	1	5	—	—	0
Total	295	21		172	12		100	11		72	6		615	94		89	15	

2 Traffic coming within four miles of, but not entering, Manhattan below 65th Street[a]

Distance	Q	V	M	Q	V	M	Q	V	M	Q	V	M	Q	V	M
				Included in non-rush hour traffic									Included in non-rush hour traffic		
0 to 1	2	1	5	1	—	0	1	—	0	7	4	0	1	—	0
1 to 2	4	1	5	2	1	5	1	—	0	16	7	0	4	2	0
2 to 3	6	2	5	3	1	5	3	1	0	22	9	0	4	2	0
3 to 4	6	1	5	3	1	5	2	1	5	19	6	0	4	1	0
4 to 5	6	2	5	3	1	5	2	1	5	17	5	0	3	1	0
5 to 6	6	2	10	3	1	5	3	1	5	17	5	5	3	—	0
6 to 8	8	2	10	4	1	10	3	1	5	24	6	5	4	1	0
8 to 10	5	1	15	3	1	10	2	—	5	16	3	5	2	—	0
10 to 15	2	—	15	2	—	10	1	—	5	5	1	5	1	—	0
Over 15	—	—	15	—	—	10	—	—	10	—	—	5	—	—	0
Total	45	12		24	7		18	5		143	46		26	7	

3 Traffic not coming within four miles of Manhattan below 65th Street

Distance	Q	V	M	Q	V	M	Q	V	M	Q	V	M
										Included in non-rush hour traffic		
0 to 3	4	3	0	2	2	0	12	6	0	5	2	0
3 to 6	10	3	0	4	3	0	26	11	0	10	4	0
6 to 10	4	1	5	2	—	0	8	2	0	2	1	0
Over 10	1	—	5	—	—	0	1	—	0	—	—	0
Total	19	7		8	5		47	19		17	7	

Note: [a]Q: Volume of traffic in millions of passengers per year. V: Variability of traffic in response to fare changes, in millions of passengers per year per five cents of fare change per passenger. M: Marginal cost per trip, in cents.

travel are separate, but, for many of the larger and of the newer lines, the controls are consolidated. Unfortunately, these data are actually tabulated by hours for only one or two days a year. For the rest of the year, they are available by stations, as daily averages for each month, and separately for weekdays and for Saturdays, Sundays, and holidays. The hourly figures, particularly for individual stations, are of course affected by the weather, special events, and also, on occasion, by substantial deviations in time of observation. They thus could be considered reliable only when assembled in considerable volume, so as to permit such effects to cancel out to some extent. In addition occasional traffic counts are taken, usually for the rush-hour period, and usually at points of maximum traffic density, of passengers in trains passing a given point. This is done by a man, stationed usually at the leaving end of the station, who attempts to estimate the number of passengers in each car as it flashes past him, and to record the results in terms of twenty minute intervals.

As for the elasticity of traffic, fortunately a fare increase, from 5 to 10 cents on 1 July, 1948, provided a rather good basis for estimating the impact of fare changes on traffic. The fare change was accompanied by the extension of free transfer privileges between the three subway divisions and the institution of a combined fare for certain trips involving both surface and subway travel. But fortunately it was possible to exclude the effect of these changes by careful selection of stations where these influences would not be important. More recently the fare was increased to 15 cents (25 July, 1953), but the results of this increase have not as yet been analyzed in the detail needed for the present purposes, though they seem to bear out in a general way the predictions based on the 1948 experience.

The results of attempting to fit a pattern of traffic and of its elasticity to the "boundary conditions" imposed by the available data are shown in table 14.1 In constructing this pattern, it was generally assumed that short-haul traffic was more elastic than long-haul; that for each day as a whole, traffic in the two directions between two given points would balance; that inbound traffic registered at turnstiles that failed to show up as passing the check point and could not be accounted for as stopping short of the check point (i.e., did not show up during the day as outbound traffic making the reverse trip) was traffic that traveled inwards to a junction point and then outwards again. It was necessary to make the rather dubious assumption that stations that segregated traffic in the two directions were representative of all stations; indeed, since the process of comparing inward registrations with the traffic recorded at the check point was possible only in a few cases (and very laboriously then), only a small sample even of the segregating stations was used in the estimates.

The volume of traffic in this table is, of course, that at the flat 10 cent fare in 1950; to obtain the pattern for other types of fare it is necessary to apply the variability coefficients to the amount by which the fare for the particular class of traffic exceeds or is less than 10 cents. Due to the rounding to the nearest million passengers, this leads to some rather extreme results for some of the smaller traffic categories. In terms of the overall picture, however, this is not serious.

The variability shown in this table is, of course, that caused by a general change in the uniform rate of fare, i.e., it represents the number of passengers who decide not to ride at all when the fare is raised by a uniform amount for all trips. If, however, a fare pattern is introduced in which there are time differentials, these differentials may well induce passengers to shift their trips from one time to another. Shifts of this character, of course, did not occur when the flat fare was raised to 10 cents, and they are not reflected in the figures in table 14.1. Indeed, there is virtually no direct evidence as to how great such a shift would be, nor would it be a simple matter to describe such responsiveness of traffic in general quantiative terms. Accordingly, in what follows attention will initially be confined to straight increases and decreases in the volume of various types of traffic, and a more or less arbitrary lump sum allowance will be made, where appropriate, for changes in the time at which passengers choose to travel.

Further, for the sake of simplicity the assumption will be made that traffic is in all cases a linear function of the fare. When carried to extremes this will obviously be absurd, but for present purposes this seems close enough, and any other assumption would have enormously complicated the calculations.

We are now in a position to evaluate the loss to the community as a whole that will result from the inefficient utilization produced by deviations of the fare from the marginal-cost level. Consider, for example, the case of counter-rush trips of six to eight miles to or from lower Manhattan, where our table shows a marginal cost of zero, a volume of traffic of 16 million passengers per year at a rate of 10 cents, and a responsiveness of 3 million passengers per year for each 5 cent change in the fare. If the fare were zero, 6 million additional passengers would be carried who were presumably not willing to pay 10 cents for these trips, but who are apparently willing to pay something. From our assumption of linearity of the demand function, we can assume that on the average these passengers would have been willing to pay 5 cents; the value of these 6 million additional trips can be set at $300,000, and this is then the measure of the inefficiency involved in setting the rate for this class of trip at 10 cents rather than zero. Or conversely, for the same trip in the reverse direction, with the peak of the rush, the table gives a marginal cost of 20 cents, a volume of traffic at 10 cents of 72 million passengers, and a variability of 5 million. Raising the fare to the marginal-cost level would thus cut this traffic to 62 million. The 10 million passengers who would thus drop out are presumably willing to pay 10 cents for the ride, but are not willing to pay 20 cents. They value the ride at something between 10 and 20 cents, and again, from our linearity assumption, one can say that on the average they value the trip at 15 cents, or altogether $1.5 million. But these trips are costing 20 cents each, at the margin either in terms of actual cost of providing the service or in terms of imposing more irksome conditions on other passengers – or perhaps a combination of both. On balance, for each of these passengers that is kept off the system there is a gain of 5 cents, or $500,000 in the aggregate. In general, the loss in efficient utilization resulting from a fare structure deviating from the marginal-cost level will equal the product of one-half the deviation in fare and the difference in volume of traffic.

This analysis can fairly readily be applied to determine the loss involved in the retention of a flat fare at various levels. The process can be expedited by grouping the data in table 14.1 according to marginal-cost levels, and then applying the flat fare, with the results shown in table 14.2. It is perhaps worth re-emphasizing that this table shows only the effects of the level of fares, and does not take into account the inefficiencies related to possible shifts in the time of riding. From this table it appears that the flat fare that would minimize the loss from inefficient utilization is about 5 cents, this loss rising fairly moderately as we go in either direction to 10 cents on one side or to free service on the other, and that the loss mounts rapidly as we push on to 15 or 20 cents. This indeed, is what might be expected, for in general, for any particular class of traffic, the loss tends to vary with the square of the deviation in fare from the marginal-cost level.

Particular interest attaches to the free service figure. We noted above that fare collection involved costs of the order of $12 million per year. If the elimination of these costs is credited to the free service figure (or, perhaps more directly, if the cost of fare collection is added to the loss from mal-use), free service turns out to be some $4 million better than the best flat fare in terms of efficient utilization and cost of collection combined. If obtaining revenue for the city were of no importance, free service would thus be a better mode of operation than any flat fare.

It is also fairly simple to examine the loss resulting from setting the fare uniformly 5 or 10 cents above the marginal-cost level. Table 14.2 shows that for each 5 cent fare change total traffic changes by 274 million, so that the loss from a 5 cent differential would be 2.5 cents times 274 million passengers, or $3.4 million. Raising the differential to 10 cents quadruples the loss, bringing it to $14.7 million.

Alternative Fare-Collection Schemes

We are now in a position to investigate more precisely what possibilities there might be for fare collection schemes aimed at economizing collection costs. We

Table 14.2 *Analysis of Results by Marginal Cost Levels*

	Marginal cost, cents per trip						Total
	0	5	10	15	20	25	
Passengers at 10¢ fare, millions	414	724	224	132	52	144	1690
Variability, millions of passengers per 5¢ fare change	117	114	22	8	4	9	274
Passengers at marginal cost fare, millions	648	838	224	124	44	117	1995
Over or under use at 10¢ fare, millions of passengers	−234	−114	0	8	8	27	
Average loss per passenger, ¢	5	2.5	0	2.5	5	7.5	
Amount of net loss, $million	11.7	2.85	0	0.2	0.4	2.025	17.275
Over or under use at 15¢ fare, millions of passengers	−351	−228	−22	0	4	18	
Average loss per passenger, ¢	7.5	5.0	2.5	0	2.5	5.0	
Amount of loss, $million	26.32	11.40	0.55	0	0.1	0.9	39.27
Revenue at marginal cost rates $million	0	41.9	22.4	18.6	8.8	29.2	120.9
Rates 5¢ above marginal cost	5	10	15	20	25	30	
Passengers, million	531	724	202	116	40	108	1721
Revenues, $million	26.6	72.4	30.3	23.2	10.0	32.4	194.9

have already seen that the elimination of fare collection costs through the provision of free service has its attractions. Furthermore, the traffic with high marginal cost, which accordingly needs most to be controlled through the collection of a fare, is largely traffic that either travels to the downtown area in the morning or leaves from the downtown area in the evening. This observation leads immediately to the suggestion that fare collection facilities be confined to the downtown area, and that passengers who do not enter the downtown area be allowed to ride free.

In its most extreme form, this central collection scheme would involve having turnstiles only in the downtown area and in a zone two or three miles wide around it, with the turnstiles arranged so that in the morning fares would be collected from passengers leaving the subway, while in the evening fares would be collected as passengers enter the subway. Turnstiles would be arranged so that the fare could be changed from time to time, being a maximum of perhaps 20 cents within the downtown area at the peak of the rush, the fare being reduced as the time moves away from the rush and as the location moves away from the downtown area. No fare would be collected at any time at outlying stations, and no fare would be collected anywhere during nonrush hours.

Such a method of collection would eliminate two-thirds or more of the fare-collection costs, since less than half of the stations would require collection agents at all, and even those would require agents for around eight hours a day, weekdays only. And while some wasteful over-or-under-utilization would occur, it would involve relatively little loss, since most of the trips for which no fare is collected have very low marginal cost in any case. There would be some undue stinting of short-haul riding in the downtown area during the rush, and there would be perhaps some excessive riding during the rush through the downtown area and out in the opposite direction, for which no fare would be collected even though the cost is at a maximum. Rough estimates give for this scheme a collection cost of $4 million, and loss from over or under use of $5 million; even if, in addition, we add $2 million for the loss from travel at the wrong time, the total is still only $11 million; whereas, for the zone-time fare, the cost of collection above is estimated to amount to $15 million. From the point of view of efficiency and collection cost combined, therefore, the central collection scheme is the best of those that have been considered.

Other fare schemes can also be evaluated in terms of their efficiency. A fare approximating a fixed rate per mile is often advocated as being more equitable than the flat fare. Efficiency-wise, however, it seems to be so little better than the flat fare that the extra costs of collection, which are substantially the same as for the zone-time fare, absorb most if not all of the gain. This is because the costs do not in general tend to vary proportionately with mileage, and a straight mileage fare overcharges the long-haul rider almost as much as the flat fare undercharges him. Some improvement is possible if the fare is graduated according to distance, with the longer hauls paying less per mile. The real factor affecting cost, however, is the degree to which the trip involves congested portions of the system. If a fare is wanted that depends only on the points between which the passenger travels and not on the time, then it is possible, by charging more for portions of trips in the congested areas than for portions of trips in the outlying or uncongested areas, to achieve a worthwhile improvement in efficiency as compared to the flat fare. The results, however, remain substantially inferior to those obtainable with the zone-time fare, and if one is going to go to the expense of putting in the type of

Table 14.3 *Efficiency versus Revenue for Various Fares. All entries are in millions of dollars*

| Fare scheme | Amount of inefficiency | | | | Revenue gain or loss compared to 15¢ flat fare |
	Cost of collection of fare	Over or under use	Untimely use	Total	
Free service	0	14.1	16.6	30.7	−200
Flat fares:					
5¢	12.5	8.8	14.0	35.3	−130
10¢	12.5	17.2	12.0	41.7	−52
15¢	12.5	39.3	10.0	61.8	0
20¢	12.5	75.0	8.0	95.5	+25
Zone-time fares					
At marginal cost	15.0	—	—	15.0	−93
5¢ above marg. cost	15.0	6.8	—	21.8	−19
10¢ above marg. cost	15.0	27.4	—	42.4	+25
Central collection:					
5–20¢; 8 hr	3.5	4.8	2.5	10.8	−127
5–20¢; 18 hr	5.0	3.2	3.0	11.2	−110
5–25¢; 18 hr	5.0	6.3	3.0	14.3	−73
5–35¢; 18 hr	5.0	11.7	2.5	19.2	−63
5–25¢; 5¢ minimum	13.0	7.6	2.5	23.1	−45
Mileage rates:					
1.0¢ per mile	14.5	11.1	14.0	39.6	−92
1.5¢ per mile	14.5	14.0	12.0	40.5	−47
2.0¢ per mile	14.5	22.0	10.0	46.5	−16
2.5¢ per mile	14.5	35.0	8.0	57.5	+1
Graduated distance:					
3¢–1¢ per mile	14.5	25.2	10.0	49.4	−7
Differentiated mileage:					
3¢–1¢ per mile	14.5	16.1	11.0	41.6	−14
4¢–1¢ per mile	14.5	26.6	10.0	51.1	+18

exit turnstile required for a zone fare of any kind, it would seem desirable to incur the relatively slight additional cost of arranging for variation of the fare according to time of day.

If the need of the city for revenue were not a factor, so that, in effect, a dollar in the hands of a passenger is as good as a dollar in the city treasury, one could perhaps base the selection of a fare structure on efficiency and collection costs and decide for the central collection scheme, among those presented here. But the city has no painless method of securing money from its citizens, and, in effect, to secure a dollar for the city from other tax sources will usually require the citizens to give up more than a dollar, directly or indirectly. Indeed, a very appropriate way to express the intensity of the city's needs for revenue is to estimate how much citizens will probably be required to give up, directly or indirectly, for each additional dollar of net revenue that the city secures by increased taxes or sources other than the transit system. While such a figure will undoubtedly be subject to a wide margin of error, it is a reasonably objective way to describe the aspects of the situation that are important in the present context.

Indeed, if we are given such a figure, it will then be possible for us to examine our data in order to determine how far the fare structure should be pushed in the direction of providing more revenue for the city, if we are to minimize the aggregate loss (including in this aggregate the losses resulting from the imperfections and necessary ill effects of the city's tax system, as well as the losses from inefficient utilization of the transit system).

It is one thing, however, to state that in principle such a figure should be used as a basis for the computation, and quite another to find a concrete figure to use in a given instance. Such a figure represents a fairly novel concept to most people who are concerned with taxation. Since this figure is based to a considerable extent on secondary and hidden effects, there are likely to be wide variations in judgment expressed as to its magnitude, particularly as the figure would imply – at different levels – different attitudes towards the whole spectrum of public activities as against private enterprise. In the context of New York City, the situation is additionally clouded by the far from cordial relations existing between city hall and Albany concerning the city finances.

Nevertheless, to avoid stalling on this point, I can perhaps set forth a few hunches as to what such a figure would be under various circumstances. At one extreme, even for a city whose finances are in good shape – with a tax system consisting of well-conceived taxes efficiently administered – it is probable that for every dollar added to the net tax revenues of the city it can be expected that there will be at least 10 cents' worth of damage done somewhere in the city's economy – in addition to the direct transfer of purchasing power from the taxpayer to the city. On the other hand, if the cost of net revenue to the city should rise as high as 50 percent, I would be inclined to suspect that city of being in very grave trouble indeed. As a figure to work with, perhaps we can split the difference and use 30 percent as a figure that is probably higher than it ought to be, but may represent what exists.

Introducing the revenue consideration changes the relative standing of the various fare systems considerably. One method of getting more revenue out of the

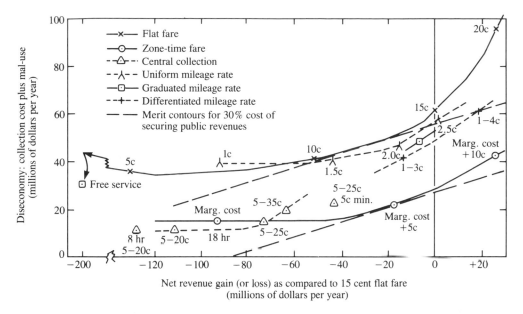

Figure 14.1 Revenue in Relation to Diseconomy for Various Fare
Structures

central collection system, for example, is to extend the hours of collection to cover eighteen of the twenty-four hours, collecting on a pay-as-you-leave basis from, say, 6 a.m. to 2 p.m., and on a pay-as-you-enter basis from 2 p.m. to midnight, the rate being 5 cents for the nonrush hours. This increases collection costs somewhat, but does cut down on the excess use to an extent sufficient to offset this cost, leaving the additional revenues as gravy. Pushing the central collection system much beyond this, however, makes the efficiency drop much more sharply than for the zone-time fare, since the revenues must be obtained from a smaller proportion of the total traffic, and there is less discrimination between the high-elasticity, short-haul traffic and the long-haul, low-elasticity traffic. Thus, by the time we push central-collection rates up to a maximum of 35 cents, the overall efficiency is no better than that for the zone-time schedule producing approximately the same net revenue. This is shown in figure 14.1, where an attempt has been made to indicate in a general way the relations between the losses from inefficient utilization and fare-collection costs, and the impact on the city finances for different types of fare structure at varying levels of fare.

Figure 14.1 enables one to determine, for any given type of fare, and for any given level of financial stringency expressed in terms of a marginal cost of public revenues, what the appropriate level of fare is. If the marginal cost of public revenues is 30 percent, for example, the best fare structure of those shown is a zone-time fare pitched at a level about 7 cents above marginal costs (possibly with a maximum fare of 25 cents to permit the use of a quarter as entrance coin, and to quiet political outcries that might be provoked by a higher fare). If on the other hand the marginal cost of public revenues is down to a 10 percent level, the best fare structure would be a central collection system on a 5–25 cent basis, eighteen hours a day. If one is restricted entirely to flat fares, the appropriate level for a 30 percent degree of financial stringency is 12.5 cents, the 10 cent fare being appropriate to a 10 percent level of financial stringency. At the present 15 cent fare level, every additional dollar collected by the Transit Authority from subway riders is costing the riders nearly $1.60.

Distribution of Income Considerations

The above analysis is still incomplete in that it neglects the effect of the fare structure on the distribution of income. If, indeed, the city were completely indifferent as to the income groups from which it derives its revenues, the above analysis could stand. And there are those who would claim that the distribution of income is no concern of government generally; or, perhaps, merely that this is primarily the concern of federal and state governments that are able to levy progressive income and estate taxes, and that it should be no concern of local governments. Nevertheless, there are certainly those who would take issue with this point of view and would hold that insofar as it can do so without undue prejudice to other objectives, city revenues should be as progressive as possible in their incidence.

Viewed as a source of city revenue, an increase in transit fares is about as regressive a tax as can well be imagined. It falls on nearly every income class in an almost flat per capita amount, regardless of income, with the exception perhaps of the unemployed and the indigent at one extreme and the wealthy who use taxicabs and automobiles at the other. Accordingly one can well be less than completely indifferent as between such a source of revenue and others available to the city, and be willing to incur costs of 30 percent or more in securing revenue elsewhere, before being willing to incur costs of say 20 percent in the collection of revenue from such a regressive source.

How far to go in this direction can of course be only a completely subjective matter, depending as it does almost entirely on the underlying attitudes of the individual concerning the distribution of income. If there were some major source of revenue used by the city that did, in fact, have an incidence as regressive as the transit fare increase, then it would be possible to take the marginal costs associated with such a revenue as an indication of how far the public generally is willing to go in obtaining revenues from a regressive source. But even the most regressive type of sales tax falls considerably short of the regressivity of a fare increase; the only substantial tax that seems to come at all close is a tax on cigarettes. A cigarette tax appears to have a very low marginal cost associated with it, at least if only the interests of the local community are considered.

Thus about all that can be said with any definiteness on this score is that considerations of distribution of income would lead to the selection of a somewhat lower level of fare than would otherwise be the case, but by how much is open to debate.

Distributional considerations enter the picture in another way when we come to comparing flat fares with zone-time fares, or indeed any fare varying with time. It is often alleged that rush-hour riders are predominantly workers with lower income than the nonrush-hour riders – said to be predominantly persons of leisure – and that, hence, the change to a zone-time fare would shift the burden to lower incomes. If it were true that rush-hour riders actually have on the average lower incomes than the nonrush-hour riders, rather than merely being predominantly members of vocal and politically influential labor unions, this would be a factor to be weighed. But it is by no means clear that this is the case. Rush-hour riders are predominantly persons who have jobs at reasonably standard wage rates, whereas many low-paid occupations such as domestic servants, charwomen, night watch-men, and the like involve odd hours or outlying places of work, so that these low-paid groups become part of the nonrush hour traffic. Many nonrush-hour riders are wives or dependents, so that the zone-time fare would shift the burden to the benefit of large families, which, in turn, are often less well off economically in terms of their greater needs. Moreover, since most impoverished residential areas are fairly close to the downtown area, the differentiation of fare by distance will tend to favor the lower income groups: this factor argues for adopting the zone-time plan rather than the central-collection one.

What does seem likely is that the groups whose fares would be increased under a zone-time plan are much more homogeneous as to income than the remaining riders, and that even if the average income of the two groups were about the same, there would be a tendency for the change to zone-time to shift the burden of transit costs from both ends of the income distribution toward the middle. Offhand, most persons would probably be inclined to give more weight to the desirable shift from the low-income groups to the middle-income groups than to the undesirable shift from the upper-income groups to the middle-income groups. This would be true on the ground that the amounts involved will be more crucial to the lower-income groups than to either of the others, and that adjustments elsewhere in the tax system can usually be made more readily as between middle- and upper-income groups than between middle and lower.

In any case the effect of the change in fare structure on the distribution of income is likely to be extremely mild compared to the effect of the overall changes in volume of revenue secured from transit riders. It is almost certainly not of sufficient importance to be seriously considered in the selection of a fare structure, as distinguished from the setting of the fare level.

Popular Acceptance

The fare structures thus indicated on grounds of efficiency, collection cost, revenue, and income distribution may turn out at many points to go counter to popular notions of what is equitable or proper. In particular there will be considerable criticism of a scheme that requires the crowded rush-hour standee to pay more for his ride than the nonrush-hour rider who rides in relative comfort. A more serious paradox is that if fares are varied according to the degree of congestion on the individual lines, then the construction of a new line into an area will be the occasion not only of an improvement in service, but also for the lowering of fares in that direction; residents of areas not so favored will feel that it is adding insult to injury not only to leave them with inferior facilities but also to charge them a higher fare to boot. Indeed, this feeling may be so strong as to make it politically imprudent to carry marginal cost pricing to this length; accordingly fares might be made more or less uniform in relation to the downtown area, the only geographical discrimination then being in the radial direction rather than a circumferential one. A possible exception to this general rule could probably be made in New York in the case of the 3rd Avenue "El": this facility happens to be relatively underutilized; but it is also generally considered to give inferior service. Charging a lower fare on this line than on the parallel Lexington Avenue line might not only be politically acceptable, but it also would be in line with cost differentials, thereby serving the useful purpose of diverting traffic from Lexington Avenue to Third Avenue, and so relieving the fairly intense rush-hour congestion that occurs on the Lexington Avenue line.

Ecology and Sociology

The study of the effects of such a fare change on the location of various economic activities, on hours of work, and the whole pattern of life of the city is too complicated a matter to be gone into at length here; an adequate discussion would involve a rather intricate study of city planning. One can indicate, however, the tendency of such a fare plan to encourage the establishment of places of employment in peripheral areas, so as to take advantage of the counter-rush fares; incentives to move working hours, so as to avoid the transit peak; and possibly the deferment of new transit construction until it is really needed as well as the more rapid development of an area such new lines serve when they *are* built. Most of these tendencies seem, if anything, to be desirable on other grounds besides those of transit costs. But if not, the fare structure would limit the incentive to the magnitude appropriate to the differences in transit cost, and would avoid the danger involved – where these objectives are promoted through regulation, public campaigns and pressures, and the like – that the mark will be overshot. That is, that in obtaining the desired relief to transit peaks, other overlooked losses will be occasioned that outweigh the transit benefits. With the incentive provided by the appropriate fare differential, if other losses outweigh the transit gains, the incentive of the fare differential will presumably be insufficient to bring about the change.

There is thus a presumption that fares at marginal cost are at a level tending to bring about an economical location of industry and organization of economic activity, at least insofar as the influence of these arrangements on the cost of transportation is a consideration. If such fares do not actually exist, it may even be desirable for city planners to compute such fares and have them in mind as a convenient means of treating transportation costs in their plans.

However, when it comes to considering the effects of fare structure changes on the use of alternative methods of transportation, the effects are direct and important enough to warrant special consideration. First, we may note that if the cost to the users of such alternative facilities happened to reflect, reasonably accurately the social costs occasioned by increments of such use, then the level of transit fares that would furnish potential travelers with a proper guide as to which means to use – taking into consideration both their own convenience and the effects on others in the community – would be the marginal-cost level. And the social loss or waste occasioned by departures of fares from the marginal-cost levels will be properly measured by half the product of the departure from marginal cost (and the change in traffic that this brings about, as developed above). It may well be argued that users of private cars and taxis, and perhaps also of buses, do not, by and large, bear costs commensurate with the increment of costs that their use imposes. This is particularly likely to be true of travel in congested areas during rush hours; and, if it is, this would be an argument for keeping transit fares somewhat lower than otherwise, particularly for travel that competes with congested surface travel. To some extent the peak of street traffic congestion occurs at different times and places than the peak of transit conges-tion, so that the effect of this consideration would not be uniform. In particular, morning rush-hour street traffic is in many areas relatively lighter compared to transit traffic than is the case in the evening. Probably the main consideration of this sort would be the possibility of recapturing some of the short-haul taxi riders, especially groups, and for this purpose the shift to graduation according to distance is especially important. Without further study, however, it is not at all clear just what effect considerations of this sort would have upon the optimum-fare schedule, except that they do not seem to argue for any very substantial modifications of the proposed patterns.

Summary

We can see thus that consideration of the effects of the fare structure on the efficiency with which transit facilities are utilized leads to a fare structure rather drastically different from those now generally in use, and generally at a level which would yield revenues falling considerably short of covering total costs. If due consideration is also given to costs of collection, the need for revenue, and the distribution of income, the appropriate fare structure is modified somewhat, but still retains the salient features of higher fares for rush-hour trips over congested sections, and a revenue yield falling substantially short of covering the total costs – at least in the case of rapid transit service of the character of the New York subways.

One further salient point may be noted, and that is that an analysis of this sort implies rather strongly that operation of a transit system on a self-liquidating or cost-covering basis, either by a private utility company or by a public authority, will inevitably fall considerably short of arriving at an optimum adjustment. Any governmental unit whose finances are in reasonably good shape can materially improve the overall welfare of its residents by raising the rates of some appropriate taxes and lowering transit fares to a level conducive to more efficient utilization of the transit facilities. Benefits of this sort are nearly always possible, to some degree, even if the level of fares is reduced without changing the pattern of the fare structure; moreover this holds true for nearly all types of transit operations, whether subway train, trolley, bus, or moving belt contraptions.

On the other hand, even if a self-liquidating basis is retained, either with private or public operation, modification of the fare structure in the general direction of the zone-time fare basis while keeping net revenues constant will often be capable of greatly increasing the value of the service to the public, even though it may not be capable of doing very much for the revenues of a hard-pressed operating unit.

15

·

Pricing in Urban
and Suburban Transport

I will begin with the proposition that in no other major area are pricing practices so irrational, so out of date, and so conducive to waste as in urban transportation.

Two aspects are particularly deficient: the absence of adequate peak-off differentials and the gross underpricing of some modes relative to others.

In nearly all other operations characterized by peak-load problems, at least some attempt is made to differentiate between the rates charged for peak and for off-peak service. Where competition exists, this pattern is enforced by competition: resort hotels have off-season rates; theaters charge more on weekends and less for matinees. Telephone calls are cheaper at night, though I suspect not sufficiently so to promote a fully efficient utilization of the plant. Power rates are varied to a considerable extent according to the measured or the imputed load factor of the consumer, and in some cases, usually for special-purpose uses such as water heating, according to the time of use. In France, this practice is carried out logically by charging according to season and time of day for all consumption but that of the smallest domestic consumers; rate changes at the consumers' meters are triggered by a special frequency signal actuating a tuned relay which connects or disconnects auxiliary registers. But in transportation, such differentiation as exists is usually perverse. Off-peak concessions are virtually unknown in transit. Such concessions as are made in suburban service for "shoppers' tickets" and the like are usually relatively small, indeed are often no greater than those available in multi-trip tickets not restricted to off-peak riding, and usually result in fares still

American Economic Review, 53 (1963); reprinted in *Public Policy and the Modern Corporation*, Grunewald and Bass, Eds. (Appleton Century Crofts, 1966), pp. 168–81; also in *Readings in Urban Transportation*, George M. Smerk, Ed. (Indiana University Press, 1968), pp. 120–33; also in *The Modern City: Readings in Urban Economics,* David W. Rasmussen and Charles T. Haworth, Eds. (Harper and Row, 1973), pp. 179–89.

far above those enjoyed by regular commuters who are predominantly peak-hour passengers.

In the case of suburban railroad fares, the existing pattern is even contrary to what would be most profitable in terms of the relative elasticities of demand. Both on a priori grounds and on the basis of the analysis of the historical experience recently made by Elbert Segelhorst in a forthcoming Columbia dissertation, it is clear that the price elasticity of the off-peak traffic, at current fare levels at least, is substantially higher than that of peak-hour traffic. If, for example, the average suburban family spends $300 per year for commuting and peak-hour trips and $50 per year for occasional off-peak trips and the commutation fares were increased by 5 percent, causing a 1 percent drop in this traffic, while off-peak fares were reduced 40 percent, with a 30 percent increase in traffic, gross revenues per commuting family would go up from $350.00 to $350.85, with operating costs if anything reduced slightly, since nearly all costs are determined by the peak traffic level. The riding public would on the average be substantially better off: the above typical family, if it maintained the same pattern of usage, would pay only $315 + $30 = $345 instead of $350 as formerly, and any adaptation that it chose to make to the new rates would represent a further benefit, since the alternative of no change would still be open to it if it preferred. Things may not work out quite this neatly in practice, but the potential for substantial gains from even more drastic revisions in the rate structure is certainly there.

Fare collection procedures are sometimes urged as an excuse for not going to a more rational fare structure, but here there has been a deplorable lag behind what a little ingenuity or modern technology makes possible. There would be relatively little difficulty in devising apparatus for collecting subway fares on as elaborate an origin, destination, and time basis as might be desired, simply by dispensing a coded check at the entrance turnstile against the deposit of an interim fare, this check being deposited in an exit turnstile which will then either refund any excess or release only on the deposit of the remainder of the fare. Bus fares represent a problem that has yet to be satisfactorily solved, but considering the vast waste of the time of operators and passengers through delays caused by present fare collection methods, a concerted attack on this problem should yield high dividends. For commuter railroads, the possibility exists of issuing machine-readable subscriber's cards, with passengers making a record of their trips by inserting the card in a register at the origin and destination stations and being billed according to the time, origin, and destination of the trips actually made by the subscriber, his family, and guests. Something like this seems to be in the offing for the new San Francisco system, which in many respects is more of a commuter service than an urban transit system. Actually, it is not even necessary to enclose the stations in order to use such a system: proper registering at the stations can be enforced by dispensing a dated seat check to be displayed during the trip and deposited in registering out at the destination.

Even short of such mechanization, existing ticketing arrangements are needlessly clumsy, involving in many cases a duplication of effort between station agent and conductor and fairly elaborate accounting and auditing procedures. The New York Central has recently taken a step forward in this respect by arranging to mail monthly commutation tickets to patrons and receive payment by mail. Gross delinquency appears to be running appreciably less than the saving in ticket agents' time, and the net credit loss is undoubtedly much less than this, since many who fail to return or pay for their tickets in fact do not use them, as when they die or move away. Another wrinkle worth trying would be the use of a universal form of multi-ride ticket, to be sold by ticket agents or conductors at a flat price of $5.00 or $10.00, validated for bearer and those accompanying him, with a liberal time limit, for a number of rides or trip units depending on the stations between which it is designated to be used by appropriate punches at time of sale. An off-peak differential could be provided in conjunction with this type of ticket by providing that two units would be charged for an off-peak ride as against three units for a peak-hour ride. The ticket itself, for a typical suburban route, need be no larger than an ordinary playing card. Accounting would be greatly simplified, conductors' cash fare transactions would be both simplified and greatly reduced in number, and the use of the service would become much more convenient for passengers. Such a ticket would provide a more effective off-peak differential than the shoppers' type of ticket, since those who are either going or returning during the peak or are returning at a later date cannot usually avail themselves of such tickets.

But while suburban and transit fare structures are seriously deficient, the pricing of the use of urban streets is all but nonexistent. Superficially, it is often thought that since reported highway expenditures by the state and federal government are roughly balanced by highway tax and license revenues, the motorist is on the whole paying his way. But what is true on the average is far from true of users of the more congested urban streets. Much of the expenditure on such streets is borne by city budgets supported slightly if at all by explicit contributions from highway sources, in most states. More important, much of the real economic cost of providing the space for city streets and highways does not appear in the accounts at all, being concealed by the fact that this space has usually been "dedicated" to the public use at some time in the past. It is extremely difficult to make close evaluations from the scanty and scattered data available, but very roughly it appears to me that if we take the burden of all the gasoline and other vehicular taxes borne by motorists by reason of their use of city streets, this amounts to only about a third of the real economic cost of the facilities they use. In current terms, the high marginal cost of increased street space becomes painfully apparent whenever a street widening scheme is evaluated. Even in terms of long-range planning, urban expressways cost many times as much as expressways in rural areas built to comparable specifications, and while the flow of traffic may be greater, this is not enough to come anywhere near amortizing the cost out of the taxes paid by the traffic flowing over the urban expressways. Even when tolls are charged in conjunction with special features such as bridges or tunnels, these seldom cover the cost of the connecting expressways and city streets. And except where the street layout is exceptionally favorable, such tolls usually have an unfavorable effect on the routing of traffic.

The perversity of present pricing practices is at its height, perhaps, for the East River crossings to Long Island and Brooklyn. Here the peculiar political logic is that the older bridges are in some sense "paid for," and hence must be free, while tolls must be charged on the newer facilities. The result is that considerable traffic is diverted from the newer facilities that have relatively adequate and less congested approaches to the older bridges such as the Manhattan and the Queensboro bridges, which dump their traffic right in the middle of some of the worst congestion in New York. The construction of the proposed expressway across lower Manhattan from the Holland Tunnel to the Manhattan and Williamsburgh bridges would be at least less urgent, if not actually unwarranted, in view of its enormous cost, if, as would seem possible, traffic could be diverted from the Manhattan Bridge to the Brooklyn-Battery tunnel by imposing tolls on the Manhattan and other East River bridges and reducing or removing the toll on the tunnel. The delusion still persists that the primary role of pricing should always be that of financing the service rather than that of promoting economy in its use. In practice there are many alternative ways of financing; but no device can function quite as effectively and smoothly as a properly designed price structure in controlling use and providing a guide to the efficient deployment of capital.

The underpricing of highway services is even more strongly pronounced during peak hours. Even if urban motorists on the average paid the full cost of the urban facilities, rush-hour use would still be seriously underpriced; moreover, this underpricing would be relatively more severe than for transit or commutation service. This is because off-peak traffic on the highways and streets is a much larger percentage of the total than is the case for either transit or commutation traffic; and therefore in the process of averaging out the costs, much more of the costs properly attributable to the peak can be shifted to the shoulders of the off-peak traffic than can be thus shifted in the case of transit or commutation service. The effect of this is that while the commutation fare problem is chiefly one of the overpricing of off-peak travel, and to a minor extent if at all one of underpricing of peak travel, the problem of the pricing of automobile travel is chiefly that of remedying the underpricing of peak travel, and to a relatively minor extent if at all of the overpricing of off-peak travel. These two relationships combine to give the result that even if motor traffic and commuter train traffic each on the whole fully paid their way on the basis of a uniform charge per trip, the proportion by which the peak-hour motorist would be subsidized by the off-peak motorist would be far greater than the proportion by which the peak-hour commuter is subsidized by the off-peak commuter.

A quantitative indication of the seriousness of the problem of peak-hour automobile traffic is derivable from some projections made for Washington, DC. Two alternative programs were developed for taking care of traffic predicted under two alternative conditions, differing chiefly as to the extent to which express transit service would be provided. The additional traffic lanes required for the larger of the two volumes of traffic would be needed almost solely to provide for this added rush-hour traffic, the less extensive road system being adequate for the off-peak traffic even at the higher overall traffic level. Dividing the extra cost by the extra rush-hour traffic, it turned out that for each additional car making a daily trip that contributes to the dominant flow, during the peak hour, an additional investment of $23,000 was projected. In other words, a man who bought a $3,000 car for the purpose of driving downtown to work every day would be asking the community, in effect, to match his $3,000 investment with $23,000 from general highway funds. Or if the wage earners in a development were all to drive downtown to work, the investment in highways that this development would require would be of the same order of magnitude as the entire investment in a moderate-sized house for each family. It may be that the affluent society will be able to shoulder such a cost, but even if it could there would seem to be many much more profitable and urgent uses to which sums of this magnitude could be put. And even if we assume that staggering of working hours could spread the peak traffic more or less evenly over three hours, this would still mean $8,000 per daily trip, even though achievement of such staggering would represent an achievement second only to the highway construction itself. At 250 round trips per year, allowing 10 percent as the gross return which a comparable investment in the private sector would have to earn to cover interest, amortization, and property and corporate income taxes, this amounts to over $3.00 per round trip, or, on a one-hour peak basis, to $9.00 per round trip, if staggering is ruled out. This is over and above costs of maintenance or of provision for parking. When costs threaten to reach such levels, it is high time to think seriously about controlling the use through pricing.

It is sometimes thought that pricing of roadway use would apply chiefly to arterial streets and highways and that it would have no application to streets used mainly for access, which should allegedly be paid for by property taxes on the abutting property to which access is given. But the relevant criterion is not the function performed, but the degree of congestion that would obtain in the absence of pricing. To be sure, there would be little point in levying a specific charge for the use of suburban residential side streets or lightly traveled rural roads, since the congestion added by an increment in traffic is virtually nil in such circumstances and the wear and tear usually negligible. In effect, at these levels of traffic the economies of scale are such that marginal cost is only a small fraction of the average cost. But this does not hold for roadways used for access at the center of a city. A truck making a delivery on a narrow side street may cause as much congestion and delay to others as it would in many miles of running on an arterial highway. Even in the case of a cul-de-sac that is used exclusively for access and carries no through traffic, a firm with frequent deliveries will make access more difficult for his neighbors; only by specific pricing of such use can the firm requiring much access be differentiated from firms requiring relatively little, and encouraged to locate where its activities will be less burdensome to the remainder of the community; or to receive and ship goods at times when less congestion is generated. Some of the worst traffic congestion in New York occurs as a result of the way access is had to firms in the garment district; restrictions on truck size and exhortations have produced only minor improvement. It seems likely that a suitable charge for such use of road space would be more acceptable than an arbitrary and drastic ban, and that with a definite financial incentive methods might be found to avoid the creation of congestion.

Talk of direct and specific charges for roadway use conjures up visions of a clutter of toll booths, an army of toll collectors, and traffic endlessly tangled up in queues. Conventional methods of toll collection are, to be sure, costly in manpower, space, and interference with the smooth flow of traffic. Furthermore, unless the street configuration is exceptionally favorable, tolls often contribute to congestion over parallel routes. However, with a little ingenuity, it is possible to devise methods of charging for the use of the city streets that are relatively inexpensive, produce no interference with the free flow of traffic, and are capable of adjusting the charge in close conformity with variations in costs and traffic conditions. My own fairly elaborate scheme involves equipping all cars with an electronic identifier which hopefully can be produced on a large-scale basis for about $20 each. These blocks would be scanned by roadside equipment at a fairly dense network of cordon points, making a record of the identity of the car; these records would then be taken to a central processing plant once a month and the records assembled on electronic digital computers and bills sent out. Preliminary estimates indicate a total cost of the equipment on a moderately large scale of about $35 per vehicle, including the identifier; the operating cost would be approximately that involved in sending out telephone bills. Bills could be itemized to whatever extent is desired to furnish the owner with a record that would guide him in the further use of his car. In addition, roadside signals could be installed to indicate the curent level of charge and enable drivers to shift to less costly routes where these are available.

Other methods have been devised in England, where the country can less well afford the vast outlays demanded by our rubber-tired sacred cow, and where street layouts are such as to make provision for large volumes of vehicular traffic both more costly and more destructive of civic amenities. One scheme suggested for use in a pilot scheme for the town of Cambridge involves the use of identifiers to actuate a tallying register, the rate of tallying being governed by impulses the frequency of which would vary according to the degree of traffic congestion existing in the zone in which the car is reported to be. Another extremely simple and low-cost but less automatic device would consist of a meter installed in each car so as to be visible from outside, which could be wound up by the insertion of a token sold at an appropriate price – the token being subject to inspection through a window and being destroyed when the subsequent token is brought into place. The driver can control the rate at which the meter runs down by a lever or switch which simultaneously displays a signal which will indicate to outside observers the rate currently being charged. The driver is then required to keep this signal set to correspond with the rate in effect in the zone in which he is driving as indicated by appropriate wayside signals. Extremely simple methods of varying the rate at which the meter runs down have been devised in England, which for the time being I must treat as confidential. The rate can appropriately be a time rate rather than a distance rate, since the greater the congestion the greater is the appropriate charge, so that no connection to the wheels is needed and the whole meter can be extremely compact, rugged, and cheap. The chief difficulty with this method is the likelihood that drivers will "forget" to turn the rate of the meter up promptly on entering a higher rate zone, but given a reasonable amount of policing this difficulty might be overcome after an initial period of habituation.

A slightly more elaborate version of this method would call for the changes in the meter rate to be actuated automatically in response to signals emitted from wayside equipment at the boundaries of the various zones. This would probably raise the cost to something above the level of the response block method. On the other hand, both this and the previous method are somewhat better adapted to serving to assess charges for parking as well as for moving about within an area, so that the cost of servicing and installing parking meters could be properly credited against the cost of the new system.

Another version would call for the meter to be run down by pulses emitted from cables laid along the roadway, with the pulse rate varied according to traffic density and other factors. Alternatively, the cables could be arranged to emit continuously and located across the roadway – the number of cables turned on at any one time being varied according to traffic conditions. Reliability of operation can be assured by using two alternative frequencies in alternate cables successively. The cables need not be spaced evenly, but for economy in operation may be placed in groups so that they can be energized from a single source. With either of these methods, any failure of the meter to operate could be checked by requiring the meter to be placed in plain view and arranging for a visible signal to be changed cyclically as the meter is actuated.

Adequate methods for enforcement of each of the schemes seem available which are reasonably simple, with the possible exception of the manual system, where minor negligience might be difficult to check and lead to major negligence. With identifier methods, the registering of the proper vehicle number could be checked by having a few of the detector stations equipped with apparatus to display the number being registered, which could be compared with the license plate by observers. Errors due to malfunction, as well as most fraudulent tampering, would show up as a matter of course during the processing of the records, as each record showing a car entering a zone must match the immediately succeeding record for that car leaving that zone. Cameras can also be arranged at some locations to take pictures of cars not producing a valid response signal. With meters, arrangements can be made to hold used and mutilated tokens in a sealed box; these could be inspected and their number compared with a nonresettable counter with a capacity not likely to be exceeded during the life of the car, as a part of an annual safety inspection program.

Ultimately, one would expect that all cars in an entire country would be equipped with meters or electronic identifiers. Initially, however, it would be necessary to make some provision for cars from other areas. Cars in transit or making infrequent visits to the congested area could be given the freedom of the city in a spirit of hospitality. Cars making a longer stay or more frequent visits would be required to equip themselves – say at cordon points established along the major arteries entering the controlled area. Unequipped cars would be prohibited from using the minor streets crossing the boundary of the controlled area. Such provisions would be particularly easy to enforce with electronic identifer methods: unequipped cars passing major control points would set off a camera; unequipped cars using routes prohibited to them would set off an alarm signal, facilitating their apprehension. With a meter system, checking on unequipped cars would have to be largely a manual operation and would probably be considerably less rigorous. Actually a similar problem occurs at present in enforcing provisions against the use of out-of-state license plates in a given state for longer than a limited period.

Such charging for street use could have a far-reaching impact on the pattern of urban transportation and even on the patterns of land use, by promoting a more economical distribution of traffic between various modes, the various modes being used in accordance with their suitability for the particular trip in the light of the costs involved, instead of, as at present, being chosen to suit the preferences and whims of the individual regardless of the impact on others. Motorists will no longer be manoeuvered into the position of being forced to pay for a luxury that they can ill-afford. Mass transportation will have an opportunity to develop in line with its inherent characteristics, eventually developing a quality and frequency of service that will in many cases be preferred even to the spuriously low-priced private car transportation that might be provided in the absence of a system of specific charges. Traffic-generating activities will tend to be located more rationally in relation to real transportation costs. For example, appropriate transportation charges might have been sufficient to have inhibited the construction of the Pan-American subway-jammer over Grand Central. Rapid vehicular transportation within congested areas, not now available at any price, will be generally available for meeting emergency and high priority needs where the cost is justified. Traffic will be routed more efficiently, so as to provide a smoother functioning of the roadway system as a whole. The levels of charge required to balance marginal cost and marginal benefit in the short run will provide a much more definite and reliable guide than is now available as to where and to what extent the provision of additional facilities can be justified. One can cite, for example, the extra half hour that the airlines have to allow during rush hours for the trip from East 38th Street to Idlewild, in spite of the fact that this route is almost entirely over grade-separated expressways.

One effect of such charging would be to change the relative attractiveness of different forms of mass transportation. Under present conditions, buses are involved in the same traffic tangle as the private car and are often further handicapped by their inferior maneuverability. It is then difficult to make a bus service sufficiently attractive relative to use of a private car to attract a sufficient volume of traffic to make the frequency of service satisfactory. In order to give the transit facility a chance to compete with the private automobile, it becomes necessary to provide some sort of reserved right of way. With buses this in theory takes the form of a lane reserved for them, but in practice this faces formidable problems in dealing with intersections and pickup points, and at best means that the lanes thus provided are likely to be underutilized, since it is seldom desirable to schedule just enough bus service to fully utilize a whole lane of capacity. These difficulties provide a strong argument for going to the very substantial expense of a rail rapid transit system.

With street use controlled by pricing, however, it is possible to insure that the level of congestion is kept down to the point at which buses will provide a satisfactory level of service, and rail rapid transit systems will be required only where a volume of traffic arises that will warrant their high cost on the basis of superior service and operating economies.

But while the most dramatic impact of street use pricing would be to permit the economical allocation of traffic among the various modes, it would be of great importance even in cases where the intermodal substitution is not a factor. Even in a community entirely without mass-transit service, street pricing could have an important function to perform. For example, traffic between opposite sides of town often has the choice of going right through the center of town or taking a more circuitous route. Left to itself, this traffic is likely to choose the direct route through the center, unless indeed the center becomes so congested as to make it quicker to go the longer way around. In the absence of pricing, one may be faced with the alternatives of either tolerating the congestion in the center of town, or if it is considered mandatory to provide congestion-free access to the center of town, of providing relatively costly facilities in the center of town adequate to accommodate through traffic as well. With pricing it becomes possible to restrict the use of the center streets to those having no ready alternative and provide for the through traffic on peripheral roadways at much lower cost. Without pricing, bypass routes, though beneficial, often attract only part of the traffic that they should carry for the greatest overall economy of transport.

Pricing of street use can in the long run have significant effects on the whole pattern of development of urban communities and on property values. While on general principles one can hardly imagine this impact to be other than beneficial, it is a little difficult to discern the net direction in which it would tend – for example, whether the concentration of activity at the center would increase or decrease. In order to gain insight into this problem I have been toying with a model which attempts to incorporate the essential element of choice of route, but in spite of drastically simplified structure and assumptions this model has so far resisted an analytical solution and will probably have to be worked out by simulation and successive approximations on a large electronic computer.

The model is as follows: Consider a community with a system of streets laid out in a circular and radial pattern; for simplicity, assume that the mesh of this network is small enough to be negligible; that is, that we can travel from any point in a radial and in a circumferential direction, but not at an angle. Thus any trip must be made up of radial segments and circular arcs. In effect, we assume perfect divisibility of road space, or that the capacity of a street is directly proportional to its width. In the neighborhood of any given point at a radius r from the center, a proportion of $w(r)$ of the area is devoted to streets, the remainder being devoted to business activities that generate one unit of traffic for each unit of net area; i.e., one unit of gross area originates and terminates $[1 - w(r)]$ units of traffic. The traffic originating at any one point has destinations distributed at random over the remainder of the business area; i.e., any tendency of related businesses to group themselves close together is neglected. The average cost of transportation per ton-mile (or passenger-mile) is given by some functional relation in which the density of traffic per unit roadway width is an argument. For example, we may put $x = A + B(t/w)^k$, where t is the volume of traffic in tons per hour and w is the width of the roadway in feet, A, B, and k being constants. A may be thought of as the operating cost of the vehicle, where the volume of traffic is negligible, the second term being the additional costs experienced due to delays resulting from congestion; k is the elasticity of this congestion cost, which can be thought of as being proportional to the number of added minutes required to cover a given distance as compared to the time required in the absence of conflicting traffic. A relation of this form was found to fit data from the Lincoln tunnel extremely well up to close to the point where a queue begins to accumulate with a value of k of about 4.5, so that the marginal congestion cost is some $k + 1 = 5.5$ times the average congestion cost per vehicle. In other words, according to this data, an individual who has to take ten minutes longer to make a given trip than he would if there were no interference from other traffic causes forty-five vehicle minutes of delay in the aggregate to other vehicles with whose movements he interferes. Unfortunately, comparable data for the more interesting case of travel over a network of city streets could not be found, but something of this order of magnitude is generally to be expected.

It can readily be shown that optimum allocation of the street space in a given small area between radial traffic and circular traffic calls for the space to be allocated in proportion to the traffic so that the average and marginal costs are the same in both directions. We can thus combine the circular traffic and the radial traffic and speak of the relation of costs to traffic in terms of aggregate ton-miles of traffic in both directions per acre of street area. Thus the cost per ton-mile can be taken to be $x = A + B(t/w)^k$, with x in cents per ton-mile, t in ton-miles per gross acre of land, and w the fraction of the land devoted to streets, in the particular neighborhood.

Given the density of traffic as a function of r, it is possible to determine the least-cost route for any given trip on an average-cost basis in which the shipper bears only the delay costs experienced by him, and alternatively on a marginal-cost basis where he must pay in addition a toll corresponding to the delay his trip imposes on others. By imposing the condition that the traffic distribution thus generated shall be one which produces the cost structure leading to the traffic distribution, one gets a differential equation which in principle can be solved to give equilibrium traffic patterns. The cost of this equilibrium traffic pattern can then be integrated over the entire area to give the total cost of transportation, and this can be done both for the marginal-cost case and the average-cost case to get the total saving in transportation cost over a given street network brought about by the pricing of street use.

Unfortunately, the differential equation that results is of the second order and third degree, and I suspect does not admit of an analytical solution in terms of well-known functions. The next step is recourse to solution of specific cases by successive approximations.

As a byproduct of this calculation, one could then also derive the equilibrium rentals that would be paid by businesses at various distances from the center, on the assumption that rental differentials would correspond to the differentials in the costs of transportation borne by the business; because of the symmetry of origins and destinations, it would make no essential difference whether shipping costs were borne entirely by shipper, entirely by consignee, or shared between them.

A further step in the analysis would be to take total cost as determined by the distribution $w(r)$ of land between business and transportation uses at various distances from the center and treat this as a calculus of variations problem of choosing the function $w(r)$ so as to minimize the total cost of transportation. In this way one could compare the pattern of land allocation that would be optimal without pricing to that which would be optimal with pricing. Considering the complexity of the problem, I hesitate to make any guesses as to the nature of this difference, except to speculate that it is likely to be somewhat surprising to many of us.

I will wind up by laying before you one final piece of unfinished business, which is the problem of developing criteria for determining how much of the area in a particular neighborhood should be devoted to transportation, given the pattern of rents in the area. Conventional cost–benefit analysis, if employed here at all, would tend to take the form of comparing the rent which private business would pay for the space with the reduction in transportation cost which would result from increasing the area used for transportation and decreasing the effective density of traffic. But in connection with the present model, this rule fails to yield optimal results. Let us imagine, to make things a little more explicit, that a Comprehensive Transportation Authority stood ready to rent or lease land, to be converted from or to transportation use, to or from private business, at a price reflecting the marginal productivity of land area in a particular location in reducing the total cost of carrying out a given number of ton-miles of traffic within a given neighborhood. In terms of our cost formula, the rental would be given by the partial derivative of total cost per unit area xt with respect to changes in the proportion of total area devoted to transportation w, the density of traffic t remaining unchanged. Thus

$$-\frac{\partial(xt)}{\partial W} = \frac{-\partial}{\partial w}\left(At + Bt^{k+1}w^{-k}\right) = +kBt^{k+1}w^{-k-1}.$$

A business will then move to a higher rent location only if the saving in transportation costs borne by the particular business is greater than the difference in rent. However, since transportation costs are in this model borne in part by the firms with which a given firm deals, only half of the change in the transportation costs of the goods he receives and ships resulting from his change in location will be felt directly by the firm making the change, so that on the whole a firm will fail to move unless the saving in the costs of the shipments to and from the firm is twice as great as the net increment in the costs of transportation resulting from the reapportionment of the space devoted to transportation. In other words, the conventional cost–benefit analysis in terms of going rents has a strong tendency to leave business uneconomically dispersed and to result in too much space in the center of the city being devoted to transportation.

This conclusion is derived from an admittedly highly simplified model, which neglects such factors as the clustering of interrelated firms, the wide variations in the ratios of land to transportation requirements of various activities, and the possibilities for creating additional space by construction of multi-story buildings, or for that matter, multi-level highways. But the model can plead not guilty to the charge of having ignored the journey to work and other passenger transportation, for, input-output analysis style, we can regard labor as the product of the household sector, and, Clayton Act to the contrary notwithstanding, as an article of commerce with a peculiarly high transport cost. The essential difference between this model and classical space economics models such as those of Von Thunen is that the latter imply a well-defined shadow price for each commodity at each point in the space, with transport taking place only between points where the price differential balances the transportation cost, whereas the present model allows for crosshauling and a certain amount of particularism in the relations between economic units. The real world presumably lies somewhere in between these two extremes. Study of journey-to-work patterns seems generally to reveal a situation a fairly long way from the Von Thunen extreme, with a great deal of cross-hauling of labor of roughly comparable skill. According to this, a cost–benefit analysis can justify devoting land to transportation only when the savings in transportation costs yield a return considerably greater than the gross rentals, including taxes, that private business would be willing to pay for the space. This in turn means that an even greater preference should be given to space economizing modes of transport than would be indicated by rent and tax levels. And our rubber-shod sacred cow is a ravenously space-hungry, shall I say, monster?

16

·

Congestion Theory
and Transport Investment

"Deepening" and "Widening" of Transport and Investment

Investment in transport facilities necessarily begins by being largely investment in the provision of new routes or new services under conditions of substantial indivisibilities and increasing returns to scale. Under these conditions the usual profitability tests for determining the desirability of specific investments lead generally to under- rather than to overinvestment in transportation facilities. At this stage, cost–benefit analysis needs to include substantial elements of consumers' surplus on the benefit side in order to arrive at correct evaluations.

As investment proceeds, however, larger and larger proportions of transportation investment are made primarily, or at least in large measure, to relieve congestion on existing routes and to expand overall capacity. In such instances criteria based on apparent profitability may be seriously misleading in the opposite direction, and when notions of consumers' surplus are narrowly applied, without regard to the overall situation, the errors may be compounded. This is especially likely to be the case where charges levied for the use of the existing and prospective competing facilities are far wide of the mark of representing marginal cost, as they often tend to be. It is this latter type of investment, designed to relieve congestion, with which this paper is concerned.

Types of Congestion

For purposes of economic analysis it is useful to distinguish at least six types of congested situations, though they are in fact often encountered in various

American Economic Review, 59 (1969) pp. 251–60; reviewed in *Traffic Systems Reviews and Abstracts* (1970), T–1072–EF.

combinations. These can be designated simple interaction, multiple interaction, bottleneck, triggerneck, network and control, and general density.

Single interaction occurs whenever two transportation units approach each other closely enough so that one or the other must be delayed in order to reduce the likelihood of a collision, no other units being sufficiently close to be immediately affected. This is the chief form of congestion encountered in light traffic. Total congestion delay tends to vary as the square of the volume of traffic; thus a motorist deciding on a trip under light traffic conditions will thereby inflict on others an amount of additional delay roughly equal to that which he himself will experience. (To be sure, for some types of vehicles the effect may not be symmetrical: slow-moving vehicles may tend to be relatively little delayed and fast-moving vehicles relatively more. The above relationship holds for an average vehicle.)

Multiple interaction tends to take place at higher levels of traffic density, short of capacity flows, where one can expect the average speed s to be a function of the flow of traffic x: $s = f(x)$. For traffic volumes ranging from about 0.5 to 0.9 of capacity, one can often fit a function of the form

$$z = t - t_0 = \frac{1}{s} - \frac{1}{s_0} = ax^k \tag{1}$$

where t is the time required to go a unit distance under actual conditions, t_0, is the time required under very light traffic conditions, z is the average delay per vehicle, and a and k are constant parameters. For a relationship of this form, the total increment of delay given by

$$\frac{d(zx)}{dx} = z + x\frac{dz}{dx} = ax^k + xak\,x^{k-1} \tag{2}$$

$$= (1 + k)z$$

that results from a unit increment of traffic thus works out to $k + 1$ times the delay experienced by the vehicle itself. That is, for every minute of delay directly experienced by the added vehicle, k minutes of delay are inflicted on the remaining traffic. For situations where considerable congestion exists, k is likely to be in the range of from 3 to 5 or even higher. The previous case is essentially that where $k = 1$.

The pure bottleneck situation, which is the one that will chiefly concern us here, is one where a relatively short route segment has a fixed capacity substantially smaller relative to traffic demand than that of preceding or succeeding segments. There is thus relatively little delay as long as traffic remains below the capacity of the bottleneck, though small amounts of delay may occur as a result of stochastic variations in the level of traffic flow when the average flow is just below capacity.

The important delays will occur when desired traffic flow continuously exceeds the capacity of the bottleneck for substantial periods. We then find that queues accumulate until either a period is reached when traffic demand is below capacity, or the prospect of waiting in the queue reduces the traffic demand by diverting it to another time or route or by suppressing the trip entirely.

A triggerneck situation develops from a bottleneck situation whenever the queue backed up from the bottleneck interferes with the flow of traffic not itself intending to use the bottleneck facility. The onset of incremental congestion may be quite sharp, and indeed in extreme circumstances a circular chain of triggerneck situations may bring traffic to a complete standstill, requiring that at least some of the vehicles involved actually back up before a forward movement can be resumed.

Network and control congestion results whenever the levels of traffic during the peak are reached requiring the application of additional control measures, whether in the form of regulations, stop signs, routing limitations, traffic lights, train controls, flight patterns and rules, or otherwise. Aside from the cost of these measures in themselves and even assuming that they are invoked only when the circumstances without them would be demonstrably worse, either from the standpoint of safety or delays, it is generally true that they cannot be applied with complete selectivity as to time and place, so that in most cases control measures required to take care of the most severe conditions will result in more delay under less severe conditions than would occur in the absence of controls, or with less restrictive controls adapted to the less severe conditions. Thus some of the delay experienced by off-peak traffic is in a medium–long-run sense caused by the increase in the peak traffic that made the controls necessary.

Finally there is a sense in which congestion costs in the long run are a function of the overall density of transportation flows in a given area for all modes combined and over all routes, even though some modes may contribute less to the total overall congestion relative to its traffic volume than other modes. Even if route separations are such that traffic on one mode has no immediate impact on traffic on the other modes, the construction of facilities to accommodate additional traffic on the one mode or route will not only encounter increased construction costs by reason of other existing facilities that cross its path, but such construction will at the same time be increasing the cost of constructing any other transportation facilities across its path in the future. In highly congested areas there is a very real sense in which long-run increasing costs may be encountered. It is very rarely that any account is taken, in the estimating of the cost of constructing facilities for a given transportation route and mode, of the increased costs of such future crossings by other links, even though good technical planning may sometimes make provision for such future crossings in the design.

Accidents as a Cost of Congestion

In addition to the cost of delays, the cost of accidents constitute an often overlooked element in the costs of congestion. While the incidence of traffic accidents does not rise with traffic density quite as rapidly as do time delays, one does expect, a priori, that as vehicle interactions per vehicle-mile increase, accidents per vehicle-mile will also increase. There is, indeed, a certain amount of empirical evidence that in a significantly wide range of situations this increase in accident rates with increasing traffic densities does in fact occur: for grade-separated limited access highways in California, it was found that the marginal increment in the number of accidents associated with an increment of traffic on a given type of highway was approximately 1.5 times the average accident incidence per vehicle-mile.[1] Thus whatever may be the effect on accidents of shifting traffic from other highways to grade-separated expressways, there is in addition a favorable effect on accidents of building roads of the same type to more ample dimensions and greater capacity, and an adverse effect on the accident rate per vehicle-mile of increasing the flow of traffic on a given roadway.

Before taking full credit for this benefit, however, it is necessary to examine the net safety effects of increasing total traffic flow overall, and of attracting traffic from other safer modes, such as rail transit. Doing too much in the name of safety considered in a narrow context can actually increase the overall death rate.

Construction to Ease Bottlenecks

Although the pure bottleneck situation is not typical of the general congestion picture, it is an important element in many cases of severe congestion and its relatively simple analysis does provide some valuable insights into the nature of the overall congestion problem.

Assume a situation in which $N = 7,200$ commuters want to make a daily trip via a given bottleneck, and that in the absence of congestion their times of passing the bottleneck point would be distributed evenly over a period between $t_a = 8:00$ a.m. and $t_b = 9:00$ a.m., this permitting each commuter to arrive at his downtown destination at a desired time. If the capacity of the bottleneck were to be enlarged to

$$v_m = \frac{N}{t_b - t_a} = 120 \text{ cars per minute,}$$

[1] See William Vickrey, "Automobile Accidents, Tort Law, Externalities, and Insurance," *Law and Contemporary Problems* (Summer, 1968), pp. 467–8.

then of course the capacity would just meet the requirements and no queue other than that due to stochastic variation would occur.

If the capacity is kept smaller than this, i.e., $v < v_m$, then it becomes impossible for all the commuters to arrive at their destinations just at the desired times. Some, at least, will have to arrive either late or early. In the absence of tolls the steady state that results will involve varying degrees of queuing, with those arriving at their offices closest to their desired times generally having to spend relatively more time in the queue than those who choose to push their arrival time further away from the desired time.

To keep the model simple, let us suppose that all commuters uniformly value time spent at home at $w_h = 2$ cents per minute, and time spent at the office at w_o, which for time prior to the desired starting time we suppose is $w_o = w_p = 1$ cent per minute, and for time after the desired starting time is $w_o = w_j = 4$ cents per minute. Time spent in the queue has a value of $w_q = 0$. It is readily seen that if an individual is to be maximizing the overall value of his time, he must be leaving the bottleneck point, subsequent to any queuing he may have had to endure, at a time such that

$$\frac{dq}{dt} = \frac{w_h - w_o}{w_h - w_q} \tag{3}$$

$$= \begin{cases} 0.5 & \text{for } w_o = w_p = 1 \text{ cent/min} \\ -1.0 & \text{for } w_o = w_j = 4 \text{ cents/min} \end{cases}$$

where $q(t)$ is the amount of waiting in the queue required in order to leave the bottleneck point at time t. A fraction

$$r = \frac{w_j - w_h}{w_j - w_p} = \frac{2}{3} \tag{4}$$

of the commuters will pass the bottleneck during the period of queue buildup and arrive at work at or before the desired starting time, the remaining fraction $1 - r = \frac{1}{3}$ of the commuters will leave the bottleneck after 8:40 a.m. during the working off of the queue and arrive at or after the desired time. The total time required for the commuters to pass the bottleneck will be $N/v = 7200/v$, which will also be the length of time that a queue will persist, as long as $v < v_m$.

The length of the queue will build up linearly from zero at time

$$t_i = t_a - r[(N/v) - (t_b - t_a)] \tag{5}$$

$$= 8:40 - 4800/v$$

to a maximum wait in the queue of

$$q_p = \frac{N}{v} (r) \frac{w_h - w_p}{w_h - w_q} = \frac{2400}{v} \tag{6}$$

for cars leaving the bottleneck at

$$t_p = t_a + r(t_b - t_a) = 8\!:\!40 \text{ a.m.} \tag{7}$$

after which it will again decline linearly to zero at

$$t_j = t_b + (1 - r)[(N/v) - (t_b - t_a)] \tag{8}$$

$$= 8\!:\!40 + \frac{2400}{v}.$$

There will be a sharp discontinuity in the amount of delay experienced as the capacity of the facility is expanded past the point where $v = v_m = 120$ cars/minute. Below v_m, delay is inversely proportional to the capacity v, while at and above v_m the delay from queuing is zero. To be sure, matters will not usually work out as sharply as this, for there will usually be some variation in the desired rates of traffic flow near the peak rather than a peak that has an absolutely flat top, as has been assumed here for the sake of simplicity. Moreover, there will usually be some elasticity of traffic demand with respect to queuing time such as to suppress some traffic entirely rather than merely to shift its timing. Nevertheless, sharp discontinuities such as this emphasize the need for careful analysis of practical situations.

In practice, too, we are usually dealing with a dynamic situation in which traffic levels are generally growing at a substantial rate, while construction of additional facilities takes time and usually involves substantial lumps of additional capacity. In the face of such substantial penalties for either over- or underinvestment, substantial waste is likely unless some form of control over the use of the facilities is applied, such as is available through pricing, and which does not involve the wastes of queuing. Unlike the construction of additional capacity, prices can be adjusted upward or downward, as proves to be desirable, on relatively short notice and by relatively small increments.

Indeed, in the above situation one can readily compute the price structure that would just eliminate the queue and lead to efficient use, at least in the short run, of whatever facilities are actually in place. This will consist of a toll rising linearly from 0 at t_i to

$$p_p = \frac{Nr}{v}(w_h - w_p) = \frac{4800}{v}, \tag{9}$$

at t_p and then declining linearly to zero at t_j. With this pattern of tolls, each commuter will find that he can do no better for himself than to set out in time to pass the bottleneck at the same time that he would have left it after waiting in the queue in the zero (or constant) price situation. If traffic should fail to adjust its movement in such a fashion as to eliminate the queue, those finding themselves in the queue would have a motive to shift their travel time in such a way that the queue would be eliminated.

In the short run, the commuters are just as well off paying the variable toll and having no queue as they were before with no toll but with an equivalent queue; moreover there is no change in the pattern of arrivals at the city center. The revenue derived from the charges thus represents clear gain. We thus have an example of tax revenue that not only has no excess burden, it has no burden at all! To the extent that any of the revenue from the variable toll is used to reduce a pre-existing flat toll, the motorists will be better off.

Obviously this does not mean that expansion of the capacity of the facility is never justified, but it does mean that the justification for such investment must be considered in an entirely different light if congestion charges are a possibility than if they are not. In the absence of congestion charges, a decision to expand facilities may have to be taken on an all or nothing basis. Expansion inadequate to take care of the entire traffic demand may result in a relatively slight improvement in conditions and may turn out to be hardly worthwhile, while a just slightly larger expansion might clear conditions up rather dramatically. Unfortunately, in a dynamically changing situation it is difficult to predict just what size of an improvement will in fact get over this threshold and for how long. It is easy to think of cases where an expansion of capacity felt to be quite ample when planned has turned out to serve merely to attract additional traffic until conditions are almost as bad as they were originally.

If, under conditions similar to the above, the levying of congestion charges is either an actuality or an alternative under consideration, benefits from the expansion of capacity are likely to be both smaller and less capricious in their behaviour than if no pricing is contemplated. The net gain from the expansion of the bottleneck, assuming the adjustment of charges both before and after so as to just eliminate queuing, consists not of any reduction in queuing time (since there isn't any queuing) nor still less of the reduction in tolls, since this is merely a transfer from the government or operating agency to the users (and may entail substantial costs involved in securing an equivalent revenue from other sources), but simply in the fact that users will be traveling at times closer to the preferred times. The value of this shift in time may be measured by the difference in the value they place on their time at the two ends of the journey, i.e., $w_h - w_p = 1$ cent/minute for reductions in the amount by which commuters travel, in advance of the preferred time, and $w_j - w_h = 2$ cents/minute for reductions in lateness. The total value of this delay, under optimum charging and no queue, is given by

$$NR(t_a - t_a)(w_h - w_p)/2 + N(1 - r)(t_\beta - t_b)(w_j - w_h)/2 \qquad (10)$$

Table 16.1

Capacity (cars per minute)	Equivalent number of lanes	Duration of queue or toll (minutes)	Maximum wait in queue (minutes)	Average toll rate (cents)	Congestion cost ($/day)		
					Displaced arrival	Waiting in queue (=toll rev.)	Total without pricing
50	1.67	144.00	48.00	48.0	2016	3456	5472
60	2.00	120.00	40.00	40.0	1440	2880	4320
70	2.33	102.9	34.29	34.3	1029	2469	3498
80	2.67	90.0	30.00	30.0	720	2160	2880
90	3.00	80.0	26.67	26.7	480	1920	2400
100	3.33	72.0	24.00	24.0	288	1728	2016
110	3.67	65.6	21.91	21.9	131	1571	1708
115	3.83	62.6	20.87	20.9	63	1503	1566
118	3.93	61.0	20.33	20.3	24	1464	1488
119	3.97	60.5	20.17	20.2	12	1452	1464
119.999	4.00−	60.0	20.00	20.0	0.12	1440	1440
120.001	4.00+	0	0	0	0	0	0

$$= N^2 r \frac{1-r}{2}(w_j - w_p)\left[\frac{1}{v} - \frac{1}{v_w}\right]$$

$$= \$1440 \frac{120 - v}{v}.$$

Where queuing results from the absence of tolls, the average queuing time is half the maximum, or $q_p(\frac{1}{2}) = 1200/v$, which when evaluated for 7,200 cars per day at w_h 2 cents/minute amounts to $172,800/v$.

The results, for various values of v, are summarized in table 16.1

Imposition of the optimal variable toll in each case eliminates queuing and results in toll revenues equal to the cost of the eliminated queuing. The displaced arrival cost will be the same whether or not the optimal toll is imposed, as this depends only on the capacity of the facility.

If we now suppose that initially we have a two-lane bottleneck with $v = 60$ cars per minute, then without the control provided by the variation in the toll rate congestion costs will total $4,320 per day. Without help from toll adjustments, opening up a third lane at a cost of $2,000 per day would reduce congestion costs by only $1,920, and so would not be worthwhile, although opening up two new lanes at a cost of $4,000 would eliminate the entire $4,320 worth of congestion and yield a net gain of $320. On the other hand the institution of variable tolls according to an appropriate pattern would cut congestion costs of the two-lane bottleneck by ⅔ to $1,440 and result in a budget inflow of $2,880 instead of a budget outflow of $4,000 if the additional two lanes were built. If the overhead costs of obtaining public funds from other sources were as much as 10 percent – a not unreasonable figure if all of the unfavorable results of increased tax rates are allowed for – this budgetary shift would constitute a further gain of $688, for a total gain of $2,880 + $688 = $3,568, a substantially better result than any that can be obtained without toll variation, and much better, in particular, than the $320 gain from the two-lane expansion.

If on the other hand the cost of expanding the bottleneck is relatively low, say $20 per day for each vehicle per minute of increase in capacity, so that some addition to capacity will be worthwhile in any event, variable tolls can still play a role in reaching the optimal result. In the absence of any tolls the best available alternative would again be to expand capacity to slightly above $v = 120$ cars per minute, so as to eliminate congestion entirely. If toll controls are available, however, it would not pay to carry the expansion much beyond $v = 90$, since expanding from $v = 90$ to $v = 100$ would reduce losses from displaced arrival by only $192, as compared with the cost of $200 for this expansion. In addition, such an increase might entail an increase in budgetary problems by the difference in revenues of $392.

The use of congestion tolls as an element in developing an efficient transportation system is thus not only a means of providing optimal adjustment in the short run but is likely to remain an important element even in the long run. It is only if the increment to capacity is provided in a manner that incidentally provides a substantially new and different route or a shorter origin to destination time for a substantial amount of traffic, or possibly where incremental costs of adding facilities for the collection of congestion charges *de novo* bulk large, that it would be possible to omit such charges from an optimally efficient scheme.

In practice, of course, most bottleneck situations are not as simple or as clear cut as the above case. The desired times of passing the bottleneck are not usually uniformly distributed, individuals vary in the values they assign to time spent in various places at various times, and to some extent the total number of trips made through the bottleneck would be affected by the tolls or the congestion conditions, probably in different ways for different users. These complications tend to lessen the sharpness with which critical capacity is determined, but in other ways they may enhance the effectiveness of appropriately graduated tolls and charges improving the efficiency of whatever facilities are constructed.

Expansion of Routes in the Presence of Alternative Routes

One situation that makes appropriately graduated charges even more essential is where a significant part of the traffic has closely competing alternative routes available to it. The classical paradigm of this situation is one where the alternative to the bottleneck route is, for a substantial portion of the traffic, a more circuitous or slower route of ample capacity. In the absence of any charges, the traffic will divide between the two routes so as to equalize total travel costs per vehicle, including travel time and also the queuing time on the bottleneck route. An enlargement of the bottleneck under these conditions will, if it falls short of being able to accommodate all of the traffic, simply result in enough traffic being diverted from the circuitous route to the enlarged bottleneck route to maintain the queue at the former level. The enlargement may thus produce no improvement in travel times at all, at least during periods of peak traffic. In a sense, such a costly enlargement proves worthless precisely because it is free.

In a more general vein, traffic often behaves like population. It has been said that if nothing stops the growth of population but misery and starvation, then the population will grow until it is miserable and starves. Similarly, if the use of private automobiles for access to the cores of large metropolitan areas is so attractive, under uncongested toll-free conditions, relative to other modes, that in effect nothing stops the growth of such traffic but congestion and delay, then such traffic will grow until sufficient congestion and delay are generated to constitute a deterrent, or until the core begins to suffer from gangrene, at which point a cumulative decline may set in that may be difficult to reverse, even with a belated introduction of appropriate toll graduation.

In practice a situation not too far from the classical paradigm often presents itself where attempts are being made to improve access to the core of a metropolitan area. In the absence of pricing, the alternatives may consist of (1) the *status quo*, (2) building an access facility sufficient for the traffic bound for the center, but which will immediately become so clogged with through traffic as to provide only moderate improvement in the speed and convenience of access to the center for a substantial part of the day, and (3) building a huge artery sufficient to take care not only of all local traffic but of any through traffic for which circumferential routes cannot be made sufficiently attractive to divert traffic from the central artery under uncongested conditions, and at the same time trying to bring the circumferentials close enough in and of such high grade as to divert as much of this traffic as possible. This third alternative is likely to prove astronomically expensive as well as disruptive of community amenities; the second alternative may in the end yield a very low return on the investment cost in terms of improvement of traffic conditions. Thus on balance the prospects of a net gain over the *status quo* may be rather dim whatever is done.

The availability of pricing opens up a new alternative of constructing central access facilities scaled to the requirements of traffic actually requiring to go to or from the center, with through traffic during the peak period being fairly thoroughly diverted to the circumferential routes by the charges imposed for the use of the central route. In some instances circumferentials that might not be worth their cost in the face of the difficulty of locating them so as to attract a sufficient volume of traffic in the absence of toll controls will become more worthwhile if pricing is available to help in the optimum distribution of traffic. With pricing such circumferentials may also be more readily located where construction is cheaper and less disruptive of amenities, and possibly also better suited for that part of their traffic that is not in any case tempted to use the central route, without fear that impairing their competitive relation to the central route would lead to undue congestion on the latter.

Variations in the Value of Time

An important but not essential element in the strategic importance of pricing as a factor influencing investment decisions is the existence of variations in the value of time, not only for different persons at the same time, but for the same individual at different times. In the absence of pricing, expansion of capacity must provide indifferently for individuals for whom the improvement will be worth relatively little as well as for those for whom it may be worth a good deal more. Pricing makes it possible to exclude the low-value uses and base the magnitude of the improvement primarily on the uses that are valued sufficiently highly so that they warrant the marginal cost of the final increment to the magnitude of the improvement. The selective effect of pricing on the costs of congestion would be to reduce still further the figures near the bottom of the "Displaced Arrival" cost column of table 16.1, enhancing the gains from the earlier increments to capacity and reducing the potential gains from the final increments. Potential improvements in efficiency and savings in construction costs are thus increased significantly over the amounts calculated on the basis of a uniform value for time.

There is, to be sure, likely to be an outcry at this point that pricing discriminates against the poor by forcing them off the congested highways. Actually the number of really poor individuals who are under any strong compulsion to drive cars with any regularity on the congested highways at peak hours appears to be quite negligible. The poorest among those significantly affected by a program of congestion charges are likely to be still somewhat above the poverty line. To the extent that this level of incomes is considered to be in need of a subsidy, there are surely better ways of determining needs than the amount of congested driving done.

A somewhat parallel outcry against the use of appropriately graduated landing fees as a means of controlling congestion at busy airports is even more difficult to justify. It is bad enough when a facility used primarily by the well-to-do is subsidized from tax revenues derived at the margin in large part from taxpayers of lower incomes; at uncongested airports this has at least the virtue of promoting better utilization. But when landing fees geared to congestion costs would substantially improve utilization while costing relatively little to assess and collect, even this excuse is lacking. In the airport case, moreover, those who would be charged the highest tolls, on a per capita basis, would be primarily general aviation planes operated in many cases for company executives and the like or private planes used for recreational and other purposes. Such users would in general be far better able to find acceptable alternatives, such as use of some of the smaller airports, if they are unwilling to pay the appropriate charges, than the patrons of the scheduled airlines. Landing fees reflecting congestion costs at various times could bring about a coordination of use that might well defer for a considerable time the need for resort to costly additional construction, often at less convenient locations. This can come about in part through the diversion of general aviation flights to other airports, through adjustment of airline schedules to reduce the concentration at the peak hours, by the use of larger planes and by scheduling for increased load factors, even without adjustment in the fare structure. If in addition some of the congestion charges can be shifted forward to passengers through the fare structure, some diversion of travel to less congested times and via less congested interchange airports may also aid in alleviating congestion. Such fare adjustments may also be essential if the best allocation of traffic between short-haul air travel and ground transportation, high-speed or otherwise, is to be achieved. A rush to construct additional airports to take care of threatened congestion may prove particularly costly at the present juncture in that improved navigational and flight control methods seem to be on the verge of substantially increasing the capacity of present airports.

Evaluation of Investment in Congestion Relief

Finally, the information provided by a system of congestion control through pricing has an essential role to play in the evaluation of investments designed to afford relief from congestion. In the absence of congestion pricing, very little solid data exists on the value of varying degrees of congestion alleviation, and much of what exists is subject to considerable bias in the direction of overestimating the value of such improvements. For example a recent study of changes in street use and traffic patterns in central London over the period from 1960 to 1966 came to the conclusion that what was widely touted as a significant improvement in traffic flow was actually no net improvement and possibly a deterioration from the standpoint of origin-to-destination volumes and times.[2] Many of the "improvements" during this period consisted of conversion to one-way traffic and the prohibition of certain turns involving crossing other traffic flows. Although average speeds and flow volumes of vehicles passing given points may have increased, these increases appear to have been used up in traversing more circuitous routes between given origins and destinations. In a similar way, higher speeds and volumes of traffic recorded on turnpikes and expressways often significantly overstate the increase in the transportation service accomplished as a result of their construction in terms of delivery from a specific origin to a specific destination. This is because distances, especially for shorter trips, are often longer via the new routes than via the old, though perhaps not as much as in the London example just cited.

If, indeed, all routes were subject to appropriate congestion tolls, the level of these tolls would then be a good initial approximation to the value of the congestion relief afforded by investment in increased capacity, at least for small increments. For larger increments one could also then rely, to some extent, on estimates of consumers' surplus under each demand curve separately. But where charges for the use of alternative routes fail to reflect congestion costs at the margin, the problem becomes much more complicated. Not only must allowance be made for the indirect effects on competing routes but consideration must be given to the possibilities for improving efficiency through introduction of appropriate patterns of user charges. In the absence of the information that would be provided by the charging of appropriate tolls, planning of investment in expanded transportation facilities is half blind, and resort is sometimes had to arbitrary rules of thumb, such as that of providing capacity adequate to handle the traffic during the thirtieth heaviest hour of traffic out of the year. The capriciousness of such a rule should be fairly obvious.

Appropriate patterns of congestion tolls are thus essential, not only to the efficient utilization of existing facilities, but to the planning of future facilities.

---

[2] J. M. Thomson, "The Value of Traffic Management," *Journal of Transport Economy and Policy* (January, 1968), pp. 3–32.

PART V

·

Urban Economics

Urban land rents are, fundamentally, a reflection of the economies of scale of the activities that are carried on within the city, and [the] efficient organization of a city, or even of the urban life of a nation as a whole, requires that these land rents, or their equivalent, be devoted primarily to the financing of the intramarginal residues that represent the difference between revenues derived from prices set at marginal cost and the total cost of the activities characterised by increasing returns . . .

Use of land rents, or, at least, of a major fraction of them, for public purposes is therefore not merely an ethical imperative, derived from categorization of these rents as an unearned income derived from private appropriation of publicly created values, but is, even more importantly, a fundamental requirement for economic efficiency.

The Economics of Public Services,
M.S. Fedelstein and R.F. Inman, Eds. (Macmillan, 1977), p. 343.

Urban economics comprises four principal subject areas: location and land use, transportation, housing, and local public finance. Until the 1970s the literatures in these four subject areas evolved more or less independently. In the 1970s the "new urban economics" emerged, which achieved an integration of the four subject areas via the monocentric city model.

Vickrey's principal contribution to urban economics is his pioneering work on urban transportation, which was covered in the previous part. He lay the foundations for modern urban transport theory, with seminal work on congestion theory, the application of marginal-cost pricing to urban transportation, and the choice of transport infrastructure. He also undertook, in the 1950s, the first modern urban transport policy analyses, one for the New York subway system, the other for the Washington, DC transport system. These were noteworthy for Vickrey's intelligent application of marginal-cost pricing, his incorporation of second-best considerations, and his attention to the technology needed for the application of marginal-cost pricing. Over the years he has had a major impact on economists' thinking about urban transportation through his persistent, eloquent, and perceptive advocacy of pricing solutions to problems of urban transportation.

While some of his earlier work anticipated the "new urban economics," he was a major contributor to only one aspect of its development – the incorporation of transport congestion. Beyond that, his contributions in urban economics relate to local public finance, especially the financing of urban public services, and to the strategic aspects of firm location.

His first paper in urban economics, outside transportation, is "General and Specific Financing of Urban Services" (chapter 18), published in 1963. This is a justly celebrated paper that discusses practical aspects of the application of marginal-cost pricing to urban public services. The paper starts off with a general discussion of the principles relating to whether a specific public service should be financed from user fees or from general revenue. The paper then goes on to discuss the application of marginal-cost pricing to specific public services. The paper is remarkable for its ingenuity and the quality of its reasoning. Vickrey argues, for example, that the fee for residential fire protection should be based on lot area. Since the cost per fire station is essentially fixed and since all houses must be within a given distance of a fire station, residential fire protection costs are approximately proportional to the residential area.

His next major contribution to urban economics, outside transportation, was a section of his 1964 *Microstatics* textbook on spatial competition. Unknown even to experts until recently, this section anticipates many of the major contributions to the subject over the next twenty-five years.

One of the most celebrated results in urban economics is the Henry George Theorem. The best-known variant of the Theorem states that in a city of optimal population size, where the source of agglomeration is a localized pure public good, urban (differential) land rents equal expenditure on the public good. Thus, a confiscatory tax on land rents is the single tax necessary to finance the public good. The explanation for the result is as follows: In a city of optimal population size, the average social cost of providing residents with a given level of utility is minimized. At the point of minimum average cost, there are locally constant returns to scale so that the product exhaustion theorem holds. With marginal-cost pricing, the profits generated from the decreasing returns to scale activities equal the losses from the increasing returns to scale activities. In the current context, the profits take the form of land rents and the loss is the expenditure on the local public good. The Henry George Theorem was discovered independently by Serck-Hansen (1969), Starrett (1974), Flatters, Henderson, and Mieszkowski (1974), and Vickrey. Vickrey delayed publication and was the last into print. Unfortunately, therefore, his 1977 paper on the Theorem, "The City as a Firm" (chapter 17), has not received the recognition it deserves. In any event, the paper provides an elegant formulation of a variant of the Theorem and an insightful explanation and discussion of it.

Vickrey's work in urban economics and in other fields has a quite distinctive character. It is guided by two related principles. First, theory is valuable in providing the basis for intelligent policy design rather than for its own sake. And, second, public policy design should be based on the consistent application of economic principles, appropriately tempered by practical consideration of administrative feasibility and political acceptability. Adherence to the first principle has meant that Vickrey has never systematically developed a line of theoretical thought. Rather he has developed theory, piecemeal, as he needs it in thinking about policy problems, and he has been content to leave important insights undeveloped if they are peripheral to the public policy at hand. Consequently, from the theorist's perspective, the most important contributions in Vickrey's papers are often to be found in asides. There is no doubt that Vickrey's adherence to theory for policy's sake has been a loss for economic theory. Vickrey is an extremely intelligent, creative, and clear-thinking theorist, and if he had had the inclination would most likely have been one of the leading theorists of his generation. But theory's loss has been public policy's gain. The clarity, rigor, and economic intelligence of his thinking on issues of public policy has set a standard for the profession.

Many of Vickrey's schemes are dismissed as unrealistic, but since the logic underlying them is always impeccable, one should ask what in our economic theory is missing that has led Vickrey to advocate a policy that common sense suggests is impractical. One case in point has been Vickrey's advocacy of electronic toll assessment on urban streets. The technology is there at reasonable cost. Why then is one's gut reaction that such fine tolling, in this context, is not sensible? Another example is site value taxation. There are strong theoretical arguments in favor of land taxation. The most familiar is that land taxation should entail no excess burden because land is inelastically supplied. Another is based on the Henry George Theorem. If a city is of optimal population size, then Pigouvian user fees for the congestible public services, including transportation, plus differential land rents raise just the right amount of revenue to finance public services. Does the Henry George Theorem provide a basis for practical policy? If not, why not?

The final paper in this part, "The Impact on Land Values of Taxing Buildings" (chapter 19), is included for two reasons. First, it indicates that, to some extent at least, Vickrey anticipated the new urban economics. Second, it shows, as do many other of his papers, that his thinking resembled that of the modern urban economist in that he considered the interdependence between urban spatial structure, transportation, housing, and local public finance.

The informed reader will be surprised that "Land Use in a Long, Narrow City," (*Journal of Economic Theory*, 3 (1971), pp. 430–7) co-authored with Robert Solow, is not included in the selection of papers in urban economics. Vickrey requested that it not be, claiming that he did little more than pose the model. But his conceptual contribution to the paper is clear from the concluding section of his 1963 paper, "Pricing in Urban and Suburban Transport." Whatever the extent of Vickrey's contribution, the paper is one of the classics in the new urban economics. It is the first to introduce congestion into the monocentric city model, and the first to investigate the effects of the underpricing of urban auto congestion on urban spatial structure.

In conclusion, while Vickrey's contributions to urban economics outside urban transportation are not of the same order as his contributions to urban transport economics, they are nonetheless significant. And his contributions to urban transport economics demonstrate a breadth and depth of vision of the urban economy that matches that of the best urban economists.

References

Flatters, F., Henderson, V., and Mieszkowski, P., "Public Goods, Efficiency and Regional Fiscal Equalization," *Journal of Public Economics*, 3 (1974), pp. 99–112.

Serck-Hansen, J., "The Optimal Number of Factories in a Spatial Market," in H. Bos, Ed., *Towards Balanced International Growth* (Amsterdam: North Holland, 1969).

Starrett, D.A., "Principles of Optimal Location in a Large Homogeneous Area," *Journal of Economic Theory*, 9 (1974), pp. 418–48.

17

The City as a Firm

Introduction

The purpose of this paper is to develop a rigorously optimizable model of a city, incorporating in this model two elements that seem to be vital to the development of large modern cities: transportation costs and economies of scale in the activities carried on within the city. If there were no transportation costs, so that goods and persons could be moved anywhere instantly and at no cost, and if there were no positive neighborhood effects, then activity could be indiscriminately scattered over the landscape instead of being concentrated in large urban complexes. Again, if there were no economies of scale, so that each activity could be carried on efficiently on as minute a scale as would be desired, activity could be organized in hamlets or small towns, each with a suitable complex of activities carried out on a small scale, with no need for the costly infrastructure characteristic of our large cities. Some degree of concentration into small cities might be accounted for by positive neighborhood effects of the kind that involves direct influence not mediated through a market transaction. The forces that bring our large cities into being are, however, predominantly those mediated through the purchase and sale of goods and services, so that the important positive externalities are of the market type, involving, in general, substantial economies of scale in at least some of the activities involved. Again, while some cities owe their location to an economically important natural feature of their site, such as a harbor or a mineral deposit, the size of the city that would coalesce around such a natural feature

The Economics of Public Services, Martin S. Feldstein and Robert F. Inman, Eds., Proceedings of a conference held by the International Economic Association at Turin (London: Macmillan; New York: Wiley, 1977), pp. 334–43.

would, in the absence of economies of scale, be far smaller than those we actually observe.

The existence of economies of scale within the activities involved immediately precludes an analysis based on perfect competition. On the other hand none of the manifold models of imperfect competition readily lends itself to incorporation in a precise model; and all of these models lack the optimizing properties that are being sought here. We shall, therefore, examine the problem of the optimal organization of a city in terms of some form of overall management structure, in effect regarding the city as a firm attempting to maximize some objective function. Even so, the inherent complexity of the situation dictates that on the one hand we keep the model stripped down to its barest essentials, and on the other that even then we stop somewhat short of full rigor of analysis, relying to a considerable extent on heuristics derived from classical models of perfect competition, or, perhaps, of a type of decentralized management derived from the analysis of Walras, Lange, and Lerner.

Littoral City

To construct a model stripped of all but the barest essentials while still retaining the essential elements of transportation cost and economies of scale, we consider a city laid out on a strip of land of uniform width along a shore. This strip will be considered to be long enough to contain all the activities to be carried out in the city, while leaving a vacant margin at either end, yet not long enough to enable a second city to be established on the adjacent portion of the strip. The sections of the strip not occupied by the city have no alternative use. While the land, if any, behind the strip is unusable for any purpose. Imports from, and exports to, other cities can be landed or loaded indifferently at any point along the strip at a uniform, delivered, or free-on-board price, while coastal ("intracity") transportation is handled at a constant cost per mile per unit of output of the ith commodity, t_i.

The character of the city is determined by the selection of a set of n activities to be carried on within the city, designated $i = 1, \ldots, n$. The level at which each activity is carried on is defined in terms of the volume of its single output, q_i. Economies of scale are represented by the fact that each activity requires a fixed quantum of imports f_i, measured in terms of aggregate delivered cost, in addition to a variable quantum of imports $m_i q_i$ proportional to the output q_i. The fixed element f_i is assumed to be large enough to assure that it will be nonoptimal to establish a second unit of activity i within the city. The extra fixed cost of setting up a second establishment would outweigh any saving that might be made in transportation costs within the city if a second and, possibly, closer source of supply for some users were provided. Each activity further requires the occupancy of $a_i q_i$ units of land, which, if the width of the strip is taken as unity, also implies the occupancy of a frontage equal to $a_i q_i$. In addition, each activity i may require as inputs amounts of the outputs of other activities, j, given by $b_{ji} q_i$. Inputs must be transported to, and outputs must be available at, the midpoint of the stretch of coastline occupied by each activity. The complication of the transportation cost of the inputs to the transportation process is avoided by stipulating that all of these inputs be imported. Finally, some or all of the output of an activity q_i may be exported at a net realization of $x_i p_i$, x_i being the amount exported and p_i the net price.

The optimization problem may be defined as one of maximizing

$$S = \sum p_i x_i - \sum f_i - \sum m_i q_i - T \tag{1}$$

where

$$T = \sum_i \sum_j (t_i \, d_{ij} \, b_{ij} \, q_j) \tag{2}$$

is the total transportation cost, and

$$d_{ij} = (a_i q_i + a_j q_j)/2 + \sum_{s_i \leq s_k \leq s_j} (a_k q_k) \qquad d_{ii} = 0 \tag{3}$$

is the distance between the centre of activity i and the centre of activity j, with s_i representing the sequence order of the ith activity along the strip, subject to

$$x_i + \sum_j b_{ij} q_j \leq q_i \qquad q_i > 0, \, x_j \geq 0 \tag{4}$$

$s_1, s_2, \ldots, s_n$ is a permutation of $1, 2, \ldots, n$.

Mathematically, the solution of this problem for any given permutation of the activities along the strip is a fairly straightforward quadratic programming problem. Determining which of the permutations is the optimal one presents more of a problem, although, since the number of permutations is finite, the problem is, in mathematical principle, solvable, even though carrying out a solution by examining all permutations would very rapidly become infeasible for any large number of activities. The problem of developing an algorithm that would shorten the process is an interesting one, but is not the main concern here. In any case, sufficiently close results could probably be obtained by testing interchanges of each pair of adjacent activities, performing the interchange where an improvement is noted, and proceeding until further interchanges show no gain. If, when this stage is reached, further tests are made for the interchange of any two nonadjacent activities, and then, possibly for the removal of an activity from one place in the order to another, one might be fairly confident of being close to the optimum; but, unless some rather difficult theorem to this effect can be demonstrated, one could not be absolutely sure of a full optimum.

Decentralized Solution

For the present, more interest attaches to a solution by *tâtonnements* along the lines of a Lange–Lerner decentralized socialist state, in which each activity is in the hands of a manager instructed to behave in a pseudo-competitive manner, and in which the role of the city manager is limited to the determination of the sequence in which the activities will be located and of the rents that the activities will be required to pay for the space they occupy. Rents will be set equal to the marginal social cost of land occupancy, which in this case consists of the increase in transportation costs involved in the occupancy of more land. Indeed, if a given activity manager wishes to occupy more land, the consequence will be that all traffic that formerly traversed his frontage will now have to go that much further, assuming that, in effect, all facilities used by an activity can be freely shifted along the strip. The land rent of each activity will then be equal to the cost of the transportation carried out in front of the area that it occupies, and total transportation costs will be equal to total land rents. (This compares with the more familiar result for the two-dimensional case that transportation costs are twice land rents.) Determination of the proper sequence for the activities is a less automatic process, but we shall assume that by some means it is satisfactorily accomplished. Starting from some arbitrary set of prices, rents, land-occupancy levels, and output levels, each manager will determine his own marginal cost on the basis of these prices, rents, and the costs of transportation over the distances indicated by the intervening levels of land occupancy; add to his output for export if this cost is below the world price; determine his demand for the outputs of other activities; and report the results. These are fed into a second round, in which each manager aggregates the demands made by other managers, so as to determine his own level of output for domestic consumption; adds, where appropriate, an amount for export, to get his new level of output; and recomputes his marginal cost. This is repeated until an equilibrium is reached in which the price of each output is equal to its marginal cost, and is either equal to the world price (where the item is being exported) or equal to or greater than the world price (where it is not being exported). The city manager can then test whether an interchange is desirable by examining the total per-mile freight costs of the items of input into two adjacent activities, i and j. If the costs for the inputs that are brought to i past j and to j past i are more than half of the total per-mile freight costs of all inputs to

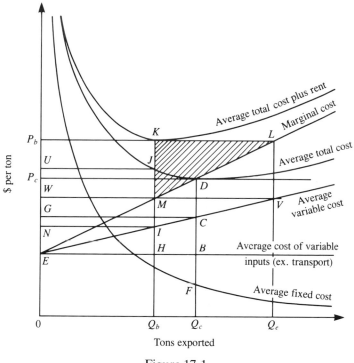

Figure 17.1

these activities (other than between *i* and *j*), the exchange should be made, but otherwise it should not.

Competition Between Cities

Although not all cities are of the same type (i.e., carry on the same mix of activities), it would seem reasonable to assume that there is a sufficiently large number of cities of each type, equally advantageously located with respect to world markets, and with no lack of additional vacant strips of land on which other cities might be established, to allow us to subject the city to the analysis developed for the firm in perfect competition. If, for simplicity, we assume that each city type exports only one commodity, we can represent the situation as in figure 17.1 in which the volume of the exported commodity is on the horizontal axis and costs per unit are measured vertically. The total average cost is made up of three components, corresponding to the last three terms of equation (1). We have, first, the constant variable cost other than transportation, represented by $\Sigma\, m_i q_i$ in the equation and shown as $0E$ in figure 17.1, and the horizontal line EHB.

The transportation-cost term, T, is homogeneous of second degree in the q_i, so that the average transportation cost is proportional to the level of activity and to the level of export x_i, and can be represented by the difference between the straight lines EHB and $EICV$. $EICV$ is then the average variable cost including transportation. The corresponding marginal cost is $EMDL$, with $BD = CD$, and so on. The fixed-cost term yields the equilateral hyperbola through F as the average fixed cost. When added to the average variable cost, this yields the average total-cost curve JD, intersecting the marginal-cost curve at its minimum point, D.

Then, if we have an unlimited number of cities of each type, with free entry for new cities and perfect competition operating among the various cities, equilibrium should establish itself with the price of the exported commodity settling down to the level P_c relative to the cost structure, with price equal to marginal cost equal to average cost, from the standpoint of the city as a whole. However, from the standpoint of the individual firm within the city, the picture will look slightly different. The price that it will be quoting (calculated at marginal cost, other prices being considered fixed) will cover the delivered cost of the variable inputs plus the rental charged for the land it occupies, but will not cover the fixed costs, f_i. For this the firm will need a subsidy from the city manager. For any individual activity, there need not be a relation between the amount of land rent paid to the city manager and the amount of the subsidy needed to cover the fixed costs.

However, for the city as a whole, rents will just balance the subsidy, as can be seen from figure 17.1 where the transportation costs given by the rectangle $EBCG$ are equal to the fixed costs represented by $GCDU$, by virtue of the fact that $BC = CD$. But we have seen that the rents on each piece of land are equal to the marginal social opportunity cost represented by the transportation costs incurred in front of the property; hence, total land rents are equal to total transportation costs. In the aggregate, then, aggregate land rents at rates representing the marginal social cost of land occupancy will be just sufficient, and no more, to pay the subsidies required to permit the individual activities to lower their prices to marginal cost. Thus, to the proposition of Henry George that, as a matter of justice, the land rents that have arisen through no effort on the part of any individual land-owner should be appropriated for public purposes, and the suggestion of Harold Hotelling that taxes on land rents would be an appropriate means of financing the intramarginal cost residues of increasing-return industries pricing their output at marginal cost, we add the following theorem, which we call the "GHV" theorem.

> *In an economy of efficiently organized cities in a state of perfect competition with each other, the aggregate of the land rents (calculated as the marginal social cost of holding land) generated by the urban*

> *agglomeration produced by the existence of activities with economies*
> *of scale within the city will equal the subsidies required to enable these*
> *activities to sell their output at prices equal to their respective marginal*
> *costs.*

In other words, if a perfectly efficient world is to be organized on a classical decentralized basis, it is necessary that all of the land rent generated by the presence of the city be appropriated to the subsidy of the decreasing-cost industries within the city. If any of these land rents are appropriated by private landlords for their own purposes, this action will preclude the achievement of complete efficiency.

The Scope of the GHV Theorem

Thus far, this theorem has been illustrated rather than proved, but there is reason to believe that it is valid well beyond the rather oversimplified example given above. For example, it would seem that going from a one-dimensional to a two-dimensional, or even a three-dimensional, model would not destroy the validity of the theorem. In a two-dimensional model, transportation costs per unit of output would tend to vary as the square root of the volume of output, and marginal transportation costs would then be 3/2 of average transportation costs. In terms of figure 17.1, we would replace the line *EIC* with a parabola with axis *EB*, and *EDL* would be another parabola, with *BD* = 3/2 *BC*. At the minimum-cost point *D*, the fixed cost would thus be equal to half the transportation cost. There are also a number of models that, for a two-dimensional case, produce an equality between transportation cost and twice the total land rents. Thus, again, we have land rents equal to the fixed costs. If we allow for the possibility of expanding vertically, say by thinking of the city as being, in effect, constructed in a k-dimensional space, with $2 < k < 3$, then we can have $T = kR = kF$, with, again, $R = F$, though in this case T may have to be thought of as including the cost of lifts, stairs, and the like.

Again, the assumption of a linear production function with a constant term does not appear to be critical, since any production function can be approximated, in the neighborhood of the optimal point, by a linear function tangent to the actual function at the equilibrium point, with a constant term that can be taken as the effective intramarginal residue. Similarly, the fact that transportation costs do not vary simply in proportion to distance, but vary in a curvilinear fashion, may be allowed for by replacing the actual transportation-cost function with one that is a linear function tangent to the actual one at the equilibrium point, and by taking the element of cost represented by the intercept and incorporating it, as packing or loading costs, in the costs of the shipping activity. Among the matters that are not so simple to deal with, but that probably can be handled along analogous lines, is the possibility that part of the fixed costs of activities may take the form of a fixed land requirement, or that inputs to the transportation service are locally produced.

An element that may be more likely to disable the theorem is the fact that, in practice, much transportation does not take the form of a direct origin-to-destination shipment, but is multi-purpose in character, as when an individual stops at the barber on his way to work, or, more importantly, when a delivery truck drops off or picks up shipments at various points along a route. Computing a relevant marginal cost under these circumstances is difficult, and it is not even clear that there will be any simple algorithm for determining the optimum pattern on a decentralized basis (consider the travelling-salesman problem).

Another caveat to be kept in mind is that the theorem applies only to the intramarginal residues occurring in those industries that are either entirely local in their markets or are replicated in similar cities. A local newspaper or a television station, for example, is a factor in the agglomerative power of a given city, and the land rents generated by this agglomerative power will cover the intramarginal costs of these activities. On the other hand whereas publication in a given city of a unique book with a worldwide distribution may add, in some degree, to the agglomerative power of the city, it is unlikely to do so to a degree that would cause land rents to rise sufficiently to cover the writing, typesetting and preparation costs involved. In effect, the theorem applies to local economies of scale, not to global ones. However, the economies of scale involved are not necessarily manifested in large organizations: the factory that makes buttons of a given model more cheaply in lots of 600 than in lots of 300 is operating under conditions of economies of scale, even though there would be no reduction in average cost if it produced 500 buttons in each of 200, instead of 100, models.

Optimizing in an Environment of Nonoptimizing Cities

A more immediate question, given the remoteness of a fully optimized situation, is how a city might optimize in a context in which other cities are behaving in a nonoptimal manner, and what the consequences of such action might be. This involves, first, defining a specific nonoptimal type of behavior that is to be ascribed to the outer universe of cities. Given the possibilities for various varieties of imperfect competition inherent in the prevalence of economies of scale, this is a wide-open opportunity for variation. Since we are concerned with the relation of land rents to city efficiency, let us assume that the one constraint against optimality is that land rents, instead of being used to subsidize the decreasing-cost activities so as to permit marginal-cost pricing, are used by landlords for their own private purposes (for instance, consumption of additional imports). This will mean that individual activities will have to be financed from their own receipts without subsidy, and that prices must cover the full average cost, inclusive of purchased inputs, land rents, and fixed costs. Let us assume, further, that land rents are optimally set so as to reflect the marginal cost of land occupancy, as determined by the cost of transportation. The average variable cost will then be *0E* plus twice the transportation cost, or *EMDL*, and the average total cost, inclusive of rent, will be indicated by the curve through *K*. We may then suppose the world price relationships to be set at the level represented by P_b, the output being at the level represented by Q_b. Of the total proceeds $0P_bKQ_b$, $0ENQ_b$ represents variable direct imports, *NIHE* the imports for transportation, *NIMW* is the rents consumed by landlords, and WP_bKM the fixed costs.

If, now, in the context of such inefficient cities, a given city wishes to optimize its own operations, it should operate at the point where marginal cost, net, equals the world price, or at *L*. Expansion from *K* to *L* produces additional revenues of KLQ_bQ_e against additional costs of MLQ_eQ_b, leaving a net gain of *MKL*. This gain, in the linear case, is equal to the former level of rents, with $Q_e = 2Q_b = 1.414Q_c$. For the *k*-dimensional case, the corresponding results are

$$Q_c = \left(\frac{kF}{t}\right)^{k/(k+1)}$$

where *t* is the transportation cost involved in a city producing one unit of output

$$Q_b = Q_c \left(\frac{k}{k+1}\right)^{k/(k+1)}$$

and

$$Q_e = \left(\frac{k+1}{k}\right)^{k} Q_b = Q_c \left(\frac{1+k}{k+1}\right)^{k^2/(k+1)}.$$

The land rents to be collected at *K* will be

$$L_b = F\frac{k}{k+1}$$

and the total surplus available at *L* will be

$$S_e = F\left[\left(\frac{k+1}{k}\right)^{k} - 1\right].$$

At L, however, land rents at the social opportunity cost would be

$$F \left(\frac{k + 1}{k} \right)^k$$

so that the surplus is insufficient, by the amount F of the fixed costs, to cover these rents.

In effect, if the landlords constitute the ruling class of the city, it would be in their own long-run interests, with world prices at P_b, to levy against their rents to subsidize to the extent of F, inducing in the long run (assuming that no other cities do likewise) an expansion to L and an increase in the gross land rents by more than the subsidy F. Of course, this process would take time. Indeed, at the initial point K, land rents are less than F, and would be insufficient at that point to do the whole job. It is only as the city expands beyond the output Q_c that land rents become sufficient to cover the entire intramarginal costs of the decreasing-cost industries.

Surplus and Efficiency

Of course, if all cities started to do this simultaneously, one might ask in what sense a shift from K to D is an increase in efficiency, since it eliminates surplus. The answer is to be found in what happens to the returns available to whatever are, ultimately, the scarce resources in the universe under discussion. An overall shortage of suitable sites for cities would lead, of course, to a surplus rent. A more interesting concept would be that of a limited labor force, freely mobile among cities. Expansion of the scale of cities, and, possibly, the establishment of new cities, would lead to an increase in the demand for labor, and an increase in its wages, represented in this model by the level of the input coefficients to the labor supply activity, representing an increase in the supply of consumer goods necessary to produce a unit of labor for use in the other activities in the city. Full competition among cities would, in this instance, lead (a) to the elimination of any new land rents to landlords, over and above the amounts taken to finance the fixed costs; and (b) to the transfer of this surplus, plus the additional surplus generated from the increase in efficiency to labor, at least in the case where there is no shortage of city sites and, hence, conceptually free entry for additional cities.

Summary

While it is dangerous to extrapolate too freely from admittedly oversimplified and even caricatured models (such as the above) to the complexities of the real world, it seems not too rash to draw the conclusion that urban land rents are, fundamentally, a reflection of the economies of scale of the activities that are carried on within the city, and that efficient organization of a city, or even of the urban life of a nation as a whole, requires that these land rents, or their equivalent, be devoted primarily to the financing of the intramarginal residues that represent the difference between revenues derived from prices set at marginal cost and the total cost of the activities characterized by increasing returns. This means that revenues derived from these rents must defray not only those overhead costs of government and public services that are not marginally attributable to specific outputs, but also the intramarginal elements of most public utility costs, as well as those of a considerable range of activities ordinarily thought of as belonging to the private sector. Such a subsidy is especially crucial for mass transit and for other forms of transportation where economies of scale are significant, given the special relationship existing between transportation and land values.

Use of land rents, or, at least, of a major fraction of them, for public purposes is therefore not merely an ethical imperative, derived from categorization of these rents as an unearned income derived from private appropriation of publicly created values, but is, even more importantly, a fundamental requirement for economic efficiency. Cities that take the lead in such public use of land rents may find that in the long run the subsidy is self-financing through the enhancement in land values that results, while cities that lag may find that in the long run they are unable to compete in national or world markets with the cities that manage to organize themselves more efficiently through the use of land rents to cover intramarginal residues. There will, of course, be many an agonizing slip between abstract economic analysis and cold political and economic reality. Lack of comprehension, political intervention, strategic recalcitrance, and the inertia associated with heavy commitments of fixed capital in what the French so aptly term *immeubles* may slow the processes involved to a glacial pace. But the fundamental tendencies and requirements inherent in the very nature of the city can be ignored only at great peril to its economic health.

18

General and Specific Financing of Urban Services

The purpose of this paper is to re-examine the degree to which municipal services are financed from (1) general purpose taxes, levied without close attention to the way in which the taxpayers benefit from public services, or affect the costs of rendering them, and (2) specific taxes, fees, and prices that attempt to reflect these costs and effects more closely. To some extent the concern with bringing payments more closely into line with costs and benefits is related to concepts of equity, in that it is conceived to be in some sense proper that those who enjoy benefits or give rise to costs should, in the absence of countervailing consider-ations, pay accordingly. But more weight, on the whole, is given in the current investigation to the possibility that such correlation of charges with costs and benefits can be made to increase the efficiency with which services are utilized, prevent waste, and in general improve the patterns along which our mushrooming metropolitan areas will grow. Indeed, it is this latter consideration that leads to a dissatisfaction with a mere statistical or average balance or proportionality between benefits and contributions and an insistence on a greater precision of detail: situations can easily arise in which groups of more or less similarly situated individuals share a cost equally and hence no individual is in fact treated unfairly, yet if the institutions are such that no one person can reduce his share in the cost by suitably economizing or restraining himself, the amount of the service demanded and supplied may be grossly excessive.

Public Expenditure Decisions in the Urban Community, Howard G. Schaller, Ed. (Resources for the Future, 1963), pp. 62–90; reprinted in part in *Readings in Welfare Economics,* K. Arrow and T. Scitovsky, Eds. (Irwin, 1969), pp. 561–87.

General Criteria

In determining whether an attempt should be made to pay for a municipal service by means of a specific charge, a number of general principles or criteria can be referred to; their specific impact varies, of course, from case to case. One of these concerns the distributional impact of the charge relative to that of the general tax that it might displace. In many cases this differential will be small enough or uncertain enough in its direction to be considered a wholly secondary matter, but in particular cases it is important and even paramount. In New York, for example, a straight increase in transit fares can be considered almost tantamount to a poll tax in its incidence, and certainly far more regressive in its distributional impact than even a sales tax. The distributional impact of an attempt to finance educational, hospital, or welfare services entirely by direct charges would obviously be so unacceptable as to preclude such a solution, at least in its simple and direct form.

Another general principle that can be appealed to is the extent to which the proposed charge can be related to benefits derived from the service in a way which will appeal to concepts of equity. This immediately raises the question of how to measure the benefit: should it be in terms of the cost of providing the service to the individual concerned or in proportion to the amount that the individual would pay rather than go without the service altogether? To what extent, for example, should water charges be based on the income of the user, or be differentiated according to the cost of his obtaining water from another source? It seemes fairly clear that answers given to such questions will vary widely from case to case and that the variation will have to be explained on grounds other than a general adherence either to cost or to utility as a basis.

Indeed, one factor that will often enter into the general attitude taken is the nexus, as perceived by the public, between the payment made and the benefit received. In many cases this perceived nexus will be significantly influenced by historical development. A new service accompanied by a new charge is likely to generate a vivid conception of a *quid pro quo*; a new charge made for a pre-existing service is more likely to create a feeling of inequity, even if the charge is a necessary means of preserving the value of the service, as in the case of the ferry that is worthless as long as it is free (because then queues accumulate until it is just as quick or convenient to detour via a bridge or tunnel), or where transit services are subsidized in part from funds obtained from highway use charges. Another element in the perception of this nexus is the manner of payment: a toll is immediately visible as an out-of-pocket cost financing a distinctive service; a gasoline tax is slightly less so; payment for a sewer connection may evoke different attitudes, even though computed on the same base, according to whether it is merely included in a global tax bill to a municipality performing all of the various functions itself, or paid as a separately itemized item on a consolidated tax bill or paid separately as an entirely distinct transaction. All of these may have a significant effect on the way in which the relation between benefit and burden is perceived by the general public and in the degree of acceptance of this relationship.

More attention is to be paid here, however, to the matter of allocational efficiency. This in effect means extending the concept of marginal cost pricing as far as possible into the realm of municipal services with the intent of attaching, to each choice by individuals that affects municipal operations or that has an impact on others in the community, a differential charge that will properly represent these impacts to the individual. Ideally, this charge would serve to coordinate decentralized decision-making on the part of individuals into a harmonious whole. In many areas, however, it will be an adjunct, though an important one, to more centralized planning activities as represented by building codes and zoning ordinances.

Moreover, even in the absence of pressures arising from considerations of progressivity and of equity perceptions, it will in practice be impossible to approach even very closely to this theoretical ideal. The relative social costs occasioned by alternative choices contemplated by individuals cannot be measured, in many cases, with anything like complete accuracy, and in other cases the costs of carrying out the measurements would be such as to outweigh the benefits. Even where the costs can be ascertained with adequate accuracy, the costs of assessing the corresponding charges may be great, and in some cases the terms of the assessment might tend to become so complicated as to be beyond the comprehension of the individual making the decision, and thus be ineffective in securing the improvement in the allocation of resources that was the original *raison d'être* of the more elaborate assessment. And finally the fact that in nearly all cases, even with the fullest possible utilization of specific charges, municipalities are almost always in such pressing need of funds that they must have recourse to general taxes that themselves have adverse effects on allocation. Consequently, by virtue of the general principle of "second best," if any specific charges are to be made, they should in nearly all cases be designed in part to contribute to the public treasury over and above the amount that would flow in on the basis of charges strictly reflecting marginal costs.

Specific Cases

General principles are seldom as enlightening in the abstract as in their application to specific cases, and accordingly some specific examples are discussed in the remainder of the paper which will serve to illustrate their application and explain their meaning. In considering specific cases, we will include on the one hand some items that may not ordinarily be thought of as municipal services, but which would lend themselves to financing by methods ordinarily associated with municipal finance; and on the other hand some municipal services, including some of the more important ones, will not be considered because of the inherent difficulty of applying to them the methods being considered here.

Fire Protection

Fire Protection accounts for some 7.6 percent of all general expenditure by cities. It serves here as a striking example of the difference between benefit and cost as a basis for charging.

Actually, fire protection is considered most appropriately paid for on the basis of property assessment, and in terms of benefit this is a fairly good basis. Benefit can be roughly measured in terms of the reduction in insurance rates on protected as against unprotected property, and in terms of the enhancement of land values in view of the provision of the protection to any structures built on the land. The value of land plus improvements would accordingly seem to be a good measure of benefit. Even here, of course, there are cases where increased property value fails to indicate increased benefit: replacing an old, obsolescent building with a modern fireproof one may lessen the amount of benefit obtained from fire protection even though the value of the property may be increased.

Viewed from the cost side, however, the picture is entirely different. Providing a given grade of fire protection to an area is almost entirely a matter of providing an engine company within a suitable distance of the property, or more operationally, within a suitable number of minutes of travel time. The National Board of Fire Underwriters, in setting standards for fire protection, requires as a rough rule of thumb that in residential areas a company be stationed within about 1.5 miles for a property to be considered adequately protected; for industrial and commercial property, apartments and the like, the distance is shortened to 0.75 mile, while for areas containing only widely scattered residences a distance of up to three miles is tolerated. There are in addition minor differences in the cost per engine company: in business and industrial areas a complement of seven men on duty is considered normal, whereas in residential areas five men on duty may be considered sufficient; in addition, the property occupied by the fire house may be more valuable in the former case. Roughly speaking, therefore, the ratio of the cost of protecting an acre of residential area and that of protecting an acre of business area may be about one to five (leaving the fringe areas out of consideration, for the moment). This is a much smaller range than the corresponding range in assessed values, in most cases.

From the point of view of resource allocation, however, it would not be sufficient to remain content with property values as the basis for paying for fire protection even if it could be shown that these costs in fact varied in proportion to assessed value. An increase in the value of the improvements in a given area, through new construction or otherwise, does not in any significant way increase the cost of furnishing a *given grade* of protection to the property already there, even though it may make it worth while to provide a higher and more costly grade of protection. Even though in principle the construction of new buildings in a given area may increase the frequency of fires within the area and thus might increase the probability that the equipment might be out on another call when a fire breaks out in a given property, this is normally a very minor factor, made quite negligible in most cases where alternate protection is normally available from adjacent fire companies. The basic act that is causally related to the need for added fire protection is the occupancy of land in the protected area. It is the exclusive occupancy and not the nature of the occupancy that counts; if an acre of land is used for tennis courts or a clay products depot, involving of itself almost no fire hazard, the displacement of the occupancies that might have used this land to outlying areas where new fire protection will have to be provided is a cost that should properly be assessed against such uses. Similarly it makes no difference to the cost to be assessed against a given acreage whether it is developed with residences on half-acre lots or row houses cheek-by-jowl, even though this might make a difference to the way an insurance company might rate the hazard.

Accordingly, the appropriate way to charge for fire protection would be on the basis of area. Possibly some gradation in the charge might be made in terms of distance from the fire house, but in most cases this would be a negligible factor. An exception might be made where the protected area dependent on a given fire house includes both residential and business property: areas zoned for business and located within the 0.75 mile distance might be assessed at a higher rate based on the higher degree of protection offered and the need of business for this higher grade of protection if it is forced to locate elsewhere by inferior occupancy of the business-zoned area. In this case it would be the nature of the zoning rather than the nature of the occupancy that would be the appropriate basis for the distinction in the charge. Moreover there is in a sense a joint product problem here: a given fire house required to provide a residential-grade protection for the 1.5 mile radius necessarily provides incidentally for business-grade protection within its 0.75 mile radius. On the one hand if the inner zone thus generated is greater than the demand for business sites, the business-grade protection is a byproduct to be provided at no marginal cost, the residential occupancy bearing the full burden; on the other hand if the business demand increases so as to require the provision of an additional fire house, the additional residential protection, if enclosing some unoccupied but developable land, is likewise a byproduct, and the full cost of such a fire house should be borne by the business protection area.

Translating the charges thus indicated into an actual tax is of course another matter. In the long run it would probably not make too much difference if the assessment were made on the basis of land value rather than land area, as any difference between the two forms of charge could readily be capitalized into the land value. In the short run transitional effects would arise, but consideration of these effects will have to be relegated to another analysis. In any event it is clear that on a cost basis, the basis for assessment is clearly land value, exclusive of improvements, in spite of the fact that at first glance the benefit basis would seem to indicate that it is improvements that should be assessed.

Another factor associated with fire could be the basis for the assessment of charges – the external economies associated with what are technically termed "exposure fires," i.e., fires not starting on the premises under the same ownership. Individuals who take precautions against fire are not only reducing their own risk, but that of their neighbors. To the extent that they are reducing their own risk in recognizable ways, they may qualify for lower insurance premiums, but since neighboring properties are insured by independent companies, and indemnities are paid regardless of the source of the fire, these rating allowances of necessity include no allowance for reductions in the likelihood of contagion or exposure losses. It would accordingly be of some merit for property tax assessments to make some small concession to structures that are fireproof or are sprinklered or are otherwise protected, over and above what building codes may make mandatory. The tax concession could even be more widely applied than building codes, since the latter are often full of grandfather exceptions; in some cases the tax concession might even motivate an improvement where otherwise the owner would be willing to hide behind an excepting clause.

Too much should not be made of this, however: over the period 1953–9 the property loss claims from exposure fires amounted to $221 millions, which is 7.2 percent of losses from known causes, which in turn was 45 percent of total losses. Since exposure fires probably constituted a relatively low percentage of the "causes unknown" category, such losses probably amounted to not more than 4 percent of the total. Though the principle may be applicable, the practical consequences are *de minimis*.

Water Supply

In the water supply we are faced with a wide range of situations as to source of the bulk supply, but the overall characteristics of distribution tend to be somewhat more uniform, and we will discuss the latter first.

In some fortunate areas, reasonably pure water may be available from a nearby source in ample quantities, so that the main problem is one of distributing this supply to users. Moreover the economies of scale in water main size are so substantial that it is only a minor oversimplification to say that the cost of the mains is proportional to their length and relatively independent of the required volume of flow. Another factor tending to warrant such simplification is that for fire protection purposes a certain minimum size main is required to provide the flows needed for fire-fighting purposes.

The problem is how to relate the total length of main required to the nature of the occupancy of the area. It is tempting to say again that area is the critical factor, but this is overruled by the observation that if we take two communities that are laid out in a similar pattern, but on different scales so that streets and mains are twice as far apart in the one community as the other, while lots are four times as large, the second community will only require twice the length of mains. The simplest rule would be to use the front foot as the unit; this however produces awkward results when applied to corner lots, but even so is perhaps the best simple rule available. One can of course expect any minor variations in the system of charges to become capitalized in the price of the lots, in this case, so that the corner problem is perhaps not a crucial one. The same is true of variations in the relative amount of frontage associated with various lots due to odd shapes, curves in the street, and the like. It would be tempting to try some more general linear measure of lot size, such as the square root of the area, or the maximum diameter, but these would produce results that make the aggregate charge for a group of lots vary according to the way the total area is subdivided in ways that bear no very close relation with the length of mains required.

In smaller communities endowed with an ample source of supply this may be all that marginal-cost pricing requires: there would remain, in addition to the cost of the mains, the cost of the collection and purification system and the transmission aqueduct from the source to the edge of the community. In many cases the incremental cost of added capacity may be so low as not to warrant the cost of installing and reading water meters. These intramarginal costs not covered by explicit charges for mains can then be covered out of general revenues, or from any other source on the basis of "least harm." One source would be surcharges on the cost of the mains; not only would this probably not be too much of a distorting influence, but it would have considerable public appeal on equity grounds. Actually, data for 1959 indicate that overall expenditures for water supply amount to $1,423 million as against revenues of $1,201 million, indicating some support from general revenues, though since expenditures are largely on a cash rather than an accrual basis, with considerable confusion between current and capital outlays and probably a considerable understatement of real interest and amortization charges, this conclusion should be made with caution.

In many cases, however, especially in the more densely populated areas and arid regions, the incremental cost of the gross supply will be a significant factor. The problem is complicated by the large size of the lumps in which increments to supply are often available, the great durability of the facilities, and by the significant seasonal and random fluctuations in the supply furnished by given facilities. Under such circumstances charges according to the amount of water used are obviously in order, but have in the past been justified far more on grounds of equity than on grounds of controlling the use. Indeed, the idea of using water charges to ration use seems quite at variance with typical attitudes of water supply engineers, who seem to view their function as one of providing an ample supply almost regardless to the cost of meeting whatever standard they decide to set, and limiting the charges to the user to whatever minimal rates prove necessary to finance the scheme overall, regardless of what the incremental cost of the particular supply involved happens to be.

Reluctance to use water charges as a means of rationing use is illustrated in the fact that rates generally remain much the same from one season to another and from one year to another. To some extent this is the result of sheer administrative inertia, but to a considerable extent it represents the view that to raise rates at a time of shortage represents exploitative profiteering that is considered undesirable and even immoral, regardless of whether the beneficiary is a private individual or a public body. Nevertheless to an economist, at least, the possible improvement in the allocation of resources through such variation in rates should be fairly obvious, the main question being how difficult such variation would be and how important the benefits that would result.

Variations in supply may arise either as a regular seasonal phenomenon, or irregularly as a result of variations in rainfall or large accretions of capacity. In all three cases variation in rates would improve resource allocation, but the difficulty of applying the changes varies considerably. One difficulty common to all three situations is that meters are usually read quarterly, and often on a rotating schedule, so that it would be difficult to bring the impact of the rate change to bear on all consumers simultaneously. In a system having large reserves, where a situation of shortage or abundance can be expected to persist over several quarters, or in the case of the addition of large increments of supply, it may be sufficient to continue a quarterly pattern, simply prorating the consumption indicated for a given quarter into the portions of the quarter falling into the low- and the high-rate periods. This works fairly well with utility bills at present, where rate changes occur, but in such cases the rate changes are relatively minor and the principal issue is one of equity; it would be relatively less satisfactory where rate changes are of a magnitude intended to be sufficient to affect consumption. Then the discriminations would be somewhat more severe and the dilution of the incentive to economize during the latter scarcity part of a quarter, by reason of the fact that such consumption would be prorated back to the earlier or abundance part (and vice versa in the case of rate reductions), would be of significant concern. Ideally, extra meter readings should be arranged as nearly as possible to the time of the rate change, so as to minimize this prorationing effect; possibly this might be done economically by combining them with electricity and gas meter readings. Self-reporting by the consumer, such as is often practiced either for interim readings or where the regular reader was not able to gain access to the premises, would seem somewhat less feasible here than where no rate change is taking place: with constant rates there is ordinarily no significant incentive for the consumer to falsify or fudge his report of the meter reading, and even where there is, the consumer would often have to be fairly sophisticated and prescient about his future consumption to take advantage of the opportunity; where a substantial rate change is involved, both the magnitude of the incentive and the clarity to the consumer of the direction in which it is to his advantage to misreport would operate to make misreporting more of a problem.

One objection to fluctuating rates is that they make it more difficult for the consumer to budget, particularly with rates that fluctuate with unpredictable variations in rainfall. The problem would be less significant with predictable seasonal fluctuations in rates. Unlike a private utility, a municipality is in a position to offset changes in water charges with changes in the general property tax rate, so that what the average consumer would gain on a given occasion in lower water rates he would lose in higher property taxes, and vice versa; the incentive for conservation of water in times of shortage would remain. In effect, a substitution effect is generated while the income effect is minimized.

With water more than with most other utility services, the tenant who turns the tap is often insulated from the impact of water rates by their inclusion in his overall rent, and for this reason rate variations may be less effective here than with other services. Such use is however relatively inelastic to price in any case, and control at such points is hardly worth while. There remains, in any case, the incentive for the landlord to pay special attention to leaks and other outright wastage and for economizing in large-scale industrial use, lawn watering, and the like.

One need not necessarily maintain that rate changes can entirely take the place of water conservation campaigns in times of threatened shortage, but high water charges should provide a significant reinforcement for such campaigns, if they become necessary. Certainly such charges provide a more efficient means of rationing than such methods as the prohibition of certain uses at certain times, or in extreme cases the shutting off of the supply in various areas at various times, with the attendant danger of contamination and increased fire hazard.

Variable rates should permit considerable economies to be made in scheduling expansion of supply. Given a means of efficiently controlling the demand in cases of drought of rare intensity, it will be less necessary to expand supply quite so far to take care of such contingencies. Similarly, it will be less necessary to plan new additions to supply quite so far in advance, since a faster than anticipated growth in demand or shortage due to subnormal rainfall can be adapted to more effectively. On the other hand, new additions to supply can be used more fully and more promptly upon their completion if charges are reduced or eliminated as long as the supply is ample.

However, a policy of raising charges prior to the completion of a new project and lowering them when it is brought into production means a drastic change in traditional modes of financing public works. To the extent that funds are accumulated out of the earlier high rationing charges, the project will be more nearly on a "pay-as-you-go" basis; on the other hand there will be no funds flowing from water charges to pay off the balance of the cost until such time as the new addition is being fully utilized and rationing charges are again needed. Whether or not this pattern can be followed in its pure form will of course depend on the overall fiscal and financial pattern of the municipality, but substantial changes in financial procedures are indicated in any case, even if the limiting situation is not a feasible one.

There is one further difficulty with drastic variation in rates over fairly long periods: consumers may be induced to install water-using equipment, such as nonrecirculating cooling equipment, on the basis of current low rates only to find that when rates are later raised their investment turns out to have been unprofitable. In principle, of course, consumers should be put adequately on notice of the likelihood of water rates being increased in the future. Fortunately, most decisions of this sort that involve substantial fixed capital and that would be significantly affected by water rates are of a commercial or industrial nature. In such instances the decision-maker can be presumed to be sufficiently sophisticated to take account of such a prospect.

Transportation Facilities

The overall picture of the finances of urban transportation conceals a great deal of inefficiency and distortion within an aggregate picture that seems spuriously close to being in balance. Aside from a few outstanding instances of substantial subsidy, such as the New York subways and rail commuter service, it appears superficially that the transit rider is about paying the costs of the service he uses. Likewise, for motor traffic as a whole, revenues from user charges seem to be roughly in balance with outlays on facilities: in 1957 total tax revenue from all motor vehicle related sources, including licenses, fuel taxes, manufacturer's excises, tolls and parking meter revenues amounted to $8,162 million; expenditures directly on highways amounted to $7,931 million, not counting that part of local police expenditures of $1,290 million that could be regarded as spent for traffic control (roughly one-tenth, judging from the number of police assigned to traffic duty in

New York City), or the portion of the $562 million of "other sanitation" expenditures that could be regarded as spent for snow removal and other traffic-related purposes.[1] On this basis one would be inclined to doubt whether there is any large-scale misallocation of traffic between various modes, or substantial under- or overutilization of facilities.

When looked at in more detail, however, the picture is quite different, especially when full economic costs not represented adequately in the financial accounts are added in. If we attempt to separate out the urban component of the motor vehicle revenues and expenditures, we find that in 1960 the forty-three largest cities spent $600 million on highways, exclusive of police and sanitation expenditures for traffic related purposes. Of this only $289 million was financed from vehicle user charges in terms of any explicit flow of funds: $155 million from state highway grants and $134 million from city licenses, parking fees, and user charges, leaving $311 million, or 52 percent of the total outlay to be defrayed out of general revenues.[2] In 1957, all cities spent $2,941 million on streets and highways, of which only $1,471 million, or just over 50 percent, was derived specifically from use-related charges.

To get closer to the allocation of resources, however, we cannot stop here for the relevant matter is not through what channels the funds flow, but whether, on balance, the charges the motorist pays, to whatever governmental agency, correspond to the costs they occasion, in whatever form and by whatever agency these costs are borne. (Indeed, one could argue that the general purpose grants from state to local governments include some highway funds.) Figures of this sort are harder to come by. However, in a recent study of the Philadelphia metropolitan area, it was found that in 1957 total motor vehicle tax charges allocable to use of motor vehicles in the city of Philadelphia amounted to $30 million to all levels of government, but that motor vehicle expenditure by all levels of government within the city amounted to $46 million. Thirty-five million dollars of this was spent by the city itself, of which only $6.5 million was financed by grants from federal and state highway funds, and by user charges (chiefly parking meters), leaving $28.5 million to be financed from general revenue sources.[3] While this is only one instance, there is no obvious reason to suppose that the total cost of facilities being provided in Philadelphia is significantly higher relative to use than in other metropolitan areas, nor that the level of charges being paid by motorists is significantly lower. On this basis motorists in large cities appear to be paying only about two-thirds of the current expenditures made for the facilities they use.

---

[1] US Bureau of the Census, *Census of Governments, 1957* (federal excise taxes added).

[2] US Bureau of the Census, *Compendium of City Government Finances in 1960.*

[3] Philadelphia Bureau of Municipal Research, *Improved Transportation for Southeastern Pennsylvania* (May, 1960), pp. 294, 314

To obtain the true economic cost of urban traffic facilities, however, it is necessary to go even further than this and substitute, in place of current capital outlays, an appropriate rental charge representing interest and depreciation or amortization on the value of the facilities used. The current capital outlays to be substituted for, as representing provision for future use rather than for current use, amounted to $351 million out of a total of $600 million for the forty-three largest cities; for all cities in 1957 the figure is $754 million out of $1,753 million. But what to put in place of these figures is something of a problem. Farrell and Paterick, of the Bureau of Public Roads, put the value of the depreciated investment in urban street and highway improvements at $10.2 billion as of 1 January, 1953; $11 billion would seem a reasonably rough figure for 1957.[4] A figure of $8.25 billion for the value of land in city streets was produced by the Federal Trade Commission for 1922;[5] a more recent estimate appears not to be available but by considering trends in property values, a 1957 value on this basis of $21 billion seems roughly reasonable. At 4 percent interest on the total value of $32 billion, plus 2 percent amortization on the depreciated improvements, this gives $1,500 million to be substituted for the $754 million of current capital outlays in figuring true economic cost. The full annual economic cost of city street use thus comes to $2,319 million, as compared with actual outlays of $1,573 million, exclusive in both cases of police and sanitation. Even at this, the computation includes no equivalent for property taxes or corporation income taxes that would be covered by rental payments for the use of privately constructed property requiring comparable amounts of land and construction. If property taxes were figured at 1 percent on the full value (in 1956, assessments of $280 billion were estimated to represent 30 percent of full value, or about $930 billion; property tax collections were $11.7 billion)[6] $326 million would be added to the bill; in addition if as little as 20 percent of the investment were financed by equities, with a net return to equity holders of only 4 percent, the corresponding corporation income tax of 52 percent would add $277 million to the cost. With these elements added in, urban vehicular traffic is found to be paying $1,050 million in charges as compared to roughly $2,916 million that users of comparable resources in the private sector of the economy have to pay.

Obviously, if there is a way in which the cities can collect an additional $1,866 million from urban vehicular traffic so as to bring the charges more nearly in line with the costs, it would not only help to improve the resources allocation pattern but would ease the financial pressure on municipal governments very substantially. (Total city revenues from all sources were $13,748 million in 1959).

---

[4] Proceedings of the 32nd Annual Meeting of the Highway Research Board (January, 1953).
[5] National Bureau of Economic Research, *Studies in Income and Wealth*, (1950) Vol. 12, p. 547.
[6] US Bureau of the Census, *Statistical Abstract of the United States, 1961*, pp. 403, 418, 419.

Unfortunately, there has hitherto been no easy way to approximately triple the charges payable by the urban motorist without excessive interference with the smooth flow of that part of the total traffic that has a legitimate and urgent need for the use of the city streets. It appears, however, that with the aid of modern electronic equipment it is now feasible to equip each car using the urban streets with a cheap and rugged response block by virtue of which a record can be made each time such a car crosses a zone boundary, without interfering with the flow of traffic, and these records can be processed on electronic computers to produce a bill which can be made to vary appropriately with the costs occasioned by the movements of the car. It remains to be seen, however, whether what is economically sensible can be made politically palatable.

Some demurrer to the assignment of all city street costs to vehicular traffic is often entered on the ground that in addition to carrying through traffic such streets also serve as "access" to the adjacent property, and that the cost of such an access function is properly chargeable against the property owners rather than against the users as such. To be sure, if conditions are such that the roadway is no more elaborate than that which would be required to provide a mere access, and if traffic conditions are such that there is in fact no interference with other users of the roadway during such "access," then the marginal cost of such use is effectively zero in the short run, and charging the entire cost of the access street against the property owner would be conducive to unrestrained use of the uncongested facility, so that efficiency would be served. The bulk of the cost, however, particularly in view of such factors as the use-related character of much of the outlay for renewal of pavement and the high proportion of the property values accounted for by the downtown areas, is more nearly chargeable against users than abutting property owners. Even when a vehicle is performing an access function, its impact on traffic and on costs may be substantial; the amount of these costs is a function of the movement of the vehicles performing the access function and is not related in any direct way to the value of the property accessed. While some allowance might legitimately be made for the access function of low-traffic residential streets, this allowance would be small. Moreover, even on equity grounds, one could well raise a question as to whether the charge for the provision of common access facilities would not be more fairly allocated according to amount of use, rather than according to the value of the property accessed.

For example, even where a cul-de-sac is used almost solely for access purposes, with no traffic movement other than that destined to one of the abutting property owners, if conditions of use are such that there is interference between users, some means of bringing the cost of this interference home to them directly is needed. This can be done conveniently if the costs associated with providing the area and the pavement are assessed against users in proportion to use. It is both inequitable and inefficient to charge these costs to the abutting property owners under these circumstances, making the abutting occupant whose business requires relatively little use of the access facility pay just as much as his neighbor whose operations seriously interfere with the ease of access of the adjacent occupants. Some of the most serious congestion in New York is the result of the way in which "access" is had to firms in the garment district.

The special problem of the rush hour   The disparities in treatment between various forms of transportation are even further aggravated by the nature of rush-hour conditions. Nearly all forms of rush-hour transportation are grossly underpriced. In 1951, at a time when the fare of 10 cents on the New York subways was just about covering operating expenses, it was estimated that the marginal cost of a moderately long rush-hour ride was somewhere between 20 and 40 cents, possibly even higher in some cases. The differential between rush hour and nonrush hour or between rush-hour costs and average overall costs varies widely as among alternative forms of service, so that even if various forms of transportation were on an equal footing over the entire week, either each paying its way or being subsidized by about the same proportion, this still would not bring about an economical allocation of traffic among the various modes during the peak hours. For one thing transit systems can handle overloads in general much more readily than highways, by putting more persons into the same vehicle, and while this causes some deterioration in the service, sometimes to a truly inhumane degree, there is no complete breakdown. On the highways on the other hand there is no mechanism whereby increased traffic flow results in more persons riding per car, and there is a rather strong tendency for the system to jam up once a critical flow has been reached. Another and more important factor is the distribution of traffic through the day. At one extreme, commuter railroads handle half of their total traffic during the fifteen peak hours per week; for subway traffic the figure is about one-third, while for expressway traffic on routes to and from the central city the proportion is about 18 percent. This means that when costs are averaged over the entire traffic flow, the rush-hour traveler, who should bear the bulk if not the entire amount of the cost for providing the capital facilities, is able to shift over four-fifths of this burden to nonrush riders if he is an auto rider, but only two-thirds if he is a subway rider and only half if he is a rail commuter. Differentiation of the charge between peak and off-peak use is thus not only a matter of encouraging peak use and discouraging off-peak use, but it is also a matter of inducing the selection of a suitable mode of transportation given the time and volume of travel.

Accordingly, there can be no efficient solution to the urban traffic problem that does not include provision for charges on automobile use that are differentiated according to time of day. The most straightforward way of doing this is of course the direct recording of the passage of vehicles. It might also be possible to accomplish something indirectly through cordon tolls at the edge of the congested area, in combination with specific parking controls. This, however, is likely to balkanize the area, providing an artificial separation of economic activity on the one side of the cordon from that on the other. Tolls at an adequate level limited to main thoroughfares might reduce this balkanization somewhat, but at the cost of producing severe "shun-pike" congestion on the parallel minor streets. Special license fees imposed on city street users, in the form of a flat monthly or annual charge, hardly meet the problem: it is difficult if not impossible, without rather elaborate checking mechanisms, to distinguish between occasional use by suburban and out-of-town vehicles, which could appropriately be exempted entirely, and regular commuting for which the maximum charge would be appropriate. The usual basis for special local license fees is the location where the vehicle is customarily garaged, which is almost entirely inappropriate. For example, a vehicle which is kept in an off-street parking facility privately paid-for, and is used only for week-end excursions may be responsible for relatively little congestion, even making full allowance for the week-end parkway congestion.

Parking   Whether in connection with a cordon toll or in connection with a comprehensive electronic toll system, it will be desirable to have a closer check on the time at which cars enter and leave the traffic stream from parking space. Attended parking lots may presumably be required to provide this information in suitable form, possibly not without some resistance; on-street parking may at first appear to present a more formidable problem. The proposal formerly advanced by the writer for parking meters to be operated on a post-payment basis in which the rate of charge would be varied according to the number of parking spaces occupied and such that the deposit of coins would be required to recover the parker's key seems inadequate for this purpose.[7]

A proposal for curb parking control more in keeping with the above requirement is one in which a record is made of the time of parking and unparking as follows: for each local vehicle there is issued a parking card; on parking his car the operator inserts his card in the parking meter, presses a lever on the meter down against a spring, and withdraws a key belonging to the meter. This operation locks the lever down and the card inside the meter, where it can be inspected through a window; simultaneously a record is made of the time and the serial number of the card by imprinting an embossed serial number from the card and a time indication from a clock inside the meter through a carbon onto a paper strip. Subsequently, on the return of the operator, he reinserts the meter key, which releases the lever, causing a second imprinting of time to be made and the

---

[7] William S. Vickrey, "The Economizing of Curb Parking Space," *Traffic Engineering* (November, 1954), pp. 62–5.

card returned to the operator. The resulting paper tapes are periodically collected, the imprinted data read photoelectrically and converted to magnetic tape, then processed on a computer, either separately or in conjunction with records made automatically as cars cross zone boundaries.

By feeding the parking data for an area into the computer first, the occupancy rates for each group of parking meters at various times could be ascertained, and on the basis of these occupancy rates appropriate charges could be assessed for each parking of a car; the data can then be sorted by car number and matched with data for the zone boundary crossings to produce appropriate charges for the trip from the zone boundary to the parking spot, or from one parking spot to another. All the charges for any given car can then be combined, modfied where indicated by a factor relating to the nature of the car, combined with any outstanding charges and a bill sent to the owner, together with a card valid for the succeeding period for those not in arrears. Payment would be enforced in considerable measure by withholding of cards from delinquent owners: it could be made unlawful to operate a locally registered car in the area without a current parking card displayed appropriately in a holder on the windshield or elsewhere.

If corresponding records can be made for cars entering and leaving private parking lots and garages, and, perhaps more difficult, for cars parking in nonmetered outlying areas, it might be possible to achieve a fairly efficient system of charges by combining these records with a record made of cars entering and leaving the metropolitan area at some cordon line, without having to equip cars with any sophisticated electronic or other apparatus. Cars coming off the street into a private facility would be able to register "off" by inserting the card in a receptacle similar to a parking meter, and from which it could be retrieved only by again registering "on." This would enable all cars making trips fairly directly from one registration spot to another to be accounted for fairly accurately. There remains the problem of taxicabs, delivery trucks, and similar vehicles making devious and irregular trips. This could be taken care of, though somewhat awkwardly, by simply assuming that in the absence of evidence to the contrary, such vehicles registered as "on" the streets would be assumed to be circulating in the most congested areas subject to the highest rate of charge per minute, and providing opportunities in the outlying areas for such vehicles to register so as to qualify for an appropriately lower rate, e.g., by registering in an unused parking meter, or at extra registers provided for the purpose at convenient locations; it would only be necessary to register once for each more or less direct trip or trip segment beginning or ending in an outlying location.

There seems to be no easy way to deal with nonmetered parking within the cordon, however, so that the necessity for having all parking within the cordon metered is likely to require that the cordon line be put rather closer in than is altogether desirable, both from the point of view of a reasonably complete coverage of significant congestion and from the point of view of locating the cordon itself at a point where the required operations would not themselves be a congestion factor. On the other hand with a little ingenuity it should be possible to avoid the necessity for "toll-plaza" operations if space is at all scarce. Outbound, it is to the operator's advantage to register, so that a number of registration stations can be set up in tandem, with the driver being left free to register at any one of the stations. Inbound, while failure to register can be adequately penalized in those cases where the vehicle is going to "roost" somewhere within the cordon, there would be the possibility of evasion by those driving on through or making stops "on the run". But even here, since the operation is simply one of inserting the card in a slot, with no occasion for receipts or change requiring a human agent, it would be relatively easy to arrange for registers to be used in tandem, with signals to coordinate the sequence of use and indicate failure to register.

There remains the out-of-town vehicle. Where such vehicles are frequent visitors, it seems clear that they should be required to obtain cards on the same basis as local cars. For the occasional visitor or transient, this involves a relatively large administrative cost; moreover there is relatively little price elasticity to this particular category of use, and a considerable sentiment, arising both from commercial motives and traditions of "hospitality" in favor of generous treatment. Accordingly it seems entirely proper to arrange for such visitors to be given the "freedom of the city" insofar as street usage is concerned, to a suitably limited extent. This can be implemented by providing stations at a suitable distance outside the cordon where incoming visitors and occasional cars can obtain guest cards, valid for from two to ten days, showing conspicuously the license number of the car for which it was issued. A record is made of this license number when the card is issued, and this record is eventually checked to see that no more than the allowed number of guest cards are issued for any one car. It would probably be worth while to man the busier stations during hours of heavy traffic, particularly as they could be made to serve as general information booths as well; for light traffic routes and slack periods, the issuance of these cards could be automatic: for example, the applicant could be asked to write the license plate number through a plastic window and a single-use carbon on to the guest card, the carbon retaining the record; as the guest card is withdrawn, a transparent contact adhesive film is pressed over the license number imprint to prevent further alteration. The guest card may also contain an embossed serial number, similar to those on regular cards, for further identification. Even though a guest card was issued as valid for, say, ten consecutive days, the subsequent processing of the records would show for how many days it was actually used, and it would be possible to specifiy that an occasional visitor was entitled, say, either to ten consecutive free days a year, or perhaps to six free days scattered through the year. It may be necessary to require the deposit of a dime for each card in order to prevent frivolous withdrawal of cards.

As compared with the cash post-payment type of parking meter the present charge account type has one major disadvantage in that the time lag in the feed-back of information to the vehicle operator as to how great the charge was for parking at a particular time and place is comparatively long, so that his response to a given level of charge may be considerably delayed. Major changes in patterns of vehicle use will probably take considerable time, however, in any case, so that this may not be as serious as it might seem at first glance. As compared with cash post-payment, the problem of the operator returning to the parked car with insufficient change to pay the accumulated charge would be avoided. The meter mechanism should on the whole be less costly, particularly as there would be no direct interconnection among meters: assessment of the level of demand in the area would be by the computer program, not by interconnecting the meters; this would be not only a considerable saving in installation costs, but would make it possible to appraise the aggregate demand with much great flexibility and over a much wider area, so that the charges would not have to vary by such severe increments and a more stable equilibrium would be obtained. It would probably be necessary to make the release of the meter key conditional upon some pattern of holes or notches in the parking cards, otherwise there might be trouble from mischievous improper removal of meter keys; since there would be no gain to be obtained from such action, the keying need not be highly sophisticated and the meter mechanism can be kept reasonably simple.

Peak/off-peak transit pricing   The problem of suitable pricing of transit service to take account of the variations in cost between peak and off-peak service is relatively simple, at least for subway and commuter lines, and need not concern us here. Suitable automatic schemes for collection of sophisticated fare structures have been available, at least on paper, for some time. Recent developments in the direction of the use of subscriber cards and monthly billing (instead of cash payment, with or without refunds, as under former proposals) have been proposed for the San Francisco Bay Area Transit System, and seem well adapted to cases where the unit of sale is fairly large, as in systems that cater predominantly to medium-haul suburban traffic, as would be the case, for example, with railroad commuter service as distinct from local subway service. Also the clientele is of a character that would give rise to less difficulty in collecting on the basis of monthly bills. The principal unsolved problem is for local bus service, where lack of space and low levels of utilization militate against the use of complicated fare collection machinery, while any complication in the fare structure tends to overload the driver and slow service. The recent abolition of bus transfers in New York is a case in point, for while it does involve discriminations of a somewhat arbitrary sort between persons whose trips happen to be catered to by single long bus routes as compared to those having relatively shorter trips requiring the use of two different routes, it does significantly ease the burden on the operator.

An interesting suggestion has been put forth in connection with subscriber fare systems for suburban service: it would be at least conceivable that the agency furnishing the service should be set up as a membership organization along cooperative lines, and if so, one might argue that the subscribers should be entitled to deduct that part of their payments representing interest on capital and taxes, somewhat as owners of cooperative apartments do. The deduction would have at least this much rationale: commuting to relatively low rent suburban housing is a more or less direct substitute for the payment of higher rentals in close-in housing. Indeed, one could present the further case that with the commuter service the efficiency of allocation of resources is being fostered rather than otherwise by the discrimination, in that the service is one offered under conditions of decreasing costs; this much cannot be said of the deductions for interest and taxes on dwellings. But this is admittedly stretching matters pretty far.

Financing the intramarginal residue in urban transportation   While the most urgent need is to increase charges on rush-hour service of various kinds, especially motor vehicle usage, there will remain, ultimately, a fairly substantial portion of the cost of urban transportation that cannot be fully allocated on marginal-cost principles. On equity grounds many would argue for allocating this residue as a charge added to marginal costs and paid by the users, and the second-best principle would support this treatment at least to some extent. Thoroughness, however, requires that some attempt be made to trace out the way in which the assessment of transportation costs affects urban land use.

In this area more than most, extreme models produce paradoxical results. Land values are widely held to be created, or at least enhanced, by transportation developments, particularly those that produce changes of mode or nodes in the transportation network. Indeed at times it almost seems as if it is imperfections in transportation that create land values. Where transportation has uniform costs, models seem to indicate that the better transportation is, the lower land values will be, as for example with the assertion often made that if transportation could be made instantaneous and costless, site value would disappear. Even with less extreme models, if demand for urban land as a whole is considered to be completely inelastic, and if rents are made to vary so that for all developed urban land the sum of rents and the transportation costs of the activities carried out on the land to and from the center of the model are constant, then land rents are proportional to total transportation costs, and cutting transportation costs in half will preserve the same geographical pattern of activity with rents likewise cut in half.

A considerably different model emerges if we admit some elasticity into the demand function for access to the urban center, the amount of access being measured by the area of land occupied and the price of access being the sum of land rent plus the cost of a uniform amount of transportation per unit of land from the site to the center. If for simplicity we assume that all land uses have the same transport-to-the-center requirement, and that the demand function is unity, then the total price paid in terms of rent plus transportation cost is constant, and of this total price one-third is rent and two-thirds is transportation cost. The total cost can be thought of as a cylinder of height $h = tr$, where r is the radius of the developed area, and t the transportation cost per unit distance; at the edge of the cylinder transport cost is tr and rent is zero; at the center transport cost is zero and rent is tr; total rent can be represented by the cone fitting into the cylinder, which will have one-third of its volume. As the transport cost t increases, r shrinks (as the cube root of the transport cost rate), rents at the center rise, but the developed area shrinks, so that outside the developed area rents fall to zero. With a more elastic demand curve for access to the center, total rents would increase as transportation costs fall, but rents at the center would still fall, the increase being accounted for by enlargement of the developed area.

In order to produce a model in which improvement in transportation raises rents at the center, it would be necessary to produce a demand curve for access to the center which is in a sense perverse, i.e., in which the larger the aggregate, the more a given buyer is willing to pay for access to the center, and in which this effect is so strong as to outweigh the diminishing marginal utility of access to a center of a given size to successively less eager buyers. In other words if the Nth renter is willing to pay R for access to a center of size N, then even though the $N + 1^{st}$ renter would be willing to pay only $R - \delta$ for access to a center of size N, the Nth renter is willing to pay $R + \delta + \varepsilon$ for access to a center of size $N + 1$, and the $N + 1^{st}$ renter is thus willing to pay $R + \varepsilon$ for access to a center of size $N + 1$. Such an upward sloping demand curve would indeed imply that a decrease in transportation costs would increase the marginal value of access to the centre, and hence increase rents throughout the developed area. Thus it is possible for an improvement in uniform transportation to increase property values at the center; but whether the economies of scale in urban aggregations of the present size of most of our large cities are still significant enough to bring about this result would seem to be unlikely on an impressionistic basis.

On balance it seems likely that improvements in uniform transportation, as exemplified by travel in private automobiles over a standardized network of city streets, would benefit owners of outlying property more than owners of centrally located property, and that if intramarginal highway costs are to be charged against property values at all, they should be charged primarily against peripheral property values rather than against central ones. Indeed some of the deterioration observed in downtown areas over a period coinciding with the growth of the automobile relative to transit's decline is rather suggestive of the agreement of reality with some of the above models; this result may not be an adventitious one resulting from strangulation by inadequate development of facilities, but may be an inherent property of a non-focusing transportation system.

Models reflecting node effects   Models which will reflect the focusing effect of a transportation system with pronounced nodes are rather hard to come by, and it seems reasonable to suspect that a number of other facts, such as the variation in the relative demand of activities for space and for transportation, the possibility of linkages that do not pass through the center, the possibility of creating space through building upward, and the effect of the aggregate magnitude of activity on the demand for space would all interact with the existence of transportation nodes in affecting the pattern. To illustrate the lines on which analysis might proceed, I venture to suggest the following outline for a model, though without necessarily implying that the model can be worked through satisfactorily short of using successive approximations on a computer.

1   All transportation takes place along the lines of a rectangular grid, which however is dense enough to allow one to neglect the spacing between transportation lines. Initially the cost of transportation is uniform per unit of distance, with the result that the developed area takes the form of a tilted square, the diagonals of which are two of the transportation routes at right angles to each other. In subsequent stages improvements are made in transportation facilities along these two main axes, so that the marginal cost of travel along them is reduced as compared to travel off these axes. The result is to spread the developed area out in a four-pointed star.

2   A unit of activity is defined as an activity originating and terminating one unit of traffic. For simplicity the amounts of traffic originated and terminated are assumed to be equal. Activities vary according to some simple distribution as to the amount of space they require per unit of activity.

3   The frequency with which a unit of transportation is carried on between any two units of activity is inversely proportional to some power of the cost of the transportation (the so-called "gravity" model).

4   Space can be provided at a given location by constructing buildings of varying height and lot coverage, at (linearly) increasing marginal cost of additional space as the ratio of space to ground area increases.

Specifying the conditions of equilibrium is a fairly straightforward matter, buildings being constructed to a height at which space rent equals marginal cost, the difference between marginal and average cost appearing as ground rent, which, on this basis, is proportional to the square of the building height. Activities presumably locate in such a way as to minimize the sum of rent and transportation cost; there is, to be sure, some question at this point whether the transportation cost considered to be paid by an activity should be the one-way transportation cost or the two-way transportation cost: in principle it should be the two-way cost, but one might want to consider contexts in which it is more likely that an activity bears only the costs of outgoing transportation and incoming transportation is fully pre-paid by the shipper, or vice versa. Presumably, also, each activity would want to minimize not the cost of reaching a given set of correspondents by transportation, but the cost of transportation as adjusted for such shifts of correspondents as would be induced by the application of the gravity rule.

I have not had time to develop this program fully so I merely offer it as a suggestion to anyone who may be possessed of the computer programming facilities and mathematical skills required. Without going into the matter further a guess at the results is risky, yet one might hazard the guess that significant differences would emerge between the patterns that result when transportation costs are uniform as compared to what they are when transportation along certain channels is specially favored. If this expectation is substantiated this would be a further reason for using property tax revenues to subsidize node-creating transit rather than unfocused motor vehicle transportation.

Rationales for subsidy of one mode by another   If for one reason or another outside financing cannot be obtained to meet the intramarginal residues of transportation as a whole, there still may be sound justification for financing the intramarginal residues of mass transit by the levying of charges on urban motor traffic, even if these charges cannot be made to vary closely with the diurnal and other variations in congestion. In one sense, such a use of motor vehicle revenues for the finance of transit would be merely the equalization of the subsidy that now is given to the urban motorist, partly in the financing of actual outlays on streets out of property taxes, and partly in the failure to account at all for the rental value of the space the motorist occupies.

In some cases a politically more acceptable rationale can be derived from adventitious historical circumstances, as when it is proposed to turn some of the San Francisco Bay Bridge toll revenues over to the Bay Area Transit Authority, on the ground that originally the bridge did carry rail transit cars of the Key System, and the tracks were later removed to make way for additional roadways. The plea is made that this diversion of tolls is in lieu of the recapture of the bridge space for rail transit use. Actually while use of the bridge would be considerably cheaper in capital cost than the present plan to construct a new tunnel for the transit system under the bay, use of the bridge would be rather less satisfactory because of the awkward approaches that would be required and the severe speed restrictions that seem inevitably to apply to rail equipment operating over suspension bridges.

A more basic argument for subsidy of this sort can be derived from the following example, however, which illustrates how far off the "every tub on its own bottom" philosophy can get when misapplied to what seem superficially to be aggregates of similar tubs (even without an introduction of decreasing costs!). Suppose a facility of type M attracts rush-hour and nonrush-hour passengers in the ratio of 1 to 4, and costs $1.00 for each rush-hour passenger provided for and $0.20 for each nonrush-hour passenger. On the other hand a facility of type T costs only $0.75 for each rush-hour passenger and $0.15 for each nonrush-hour passenger, or uniformly 25 percent less; however, it attracts only one nonrush-hour passenger for each rush-hour passenger. If no differentiation between rush-hour rates and nonrush-hour rates is possible, facility M can break even with a charge of [$1.00 + 4($0.20)]/5 = $1.80/5 = $0.36; for facility T the break-even fare is [75¢ + 15¢]/2 = 90¢/2 = 45¢. Thus with each facility required to be self-liquidating, the passenger is offered a 9 cent fare differential in favor of facility M, alike in the rush hour and in the nonrush hour, whereas the consequence of his choosing facility M rather than T is to increase the costs, by 25 cents in the rush hour and 5 cents in the nonrush hour.

Of course, if it were true that if five rush-hour and five nonrush-hour passengers were to shift from T to M, they would automatically convert themselves in some way into two rush-hour and eight nonrush-hour travellers, then the 9 cent reduction in fare that they would obtain would be justified. But there is no reason to expect any effect in this direction, and an effect of even a fraction of this magnitude would be a highly unlikely occurrence. Actually, if peak–off-peak differentiation in charges is impossible for one reason or another, the next-best thing would be to reverse the relationship between the charges, and raise the charges on M to 45 cents and lower the charges on T to 35 cents, resulting in a subsidy of about 25 percent to T from excess revenues of M. If for the M facility we read streets and highways and for T we read suburban rail service, the correspondence with the typical facts is reasonably close. Thus if charges for peak use are ruled out, there is an even stronger case than would exist otherwise for subsidizing mass transportation at the expense of vehicular traffic.

Police and Custodial Service

Police expenditures amount to slightly over 10 percent of city expenditures, ranking below education and sanitation, but are perhaps less amenable than most other services to financing by means of specific charges. There is nevertheless something to be gained by an examination of the ways in which the revenue structure can be brought more closely in line with the costs of performing this service.

Unfortunately, not very much is as yet known concerning the specific factors that influence or should influence the level of police service provided. In New York City, under a "Post Hazard Plan" promulgated in 1955 and subsequently revised, an index of the relative volume of police problems in the various areas is used as an aid in allocating personnel. The index uses the following items with corresponding weights: Crimes of personal violence, 0.25; other crimes and offences, 0.20; juvenile delinquency, 0.15; accidents and aid cases, 0.10; population, 0.10; area, 0.05; business establishments, 0.05; school and recreation areas and crossings, 0.05; and radio alarms transmitted, 0.05. Obviously, at most 0.20 of the total weight is assigned to factors that could be made the basis for some form of tax, and even here the basis is impressionistic rather than based on any rigorous study.

There would seem to be a relatively close relationship between the characteristics of buildings in an area and the magnitude of the policing problem. But even if this can be substantiated, it is not clear how this relationship could be converted into a tax base and whether it would be desirable to do so if it could be done. Buildings converted to single room occupancy may appear to increase the policing problem, but it is at least possible that a tax on such occupancy would only result in the tax being passed on very largely to tenants. Indeed, to the extent that police problems are most intense in low-income neighborhoods, it may be almost inevitable that any attempt to levy a tax in proportion to some factor that seems to be causally related to policing costs will result in a severely regressive levy. This can be illustrated, for example, if it is proposed to allow some sort of tax credit for the provision of doormen, full-time janitors, and the like, whose presence would tend to reduce the policing problem.

There is, indeed, a whole array of situations where the line between private and public policing is unclear. At one time it was the practice in New York for city police to be detailed as guards to accompany payrolls and other similar transfers. This had serious ill-effects: gratuities were often offered in connection with this service, to the detriment of morale; the gratuities failed in most cases to cover the full cost, so that in effect an incentive for converting to a payment-by-check basis that should have been brought to bear was held off. A further effect was the diversion of unduly large numbers of police to this duty at peak periods near week-ends. In some instances police are hired to perform such duties during their off-work hours; this also may lead to abuses. Similar difficulties occur in conjunction with sporting events and other occasions where large numbers of persons are assembled. The range over which this problem of drawing the line between that for which the public police department will be responsible and that which is a private responsibility is a wide one. At one extreme, the Morningside Heights Association has recently arranged for a corps of private police to patrol the area as a supplement to the city police. At the other there is said to be least one case where the municipal police deliver the morning newspapers as a part of their early morning patrol. While this could obviously cause difficulty if carried too far, there are obvious complementaries between patrolling an area and performing other functions that may be worth taking advantage of, and of course if police are involved in such activities, the possibilities for obtaining revenues by appropriate charges should not be overlooked. But on the whole there is at this stage little that can be said definitely about appropriate modifications of revenue structures on the basis of their impact on police expenditures.

Recreational Facilities

Expenditures on recreational facilities account for about 5 percent of general expenditures, or about one-third as much as highways (in terms of cash outlay). In terms of the nature of the benefit, one could argue that here is an even stronger case for the levying of specific charges. However, it is rather more difficult to isolate a marginal cost that makes very much sense because in many cases the amenity provided by a park is enjoyed by occupants of abutting property, even if they impinge in no way upon the enjoyment of others. Some uses are joint rather than exclusive, in that one goes to an event in part in order to be part of the multitude. Even where the use is definitely exclusive, as in playing golf or tennis in periods of heavy demand, and accordingly efficient allocation would definitely call for the levying of a specific charge sufficient to equate demand and supply, there is a case to be made on distributional grounds for rationing by queue rather than by price. Many groups have more time than money, and it can be argued that it is desirable to preserve a reasonably wide variety of areas in which those who possess little coin of the realm can cash in that coin of which they have relative abundance.

Thus while a professor of economics, accustomed to value time highly and to think of queuing as an essentially wasteful process may at first take a dim view of a system where people line up for hours to get on a public golf course, this may not accurately reflect the feelings of those who do the lining up. Existence of a queue, to be sure, is *prima facie* evidence of inefficiency, in that if somehow reservations could be handed out to approximately the same group of persons who eventually play, the waiting, at least, could be eliminated. The cost involved in handling the reservations, however, may be greater than that of waiting (this is essentially the analog of the former situation with respect to vehicular traffic, where it was maintained that the cost of toll collection would be greater than the cost of the congestion it was to eliminate). Permitting nontransferable reservations to be made on a first-come, first-served basis involves an alternate waste of induced excessive precommitment to a specific plan of behavior some time in advance, on pain of forfeiting the privilege represented by the reservation. Again at first glance one might suppose that this waste could be eliminated by making the reservations transferable, to the mutual benefits of transferor and transferee, but this would only make the reservations either an attractive area for speculators to operate in, or require the application of some prior criteria for the issuing of the reservations.

Where the capacity of the facility is fairly rigid, as with tennis courts, and the demand somewhat unpredictable, because of the influence of the weather if for no other reason, it will in any case be almost impossible to clear the market with any degree of precision through pricing alone, and in such cases a combination of pricing and queuing is likely to occur. In the absence of distributional considerations, a proper balance is to be sought between the wastes of queuing and the wastes of underutilization of the facilities: the higher the price the less the queuing but the greater the underutilization in periods of unusually low demand. On the other hand the lower the price, the lower the revenues over the range of prices that is relevant here, while the greater, presumably, is the favorable effect on the distribution of income.

The outcome of the balance of these considerations is not a cut-and-dried matter, in any particular case. In considering the weight to be given to the losses of queuing, however, it is appropriate to consider the degree of compulsion involved in the queuing: if the associated service is one easily dispensed with or for which there are reasonably close substitutes available, as for example where private facilities are available at moderate fees, then the queuing losses can be assigned a relatively low value in the appraisal of alternatives, whereas if the queuing is more nearly associated with a necessity, with only relatively remote substitutes available, the costs of the queuing are likely to weight more heavily in the decision.

The same principles apply to the case where there is a temptation to continue the same fee that is inadequate to eliminate queues in peak periods over into periods of slack demand where the facilities are lightly used. In these cases the argument seems to be that the demand is highly inelastic over the range of prices in question anyhow, and that the redistributive effect of reducing the fees is less likely to be favorable, partly because of the absence of the selective effect of the queue, and partly on the ground that possession of leisure during the off-peak period is evidence of economic prosperity. There is also the problem of whether in view of the relatively low level of demand the facility should be closed down entirely during off-peak periods, or whether, contrariwise, only the fee collecting element should be closed down. This is not an important problem, but it is one that often seems to have been resolved more in terms of administrative convenience than in terms of any serious economic appraisal of the situation.

Education

Education is by far the largest single item in local government budgets, and there is no dearth of material on its financing. This is not the place to attempt a review of the volumes that have been written, but rather to sketch out new avenues of approach that might follow from an examination of the economics of the problem.

If provision of a uniform minimum standard of educational opportunity for all were more nearly a fact, rather than the rather remote aspiration that it actually is, the problem might be considered relatively simple. In fact, communities differ widely in their ability as well as in their willingness to provide a high grade of education. While intrastate differences in ability are met to a moderate degree by state aid formulae, the degree to which interstate differences in ability are met by federal aid is as yet minimal. The desire to provide adequate or even superior educational facilities thus often is severely constrained by the lack of adequate public revenue resources.

The problem is aggravated to a certain degree by the imbalance of internal migration. Regions that are net exporters of educated personnel fail to realize the tax base that would ordinarily result from the activities of the persons the, educate, a process that has certain vicious circle elements in it as areas with high educational aspirations relative to their tax base fail thereby to attract the base necessary to support the aspirations without recourse to burdensome rates. It is easy to exaggerate the importance of this, but it seems clear that some means of breaking through this situation is needed. The essence of the problem is that the opportunity for a profitable investment in education is being missed because the parents of the children involved may be unable to finance the education, either individually or collectively, while the community finds it very difficult to finance an investment from which the returns will accrue elsewhere. The problem is how to arrange for the repayment to the investing community of some of the returns generated by that investment in education.

The somewhat exotic proposal that these considerations seem to point to is as follows. Each federal income taxpayer should be required to report on his income form the state (or school district) in which he received his public education, if any. A portion of his tax would then be turned over to the state (or school district) so indicated. The intended effect would be primarily one of making "educational export" regions more willing to upgrade their educational standards in view of an expectation that even though the region might not benefit directly from the better education of those who leave, the region would nevertheless get a return in this form.

Such a principle is of course capable of great modification in detail. It could, for example, be applied only prospectively, to taxpayers in the future that are now getting educated; presumably the incentive to educational export regions to upgrade their education would remain as strong, even though they might have to borrow to do it on the strength of the expectation of these revenues. They merely would not obtain an unexpected windfall from the incomes of their previous students. However, this would be subject to the perennial problem of the inability of any government to commit itself effectively to a program that would have to extend for so many years into the future if it were to be effective at all and in the absence of some mechanism of effective commitment, the incentive effect on current expenditures on schools might not be realized. Also, it would be possible to limit the distributions in some way to those educational systems that represent a high degree of effort in relation to the revenue resources available. Another possibility would be to vary the amount of the income tax payable by the individual according to the degree to which his income might be considered to be the result of superior or inferior educational facilities, the variation in tax above the minimum level being the amount available for redistribution back to the educational agencies.

The difficulties of putting any such plan into practice are obvious and probably insurmountable, and accordingly it must be considered as being presented as an aid and stimulus to discussion rather than as a serious proposal. Possibly a more likely, but less effective, variant would be to propose that some of the federal grants in aid to states might be calculated on the basis of their being, in effect, *ex post* compensation to the exporting states for the loss of human capital they experienced as a result of net migration in the past, insofar as this capital export could be considered to reflect the value of the education given. Another way of doing it would be to make current and future migration patterns the basis for grants, without attempting to relate the grants to the income actually yielded by the investment in education.

Health and Hospital Services

The main element that is peculiar to health and hospital services is the close interrelationship between municipally financed services and services covered by insurance, and the presence of a "moral hazard" element, by which is meant the tendency to make unjustified use of the facilities because they are either free or covered by insurance. In a sense the "moral hazard" here is only an acute form of the general tendency to overuse a facility that is underpriced; if a difference exists it is mainly that here the justification for use is supposed to reside more in objective medical facts and less in individual preferences, and the moral hazard arises because the objective medical facts are never quite as objective as the concept of a welfare standard or an insurance indemnity would like them to be. The moral hazard arises from many motives, from the doctor's desire to have the patient where it is easy to visit him, or the use of the hospital as a refuge, or to the desire to take advantage of section 105(d) of the federal income tax, which allows a deduction for sick pay for the first seven days of illness only if the employee is hospitalized during that time. The problems are so diverse that about all that could be done here is to simply list the area as one in which there is the possibility of some financing by fees.

Public Utility Services

Although such public utility services as electricity supply, telephone service, gas distribution, mail service, parcel delivery, and even newspaper delivery are not ordinarily included among the services considered as part of the standard pattern of governmental activity at the local level, the lines between these services and those such as water supply, garbage collection, and sewage disposal, that more typically are so considered, are to a degree arbitrary. Of these, the one that is most frequently added to the list of municipal activities, electricity supply, is perhaps the one for which the special powers of the municipality are least needed.

Dissatisfaction with the results of public utility regulation of private utilities, plus the attractions of the availability of relatively low-cost capital and certain other tax advantages relative to federal and state taxes are among the major factors which have led to the entry of municipalities into the business of supplying electricity, but these factors are common to the other utilities as well. In some cases the establishment of a municipal electricity service is the result of such special stimuli as the TVA and other public power agencies. But to a large extent the fact that these forces were effective with respect to electricity but not to other utility services can be laid to the fact that of all of the predominantly privately supplied ones, electricity is the one that is most nearly an absolute necessity for the typical urban resident. Actually, it is precisely this characteristic that would make it possible for a privately operated utility to come reasonably close to an optimum allocation of resources through the adoption of a schedule of charges that will closely reflect marginal cost and yet at the same time extract a sufficient additional revenue from the intramarginal consumption to earn a normal return on its investment. There are several ways of doing this, but the most appropriate would be to charge rates for kilowatt-hours at the appropriate marginal cost, and assess in addition a front-foot charge to cover the basic cost of the distribution system. The front-foot charge could be expressed, if need be, in the form of a higher rate per kilowatt-hour for the first x kilowatt-hours per month per front foot; since practically all consumers would be using more than this initial block, the result would be essentially marginal-cost pricing. This device is available to the electric power company primarily because the use of electricity is so nearly universal that no customers to speak of would find it advantageous to refuse service because of this initial rate.

With nearly all of the other services, however, an attempt to charge for the service according to front feet, to cover the basic costs of traversing the streets so as to cover the area effectively, would result in many potential customers refusing the service in order to escape the cost, and it does not seem likely that a privately operated service would be empowered to assess charges on property owners who do not take the service. It is here that there is a definite opportunity for improvement in the efficiency of allocation of resources through the collection by the municipality of a special frontage tax to defray the basic traversal costs of these various services, and then make available to the residents these various services at rates that would be fairly close to the incremental cost of rendering the service. It would not be absolutely necessary for the municipality to render the service on its own account: this could be done by contract, though of course in this case care would have to taken lest abuses occur, and if anything of this sort were to be done at all, many would be inclined to favor some method that would not result in the subdivision of responsibility and the introduction of opposing monopolistic interests. Including mail delivery in this list is perhaps a bit quixotic in view of the firm preemption of this field by the federal government, yet it is technologically no more unreasonable to contemplate the local handling of mail that is transmitted nationwide by a national service than it is to contemplate local distribution of electric power generated and transmitted over a wide area by a federal agency.

Specific Financing and the Overall Fiscal Picture

In considering the extent to which specific charges should be used in each instance, some attention must of course be given to the relation of the costs and revenues in that area to the overall fiscal picture of the governmental unit, both as to the aggregate amount and as to the distributional impact of the costs and revenues. The first of these elements can be adequately represented for most purposes by introducing as a parameter the "marginal cost of public funds."

The Marginal Cost of Public Funds

The marginal cost of public funds is defined as the net reduction in the overall allocational efficiency of the economy resulting from the raising of an increment of revenue from a given source, expressed as a ratio or percentage of that increment in revenue. It includes, overall, the loss in consumers' surplus, the loss

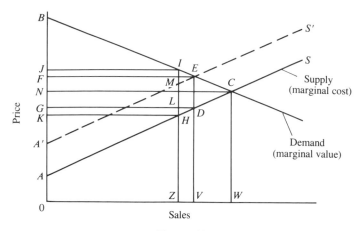

Figure 18.1

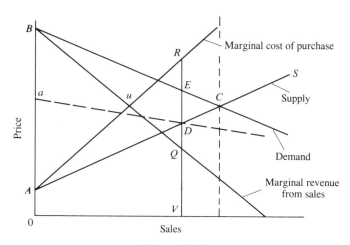

Figure 18.2

in producers' surplus or economic rent, the marginal costs of administration, and the marginal costs of compliance. If we are considering an established set of taxes and charges and only the rates are under consideration, the compliance and administrative costs may be approximately constant, so that they can be neglected, and we can focus our attention on the effects of the rate changes on surplus.

The simplest case to analyze is that of a simple excise tax on a commodity produced under conditions of constant or increasing costs. In figure 18.1, AC is the supply curve, BC is the demand curve, C is the price and quantity resulting

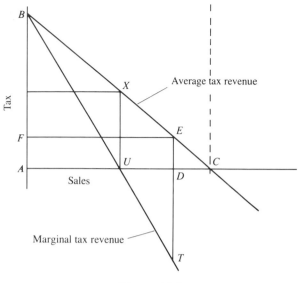

Figure 18.3

under competition with no tax, and *ACB* is the net social gain generated as a result of the production of the commodity in question, divided into consumers' surplus *CNB* and producers' surplus or rent, *ANC*. If a tax equal to *DE* is imposed, per unit of output, the supply curve inclusive of tax moves from *ACS* to *A'ES'* there is a tax revenue of *EDGF*, the consumers' surplus is reduced to *EFB*, producers' surplus is reduced to *AGD*, and there is a net loss of potential surplus to the community as a whole of *DEC*, representing the excess of the value *VECW* of the output that is no longer being produced *VW*, over what it would cost to produce it, *VDCW*.

Suppose that now the tax is increased to *HI*. Consumers' surplus is now *IJB*, revenue is now *HIJK*, and producers' surplus is now *AKH*, the total loss of potential surplus now having increased to *CHI*. The net increase in this loss, *EDHI*, is what is to be compared to the increase in revenue, which is *HIJK – DEFG*. This comparison can be made in terms of the somewhat simplified figure 18.2, in which we in effect regard the tax as the margin which the government acting as a monopolist adds to what it pays for the total supply to determine the price at which the total amount will be sold. *BC* is the demand curve as before, and *BQ* is the corresponding marginal revenue curve (in the case of straight line demand curves it is twice as steep as *BE*), representing the net increase in gross revenues from the sale of one or more units at the correspondingly lower price. Similarly, *AR* is the marginal cost of purchase curve, representing the cost of buying one more unit, allowing for the fact that buying one more unit will raise the price which must be paid for all units in the open market. The difference RQ is then the loss in net revenue resulting from the purchase of one more units at an overall additional cost of VR and its sale at an overall additional revenue of VQ; this is what is to be compared to the loss of net social surplus represented by ED, the difference between the value VE the buyer would place on the additional unit and the cost of producing it, VD.

A third way of presenting the situation is to subtract the supply curve AC vertically from the demand curve BC to get the curve BC in figure 18.3 which shows the relation between the tax rate and the amount sold. This can be regarded as the net demand for the government's (costless) services in transferring the product from sellers to buyers. The total surplus generated if there is no tax is ABC, as before, and the amount that is sacrificed if a tax of DE is imposed is DEC, the total tax revenue being $ADEF$. The marginal government revenue curve BUT being the marginal curve corresponding to the average revenue or tax rate curve BEC, represents the net revenue from arranging for the sale of an additional unit. Increasing the tax to reduce the sales by one unit thus increases revenues by DT (the negative marginal revenue), and increases the net social loss by DE. It is the ratio ED to DT that is the marginal cost of public funds; this obviously begins at zero for no tax at C and increases steadily as the tax rate is increased, becoming infinite as the tax is raised to the point UX, where the revenue is a maximum.

If taxes are being raised from several such sources at once, the optimum arrangement is one in which the ratio ED/DT is the same in all cases. It can be shown that for excise taxes this relation obtains if the ratio of tax to price for each commodity taxed is proportional to the sum of the (absolute) inelasticities of demand and of supply, provided that we measure the inelasticity of demand net of the tax (i.e., as though the demand curve had been shifted downward by the amount of the tax; inelasticity is the reciprocal of the elasticity).

It is tempting to apply this analysis directly to the case where the government is itself the supplier. This is correct if the supply is obtainable at constant costs, but in the case where the service is subject to increasing or decreasing costs it is necessary to allow for the fact that the government is in effect the recipient of the producers' surplus that in the excise tax case accrued to private individuals, at least in the more usual case where the increasing costs of the government service arise within the service itself and is not a result of pushing the prices of factors of production on the market up. Thus in figure 18.2, the loss from reducing the consumption by one unit as a result of raising the price is still ED, but the accompanying change in revenue is the saving in cost, indicated by the marginal-cost curve which would be the supply curve in the former case, or VD, less the reduction in revenue, indicated by the marginal-revenue curve VQ. Thus in this case the marginal cost of obtaining public funds by raising the price is ED/QD. The "tax" DE, in this case representing the excess of the price over marginal cost, is, as a percentage of the price VD, to be made proportional only to the inelasticity of demand, the inelasticity of supply for this purpose being taken as zero. The same analysis applies if the service is supplied under conditions of decreasing cost, as would be indicated by the dotted curve aD.

Marginal Redistributional Coefficient

Similarly it would be nice to have a coefficient of redistribution that could be applied, to indicate more or less how much misallocation the community was willing to tolerate for the sake of how much redistribution. In principle, it would be just as inconsistent to have two alternative systems which show an equal marginal cost of public funds but a widely varying marginal impact on distribution. Distribution, however, is not something that can easily be reduced to a single parameter, and in addition opinions vary so widely on the desirability of income redistribution that anything that could be done along this line would be highly subjective. In view of these difficulties, the matter is left with this brief mention.

Summary

Enough has been said to indicate that even though the decision to provide a given facility or service may well require a weighing of costs and benefits, benefit may not provide a suitable basis for the assessment of charges to defray the costs. The decisions made by governments in deciding whether to offer a service and of what extent and character, and those made by individuals in availing themselves of whatever service is provided are of a different scope and often of a different dimension, so that the comparisons that are pertinent for the one decision are not always relevant for the other. Generally speaking, the considerations adduced in considering appropriate charges lean rather more toward the taxation of land rather than improvements, not necessarily in terms of its market value, but rather in terms of such parameters as area and frontage. Even where benefits seem to be most closely measurable in terms of improvements, the causal nexus is found to be more nearly independent of actual improvements and to relate more to the fundamental site-determined characteristics. Finally, a comprehensive approach to the pricing of municipal services may lay the groundwork for a new and more fruitful approach to overall urban planning in terms of economic costs as well as of architectural design.

19

The Impact on Land Values of Taxing Buildings

The conventional wisdom concerning the shifting of property taxes has it that taxes on land values or ground rents are borne by the owner of the land and are capitalized in the value of the land, while taxes on improvements are shifted forward to the tenants. There remains the possibility, however, that the impact of the tax on improvements may be felt in one way or another by the landlord, through changes in the overall demand. The supply of land, indeed, may be highly inelastic and not susceptible to substantial influence by taxation. The demand for land, however, may be so influenced, and if it is, the impact may be of significance. The present paper is an attempt to explore these relationships more fully with the aid of a somewhat drastically simplified mathematical model.

Suppose that the annual cost for financing and maintenance for a structure of mean height h is given by

$$C = (1 + x)f(h) = (1 + x)bh^a , \qquad (1)$$

where the structure occupies a unit area of land, h is the ratio of where the standardized rentable space to land area, b and a are constants, with $a > 1.0$, and x is the effective rate of tax on the improvements. The city is built up in a circularly symmetrical pattern around a center, and prospective tenants all have a uniform pattern of a given amount of travel to or from the center per unit of rental space occupied. Preference for a central location is entirely accounted for by this transportation cost, so that the rental at a distance r from the center can be set equal to $t(R - r)$, where t is the cost over a unit distance of the amount of transportation with the center associated with the occupancy of one unit or rental

Proceedings of the 62nd National Tax Conference (Columbus Ohio: Tax Institute of America, 1969), pp. 86–9.

area, and R is the radius of the built-up portion of the city, space being available beyond the radius R at zero rent. The height of construction at any distance r from the center is then, in equilibrium, given by equating the marginal cost of added space through increasing height with the value at which the space can be rented, or

$$\frac{dC}{dh} = ab(1 + x)h^{a-1} = t(R - r) . \tag{2}$$

Solving for h, putting $B = b(1 + x)$, $q = R - r$, $k_1 = (t/a)^c$, $c = 1/(a - 1)$, we have

$$h = k_1 B^{-c} q^c$$

The total space available within the outer radius R is then

$$S = \int_0^R 2\pi r h \, dr = B^{-c} 2\pi k_1 \int_0^B (R - q) q^c dq = k_2 B^{-c} R^{c+2} , \tag{4}$$

where $k_2 = 2\pi k_1 [1/(c + 1) - 1/(c + 2)]$.

The total cost of occupying space is uniformly tR, this being the rent at the center where there is no transportation cost, and the transportation cost at the rim where there is no rent. We can then suppose that the demand for space is given by

$$S = A \, tR^{-e} , \tag{5}$$

where e is thus the elasticity of demand. Initially at least, we assume that all persons are uniform in their relative need for transportation to the center, and that their degree of preference for a central location is also uniform, so that at the equilibrium prices each person is indifferent, given the rents, as to where he locates.

Putting (4) and (5) together, we have $k_2 B^{-c} R^{c+2} = At^{-e} R^{-e}$, which gives

$$R^{c+2+e} = (A/k_2) t^{-e} B^e \quad \text{or} \quad R = k_3 B^{c/(c+2+e)} \tag{6}$$

where $k_3 = ([A/k_2] t^{-e})^{1/(c+2+e)}$.

Thus in this model, as the tax rate on improvements, x, increases, and thus $B = b(1 + x)$ also increases, so does R. Taxes on improvements are thus a factor tending to increase urban sprawl, leading to increased ground rents near the perimeter.

The impact may be considerably different near the center, however. Ground rents at a distance r from the center are given by

$$g(r) = h \frac{dC}{dh} - C = aBh^a - Bh^a = (a - 1)Bh^a = (a - 1)C . \tag{7}$$

Thus by virtue of the cost function selected, ground rents are a fixed proportion of total rent and bear a constant proportion to improvement costs. This is in conformity with the frequent practice of appraisers of expecting a "normal" relation between the value of land and improvements to be fairly constant. Using (3) in (7), we have

$$g = (a - 1)B(k_1 B^{-c}q^c)^a = k_4 B^{-c}q^{c+1} \tag{8}$$

where $k_4 = (a - 1)k_1{}^a$, since $ac = c + 1$. At the center, $q = R = k_a B^{c/(c+2+e)}$, from (6), so that

$$g(0) = k_5 B^{-c(e+1)/(c+2+e)}, \tag{9}$$

and increasing the tax on improvements will lower the ground rent at the center.

The total ground rent is given by $G = \int_0^R 2\pi r g \, dr$, or

$$G = \int_0^R 2\pi k_4 B^{-c}(R - q) \, q^{c+1} \, dq = k_6 B^{-c}R^{c+3} = k_7 B^{c(1-e)/(c+2+e)}, \tag{10}$$

The effect of tax change on total ground rent thus depends on the elasticity of demand for urban space, in this model: an elastic demand results in an increase in total ground rents with decreasing improvement tax rates, and vice versa. Indeed, in this model, ground rents, structure costs, and transportation costs make up the total cost of space occupancy in constant proportions, and ground rents are in effect varying in proportion to the total expenditure on space.

One interesting possibility suggested by this model is that if the demand for space is sufficiently elastic, it would be possible to reduce or eliminate the tax on improvements and recoup the revenue out of the increase in ground rents or land values. The difficulty would be that this could not be done by a uniform tax on ground rents or land values, since land values near the periphery would go down rather than up, so that a uniform increment in the land tax would leave some property owners worse off. Only some form of tax on value increments, coupled with a compensation for those whose property values declined, could produce a situation where everyone was made better off.

Another suggestion presented by this model is that if a shift is made from taxes on improvements to taxes on land, land values in the center will rise relatively to those in the suburbs, and indeed values in the suburbs may decline.

Even these notions are based on what is an extremely oversimplified model. In reality the assumption of a constant elasticity of cost with respect to height or density of coverage is probably not fully realized, although I would hesitate to say at this point in which direction reality diverges or what effect this would have on the model. Another and more one-sided assumption is that all users of space have uniform space-transportation ratios, whereas actually there will be a concentration at the center of those who, for one reason or another, find separation from the center more expensive.

Still another factor that calls for consideration is that demand for space near the center tends to be in some degree autocatalytic: the demand for space is enhanced by the concentration of space near the center.

Representation of these complications even in the simplest possible form leads to a much more complex model about which it is difficult to say anything very precise without more anaylsis than there has as yet been time for. All that is clear at the moment is that the classical assumption that the incidence of the tax on improvements is on the tenant and that land values are affected only by the capitalization of the land tax need to be considerably modified if a reasonably complete analysis is made, and that the issue of land taxation versus the taxation of improvements may have fairly substantial repercussions on the relative finances of the core city as compared with the suburbs.

PART VI

———————————— · ————————————

Macroeconomic Policy

In effect, the economy can be thought of as having three major parameters that we would like to control: the level of employment of human and other resources, the price level, and the division of the resulting total product between provision for current wants and investment in growth and the future. At the same time, we have only two major policy tools: monetary and fiscal policy. In an era when inflation was not a threat, one could think of these two tools as controlling the level of employment and the rate of growth ... However, with a need to control inflation as well, relying on only two dimensions of control is like trying to fly an airplane without ailerons, which were the third dimension of control that was the key to the success of the Wright brothers. A new tool is needed.

American Economic Review, 1 (1993) p. 7.

This part of the volume differs from the preceding ones in an important respect. William Vickrey wrote systematically and recurrently about taxation and public utilities. His work had a significant intellectual influence on social choice theory and mechanism design. No such claims can be made about his writings on macroeconomic policy. The significant aspect here is that, *since the mid eighties, Vickrey's attention has been very much focused on the problem of unemployment.* The main purpose of this part of the volume is to bring out the turn taken by Vickrey's interests over the past decade, and to lay out his views about today's policy agenda.

Macroeconomics and fiscal policy had retained his attention all along, in part no doubt due to his concern about public policy in general, in part due to his involvement in teaching general theory. For many years, Vickrey taught a two-semester graduate course at Columbia in economic theory, the special flavor of which is partly encapsulated in the two volumes published in 1964 under the respective titles of *Microstatics* and *Metastatics and Macroeconomics*. The second volume is a nonmathematical presentation of *general equilibrium in a monetary economy*.

Because few of us would naturally turn for inspiration to a textbook written thirty years ago, it is appropriate to quote briefly from the Preface to that second volume:

Microstatics covers the usual neoclassical theory of consumption, exchange, production, competitive equilibrium, monopoly, and imperfect competition, with considerable emphasis on the use of indifference curves as a technique and on welfare economics as a motivation. There is also a brief introduction to game theory as an illustration of the difficulties encountered in pushing very far with a priori theoretical analysis into the area of imperfect competition.

. . . Under the heading of "metastatics," in which the element of uncertainty is excluded, are discussed the notion of general intertemporal equilibrium in a hypothetical "futures" economy, the general analytical framework for capital formation, growth, and progress, including some tentative remarks concerning population problems, the application of the theory to anticipated fluctuations, and the Bernouillian theory of risk. The basic elements of monetary theory are presented as a prerequisite to the formulation of complete macroeconomic models . . . As a second prerequisite, the basic concepts of national income accounting are presented, a special attempt being made to relate the aggregates encountered in practice to underlying analytical concepts.

The greatest attention in this volume has been focused on the problem of presenting the Keynesian and the classical modes of general equilibrium analysis in a manner that will permit the student to arrive at a synthesis in which the salient elements of each approach are given their due share of emphasis. Indeed, this part has been considered sufficiently important to warrant the presentation of two complete alternative forms of the analysis.

. . . Although there may be little here that can claim to be entirely new, some of the presentation, including the methods of representing graphically the integration of classical and Keynesian analysis, may be sufficiently novel to merit the attention of many of whom the basic ideas have long since been familiar.

Given the amount of thought put by our friend Bill into this one figure, we take pleasure in reproducing it opposite, for the benefit of those whose attention it merits.

In the same chapter on "Macroeconomic Equilibrium," several sections are of more direct relevance to the papers selected for this volume, in particular the sections entitled "Nature of the Capital-Market Equilibrium", "Difficulties with the Classical Mechanism" and "The Mechanism of Interest Determination." Some of the problems labeled "recycling of savings" in what follows were expounded systematically in the textbook.

The preoccupation with the ineffectiveness of monetary policy at very low nominal rates of interest, which is central to chapter 20 below, is also documented in that chapter of the textbook.[1] In addition, chapter 20 reveals Vickrey's familiarity in the fifties with the argument that "any limitation of the supply of [fiat] money can be regarded as leading to a waste of real resources in the form of . . . extra trips to the bank, extra financial transactions, telegraphic transfers, and the like, all of which . . . attempt to economize a good which has a cost of production of zero." That argument, which is central to Friedman's approach to *The Optimum Quantity of Money*,[2] is regarded by Vickrey as superseded by the drawback of monetary policy ineffectiveness when nominal interest rates approach zero.

---

[1] The ideas presented in chapter 20 were developed formally in a 1954 paper, "Stability Through Inflation," which appeared in *Post Keynesian Economics*, K. Kurihara, Ed. (New Brunswick: Rutgers University Press.)

[2] Chicago: Aldine, 1969.

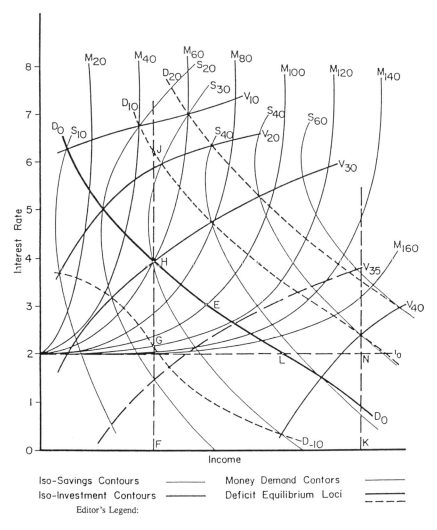

Iso-Savings Contours   ———   Money Demand Contors   ———
Iso-Investment Contours ———   Deficit Equilibrium Loci ====

Editor's Legend:

$S_{20}, S_{30}, \ldots$: loci of income–interest pairs with "constant *ex ante* savings" (at levels 20, 30,…).

$V_{20}, V_{30}, \ldots$: idem for "constant planned investment."

$D_0 - D_0$: locus of balanced-budget equilibrium pairs (at H, savings=investment=30, etc.).

D_{-10}, D_{10} : constant–deficit equilibrium loci (D_{-10} means a surplus of 10, D_{10} means a deficit of 10).

$M_{20}, M_{40}, \ldots$: loci of income–interest pairs with "constant money demand" (at levels 20, 40,…) (to be used when money supply rather than interest is controlled).

The central chapter in this part of the volume is the last one, Vickrey's 1993 Presidential Address to the American Economic Association entitled "Today's Task for Economists."[3] The remaining two chapters, one of which goes back to 1986, are developments of themes that figure prominently in the Presidential Address.

There is a clear indication here of "responsive thinking" by a responsible economist. Vickrey's concern with economic efficiency at the service of human welfare is obvious throughout his career; the section entitled "The Allocation Task of Yesteryear" in the Presidential Address provides a bird's eye reminder of how that concern expressed itself over the years. Today's task is clearly identified. When comparing the social costs of inflation and unemployment, Vickrey writes:[4] "Actually, inflation anticipated with certainty is in the not-too-long run merely a minor inconvenience in the making of transactions. Unanticipated changes either up or down in the rate of inflation are largely a matter of inequitable redistribution, a kind of widely distributed embezzlement, as contrasted with unemployment, which in terms of its impact on the aggregate product is akin to vandalism, and which in addition has severe social impacts on homelessness, drug addiction, and crime."

The message of the Presidential Address is a forceful one: "we have not had anything approaching real full employment since the Korean War, or indeed in peacetime at any time since 1926 . . . I lay before you a plan I believe can accomplish this . . . If you don't think that something like this can be made to work, then it is up to us to find something that will." The dedication of Columbia's white-haired crusader is as fierce as ever.

There is no point in summarizing the "plan" here: the Address is short enough and should be read by any user of this volume. Perhaps it should be read twice: a first time to understand the general argument; a second time, after having attempted to fit the argument into one's customary mental framework and having thought up possible objections, to reflect on the research priorities best suited to "find something that will work." In the process, the reader should verify that he follows Vickrey in enlarging the customary "inflation–unemployment" trade-off into the broader "inflation–unemployment–*accumulation*" trade-offs.

Chapter 22, entitled "Necessary and Optimum Government Debt," deserves a special comment. When the plan to publish this book was presented to William Vickrey in October, 1992, he quickly gave his unequivocal approval, and then

---

[3] Actually, chapter 23 is a revised version of the Presidential Address, dated February 1993; see "Prologue," p. 432. When we asked Vickrey to approve the contents of this volume, he suggested substituting this revised version for the earlier one, published in the *American Economic Review*. There are interesting nuances, revealing not only the "activity of the little grey cells," but also the seriousness of Vickrey's concern about today's wasteful unemployment.

[4] In "Meaningfully Defining Deficits and Debts," *American Economic Review* (1992), p. 310.

asked whether he should write a Preface. The editors suggested that he might instead contribute a "Postface," addressed to the readers who had already familiarized themselves with the contents of the volume. As it later turned out, the Presidential Address (chapter 23) serves naturally the purpose of a Postface. So Bill offered instead to write a new chapter, developing some aspect of current interest for which the format of the Presidential Address did not permit adequate treatment. Chapter 22, dated 16 March, 1993, develops the idea that budget deficits may be indispensable at this time to recycle the excess of private savings over private investment. This leads to a definitely unconventional approach to government debt. For a citizen of Belgium, a country where a public debt amounting to 130 percent of GDP currently imposes on the government budget gross service charges in excess of 10 percent of GDP at a real interest rate of some 5 percent and at a time of budget contraction, the views expressed in chapter 22 seem rather optimistic. Of course, these views are developed for the US, not for a very small and very open economy. Still, even to a Belgian, the different approach offers food for thought.

As William Vickrey approaches his eightieth birthday, he has learned from experience that simple logical ideas, conducive to innovations of great practical significance – like cumulative averaging or congestion charges – may fail to gain wide acceptance; whereas other ideas, initially addressed to theorists rather than to practitioners – like demand revealing mechanisms – may receive enthusiastic recognition. "Marketable Gross Markup Warrants" might look like a candidate for the first category. However, unsolved problems keep pressing their demands, while intellectual and technological progress shifts the feasibility frontier. Electronic Vehicle Identifiers may have seemed futuristic in 1959; they have now been tried, the technology is being developed, and significant applications are bound to emerge under the growing pressure of traffic congestion. The inflation–employment–accumulation challenges should put mounting pressure on economists to "find something that will work" toward "a major reduction of the ills of poverty, homelessness, sickness and crime." Economists of the current generation will no doubt consider seriously the task laid before them, on the basis of fifty-five years of experience, by a particularly insightful and dedicated member of the profession.

20

The Optimum Trend of Prices

Traditional approaches to macroeconomics have often taken for granted as a norm some kind of stable price level, either as a state of affairs that would come about naturally if no sins were committed against the canons of sound finance and sound money, or as a goal to be pursued through various monetary and fiscal measures by reason of its presumed advantages. Probably few if any are now left who would have much confidence that such a state would be reached without deliberate intervention by appropriate agencies, but there remain many who are willing to accept a stable price level as a desideratum without adequate inquiry into the specific advantages and disadvantages of this as compared with some other regime. It is time, I think, that we broadened the field of alternatives among which we choose, and give more deliberate attention to the possibilities that are opened to us if we are willing to consider the deliberate choice of upward or downward trends in the price level as alternatives worthy of serious consideration rather than as heresies to be dismissed offhand.

Traditional arguments in favor of a constant price level have included arguments that such a state, or a reasonably close approach to it, is a necessary prerequisite for general economic stability; that a stable price level favors correct economic calculation; and that it is necessary to the preservation of equity as between debtors and creditors and between differently situated economic groups generally. Upon examination, it turns out that given suitable auxiliary conditions, none of these advantages is exclusive to a stable price level, and that the decisive factors may be quite different in character.

Indeed, the concept of the stable price level has itself been given different interpretations. Some have written in terms of a stable level of product prices, or

Southern Economic Journal, 25 (1959), pp. 315–26.

of a stable level of the cost of living; others have spoken in terms of a constant level of factor prices. Given some form of technological progress, the two necessarily give different results. Sir Dennis Robertson, for example, has on occasion expressed himself in favor of the stable factor price level, in part because he conceives that this would give the rentier and pensioner a greater share in economic progress. Keynes' use of the wage-unit as a numéraire in much of his analysis is another indication in the same direction, though this would not necessarily commit him to favoring factor price constancy. Most modern economists, however, tend to express themselves in terms of product price constancy, either because of the greater conceptual precision of the cost of living index and the focusing of attention on it generally, or from a recognition that in terms of labor union pressures for ever higher money wage rates and the other political realities of the current situation this is a more readily attainable goal than that of factor price constancy. There are thus already at least two major alternatives, and it is not too much of an extension to bring under consideration the whole gamut of possible price trends.

The argument will be easier to follow if we have explicitly in the background a specific simplified model, which can be called the "metastatic model." In such a model there is change and development through time, but no significant uncertainty. Mathematically speaking, it is a model exactly similar to a static model, except that the number of commodities and services has been multiplied by the number of time periods under consideration, so that in effect a given commodity at two different times is treated as two different commodities; storage of a commodity is a productive process converting the input of a commodity at the earlier time into an output of the physically identical but economically distinguished commodity at a subsequent time.

As a concrete realization of such a model, one can imagine, perhaps, a state where all producers and consumers have perfect knowledge of their own production possibilities and consumption preferences relating to inputs and outputs for all periods from the present to the indefinite future (or perhaps to some "horizon"); that an initial set of prices is announced for all goods both for present and for future delivery, implying specific rates of exchange between present and future commodities; that each consumer or producer then calculates his proposed purchases and sales at these announced tentative prices; that these plans are then assembled, aggregated, and compared, and the discrepancies between aggregate supply and aggregate demand for each commodity at each time made the basis for a change in the announced prices. This process is then repeated, before any production or trading actually takes place, until by this series of Walrasian *tâtonnements* the system is brought into equilibrium, at which time contracts are confirmed for the future delivery of all commodities and services, the economic process is concluded, and nothing remains but the carrying out of these contracts. Given the absence of fraud, uncertainty, and ignorance, the plan so arrived at should be capable of being carried out; given further appropriate assumptions, not relevant here, the result should be Pareto-optimal.

In such an economy it is obvious that the real equilibrium will be unaffected by the choice of the numéraire in which the prices are expressed, or indeed if no one commodity is singled out for this role, provided that the system of exchange ratios announced is connected, so that an exchange ratio is implied between any two given commodities for delivery at any two respective dates, and consistent, so that no profitable arbitrage is possible. To make the model more closely relevant to a discussion of price levels and interest rates, we can specify that all intertemporal exchanges are performed through the medium of a "money" intermediary. That is, an exchange of commodity x to be delivered at time s, which we will call x_s, for commodity y to be delivered at time t, or y_t, is accomplished by first converting x_s into cash to be delivered at time s, or m_s, then trading m_s for m_t by lending or borrowing money, and finally buying y_t with m_t. The rate of exchange between m_s and m_t can be expressed in terms of a money rate of interest for the period from s to t; the rates of exchange ruling between x_s, y_s, z_s, etc., and m_s are components of the price level for time s, and similarly for time t. If m is pure money, having no intrinsic utility of its own, then the equilibrium is obviously unaltered if all prices at time s are multiplied by a factor f, all prices at time t are multiplied by a factor g, and at the same time the rates of interest are altered so that the price of m_t in terms of m_s is increased proportionally to f/g, provided that storage of money is either prohibited or always unprofitable: money in this case is purely a money of account and not a currency or a medium for savings.

As long as money is purely a money of account, there is no particular difficulty in using that variant of the model in which money rates of interest are zero, with future price levels adjusted so as to preserve the same overall ratio of exchange between present and future commodities. Indeed, such a realization of the model would have a certain advantage in that price computations would be simplified.

As soon as money becomes a currency, however, the picture becomes slightly different. Depending on the particular financial institutions prevailing in a given economy, the holding of a stock of money over time may be necessary or convenient for the carrying on of trade, and there may be varying degrees of convenience and saving in expense in holding a larger stock than the minimum essential. If we adopt for the moment the assumption that money so held earns no interest, the money rate of interest is a measure of the cost of holding money rather than earning assets. A useful element to incorporate in the model at this point is Baumol's "inventory" treatment of the demand for cash balances,[1]

---

[1] William J. Baumol, "The Transactions Demand for Cash: An Inventory Theoretic Approach," *Quarterly Journal of Economics*, 66 (November, 1952), p. 545.

according to which a rational consumer or producer will adjust his cash balances so as to minimize the sum of the loss of interest on these cash balances and the cost of the financial transactions[2] needed to reduce this average cash balance by shifting into and out of earning assets. The loss of interest will in turn vary with the price trend selected as the norm, since this would in turn affect the (short-term) money rates of interest.

Thus while the overall equilibrium of an economy with a constant price level and a 5 percent interest rate, corresponding to a 5 percent "real marginal productivity of capital" in equilibrium with a 5 percent "real marginal time preference" of consumers, might be roughly very similar to the overall equilibrium attained with a rising price level of 10 percent per annum and a corresponding money interest rate of 15.5 percent, or on the other hand to that attained with a zero money rate of interest and a price level falling at a rate of about 5 percent per annum, the handling of cash balances will differ. In the inflationary economy, cash balances will be low, and considerable effort in terms of real resources will be expended in keeping them low; in the deflationary economy, financial transactions will be at a minimum, in that there will be nothing to be gained by putting cash into nonspeculative investments. The liquidity preference curve can be viewed as a demand curve for cash in somewhat the same sense that we use in considering a demand curve for, say, cash registers and the area beneath the curve can be considered to be a form of consumers' surplus representing the benefits obtained from cash holdings over and above the interest price paid. Or in other words this curve can be thought of as a marginal productivity curve for cash, the productivity of an increment to the supply of cash being the saving in resources devoted to financial transactions that can be avoided if cash is more plentiful, or extra resources consumed in the speeding up of transactions through cable rather than mail transfers, and the like.[3]

When money is strictly a commodity money, efforts made to economize cash are productive in that they release capital resources for other uses that would otherwise be tied up in the costly money supply. The balance at the margin between the productivity of investment in additional monetary stock and investment of a corresponding amount in productive plant will vary according to whether the monetary commodity is one tending to increase in relative value (e.g., copper), and thus producing a falling price level, a low interest rate, and a large immobilization in monetary stocks with correspondingly low current

---

[2] Financial transactions are those engaged in for the purpose of adjusting cash balances or changing investment portfolios as distinguished from production transactions that are necessary to the securing of factors and the sale of products in a given institutional context.

[3] See Martin Bailey, "The Welfare Cost of Inflationary Finance," *Journal of Political Economy*, 64 (April, 1956), p. 93; we are here concerned with more moderate rates of inflation or deflation than those which Bailey discusses, though the difference is to some extent only one of degree.

expense of financial transactions, or whether the monetary commodity is one tending to fall in relative value (e.g., aluminum); the problem of what type of commodity to select for a monetary medium in such circumstances is an interesting one, but as it is irrelevant to the current situation, it need not detain us here.

The successive invention of partial reserve banking and fiat currency have, however, created the possibility of expanding the supply of cash at substantially zero marginal cost. Under these circumstances any limitation of the supply of cash can be regarded as leading to a waste of real resources in the form of expenditures by individuals to conserve their limited supply of cash, such as extra trips to the bank, extra financial transactions, telegraphic transfers, and the like, all of which can be regarded in these circumstances as being unproductive, since they attempt to economize a good which has a cost of production of zero. The situation is analogous to that which arises when a tax is imposed on the consumption of an item which in the absence of the tax would be a free economic good. The area under the tail of the liquidity preference curve, from the ordinate representing the money supply out to the saturation point, can be considered a measure of this economic waste. To this extent, the lower the money rate of interest and consequently the higher the holdings of cash, the smaller will be the quantum of real resources needlessly used up in this attempt of individuals to economize cash, and the higher will be the real net product of the community from a given full employment input of factors. The effect is no less real, though presumably somewhat milder, if the loss imposed on the holder of cash is of the order of 3 to 5 percent per annum rather than the more drastic rates of up to 200 percent per day considered by Bailey.

Pushing this to the limit, however, leads to trouble from another direction. If the money rate of interest falls to zero, there is no incentive for individuals to hold gilt-edged securities rather than cash. To be sure, in the futures economy, this merely means that an individual who with a positive rate of interest would be actually lending to borrowers will instead tend merely to hoard his cash, so that to preserve an effective supply of money to would-be borrowers at a zero rate of interest some separate mechanism would have to be instituted. The only significant difficulty that would arise in the strict futures model is that the price adjustments that will be required in the course of the Walrasian *tâtonnements* will now have to be made in terms of raising or lowering the entire set of prices in effect for deliveries at a given time so as to adjust excesses or deficiencies of aggregate demand at that time, rather than by adjusting the rate of interest, i.e., the rate of exchange between cash for different delivery rates.

If, however, we turn to a slightly more realistic model in which the adjustment of interest rates has a role to play in the equilibrating process, the attempt to economize on transaction costs by expanding the money supply to the point where interest rates fall to zero is likely to create difficulties. Consider for example a model in which instead of assuming that the future is known with certainty, we merely assume that expectations have a "certainty equivalent," i.e., that there is some pattern of expectations such that it would be rationally consistent with the observed behavior of individuals that they should hold these expectations with complete certainty. This certainty equivalent expectation may, in the event, not be realized, but we assume for the purpose of this model that repeated failure to realize what was previously expected with certainty nevertheless fails to discourage the formation of certainty-equivalent expectations with respect to the future, i.e., that no hedging against possible surprise takes place. Suppose further that the money supply for all future dates is rigidly and exogenously determined, and that we start from an equilibrium in which price expectations and this programmed money supply are compatible with a zero rate of interest.

If now there is any accidental occurrence that leads to an upward shift in short-run price expectations, i.e., a reduction in the rate at which prices are expected to fall, this would tend to result in the acceleration of all kinds of purchases, ranging from investment to advance consumer buying. Given the very large supply of money with which the system would be starting, this increased volume of purchases would be possible with only very slight absolute increases in the velocity of circulation, and would encounter little if any restraint through increased interest rates or other forms of credit restraint. In the absence of adequate corrective measures, this increased demand would tend to touch off further upward deviations in prices from the long-term norm that would be likely to get completely out of hand unless counteracted by extremely prompt and well-calculated monetary or fiscal measures.

To be sure, a similar self-reinforcing movement is also possible starting from equilibrium situations higher up on the liquidity preference curve with higher interest rates, but in this region the demand for money is less elastic, and the amount of money in circulation is relatively smaller, so that shortages of liquid funds, tightening of the money market, and rising interest rates would be likely to contribute substantially to the dampening of the surge, and less drastic corrective measures may suffice to restore equilibrium.

On the downward side, starting again from a zero-interest equilibrium, development of abnormally pessimistic expectations (i.e., more pessimistic than the standard downward trend) would lead to even greater difficulty. There would be no possibility for the resulting contraction of demand and further downward deviations to be corrected or even abated by further easing of the supply funds or reduction of interest rates, given institutional arrangements in which a significantly negative money rate of interest is not possible. While it is conceivable that a fiscal policy operated with the utmost flexibility and sophistication might be able to keep the economy in balance along this zero-interest tightrope, prospects for this in practice would be almost nil even under the most favorable conditions. Even if it could be done, the constant revision of tax rates or government expenditure programs that this would require would give rise to a confusion more costly than the transaction expense that the zero interest rate is intended to economize.

It may be remarked in passing that while few economists have directly considered a zero-money-interest economy as a desirable or feasible norm in any proximate time period, it is at least theoretically conceivable that a policy of constant factor prices, which some have actually considered as a possible norm, might run into substantially similar difficulties. For example, if progress from innovation is sufficiently rapid and sufficiently capital-saving to bring the marginal productivity of capital, in constant product price terms, down to below the rate of increase of real factor incomes, then the marginal productivity of capital expressed in terms of constant factor prices would be negative! In theory, at least, this could happen even if aggregate savings and net capital formation were themselves zero or even negative. Even though in the world as it happens to exist today a constant factor-price level economy might be reasonably workable and lead to a positive rate of interest, the fact that it is possible to imagine circumstances where this standard would become unworkable casts considerable doubt on the desirability of insisting on adherence to this standard.

Even if it were possible to conceive of fiscal policy as being able ultimately to keep the economy moving along the zero-interest path in a reasonably steady manner, it is to be doubted whether the mere economizing in financial transactions is a sufficiently important objective to justify the other sacrifices involved. For example, if such a course were followed, monetary policy as a control over the course of the economy would have to be very largely given up. This would be a grave disadvantage, not only from the point of view of the relative flexibility and ease of application of monetary as compared with fiscal controls, but also from the point of view of preserving certain desirable differential effects obtainable by judicious combinations of monetary and fiscal policy.

The level of normal money interest rates has indeed a crucial influence on the effectiveness of monetary policy. It is not unreasonable to maintain that the main effect of monetary expansion or contraction on the economy is felt through the consequent changes in interest rates and their influence on *ex ante* savings and investments; or at least that the intensity of any direct effect through the tightening or loosening of other terms of credit is in fairly direct proportion to the tendency of such changes to produce changes in interest rates. Monetary policy can always ultimately check a boom if pursued vigorously enough, but only at the risk of not being able to stop a collapse if the mark is overshot; monetary contraction can push monetary interest rates up almost without limit, and can thus drastically inhibit investment, but monetary expansion cannot push interest rates below zero, or indeed below a figure somewhat above zero, so that the encouragement that it can give to new investment is strictly limited.

Now the lower the normal money interest rate, the more elastic the demand for money, and the greater the volume of monetary action required to produce a given interest rate differential. More important even, the lower the normal money interest rate, the smaller will be the possible range of reduction in interest rates which constitutes the margin of action available for the correction of downward tendencies, and the greater the likelihood that a downward tendency will develop a momentum too great for this margin of action to counteract, before the monetary controls can be brought to bear. Preservation of the effectiveness of monetary policy on the downward side and of the possibility of delivering an adequate monetary stimulus to the economy requires that the normal money rate of interest be kept high enough to keep a sufficient margin for stimulating action. Moreover, readiness to use monetary action freely against upward deviations may depend in large measure on the effectiveness of a reversal of policy in case the mark is overshot. Given the real situation of the economy, with a given real rate of interest, monetary policy will be more effective with a rising price level as the normal program, with its consequent high money rate of interest, than if the norm is a constant price level with a rate of money interest equal to the real marginal productivity of capital, and similarly more effective where the norm is a constant price level than where the norm calls for a falling price level.

Monetary policy is not only easier to apply on short notice than fiscal policy, it has important differential effects. The objectives of social policy involve several parameters, such as full employment, the appropriate division of activity between private and government enterprise, and a desired division of the national product between current consumption and capital formation. To permit control over all of these parameters, a corresponding number of control parameters must be available. In this case we can exercise control over the quantity of money (or the rediscount rate and the price of government bonds, but not both), the deficit on current account, and the volume of public expenditure. Monetary policy cannot be surrendered as an effective tool of control without restricting the range of attainable objectives.

For example, full employment can be achieved either with a level price trend, a large budget surplus, and low interest rates, or with a level price trend, a large deficit, and high interest rates. Private capital formation will be higher, and consumption lower, in the first case than in the second. If monetary policy and fiscal policy are both effective, a choice can be made between the two allocations of real output. But if the price level is to be kept constant, there is a limit to the degree to which policy can be shifted toward lower interest rates and a correspondingly higher budget surplus without impairing the effectiveness of monetary policy, and a somewhat broader limit to what can be brought about at all. Thus there are limits to the magnitude of the budget surplus (or minimum deficits, under some circumstances) that cannot be transgressed without making the maintenance of full employment difficult if not impossible. It is quite possible that insistence on a level price trend as a norm may greatly restrict the choices that can be made on matters of real significance, i.e., that it may impose a limit on the amount by which resources can be directed to capital formation through private channels, and a much more severe limit on the extent to which this can be done without impairing the promptness and reliability with which the available controls can correct deviations from the desired path resulting from random or exogenous shocks to the system.

There may thus be considerable advantage in having an economy geared to a constantly rising price level, in that a wider range of choice is possible concerning the proportion of the national income to be devoted to capital formation. And even if the desired rate of capital formation happens to fall within the range of rates attainable with a level price trend, a rising price trend norm with the same real disposition of the economy may be more stable and more amenable to the use of the more flexible monetary controls.

It can of course be argued that in practice no one would want to promote capital formation to such a degree that under full-employment conditions the real marginal productivity of capital would be brought down to levels where mainten-ance of a constant price level would imply that monetary policy would lose its effectiveness. This may in fact be the consensus, but to foreclose the issue by insisting on a level price trend is to risk forcing the decision on the wrong basis. It may be, to be sure, that it would not be desirable to continue investment to the point where the marginal efficiency of investment drops to zero, and it might be maintained that the lower limit of the money rate of interest is so close to zero as to make little difference. But even if one were satisfied that the level of investment should be pushed only to the point where the marginal efficiency of investment is 3 or 4 percent, this is not the whole story, for the marginal social efficiency of investment may exceed substantially the marginal private efficiency. This would be the case generally, for example, where competition is imperfect and the demand for the products of the investment less than perfectly elastic; moreover, even under perfect competition, there may well be a generalized tendency for investment to involve significant external economies. To be sure, where there are specific external economies that involve investment, it may be possible for a government to deal with this more specifically and directly by appropriate subsidy. It is likely, however, that a general subsidy to investment such as through low real rates of interest associated with the promise of a rising price trend would be at least as appropriate as any other form of general subsidy, and in many cases easier to administer, less discriminatory, and more pervasive in its effects. Certainly the opponents of centralization and of the extension of specific government control have reason to prefer this method to that of specific subsidy or to that of direct government investment in public enterprise. Not, again, that these should necessarily be excluded, but rather that the decision between public operation, specific control, or general stimulus should be made on the merits of these respective policies in their own areas, and should not be preconstrained by prejudices as to appropriate norms of price trends.

These considerations are particularly pertinent to the situation of many underdeveloped countries where very high targets of capital formation are aimed at, justified by the pressure of population and the need to surmount the Malthusian hump. One of the attractions of Communism to such countries is that it permits a higher rate of capital formation, relative to the national product, to be maintained than can be achieved in terms of the traditional formulae of liberal capitalism. If free enterprise is to compete with Communism on this score, or even if a mixed economy is to be operated in a rational and integrated manner, acceptance of a rising price trend as a permanent and deliberate policy may be an essential prerequisite. A further contributing factor related to the need for a rising price trend in these countries is the fact that capital markets are relatively poorly organized and investors have relatively fewer facilities for evaluating the risks attached to various investments, so that the limits below which it is difficult to push interest rates are considerably higher than in more highly organized countries. Since risk of loss to the investor is often not entirely a reflection of risk of social loss from an investment, low real interest rates are again more likely to require a rising price trend to make them effective.

It is worth emphasizing again what was perhaps only implicit in the metastatic model upon which all this is based: that it is a planned, announced, and as far as possible guaranteed rate of inflation that is in question here. Inflation that is the mere byproduct of the inadequacy of half-hearted attempts to halt an inflation that is publicly condemned as unwanted will not do, since then investors in equity interests merely reap a windfall that they had no very clear expectation of obtaining and which played relatively little role in inducing them to invest. Rather, what is wanted is the announcement to the investor, and so far as possible the guarantee to him, that he will be able to sell his product in a market in which prices generally are rising steadily, and that if he borrows to expand his investment he will be able to repay principal and interest in gradually depreciating currency.

There are of course certain mechanical objections to a price trend that is rising too rapidly. If inflation requires the revision of price lists more frequently than is otherwise appropriate, then the cost of this operation, which may in some cases be considerable, is a disadvantage; of course, a mere percentage adjustment is not so serious a matter as a general revision, but it may be a nuisance. More serious is the matter of conventional prices: candy bars, coin machines, and the like, where a substantial price trend would involve frequent adjustments at considerable expense. Economic calculation also tends to become more difficult for the average consumer if there is a continual revision of the level of prices going on so that he must be continually revising his conception of what an appropriate price for a given item is. For economists, statisticians, and accountants, there is the resulting greater need for general deflation of money figures in order to obtain a picture representing the underlying real phenomena. And over the long pull there is the cost of revising the coinage.

So far we have passed over lightly what most discussions of inflation take to be the most important and even crucial point: the devaluation of savings. Under the assumptions of the metastatic model, however, interest rates are adjusted, and all contracts are entered into in the light of the fully anticipated inflationary price trend, so that there is no inequity involved. There may, to be sure, be some redistribution of income as between property owners and recipients of earned income, as the real rate of interest may be adjusted in accordance with the changed equilibrium involving a lower marginal productivity of capital, but this is a general adjustment between property and labor as such, and involves no discrimination between debt and equity holders, nor any greater disappointment of expectations than occurs with a level price trend.

Actually of course one must start from an existing situation, where in general there will be multitudes of long-term contracts in force calling for the payment of money at future dates, most of them entered into on the basis of a tacit assumption of a reasonably level price trend, and a policy change must at least consider this initial state. There are at least three possible courses of action: the simplest but least equitable would be to go ahead with a deliberately inflationary policy without any adjustment of contracts, and so ignore the resulting inequities. A second possibility would be to require, at the time the deliberately inflationary policy is inaugurated, that all contracts for future payments of money outstanding shall be adjusted to take account of the changed policy regarding the future value of money. A third is to postpone the onset of the inflationary price trend to a set future date, with the hope that payments after that date involved in presently outstanding contracts would be sufficiently unimportant to be ignored, and the assumption that contracts entered into after the announcement of the policy, even though prior to the onset of the inflation, would take full cognizance of the proposed change in policy. None of these alternatives is particularly attractive. The inequities produced by the first alternative would be serious, at least if the rate of inflation adopted were fairly substantial; the second involves a rather formidable accounting adjustment at a particular time, and might be difficult to get carried through in any uniform or smooth manner, while the third involves a commitment a long time in advance to make a specific change in policy at a specific future date, a commitment that it would be difficult to make in terms that would not only ensure its being in fact carried out at the appointed time, but would also inspire general confidence as to its being carried out.

There is perhaps a fourth possibility to be explicitly considered, which is that a gradual shift may take place from a policy of stable prices to a policy of allowing a certain amount of inflation to take place by default, resulting in a poorly defined but generally rising trend of prices over a period of years, so that disappointment of expectations would be spread out over a sufficient period of years to be tolerated, with the eventual result of an established rising price trend that is fully anticipated. Something of this sort may indeed have happened in some Latin American countries, and this experience is not to be written off as unlikely elsewhere. Such a development may in many countries be considered the most likely alternative to a continued and partially successful attempt to preserve a stable price level.

The above has been in terms of a closed economy. An open economy that attempts a policy of deliberate inflation for the sake of better control over the course of domestic affairs will, of course, have to permit exchange rates to have a similar trend, which might cause difficulty in view of present prejudices against devaluation as an unfair means of competing in international trade. A far more serious difficulty occurs if an attempt is made at the same time to stimulate investment in the domestic economy to the extent of driving the real marginal productivity of capital domestically down to a low level. If this is done there will be a tendency for domestic capital to move abroad. In the context of a perfectly competitive system there would perhaps be no objection to this: indeed, the profits that such capital could earn abroad would presumably be greater than the profits obtainable domestically, and the net result would be a greater increase in the national income inclusive of the earnings on foreign investment, than would have been obtained through strictly domestic investment. But in the absence of such perfect competition, and especially in underdeveloped countries, the tendency for such capital to go abroad would forefeit the indirect benefits accruing from the external economies that would flow from the investment of such capital domestically. This result would, however, tend to follow any program that attempted to push investment farther in one country than in the rest of the world to the extent that the marginal private productivity of capital falls below the yields obtainable elsewhere.

Even if one is dealing with a virtually closed economy, such as the United States, and were planning on a *tabula rasa* where there are no outstanding contracts for future payment of money, it is by no means clear what should be recommended. The advantages of a high money rate of interest for stability purposes are to be offset against the real costs of the resulting needless attempts to economize cash balances and the costs of more frequent price adjustments. Moreover a level price trend is unique in a way that no other price trend is; it has a certain air of rightness about it that is perhaps the modern counterpart of the aura attached to the gold standard. Politically and practically it may be far easier to resist temptations to allow deviations from a level price trend than comparable deviations from an established rate of inflation, and particularly it may be easier to inspire confidence in a money that is to be kept at a constant purchasing power, than to inspire a comparable degree of confidence that a rate of inflation will be maintaned within comparable limits, even though in fact the resources available for maintaining the stipulated rate of inflation are more effective than those available for maintaining a stable price level.

There is a way of partially reconciling the opposite aims of a high money rate of interest for control purposes and a large supply of cash to minimize the cost of financial transactions, and that is to allow interest to be paid on cash balances. This cannot be done with currency, but there is no particular difficulty to allowing interest on checking accounts; indeed a form of interest in kind is in effect allowed now in terms of the way service charges are computed. Costs involved in the economizing of currency are probably inevitable, but those involved in the economizing of checking account balances are probably minimizable in some such way as this. In any case the demand for currency is probably much more nearly controlled by the risk of theft or loss than by the loss of interest involved, and it is doubtful whether there would be much of a reduction of the currency in circulation if interest were paid on checking account deposits but not on currency.

Deliberate and planned inflation is in a sense merely another way of looking at the same problem as was tackled by Gesell, Dahlberg, and others in proposing various forms of "demurrage money." If money is thus made perishable, it becomes possible to drive the money rate of interest below zero, and monetary policy regains its effectiveness without involving any of the equity questions that arise with the introductions of an inflationary price trend. The practical difficulties of a demurrage money seem insurmountable, however, in that most schemes for collecting a tax on cash holdings seem to involve so much trouble as to greatly impair the usefulness of currency as a medium of exchange.

However the problem is approached, the difficulties are certainly such as to cause us to be cautious in our approach; I would certainly not want to recommend the start of a program of deliberate inflation tomorrow, or even a year or two from now. But it is high time that we broaden the scope of the programs we are willing to entertain as respectable candidates for adoption. The desideratum is not necessarily a level price trend, but a price level whose future course can be predicted with as small a margin of uncertainty as possible. An inflationary price trend may well turn out in the long run to meet this requirement better than a stationary one.

21

Design of a
Market Anti-Inflation Program

Difficulties with Specific Price Controls

Direct price and wage controls, such as have often been used in wartime, tend to be unsatisfactory as semipermanent measures for use under more normal circumstances. In wartime a certain amount of patriotically motivated cooperation is available that tends to be lacking in peace time. If the duration is generally expected to be short, there is less time for prices based on historic patterns to get badly out of line, and the rate of introduction of new products that cause difficulty is less. Where specific items become scarce, rationing can be resorted to.

For use as a long-term peace-time measure, historically based price controls tend to become more and more inappropriate, requiring constant administrative adjustment that is likely to be slow and inaccurate. New products are introduced with a frequency considerably enhanced by attempts to use spurious novelty as a means of defeating the price controls. Any attempt to prevail over these obstacles would require a vast, expensive, and cumbersome bureaucracy. And most important politically, the whole project is likely to be opposed by labor representatives who fear with some justification that wage and price controls would turn out to be considerably more effective in controlling wages than in controlling prices.

Attempts to avoid the bureaucracy by resort to guidelines, exhortation, and "jawboning" have proven to have little effectiveness, except possibly as a short-term expedient. Specific wage and price controls would seem to have little to offer as a long-term solution to the problem of persistent inflationary pressure.

Incentives-Based Incomes Policies, David C. Colander, Ed. (Ballinger, 1986), pp. 149–58.

Tax Incentive Plans (TIPs)

Many proposals have been advanced for applying anti-inflationary pressure in the form of credits or surcharges on existing taxes. These plans also suffer from the difficulty of evaluating a measure of price change that can be used to determine the surcharge or credit. In addition, in many cases they operate somewhat capriciously, depending as they generally do on the existence of a liability for the tax. This is especially true of those TIPs that are based on the corporation income tax, as a fairly large number of corporations will have no net income and no tax liability for any given year. It is of course possible to circumvent this difficulty to some extent by the use of a "refundable" tax credit.

There is a further difficulty not often emphasized, which is that in adding yet another special provision to a tax law already riddled with special provisions it is difficult to predict how the new TIP will intereact with these other provisions in various combinations. Ten special provisions can intereact in $2^{10} = 1,024$ possible combinations. Tax lawyers and accountants can be relied on to take advantage of these interactions to produce strange and wonderful results not at all consonant with the basic purpose of the TIP. As an example, when charitable gifts of appreciated property were allowed to be deducted at current value rather than at cost, tax practitioners worked out schemes for giving just the gain rather than the entire property, so that frequently the taxpayer came out better off than if he had sold the property and kept the proceeds. It is almost impossible to predict the outcome of adding a new proviso to the tax code.

Finally, a TIP, being basically a tax measure, must, in the United States, be embodied in legislation that is constitutionally required to originate in the House of Representatives and work its tedious way through the Ways and Means Committee, the House, the Senate Finance Committee, the Senate, the House, the Conference Committee, the House again, the Senate again, and finally the White House. As conditions change, the lags between the perception of the need for a change in the rates of the TIP and the effective enactment of the change are likely to be excessively large, even under a speeded up procedure such as was characteristic of the early days of the New Deal.

While in principle it would be possible for the Congress to delegate to the executive branch the authority to adjust the rates in the TIP according to current conditions, much as the Federal Reserve System has enjoyed the power to adjust the rediscount rate, the Congress and especially the House have in the past shown themselves exceedingly jealous of their constitutional prerogative in this matter and are unlikely to assent to such a delegation of authority, even assuming that the Supreme Court would declare such a delegation to be allowable under the Constitution. On the whole the prospects for a workable and effective TIP plan along the lines so far explored appear to be exceedingly slim.

The Concept of a Market in Rights to Raise Prices

One way to assure a specified trend in the general price level without having to guess in advance what level of incentive will do the trick is to arrange for the required level of incentive to be determined to a market. In effect, rights to raise prices (and their opposite, obligations to lower them) could be required to be traded in a market in which the price of these rights would converge to a level such that the balance of increases and decreases in prices would in the aggregate be just what is required to produce the desired overall price level. The equilibrium price of these rights so arrived at would provide just the right degree of incentive to yield the desired result.

However, one difficulty with a MAP scheme defined directly in terms of prices is that like many forms of TIP it requires the determination of by what amount prices have been increased or decreased in the face of changes in quality, proportions, and the ancillary terms of sale. The problems that would be encountered in attempting to administer a program couched in these terms would be formidable, though possibly they could be overcome if the need were sufficiently urgent.

A more fundamental difficulty is that if the program is based solely on sales prices of outputs at all levels, pyramiding problems would occur in that more stringent restraint would be imposed on products that are produced in several stages and pass through several hands on the way to the consumer as compared to those where there are fewer stages or a greater degree of vertical integration. To be sure, this problem might prove transitory if it turned out that the restraining pressure would need to be substantial only during a brief initial period in which the pre-existing inflationary expectations were being dealt with. But in any case, once this problem is recognized, it should be possible to come up with a better solution.

Implementation of a MAP in Terms of Mark-ups

A MAP as an Excess Gross Mark-ups Tax

An approach that appears to avoid much of the above difficulty is to formulate a MAP in terms of the relations between *gross mark-ups*, or the excess of gross sales over the cost of inputs other than primary factors. Each agent would be given an entitlement to gross mark-ups based on that agent's past history of gross mark-ups adjusted by changes in the inputs of capital, labor, and other prime factors.

One way to think of the proposal is as an excess value-added tax with transferable entitlements, somewhat analogous to the wartime excess profits tax –

the differences being that the base is akin to value added rather than net profits and that the "entitlement" to value added, unlike "normal profits," is capable of being modified by direct purchases from, or sales to, other agents, whereas under the excess profits tax transfers of entitlement to normal profits were possible, if at all, only through mergers or spin-offs. In addition, the entitlement to normal profits was adjusted mainly with respect to investment or disinvestment since the base period, whereas with the excess gross mark-ups tax adjustments would also be made with respect to changes in labor and other prime inputs.

Another way to relate the proposal to existing institutions is to regard it as a modification of the value-added taxes prevalent in the European Common Market. The main additional administrative requirement is the determination of the entitlements to gross mark-ups, which indeed is likely to prove the critical element in the feasibility of the plan.

The term *gross mark-ups* is used in preference to *value added* or *net sales* in order to emphasize the price control effects of the plan, whereas *value added*, to the extent that it is sometimes defined as the sum of prime factor payments, has more of a connotation of income control. But this is a mere matter of euphemistics, which – while it may have political importance in gaining acceptance of the proposal – is not an essential difference.

Ideally the purchases and sales of entitlements to gross mark-ups would be handled through some kind of organized market. Indeed the primary incentive impact of the scheme would be through the market price of entitlements rather than the tax itself, which might raise relatively little revenue, if any. The chief purpose of the tax would be to provide the back-up incentive for firms to provide themselves with an adequate amount of entitlement to cover their operations, and in most cases tax would become payable only as a penalty for failure to comply with the requirement. The strength of the incentive to keep prices down would vary automatically with the market price of entitlement and would not require adjustment by an act of Congress. The exact level of the tax rate or tax schedule, if it were graduated in some way, would be relatively unimportant, and it could be adjusted, if necessary, at longer intervals without significant change in the adaptability of the scheme to short-term changes in the economic environment.

Indeed, it would be possible to couch the enforcement part of the scheme in terms of requiring any deficiency in entitlement revealed at the end of the accounting period that could not be met in the market (the firms with a shortage of entitlement being in effect "cornered") to be made up by the purchase of additional entitlement issued by some such agency as the Federal Reserve System much as deficiencies in bank reserves can be made up by borrowing at the rediscount window. But whether the Congress would be willing to delegate authority to determine the price to be paid for this "make-up" entitlement remains to be seen.

Still another possibility for dealing with firms with a deficiency of entitlement at the end of the accounting period would be to permit borrowing against future entitlement at a suitable discount rate. In this case it would be necessary to provide some restriction to prevent the scheme being vitiated by indefinitely continued rollovers. It might even be possible to dispense entirely with the explicit tax element of the plan.

But whatever method is used to induce compliance, it is the market price of entitlements that is the decisive element, and the tax, if there is one, is a purely secondary back-up element.

Adjustment of Entitlements for Changes in Capital

For existing firms, entitlement to gross mark-ups would be determined on the basis of starting with the gross mark-ups for some appropriate past period and adjusting this to take account of changes in capital invested in the firm, employment, and possibly other prime inputs. The base period should preferably be one prior to the start of serious consideration of the scheme so that anticipation of the application of the scheme will not lead to a spate of price increases as sellers attempt to establish a higher basis for the computation of future entitlements.

Adjustment for changes in investment is fairly straightforward. One can, indeed, follow the precedents established for the excess profits tax, though there may be reasons for a different treatment in some cases. The chief problems involve the treatment of inventories, depreciation, and distinguishing between purchases of inputs on current account and on capital account. If only the income tax were on a sound basis instead of being full of special provisions such as accelerated depreciation and the like, one could simply take net income minus distributions, plus net receipts from loans and sale of equity, and adjust entitlement by a percentage of this change in investment. As it is, it may become desirable to make adjustments to net income to reflect normal accounting for purposes of determining entitlement.

Adjustment of Entitlements for Employment Changes

How entitlements should be adjusted for changes in employment is one of the more critical problems for a MAP scheme. To adjust entitlement on the basis of changes in total payrolls or labor costs would largely vitiate the scheme, since then there would be no disincentive to raising labor compensation together with prices without limit. At the other extreme, to allow only a flat amount per additional employee hired would involve a rather sharp discrimination against the hiring of the more highly skilled employees. While under current circumstances there would be much to be said for a discrimination in this direction, given the concentration of unemployment among the unskilled, this may be thought of as going too far. It may be satisfactory to adopt some intermediate compromise by allowing a flat amount per additional employee plus a fraction of the payrolls in excess of this fixed amount. Unfortunately there seems to be no clear principle to appeal to as to where this compromise should be struck, leading to a possibility for debate and even filibuster over the issue.

Such a plan would tend to discriminate in favor of shorter hours and part-time employment, again possibly a not undesirable discrimination in the light of the current relative scarcity of part-time employment opportunities. To attempt to eliminate this discrimination would pose formidable administrative problems, given possibilities for disguising shorter hours as simply lax enforcement of flex-time, for example. It would, however, be appropriate, where the wage paid is less than would be paid for full-time work at the minimum or standard wage, to limit the adjustment to entitlement to the actual payment.

One should beware of insisting on too sophisticated adjustment to entitlements, given the likelihood that the market price of entitlement would decline rapidly to a very low level as the operation of the scheme reduces inflationary pressures by eliminating inflationary expectations. The degree to which this would occur would depend to some extent on the speed with which an attempt is made to reach full employment.

The Calculation of Gross Mark-ups

The calculation of gross mark-ups, though a simpler matter than the calculation of net income, is not as simple as it might seem at first blush. In principle, purchases and sales of capital assets must be distinguished from purchases and sales on current account and treated as adjustments to investment rather than to mark-ups. The distinction can in some cases be difficult and even arbitrary. Increases in inventory must likewise be excluded and decreases in inventory included in the nonprime factor cost of goods sold. Inventory for this purpose must include not only stocks in storage but work in progress. Depreciation needs to be treated in a similar fashion, with the difference that determination of the appropriate value of depreciation is open to much greater uncertainty than the valuation of inventory changes.

While for income tax purposes errors in evaluating these items may make only a relatively modest difference, since the result in most cases is merely to shift income from one accounting period to another, for MAP purposes the stakes are higher, at least in the initial phase of the scheme, since the market price of entitlement may be expected to fall off rather sharply as inflationary expectations abate. This is not the place to try to specify in detail how these separations are to be made in particular cases, but the problem will eventually have to be faced.

Coverage

Coverage of the MAP plan could exclude a significant part of the economy without losing much if any of its effectiveness as an anti-inflationary weapon. Accordingly the administrative burden can be substantially eased by excluding small firms up to a fairly substantial size. This could be accomplished without introducing discontinuities by providing each firm with a minimum fixed amount of nonmarketable entitlement – for instance, up to $100,000 for incorporated firms and $200,000 for unincorporated firms. The smaller amount for the incorporated firms is in recognition of the fact that they are more likely to have well-developed accounting systems in place. This would be alternative, not in addition, to an entitlement as calculated in the standard manner. Care would have to be exercised in defining the exclusion in a manner that would avoid opportunities for abuse.

It is not clear, either, to what extent one would want to exclude certain types of enterprise from the operations of the scheme. Regulated public utilities might be excluded on the ground that since their rates are regulated in any case they have little or no capability to respond to the incentives provided by the program. Similarly nonprofit entities, cooperatives, and mutual companies might be considered to be properly exempt, especially if sales of commodities or services constitute a small part of their activity, though in some cases there would be an outcry from competing stock companies that they would be subject to unfair competition. Banks, financial intermediaries, and insurance companies might be granted exemption on the ground that the services they supply are defined in monetary terms and thus stand somewhat to one side of the main concern with inflation of commodity or service prices. Interest rates as the price of money can be considered to be the special preserve of the Fed. Difficulties would arise with conglomerates whose operations span the exempt and the nonexempt areas, and this may argue in favor of a more comprehensive approach.

International Transactions

There is little special difficulty with the ordinary company buying from or selling to foreign trading partners on the assumption that the transactions are at arm's length. Problems arise, however, where multi-national corporations trade with related foreign companies in circumstances under which the assumption of arm's length trading cannot be relied on. The problem is comparable to that encountered under the income tax, where the determination of where income shall be deemed to arise requires the establishment of appropriate "transfer prices" for international transactions within and among related companies.

Here again the simplest solution would probably be one of accepting the transfer prices established for income tax purposes. Yet it must be recognized that these transfer prices are themselves far from satisfactory, involving as they do attempts to apply a number of *ad hoc* solutions, such as the use of arm's length prices for comparable goods, the use of a mark-up over a "fully allocated" cost concocted by accountants using arbitrary rules for the apportionment of joint costs, or a discount from final sale price, the tracing of transactions through a whole sequence of subsidiaries located in various countries, and in many cases litigation stretching over many years.

In the comparable problem of allocating income among the states for state income tax purposes, most states have decided to cut the Gordian knot by the use of somewhat arbitrary formulas, a typical one being the so-called Massachusetts formula

$$B_{ij} = [(S_{ij}/S_i) + (K_{ij}/K_i) + (W_{ij}/W_i)] [B_i/3]$$

where i refers to the firm, j to the jurisdiction, B is the tax base, S is sales, K is property, and W is payrolls. This formula is seriously defective, however, for it fails to give due weight to the relative importance of the three factors in the determination of the income of any given company. For example, if a consulting firm located in New York and renting its premises and equipment, so that is has very little capital, should want to get nearly a third of its income allocated to Vermont, all it would have to do would be to buy a small summer camp as a vacation spot for its employees and presto! the formula puts a third of the firm's income in Vermont and only two-thirds in New York. A better formula would be

$$B_{ij} = B_i [aS_{ij} + bK_{ij} + cW_{ij}] / [aS_i + bK_i + cW_i]$$

where the coefficients *a, b* and *c* are derived from a regression of total tax base on total factors for a suitably chosen set of firms (which might include all firms doing business in a given jurisdiction)

$$B_i = aS_i + b K_i + cW_i + u_i.$$

It may be a bit more difficult to get the data by which to apply a formula in an international case than in the interstate case, although several states are beginning to apply formulas to assess multi-national corporations on a "unit rule" basis, over strong objections by the multi-national corporations, but with recent approval by the Supreme Court.

Periodicity

From the standpoint of getting faster results from the introduction of a MAP, the shorter the time period on the basis of which the program is operated the better, but minimizing compliance and administration costs would call for a longer period. Probably the shortest period for which accounts are drawn up with any generality is the quarter, while many firms will compile their accounts only annually. It might be possible to work on a quarterly basis for the larger firms and an annual basis for the smaller firms. No final judgment here is possible without more data than is readily at hand.

Full-Employment Policy With MAP

Once MAP has provided assurance that inflation will be brought under control, fiscal and monetary policy can be applied unstintingly to provide a level of full employment at which a balance will be struck between full utilization of resources and flexibility. This could be in the range of 1–3 percent rather than the much higher levels often talked of as the best that could hope to be achieved in the absence of a program such as MAP. Fiscal policy would be fully effective, since it would no longer be frustrated by monetary contraction motivated by fears of excessive inflation. And monetary expansion would be effective in lowering interest rates to the extent needed to stimulate the desired level of investment, assuming that the financial markets could be persuaded of the effectiveness of MAP so that they would no longer be anticipating that higher interest rates would eventually have to return.

In this atmosphere it would be possible to choose deliberately how much of the full-employment national income would go to current consumption and how much to investment to provide for economic growth and enhancement of the heritage to be left to future generations. A larger fiscal deficit coupled with high interest rates would produce higher disposable incomes and consumption on the one hand and less investment and growth on the other, while a lower deficit or even a surplus with low interest rates would result in restricted consumption and the devotion of a larger portion of available resources to investment stimulated by the lower interest rates.

Optimum Price Trends

Equity to Debtors

In addition to permitting a choice to be made between alternative growth rates, a MAP program will allow a choice as to the rate of inflation to be allowed in the future, by suitably adjusting the way entitlements to gross mark-ups are calculated. While the conventional wisdom has it that an anti-inflation policy should aim for a stable price policy involving a zero rate of inflation to be achieved as rapidly as possible, it is not at all clear that this is indeed the optimum policy. From an equity standpoint, indeed, it might well be considered best to aim for something closer to the average level of prices expected at the time outstanding contracts were entered into. To go immediately to a zero rate of inflation would impose windfall losses on debtors who have entered into long-term contracts on the assumption that prices would rise significantly above their current levels.

Impact on Developing Countries

The equity aspect may be especially acute with respect to the indebtedness of Third World countries. In many cases these countries borrowed heavily with the expectation that the debt could be serviced from continued sales of exports at rising prices to developed countries. Abatement of inflation and economic recession have caused the dollar value of exports out of which debt service must eventually be financed to fall way below earlier expectations and have produced a financial crisis in many of these countries. A further rapid reduction of the inflation rate to zero would further exacerbate this problem. While the return of full-employment prosperity that could be expected with a MAP program would alleviate the problem somewhat by offering enlarged markets for exports from developing countries, as would also the availability of funds at low real interest rates for refinancing, especially if a high-growth low-interest-rate policy is adopted, considerable alleviation of the burden of the outstanding debt would result from a policy of retaining a moderate rate of inflation, at least for an interim period.

Widening the Range of Growth Policy Options

On another front there is a case to be made for a mild rate of inflation to be continued into the indefinite future as a means of widening the range of options available with respect to the growth rate. Monetary policy cannot in general push money interest rates below a certain level termed by Keynesians the *liquidity trap level*. With a stable price level this imposes a limit below which real interest rates cannot be pushed and so places a limit on the amount of private investment that can be encouraged through low interest rates. And though other methods of stimulating investment are available, there may be less of a likelihood of misallocation if it is mediated through a uniform market rate of interest. A mild rate of inflation would make it possible for the monetary authority to push real rates of interest to a lower level than would be possible without the inflationary trend. Whatever course is chosen, it is appropriate that the policy be announced as far in advance as possible and adhered to, in the absence of major unforeseen developments.

22

·

Necessary and Optimum Government Debt

The national debt, if it is not excessive, will be to us a national blessing.

Alexander Hamilton, in a letter to Robert Morris, April 30, 1781.

Government Debts as Private Assets

Alexander Hamilton may not have had the benefit of modern macroeconomic analysis, but his instincts seem to have been far more insightful than the conventional wisdom of those who currently preach austerity and deficit reduction, usually from vantage points safely distant from the more intense burdens of the recommended austerity. The failure of successive administrations in most developed countries to embark on any vigorous policy aimed at bringing down unconscionably high levels of unemployment has been due in no small measure to a "viewing with alarm" of the size of the national debts, often alleged to be already excessive, or at least threatening to become so, and by ideologically urged striving toward "balanced" government budgets without any consideration of whether such debts and deficits are or threaten to become excessive in terms of some determinable impact on the real general welfare. If they are examined in the light of their impact on welfare, however, they can usually be shown to be well below their optimum levels, let alone at levels that could have dire consequences.

To view government debts in terms of the "functional finance" concept introduced by Abba Lerner, is to consider their role in the macroeconomic balance of the economy. In simple, bare bones terms, the function of government

Previously unpublished manuscript, 16 March, 1993.

debts that is significant for the macroeconomic health of an economy is that they provide the assets into which individuals can put whatever accumulated savings they attempt to set aside in excess of what can be wisely invested in privately owned real assets. A debt that is smaller than this will cause the attempted excess savings, by being reflected in a reduced level of consumption outlays, to be lost in reduced real income and increased unemployment. This continues until the demand for assets corresponding to the reduced income has been brought down to equality with the supply provided by the private capital stock plus the government debt.

This is the opposite of the conventional view that treats the amount that the public is willing to hold as assets rather than spend on consumption as a given, independently of the level of income, so that government debt "crowds out" private investment. This conventional wisdom was derived from neo-classical economics where it was assumed that equality between savings and wealth accumulated by individuals for various private motives on the one hand and investment in real privately held capital goods as decided upon by others in terms of opportunities for profit, would be achieved automatically through the operation of a capital market. But there is no law of economics that guarantees that there will always be a feasible and acceptable state of the capital market that will accomplish this, nor any mechanism that will in an adequately prompt way automatically converge on and maintain such an equilibrium if it were to exist. Indeed, current situations tend to be such that the desire of individuals to save and accumulate have been augmented by longer anticipated periods of retirement and higher costs of desired levels of care for disabilities, and increased exposure to the hazards of unstable industrial economies, while capital-saving innovation and the shift of economic activity from heavy, capital-intensive sectors to less capital-intensive light industry and service sectors, together with rapid rates of depreciation and obsolescence, have decreased the scope for profitable net new private-sector investment, even at very low interest rates. The classical full-employment equilibrium without government intervention, precarious at best, has become an impossibility.

Government Debt in the Absence of Capital

To put the matter into sharper focus, let us start with a hypothetical simple economy of nomads where all commodities deteriorate fairly rapidly over time and the amount of capital investment is fairly strictly limited, household appurtenances beyond a fairly limited quantity being more of a nuisance to carry about on migrations than they are worth. Trade is by barter, possibly facilitated by the use of some such unit as the bushel of grain as a numéraire. The marginal productivity of capital is zero or negative, and adequate individual accumulation for remote future needs is hardly feasible.

Under such circumstances provision for old age has typically taken the form of relying on the younger members of more or less extended family units to take care of the older family members. At best, however, this is unsatisfactory on two counts. First, the safety net may develop holes through infertility, capricous mortality, or estrangement that results in a satisfactory level of care not being forthcoming. There are indeed reports of nomadic tribes where those too weak to keep up on the migration are simply left to expire by the wayside, however regretfully. Second, the level of retirement care provided is not subject to the individual's control: some may indeed find fulfilment in hiking in the woods, sitting by the fireside reading or watching TV, or baby-sitting the grandchildren, but others might prefer to plan in terms of frequent luxury cruises to exotic destinations or attendance at sports events or the theatre. Without the opportunity for individual saving the level of retirement care will be largely mandated by custom, without regard to individual preferences.

The next step could be the introduction of a currency in the form of certificates redeemable in terms of commodities. One way of keeping the value of the certificates from undue fluctuation in the event of a substantial disturbance in the market for a particular commodity (such as the Spanish conquest in the case of gold and silver) would be to specify the amounts of a moderately wide range of staples in terms of which the certificates could be redeemed, the terms of redemption being that on request for redemption the issuer could exclude up to a specified number of commodities from the list that at the time are in relatively short supply, the holder being then allowed to specify which of the remaining commodities he wishes to get for his certificate. This will keep the value of the certificates from being unduly affected by changes in the market for particular commodities, and also avoid the inconvenience of the redeemer having to accept a bundle of commodities inconvenient for him to handle. If there is a sufficient overlap in the seasonal pattern of the various commodities, much of the reserve can consist of normal seasonal storage, reducing the real cost of maintaining the reserve. The above is for illustrative purposes only; for what follows the exact nature of the currency is not important.

The amount of these certificates that will circulate in daily commerce, Mc, is a noninterest-bearing debt of the issuing government. The excess of Mc over the necessary reserve R can be distributed as a social dividend, or used to subsidize the provision of wells or other public goods. What is important here is that it now becomes possible for individuals to hoard these certificates to provide for their old age, possibly as a supplement to what is forthcoming from the younger members of the family. In order to prevent a stifling of current trading, any amount so hoarded Mh must be replaced by issuing additional certificates, spending them on the resources otherwise used to provide goods and services bought by the hoarders, thus maintaining the overall level of activity.

As the amount Mh becomes large, it might become necessary to increase the reserves R to guard against the possibility of not being able to meet a spate of demands for redemption. To avoid this one might then issue bonds to replace the hoards, bearing interest at a rate sufficient to make them more attractive, subject to restraints against redemption on demand. We are thus into a regime with a national debt that has become necessary because of the opportunity that a monetary economy gives to individuals to save against future needs without reference to any opportunities for profitable private investment. Failure to increase the national debt to accommodate individuals' desire to save would in this model simply result in the draining of Mc funds into Mh funds and a reduction in the volume of trade, absent an increase in the velocity of circulation of Mc which there would be no reason to expect.

What would be the magnitude of such a debt in long-term equilibrium? For purposes of a gross, order-of-magnitude estimate one might assume a constant population with an average lifespan of eighty-four years divided into four periods, a growing period up to twenty-one, a parenting period from twenty-two to forty-two, during which people beget and raise their children, an accumulating period forty-three to sixty-three during which unspent income is either devoted to the care of the elderly in the family-style economy or is accumulated for retirement in the individualistic economy, and a period averaging twenty-one years from age sixty-four on in which one is either taken care of by younger family members or lives on the individually accumulated annuity. Focusing on the latter two periods, if we assume that individuals aspire to the same standard of outlay in the final two periods, they will save half of their income during the accumulation period, having at the end an accumulation of 10.5 years of income, so that over the final forty-two years the average capital accumulation is 5.25 times income, and if there is no accumulation of nonhuman capital in the first forty-two years, the accumulation of those in the final forty-two years of life will be 2.625 times the national income. This would be in addition to whatever accumulation is bequeathed to heirs, or is accumulated temporarily in earlier years to finance higher education and similar purposes. There is, in any case, no relation between individual accumulation of claims and any real creation of productive capital.

Whether there is any intertemporal or intergenerational transfer involved depends on the way in which the resources given up by cohort B aged forty-two to sixty-two at the time of the change and purchased by government with the proceeds of the bonds they purchase are distributed. If they are distributed in retirement benefits to the preceding cohort A, then what occurs is merely the formalization of the previous social obligation of cohort B to care voluntarily for the retirement of cohort A, plus a mutually desirable trade among the members of cohort *B* whereby the savers among them give up consumption in favor of the spenders in *B*, subject to a compensating reverse transfer during their later retirement. If on the other hand the proceeds of the bond sales are spent on public goods enjoyed by all, cohorts *C* and *D* would tend to gain at the expense of cohorts *A* and *B*, the way the burden is distributed between cohorts *A* and *B* depending on the degree to which cohort *B* continues to honor its social obligation to take care of cohort *A*. In this case the result is a benefit to later generations, contrary to the notion that borrowing is a burden on the future.

Secular Changes in the Demand for and Supply of Assets

In reality, of course, up to and into the heyday of the industrial revolution, provision for retirement remained largely on a family rather than an individualistic basis; moreover the weight of such provision was lighter given the shorter life expectation. Major accumulations of savings and wealth were more often made by individuals closely associated with the creation and use of real capital assets. Savings and wealth accumulated without reference to the capital assets in which they would be realized played a relatively minor role and could readily be accommodated by private capital formation without the necessity for a government debt. This remained true for a while even as the shift from family provision for retirement to individualized provision was institutionalized in the growth of savings banks, life insurance companies, and pension funds.

Over most of the past century, however, the situation has changed, gradually but radically. Desired accumulations to provide for old age have increased dramatically, for a number of reasons. The shift from extended family patterns to nuclear families, and to broken families and single individuals, has greatly increased the need for individualistic provision for old age. Pension plans, flawed as they often are, have become widespread, and if properly handled require large accumulations of assets. Increased longevity and increases in the costs of caring for the infirmities of old age have added to the cost of adequate provision. This is in addition to savings motivated by a desire to provide reserves for contingencies, to leave bequests to heirs, to provide for increasingly expensive higher education, to establish an industrial empire, or simply to acquire chips with which to play financial games.

On the other hand as industrial economies have matured, while it is perhaps too much to say that investment is reaching a saturation point, opportunities for profitable net investment appear to have declined substantially relative to aggregate output. Accumulated past investment throws off an increasingly large flow of depreciation charges and other capital consumption allowances that must be reinvested before any net investment can be registered. Capital-saving innovations replace the functions of old capital at much lower cost, often allowing for increased output on the basis of a smaller net investment. The general shift in emphasis away from capital-intensive heavy industry such as mining, steel mills, and railroads to electronics, trucking, and services also implies a reduction in the overall capital–labor ratio. Increased sophistication of equipment and rapid technological change reduce the economic life of investments to the point where changes in the rate of interest become relatively insignificant in determining the profitability of investment.

In terms of the current situation in the US at least, the net result seems to be that for the foreseeable future, desired savings and wealth accumulation out of a full employment level of production and income are likely to be substantially in excess of what can be taken up and recycled into purchasing power by private profit-motivated capital formation. The difference must be supplied by government deficits and debt. But how great do these balancing items have to be in order to make full employment possible, how great can they get before dire consequences impend, and is there any way of defining an optimum position within these limits? And can the fears of the alarmed viewers be put to rest?

Types of Capital

From the standpoint of their relation to production and employment, it would be useful to distinguish various types of real capital. The most important category is productive plant and equipment, which is indeed what comes first to mind. A related category is that of growing crops, goods in process and in transit, a quantity that varies almost automatically with the volume of production. This must be distinguished, however, from sales inventory, where saving in the form of reduction in the purchasing of tangible consumer goods does result in an immediate short-run investment of the savings in the inventory, but an investment that will tend to be cancelled almost immediately by a cut-back in orders from the producer and a reduction in employment. Another category is depletable natural resources, where one would have to distinguish between predictable changes in value by lapse of time, or by depletion, related to a rational production plan, from adventitious changes produced by market fluctuations. Still another category is that of nondepletable, nonreproducible assets such as land (in terms of site value as distinct from improvements), Renoirs, Rodins, stamp collections, and Micky Mantle's uniform.

Another more subtle form of capital is what sometimes goes by the name of "good will," or, for tax assessors, "corporate excess," being the difference between the market value of a firm as a whole over that embodied in its underlying assets valued separately. In some cases the term serves as a cover for monopoly position or reputation acquired by collusion or misleading advertising and is thus not a contributor to national welfare, but in others it could be described as "organizational momentum" consisting of contacts, clientele, and coordination and training of a work force developed as a result of genuinely productive outlays of resources. While it is possible to recognize that there is in principle a real value in such an element, both as the result of resource use and the recycling of savings into purchasing power on the one hand and as a contribution to productive capacity on the other, it is extremely difficult to specify this value or distinguish it from other elements that would fail this test.

Another related issue is that of capital embodied in patents, copyrights, and trademarks. From a prospective point of view, the welfare economics of a right to exclude others from making and distributing a given drug is no different from a grant of exclusive right to produce and sell salt. The restriction is an asset to the grantee, but an impairment of economic efficiency. The problem is one of providing appropriate incentives for the outlays involved in the development of new products. The strength of the incentive provided by monopoly grants is quite capricious and its cost to society often much greater than the value to the innovator. Ideally the incentive would be provided through a system of prizes granted to successful innovators, but the problem of devising a desirable procedure for the awarding of such prizes is intractable. Also intractable is how such capital should be treated in a macroeconomic model. For present purposes, the capital value of such rights is a poor measure of the amount of labor and other resources employed directly and indirectly in their development. For better or worse, the inherent uncertainties in such models tend to overshadow any error in the treatment of this item.

Types of Income

There are also difficulties in specifying the relationship between disposable income and its division between income generating expenditure and savings that must be independently recycled, if they are not to disappear. For example changes in the value of capital assets are included in the Haig–Simon–Schantz definition of individual income. Use of this definition is indeed necessary if one is to avoid the need for essentially arbitrary administrative distinctions in the assessment of income taxes, or create incentives for undesirable manipulations by taxpayers. This does not, however, preclude the making of distinctions for analytic purposes where tax avoidance considerations are not involved.

Indeed for purposes of macroeconomic analysis there are important qualitative distinctions to be made among various types of income, in terms of the way in which income is likely to be allocated between consumption and savings on the one hand and in terms of the impact of government finance on their magnitude on the other. Changes in wages and salaries, for example, tend to be regarded as moderately permanent, leading to relatively large immediate changes in consumption and smaller changes in savings; changes in profits are likely to produce relatively smaller changes in consumption, and capital gains and losses still smaller. Government recycling, measured as the excess of government payments having the effect of adding to disposable income over receipts that diminish disposable income, if in the form of wages, salaries, interest, pensions, or welfare payments, will be spent on consumption to a larger extent than purchases of goods and services that contain an element of profit.

In the light of the above rather imprecise qualitative considerations, any assertions that one can make about the levels of government recycling and eventual levels of national debt required to move from current levels of unemployment to a full employment economy over a period of two or three years and maintain full employment thereafter, assuming that adequate means are available to keep inflation under control, must be considered, subject to a wide range of uncertainty. A preliminary look at rough orders of magnitude, however, should be useful in demonstrating that major changes in the general direction of current policies are urgently needed.

Projecting Debt Needs for the US Economy

Looking first at the required ultimate level of the national debt, which is the underlying concern of the viewers with alarm, in a closed economy this could be set equal to the excess of desired nominal personal wealth over domestic privately owned wealth. Starting from the recent situation in the US, as an indicator of the desired level of individual assets we can observe that the ratio of privately owned wealth (estimated as the sum of private real industrial wealth, consumer durables, and federal, state and local debt) to disposable personal income for the period 1960–90 ranged from a low of 3.631 for 1971 to a high of 4.133 for 1990, with a fairly substantial upward trend from 3.767 for 1984 to 4.133 for 1990. As an indicator of private recycling we can observe that the ratio of private real capital (inclusive of consumer durables) to gross domestic product ranged from a low of 1.878 for 1966 to a high 2.323 for 1982 and back to 2.202 for 1990, the downward trend for industrial capital being partially offset by an upward trend in the consumer durables component.

Taking 1997 as a year by which the maintenance of an unemployment rate of 1.5 percent would have been established, real gross domestic product will have grown by 3 percent per year to allow for productivity and labor force increases, and by another 15 percent to allow for the reduction of unemployment by 6 percent from 7.5 percent to 1.5 percent, using Okun's figure of 2.5 for the elasticity of GDP with respect to measured unemployment. From a base of 4.821 trillion 1987 dollars the GDP will thus have to increase to 6.620 trillion 1987 dollars. If inflation were to continue at about 3 percent so that the CPI for 1997 would be 143.1, GDP would be 9.473 trillion current dollars.

If we assume that the asset–disposable-income ratio tops out at 4.500 years, this will be, using a 0.7171 disposable income to GDP ratio, 3.227 years of GDP; if the private capital to GDP ratio bottoms out at 2.150 years this leaves the government debt requirement at 1.077 years of GDP, or 10.202 trillion current dollars, as the amount necessary to satisfy the need of individuals for assets into which to put their savings so that they will be recycled into the income stream and not lost. Comparing this with the 1992 figure of 5.160 trillion, we have a total deficit for 1993 through 1997 of 5.042 trillion, or an average of 1.008 trillion per year. This would not be spread evenly: one would want to start with a recycling stimulus of the order of perhaps 2 trillion for an initial year, followed by a couple of years of 0.5 trillion as private investment gears up to full employment, followed again by larger deficits as private investment reverts to a level appropriate to a 3 percent real growth rate.

If thereafter inflation continues at 3 percent and real product also grows at about 3 percent, producing an annual growth in nominal GDP of 6.09 percent, and the coefficients stabilize at the assumed levels of 4.50 years for desired assets in terms of disposable income and at 2.15 years for private capital in terms of GDP, the debt will likewise have to grow at 6.09 percent. If the nominal interest rate on the debt of 1.077 years of GDP is 9 percent per year, this leaves a net charge to be financed out of current revenues of 2.81 percent of the debt or 3.03 percent of the GDP, which while substantial, is not enough of a burden relative to government budgets on the order of 25 percent of GDP to be a cause for alarm. As for the required annual recycling through the budget, roughly equal to the deficit as currently defined somewhat arbitrarily, this will be equal to the increase in the debt requirement, or deficit levels; this is not disproportionate to the advantages secured by genuinely full employment. The main problem will be one of keeping inflation down to the supposed 3 percent in the face of a tight labor market. This will call for the institution of some additional control measure such as the marketable markup warrants program discussed elsewhere in this volume.

Actually, if there exists a fully effective control over the rate of inflation, the rate of inflation might with advantage be allowed to rise to 5 percent while monetary expansion is used to drive the money rate of interest down to 6 percent, leaving a real rate of interest of 0.951 percent. Nominal GDP and the nominal value of the debt would be increasing at 8.15 percent, leaving a net inflow of funds from capital operations to the operating budget of 2.15 percent of the debt or

0.0232 of the annual GDP. If there is any "burden on the future" beyond 1997, it would be infinitely deferred.

An Unlikely Extreme Alternative Scenario

The results are of course significantly dependent on the assumptions made. To push rather drastically in the direction of a lower debt requirement, one might suppose that by reason of heavier depreciation and obsolescence charges, and larger government expenditures financed out of taxes, the ratio of disposable income to gross domestic product is reduced from 0.7171 to say 0.6, that by reason of a more equal distribution of income, whether resulting from progressive taxation or resulting from a shift in income from profits to wages, or from reductions in interest and profit rates, the asset–demand ratio is reduced from 4.5 to 3.5, and that innovation again becomes capital intensive, so as to raise the capital–output ratio to 2.5 instead of 2.15. If indeed by some set of revolutionary developments all of these changes occurred, one would have a government capital surplus at full employment equal to $2.5 - 0.6(3.5) = 0.4$ times GDP, required to sustain capacity growth. Alternatively, monetary stringency could be applied to raise interest rates sufficiently to limit capital formation to the available private savings, with a correspondingly slower rate of growth. This may be the sort of world budget balancers have in mind, but it is very far from current reality.

In an open economy there is also the role played by the foreign trade balance: currently the trade deficit is in effect an addition to the foreign component of the total demand for domestic assets; its effect is implicitly included in the above calculations. The estimates would be modified by a change in the trade balance: eliminating the trade balance deficit or shifting to a surplus would constitute an increase in the assets available to absorb domestic savings, correspondingly reducing the need for government debt. What is clear in any case is that the debt required to produce full employment is issued to absorb the savings of residents, and the notion that a large debt of this kind would involve a burdensome payment to unfriendly foreigners is simply incorrect.

Thus whatever a fuller analysis than there has been time for here may reveal concerning the relevant parameters, it is clear that it is possible to attain a state of genuinely full employment, with all the benefits in terms of human and social values that this would entail, without major burdens on posterity. Indeed, the real heritage left to the future in terms of the additional private capital brought into being to meet enhanced demands would far outweigh any net burden involved in making transfers from taxpayers to resident bondholders. To be sure, legitimizing large deficits may widen the temptation to engage in pork-barrel largesse, such as paying three times the market price to producers of mohair, providing scarce water at way below market price to producers of rice, cotton, and alfalfa, and protecting cane sugar producers on the fringes of the Everglades with disastrous ecological consequences, to say nothing of the burden on the American consumers and Latin American producers. But the remedy is surely not to strangle government in a budgetary straitjacket but to bring sanity, discipline, and a knowledge of relevant economic facts and principles to the halls of legislatures.

23

---·---

Today's Task for Economists

Prologue

The established protocols of this association decreed that the copy for this address should be in the hands of the editors of the *AER* by 15 October, but they could not decree cessation of activity of the little gray cells even of the oldest occupant to date of this podium, nor stay the course of economic history over the subsequent ten weeks. At the risk of considerable hubris I feel impelled to offer today a rather radically altered version of the address that those of you who read such things will find in the March issue of the *AER*.

Briefly, the experience of the past few weeks has left me aghast at the willingness of the great bulk of that part of the profession close to the seats of power to remain content with modest palliative measures constrained by a supposed need to reduce the so-called budget deficit, if not immediately then in some future state of affairs, usually to a state of "balance," and by a less actively articulated but possibly better justified fear of rekindling inflation. What is urgently needed is to bring the economy rapidly to a point of genuine full employment and keep it there. By genuine full employment I mean a situation where there are at least as many job openings as there are persons seeking employment, probably calling for a rate of unemployment as currently measured of between 1 and 2 percent. On an individual level, the objective is that the situation should be such that any reasonably responsible person who is not too choosy about the kind of work can find a job within forty-eight hours at a living wage.

Presidential Address to the American Economic Association, 6 January, 1993 (revised 3 February, 1993; original version published in *American Economic Review*, March 1993, pp. 1–10).

This would have salutary consequences not only for the level of production but also in terms of reduced budgetary drains for unemployment insurance benefits, welfare payments, and the like, and significant beneficial impacts on levels of poverty, homelessness, drug addiction, and crime. Full employment would also substantially ease tensions over such issues as defense cutbacks, race relations, free trade, and immigration, as well as over many labor-management issues such as featherbedding, demarcation, seniority, and job tenure. Genuine full employment would allow qualified workers to move upscale out of low-skill jobs to jobs more suited to their potential. Under these conditions training would become effective in increasing overall productivity, whereas under present conditions training programs, while they may be microeffective in moving the selected trainees to the head of the queue of job applicants, nevertheless are largely macroineffective in reducing the size of the queue. This upscaling of potentially qualified labor out of the low-skill market would in turn tend to raise the wage level and esteem of socially necessary low-skill jobs so as better to integrate those performing them into the life of the wider community.

Compared to the manifold benefits accruing from genuinely full employment, the problems involved in dealing with any debt that might have to be accumulated in the process of obtaining full employment will pale to relative insignificance. Inflation is a more serious matter that I will deal with in due course. But it is high time we gave human values a deserved priority instead of staying mesmerized by figures on balance sheets. It's not "the economy, stupid," as one cartoonist had it, if by the economy one means the usual financial numbers such as the Dow Jones, bond prices, or even the gross domestic product; the three most important problems of today are "unemployment, employment, and jobs."

The Allocation Task of Yesteryear

Nearly two score years ago, on the occasion of Columbia's bicentennial celebration, Sir Dennis Robertson gave an address entitled "What do Economists Economize?" the burden of which was that since presumably economists are the most expert economizers, they should economize the most precious thing in the world, namely love, or altruism. This would be done in part by so arranging things that in the ordinary conduct of life individual choices made on the basis of self-interest in terms of market prices would at least be consistent with maximizing social welfare, so that the exercise of scarce resources of altruism could be concentrated on situations where Adam Smith's unseen hand could not be made to serve. To me one implication of this was that economists should see to it that market prices correctly reflect the relevant marginal social cost of various alternatives. I have devoted a major part of my career to the promotion of such marginal-cost pricing, but thus far with a notable lack of practical success outside academia.

At that time, indeed, there was a certain euphoria prevailing among at least part of the economics profession over the prospect of curbing the business cycle and maintaining a high level of economic activity through Keynesian fiscal policy. Under these circumstances it was reasonable to think that the chief remaining job of the economist was to assure as near an approach as possible to a Pareto-efficient allocation of a given aggregate of resourcs. The event, however, proved otherwise. The conventional wisdom of regarding budget deficits as improvident prodigality, and government debt as the legacy of a craven deferral of burden to the future, resumed command.

One eminent economist is said to have remarked, in effect, that it was the function of the science of public finance to see to it that nothing of importance is ever done or left undone merely for financial reasons. Alas, the financial reasons have thus far carried the day, and we have not had anything approaching real full employment since the Korean War, nor indeed in peacetime at any time since 1926 if then.

In the Eisenhower years, the conventional wisdom held sway in spite of the absence of serious contra-indications to the Keynesian prescription. In effect, the dominant thinking reverted to that of the Coolidge–Hoover era, with a naïve faith that a self-equilibrating free market would somehow work to produce a satisfactory equilibrium, and if business cycles occurred, this would be a small price to pay for the wonderful benefits of *laissez faire*.

The Way Savings and Investment Actually Interact

In the background there still seems to lurk the notion that capital markets work like a market for potatoes. In a potato market, if the price happens to be higher than that equating demand and supply, the presence of unsold potatoes will cause the price to fall, and in the reverse case the clamor of unsatisfied customers will cause the price to rise. But in the capital market it doesn't work that way. If interest rates initially equate intended capital formation and intended savings, and I decide to save an additional $8 by not having my hair cut, thus in the classic diagram moving the "supply" of savings to the right, nothing happens to lower the rate of interest to the new equilibrium point. There will be $8 more in my bank account, but $8 less in the barber's account; his income is reduced, he is partially unemployed, and there is nothing that makes it any easier for anyone to obtain funds with which to create capital, nor anything that makes the prospects for capital formation more attractive. As Gertrude Stein remarked, "the money is always there, it's the pockets that keep changing." If the barber reacts by curtailing his consumption, this further reduces national income and saving, in a downward cumulative process. I may succeed in my attempt to save, but only by reducing the saving of others by even more. Savings are an extremely perishable entity. Say's law ("supply creates its own demand") fails as soon as part of the income generated in the process of producing the supply is shunted off into savings that fail to get converted into an increase in the stock of capital goods.

Essentially the same results obtain, somewhat less instantaneously, if I save $10,000 by not buying a car: the $10,000 less in the dealer's balance represents say $2,000 of reduction in his gross margin, and an $8,000 increase in his bank loan to cover his inventory. There is, indeed, investment in inventory, but this will be transitory as the dealer cuts back on his orders from the factory, and unemployment on the assembly line results. Unless attempted savings are recycled into the stream of purchasing power by some coincidental, nonautomatic action, they simply vanish in reduced income and reduced realized savings.

On the other hand if some genius invents a new product or process and obtains a credit or borrows the funds needed to finance the capital involved in its production, this added real wealth is, ipso facto, someone's saving. Instead of Say's law we have "capital formation creates its own saving." Indeed since much of the income generated by the capital formation process will be spent rather than saved, there will be a multiplier effect, in which income is ultimately increased by enough so that out of it the increased savings will equal the increased investment. Either way, there is no automatic equilibrium at reasonably full employment. Rather, if savings at full employment would exceed investment, income would tend to fall, so that if savings fall off more rapidly than investment a low-employment long-run equilibrium is established, possibly only as an average around which cycles fluctuate.

The Biases and Limits of Monetary Intervention

To mitigate this unsatisfactory state of affairs a *deus ex machina* is introduced into the classical model in the form of a monetary authority charged with the task of adjusting interest rates and other aspects of the capital market so as to allow a balance between planned saving and planned investment to occur at a satisfactory level of employment. Unfortunately, monetary authorities seem to be afflicted with an inherent constitutional bias stemming from the close association of those responsible for monetary policy with financial interests, and their relative remoteness from the grim realities of unemployment. For fear of disturbing the smooth functioning of financial markets, adjustments on the down side tend to be too little and too late, while a stance is maintained of being prepared to slam on the brakes at the first signs of a recrudescence of inflation regarded as a sacrilege against the monetary standard in terms of which they measure all good and evil.

Moreover, monetary authorities tend to confine their activities to the short-term end of the capital market, and appear relatively reluctant or unable to do very much directly about longer-term interest rates, which are the more important rates from the standpoint of influencing saving and capital formation. A perceived readiness to put short-term rates back up promptly should inflation begin to threaten is not an atmosphere conducive to the financing of the creation of durable capital. Indeed, to the extent that interest rates are raised in an attempt to check inflation, sellers will regard the increased interest charges as a cost justifying an increase in prices, giving inflation an additional expiring flip as a result of the attempt to control it through monetary policy.

Special Measures to Promote Capital Formation

Various supply-side measures to promote investment have been proposed, but the ones most actively promoted seem unusually weak compared to many that could be advanced on this ground. Enterprise zones seem to result more in the shifting of investment to even out the geographical distribution of unemployment rather than to increase total employment. Investment tax credits, that look so attractive from a distance, become an administrative nightmare as soon as one begins to inquire about the details of which investments are to be eligible, and at what time, whether at the time of conception, of commitment, of manufacture, of purchase, of installation, of payment, etc. Empirical evidence of their effectiveness at the modest rates effective in the past is at best inconclusive.

Concessions to capital gains, if enacted with adjustments to regular income taxes on a revenue-neutral basis, may actually depress economic activity. Additional savings out of the capital gains tax reduction are likely to be greater than the reduction in savings from the increase in other taxes, requiring an increase in savings recycling. This may well exceed the additional capital formation induced, especially as the inducement to capital formation is in terms of a tax reduction in a relatively remote future subject to legislative vicissitudes. At best special treatment of capital gains greatly increases the complexity of the tax law, and diverts investment flows from their most efficient use. There is nothing to indicate that investments likely to yield returns in forms defined by the tax code as capital gains will have any superior social value: gains from land speculation, in particular, add nothing to the real availability of resources, and many of the legislatively prescribed inclusions in the capital gains category are essentially pork.

Other far more effective supply-side measures for stimulating the economy and improving the allocation of capital investment exist, but have for the most part been ignored by reason of their political unpopularity. One such measure would be the abolition of the corporation income tax, which is by far the most serious hurdle in the way of private capital formation of a kind requiring equity funding. Unlike the capital gains tax, the corporate income tax is a tax largely above or before the market, requiring a rate of return on investment sufficient to cover the corporation tax and leave a rate of return after tax comparable to other investments, whereas the capital gains tax operates largely as a reduction in the return to the investor after or below the market, comparable to the reduction of net income to the taxpayer resulting from the personal income tax on other income. In addition the corporation tax causes inefficient allocation of investment between equity-type and loan-type investments, it encourages thin equity and resulting bankruptcies and reorganizations, it lubricates takeovers and mergers of dubious intrinsic merit, and its existence greatly complicates the income tax law and regulations.

Nevertheless this tax, in spite of its many defects from the standpoint of economic efficiency, has enormous political popularity due to the fact that nearly everyone thinks that its burden falls on someone other than themselves. Indeed economists have differed widely in their assignment of the "incidence" of the tax, owing to a failure to specify, or even to consider, the macroeconomic policy changes necessarily involved in a change in the tax. Unlike most other taxes, the corporation tax inflicts a double whammy on the economy in that it both extracts income from the stream of purchasing power and reduces the recycling of saving through investment. If imposed on a revenue neutral basis it causes unemployment, while if a budgetary adjustment is made to maintain employment constant, much of its burden can be thought of as falling on future wage-earners who will have less capital with which to work, while the immediate impact will be offset by individual income increments generated by the budget recycling required to maintain a constant level of employment.

Improving the Neutrality of the Tax System

Problems of the deferral of income through undistributed profits, as well as the deferral of taxation to the time of realization of capital gains, would ideally be met by putting the personal income tax on a cumulative basis, along lines I developed while working with Carl Shoup in 1938, whereby the deferral of the reporting of income, by whatever means, merely involves the borrowing of the deferred tax at a suitable rate of interest. About two-thirds of the internal revenue code would become redundant, with the possible exception of the need to deal with the international jet set and revolving-door marriages; large numbers of tax techies would have to apply themselves to more productive employment.

In the absence of cumulative assessment, an approximation to a level playing field might be had by imposing a small annual tax on the accumulated undistributed surplus of corporations, roughly equal to the interest on the stockholders' postponed individual income tax. Similarly a surcharge could be imposed on realized capital gains, proportionate to the length of time held, to offset the gain from the deferral of the tax, though the administrative difficulties that this would entail in all but the simplest of cases give pause.

If there is nevertheless a need to cater to a political demand for something that can be labeled a corporation tax, this might be satisfied by levying a corporation tax on dividends, interest, and retained earnings at a rate corresponding to the first bracket rate of the individual income tax, and exempting such interest and dividends from this "normal" rate, going back to the pre-1934 practice of dividing the income tax into a normal tax and a progressive surtax. To even things up neatly, normal tax paid on other forms of income should be deductible in computing the base for the progressive surtax paid by a minority of taxpayers. It would still be appropriate to have an undistributed surplus tax to correspond to this surtax.

Tax-Exempt Bonds

Another measure that might slightly improve investment allocation would be to replace the exemption of interest on state and local bonds by a taxable tax credit at a rate that would maintain the market value of the bonds. Low bracket taxpayers would be little affected while nearly all the loss of revenue to the Treasury from this tax credit would accrue as a subsidy to the issuers. Upper bracket taxpayers would no longer have an incentive to invest in such bonds rather than in riskier investments more suitable to their status.

Taxing Imputed Income

A more important but politically more difficult measure would be to require the inclusion in taxable income of the rental value of owner-occupied residences. This would not only improve the equity and progressivity of the income tax but go a substantial way toward making more units available for rental and to a modest extent promoting the construction of additional affordable rental housing and abating the problem of homelessness. It would create a more nearly level playing field for alternative forms of ownership and tenancy: it is not for the love of cooperative principles that so many luxury apartments have been converted to coops and condos. Elimination of the tax discrimination would greatly ease tensions in the relations between landlords and tenants fighting over the distribution of the tax benefits from conversion.

A similar case can be made for including in the income tax base a net rental value of nonbusiness automobiles (equal to interest on the market value of the car), in this case reducing the discrimination against the use of public transit and car rental. The theoretical case for treating other consumer durables similarly is outweighed by considerations of administrative difficulty and the lack of important taxed alternatives.

Shifting Property Taxes from Improvements to Land

A measure which could provide a powerful stimulus to investment in property improvements would be to replace part or all of the property tax by a tax on land value only, a proposal that can be traced all the way back to Quesnay and the French physiocrats, and more recently associated with the name of Henry George. This would remove the very serious deterrent effect of the property tax on improvements. Unfortunately from the standpoint of a national employment policy, this tax is largely levied by local governments, which are often constrained by constitutional provisions or state laws. Nevertheless some means of bringing pressure to bear on these governments to make this change might be found. Some Pennsylvania governments are already doing this. When levied for municipal purposes, it might be appropriate to exempt from the tax a flat amount per square foot as representing the value of surrounding agricultural land for which the urban government can claim no credit; this would also mitigate discriminations at jurisdictional boundaries.

Such a shift in the basis for local taxation might not only encourage private investment in improvements, but open the door to additional public investment that could then be financed without significant excess burden, in many cases enhancing the rental value of the taxed land. In particular, it would be desirable to increase land taxes to provide subsidies to enable local utility, transit, and other services to be priced efficiently at levels closer to short-run marginal social cost. To the extent that labor and capital finance are mobile, so that their returns are determined by a wider market, the gains in efficiency would be captured by land, as the immobile factor, so that land rents would rise by more than the tax increase.

Limitations of "Supply-side" Measures

Under current conditions, however, such "supply-side" measures designed to operate by reducing the cost of capital are likely to be severely limited in their effects. As long as nearly all types of capital facilities are idle or underutilized, very little "widening" investment is likely to take place. At most, some "deepening" investment in new products or technologies may take place, or there may be corners of the economy where relatively rapid growth has kept capacity fully utilized. Even in such cases, investment in capital facilities may depend more on appraisals of an uncertain market for the product than on the cost of capital. Supply-side measures, like monetary stimuli, are aptly described as paying out on a rope, and are relatively ineffective when there is no demand-side pull at the other end.

Long-term Excess of Desired Saving over Private Investment

Supply-side measures, even if carried forward much more vigorously than are being actively advocated, are thus likely to fall woefully short of causing a rapid growth toward full employment. *There is, indeed, no principle of economics that assures that there will always be a feasible rate of interest or state of the capital markets that will equate desired savings with net private capital formation under conditions of steady full employment.* Current trends seem to be such as to make it extremely unlikely that such an equality can be achieved even by the most vigorous possible application of supply-side measures. One factor has been a spate of capital-saving innovations and practices. Fiber optics, when fully utilized, costs less per unit of service by orders of magnitude, leaving ductways planned for copper forever surplus; electronic exchanges occupy a fraction of the space formerly required by equivalent electro-mechanical exchanges; just-in-time practices reduce investment in inventory; improved communications enable more freight to be carried on a single track line with sidings than was formerly carried by a full two-track line; trucking requires less capital per employee than rail transport; assembling electronic gear with a soldering iron uses far less capital than the man in the pulpit of a rolling mill, and service industries generally seem to use less capital per employee than manufacturing, mining or transportation.

Moreover, before gross capital formation can begin to recycle private savings, it must first recycle funds set aside in depreciation, amortization, depletion and obsolescence charges, while rapid obsolescence due to accelerating technological progress makes capital formation relatively insensitive to changes in interest rates. Very low or negative interest rates may stimulate investment in escalated prices for nonreproducible assets such as land, authentic masterworks, memorabilia, and other "collectibles," but even this is limited by the possibility that speculative bubbles may burst, and in any case relatively little recycling is produced thereby, except to the extent that the enhanced asset values cause owners to feel wealthier and spend more.

On the savings side, increased longevity and the high cost of old age illness lead to increased savings through funded pensions and other provisions for retirement. For this purpose, the lower the rate of interest the greater the amount that must be put aside out of current earnings to provide a given level of retirement security. On the other hand increased incomes from higher interest and profit rates are more likely to lead to higher savings. More recently the increased concentration of income among the very wealthy, who have a high propensity to save, not so much for eventual consumption but largely to accumulate chips with which to play financial games and exercise economic power, has further added to the savings recycling problem. Some recycling may take place through investment abroad reflected in a positive trade balance and the production of goods for export, though it is uncertain how far this can be carried in the face of political instability, the danger of creating repayment problems, and the resistance of foreign governments that do not have an effective full employment policy of their own to our exporting our unemployment to them in this way.

On balance it is likely to prove impossible, for the foreseeable future, to maintain a steady state of genuinely full employment without a substantial amount of government recycling of savings, a chronic budget deficit, and a long-term increasing trend in the national debt, however distasteful this may be to those ideologically addicted to a balanced budget. It may even prove necessary for the debt to grow at a rate faster than the growth of GNP, though this ratio would presumably remain below some upper bound. The burden of servicing this debt might be kept within bounds by reducing real interest rates, close to zero if need be, though this might imply a higher level of private investment than would be chosen on its own merits. Some mitigation of the need for recycling savings might be obtained through increasing the progressivity of the tax structure, thus reducing the average propensity to save. Even contemplating such prospects calls for a significant expansion in our range of habitual thought.

Rethinking Deficits and Debt

Getting acceptance for the idea that government recycling of savings on a substantial scale will have to be a permanent feature of any full-employment economy is not going to be easy. We have the spectacle of the House voting by a substantial majority in favor of a constitutional amendment to require a balanced budget, fortunately falling short of the required two-thirds. This was done in spite of the fact that the nominal budget as currently computed is not a valid measure of any significant economic quantity. The nominal deficit would be reduced by selling the Pentagon to a life insurance company subject to a long-term lease-back and repurchase option; this at least would do no harm, unlike the sale of natural resources to private exploiters that would actually decrease the real heritage handed down to the future, on the pretext of reducing the transfer requirements embodied in the national debt.

Savings Recycling and the Deficit

Government savings recycling is indeed a concept associated with the deficit, but is not identical with it. Direct government recycling can be defined as the excess of government payments that are considered by their recipients to be income, over government receipts considered by their payors to be reductions in disposable income. Thus not all deficit financing results in recycling of savings, whether measured by the current capriciously defined nominal deficit, or by a more rational definition involving accounting for government assets. Thus the sale of the Pentagon, or the purchase of an office building currently being rented by the government, offset by bond transactions, would not involve any change in the level of recycling. Indeed, if purchase of a previously rented building is financed by taxes, recycling is diminished. And if government investment in a power plant, for example, substitutes for investment that would otherwise have been made by private enterprise, in a genuine "crowding out" as distinct from the largely spurious crowding out alleged to occur in the financial markets, there is no overall increase in net recycling.

It is worth noting that the significance of a government deficit and debt would be drastically different in a community relying exclusively on a land value tax. Such a debt would in effect be a collective mortgage on the land, especially if it can be assumed that land values in the community will vary proportionately over time. Since the interest on the community debt will generally be lower than interest charged on individual mortgages, it can be in the general interest of all the taxpayers of the community for the government to borrow as much as the market will take, even to finance current outlays, provided a suitable margin is left to deal with emergencies. On the other hand such debt financing performs no recycling of savings, there is no room for Keynesian fiscal policy, and Ricardian equivalence is in full sway. This does not detract, however, from the powerful stimulating effect of a reduction in the tax on improvements.

On the whole, however, recycling tends to vary in rough correlation with the nominal deficit, and the strength of the notion in the minds of the public and their representatives that deficits are bad and that the "budget" should be balanced may make it difficult to achieve an adequate level of recycling.

Recycling Savings through Public Capital Formation

Some help in gaining acceptance for government recycling might be derived from restating the budget in terms of distinguishing between transactions on current account and on capital account, as is done in many other governmental units. If AT+T, General Motors and households had been constrained to operate under the restrictions of the proposed balanced budget amendment, we would now have far fewer telephones, automobiles and houses. By analogy, it would be proper, even on classical principles, for a government to borrow for capital purposes, borrowing for the capital account being justified by comparisons with correspond-ing private practices and by the thought that future generations being burdened with the service of the debt would also reap benefits from the real capital passed on to them. While this may constrain choice away from what rational voters would have chosen as the optimal level of government capital formation, there might be enough scope for government capital investment to provide sufficient recycling to bring about full employment, particularly if investment in education, research, space exploration, and the like are considered eligible for treatment as capital investment, in whole or in part. Some of these projects, even if they would not stand scrutiny aside from their function in justifying income recycling, may nevertheless have the same kind of justification as the building of the Egyptian pyramids had for Keynes. On general welfare grounds, one might well prefer recycling in terms of borrowing to finance health care to borrowing to finance space stations, but if borrowing for health care is ruled out as creating an ideologically sinful current-account deficit, space stations it will have to be.

Government Recycling to Enable Individualistic Provision for Retirement

Another approach that might help in securing acceptance for adequate long-term government recycling and the associated so-called "deficits" is in terms of their role in enabling provision for retirement on an individualistic basis. In pre-capitalist economies, the needs of the elderly were generally taken care of somewhat haphazardly by the younger members of more or less extended family groups. Inevitably, life's hazards would leave some inadequately cared for and others with an unduly heavy burden. Where land was either freely available or held in common, opportunities for individuals to save for their own future were limited by the absence of scarce durable capital goods.

It would be possible to enable provision for old age to be made on an individualistic basis through government recycling of savings by issuing bonds to be purchased by individuals, directly or through intermediaries, the proceeds of this government borrowing being used for current public services, or even for the payment of a social dividend, and eventually for the redemption of previously issued bonds. Individuals would then have greater freedom of choice, both as to the size of families and the way in which they divide their consumption between middle and old age.

The industrial revolution, by opening up large opportunities for private capital investment, made it possible to shift to a considerable extent in the direction of individualistic provision for old age without having to rely on familial loyalty or requiring recourse to government recycling. In recent decades we have seen a shift to less capital intensive forms of production and a lengthening of the duration of retirement coupled with increases in the cost of caring for infirmities character-istic of old age. We thus are once again faced with a chronic need for government recycling. The government "deficit" is thus not a "burden on the future" but an opening up of choices not otherwise available, and the public debt a means whereby provision can be made for one's old age on an individualistic basis, where opportunities for investment in private industry are inadequate to serve the total need.

The Need for Inflation Control

But while adequate government recycling may be a necessary condition for genuine full employment, it is not sufficient. The stagflation that began to be experienced in the 1960s demonstrated that vigorous application of Keynesian stimuli could eventuate in the resulting increased purchasing power being dissipated in excessively rising prices rather than in expanded production. The simple Keynesian approach thus tended to lose much of what little support it had achieved. It has become necessary to develop methods of dealing with this phenomenon, which was not effectively addressed by the earlier models. Indeed, when Keynes' *General Theory* appeared in 1936, modest increases in the price level back to those prevailing in the 1920s would have been generally considered desirable rather than otherwise.

The Phillips Curve and the NIARU

For the analysis of this new phenomenon a new relationship, the Phillips curve, relating the evolution of inflation to the level of unemployment was added to the economists' tools of analysis, with its "Noninflation-accelerating rate of unem-ployment" or NIARU. This NIARU is of course not a fixed datum, but varies over time and place according to the socio-political ambience, the mechanics of the labor market, and the vigor of competition. It may have been rising over time as a result of the increased sophistication and differentiation of products, real and factitious, giving sellers, as the ones most knowledgeable about the characteristics of their product and its market, considerable leeway to raise their prices without unacceptable loss of sales. This leeway has been enhanced by high design and development costs and also by the increased cost of the advertising required to break into a market. Patents, copyrights, trademarks, quotas, and other governmentally generated barriers to entry have played an increasing part in weakening market competition. This tendency for a wage–price spiral to emerge is a process ultimately held in check only by the presence of underutilized resources, including mainly what Marxists used to call "the reserve army of the unemployed." Currently in the US the NIARU appears to be around 4 percent to 6 percent.

Callous Tolerance for Unemployment

In some quarters this NIARU has even been termed the "natural" rate of unemployment, in one of the most vicious euphemisms ever coined. One of my colleagues has even gone so far as to define "full employment" as being the NIARU, and a member of the financial establishment recently responded to my proposal by asserting that he regarded 7 percent unemployment as "full employment," while his ilk often talk as though unemployment didn't really matter as long as the markets behaved favorably.

But while 5 percent unemployment might be barely tolerable if it meant that everyone would be taking an additional two weeks' vacation every year without pay, it is totally unacceptable as a social goal when it means unemployment rates of 10, 20, or even 40 percent among disadvantaged groups, with resulting increases in poverty, homelessness, poor health, drug addiction, and crime. Yet the hard political fact is that at such a NIARU the great majority of the voting population, including most of the politically active upper and middle classes, will have relatively little personal experience of severe unemployment, while nearly everyone will have some direct experience of inflation. Many seem to feel that if only prices would stop rising they would benefit correspondingly by having their income go further, giving relatively little thought to the effect on their incomes. Even those with large mortgages or other debts who would actually gain from inflation, tend to concur in the notion that they suffer from it. It is thus extremely difficult to get political support for anti-unemployment measures that are perceived as involving a threat of inflation, at least until unemployment reaches 7 percent or more at which point unemployment becomes a more widespread threat.

The Advantages of Assured Predictable Low-rate Inflation

Actually it is the uncertainty as to the rate of inflation, and not its level, that does the damage. An assured, moderate rate of inflation can be adapted to by adjusting nominal rates of interest and the terms of long-term contracts involving money payments, and by modifying the manner in which depreciation allowances are calculated. The "menu cost" of changing price tags and catalog quotations is probably less important than the mental effort required of consumers in forming an idea of what an appropriate current price is for infrequently purchased items, such as furniture or clothing. An inflation rate assured to stay between 5 percent and 6 percent, say, might even have advantages. Monetary policy would be more powerful in stemming a downturn in that very low and even negative real rates of interest would become feasible as a stimulus to investment. It might in principle be easier to keep inflation within a 1 percent range between 5 percent and 6 percent, than to keep it within a 2 percent range between minus 1 percent and plus 1 percent, given the smaller real value of noninterest-bearing moneys in circulation and the greater scope for monetary policy, even allowing for the superior political focusing power of a target of 0 percent as compared to one of 5.5 percent.

The base of the income tax would be broadened, also, making it possible to have a tax that is more progressive and more productive of revenue with lower marginal rates and less of a distortionary effect. A tax based on nominal accrued income would in effect be a tax on a base consisting of real income plus a percentage of net worth. While this is not what is meant by an ideologically pure income tax, in terms of its practical effects it can be deemed a superior tax. Indexing of capital gains, especially, not only suffers from the disadvantages of a general indexing of capital income, but involves an administrative nightmare of defining the relevant dates in complicated transactions, and provides a field day for tax techies in finding various ways around the regulations to arbitrage against the revenue by offsetting indexed gains with nonindexed deductions.

Inflation versus Unemployment

It is the possibility of substantial changes in the rate of inflation, either up or down, that does the damage. Such changes involve a disappointment of expectations and a redistribution of wealth and income derived from a given national product that is capricious and often inequitable, but it does not of itself substantially reduce the amount to be distributed. Unemployment, on the other hand directly and substantially reduces the total product to be distributed. Unanticipated changes in the rate of inflation, up or down, may be considered to be a form of legitimized embezzlement, or perhaps involuntary participation in a lottery, whereas unemployment is vandalism.

The Apotheosis of the Bottom Line

Nevertheless, the stance of the politico-financial establishment is still to look at the bottom line as the ultimate reality, whether of the corporation or the national budget, and since money is the measure of all good and evil in this kind of calculus, anything that impugns the value of money is viewed as a kind of sacrilege. Deficit financing, often vaguely identified with printing of money and "inflation" of the currency, is anathematized.

This is likely to be true not only of deficit financing but even more of direct monetary policy. In any attempt to emerge from present rates of unemployment, even only down to the NIARU, within any reasonable time period, monetary policy is likely to prove a weak reed, sometimes aptly described as pushing on a string. The main difficulty is that monetary policy bears primarily on short-term interest rates and credit availability, and in its usual practice does not directly control long-term rates, which are what are important for most decisions involving real durable capital formation. The posture of the Federal Reserve System in holding itself ready to slam on the brakes at the first sign of resurgent inflation is poorly adapted to bringing long-term rates down. It does not appear that the Fed has either the will or the resources to do enough about long-term rates to do very much to increase capital formation, especially when idle and underused capacity pervades much of the economy. At least in the initial phase of getting a desirably rapid start out of a depression, the main reliance will have to be on recycling through fiscal policy.

The Need for Direct Inflation Control

Long before the economy reaches a really satisfactory level of full employment, however, as employment gets to the NIARU level, and inflation threatens to accelerate, the Fed is likely to try to restrain credit expansion and raise interest rates, while demands for a more stringent budget balancing and cut-back of "government waste" are likely to be heard in the halls of Congress. To get anywhere near a satisfactory level of unemployment, some method of dealing with inflation will have to be devised. We are short of tools.

In effect, the economy can be thought of as having three main macroeconomic parameters that we would like to control: the level of employment of human and other resources, the price level, and the division of the resulting total product between provision for current wants and investment in growth and the future, whereas we have only two major policy tools, monetary and fiscal policy. In an era where inflation was not a threat, one could think of these two tools as controlling the level of employment and the rate of growth, with low interest rates combined with a deficit or surplus sufficient to maintain full employment leading to high investment and growth, and conversely. But with a need to control inflation as well, relying on only two dimensions of control is like trying to fly an airplane without ailerons, which were the third dimension of control that was the key to the success of the Wright brothers. A new tool is urgently needed.

Over the past three decades a number of proposals for direct control of inflation have been made, notably by Arthur Okun, Eli Wallach, and others, but none has achieved general acceptance. Wartime control of specific prices, accompanied by rationing, was accepted as an emergency measure and worked in part because of patriotic willingness to conform and in part because, being temporary, many past prices could be continued without becoming absurd, while relatively few new or substantially altered commodities were being introduced. As a permanent scheme this is probably unworkable and certainly unacceptable. More recent schemes have involved tax incentives of various kinds to provide a countervailing downward pressure against the inherent inflationary tendency of an imperfectly competitive system. Such schemes have generally suffered from difficulties in measuring price changes at an individual product level, capriciousness of results when tied to such taxes as the corporation income tax, and possible time lags in adjusting the strength of the incentives to changing circumstances.

Market-based Inflation Control Plans

A few years ago David Colander came to visit me and reported on a proposal by Abba Lerner for a market in rights to raise prices. Those wishing to raise their prices would be required to purchase the right from those prepared to lower their prices, in a manner analogous to proposals for tradable pollution allowances, thus assuring a constant overall price level. While this neatly circumvents the problem of adjusting the strength of incentive to changing inflationary pressures, the problem remains of how to measure price changes in the face of quality changes, new products, and variations in the terms of sale such as delivery, reliability, service, credit terms, tie-in sales, and the like.

More pregnant was the question of how to deal with cases where prices paid to suppliers have risen. A somewhat similar problem arises with gross receipts taxes, which discriminate in favor of vertically integrated operations and against situations where the product passes through several hands on the way to the market. In Europe this problem has been solved by shifting from gross receipts taxes and sales taxes to value added taxes, which immediately suggests that instead of a market in rights to raise prices we have a market in rights to value added.

Control with Marketable Gross Markup Warrants

For semantic reasons I have chosen to speak in terms of "gross markups" rather than value added, as being more suggestive of something to be restrained rather than promoted. In principle, gross markups is simply the excess of sales revenue over amounts paid for nonprime inputs. In operation, warrants for gross markups for a prospective accounting period would be issued to each firm on the basis of the gross markups for a corresponding preceding period, plus or minus adjustments for changes in prime inputs such as labor and invested capital. These warrants would be issued in sufficient total face value to correspond to the value at a desired overall average price level of the output expected to be produced by the inputs against which the warrants were issued. The trend of the overall price level would thus be under firm control within very narrow limits.

Markup warrants would be freely tradable for cash in a competitive market, and if at the end of the accounting period a firm is found to have retained or acquired fewer warrants than the actual amount of its gross markups for the period, a penalty tax would be assessed. This tax would not be a substantial source of revenue, but would serve merely as an enforcement device. It could be set at a level fairly certain to be higher than the market price of the warrants.

Adjustment of the warrant issue for changes in investment could be made simply on the basis of a uniform percentage of such change. Adjustment for changes in employment is somewhat more difficult: a flat amount per employee or manhour takes too little account of variations in qualifications, while to allow adjustments equal to payrolls would run a danger of permitting inflationary wage increases. Some formula such as a percentage of payrolls plus a flat amount per employee might be satisfactory, and involve a certain bias in favor of the employment of low-skill labor, which may be considered desirable in view of the fact that that is where the unemployment problem is most serious.

Administration would seem to pose no insurmountable problems. Determination of gross markups is essentially no different than the assessment of a value added tax such as is widespread in Europe. Adjustment for investment can be made on the basis of accounts already needed for income tax purposes, while adjustments for employment can be related to the social security records. Some special methods may have to be developed for dealing with the self-employed and very small firms, and possibly some classes of firms could be excluded from the scheme as is sometimes done with the value added tax. Inflation control would probably be adequate even if significant parts of the informal and other sectors were excluded from the scheme; distortions would not be a serious problem since no substantial net revenue is being extracted.

Prospects for Rapidly Reaching Genuine Full Employment

With such an instrument in place, what can we plan for in terms of getting from where we are to full employment? Recently unemployment has been reported as about 7.5 percent, and full employment can be reckoned at about 1.5 percent, giving a slack to be made up of 6 percent. Using Okun's ratio of percent change in GNP to percent change in reported unemployment of 2.5, we have a slack in GDP of 15 percent to be made up. If this slack can be taken up within two years, this will be 7.5 percent per year; if to this we add 2.5 percent for growth in the labor force and in productivity, we get a 10 percent per year growth in GNP over two years, at which time we hit the ceiling and growth thereafter will be limited to the labor force and productivity factors, possibly between 2 percent and 4 percent.

Is public finance up to the job of reaching the goals thus defined in terms of the limits of our real resources? Possibly, but it requires breaking new ground. One would have to begin with increasing government recycling as rapidly as possible by between 6 percent and 9 percent of GNP in order to inaugurate the 10 percent growth rate. How rapidly this could be done would of course depend on the political and legislative ambience. From some points of view the fastest and easiest way to do this is by tax cuts. Unfortunately if tax cuts are temporary they tend to be viewed as windfalls to be saved rather than spent, so that only part of the tax cuts are effectively recycled, while if not announced as temporary they tend to create a resistance to later tax increases called for by full employment conditions and large debt service requirements. This is especially threatening in the context of recent political campaigning on the basis of promises of no new taxes. Perhaps the best tax cut would be a cut in the payroll taxes, say by 70 percent of taxes on the first $10,000 per year of earnings, and 40 percent of the tax on the next $5,000, as promising the maximum proportion of recycling, if this can be done in the face of outcries that this would be jeopardizing the financial soundness of the Social Security System, which ultimately depends, not on any nominal social security account, but on the willingness of future Congresses to make the financial arrangements needed to provide the promised benefits, whether through payroll taxes or otherwise.

Outlays on actual programs on the other hand are somewhat harder to start and stop rapidly, though many state and local governments stand ready to restore cuts in programs on fairly short notice. There is also the need not to get too far ahead of the effective operation of whatever anti-inflation program is put in place, whether the gross markup warrants program proposed above or some other, lest anticipatory speculation and inflation get out of hand. The exact program for the start-up period will require careful study.

What happens after the first three or six months will depend to a large extent on what Keynes called the "animal spirits" of the financial community. At one extreme there could be such horror and alarm at the violation of the fallacious conventional wisdom concerning the sinfulness of deficits as to produce a widespread hibernation and flight to foreign shores, resulting in a reduction in private recycling of savings. If this should occur it would have to be dealt with by correspondingly enlarging the amount of government recycling, rather than pandering to this timidity by cutting back on the recycling program, prolonging the depression and validating the fears that led to the flight.

More likely, once the financial community has become convinced of the seriousness of the administration's purpose to bring about full employment, and once it is anticipated that demand will shortly use up the spare capacity of existing productive facilities, private capital formation may pick up to the point of absorbing and recycling individual savings sufficiently so that less government recycling, or even none at all, may for the time being be necessary. At the same time government revenues from increased GNP will increase, outlays for unemployment insurance and welfare will decrease, so that together with the shutting down of these governmental programs that compete for real resources with private capital formation so as to avoid a real "crowding out" (as contrasted with the mythical financial crowding out alleged to occur as a result of government borrowing associated with a tax cut), a brief period of budget balance or even of surplus may be called for.

As the economy hits the ceiling of full employment, however, still another transition becomes necessary. For a while capital formation may continue on its momentum to recycle savings, but producing excess capacity that either cannot find labor with which to operate or cannot find markets in which to sell its product. Within a short time after hitting the full-employment ceiling, capital formation will inevitably drop from that appropriate to a 10 percent growth rate to that called for by a far slower growth rate. At this point attempted savings will almost certainly exceed by a substantial margin what can be absorbed by private capital formation, even at very low rates of interest. Other ways to recycle the excess will again become necessary, one of which will be renewed government recycling.

The Need for Flexibility

It will not be possible to predict reliably the optimum time path of the necessary government recycling: any econometric models will necessarily have to be calibrated on the basis of past experience, whereas the proposed program forges ahead into new territory to which past experience will be an imperfect guide. Accordingly it will be desirable to retain the ability to respond promptly to developments as they occur: it is more a matter of maintaining flexibility than of a "fine tuning" of longer-term forecasts. Some flexibility might be exercised by adjusting the coefficients used for the adjustment of the markup warrant issue; this would argue for the use of shorter, say quarterly rather than annual, periods for the markup warrants. On the whole it would seem to be desirable for any error in the amount of recycling to be on the high side rather than the low side: excessive recycling would show up as abnormally low inventories, as well as possibly in high market prices for markup warrants. This could be taken as a signal for monetary authorities to restrain credit expansion and possibly increase interest rates, extending as far into the long end of the market as is feasible.

The Socially Optimal Term Structure of Government Debt

At this point the Treasury could help by giving up its objective of arranging the term structure of its debt to minimize its interest costs, by giving up its monopolistic exploitation of its more dominant share of short-term markets. Since there is no difference between the supply-side social cost of providing capital funds on a short- versus a long-term basis (as distinguished from the demand-side differentials in risks associated with real investments of varying durability), overall efficiency would be best served by the Treasury arranging its financing to equate the various long-term rates with the effective average of the expected short-term rates over the same periods, even if this results in an increase in its total interest charges. This would serve to make it easier for monetary authorities to influence medium- to long-term interest rates. It would also help to quiet those who hold that government borrowing "crowds out" borrowing to finance private capital formation.

Focus on Unemployment Reduction, not Bookkeeping

In any case what is necessary is to focus on achieving the amount of recycling required to produce the speediest possible approach to full employment, and get out from under our obsessive concern over the supposed need to reduce the deficit and to reduce inflation to zero. If we can move rapidly to full employment and stay there, any consequences in terms of higher national debt will be a minor problem compared with those that would be involved with continued unemployment. A ten trillion debt in a context of full employment, low demands for redistributive payments, and a productive revenue system will be easier to handle than a five trillion debt in an economy wallowing in the doldrums.

At the very least, we must not be lulled into being satisfied with less vigorous measures by the recent improvements in the economic outlook. Much of this upturn has been created by the increasing likelihood of a change in administration and by expectations that the new administration would take effective steps to stimulate the economy. It would be highly perverse for the new administration to do less because of an upturn produced by expectations that it would do more.

The Task Before Us

This, then, is the challenge I lay before the economics profession. There is no reason inherent in the real resources available to us why we cannot move rapidly within the next two or three years to a state of genuinely full employment, and then continue indefinitely at that level, with all the reduction in the ills of poverty, homelessness, sickness, and crime that this would entail, together with a reduction in the resistance to reductions in military expenditure to more rational levels, to liberalization of trade and immigration policy, and to conservation and environmental protection programs. Dealing with whatever debt emerges in the process will then be a relatively trivial problem.

I lay before you a plan I believe can accomplish this. It involves government recycling of whatever excess of private savings over private investment can be expected to emerge from a real national income planned to reach genuine full employment as rapidly as possible, plus a method of keeping inflation under control. I believe such a program can do the job while preserving the essentials of a free market system. There may be some details to be worked out, but I am confident that the basic concept is sound and workable.

There is too a free lunch out there, in the form of underutilized resources of labor and capital. The various forms of belt tightening urged on us in the name of fiscal rectitude, mostly by those who are in little danger themselves of sharing in the hardship, are not only cruel but unnecessary. We simply cannot continue on as we have been doing without falling apart as a community and losing what is left of our status of world leadership. If you don't think that something like this can be made to work, then it is up to us to get together to find something that will. Otherwise if we continue to tie our hands with financial shibboleths and models that tacitly assume a fixed total of resource utilization, we are no better than the feckless castaway whose contribution to the solution of the problem of dealing with cases of canned goods was "let's just assume we have a can-opener." Let's go to it!

PART VII

---·---

Miscellany

Economic theory, in its purest and most abstract form, can be treated as a system of logic, having no more immediate ethical content than a proposition in Euclidean geometry. And even with applied economics, it is possible to approach the study with the detachment of an entomologist observing an anthill. Yet no scientific investigation, however abstract or detached, can entirely escape the probability of having ethical consequences . . .

Economics, as a social science, deals with human beings directly, rather than with inanimate objects or even the lower organisms whose development can be considered of relatively negligible intrinsic significance. Economics studies in complete abstraction from all human values would be an insubstantial discipline, for economics is pivotally concerned with values.

"Goals of Economic Life: An exchange of Questions between Economics and Philosophy," A.D. Ward, Ed., *Goals of Economic Life* (National Council of Churches, 1950).

There is a common theme to almost all of Vickrey's corpus of research – the design of public policy to improve the functioning of the economy. The philosophical basis for his work is captured in two quotes from "An Exchange of Questions between Economics and Philosophy," (1950).

Our best hope is probably to make the self-interested part of our economic system as smooth running as possible, so that more and more of our conscious effort can be directed towards the solution of those problems that cannot be resolved without explicit ethical considerations. (p. 62)

[W]hile it is possible for an economist to maintain an Olympian aloofness and declare that he is merely studying the techniques of adapting limited means to multiple ends, without in the least concerning himself with the source or justification of these ends, such economics is likely to prove limited and sterile. (p. 36)

While the bulk of his work has been devoted to the subject areas treated in the previous parts – social choice and allocation mechanisms, taxation, marginal-cost pricing, urban transportation, and urban economics – he has also written papers on a wide variety of other topics. All of these papers too relate to public policy, but some focus on the philosophical or methodological basis of economics, while others focus on more technical aspects of economic policy analysis.

The policy papers cover topics ranging from student loans, philanthropy, the poverty gap, and gerrymandering, to the resolution of international disputes. All are remarkable for the novelty of their perspective, as well as for their ingenuity and logical rigor. Two of these papers are presented in this part. The first (chapter 25) proposed an algorithm for the drawing of electoral districts that leaves little if any scope for gerrymandering.[1] The essential feature of the algorithm is the introduction of randomness, which makes the outcome unpredictable . . . The second, "One Economist's View of Philanthropy" (chapter 26), is, according to Martin Feldstein (1976), "the first fundamental study of the economics of charity," and remains the cornerstone of the growing literature on the subject. The paper is wide-ranging but focuses on the motives for charity and its redistributive impact.

Vickrey's inventiveness and originality in applying economics to public policy is illustrated by the following quote, taken from his Presidential Address to the Atlantic Economic Association (1993), which discusses innovations to the political process, including the application of demand-relevation mechanisms to Congressional decision-making:

Given the failure of the political process to produce sensible economic solutions, perhaps the time has come for economists to exercise a little disciplinary imperialism and propose innovations to the political process. It is absurd, for example, to attempt to achieve minority representation by gerrymanders compared to which the original salamander-shaped district was a convex set, rather than to go directly to multi-member constituencies with some form of proportional representation. If members of a legislative body were accorded voting weight in proportion to the support they obtained in their district, a good approach to proportionality might be obtained even with only a small number of representatives per district. That one's vote will have the effect of enhancing the influence of one's representative even when his election is a foregone conclusion would be a significant incentive for voters to turn out.

One might even contemplate continuous instead of periodic elections, in which each voter would register his vote initially, but would be free to change it at any time he is dissatisfied with his representative, or finds a preferred candidate. The representative would then be replaced whenever his support falls below a critical level. Modern electronics should make it possible to arrange this in a convenient and reasonably fraud-proof manner.

The other main problem with current democratic institutions is the practice of decision making within the legislature by sequential pairwise majority rule, which generates opportunities for all kinds of manipulation and inconsistent results. While in principle the Supreme Court may be considered to be charged with the duty of protecting minorities against tyranny by a majority, the Court has not always measured up to this obligation, and moreover cannot be expected to involve itself in minor infringements of the interests of minorities, as distinct from their "inalienable rights," nor to have the ability or the mandate to decide issues on the basis of a nice balancing of gains and losses.

Another main difficulty is that as Congress is organized, committees in which appropri-

---

[1] *Webster's New Collegiate Dictionary* (2nd edn, 1957) "Gerrymander: [Gerry and salamander, after Gov. Eldridge Gerry, whose party in 1812 divided Essex Co., Mass., so as to form a dragon-shaped district]. To divide (a state, county, etc.) into election districts or other civil divisions in an unnatural or unfair way, especially to give a political party an advantage over its opponent."

ations are discussed are seldom empowered to specify where the money is to come from, and committees concerned with revenues operate largely without regard to how the money is to be spent. Some improvement has been made recently in requiring measures to be revenue neutral or for outlays to stay within a given budget constraint, but at best the putting together a balanced package that makes sense is difficult.

Kenneth Arrow has of course shown that no system that relies on ordinal preferences and eschews information about the intensity of preferences can be free of inconsistency. Outcomes will depend capriciously on the sequence of submission of alternatives, through amendment and otherwise, and on arbitrary stop rules. It is necessary to have a numéraire in terms of which intensities of preference can be registered. Such a numéraire might consist of a number of voting units allotted to each member for each session or part of a session, possibly according to the voting support garnered by the member in his district. It is Arrow's "independence of irrelevant alternatives" postulate that precludes reference to such a numéraire.

A decision-making procedure in terms of such a numéraire could use a demand-revealing technique, as follows: A suitable agenda is set up consisting of alternative, self-contained measures falling within a suitably defined area, each containing a specification of the way in which any outlays involved are to be financed (including eventual service of any debt to be incurred). Opportunity is provided for anyone to add to the agenda. Once the agenda is set, and a suitable period of discussion allowed for, each legislator would be allowed to indicate the intensity of his preferences for the various alternatives in terms of his voting units. The alternative with the highest number of votes is declared enacted, and each legislator is then charged against his quota of voting units the value of the outcome to the others. In the absence of collusion, this serves as a form of "marginal-cost pricing" giving each legislator an incentive to report his preferences honestly. (pp. 8–9)

Vickrey's more technical papers cover such topics as cost-of-living indices, equivalence scales, and sorting theory. The 1949 paper on equivalence scales, "Resource Distribution Patterns and the Classification of Families" (chapter 24), has been selected for inclusion in this part. It examines the appropriate aggregation of different family sizes for measurement of the distribution of income, the propensity to consume, and the distribution of the tax burden. This paper influenced Modigliani and Brumberg (1954) in their analysis of the consumption function, and Friedman (1957) in his thinking about the permanent income hypothesis. It also anticipates the modern literature on equivalence scales and the measurement of inequality and of tax incidence.

A strong moral sense, commitment to social justice, and concern for social improvement permeate Vickrey's work. Indeed, Vickrey is one of the few major figures in modern economics who could be labeled a "moral philosopher." It is not surprising, therefore, that his more philosophical papers are so thoughtful, articulate, and rich in ideas.

It is interesting that Vickrey, despite a strong commitment to social betterment, has focused on efficiency rather than equity in his work. For example, while much of his work on taxation is concerned with progressivity, he devotes more attention to the efficient achievement of a given degree of progression than to the case for more progression. In his work on macroeconomics, his objection to high unemployment is based more on the human waste it entails than on its adverse distributional impact. And in his work on the pricing of urban transportation, equity concerns play a decidedly secondary role. Perhaps he is agnostic concerning the optimal degree of progression. Perhaps he finds it distasteful to impose his ethical views on others; he is willing to admit value judgments in analyzing the theory of public policy, but may feel that going further is going too far.

Another distinctive feature of his work is his inattention to attribution. This is certainly not due to any desire to claim paternity for borrowed ideas since Vickrey is singularly generous of spirit. Rather it reflects an attitude that ideas are common property to be used in the social interest.

An endearing feature of Vickrey's work is its lack of cynicism and bitterness and its almost naïve idealism. He is sometimes frustrated that specific proposals of his have not been adopted or even given serious consideration. But the faith remains, despite the short-sightedness, illogic, self-interest, and chicanery of actors in the policy process, that clear thinking and wise policy will ultimately prevail.

References

M. Feldstein, "Charitable Bequests, Estate Taxation, and Intergenerational Wealth Transfers," in R. Grieson, Ed., *Public and Urban Economics: Essays in Honor of William S. Vickrey* (Lexington, Mass: Heath, 1976).

F. Modigliani and R. Brumberg, "Utility Analysis and the Consumption Function: An Interpretation of Cross-Section Data," in K. Kurihara, Ed., *Post-Keynesian Economics* (New Brunswick, N.J.: Rutgers University Press, 1954), pp. 388–436.

M. Friedman, *A Theory of the Consumption Function*, National Bureau of Economic Research (Princeton: Princeton University Press, 1957).

W. Vickrey, "Goals of Economic Life: An Exchange of Questions between Economics and Philosophy," A.D. Ward, Ed., *Goals of Economic Life* (National Council of Churches, 1950).

"My Innovative Failures in Economics," *Atlantic Economic Journal* (1993), 1–9.

24

--- · ---

Resource Distribution Patterns and the Classification of Families

In all the voluminous discussions and statistics on how the nation's resources are distributed among its citizens, far too little attention has been paid to the basis on which various groups of the population are classified. Consequently, much of the statistical material is poorly adapted to the purposes for which it has been produced and used, and many of the conclusions that have been drawn are without solid foundation, if not actually erroneous. The object of this paper is to investigate the effect of various methods of classification on the distribution of income and on the conclusions to be drawn concerning tax burdens, consumption patterns, and the propensity to consume.

The Reporting Unit and the Classification Basis

The basis of classification and the unit to be studied are separate questions. One may choose as a unit the family, the household, the individual, or the residents of a structure; the chief basis for the choice is ordinarily the ease with which the affairs of one unit can be disentangled from those of another. Provided the methods of classification are suitable, the results should not be greatly affected unless the unit is so large that the dispersion is substantially reduced by averaging within the unit. But too frequently some aggregate attribute of the unit, such as its income or wealth, becomes the basis for classification and no adjustment is made for the size of the unit or its characteristics; when this is done, the choice of a unit may incidentally involve a considerable difference in the method of classification and hence materially affect the final results.

Studies in Income and Wealth, 10 (National Bureau of Economic Research, 1949), pp. 266–97.

However chosen, the unit should be classified according to some property relevant to the conclusions to be drawn. If such a property is not susceptible of direct measurement, it is necessary to select some readily available statistic that will correspond closely to the desired property. For example, if the fundamental purpose of a tabulation is to find out how many persons are at various levels of economic welfare, we can take income or expenditure levels as an indicator though we may not be able to measure welfare or even agree precisely on its meaning.

In practice, almost all the figures on the distribution of income and expenditure for the entire population are by classifications derived more by following the line of least resistance than by formulating a base pertinent to the purpose at hand. An aggregate of some quantity for the reporting unit is usually taken for the classification parameter with no adjustment for the relative size or importance of the unit. In *Statistics of Income*, returns are classified primarily by net income per return, a classification that corresponds neither to the economic welfare level of the taxpayer nor to the bracket in which his income will be taxed. In the studies of the National Resources Committee for 1935–6 the unit is logically enough the "consumer unit" or the family household, but a consumer unit is classified according to its total income, regardless of whether it consists of a family of seven or only of a single unattached individual.[1] Accordingly, the statement that the "lowest third" of the consumer units receive 10 percent of total income does not mean much, for this lowest third includes single unattached persons with incomes of $750, but excludes large families with incomes of $800, who will in general be much worse off. To be sure, *Statistics of Income* classifies returns by family status, and some adjustment can be made to allow for differences between returns representing different numbers of individuals and entitled to different personal exemptions. But the adjustment is at best tedious and approximate, and would be more adequate if made by a proper classification in the first instance. The present classification is entirely unrelated to any of the many purposes to which the figures might be put: the most that can be said for it is that it preserves a certain degree of formal continuity from year to year. Again, the National Resources Committee studies have some tables with distributions by family size. But this is done for only a few data, and unless the user is prepared to undertake the monumental work of either treating each family size separately or recombining the figures in some way, he must accept data in which figures for a family of two with an income of $1,612 spending $429 for food are combined with families of seven or more having an income of $1,624 but spending $721 for food. By combining families at widely different welfare levels and having different spending patterns, merely because

<hr />

[1] *Consumer Incomes in the United States* (National Resources Committee, 1938); *Consumer Expenditures in the United States* (1939); *Family Expenditures in the United States* (1941).

their aggregate income is the same, the differences in the spending patterns at different welfare levels are partly glossed over.

The possibilities of correcting for this combination of families of dissimilar habits and welfare levels in the same income groups are still fewer in the case of the 1941 consumer income and expenditure studies.[2] The size of the sample precluded tabulating different family sizes separately; and only family units and single consumers are segregated. Some improvement is possible through recombining single persons with families having, say, 2.5 times the income of single persons, but, as we shall see later, this procedure eliminates only a small part of the total bias arising from the method of classification.

Again, if an individual wishes to know where he stands in relation to the rest of the population, present tabulations give him no real answer. If *A*, who is a member of a family of two with an income of $2,000, consults the tables, he may find, for example, that 53 percent of the families have incomes of more than $2,000. But *B*, who is a member of a family of six with an income of $2,000, will come to the conclusion that he also is at the 53rd percentile of the population, though he is obviously not nearly so well off as *A*. While this difference may be considered minor if the extra members of *B*'s family are small children, the difference is striking if these other members are themselves wage earners.

Allowing for Size of Family

The desirability of some allowance for the size of the family has long been recognized, but it has been difficult to decide upon a formula. Merely putting the figures on a per capita basis will not do, for individuals, particularly children, vary widely in their needs. A partial remedy has been sought by setting up for each member of the family a weighting factor reflecting his consumption needs relative to those of an adult gainfully employed male; by adding these weights for the various members of the family, a rating of the family's needs in terms of adult male maintenance units, "ammains", can be obtained.

The difficulty, of course, is in agreeing upon a schedule of weights. Possibilities of deriving such weights from objective data are limited, and it seems almost inevitable that the coefficients should rest on some a priori notions of the relative needs of individuals of different ages, sexes, and occupations. To be sure, attempts have been made to compute the coefficients on the assumption that families spending a given fraction of their budget for the basic necessities such as

---

[2] *Income and Spending and Saving of City Families in Wartime* (Bureau of Labor Statistics, Bul. 724, September, 1942); *Rural Family Spending and Saving in Wartime* (Department of Agriculture, Misc. Publication 520, June, 1943).

food are on the same level of welfare. To be workable, this method requires that the proportion spent on the less essential categories increase uniformly as the level of welfare rises. On this assumption, one could plot this percentage against total outlay separately for each family composition, and a comparison of the total outlay at which a given percentage goes to necessities for the various types of family would yield a clue to relative needs. The difficulty is that it is impossible to draw a sharp line between necessities and luxuries, and the results will depend upon where the line is drawn. For example, if the proportion of outlay for food alone were taken as the index of welfare, the results would differ from those which would be obtained if rent were included among "necessities," for it seems logical to assume that a large family will naturally spend a bigger proportion of its budget for food and less for rent than a small family, even at the same level of welfare. Again, the relative shares of the family members in the family resources may vary considerably from one welfare level to another, so that a coefficient appropriate at one level might not be appropriate at another; thus a single set of coefficients would probably be inadequate to give the complete picture.

Attempts have also been made to compute coefficients by setting up budgets designed to provide a given standard of health. This approach is most applicable to food: the cost of achieving certain dietary standards can be ascertained and used as a basis. However, this method is applicable only to a small part of the total budget, and in any case must be qualified by the observation that in practice families do not feed themselves scientifically but in accordance with many prejudices and customs. These can be taken into account in setting up the hypothetical budgets, but the results are likely to be correspondingly less precise.

Some expenditures are fairly clearly for the benefit of individual members of the family. One example is clothing, and it may be possible to set up schedules of relative clothing needs by actually observing the amount spent on the clothing worn by the various members of the family. But even here, where there is a substantial amount of handing down and remodeling, this method may have to rely to a considerable extent on arbitrary allocations of the cost of clothing worn by more than one person.

For a large part of family expenditure, however, there is no ready method of apportionment among the family members, especially of rent and household operation items. It appears therefore, that the weights assigned the various members must remain in considerable measure a matter of subjective appraisal.[3] But the fact that subjective appraisal is involved in making an allowance for family size is no excuse for making no allowance at all under the pretext of preserving a

[3] For a discussion of consumption scales as a measure of size of family see Robert Morse Woodbury, "Economic Consumption Scales and their Uses," *Journal of the American Statistical Association*, 39 (December, 1944), p. 455.

spurious objectivity. Any allowance, no matter how arbitrary, is preferable to a patent absurdity, if the allowance is even remotely reasonable.

One notable attempt to classify families by economic welfare level was the 1934–6 "Study of Money Disbursements of Wage Earners and Clerical Workers."[4] The families were classified according to "annual unit expenditure." Separate family size factors were set up for food, for clothing, and for all other expenditures. Scales of relative consumption needs for the first two items were based on standard budgets, but for other expenditures all persons were treated as equal units. The final number of consumption units in the family was an harmonic mean of the three measures, weighted by the actual expenditure of the family for the three types of consumption.

Unfortunately no such procedure has ever been applied to a complete sample. Failure to apply this procedure or an improvement of it to subsequent studies is probably in part due to the fact that it was fairly complex: it was somewhat difficult for persons accustomed to thinking in terms of family income classifications to grasp the significance of the figures. These fundamentally more meaningful figures might have been more widely accepted had the classification been simpler, and had greater prominence been given to the average family incomes and average family sizes of the families classified in a given unit expenditure group.

Nor does the complexity of the method used for determining family size seem to be justified by any superiority of the results: the procedure adopted implies that two families of identical composition may differ in the number of consumption units merely because they divide their consumption differently among food, clothing, and other items; e.g., if one family does its own baking using purchased fuel instead of buying bakery products, it would in general be considered to contain more consumption units. Since the family size obtained by this method depends upon the distribution of expenditure within the family, it cannot be ascertained merely from figures on the composition of the family by age, sex, and occupation. It is thus difficult for the average person to appraise the number of consumer units represented by his own family, and also to compare the figures so gathered with figures obtained from data that do not admit of such a complicated method of appraising family size.

The assumption that all family members shared equally in expenditures other than for food and clothing is particularly open to question, but can well be accepted on the grounds of simplicity and in the absence of any objective alternative. Even here, however, a set of factors, no matter how uncertain, would have been preferable. It does not seem likely, for instance, that outlays other than for food and clothing for a family consisting of husband, wife, and four children

---

[4] Bureau of Labor Statistics, Bul. 638, pp. 362–6, 56–65, and various tables.

would be double those of a family consisting of husband, wife, and one child, at the same welfare level. While considerable subjective judgment might be involved in setting up factors for such expenditures, such factors would be preferable to an arbitrary assumption that all persons of whatever age count equally.

In any case, it is almost impossible to correct the more comprehensive figures by this partial sample, for it specifically excludes the unemployed, the self-employed, and families having substantial property incomes. As the fluctuations of income experienced by these other groups differ greatly from those experienced by the rather drastically restricted sample, the extension of the results obtained in this sample to the entire population would be entirely unwarranted.

Income versus Expenditure as a Basis for Classification

Except in the 1934–6 wage earner study, the parameter used for classifying the economic units has almost invariably been a variant of income. This is natural enough in statistics derived from an income tax, and even in presenting the distribution of income. But it is at least curious that in all the more inclusive studies of consumer expenditures the classification by income is retained and that in studies purporting to measure the welfare of various economic groups, income is used almost exclusively as a basis for classification.

Classification by income would probably be innocuous enough if only the data permitted classification by income for a fairly long period so that fluctuations could be averaged. But nearly all statistics are for the income of a single year. In fact, it is extremely difficult to get figures covering a longer period. Families move, change in size, break up, form, and so on – all of which require continual adjustments. It is by no means certain how figures covering the income of individual families for a series of years should be processed even if the raw materials could be obtained.[5]

Incomes fluctuate in varying degrees from year to year, not only together with national income but also as a result of developments affecting the individual, such as sickness, unemployment, overtime work, business ventures, gains or losses on the stock exchange, the writing of a best-seller, high temporary earning as an actress or athlete, retirement, good or bad crops. Thus the income for any given year may not at all reflect the long-run prospects of an individual. If we are interested in actual standards of living, annual expenditure comes much closer to giving us what we want. Even if fundamentally we are interested in the long-run average level of income, annual expenditure may be a better indicator of relative

[5] The Wisconsin Tax Commission has published *Changes in Income of Identical Taxpayers, 1929–1935* (1939); see also *Analysis of Wisconsin Income*, by Frank Hanna, Joseph Pechman, and Sidney Lerner, a study prepared for the Conference on Research in Income and Wealth.

rank, for purposes of classification than annual income, for it at least reflects past savings and in some degree also the individual's expectations regarding his future income, as well as his actual current income.

The effect of using income for a single year rather than average income for a period as a basis for classification tends not only to blur differences in expenditure patterns through aggregating items for units at considerably different levels of economic welfare, but also to exaggerate the inequality of the distribution of income.

In effect, there are three sources of variance in annual incomes: general changes in national income, fluctuations in the income of individuals, and differences in the long-run average economic status of individuals. A classification by income for a single year eliminates the first, but retains the last two. It will show a greater dispersion of individuals than would an average income for several years. In the top income groups will be a relatively large number of persons whose income is higher than normal, and who must make some provision from this unusual income for the future when their income may be lower. In the bottom income groups will be a relatively large number of persons whose income is only temporarily low, and who will be able to maintain a fairly high standard of living by drawing on their savings.

The distortions produced by using annual income as a basis for classification are moderately important when the distribution of income is considered, and extremely serious when savings and expenditure patterns are considered and an attempt is made to derive a propensity to consume function. The savings of the lower income groups are greatly understated and their consumption overstated by including persons who maintain a fairly high level of consumption by drawing on savings; conversely, the savings of those at the top of the scale are exaggerated and their consumption understated. Consequently, the usual figures on the concentration of savings greatly overstate the savings of persons at the upper economic levels, and marginal propensity to consume figures are generally too low.

The Experimental Tabulation

In an attempt to give some notion of the magnitude of some of the biases arising from the usual methods of tabulation, 2,147 schedules from the recent *Study of Family Spending and Saving in Wartime* were retabulated: 925 representing rural nonfarm units surveyed by the Bureau of Human Nutrition and Home Economics and 1,222 representing urban families surveyed by the Bureau of Labor Statistics.[6]

---

[6] These schedules were made available to the Committee for Economic Development, under whose auspices the retabulation was carried out.

The BLS sample was designed to cover 1 in 20,000 urban families, that of the BHNHE 1 in 10,000 rural nonfarm families; accordingly, in combining the sample figures, the BLS sample was multiplied by 2, so that the combined results represent approximately 1 in 10,000 nonfarm families in the nation. Although in preparing a general distribution of income from the sample, the BLS and the BHNHE varied the weights for the several income groups somewhat, no adjustment for these variations in weightings were made in the present figures. The validity of such variations in the weights for classifications by per capita income and expenditure is at best doubtful and would tend to cancel in the reshuffling. Moreover, the present figures are but approximations at best, since no schedules for farm families were included. Even as adjusted, there is a general feeling that single persons are greatly underrepresented in the original sample. The present figures are intended to indicate differences brought about by reclassification; they are not a complete income distribution in themselves.

In setting up a figure representing family size, the following scheme was used. Persons over twenty years of age were counted as an "equivalent adult" if they worked more than thirty-four weeks during the year; as 0.9 of an equivalent adult if they worked twelve to thirty-four weeks, and 0.8 if they worked less than twelve weeks. Persons between sixteen and twenty were counted as 1 if they worked more than thirty-four weeks, 0.8 if they worked twelve to thirty-four weeks, and 0.7 if they worked less than twelve weeks. Children aged eleven to fifteen were counted as 0.5; children aged six to ten, as 0.4; and children under six years old, as 0.3. In addition, for the first child under fifteen, 0.2 was added to the total as an allowance for the initial expenses involved in setting up a household with accommodations for a child, expenses that in general are not duplicated for additional children. Thus a family consisting of a husband working full time, a wife not gainfully employed, and two children aged three and six would be assigned a "size" of 2.7 (1.0 + 0.8 + 0.3 + 0.4 + 0.2); a family consisting of a husband and wife, both working full time, and a daughter aged eighteen not working would be assigned a "size" of 2.7 (1.0 + 1.0 + 0.7). Though admittedly arbitrary, this scheme is not unreasonable and will probably produce results not greatly different from any system that might be devised from more precise data. Moreover, it is simple enough to be readily applied by an individual to his own status and to be readily understood.

The number of "equivalent adults" in each family was computed according to the above scheme, and the income and expenditure divided by this figure, to obtain the income and expenditure per equivalent adult. Tables 24.1 and 24.2 show the number of schedules, number of equivalent adults, total income, and total expenditure, by income and expenditure per equivalent adult. Tables 24.3 and 24.4 show these figures tabulated by family income and by family size.

In some cases a separation of the data into single and family schedules is available when a more detailed distribution by size of family is not. A partial correction may be attempted by adjusting the single data and combining them with the family data in such a way that single persons are combined with the family income group having the same average income per equivalent adult. As a means of ascertaining what the proper relation between single and family groups should be, the average size of families and of single individuals is compared in table 24.5.

Classification Methods and the Distribution of Income

What effect does shifting from one method of classification to another have on the apparent concentration of income? The simplest method of comparing two distributions is probably the Lorenz curve. Tables 24.6 and 24.7 show the data in the cumulative percentage form required for Lorenz curves. Table 24.6 shows the figures that result from classification by per capita income and expenditure. Table 24.7 shows the figures that result from a classification by family income, and also those that appear when the classification by family is modified by placing single individuals in the income group occupied by families having 2.5 times as much income.

Economic inequality can be expressed in a large variety of ways. In fact, three factors are involved: the method of classification (family income, per capita income, per capita expenditure, family wealth, or some other index of economic status), the economic quantity whose distribution is being studied (income, wealth, expenditure, or some other measure of economic power), and the measure of the population used (the person, the family, the equivalent adult, or some other measure of relative importance of the various economic units).

Figure 24.1 shows how the method of classification affects the results. The upper curve, showing the least concentration, is the result obtained when family income is the basis of classification – the top 50 percent of the population has 71.2 percent of the income. If an adjustment is made to include single persons in the group with families having 2.5 times as much income, the second curve is obtained – this top 50 percent of the population gets 72.8 percent of the income. If we classify families according to income per equivalent adult, the lowest curve is obtained – this top 50 percent of the population gets 75.6 percent of the income. Finally, if we clasify families by expenditure per equivalent adult, the top 50 percent of the equivalent adults get 73.8 percent of the income.

Figure 24.2 shows how the indicated inequality is affected by the unit chosen to measure the population. The lowest line, indicating the greatest concentration, is the result obtained when income per family is the basis of classification and the percentage of income is plotted against the percentage of families. Using the same

Table 24.1 *Sample Number of Schedules and Number of Equivalent Adults, 1941, by Income and Expenditure per Equivalent Adult*

Income per equivalent adult groups

Number of schedules

Expenditure per equivalent adult groups	Under $0	0 to 200	200 to 300	300 to 400	400 to 500	500 to 600	600 to 700	700 to 800	800 to 900	900 to 1,000	1,000 to 1,200	1,200 to 1,500	1,500 to 2,000	2,000 to 3,000	3,000 to 5,000	Over 5,000	Total
$0–200		245	32				2										279
200–300		35	168	54	9		5										271
300–400		9	42	162	49	5	6	1									274
400–500		7	7	43	152	84	19	6	3	2							323
500–600				16	44	140	78	25	6	4	2	2	1				318
600–700		4	2	10	19	78	107	96	7	2	17	2					344
700–800				4	2	13	54	91	66	36	23	9	2				300
800–900						7	26	36	99	50	33	5					256
900–1,000		2					5	18	26	64	62	24	8	3			212
1,000–1,200	2	2	3	3			2	11	13	24	134	88	19		3		304
1,200–1,500		2							7	7	40	83	59	14	5		217
1,500–2,000					1						3	46	69	47	9	2	177
2,000–3,000										2	5	9	2	42	5		65
3,000–5,000													2	2	16	4	24
Over 5,000																5	5
Total	2	306	254	293	275	327	290	287	238	200	316	266	162	105	37	11	3,369

Number of equivalent adults

																	Total
$0–200		669.5	74.6	1.6													745.7
200–300		84.0	447.3	133.8	14.0	2.0	4.3	0.9									686.3
300–400		18.1	112.5	459.2	150.4	17.8	11.0										769.0
400–500		15.0	14.7	116.0	411.9	212.2	42.8	14.7	8.8	1.6							837.7
500–600			2.4	42.0	150.1	377.1	207.8	63.2	16.8	8.6	2.0	5.8					875.8
600–700		7.2	1.8	18.5	10.2	193.1	265.3	255.1	51.0	37.4	45.8	9.5					894.9
700–800			1.0	20.4	11.5	28.1	122.4	250.2	171.6	90.9	60.1	15.6					771.8
800–900					11.6	13.8	46.4	92.4	249.4	120.6	87.7	21.6	7.0				650.5
900–1,000		1.6			3.4	6.9	11.9	46.1	62.7	160.4	143.3	50.8	10.3				497.4
1,000–1,200	3.6	3.2	1.6	2.6	4.5	9.2	29.6	34.0	54.5	305.2	177.7	37.6	3.6				666.9
1,200–1,500		1.6				4.8	0.8	6.6	5.0	14.5	73.6	205.3	118.4	22.1	10.8		463.5
1,500–2,000									1.6	1.6	8.0	87.2	154.6	100.3	19.0		372.3
2,000–3,000									1.6	1.6	6.8	3.6	13.6	83.5	7.4	5.6	123.7
3,000–5,000													1.6	1.6	38.8	9.2	51.2
Over 5,000																7.4	7.4
Total	3.6	800.2	655.9	794.1	774.0	861.8	712.7	759.5	607.7	489.4	729.3	575.1	341.5	207.5	79.6	22.2	8,414.1

Table 24.2 Total Income and Total Expenditures, 1941, by Income and Expenditure per Equivalent Adult

Income per equivalent adult groups

Total income (dollars)

Expenditure per equivalent adult groups	Under $0	0 to 200	200 to 300	300 to 400	400 to 500	500 to 600	600 to 700	700 to 800	800 to 900	900 to 1,000	1,000 to 1,200	1,200 to 1,500	1,500 to 2,000	2,000 to 3,000	3,000 to 5,000	Over 5,000	Total
$0–200		90,019	17,068					1,174									108,261
200–300		13,967	113,074	44,682	6,220	1,032	2,860			860							182,695
300–400		2,716	29,276	162,770	66,161	9,790	7,164										277,877
400–500		2,239	3,810	42,912	188,255	113,767	27,245	10,776	7,581	1,554							398,139
500–600		618	15,059	70,660	208,819	132,899	46,202	13,727	7,784	2,263	7,344						505,375
600–700		369	414	6,653	4,562	108,843	170,945	190,311	42,376	35,506	49,030	12,798					621,807
700–800		238	7,446	5,441	15,797	80,598	186,677	145,074	84,950	65,375	19,967						611,563
800–900					5,404	7,950	30,308	69,836	212,298	114,210	95,999	29,152	10,666				575,823
900–1,000		20			1,574	3,596	7,573	34,177	54,353	150,658	156,255	65,050	17,114				490,370
1,000–1,200	−250	582	409	957	1,950	5,164		22,486	28,679	51,385	333,958	228,009	59,652	11,872			744,853
1,200–1,500		42		542	2,000		523	4,792	4,000	13,376	83,090	276,853	191,102	48,453	34,906		659,679
1,500–2,000								1,370			8,926	121,881	257,909	245,170	76,753		712,009
2,000–3,000						840			5,700		4,000	2,068	26,084	208,603	28,462	40,286	316,043
3,000–5,000					712								3,390	137,892	65,580		207,574
Over 5,000																111,455	111,455
Total	−250	109,954	164,907	281,021	352,939	475,598	460,115	566,431	515,158	460,283	798,896	763,122	562,527	505,616	289,885	217,321	6,523,523

Total expenditures (dollars)

																	Total
$1–199		90,489	13,039					1,892									105,420
200–300		19,233	111,319	36,875	4,058	579	1,168			262							173,494
300–400		5,991	36,208	158,545	56,113	6,160	3,857										266,874
400–500		6,592	6,239	49,569	184,733	98,802	19,399	6,711	3,970	752							376,767
500–600			1,330	23,203	79,936	206,208	116,880	35,716	9,494	4,990	1,114	3,224					482,095
600–700		4,838	1,256	12,106	6,680	123,880	170,583	165,669	33,884	24,312	29,624	6,309					579,141
700–800			716	15,674	8,800	21,212	90,458	185,018	129,398	69,168	45,044	12,030					577,518
800–900					10,230	11,360	38,783	78,028	210,040	102,354	75,523	18,389	5,890				550,597
900–1,000		1,548			3,062	6,657	11,151	43,609	58,988	150,421	136,071	49,168	9,691				470,366
1,000–1,200	3,728	3,568	1,612	2,815	4,638	9,911		31,748	37,403	58,984	333,396	194,325	41,410		3,754		727,292
1,200–1,500		2,232			6,164		1,095	8,118	6,152	18,602	93,450	271,624	159,223	28,186	15,461		610,307
1,500–2,000				2,584					2,406		13,361	142,440	259,323	185,700	34,118		639,932
2,000–3,000						4,408			17,822		8,000	3,436	29,256	189,267	18,697	15,760	286,646
3,000–5,000					4,818									5,408	133,065	40,796	184,087
Over 5,000																77,033	77,033
Total	3,728	134,491	171,719	301,371	369,232	489,177	453,374	556,509	509,557	429,845	735,583	700,945	504,793	408,561	205,095	133,589	6,107,569

Table 24.3 Sample Number of Schedules and Number of Equivalent Adults, 1941, by Family Income and Size

| Income per family groups | Family size (equivalent adults) groups | | | | | | | | | | Total |
| | 0–0.8 | 0.9–1.0 | 1.1–2.0 | 2.1–2.5 | 2.6–3.0 | 3.1–3.5 | 3.6–4.0 | 4.1–5.0 | 5.1–6.0 | Over 6.0 | |
	Number of schedules										
$0–500	98	83	151	38	24	15	9	5	1		424
500–750	31	69	86	32	25	24	14	24	5	2	312
750–1,000	11	48	94	34	49	19	9	16	2	3	285
1,000–1,250	10	50	101	54	25	29	13	8	4		294
1,250–1,500		28	83	49	54	27	23	8		2	274
1,500–2,000	5	30	125	97	114	50	36	39	5	7	508
2,000–2,500	6	16	134	74	91	69	20	25	10	2	447
2,500–3,000	3	11	51	54	81	54	17	35	11	6	323
3,000–4,000	1	2	58	29	58	33	28	34	11	7	261
4,000–5,000		2	23	9	26	15	12	12	9	4	112
5,000–7,000			13	9	8	13	7	8	8	9	75
7,000–10,000			2	4	2	4	2		2	2	18
10,000–15,000	2			1	2	2	10	4		4	25
Over 15,000			5		4			2			11
Total	167	339	926	484	563	354	200	220	68	48	3,369

Number of equivalent adults

$0–500	78.4	80.9	256.9	89.8	66.3	48.7	34.4	22.6	5.1	13.3	683.1
500–750	24.8	66.8	146.7	75.6	70.2	78.4	53.1	108.2	27.6	19.5	664.7
750–1,000	8.8	46.9	164.5	81.1	133.8	61.5	33.9	72.2	10.4		632.6
1,000–1,250	8.0	49.2	178.4	126.7	70.3	97.0	49.2	35.2	20.4		634.4
1,250–1,500		27.6	149.4	115.7	148.3	89.8	86.8	36.2		12.8	666.6
1,500–2,000	4.0	30.0	225.3	230.4	310.8	165.1	137.4	170.0	26.5	45.6	1,345.1
2,000–2,500	4.8	16.0	246.2	177.4	250.6	225.6	75.7	110.5	54.0	13.4	1,174.2
2,500–3,000	2.4	11.0	94.7	129.4	225.3	178.7	64.4	155.2	62.8	42.2	966.1
3,000–4,000	0.8	2.0	109.4	69.5	160.6	109.9	105.9	146.6	60.1	45.1	809.9
4,000–5,000		2.0	43.3	21.5	72.9	49.6	44.5	53.4	49.2	29.2	365.6
5,000–7,000			23.8	22.1	22.2	43.9	26.3	37.2	44.0	60.5	280.0
7,000–10,000			3.8	9.6	5.2	14.0	7.4		12.0	12.2	64.2
10,000–15,000	1.6			2.5	5.2	6.8	36.8	18.8		27.0	98.7
Over 15,000			9.4		11.2			8.2			28.8
Total	133.6	332.4	1,651.8	1,151.3	1,552.9	1,169.0	755.8	974.3	372.1	320.8	8,414.0

Table 24.4 Sample Total Income and Total Expenditures, 1941, by Family Income and Size

Income per family groups	Family size (equivalent adults) groups										Total
	0–0.8	0.9–1.0	1.1–2.0	2.1–2.5	2.6–3.0	3.1–3.5	3.6–4.0	4.1–5.0	5.1–6.0	Over 6.0	
	Total income (dollars)										
$0–500	25,990	22,881	46,610	13,230	7,209	4,600	3,622	1,721	482		126,345
500–750	19,007	42,551	50,362	19,237	15,706	14,607	8,814	15,323	3,446	1,454	190,507
750–1,000	9,441	41,911	81,575	29,285	41,484	16,883	7,832	14,024	1,622	2,296	246,353
1,000–1,250	10,826	56,608	112,117	60,413	28,028	33,025	14,935	9,213	4,237		329,402
1,250–1,500		38,656	113,370	67,350	74,227	36,971	31,290	11,305		2,700	375,869
1,500–2,000	9,003	50,176	217,399	168,775	198,659	88,503	63,289	68,265	8,609	12,088	884,766
2,000–2,500	13,334	35,271	296,798	164,854	206,999	154,134	45,314	55,579	22,615	4,742	999,640
2,500–3,000	8,693	29,164	138,196	148,075	223,540	148,205	46,178	95,674	30,073	17,026	884,824
3,000–4,000	3,939	7,736	195,894	100,653	199,131	113,789	97,646	116,194	36,679	24,449	896,110
4,000–5,000		9,450	98,878	39,922	116,095	67,360	52,260	55,230	39,314	17,248	495,757
5,000–7,000			73,158	52,781	47,766	71,976	38,566	48,346	45,082	51,003	428,678
7,000–10,000			15,870	31,780	17,462	31,994	19,772		14,740	14,272	145,890
10,000–15,000	25,978			12,315	25,634	20,000	116,836	52,774		42,980	296,517
Over 15,000			119,857		71,486			31,080			222,423
Total	126,211	334,404	1,560,084	908,670	1,273,426	802,047	546,354	574,728	206,899	190,258	6,523,081

Total expenditures (dollars)

$0–500	40,223	25,422	59,961	17,007	8,272	5,877	3,572	1,787	504		162,625
500–750	20,972	41,915	54,417	20,358	16,973	17,368	10,898	16,911	3,245	1,353	204,410
750–1,000	7,843	40,994	90,832	31,536	45,209	16,339	7,991	15,170	2,109	2,385	260,408
1,000–1,250	9,812	56,551	113,574	67,893	29,721	33,347	14,998	9,071	4,108		339,075
1,250–1,500		35,755	113,337	71,607	72,168	38,909	30,942	11,149		2,684	376,551
1,500–2,000	9,851	45,220	206,185	163,561	189,240	86,687	59,850	68,842	8,583	12,880	850,899
2,000–2,500	8,890	28,424	288,627	155,224	202,955	153,998	42,580	56,372	23,598	10,330	970,998
2,500–3,000	8,988	25,276	123,863	138,202	204,845	159,999	44,186	95,076	34,792	17,848	853,075
3,000–4,000	3,251	5,268	173,199	81,465	171,713	102,171	90,050	112,104	38,506	23,922	801,649
4,000–5,000		8,786	82,460	40,959	107,694	64,082	45,016	50,208	39,209	18,628	457,042
5,000–7,000			45,762	37,971	37,002	62,274	32,064	40,268	38,138	50,062	343,541
7,000–10,000			6,500	24,930	16,254	30,104	14,692		15,190	10,274	117,944
10,000–15,000	14,096			4,689	7,810	20,220	91,646	38,676		44,046	221,183
Over 15,000			79,299	40,194				28,676			148,169
Total	123,926	313,611	1,438,016	855,402	1,150,050	791,375	488,485	544,310	207,982	194,412	6,107,569

Table 24.5 *Average size of families, 1941*

Income per family groups	Number of				Av. no. of equivalent adults		Ratio of family to single
	Schedules		Equivalent adults				
	Single	Family	Single	Family	Single	Family	
$0–500	181	243	159.8	523.8	0.88	2.16	2.45
500–750	100	212	91.6	573.1	0.92	2.70	2.95
750–1,000	59	226	55.7	576.9	0.94	2.55	2.70
1,000–1,250	60	234	57.2	577.2	0.95	2.47	2.59
1,250–1,500	28	246	27.6	639.0	0.99	2.60	2.64
1,500–2,000	35	473	34.0	1,311.1	0.97	2.77	2.86
2,000–2,500	22	425	20.8	1,153.4	0.94	2.71	2.87
2,500–3,000	14	309	13.4	952.7	0.96	3.08	3.22
3,000–4,000	3	258	2.8	807.1	0.93	3.13	3.35
4,000–5,000	2	110	2.0	363.6	1.0	3.30	3.30
5,000–7,000		75		280.0		3.73	
7,000–10,000		18		64.2		3.57	
10,000–15,000	2	23	1.6	97.1	0.80	4.22	5.28
Over 15,000		11		28.8		2.62	
Total	506	2,863	466.0	7,948.0	0.921	2.776	3.014

classification but plotting income against number of equivalent adults gives a markedly more equal distribution – as indicated by the dotted line. The spread between the income versus equivalent adult curve and the income versus family curve is much narrower for data classified by income per equivalent adult; also in this case it is the income versus equivalent adult curve that indicates the greatest inequality.

Figure 24.3 shows the difference between using expenditure and income as a basis for classification. The distribution is most unequal when the distribution of income is by income groups, and least unequal when the distribution of expenditure is by income groups. When expenditure groups are used, it makes only a slight difference whether the distribution of income or of expenditure is considered.

The most striking effect of methods of classification is found in Figure 24.4. For comparison, the distribution of expenditure by expenditure per equivalent adult is also shown. When the classification is by income, nearly the whole lower half of the population have dissavings or negative savings, and the actual net savings of

Table 24.6 *Sample cumulative percentage distribution of schedules, equivalent adults, income, expenditures, and savings by income and expenditure per equivalent adult, 1941*

	Cumulative percentages of total above given level				
Income per equivalent adult levels	Number of		Money		
	Schedules	Equivalent adults	Income	Expenditures	Savings
Negative	100.00	100.00	100.00	100.00	100.00
$0	99.94	99.96	100.00	99.94	100.96
200	90.86	90.45	98.32	97.74	106.86
300	83.32	82.65	95.79	94.92	108.49
400	74.62	73.21	91.48	89.99	113.38
500	66.46	64.02	86.07	83.95	117.30
600	56.75	53.77	78.78	75.94	120.57
700	48.15	45.30	71.73	68.51	118.95
800	39.63	36.28	63.05	59.40	116.56
900	32.56	29.05	55.15	51.06	115.22
1,000	26.62	23.24	48.09	44.02	107.90
1,200	17.24	14.51	35.85	31.98	92.68
1,500	9.35	7.71	24.15	20.50	77.73
2,000	4.54	3.68	15.53	12.24	63.85
3,000	1.42	1.21	7.78	5.55	40.52
5,000	0.33	0.26	3.33	2.19	20.13
Expenditure per equivalent adult levels					
$0	100.00	100.00	100.00	100.00	100.00
200	91.72	91.14	98.34	98.27	99.32
300	83.68	82.98	95.54	95.43	97.11
400	75.54	73.84	91.28	91.06	94.46
500	65.95	63.89	85.18	84.90	89.32
600	56.52	53.48	77.43	77.00	83.73
700	46.30	42.84	67.90	67.52	73.47
800	37.40	33.67	58.52	58.06	65.28
900	29.80	25.94	49.70	49.05	59.22
1,000	23.51	20.03	42.18	41.35	54.41
1,200	14.48	12.01	30.76	29.44	50.19
1,500	8.04	6.59	20.65	19.45	38.32
2,000	2.79	2.17	9.74	8.97	20.99
3,000	0.86	0.70	4.89	4.28	13.92
5,000	0.15	0.09	1.71	1.26	8.28

Table 24.7 *Sample cumulative percentage distribution of schedules, equivalent adults, income, expenditures, and savings by family income groups, unadjusted and with single person adjustment,[a] 1941*

Family Income level unadj.		Cumulative percentages of total above given level				
		Number of			Money	
		Schedules	Equivalent adults	Income	Expenditures	Savings
Negative		100.00	100.00	100.00	100.00	100.00
$0		99.94	99.96	100.00	99.94	100.96
500		87.42	91.89	98.06	97.34	108.73
750		78.25	83.99	95.14	93.99	112.08
1,000		69.69	76.47	91.37	89.73	115.46
1,250		60.97	68.89	86.32	84.18	117.79
1,500		52.84	60.98	80.55	78.01	117.95
2,000		37.71	45.00	66.99	64.08	109.80
2,500		24.49	31.05	51.67	48.18	102.91
3,000		14.90	19.57	38.10	34.21	95.27
4,000		7.15	9.95	24.36	21.09	72.53
5,000		3.83	5.60	16.76	13.60	63.22
7,000		1.60	2.28	10.19	7.98	42.73
10,000		1.07	1.52	7.96	6.05	36.00
15,000		0.33	0.34	3.41	2.43	17.87
Family income level adj.[a]	No. of schedules adj.[b]					
Negative	100.00	100.00	100.00	100.00	100.00	100.00
$0	99.94	99.94	99.96	100.00	99.94	100.96
500	91.32	91.07	93.17	98.71	98.22	105.87
750	83.90	83.64	85.96	96.59	95.72	109.36
1,000	75.83	75.33	78.55	93.31	91.84	115.01
1,250	67.79	67.47	71.32	89.08	87.09	118.33
1,500	59.16	58.80	63.24	83.53	81.08	119.57
2,000	42.88	42.83	46.95	70.18	67.33	112.12
2,500	28.39	28.79	32.70	54.94	51.36	107.57
3,000	17.66	18.14	20.82	41.11	37.07	100.49
4,000	8.62	9.05	10.67	26.54	23.06	77.63
5,000	4.70	5.05	6.07	18.41	15.06	67.72

Table 24.7 *(cont.)*

Family income level adj.[a]	No. of schedules adj.[b]	Cumulative percentages of total above given level				
		Number of		Money		
		Schedules	Equivalent adults	Income	Expenditures	Savings
7,000	1.83	1.84	2.36	10.65	8.41	43.58
10,000	1.16	1.13	1.54	8.10	6.19	36.16
15,000	0.38	0.39	0.36	3.81	4.08	20.73

Note: [a] Single persons included with families having incomes 2.5 times as great.
[b] Each single schedule counted as 0.4.

the country are accounted for by the top 18–27 percent. On the other hand when the classification is by per capita expenditure, there are no dissavings at the bottom of the scale and the distribution of savings is only moderately more unequal than that of expenditures.

.

Classification Methods and the Propensity to Consume

Such striking differences in the apparent distribution of savings suggest strongly that corresponding differences may occur in the marginal propensity to consume and the marginal propensity to save as computed from these figures. The marginal propensity to consume is defined as the percentage of an increase in disposable income that would be spent by a given income group. The usual method of estimating the marginal propensity to consume at various income levels is to assume that if the members of one income group were to have their disposable incomes increased to the average disposable income of the next higher group, they would on the average increase their expenditures to the present expenditure level of the higher-income group. The procedure then is to take the difference between the average expenditure of the successive groups and divide by the corresponding difference between their average disposable incomes.

This procedure clearly is relevant only to a long-run propensity to consume: that is, it measures what individuals would do with a permanent increase in disposable income after having adjusted themselves to the change. Or by stretching the relevance a bit, it could indicate the disposition of a temporary increase in income provided we consider not the disposition made in the

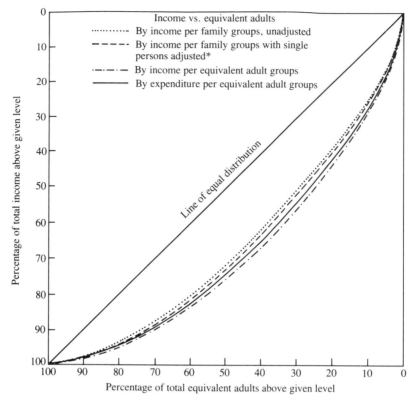

Figure 24.1 Effect of the Classification of Families on the Distribution of Income
Lorenz curves of income versus equivalent adults; classified by income per family, by income per family with single persons shifted upwards,* by income per equivalent adult, and by expenditure per equivalent adult
Note: * single persons grouped with families have incomes 2½ times as great.

immediate period but the ultimate disposition of this added economic power over a long enough period.

Obviously, only rarely will a temporary increase in income be spent immediately; most of it will be saved, at least for a brief period. But this saving may not be permanent: much of the larger income may be spent after a shorter or longer interval, and only a relatively small amount retained permanently as capital. If a suitably long period, probably five years or more, were allowed for determining what is to be done with the added income, the disposal in such a period might be considered to correspond fairly well with the marginal propensity to consume.

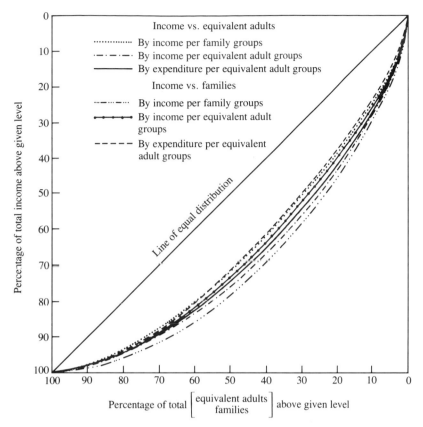

Figure 24.2 Effect of the Unit by which Population is Measured on the Distribution of Income

Lorenz curves of income versus equivalent adults compared with curves of income versus families; classified by income per family, by income per equivalent adult, and by expenditure per equivalent adult

However, a classification by annual income is inappropriate for deriving a propensity to consume by this method, for this method presupposes that the average income and expenditure of persons in the various groups is typical of those who are permanently at such a level of income. Actually, as we have seen, the top income groups contain relatively more persons with temporarily large incomes and who accordingly have more savings than persons who receive steady incomes at these levels. Conversely, the lower income groups contain many persons with temporarily impaired incomes who have smaller savings and greater dissavings than persons permanently at these lower income levels. Accordingly, differences in savings corresponding to given differences in incomes are greater

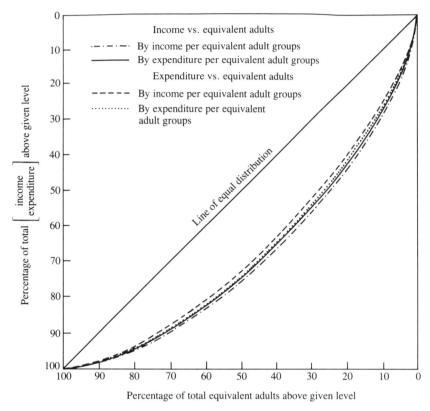

Figure 24.3 Effect of the Unit by which Resources are Measured on the Distribution Picture
Lorenz curves of income versus equivalent adults compared with curves of expenditure versus equivalent adults; classified by income per equivalent adult and by expenditure per equivalent adult

than they would be were the various groups to include only persons permanently at the various income levels, and the marginal propensity to save is overestimated and the marginal propensity to consume correspondingly underestimated.

There is on the whole good reason to believe that a marginal propensity to consume derived from a distribution classified by per capita expenditure would be closer to the theoretical long-run curve than one derived from an income classification. Annual expenditure is likely to be much more stable from year to year than annual income, and the average savings of a given expenditure group is likely to be much closer to the average savings of families who remain steadily at that average level of income and expenditure than the average savings of the corresponding income group. In other words, there is a high correlation between

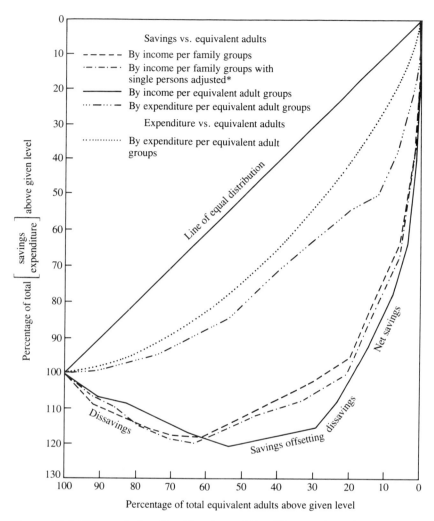

Figure 24.4 Effect of the Classification of Families on the Distribution of Savings

Lorenz curves of savings versus equivalent adults, classified by income per family, by income per family with single persons shifted upwards,* by income per equivalent adult, and by expenditure per equivalent adult; and of expenditure versus equivalent adults by expenditure per equivalent adult. *Note*: * single persons grouped with families have incomes 2½ times as great.

Table 24.8 *Marginal propensity to consume as derived from various tabulations*

1935–1936 NRC family data			
Disposable income per family (1941 $)	Marginal propensity to consume	Disposable income per family (1941 $)	Marginal propensity to consume
$452	0.775	$13,930	0.549[a]
758	0.859	19,170	0.211[a]
1,007	0.888	23,890	0.380
1,258	0.808	29,440	0.356
1,508	0.824	37,310	0.335
1,758	0.827	52,600	0.310
2,063	0.759	85,350	0.215
2,513	0.715	159,500	0.128
3,104	0.666	310,800	0.099
3,941	0.593	771,200	0.074
5,580	0.512	(15,570	0.405[a])
8,870	0.408		

1941 BLS-BHNHE tabulations			
All family units		Urban family units	
Disposable income per family	Marginal propensity to consume	Disposable income per family	Marginal propensity to consume
$790	0.868	$676	0.779
1,232	0.836	1,111	0.980
1,696	0.832	1,617	0.789
2,276	0.954	2,120	1.040
3,239	0.732	2,642	0.918
		3,384	0.750
		4,991	0.652
		9,398	0.606

the annual savings of given families in different years and their annual incomes, and this correlation produces a higher estimate of marginal propensity to save than would a comparison of the average savings of different families at different average income levels.

Table 24.8 and figure 24.5a and b compare the marginal propensity to consume

Table 24.8 *(cont.)*

| Sample tabulations of nonfarm schedules, 1941 | | | | | |
| By family income groups | | By income per equivalent adult groups | | By expenditure per equivalent adult groups | |
Income per schedule	Marginal propensity to consume	Income per schedule	Marginal propensity to consume[b]	Income per schedule	Marginal propensity to consume[b]
$515	0.911	$587	0.930	$617	0.941
919	0.944	1,095	0.998	1,127	0.943
1,492	0.830	1,578	0.845	1,662	0.906
2,095	0.983	2,003	0.888	2,097	1.035
3,089	0.783	2,455	0.795	2,487	0.937
4,955	0.649	3,078	0.838	3,359	0.799
9,019	0.684	4,144	0.622	4,442	0.931
16,040	0.553	6,325	0.504	6,756	0.852
		13,800	0.560	15,470	0.619

Note: [a] Data for $15,000–20,000 group implausible; alternative computation made with this group omitted.
[b] Computed from differences in income and expenditure per equivalent adult.

as estimated from various sources. Though the National Resources Committee data for 1935–6 are practically obsolete and rest on a relatively small sample that must be considered open to wide margins of error, they afford the only estimates in the upper ranges of income. The two estimates from the data for the $15,000–20,000 group are out of line in a way that strongly suggests a blunder of some sort in the figures. One estimate is derived from the total figures of the 1941 *Study of Family Spending and Saving in Wartime* and another from those for urban families only, as the urban figures are for higher income groups. Finally, three estimates are shown derived from the sample treated here: as derived from a classification by (1) family incomes, (2) income per equivalent adult, and (3) expenditure per equivalent adult.

The figures in table 24.8 are of course not all exactly comparable. In the 1935–6 figures, the disposable income levels have been adjusted upward to correspond to 1941 price levels. In the 1935–6 figures and in the figures derived from the BLS-BHNHE studies for 1941, the propensity to consume is the ratio between changes in consumption and in consumption-plus-savings; personal gifts are not considered on the ground that their ultimate disposition will depend upon the

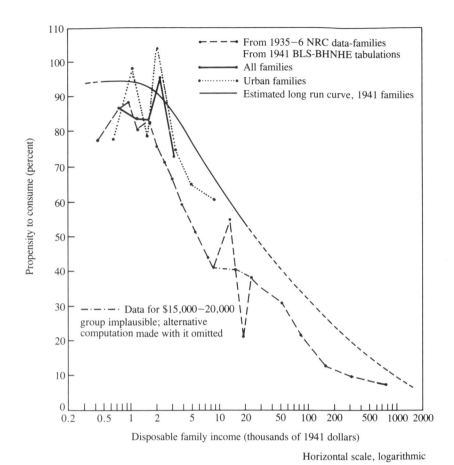

Figure 24.5a Marginal Propensity to Consume (from earlier tabulations)

action of the donee. However, the abscissa for plotting purposes is the disposable income including gifts, i.e., net income less personal taxes.

As no figures in the sample tabulations were available for taxes or gifts, they are in effect included in "savings." The difference is probably negligible except at the top of the scale; in any case the three propensities computed from these data are comparable in this respect.

In each instance the abscissa against which the marginal propensity is plotted is the geometric mean of the average (disposable) incomes of the two groups between which the marginal propensity to consume was computed.

The curve for an estimated long-run marginal propensity to consume is conceptually the result of adjusting the curve obtained from the total figures by family income groups as given by the BLS-BHNHE study for 1941 according to the difference between the figures derived from the family income classification of

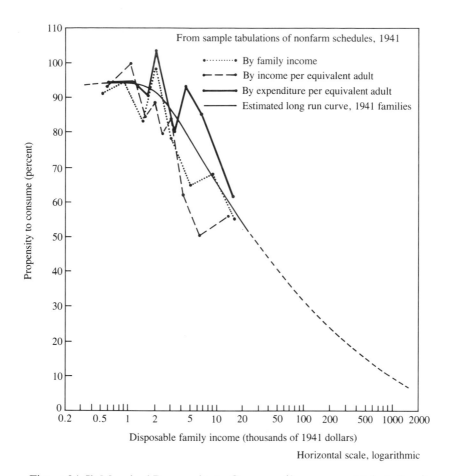

From sample tabulations of nonfarm schedules, 1941

•·········• By family income
‒ ‒ ‒ By income per equivalent adult
—— By expenditure per equivalent adult
—— Estimated long run curve, 1941 families

Disposable family income (thousands of 1941 dollars)

Horizontal scale, logarithmic

Figure 24.5b Marginal Propensity to Consume (from present tabulations)

the present sample and those derived from the classification by per capita expenditures. The figures for urban families in the BLS study and the figures from the 1935–6 study were used as a guide in extrapolating the curve beyond the upper limit of these basic figures. It will be appreciated that this curve is subject to a wide margin or error, particularly in the upper ranges. Indeed, computing a marginal propensity to consume from the detailed figures in tables 7 and 8 gave such erratic fluctuations that it was necessary to combine the groups in order to produce intelligible results; it thus appears that the basic data are subject to large random fluctuations. And in the upper income ranges the estimated curve is not only based upon doubtful data but also is obtained by rather drastic extrapolation procedures. Nevertheless, the curve is a definite improvement over figures derived solely from data classified by family income.

While it may be fairly clear that a classification by annual expenditure gives a closer approximation to the long-run marginal propensity to consume than a classification by annual income, annual expenditure does vary from year to year and so fails to rank individuals accurately according to their long-run economic status. We may thus enquire whether there are theoretical grounds for believing that the true long-run marginal propensity to consume is higher or lower than the estimates based upon a classification by annual expenditure.

The answer depends fundamentally upon whether variations from year to year in the savings of given individuals are positively or negatively correlated with variations in expenditures. If savings of given individuals tend to be higher than usual in years of higher expenditures, the average savings in the higher annual expenditure groups will be higher than the savings of persons who have steady expenditures of this amount. Indeed, the average savings of these groups will also be greater than the average savings of persons who have fluctuating expenditures but whose average expenditures equal the average expenditure of the group. Thus whether we take as the hypothetical norm persons having steady expenditures or merely want the average savings for a period of years of persons having given average expenditures, the inequality of the distribution of savings will be exaggerated, and likewise the marginal propensity to save will appear too large and the marginal propensity to consume correspondingly too small. Conversely, if there is a negative correlation between expenditure and savings the propensity to consume will be overestimated.

Fluctuations in annual expenditures per equivalent adult arise from two principal sources: changes in needs and in incomes. When the fluctuations arise from changes in income, it is reasonable to suppose that the change in expenditure will be less, and that accordingly the savings will vary in the same direction as the income and the expenditure. On the other hand, when changes in expenditure arise independently of changes in income, e.g., through expenses arising from illness, retirement, taking a long vacation, providing higher education for children, the purchase of durable consumer goods, moving from one location to another, or equipping a newly established household, savings probably vary inversely with expenditure. Moreover, any change in family need due to changes in the size of family and not reflected in the factor used to measure the size of family will also cause variations in savings to be negatively correlated with expenditure. For example, if we were to classify by family expenditure rather than by per capita expenditure, then within each class one would find varying levels of economic welfare, depending on variations in family size; one would expect to find the higher family expenditure groups relatively overloaded with families that are (temporarily or otherwise) large and that may have relatively low savings (compared to what would be the case were the families all to remain constant in size), while the lower family expenditure groups would conversely be overloaded with small families having small expenditures by reason of small needs rather than small income and accordingly having unusually large savings. Whether the propensity to consume is over- or underestimated by the use of an expenditure classification will depend on whether changes in consumption are more closely related to such changes in needs as are not reflected in the method of classification or to changes in resources.

On the whole it seems probable that in contemporary circumstances and for a classification that takes family size into consideration changes in income affect expenditures more than changes in other factors influencing consumer needs, and that accordingly savings and expenditures of given individuals in different years are positively rather than negatively correlated, and the marginal propensity to consume obtained from data classified by expenditure per equivalent adult is too low rather than too high. This conclusion, however, rests only on speculation: no data are as yet available that would permit its verification.

While it may be admitted that a classification by consumption per equivalent adult may produce a closer approximation to the long-run marginal propensity to consume, if a short-run propensity to consume is wanted, the figure produced by using data classified by annual income may be more appropriate. For example, it may be desired to know how much of a given tax increase will come out of savings in the period immediately following its imposition, say a year, rather than in the long run.

However, there is actually nothing in the annual income classification that will ensure this result. What we obtain from this classification is an average of short- and long-run propensities with unspecified weights given to the propensities for the varying periods, not a short-run propensity to save. The various income groups include not only individual families with varying incomes but also families whose income is steady for longer or shorter periods. Thus it cannot be said that the "propensity to save" figure obtained from such data pertains to a year merely because the basis for classification is the income for one year; nor can it even be said that such a figure pertains to any determinable period at all, as there is no way of telling what the "average" period of income fluctuation is.

Similar reasoning applies when the problem is to determine the marginal propensity to spend on specific items of consumption. For instance, if it is required to determine what the total expenditure for food is likely to be at a given level and distribution of national income, figures derived from a classification by expenditure groups are likely to yield a more unbiased answer. If, for example, the income is assumed to double, but the price level and the distribution remain the same, judging the consumption of the future $2,000–3,000 group on the basis of the consumption of the present $2,000–3,000 group will lead to a biased result, for the future group will contain a larger proportion of temporarily depressed incomes; in fact, if the fluctuation patterns are preserved, it may be expected that the proportion of depressed incomes will be more nearly comparable with that in the present $1,000–1,500 group. By minimizing the effect of income fluctuations, a classification by expenditure groups should greatly reduce the bias in any such estimates.

Classification and the Distribution of the Tax Burden

The proper classification of families is also of great importance when we come to estimate the distribution of the tax burden and particularly when an attempt is made to compare the progressivity of types of tax. Actually, if the tax base is closely correlated with the measure used for classification, the progressiveness or regressiveness of the tax may be exaggerated; on the other hand if the tax base varies in large degree independently of the classification measure, a spurious appearance of regressivity may result. Moreover, these biases do not necessarily depend upon the relation of the basis for classification to the standard of ability to pay adopted as a criterion for progression.

For example, consider a community of six individuals, of which *A, B,* and *C* have average incomes of $4,000 and steady annual expenditures of $3,600, *A* having a steady income of $4,000, *B* having in the current year an income of $3,000 and in alternate years an income of $5,000; while *C*'s income is currently $5,000 and $3,000 in alternate years. Similarly, *D, E* and *F* have average incomes of $3,000, and annual expenditures of $2,700, *D* having a steady $3,000 income, *E* $2,000 in the current year and $4,000 in alternate years, while *F* has an income of $4,000 in the current year and $2,000 in alternate years. If now we impose a flat 10 percent tax on expenditure, and classify individuals according to whether their current income is above or below $3,500, then *A, C* and *F* will fall in the top group and pay a tax of $990 on an expenditure of $9,900 out of a total income of $13,000. Measured against expenditure, the tax is of course 10 percent, but measured against income the tax is 7.6 percent. On the other hand *B, D,* and *E* will fall in the lower group and pay a $900 tax on a total expenditure of $9,000, out of a total income of $8,000 or 11.2 percent. Thus the burden expressed in terms of the relation of tax to income looks regressive. Actually if we classify the taxpayers on the basis of their average income or expenditure, *A, B,* and *C* will be in the top group and pay $1,080 on an expenditure of $10,800 out of an income of $12,000, while *D, E* and *F* will pay a tax of $810 on an expenditure of $8,100 out of an income of $9,000. In both cases the burden is 9 percent of income or 10 percent of expenditures, and the tax is actually proportional. Nor will the consideration of the alternate years correct this bias: for then *A, B* and *E* will be in the bottom group, and the distribution of the tax burden will be the same as in the current year. Thus a classification by annual income exaggerates the regressiveness of sales and expenditure taxes.

On the other hand if we look at the effect on the apparent progressiveness of the income tax, the reverse is true. If, for example, we have an income tax of 40 percent on income in excess of $3,500, the top annual income group will pay $1,000 on income of $13,000 while the lower group will pay nothing; however, on the average, *A*, *B*, and *C* will pay $800 per year on income amounting to $12,000, while *D*, *E* and *F* will pay $200 per year on income amounting to $9,000. On an annual basis the relative burdens seem to be 7.7 percent and zero; on the average, they turn out to be 6.7 and 2.2 percent. Thus it is apparent that the relative tax burdens computed from data derived from tabulations classified by annual income must be accepted only with reservations. Unfortunately, no data are available that would permit any close readjustment of tax burden figures.

Summary

For the study of the welfare of families, the distribution of the tax burden, propensity to consume, and many other aspects of the distribution of resources and patterns of expenditure, data based on a classification of families by expenditure per equivalent adult are evidently better suited than present classifications by family income, or even than by income per equivalent adult. Even if no close agreement is to be had on the relative weights to be assigned different members of the family, any weighting, no matter how crude, is vastly better than no adjustment for family size. Refusing to make any adjustment merely because no close agreement is to be had recalls the well-known donkey that starved to death through not being able to decide between two bales of hay.

The classification scheme adopted need not be as elaborate as that adopted for the 1934–6 wage earner study; in fact, a simpler scheme is preferable not only to permit simple exposition but also to make comparison possible with other studies in which the data are collected in less detail. It is to be hoped that in any future studies of savings and consumption patterns and size distributions of incomes there will be included in the tabulation program the production of extensive data by expenditure per equivalent adult particularly, and possibly also by income per equivalent adult.

25

·

On the Prevention of Gerrymandering

The current decennial Census brings up again the possibilities for chicanery in the redrawing of electoral districts. It is sometimes felt that gerrymandering is such an obvious form of chicanery that any political body sincerely desiring to achieve a completely equitable redistricting should have no trouble in carrying out such a purpose. It may, indeed, be possible to proscribe effectively, or at least to avoid, the more extreme manifestations of this art, by laying down rules as to contiguity, compactness, and the like. But whenever the drawing up of the boundaries is left even slightly to the discretion of an interested body, considerable latitude is left for the exercise of the art.

To illustrate with a concrete, though artificial example, suppose a rectangular area, twelve miles from east to west and six miles from north to south, which is to elect four representatives, happens to divide politically into nine subareas, each four miles from east to west by two miles from north to south, with the five areas on the diagonals being predominantly of the Red party, while the four areas in the center of the sides are predominantly Blues, checkerboard fashion. One natural districting proposal is to divide the area by bisecting it both north and south and east and west, giving four electoral districts, six miles in the east–west direction by three miles north–south. In this case the Reds sweep all four seats. Another equally natural one is to divide the east–west dimension in four, thus yielding four rectangular electoral districts of the same shape as before, except that this time the six-mile dimension is north–south, while the east–west dimension of each district is three miles. Now we find the two parties each get two seats. Yet there is no obvious geometrical criterion for distinguishing one subdivision from the other

Things are not much improved if we attempt to choose on the basis of the

Political Science Quarterly, 76 (1961), pp. 105–10.

political results. In a system of area representation, it is commonplace that the proportionate majority in the legislature will normally be considerably larger than the proportionate majority of the electorate. But how much larger? For this we have no abstract criterion. If the parties are homogeneously distributed geographically, a slight majority of the electorate can secure all of the legislative seats. However, it is extremely unlikely that any random drawing of the electoral boundaries would produce proportional representation. Thus, while a situation where the minority of the vote elects more than its proportion of the representatives can be considered *prima facie* evidence of gerrymandering, there remains a wide range of results that would at least be compatible with the complete absence of conscious gerrymandering. In the absence of any clear criterion as to what a fair result should be, it is not possible to use the results as a criterion of unfairness in the establishment of electoral districts.

If there is thus no available criterion of substantive fairness, it is necessary, if there is to be any attempt at all to purify the electoral machinery in this respect, to resort to some kind of procedural fairness. This means, in view of the subtle possibilities for favoritism, that the human element must be removed as completely as possible from the redistricting process. In part, this means that the process should be completely mechanical, so that once set up, there is no room at all for human choice. More than this, it means that the selection of the process, which must itself be at least initiated by human action, should be as far removed from the results of the process as possible, in the sense that it should not be possible to predict in any detail the outcome of the process. If this is not done, we may simply transfer the wrangling to an earlier stage and have a fight over which of several alternative processes should be designated, which would be fought not in terms of principle but rather in terms of results in the case at hand. This means that at some stage in the process a random element should be introduced which, while not affecting the general principles that are to be applied, will substantially affect the result in the particular instance, so that legislators in selecting one process rather than another will not be able to base their choice on particular detailed outcomes and will be compelled to base their choice on general principles.

As a somewhat oversimplified picture of what might be done along these lines, we might consider the following procedure. The basic data would be the census tracts with their enumerated populations. The first step would be to draw a particular unassigned census tract at random; call this tract A. The second step would be to determine which of the unassigned census tracts is furthest from A; call this B. Beginning with B, add to B the neighboring contiguous unassigned census tracts in order of increasing distance from B (measured, for example, between the centroids of the tracts) until the population quota has been reached, the population quota being at each stage the ratio of unassigned population to unassigned seats. This, then, constitutes an election district and the process can be repeated beginning with the determination again of which of the now unassigned tracts is furthest from A. If this is C, then a new election district is constructed centered on C, and so on.

The purpose of determining B, C, and so on as the tracts furthest from the randomly selected tract A is to insure that insofar as possible the process will not leave enclaves or isolated fringe areas that cannot be amalgamated into contiguous election districts: by moving from the fringe toward the center the likelihood of this happening is made sufficiently small so that on those rare occasions when an enclave does occur, the resulting construction of an election district with noncontiguous parts will be tolerable as a freak for the sake of adhering to the straightforward rule; in any case, the amount of separation that would occur between the parts of the electoral district should not be great. If desirable, it would be possible to insert a rule against the creation of enclaves, simply by stating that if the addition of a particular census tract D to an election district in accordance with the rule of adding them in order of increasing distance from the initial tract for that district, would divide the remaining unassigned census tracts into two (or in rare cases, more than two) noncontiguous parts, then instead of adding D, that census tract shall be added which is not in the same part as tract A, is contiguous with the part of the election district already assembled, and is furthest from D.

It might be felt desirable to add to the random element by specifying that a new drawing of the tract A from among the unassigned tracts should be made each time an election district is completed. This would have the advantage of making the ultimate pattern of districts even more difficult to predict. It would slightly increase the likelihood of potential enclaves, but if these are handled by the anti-enclave provision there should be no difficulty on this score.

In the above no attempt has been made to take account of political subdivisions such as towns, counties, wards, and the like. It is likely, of course, to be considered desirable to make election districts coincide as far as possible with other political boundaries. It would be simple enough to provide that whenever a tract from a particular ward, borough, village, town, or county has been included in the course of constructing a particular election district, further additions to that election district shall be made only from the corresponding political entity until either the entire entity has been included or the quota has been reached. In addition, it might be considered desirable to provide against minor overflows into neighboring jurisdictions. For example, if at any point the inclusion of the entire political unit, to which the last tract assigned belongs, would not cause the population quota to be exceeded by more than, say, 5, 10, or 15 percent (the percentage used possibly depending on the rank of the political unit), then the entire political unit may be assigned to the election district in question. On the other hand if at any point during the assignment process a new political unit is about to be entered and the population already assigned to the electoral district has already reached, say, 85, 90, or 95 percent of the quota, depending on the nature of the political unit, the political unit is to be excluded entirely from the electoral district, unless the inclusion of the political unit would bring the total population of the political unit closer to the quota than its exclusion. In case of exclusion, formation of the electoral district is to be continued, with the unassigned contiguous tract closest to *B* among those not in the excluded political unit, until either the quota has been reached or there are no contiguous political subdivisions to be included under the above rule.

This procedure, of course, means that a certain unevenness in the population of the electoral district is to be tolerated for the sake of making them more nearly coterminous with political entities, but in view of the amount of unevenness that is bound to develop in any case as a result of population shifts between redistrictings the gain may be worth the cost. The possibility that the excesses or deficiencies might cumulate so as to leave an unduly large or unduly small population in the last district to be established is obviated by the process of recalculating the quota after each district is established, in terms of the remaining number of districts and the remaining unassigned population.

Many other procedures could of course be devised having roughly the same characteristics, and the above is intended only as an example, to show that it is possible to establish mechanical rules which will eliminate the element of human discretion almost entirely from the process of redistricting, and which if followed would make gerrymandering virtually impossible. Such procedures should be capable of appealing to nearly everyone as essentially fair, while at the same time the random element is sufficiently large so that it would not be possible to develop any very serious attachment for one particular procedure over another on the basis of estimates as to the particular political consequences of applying them to the circumstances of the moment. Politicians are going to be reluctant in most cases to desist from discreet gerrymandering, but it is just barely possible that presentation of a scheme of this kind would develop sufficient support for its inherent fairness to overcome this reluctance.

But while such a scheme may satisfy demands made on it on grounds of political fairness, and thus be acceptable in a *de novo* situation, in an ongoing situation redistricting involves not only the relative political strength of parties in general but the political fortunes of present incumbents. Of course, to the extent that redistricting involves reductions in the representation of one party or the other, either because of the correction of former gerrymandering, or because of a reduction in the total number of seats allotted to the jurisdiction as a whole, this will involve the ousting of some incumbents, over and above what turnover may be caused by shifts in political strength. But the amount of such turnover may be greater under an impersonal redistricting method than under a politically motivated one. To the extent that the demand for minimizing the turnover is legitimate, it is difficult to see how it can be fully met without reintroducing opportunities to gerrymander. A strictly impersonal method would be likely to produce situations where an incumbent finds himself residing in a new district that is strongly of the opposing political complexion; often, though not always, this will be because a previous gerrymander has been undone, and it will be difficult if not impossible to devise rules for determining in which specific cases the complaint is to be catered to, nor what remedy should be adopted if the complaint appears legitimate. In most cases all that can be done nonpolitically in such cases is to consider the turnover as part of the fortunes of political strife. Politicians, however, are not likely to take such an objective view of the matter, and this may be one very serious obstacle in the way of adopting a neutral scheme.

On the other hand, there are cases where the above redistricting scheme would result in two incumbents residing in the same district. Of course, where the number of districts is being reduced, some cases of this sort are inevitable, but it would be reasonable to require that they be kept to a minimum. It is not too difficult to devise modifications of the above scheme that will accomplish this, at the expense of somewhat impairing the compactness of the electoral districts. However, if the previous districts were seriously gerrymandered, this may allow some of the effects to carry over into the redistricting, though this is likely to be of very small consequence. More serious, it is difficult to devise a scheme which will not discriminate among incumbents as to the likelihood of their surviving as the sole incumbent in their district, according either to their being near the center of the entire jurisdiction or on the fringes, or to their being relatively close to other incumbents. It would, of course, be possible to select by lot at the beginning of the procedure those incumbents whose residence location is to be disregarded in drawing up the new districts; this would be likely to further impair the compactness of the resulting districts. But even such a procedure, or indeed any impersonal procedure, is likely to run counter to what may be conceived as a political party's legitimate interest in the political survival of particular incumbents. There are, to be sure, ways of adapting to this situation, as by running the displaced incumbent for another office, or the other legislative chamber, by asking the competing incumbent to withdraw, or even by change of residence. But this difficulty is probably best regarded as one inherent in the practice of requiring a representative to reside in his district, as contrasted with the more flexible British practice.

In summary, elimination of gerrymandering would seem to require the establishment of an automatic and impersonal procedure for carrying out a redistricting. It appears to be not at all difficult to devise rules for doing this which will produce results not markedly inferior to those which would be arrived at by a genuinely disinterested commission. Nevertheless, it is likely to be some time before we put to the test the question of whether incumbents who have a natural interest in preserving an established position can bring themselves to trust their fate to an impersonal procedure, however effective, rather than continue to maneuver in terms of back-room bargaining.

One Economist's View
of Philanthropy

The theoretical economist's ideal model of the economic system is one in which each participating unit lives in its own compartment, completely isolated from all others except through the process of economic exchange. The market is such that prices are precisely determined by competitive forces as modified by taxes and other well-defined and specifically legislated provisions. Within these bounds each economic unit acts only in terms of its own direct interest, trusting in an unseen hand to bring harmony out of conflicting interests. But such a pure competitive economic system, even if it could be realized, would be far too rigid and heartless to serve as the economic basis for a tolerable society. To be viable at all, such a system must provide at least some softening of the corners and relaxation of the rigid rule of self-interest.

Some of this relaxation comes, in the earlier stages of economic development, from the sheer lack of universality in the economic system itself. Not every economic good acquires at the outset the characteristics of inviolable private property; gleaners, squatters, and scavengers eke out an existence in the interstices of the formal system. But as property rights become all-encompassing and the system becomes more complex, the interstices change in character: they are no longer the refuge of the dispossessed but rather the arena for the nimble, the venturesome, and often the unscrupulous. Whether from a growing social conscience, an advancing ethical standard, or response to the sheer importunities of the indigent, some forms of succor for the unfortunate or the underprivileged emerge as a significant element in nearly all the more highly structured civili-

Philanthropy and Public Policy, F. G. Dickinson, Ed. (New York: Columbia University Press, 1962), pp. 31–56.

zations. These range from casual almsgiving through tax-supported public welfare systems to international aid such as that under the Marshall Plan.

Voluntarism Versus Compulsion

Given that there are important functions to be performed outside the economist's marketplace, it becomes appropriate to attempt to appraise the various institutions performing them. One scale on which they can be ranged is the degree to which the individual contribution is voluntary rather than compulsory. At the one extreme lies the alms given in secret, for which there is no motive beyond the desire to respond to the promptings of conscience, and at the other is the heavy hand of the tax collector, obtaining funds for purposes which in many cases overlap considerably with those for which strictly voluntary gifts are used. Ranging in between arc contributions made under varying degrees of social or other pressure, such as the importunities of the panhandler, the sanctions of the clerical hierarchy, the threat of social ostracism, the withdrawal of such benefits as good will, or the superstitious fear of losing the favors of Dame Fortune. The history of the development of the welfare state can be told, in part, in terms of the growing need for works of public beneficence beyond the ability or at least the willingness of the public to respond voluntarily, and the substitution of tax-financed welfare disbursements for voluntary charity as a consequence. An ultrarationalist might claim that the result of this trend would be to so develop public welfare programs that there would be little or no need for private charity. While there has been a pronounced shift, in recent decades, in the relative roles of tax-supported and voluntary public welfare outlays, there are limits beyond which this trend does not seem likely to go. Under almost any conceivable development of the public sector, there will remain areas where voluntary support will be more appropriate; and in many areas, where either method of financing might be possible, voluntary financing has advantages that are not to be lost sight of.

Church and State

One of the largest areas in which voluntary giving is likely to remain the main resource is the support of religious institutions. To be sure, in a theocratic state, support of the church and support of the state are often so intermingled that the distinction between tax and tithe almost disappears. In countries with an established church, establishment usually carries with it some degree of financial support from funds collected in a compulsory manner, whether termed taxes or tithes; however, this can vary all the way from virtually complete support to a mere grant of minor special privileges.

Even where the principle of separation of church and state is the rule, various privileges accorded churches and similar institutions amount to a fairly substantial subsidy. In the United States, their property amounting to some $15 billion, is largely exempt from property tax; at effective rates averaging probably between 1.5 and 2.5 percent, this is an effective subsidy on the order of $300 million. Even greater is the subsidy in effect granted through the deduction allowed for contributions in computing the individual income tax: of $5.6 billion claimed for such contributions in 1958 returns itemizing deductions, probably $3 billion or more went to religious organizations.[1] This is deducted in returns with marginal rates averaging about 30 percent, indicating a subsidy on the order of $900 million (in the sense that, had this $3 billion not been given to churches, $900 million of additional income tax would have been collected). In the face of subsidies thus aggregating over $1 billion a year to specifically religious activities, the furor over public aid to religiously controlled or sponsored education, to say nothing of the use of public school buses by parochial school students, brings up questions of the relative digestibility of gnats and camels.

Nevertheless, separation of church and state requires, at the very minimum, that religious institutions have sufficient voluntary support to eliminate the danger that subsidization, through tax exemption or otherwise, will provide an occasion for undue interference of the state in the affairs of the religious body, or vice versa. State subsidies in the form of deductions allowed for contributions have the virtue that they are distributed with reference to the independent voluntary support that the various institutions attract, so that the question of budgetary allocation does not arise. Conversely, since the allocation is automatic, there is little likelihood that lobbying for an increased share will arise, though we have seen that where the degree of interest in specific activities, such as church controlled schools, varies among faiths, a religious issue can become intermingled with political issues.

While preserving a nation from the taint of establishment on the one hand and godless secularism on the other does require some voluntary support of religion, this support need not be completely private, as tax deductibility shows, nor need it be in all cases strictly gratuitous. Though most forms of "selling" religious services have their obnoxious features, it must be recorded that in the past considerable revenues have been obtained for religious organizations by practices that range from simony in its explicit form, through sale of indulgences, fees for marriages

---

[1] The American Association of Fund-Raising Counsel estimates that religion accounts for 51 percent of all philanthropic giving, and presumably a larger proportion of individual than of corporate and foundation giving, but possibly a smaller proportion of upper income bracket giving covered by the standard deduction.

and other rites, to pew rentals, and the like. While many of these practices represent relatively innocuous ways of obtaining church funds, the lingering taint of simony on the one hand and commercialism on the other has led to their de-emphasis. Even where fees are retained in conjunction with religious rites, either the amount is left largely to voluntary determination, or an amount is specified for the aesthetic elaboration of a ceremonial which, in more spartan form, is available without charge. While the practice is often inferior to the theory, the ideals usually expressed concerning the financing of religious institutions call for voluntary contributions commensurate with the means of the faithful, and sanctioned primarily by the urgings of the individual conscience, rather than by any threat of ostracism or of the withholding of ritual benefits.

The practical working out of the separation of church and state however, has led to many economically wasteful practices. In many instances, public educational facilities are unavailable for activities that have a religious or sectarian aspect. This is one factor in the complex of forces that has resulted in a quasi-duplication of educational facilities, one set being used five days a week for secular education and the other, generally inferior, set being used often only one-half day per week for religious education. The situation is at its extreme when, under "released time" arrangements, students are dismissed from public school ahead of the normal time in order that they be enabled to attend religious classes of a type approved by their parents, but in separate, and in some cases distant, facilities. There would seem to be a significant inconsistency in subsidizing the construction of religious facilities through tax exemption on the one hand, while on the other denying the use of alternative facilities that would otherwise be idle, on the grounds that this would involve the establishment of a religion by the state. To be sure, many religious groups would doubtless still wish to provide separate facilities that could be more closely integrated with the other activities of the congregation, but in terms of the economics involved, if they choose to do this it should only be after considering the full costs of the alternatives.

As is usually the case with special tax exemptions, those to religious bodies involve special problems, and unintended effects. Restrictions on tax exemption of church property vary from one local jurisdiction to another. In rare cases exemption is applied to all property owned by a religious organization, regardless of character or use. Where the religious organization is in a position to derive explicit revenue from the property, an exemption so inclusive is obviously open to serious abuse: its benefits are capable of being multiplied beyond all reason through the expansion of activities only remotely related to any religious purpose. Not only is the loss of revenue a problem, but in many cases there is more or less direct competition with enterprise not favored with comparable tax privileges, and there are obvious grounds for complaint.

In order to prevent such abuses, exemption is more often limited to that part of the property devoted specifically to a religious use and not operated for revenue. But this also, when applied too rigorously, leads to economic waste. A common example is that of a church, located near a suburban shopping center and railroad station, which is encouraged, if not actually required by zoning ordinances, to provide a parking lot on its property for its congregation. This lot is then kept vacant during most of the week, though neighbouring streets are parked as solid as the regulations will allow, lest the revenues that might be obtained from operating the parking space during the week be considered to forfeit the tax-exempt status of the property.

Even where appropriate adjustments are possible, so that the more obvious inefficiencies do not arise, there is a considerable bias introduced into the choice of means by which philanthropic purposes are served: land and buildings are favored with tax exemptions which do not apply to salaries.[2] To be sure, this may be regarded as merely the removal of a bias which otherwise afflicts economic activity in general, but even so, the consequences are probably inferior to what would result if a less prejudicial form of support for the activity were available.

Public and Private Contributions

Even outside the peculiarly sensitive area of religion, there are large areas where for one reason or another the more cumbersome apparatus of the state seems a less appropriate means of effecting the desired results than private contribution. In some cases this is because the activity in question appeals to a restricted class of individuals: the maintenance of a dog cemetery, or the maintenance of bird sanctuaries, or support for the climbing of Mt. Everest. Examples of this sort are, however, increasingly hard to find: Goddard's experiments with rockets could not find support through public appropriations, but we now find a million-fold expansion of his line of effort carried out with public funds. Private philanthropy very often provides limited means for initiating an activity which may later receive large public support once its value has been demonstrated.

In some cases the advantage of privately financed philanthropy arises from a greater freedom of action: the ability to discriminate in dispensing benefits, for example, may be necessary either to arrive at clear-cut results or to prevent the available resources from being spread uselessly thin; public auspices are more likely to find themselves handicapped either by beneficiaries who congest facilities, demanding a share as of right, or by sheer bureaucratic demands for some sort of uniformity. The Arrowsmith dilemma is often a vexing one, but

---

[2] Where education is concerned, this is another factor contributing indirectly to the tendency to provide bricks rather than brains.

when it occurs in a public operation the choice of long-run scientific advance rather than short-run palliative is much more likely to seem, to many, an abuse of power.

Another reason for entrusting an activity to privately financed agencies is the cumbersomeness of public agencies in dealing with relatively small-scale activities. To be sure, a considerable degree of improvement is possible in the administration of support for small projects through the establishment of subsidiary agencies, subcontracting, and the like, but there is always the basic conflict between, on the one hand, the expenditure of the time and effort of high-level decision-making bodies on matters of small magnitude in which they have relatively little basis for judgment, and on the other, the dilution of underlying accountability and responsibility to the point where there are excessive opportunities for waste or extravagance (or merely the undue promotion of the hobbies of individual administrators).

Closely related to this is the idea that activities financed through voluntary contributions are more efficiently and more economically carried out than when financed from public funds. Certainly administrators and employees of voluntary agencies who are aware that they are spending the widow's mite, or that the probability is slight that "there is more where that came from" are likely to be somewhat more concerned to use what they have carefully than where the vast resources of the state are available. An additional argument often cited is the fact that voluntary agencies are often able to secure conscientious work at wages that are considerably below the rate which comparable work would command in public employment, and below the going rates generally; in addition a considerable amount of free volunteer service is often obtainable. But too much should not be made of this: the response to the proposal for a Peace Corps indicates that under proper circumstances large amounts of volunteer effort can be mobilized under public as well as under private auspices; the ability to secure competent services at lower wage rates should properly be regarded not as an economy in the use of resources, but partly as the eliciting of an additional contribution in kind from these employees. It is possible that if these employees were to do the same work under public auspices at higher pay they would devote part of the difference to the support of other philanthropy. It is also possible that they derive more immediate satisfaction from doing the work under private auspices than they would under public; indeed, in a completely rational market this would be the necessary inference to be drawn from the fact of the wage differential.

To some extent, also, this efficiency differential may be considered a scale effect: where an activity is conducted on a large scale, and especially where it acquires a quasi-official status, as with the Red Cross, the identification of the administrator or employee with the contributor tends to diminish, and the pressure for efficiency tends to relax. Moreover, in large-scale philanthropic enterprise there is often no clear-cut criterion of efficiency comparable to that provided in a large industrial organization whose accounting procedures provide allocated profits and losses as figures of merit. To this extent, then, the argument for voluntary activity on the basis of efficiency may be applicable primarily to activities that can be carried out on a small scale rather than those which by their nature require large-scale effort.

Costs of Financing

Overall efficiency is not merely a matter of expenditure of funds, but also of their collection. Here the picture is confused and the variety of situations is great. The marginal cost of public funds can be thought of as comprising three components: the marginal administrative cost of collecting increased sums in taxes, the marginal taxpayer compliance cost occasioned by an increase in the tax burden, and the marginal misallocation cost. Misallocation cost is the loss of economic efficiency which results from the distortions introduced into the operation of the economy by increasing tax rates and which induces more and more drastic adaptations, taken either directly or at several removes, to the changes in relative opportunities which the tax increase brings about. These adaptations may or may not have as a conscious intent the minimization of the tax burden. Rough ideas of average administration and compliance cost are comparatively easy to come by; the corresponding marginal costs may be somewhat more elusive, but in most cases will be relatively modest. Of course, one must be wary of estimating marginal administrative and compliance costs on the basis of the assumption that an increase in public expenditure is automatically to be covered by a simple increase in, say, the individual income tax rates. It cannot be concluded thereby that, since the only difference is in the size of the figures on the returns, these marginal costs will be negligible. Rate increases tend to provoke elaboration of the law, the litigation of issues that otherwise would not be raised, and increased evasion which in turn calls for increased countermeasures; moreover increased pressure for revenue may induce the introduction of new taxes. But by and large these costs will be minor. The misallocation cost is the great uncertainty, and in the absence of well-grounded estimates, opinions as to the magnitude of this cost will vary widely according to political complexion. A low overall estimate for the cost of federal funds might run as low as 10 percent, whereas for a hard pressed municipality with a poorly administered tax system the marginal cost of public funds might well run as high as 50 percent.

The cost of voluntary contributions has a somewhat different composition. There is little here to correspond to the misallocation cost involved in taxation; it is difficult to think of potential contributors taking any drastic action to avoid the obligation to contribute, although some avoidance action may take place. Travelers may consciously or unconsciously avoid areas where beggars abound; in our own culture the prevalence of unlisted telephones may be, in small part, a corresponding phenomenon. But in the aggregate this is likely to be a negligible matter. Similarly, the time the individual takes in examining various appeals and discarding them or responding to them is probably far smaller in absolute amount than the effort expended in preparing tax returns, though in proportion to the total volume of contributions it may be more nearly comparable. The marginal effect may also be relatively larger: a larger aggregate of contributions probably means a larger number of appeals and responses, to a much greater extent than a larger tax burden means a more numerous array of taxes.

The cost of solicitation is another matter. In cases bordering on fraud, costs have been known to cover a major fraction of the receipts. At best, even a minimal solicitation, acknowledgment, and maintenance of lists of contributors is likely to be a substantial fraction of the cost of operation. This is particularly true of any organization that depends on the repeated contributions of large numbers of small contributors rather than the special favor of a few large contributors or foundations.

The nominal costs of solicitation may not, however, be a true representation of social costs. A considerable amount is often spent for reports and other literature produced either as an essential part or as an adjunct to the principal activity of the agency. At one extreme the value of this information to the contributor as a matter of interest or usefulness may justify the cost of its distribution, wholly aside from any incidental effect that its distribution may have in encouraging contributions. At the other extreme the literature may be of little value except as a means of inducing the contributor to maintain his contributions. Since not much is available in the way of uniform reports on the outlays of philanthropic agencies, particularly of the smaller units, the question of where particular agencies draw the line between outlays for fund raising and outlays for other activities is largely academic.

Many agencies in raising funds find it psychologically effective to affix postage stamps to the return envelopes, which constitutes a somwhat different type of expense than that involved in other costs associated with fund raising. Since this involves a lower postage rate than when business reply envelopes are used, there may even be some saving in those cases where the response rate is high. To the extent that the rate differential reflects the extra cost to the post office of handling business reply mail, this saving is a genuine one in terms of resources. On the other hand if a fairly large percentage of the postage stamps remain unused, this is in effect a diversion of some of the contributed funds to the post office, as a kind of offset to the benefits of tax exemption. To the extent that some of the addressees are induced to spend time and effort salvaging the stamps, this is then of course part of the net social cost of the fund-raising operation. If this practice is psychologically effective, however, it probably impairs rather than improves the degree to which philanthropic contributions reflect the genuine underlying interests of the contributors.

There are other methods of raising philanthropic funds which have their own peculiarities, ranging from the church bazaar through bingo to the beaux-arts ball. The varied motivations for and benefits derived from these activities in addition to the fund-raising goal resist easy generalization. At one extreme the philanthropic aspect does little more than cast a mantle of respectability over indulgences that would otherwise be condemned; too often the price exacted for this cachet is absurdly low. In other instances the benefit becomes an activity worthwhile in its own right and needing only the catalyst of charitable purpose to bring it off. But there are many cases where a cold hard look at the relation between the results and the effort and sacrifice that went into them would produce a finding that the game was not worth the candle. To be sure, all ventures, whether for profit or for charity, entail some risk; the peculiar mixture of free and costly goods and services in philanthropy makes the evaluation of the results peculiarly difficult.

Interaction in Giving

There remains, however, perhaps the largest and the most difficult element in the social cost of voluntary and of public finance: the meaning to the contributor of giving up the amount contributed, voluntarily at one extreme and compulsorily at the other. A strict positivist might claim that in the case of a voluntary contribution the donor, on balance, gains in satisfaction at least as much as he would by spending the money in other ways (otherwise he would not have made the contribution). This might be valid in the case of an atomistically motivated contribution; in practice however we are in a situation akin to that of monopolistic competition where one's own behavior is expected to influence that of others, and so in making a choice one must allow not only for direct, but also for these indirect effects. The phrase sometimes used in connection with more substantial donations "in consideration of the gifts of others" is not a mere legal form but has economic substance. Financing a given public welfare service by taxation in a community of peers could then be considered merely a formalization of this implied agreement. Even if we set up a rigorous model of the situation, including the living standards of all members of the community as arguments in the utility function of each donor, it is no longer necessary to say that a donation by A, designed to increase the standard of living of X, Y, and Z, must yield A as much utility through this effect as it would if spent to raise A's own standard of living. A will expect that B and C may also be induced by his gift to contribute to the same or similar objectives. The combined effects of *A*'s original gift plus that of the induced gifts on the standard of living of *X*, *Y*, and *Z* will provide for *A* a level of satisfaction equal to what he would have obtained had he kept the amount of his contribution for himself. Indeed, in some instances this interdependence of giving is formalized by the device of conditional or matching gifts, whereby a donor pledges to contribute a given amount provided that some specified amount is raised from other sources, or agrees to contribute in proportion to the gifts obtained from others. The donor might derive satisfaction from the direct consequences of his gift, sufficient to compensate him for making it, even without considering the effects of the gifts induced from others, but some fairly significant degree of interdependence does exist. From the point of view of welfare economics, this can be considered as a case of compounded external economies: not only do the expenditures of *X*, *Y*, and *Z* have favorable neighborhood effects on *A*, but the facilitating of these expenditures by *A* has favorable repercussions on *B* and *C*, and vice versa.

On the other side, it is not always clear that the payment of a tax or compulsory contribution is to be considered a clear net burden on the taxpayer, even before the benefits purchased with the tax are taken into consideration. If all similarly situated individuals are required to pay comparable tax increments, each taxpayer may feel relatively just as well off. In absolute terms, he may feel considerably better off than he would have felt if he had been singled out for a discriminatory levy. There is even some experimental evidence for this contention in the results of certain game experiments conducted at RAND and elsewhere. These indicate that at least in some situations in which the possibility of a competitive relationship is present there is a natural tendency on the part of individuals to maximize their relative rather than their absolute position. In the situations studied, two individuals not known to each other and having no direct means of communication with each other were asked to select on a given signal one of two actions, there being four possible combinations thus resulting. Previous to each series of trials each of the two individuals was shown a payoff matrix specifying the amounts that each player was to receive in the event of each of the four outcomes, the sum of the winnings of the two players being variable rather than constant. Results differed with variously structured payoff matrices, but the principle upon which a wider variety of the results could be rationalized than any other was that the players acted with the intention of maximizing the difference between their own winnings and those of their opponents.

There is, to be sure, a certain element of contradiction between a hypothesis that the motive of *A* is to outdo *B* and that hence *B*'s success is a negative element in *A*'s satisfaction on the one hand and that *A* can derive satisfaction from improvements in the situation of *X*, *Y*, and *Z* resulting from his gifts and those induced thereby from others. But this contradiction can probably be adequately resolved by assuming that where the individuals involved are of roughly comparable status, as A and B, the competitive or negative element may tend to predominate, particularly in a situation structured to resemble a game where success tends to be regarded as predominantly a relative matter, whereas between individuals such as A and X, comparability is so remote as to make any competitive element almost irrelevant, and the element of empathy becomes controlling.

This situation can be roughly pictured in Figure 26.1. We can think of individuals ranked along a line according to income or economic status, Y, relative to a particular individual A; the degree to which A obtains satisfaction from the welfare of others may be described in a curve $E_A(Y)$, which typically has a peak near A and tapers off in either direction, the exact shape depending on the temperament of the individual A; a secondary and fairly sharp peak may exist for some charismatic leadership group near the top of the status scale. Similarly, we can describe the influence of the typical rivalry between A and others in a curve $R_A(Y)$, somewhat similar to $E_A(Y)$, but much more sharply peaked, dropping off rapidly to a level of practically zero within a relatively short distance on either side. Rivalry being a negative interaction and empathy a positive one, by subtracting R from E we get the net interaction or neighborhood effect, $N_A(Y)$, which may be negative in the neighborhood of A, but can be thought of as having a positive peak at an income some distance below Y_A, and possibly one or two other peaks at an income above Y_A. Further, we can draw a marginal utility of income curve $U_A(Y)$, as perceived by A, representing the amount of satisfaction that A thinks individuals at different income levels will receive from an increment of income (or of expenditure on their behalf) and multiply $N_A(Y)$ by $U_A(Y)$, and also by a factor representing the "contagion effect" of A's contributions on the contributions of others (it would be very difficult to say anything specific about the variation of this contagion effect between contributions for activities benefiting different income levels); the result can be shown as a curve $M_A(Y)$, representing the marginal utility to A of a contribution by him for the benefit of persons of status Y. If a horizontal line is drawn at a level representing the marginal utility of income to A, cutting $M_A(Y)$ at V and W, and possibly also at K and L, then the individuals in the status range indicated by V and W can be considered the natural objects of A's bounty. The possible KL range can be considered to cover the case of the charwoman who knits a shawl for the princess, or more generally of the MP who as her representative votes for a substantial civil list, though cases of this sort can be fitted only somewhat awkwardly into such a scheme.

Of course, in addition to distances measured by income or economic status, there will also be distances in terms of age, race, culture, geographic location, and other characteristics to which a similar discussion might apply.

The net result of these considerations seems to be that it is not possible to say

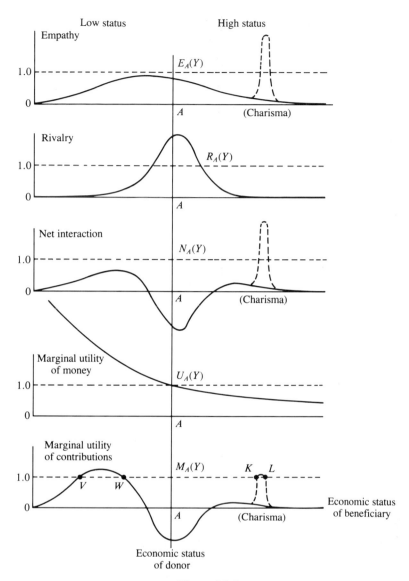

Figure 26.1

anything very definite from a strictly behavioral point of view on the relative subjective sacrifice involved in the making of a gift and the payment of a tax, though on balance the evidence may seem to point to the tax as more painful than the gift, but not by anything like the amount of loss suffered, say, if the same quantum of resources had been destroyed by some uninsured catastrophe.

Philanthropy and Redistribution

Private and public philanthropy are both often regarded primarily as instruments for the redistribution of resources so as to diminish economic inequalities. But the differences between the degree to which public and private philanthropy accomplish this are probably much more striking, in terms of the evidence available, than casual observation would lead one to expect. The analysis of the preceding section might indicate that the natural objects of philanthropy of a given economic stratum are those located only a moderate distance down the scale, rather than at the bottom. Such data as we have as to the character of giving indicate that the difference in economic level between donor and beneficiary is comparatively small. According to the 1950 BLS–Wharton School sample survey, 32.6 percent of all gifts were in the nature of family and reciprocity gifts having a minimal redistributional content; 21.4 percent were gifts for the support of individuals, including alimony, representing some redistribution, but in most cases largely among relatives and spanning a relatively narrow spread of status. Another 29.4 percent of all giving was to religious institutions, and while these might be thought of as agencies through which redistribution would take place, a very large fraction of this amount is spent for the maintenance of activities in the congregation, and only a minor fraction finds its way to the support of outside activities. Moreover, as public welfare agencies have taken over a large portion of the burden of caring for the indigent, the channeling of alms through religious agencies has correspondingly diminished in importance. Further, the ratio of gifts to religious organizations of discretionary receipts was remarkably constant over all the income levels covered by this survey. To consider that redistribution amounts to any very substantial part of this category of contribution would require the assumption that the individual's share in the consumption of religious services constitutes, in technical economic terms, a very "inferior" good indeed!

The next largest single category among objects of individual philanthropy is education. Here again, casual observation suggests that the beneficiaries tend to belong to social and economic strata not very far removed from those of the donors: private schools and colleges are supported in considerable measure by their own graduates; students at such institutions are often drawn from social strata not far removed from those of the chief benefactors, and even scholarship holders come in large measure from the middle class rather than the poorest strata in the population. Indeed, some of the giving of this kind could well be regarded as the repayment of a loan or at least of the reciprocation of a previous gift, and thus have no redistributive consequences at all.

Not enough is known about the remainder of private philanthropy to warrant much being said without further appraisal. But the overall picture would appear to remain one in which the role of philanthropy in redistribution is relatively slight.

This impression is somewhat reinforced by the examination of the figures available from income tax returns on the distribution of charitable contributions by income classes. Data on contributions are unfortunately limited to those returns of taxpayers who elect to itemize deductions; in 1958, the latest year for which data are available, such returns were only 35 percent of the total number, though they accounted for slightly over half of the adjusted gross income. As shown in table 26.1, the proportion of returns that itemize deductions increases steadily with income. It can be presumed therefore that, since a relatively large amount of contributions would be one of the factors inducing taxpayers to itemize, *ceteris paribus*, the itemizing taxpayers will, on the average within each income class, make relatively greater contributions than nonitemizing taxpayers. Nevertheless, over ranges where the proportion of itemizing taxpayers does not change too abruptly, the figures presented in table 26.1 represent reasonably well the degree to which contributions are concentrated in the upper income classes.

Column 6 shows the crude ratio of gross contributions reported to the adjusted gross income of itemizers. It is seen that in the lower income classes singling out the itemizers is highly selective of those taxpayers with relatively large contributions. This selectiveness is somewhat less severe as incomes increase; the proportion of contributions drops to a low of 3.36 percent in the $8,000–$9,000 class, thereafter rising gradually to a maximum of nearly 20 percent for incomes over one million dollars. This is a reasonably progressive showing, particularly as the maximum limit for the individual on the deduction of contributions is in most cases 30 percent of adjusted gross income.

To assess properly the effect of contributions on the distribution of income, however, it is necessary to consider the fact that only part of the gross contribution reported represents a net sacrifice to the taxpayer; depending on the marginal tax rate, a fairly substantial part of the cost of the contributions represents a reduction in the tax that would otherwise have become due. On the basis of a composite weighted mean marginal rate, derived from the marginal rates for the various categories of taxpayers in each income class, the net cost of the contributions is given in column 7. It is appropriate to consider this net cost in relation to the net disposable income the taxpayer would have had, had he made no contributions (see col. 8 of table 26.1). This is obtained by taking total income, correcting it to reflect in full the capital gains and losses reported for the current year, subtracting all allowable deductions, and also the income tax itself, and adding the cost of the contributions as given in column 7. The resulting ratios are given in column 9, where it is apparent that instead of the proportion of contributions increasing with income, there is a substantial and steady decrease in the percentage of disposable income sacrificed, except for a modest increase in the top income class.

These figures are also, of course, subject to considerable bias through the selective effect of considering only itemizing returns, but this factor is hardly

Table 26.1 Regressivity of net charitable contributions, 1958 (money figures in thousands of dollars)

Adjusted gross income class	Total no. of returns (1)	No. of itemizing returns (2)	Percentage of returns itemizing (3)	Gross contributions of itemizers (4)	Adjusted gross income of itemizers (5)	Col. 4 / Col. 5 (percent) (6)	Net cost of contributions (7)	Disposable income (8)	Col. 7 / Col. 8 (percent) (9)
None	384,258	—	—	—	—	—	—	—	—
Under 0.6	3,950,030	26,090	0.66	2,164	10,046	21.54	2,164	2,164	a
0.6 to 1.0	3,060,247	207,591	6.78	14,435	174,300	8.28	13,626	116,505	11.70
1.0 to 1.5	4,120,276	451,900	10.97	41,067	578,099	7.10	37,343	386,684	9.66
1.5 to 2	3,570,536	613,555	17.18	66,235	1,077,804	6.15	58,034	757,164	7.66
2 to 2.5	3,689,218	845,169	22.91	104,089	1,905,776	5.46	89,656	1,392,209	6.44
2.5 to 3	3,723,909	962,390	25.84	134,649	2,653,578	5.07	114,048	1,970,476	5.79
3 to 3.5	3,742,848	1,126,380	30.09	176,263	3,659,665	4.82	146,627	2,731,357	5.37
3.5 to 4	3,729,578	1,304,349	34.97	218,021	4,900,598	4.45	179,374	3,681,170	4.87
4 to 4.5	3,745,242	1,452,898	38.79	263,750	6,172,608	4.27	214,427	4,634,058	4.63
4.5 to 5	3,639,977	1,574,279	43.25	298,951	7,481,243	4.00	249,627	5,639,531	4.43
5 to 6	6,375,555	3,253,856	51.04	654,731	17,837,342	3.67	539,887	13,343,556	4.05
6 to 7	4,676,947	2,605,487	55.71	602,241	16,861,809	3.57	485,414	12,580,871	3.86
7 to 8	3,226,844	1,797,271	55.70	457,855	13,430,839	3.41	366,550	9,959,190	3.68
8 to 9	2,171,701	1,223,286	56.33	348,207	10,354,116	3.36	271,653	7,645,980	3.55
9 to 10	1,452,594	795,245	54.75	252,924	7,525,975	3.36	197,250	5,527,028	3.57
10 to 15	2,488,095	1,496,835	60.16	610,286	17,710,772	3.45	473,574	13,005,654	3.64
15 to 20	588,262	425,450	72.32	249,564	7,297,241	3.42	172,665	5,323,023	3.24
20 to 25	264,732	213,829	80.77	161,334	4,758,024	3.39	104,426	3,418,940	3.05
25 to 50	369,939	325,166	87.90	373,703	10,913,850	3.42	207,649	7,460,084	2.78
50 to 100	91,715	88,070	96.03	254,865	5,823,403	4.38	93,790	3,553,809	2.64

100 to 150	14,080	13,811	98.09	99,799	1,615,243	6.18	26,244	923,337	2.84
150 to 200	3,863	3,804	98.47	48,984	651,423	7.52	9,970	377,432	2.64
200 to 500	3,956	3,934	99.44	115,374	1,109,114	10.40	12,440	649,997	1.91
500 to 1,000	536	534	99.63	47,424	357,883	13.25	4,172	231,307	1.80
1,000 & over	244	243	99.59	96,921	498,205	19.45	8,481	353,896	2.40
Total	59,085,182	20,811,422	35.22	5,693,836	145,358,961	3.92	4,079,091	105,663,258	3.86

Note: [a] Negative disposable income.

Table 26.2 Contributions in Taxable and Nontaxable Returns, with Itemized Deductions, 1958

| Adjusted gross income class (thousands of dollars) | Taxable returns | | | Nontaxable returns | | | Ratios of gross contributions to adjusted gross income (percent) | | Ratios of net cost of contribution to disposable income (percent) | |
| | Total number | Itemizing | | Total number | Itemizing | | | | | |
		Number	Percent of total		Number	Percent of total	Tax.	nontax.	Tax.	nontax.
None	—	—	—	384,258	—	—	—	a	—	b
Under 0.6	—	—	—	3,950,030	26,090	0.66	—	21.54	—	b
0.6 to 1.0	1,296,407	67,066	5.17	1,763,840	140,525	7.97	6.76	9.07	6.51	15.56
1.0 to 1.5	2,127,075	228,159	10.73	1,993,201	223,741	11.23	6.42	7.79	6.91	13.12
1.5 to 2.0	2,111,329	389,618	18.45	1,459,207	223,937	15.34	5.94	6.51	6.31	10.63
2.0 to 2.5	2,537,591	584,426	23.03	1,151,627	260,743	22.64	5.45	5.49	5.82	7.96
2.5 to 3.0	2,807,388	744,640	26.52	916,521	217,750	23.76	5.02	5.26	5.34	7.38
3.0 to 3.5	3,062,908	948,514	30.97	679,940	177,866	26.15	4.80	4.88	5.09	7.00
3.5 to 4.0	3,232,549	1,147,777	35.51	497,029	156,572	31.50	4.37	5.06	4.59	7.09
4.0 to 4.5	3,488,552	1,339,914	38.41	256,690	112,984	44.01	4.22	4.91	4.45	6.82
4.5 to 5.0	3,465,499	1,488,801	42.96	174,478	85,478	48.99	3.97	4.45	4.32	6.39
5.0 and over	21,522,836	12,114,799	56.29	206,227	132,022	64.17	3.66	7.04	3.47	12.17
Total	45,652,134	19,053,714	41.74	13,433,048	1,757,708	13.08	3.85	5.80	3.71	8.73

Notes: *a* Negative adjusted gross income.
b Negative disposable income.

sufficient to change the general picture for income classes above $5,000. There are other biases that would tend to strengthen the trend shown: in the absence of data, no adjustment was made to include tax exempt interest and similar items in the disposable income. Nor are capital gains unreported for income tax purposes represented in the figures, whether because the assets are held to the death of the taxpayer or, more relevantly for present purposes, because they are used as the medium in which the gift is made. In this latter increasingly frequent case, not only is the gain not reported, but the full market value of the asset is used as the basis for the charitable deduction, so that the cost of the contribution is even less, on this account, than that shown in the table. While this practice is one well-known to fund raisers, there are no data available on its magnitude. Its prevalence, however, should quiet any qualms that one might have about the inclusion of realized capital gains in a disposable income figure to which the cost of the contribution is to be related.

To what extent does the tax deductibility of gifts stimulate giving? Unfortunately the data available provide very little evidence on this question. At the lower level, we do have separate data for taxable and nontaxable returns at the various income levels, but the effect of selecting only itemized returns is to make the ratio of gifts to disposable income uniformly higher for the nontaxable returns (table 26.2). Also, since the classification of returns is by adjusted gross income, returns in a given income class are more likely to be nontaxable if they have large contributions. The combined effect of these two influences is to mask completely any possible tendency for the tax deduction in taxable returns to induce a higher level of giving. Data for earlier years is available by net income classes, and without the complication of the nonitemizing return; the data for 1940 and 1941 are compared in table 26.3, showing the effect of the introduction of the standard deduction for returns under $3,000; Table 26.4 compares 1943 and 1944, showing the effect of extending the standard deduction privilege to incomes above $3,000. However, the data are open to the interpretation that the taxability of the return merely makes the taxpayer more careful to list all of his contributions, whereas the filer of the nontaxable return may simply not bother to list all of his deductions, even though his contributions may be just as large.

Other somewhat inconclusive evidence may be gleaned from estate tax returns. Here the calculation of the ratio of net cost of contribution to net disposable estate shows a definite though somewhat irregular increase with size of gross estate (tables 26.5 and 26.6). On the whole one would expect that a wealthy taxpayer, anxious to take full advantage of the tax deduction, would do his giving during his lifetime so as to obtain the benefit of the income tax deduction in addition to the avoidance of the estate tax. But of course a similar argument could be made in favor of noncharitable *inter vivos* dispositions to take advantage of the gift tax. In some cases earlier disposition during the lifetime of the donor may run

Table 26.3 *Effects of Taxability and Nonitemizing on Reported Contributions, 1940–1*

Income classes[a] (thousands of dollars)		Thousands of returns				Percentage of returns itemizing		Ratios of gross contributions net income in itemizing returns (percent)	
		Itemizing		Nonitemizing					
		1940	1941	1940	1941	1940	1941	1940	1941
0 to 1	Taxable	529	794	—	894	100	47.0	2.86	4.24
	Nontaxable	1383	1143	—	369	100	75.6	2.67	3.58
	Total	1912	1937	—	1263	100	60.5	2.73	3.90
1 to 2	Taxable	2905	3403	—	3277	100	50.9	2.68	3.21
	Nontaxable	2108	2334	—	2527	100	48.0	1.56	1.93
	Total	5013	5737	—	5804	100	49.7	2.19	2.70
2 to 2.5	Taxable	914	2317	—	1275	100	64.5	2.12	2.41
	Nontaxable	2545	553	—	958	100	36.6	0.92	1.58
	Total	3459	2870	—	2233	100	56.2	1.25	2.25
2.5 to 3	Taxable	912	1695	—	753	100	69.2	2.10	2.33
	Nontaxable	887	150	—	199	100	43.0	1.03	1.54
	Total	1799	1845	—	952	100	66.0	1.56	2.27
3 to 4	Taxable	1014	1644	—	—	100	100	2.08	2.04
	Nontaxable	6	33	—	—	100	100	1.23	1.14
	Total	1020	1677	—	—	100	100	1.93	2.02
4 to 5	Taxable	394	514	—	—	100	100	2.11	2.12
	Nontaxable	[b]	1	—	—	100	100	(1.80)	(1.27)
	Total	394	515	—	—	100	100	2.11	2.12

Notes: [a] Itemizing returns by net income; nonitemizing, by gross income.
[b] Less than 500.

up against the 30 percent limit on the deductibility of charitable contributions in the income tax, whereas no corresponding limit exists for the estate tax. On the whole, the evidence would seem to indicate that, viewed as demand for a commodity whose price is reduced by the tax deductibility, demand for "gross charity" has an elasticity smaller than one, and that, while the deductibility may increase the gross amount of contributions, it does so by less than the tax relief granted. The net effect, therefore, is to decrease the aggregate amount of net sacrifice incurred by the donors, the increase in the proceeds to the beneficiaries being a burden borne entirely by the fisc. One may well question whether it is

Table 26.4 *Effects of Taxability and Nonitemizing on Reported Contributions, 1943–4*

Income classes[a] (thousands of dollars)		Thousands of returns				Percent of returns itemizing		Ratios of gross contributions net income in itemizing returns (percent)	
		Itemizing		Nonitemizing					
		1943	1944	1943	1944	1943	1944	1943	1944
Taxable and nontaxable returns									
Negative	Nontaxable	17	192	—	—	100.0	100.0	—	b
0 to 0.5	Taxable	218	—	—	—	100.0	—	8.33	—
	Nontaxable	644	80	1601	3181	28.7	2.4	4.62	9.70
	Total	862	80	1601	3181	35.0	2.4	5.55	9.70
0.5 to 0.75	Taxable	754	131	1293	914	36.8	6.4	5.06	5.80
	Nontaxable	208	159	376	693	35.6	18.7	2.03	9.43
	Total	962	290	1669	1607	36.6	15.3	4.45	7.46
0.75 to 1.00	Taxable	1106	304	2016	2646	35.4	9.6	4.46	6.57
	Nontaxable	121	103	95	117	56.0	46.8	2.38	6.76
	Total	1227	407	2111	2763	36.7	12.8	4.25	6.61
1.00 to 1.25	Taxable	1332	412	2276	3065	36.9	11.9	4.25	6.54
	Nontaxable	128	66	111	71	53.5	48.2	1.50	8.28
	Total	1460	478	2387	3136	38.0	13.2	4.01	6.72
1.25 to 1.50	Taxable	1467	469	2313	3044	38.8	13.4	3.89	6.30
	Nontaxable	—	95	—	—	—	100.0	—	7.39
	Total	1467	564	2313	3044	38.8	15.6	3.89	6.45
Taxable									
1.50 to 1.75		1517	512	2371	2947	39.0	14.8	3.64	6.15
1.75 to 2.00		1646	523	2135	2880	43.5	15.4	3.38	5.70
2.00 to 2.25		1628	513	1842	2617	46.9	16.4	3.20	5.50
2.25 to 2.50		1579	511	1556	2359	50.4	17.8	1.86	5.33
2.50 to 2.75		1446	519	1289	2268	52.9	18.6	3.09	5.02
2.75 to 3.00		1680	495	1069	2019	61.1	19.7	2.74	4.89
3.0 to 3.5		2991	873	—	3260	100.0	21.1	2.42	4.83
3.5 to 4.0		1685	621	—	2165	100.0	22.3	2.37	4.72
4.0 to 4.5		902	422	—	1356	100.0	23.7	2.32	4.77
4.5 to 5.0		509	273	—	766	100.0	26.3	2.27	4.46
5 to 6		469	305	—	628	100.0	32.7	2.27	4.49
6 to 7		250	174	—	244	100.0	41.6	2.31	4.38
7 to 8		166	97	—	123	100.0	44.1	2.26	4.04

Table 26.4 *(cont.)*

Income classes[a] (thousands of dollars)	Thousands of returns Itemizing		Thousands of returns Nonitemizing		Percent of returns itemizing		Ratios of gross contributions net income in itemizing returns (percent)	
	1943	1944	1943	1944	1943	1944	1943	1944
Taxable								
8 to 9	120	73	—	78	100.0	48.3	2.28	3.93
9 to 10	95	58	—	54	100.0	51.8	2.25	3.85
10 to 15	231	180	—	118	100.0	60.4	2.11	3.52
15 to 20	101	93	—	14	100.0	71.5	2.12	3.21
20 to 25	54	53	—	14	100.0	79.1	2.15	3.07

Notes: [a] For 1943, net income; for 1944, adjusted gross income.
[b] Negative income.

sound public policy to thus subsidize much more heavily the charities favored by the wealthy as distinct from those appealing primarily to the poorer contributors.

Although I have not looked into this matter recently, my impression from earlier surveys is that the United States is almost unique in the degree to which charitable contributions are subsidized through tax exemption. In the United Kingdom, in order to qualify for exemption, the gift must take the form of a transfer of income, in line with the British predilection for considering only more or less repetitive transfers as entitled to consideration under the income tax. In effect, a donor must enter into a covenant with the beneficiary to pay a stated sum regularly for a period of five years or more; when he makes these payments he withholds the normal income tax, and the beneficiary as an exempt entity is entitled to put in a claim for a refund of the tax thus withheld on its income. It is not clear to what extent, if any, this has the psychological effect of inducing the donor to make a net payment of as much as the gross gift would have been without the tax, so making the tax refund a net increment to the resources of the beneficiary, or whether only the same gross gift tends to be made in any case.

The most clear-cut cases of tax-induced philanthropy seem to derive from the estate tax, where the establishment of a philanthropic foundation under friendly control may be the means of avoiding the dissolution or loss of control of a family corporate empire. It has been claimed that this was a significant factor in the creation of the Ford Foundation. While these instances are striking when they occur, they are probably relatively few in number.

Table 26.5 *Progressivity of Net Charitable Bequests, 1959 (money figures in thousands of dollars)*

Gross estate classes	Taxable and nontaxable estates			Nontaxable estates		
		Net cost of charitable bequests			Net cost of charitable bequests	
	Disposable estate (1)	Amount (2)	Percent of disposable estate (3)	Disposable estate (4)	Amount (5)	Percent of disposable estate (6)
0 to 60	450	—	—	450	—	—
60 to 70	365,685	7,138	1.95	250,625	7,033	2.81
70 to 80	426,829	7,671	1.80	192,765	7,069	3.67
80 to 90	403,697	9,303	2.30	183,464	8,353	4.55
90 to 100	386,049	6,534	1.69	180,359	5,560	3.08
100 to 120	694,739	12,846	1.85	315,741	10,399	3.29
120 to 150	825,212	17,218	2.09	153,383	12,914	8.42
150 to 200	928,677	22,930	2.47	44,413	16,805	37.84
200 to 300	1,101,702	30,580	2.78	29,005	17,784	61.31
300 to 500	1,062,246	41,110	3.87	22,598	19,233	85.11
500 to 1,000	1,111,714	57,663	5.19	19,051	16,212	83.13
1,000 to 2,000	714,490	44,834	6.27	8,737	7,544	86.35
2,000 to 3,000	280,095	35,316	12.61	5,191	3,748	72.20
3,000 to 5,000	224,218	28,731	12.81	2,421	2,382	98.39
5,000 to 10,000	205,581	22,705	11.04	4,607	1,707	37.05
10,000 to 20,000	131,592	12,466	9.47	—	—	—
20,000 and up	68,793	23,283	33.85	—	—	—
Total[a]	9,068,299	516,447	5.695	1,435,603	159,536	11.11

Note: [a] Calculated from average ratios.

If there were a substantial response of philanthropic contributions to the inducement of income tax deductibility it would seem that it would show up in a comparison of data for 1930–1, when the top combined normal and surtax rates were 25 per cent on incomes over $100,000, and 1932–3 when the rates at these income levels were more than doubled, to from 56 percent to 63 percent. But examination of this material, as presented in table 26.7, indicates no such responsiveness.

Table 26.6 Effects of Classification Basis on Charitable Bequest Ratios, 1959

| | Classification by net estate[a] | | Classification by gross estate | | | |
| Net estate classes (thousands of dollars) (1) | Charitable bequests as percentage of gross estate (2) | Average gross estate (thousands of dollars) (3) | Gross estate classes (thousands of dollars) (4) | Charitable bequests as percentage of gross estate | | |
				All estates (5)	Taxable estates (6)	Nontaxable estates (7)
Under 60	—	52.0	Under 60	—	—	—
			60 to 70	1.78	0.09	2.51
			70 to 80	1.64	0.26	3.25
			80 to 90	2.11	0.44	4.08
			90 to 100	1.55	0.49	2.77
60 to 80	1.97	102.5	100 to 120	1.70	0.69	2.96
80 to 100	3.65	132.3	120 to 150	1.92	0.71	6.90
100 to 150	2.82	173.5	150 to 200	2.34	0.80	26.49
150 to 200	3.76	248.9	200 to 300	2.86	1.38	46.91
200 to 300	3.28	340.3 }				
300 to 400	3.54	486.1 }	300 to 500	3.91	2.31	66.19
400 to 500	5.22	633.4 }				
500 to 600	11.40	801.7 }	500 to 1,000	5.44	4.06	73.13
600 to 700	4.81	907.8 }				
700 to 800	11.54	1,105.4 }				
800 to 900	4.59	1,147.5 }	1,000 to 2,000	6.77	5.82	72.55
900 to 1,000	3.97	1,250.5 }				
1,000 to 2,000	7.26	1,818.1 }				
2,000 to 3,000	13.76	3,425.5	2,000 to 3,000	14.07	12.97	76.82
			3,000 to 5,000	15.16	14.17	92.12

3,000 to 4,000	5.70	5,129.0 ⎫			
4,000 to 5,000	28.07	8,350.0 ⎬			
5,000 to 7,000	8.05	7,799.0 ⎭	5,000 to 10,000	15.36	14.84	48.68
7,000 to 10,000	7.08	11,847.0 ⎫			
10,000 to 20,000	4.06	19,246.0 ⎬	10,000 to 20,000	17.20	17.20	—
20,000 and over	0.16	31,676.0	20,000 and over	52.03	52.03	—
Total	5.10	259.5	Total	5.74	5.10	9.66

Note. [a] Taxable estates only.

Table 26.7 *Effects of Rate Increases on Contribution Ratios, 1930–3*

Net income classes (thousands of dollars)	Marginal tax rate, percent		Gross contributions as a percentage of net income				Net cost of contributions as a percentage of disposable income			
	1930–1	1932–3	1930	1931	1932	1933	1930	1931	1932	1933
100 to 150	25	56	3.68	4.41	4.87	3.60	3.01	3.86	6.02	2.81
150 to 200	25	57	3.86	4.26	5.75	3.73	3.25	4.02	6.08	3.77
200 to 250	25	58	3.89	4.87	6.04	3.92	3.28	4.56	16.34	3.24
250 to 300	25	58	4.01	4.45	4.72	3.96	3.35	4.04	5.87	2.88
300 to 400	25	59	4.29	5.03	7.37	3.44	3.53	4.55	5.89	4.08
400 to 500	25	60	4.48	5.10	6.40	3.98	3.74	4.28	6.62	3.13
500 to 750	25	61	4.39	5.79	7.00	3.97	3.61	4.95	*a*	2.65
750 to 1,000	25	62	4.90	6.28	5.37	5.62	3.98	6.60	4.45	2.90
Over 1,000	25	63	6.86	6.24	8.67	3.58	5.62	5.72	9.53	2.34
Over 500	25	62±	6.01	6.14	7.29	3.99	4.92	5.63	12.50	2.52
Over 100	25	59±	4.67	5.11	6.04	3.80	4.13	4.62	9.07	2.93
All returns			2.72	2.92	3.30	2.68				

Note: *a* Negative disposable income due to large capital losses.

External Economies and Diseconomies in Fund Raising

The pursuit of the contributor's dollar has obvious external economies and diseconomies not greatly dissimilar to those encountered in any kind of selling activity. There is, on the one hand, the likelihood that funds obtained through appeal may impinge on the funds available for other contributions, and on the other, that appeals may reinforce each other by enhancing the general level of giving. It is hard to determine just what would be the socially optimal proportion of effort to put into fund-raising activities. Aside from curbing the more extreme practices that take undue advantage of psychological predilections or that verge on fraud, it is not clear just what modifying influences would, on balance, be in the public interest.

Contributions and Macroeconomic Equilibrium

There is a sense in which the claim of the advertising industry that it is a great creator of aggregate demand has a counterpart in the soliciting of charitable contributions: to the extent that they are made out of savings and that the proceeds are immediately disbursed, the contributions tend to be a stimulus to the economy. Of course this stimulus will be desirable or undesirable according to whether the economy is or is not suffering from underemployment. If contributions were relatively higher in periods of depression than in prosperity, as seems to some slight extent to be the case, they would constitute a stabilizing factor in the economy. It may be doubted, however, whether this is more true of charitable contributions than of many forms of personal expenditure.

On the other hand to the extent that charitable gifts or bequests are made in the form of endowment funds, there may be a depressing effect on the economy; the gift may have the effect of reducing the level of expenditure of the donor or of those who would have been his beneficiaries in the absence of the charitable bequest. Probably this effect is not large enough to be a primary concern.

Summary

The main suggestion that emerges from the above discussion is that the methods and degree of public support to privately controlled philanthropy needs to be thoroughly reexamined. Complete absence of any subsidy of religion by the state is a gross fiction. Tax exemption, particularly the deduction under the income tax, seems to be much more an expression of the general predilection in this country for privately organized and controlled philanthropy rather than a significant stimulus to *net* giving. A concession that seemed moderate enough when originally introduced has grown and changed shape with increases in tax rates and the complexities of the law, so as to produce results that are not only bizarre on occasion, but in their overall pattern seem to conform to no defensible social policy. The unacknowledged and haphazard array of subsidies that result from present special tax privileges call for replacement with more uniform and explicit arrangements that can be brought into line with desirable public policy.

Bibliography of William Vickrey

Principal Fields of Interest 323 National Taxation; 613 Public Utilities.
Publications *Books*: 1. *Agenda for Progressive Taxation* (Ronald Press, 1949, 1971); 2. *The Revision of the Rapid Transit Fare Structure of the City of New York* (Fin. Project, Mayor's Comm. Management Survey, 1952); 3. *Microstatics* (Harcourt Brace & World, 1964); 4. *Metastatics and Macroeconomics* (Harcourt Brace & World, 1964).

Articles: 1. "Utility, strategy, and social decision rules", *QJE*, 74, Nov. 1960, repr. in *Readings in Welfare Economics*, eds. K. J. Arrow and T. Scitovsky (Richard D. Irwin, 1969); 2. "Counter-speculation, auctions, and competitive sealed tenders", *J. Fin*, 16, 1961; 3. "Responsive pricing of utility services", *Bell JE*, 2, 1971; 4. "The city as a firm", in *The Economics of Public Services*, eds. M. S. Feldstein and R. P. Inman (Macmillan, 1977); 5. "Optimal transit subsidy policy", *Transportation*, 9, 1980.

Principal Contributions Progressive taxation reform proposals: cumulative averaging assessment, bequeathing power succession tax, age difference graduation of succession taxes, taxable tax credit for government interest, rationalization of undistributed profits tax, of earned income credit. Theory and application of marginal cost pricing: responsive pricing, urban congestion charges, simulated futures markets in airline reservation, impacts of inflation on utility regulation, pricing and fare collection methods. Public choice theory: demand revealing procedures, auctions and bidding theory, self-policing imputation sets in game theory, social welfare functions. Land value taxation: short- versus long-term impacts and relationships with marginal cost pricing.

Who's Who in Economics (1986), p. 858.

William Vickrey:
Classified and Commented Bibliography

Entries were divided into four sections: Books and Monographs, References, Other Publications, and Unpublished, and entered chronologically within each. The works are further categorized by area of focus using the Key below.

Works with a reference code, consisting of a letter, denoting the category, and an identification number, may be ordered by writing to Professor Richard Arnott, Department of Economics, Boston College, Chestnut Hill, MA 02167, USA. Please include the reference code, title, and return address when ordering. A prepaid charge of $3.00 per item, in US funds, is requested to cover copying and mailing costs.

Key: AV   Averaging
     EP   Efficient Pricing
     GA   Games & Auctions
     GX   Government Expenditure
     MA   Macroeconomics
     MI   Microeconomics
     PC   Public Choice
     PF   Public Finance
     PL   Planning
     PW   Political Economy and Welfare
     ST   Statistics
     TR   Transportation
     TX   Taxation

Books and Monographs

TX   *Agenda for Progressive Taxation*. New York, Ronald Press, 1947, pp. xi–496.

Translated in part and published serially in, *Japanese Tax Journal*, as background material relating to the philosophy of the Shoup Mission report.

Reprinted, with an introduction, in *Reprints of Economic Classics*, Clifton, NJ, Augustus Kelley, 1972.

Doctoral dissertation, presenting a comprehensive set of proposals for tax reform. Still pertinent, in spite of the many intervening "reforms."

TR   *The Revision of the Rapid Transit Fare Structure of the City of New York*, Technical Monograph No. 3, Finance Project, Mayor's Committee for Management Survey of the City of New York, 1952, mimeo.

An analysis of various transit fare structures and their consequences emphasizing a scheme for varying fares from 5 to 25 cents, according to time, origin, and destination, including an electromechanical method of implementation.

TR   *Subway Fare Decoder Circuits*. Technical Monograph, No. 6, Mayor's committee for Management Survey of the City of New York, 1952, mimeo.

The details of the electromechanical implementation. Now made obsolete by magnetic card and computer technique.

TR   *Adapting Subway Services to Changing Traffic Patterns*. Technical Monograph No. 5, Mayor's Committee for Management Survey of the City of New York. April, 1952, mimeo.

Skip-stop scheduling through critical bottleneck stations, trains longer than platforms, etc. Never implemented, but still pertinent.

TX   *The Fiscal System of the Federal District of Venezuela*. With Carl S. Shoup and C. Lowell Harriss, Baltimore, Garamond Press, 1960, pp. xii, 162.

Also in Spanish: *Estudio del sistema fiscal del Distrito Federal, Venezuela*, Gobernacion del Distrito Federal, 31 July, 1959, 170 pp.

Survey and recommendation.

MI   *Microstatics*. New York, Harcourt, Brace and World, 1964, pp. x, 408 (Spanish translation).

A graduate-level textbook. Reprinted once, but apparently thought too difficult for widespread use and not kept in print. Contained some frustrating errors.

MA   *Metastatics and Macroeconomics*, New York, Harcourt, Brace and World, 1964, pp. x, 314.

TX   *The Tax System of Liberia*, with Carl S. Shoup, Douglas Dosser, and Rudolph G. Penner, Columbia University Press, 1970, pp. xiii, 189.

Survey of recommendations.

Reviews

R–1	TX	Kenneth James Curran, *Excess Profits Taxation*, in *Columbia Law Review*, May, 1944, pp. 463–5.
R–2	TX	Harold Groves, "Production, Jobs and Taxes: Postwar Revision of the Federal Tax System to Help Achieve Higher Production and More Jobs," in *Journal of Political Economy*, 53, 1945, pp. 92–3.
R–3	TX	Shirras and Rostas, "The Burden of British Taxation," in *Journal of Political Economy*, Dec., 1945, pp. 181–3.
R–4	MA	Horst Mendershausen, "Changes in Income During the Great Depression," in *Journal of Political Economy*, 55, 1947, pp. 490–1.
R–5	MA	Shoup, Friedman, and Mack, "Taxing to Prevent Inflation," in *Journal of Political Economy*, Dec., 1945, p. 381.
R–6	PF	Allen and Brownlee, "Economics of Public Finance," in *American Economic Review*, March, 1948, pp. 172–5.
R–7	TX	Tax Institute, "How Should Corporations be Taxed?," in *American Economic Review*, March, 1948, pp. 175–7.
R–8	TX	Henry C. Simons, "Federal Tax Reform," in *National Tax Journal*, June, 1950, pp. 187–90.
R–9	MI	Michel Brodsky and Pierre Rocher, "L'economie politique mathematique," in *American Economic Review*, 40, 1950, pp. 424–5.
R–10	MA	Kenneth Boulding, "A Reconstruction of Economics," in *American Economic Review*, 41, Sept., 1951, pp. 671–6.
R–11	TX	L. Seltzer, S. Goldsmith, and M. Slade Kendrick, "The Nature and Tax Treatment of Capital Gains and Losses," in *Accounting Review*, 27, April, 1952, pp. 267–9.
R–12	MA	Hollis B. Chenery and Paul G. Ciaro, "Interindustry Economics," in *Management Science*, 7(2), Jan., 1961, pp. 189–91.
R–13	TX	US Treasury Department, Tax Advisory Staff of the Secretary, "Federal Income Tax Treatment of Capital Gains and Losses," in *Accounting Review*, 27, April, 1952, pp. 267–9.
R–14	MA	Simon Kuznets, "Economic Change: Selected Essays in Business Cycles, National Income and Economic Growth," and Simon Kuznets and Elizabeth Jenks, "Shares of Upper Income Groups in Income and Savings," in *Political Science Quarterly*, 69, June, 1954, pp. 296–9.

R–15   PW   Milton Friedman, "Essays in Positive Economics," in *American Economic Review*, 44, June, 1954, pp. 397–400.
               "Correction," in *AER*, 45, Dec., 1954, pp. 937–8.
               A correction of the review of Friedman's work.

R–16   TX   Paul Randolph, "Taxation in the United States," in *Political Science Quarterly*, 70, June, 1955, pp. 291–2.

R–17   EP   Burnham P. Beckwith, "Marginal Cost Price–Output Control," *Kyklos*, 1955, pp. 437–9.

R–18   TX   Nicholas Kaldor, "An Expenditure Tax," in *British Tax Journal*, 1(1), June, 1956.

R–19   PW   Conference of the Universities National Bureau Committee on Economic Research, "Business Concentration and Price Policy" in *Accounting Review*, 31, April, 1956, pp. 337–8.

R–20   PW   Albert Ando, Franklin M. Fisher, and Herbert A. Simon, "Essays on the Structure of Social Science Models," in *American Economic Review*, 54(6), Dec., 1964, pp. 1130–1.

R–21   PW   Nicholas Kaldor, "Essays in Economic Policy," in *Economica*, May, 1966, pp. 235–7.

R–22   PW   Ralph L. Nelson, "Economic Factors in the Growth of Corporate Giving," in *Journal of Economic Literature*, 1971, pp. 1227–9.

R–23   TR   Ralph Turvey, "Economic Analysis and Public Enterprises," in *Journal of Business of the University of Chicago*, 46, Jan., 1972, pp. 103–5.

R–24   EP   Gabriel Roth, "Paying for Roads: The Economics of Traffic Congestion," in *The Antitrust Bulletin*, 19(3), Fall, 1974, pp. 631–42.

R–25   PW   George Stigler, "The Citizen and the State: Essays on Regulation," in *The Antitrust Bulletin*, 23, Spring, 1978, pp. 257–61.

R–26   PF   Richard M. Bird, "Charging for Public Services: A New Look at an Old Idea," in *Finanzarchiv*, 36(3), 1978, pp. 560–1.

R–27   TX   Hiromitsu Ishi, *The Japanese Tax System*, Oxford University Press, 1989, in *The Journal of Economic Literature*, 29(3), Sept., 1991, pp. 1193–4.

Other Publications

O–1   PL   *Patterns of Resource Use* (Contributor). National Resources Committee, Washington, 1938.
Some early, simple-minded, econometric models of various industries.

O–2   TX   "A Comparison of Aggregate Burdens of Federal Income Tax and State Income Tax in 11 Selected States," with Carl Shoup and Bernard L. Shimberg, in *Studies in Current Tax Problems*, Twentieth Century Fund, 1938, pp. 523–961.
Effects of combining federal and state income taxes.

O–3   TX   "Estimating Income and Estate Tax Yields," with Susan S. Burr, Ibid., pp. 141–238.
Some procedures and short-cuts for dealing with statistics of income data: now obsolete.

O–4   TX   "Averaging of Income for Income Tax Purposes," *Journal of Political Economy*, 47, June, 1939, pp. 379–97.
Reprinted: *Readings in the Economics of Taxation*, Carl S. Shoup and Richard A. Musgrave, Eds., Irwin 1959, pp. 77–92.
Developed as a result of work on the treatment of capital gains under Carl Shoup for the US Treasury. Includes a survey and critique of previous averaging methods and the original development of the cumulative averaging method, later included in "Agenda." A master stroke of simplification and tax neutralization that never caught on. See "Cumulative Averaging After Thirty Years."

O–5   PL   *The Structure of the American Economy, Part I. Basic Characteristics* (contributor); *Appendix 2, Wholesale Price Data*, National Resources Committee, pp. 186–204.
Statistical analysis related to Gardner Means' thesis of differential behavior of prices as a factor in business cycles.

O–6   TX   "The Effects of the Federal Revenue Acts of 1938, 1939 and 1940 on the Realization of Gains and Losses on Securities (Comment)," *Journal of the American Statistical Association*, 36, Sept., 1941, pp. 431–3.
A critique pointing out the failure to allow for timing shifts induced by anticipation of tax changes. Current Treasury analyses still perpetrate the same errors.

O–7   TX   "The Spending Tax in Peace and War," *Columbia Law Review*, March, 1943, pp. 165–75.
Special advantages of a progressive expenditure tax as an instrument of war finance. Response by Irving Fisher.

O–8   TX   "Insurance Under the Federal Income Tax," *Yale Law Journal*, 52, June, 1943, pp. 554–85.
Non-neutrality aspects of the individual income tax and how to deal with them. Still pertinent. Largely included in "Agenda."

O–9   TX   "An Integrated Succession Tax," *Taxes*, 22, Aug., 1944, pp. 368–74.
The bequeathing power method of achieving neutrality among methods of devolution. Quite complicated and still fails to deal with interjurisdictional transfers. Included in "Agenda."

O–10   TX   "The Rationalization of Successive Taxation," *Econometrica*, 15, July–Oct., 1944, pp. 215–36.
The mathematical treatment of bequeathing power. Included in "Agenda."

O–11   TX   "A Reasonable Undistributed Profits Tax," *Taxes*, February, 1945, pp. 122–7.
An attempt at an approximate offset to the deferral of individual income tax involved in undistributed profits. The proposal has been largely ignored, but is still pertinent.

O–12   TX   "The Effect of Averaging on the Cyclical Sensitivity of the Yield of the Income Tax," *Journal of Political Economy*, 53, Sept., 1945, pp. 275–7.
Countercyclical properties of cumulative averaging. Not very important in the current context, but seemed more relevant when simple Keynesian analysis was dominant.

O–13   PW   "Measuring Marginal Utility by Reactions to Risk," *Econometrica*, 13, Oct., 1945, pp. 319–33.
The maximization of expected utility hypothesis. Independent development of essentially the same concept as that in von-Neumann and Morgenstern's "Theory of Games and Economic Behavior," but somewhat more simple-minded and without the axiomatic underpinnings.

O–14   MA   "Fiscal Policy in Prosperity and Depression: Discussion," *Proceedings of the American Economic Association*, 60, Dec., 1947, pp. 409–16.

| | | Thoughts on the relation of simple Keynesianism to the choice between aggregate savings and appropriate consumption under full employment, and implications for the rate of economic growth. |

O–15   EP   "Some Objections to Marginal Cost Pricing," *Journal of Political Economy*, 56, June, 1948, pp. 218–38.

Answers to the objections. An early discussion.

O–16   TX   "The Effects of Integration of Corporate and Individual Income Taxes on Business," *Proceedings of the National Tax Association*, 46, 17–20 Nov., 1947, pp. 179–88.

Reprint from the proceedings, pp. 3–12.

O–17   MA   "Limitations of Keynesian Economics," *Social Research*, 15, Dec., 1948, pp. 403–16.

I suspect that my thoughts on this subject have changed considerably.

O–18   TX   "Some Limits to the Income Elasticity of Income Tax Yields," *Review of Economics and Statistics*, 31, May, 1949, pp. 140–4.

For a Pareto distribution of income in the upper brackets the built-in countercyclical properties of the income tax are relatively constant, independently of the degree of progression. Interest in this topic has waned.

O–19   ST   "Resource Distribution Patterns and the Classification of Families," *Studies in Income and Wealth*, 10, pp. 266–97 (reply, 324–9), National Bureau of Economic Research, 1949.

The meanings of statistics on the size distribution of income and expenditure is significantly more affected and often biased by methods of classification and the use of data collected on an annual basis. This problem seems largely to have been ignored, but is still pertinent.

O–20   ST   "International Comparisons of Real National Income: A Note on Methods, by Hans Staehle: Comment," *Studies in Income and Wealth*, 11, pp. 271–2, National Bureau of Economic Research, 1949.

Some fairly esoteric details.

O–21   TX   *Report on Japanese Taxation*. Joint Author; The Shoup Tax Mission, General Headquarters, Supreme Commander for the Allied Powers, Tokyo, 1949.

Issued in bilingual format on facing pages, 4 volumes pp. 227, 31, 30, 44, 68 (x2).

O–22   TX   Second Report on Japanese Taxation, Joint Author, The
              Shoup Tax Mission, Japan Tax Association, 1950.
              A new translation of the two reports, together with a
              chronology of the first mission, was prefaced with a
              preface by Carl Shoup in 1985, pp. 471.

O–23   PW   "Ethics and Economics: An exchange of questions between
              Economists and Philosophy," *Goals of Economic Life*,
              Arthur D. Ward, Ed., pp. 148–77. Sponsored by the
              National Council of Churches, 1950.
              Reprinted in *Economic Justice*, Edwin S. Phelps, Ed.,
              Baltimore, Penguin, 1973, pp. 35–62.
              Boulding's comment:

                      Oh where does economics tend
                      When ends are means and means are end?
                      Yet one Conclusion soon is fashioned:
                      Virtue is scarce and must be rationed.

              A fairly basic disquisition.

O–24   MA   "Stability Through Inflation," *Post-Keynesian Economics*,
              M. Murihara, Ed., Rutger's University Press, 1954, pp.
              89–122.
              Heavily Mathematical

O–25   EP   "The Economizing of Curb Parking Space," *Traffic Engin-
              eering Magazine*, Nov., 1954.
              An early approach to traffic problems by the application of
              short-run marginal social cost concepts.

O–26   TX   "Rate Reduction or Increased Exemptions: The Economics
              of the Question," *Proceedings of the National Tax Asso-
              ciation*, 1954, pp. 268–95. Reprint from the proceedings,
              pp. 1–8.
              Keynesian analysis applied to forms of progression.

O–27   EP   "A Proposal for Revising New York's Subway Fare Struc-
              ture," *Journal of the Operations Research Society of
              America*, 3, Feb., 1955, pp. 38–68.
              Reprinted as "Revising New York's Subway Fare Struc-
              ture," *Operations Research for Management*, Vol. II,
              Joseph F. McClosky and John Coppinger, Eds., Johns
              Hopkins 1956, pp. 101–33.
              A revised and condensed version of the Mayor's Commit-
              tee monograph.

O–28   EP   "Pricing in Transport and Public Utilities, Some Implications
              for Marginal Cost Pricing for Public Utilities," *American*

Economic Review, May, 1955, pp. 605–20.

A further development of marginal-cost pricing theory.

O–29   TX   "L'imposition des plus-values de capital," *Revue de Science Financiere*, 48, 1956, pp. 423–37.

Another critique of special concessions to capital gains.

O–30   TX   "Expenditure, Capital Gains, and the Basis of Progressive Taxation," *The Manchester School*, Jan., 1957, pp. 1–25.

Excerpted in *Public Finance*, R.W. Houghton, Ed., Penguin Modern Economics Readings, 1970, pp. 117–28.

Reprinted: "Ausgaben, Kapitalgewinne and die Gundlage Progressive Besteuerung," in *Finanztheory*, Horst Claus Recktenwald, Herausgeber, Köln, Kiepenhauer and Witech, 1969, pp. 425–33.

More on the capital gains issue.

O–31   MA   "A Note on Micro- and Macroeconomics," *Common Frontiers of the Social Science*, Mirra Komarovsky, Ed., Glencoe, Ill., Free Press, 1957, pp. 376–82.

O–32   TR   "Transit Finance: A Review," *Proceedings of the Fifty-First National Tax Conference*, Philadelphia, 27–31 October, 1958, pp. 551–8.

O–33   MA   "The Optimum Trend of Prices," *Southern Economic Journal*, 25, Jan., 1959, pp. 315–26.

O–34   GA   "Self Policing Properties of Certain Imputation Sets," in *Contributions to the Theory of Games IV*, A.W. Turner and R. W. Luce, Eds., Princeton University Press, 1959, pp. 213–46.

An attempt to develop a realistic rationale for the von Neumann and Morgenstern concept of "solution." Quite esoteric. It never caught on, and game theory proceeded in a different direction.

O–35   MA   "Defense Spending and the Business Cycle," *Challenge*, April, 1958, pp. 24–8.

Defense may provide a pretext for anti-depression deficit spending, but is not the only way to deal with the problem.

O–36   EP   Statement on the Pricing of Urban Street Use. *Hearings: US Congress, Joint Committee on Metropolitan Washington Problems*, 11 Nov., 1959, pp. 466–77.

The original proposal for finely adjusted congestion pricing with automatic vehicle identifier (AVI) units and roadside scanning points. Never fully appreciated, generally regarded as political poison, although almost adopted recently in Hong Kong. The subject is currently (1993) enjoying a revival of interset with Charles A. Donze and Earl Hilburn of Link Aviation and Paul A. Bach of Remington Rand Univac.

O–37   TR EP   "Reaching a Balance Between Mass Transit and Provision for Individual Automobile Traffic (July 1958)," Ibid., pp. 478–87.

Relations between transit fares, congestion charges, and parking fees.

O–38   TR EP   "Construction of Tentative Fare Structures for Washington, D.C. Regional Rapid Transit System," Ibid., pp. 487–507.

With Lyle Fitch and Sumner Myers.

O–39   PW   "Utility, Strategy and Social Decision Rules," *Quarterly Journal of Economics*, 74, Nov., 1960, pp. 507–35.

Reprinted in part in *Readings in Welfare Economics*, K. Arrow and T. Scitovsky, Eds., Irwin, 1969, pp. 456–61.

Arrow's Impossibility Theorem.

O–40   MI   "Resource Price Trends and Resource Scarcity; a Comment on the paper by H.J. Barnett and Chandler Morse," Resources for the Future, 1960.

Relations between price trends and scarcity under perfect geological information, competition, and constant technology, along the lines pioneered by Harold Hotelling. Unrealistic.

O–41   TX   "Can Excises Lower Prices?," *Essays in Economics and Econometrics*, R. W. Pfouts, Ed., University of North Carolina Press, 1960, pp. 165–77.

Explication and examples of the Edgeworth Taxation Paradox under competitive conditions, according to possibilities revealed by Hotelling.

O–42   ST   Statement for the Subcommittee on Economic Statistics Regarding Cost of Living Indexes. *Hearings on Government Price Statistics*, US Congress, Joint Economic Committee, May, 1961, pp. 742–5.

O–43   PC   "On the Prevention of Gerrymandering," *Political Science Quarterly*, 76, March, 1961, pp. 105–10.

The necessity of using a randomized computer process if gerrymandering is to be prevented.

O–44   GA   "Counterspeculation, Auctions, and Competitive Sealed Tenders," *Journal of Finance*, 16, March, 1961, pp. 8–37.

A much-cited article, after ten years of dormancy, attempting to develop methods of assuring Pareto-efficiency, later expanded into the concept of demand revealing procedures.

O–45 MA "The Burden of Public Debt; Comment," *American Economic Review*, 51, March, 1961, pp. 132–7.

Reprinted in *Public Debt and Future Generations*, James Ferguson, Ed., University of North Carolina Press, 1964. Superceded by later analysis.

O–46 PC "Risk, Utility and Social Policy," *Social Research*, Summer, 1961, pp. 205–17.

Expected utility maximization for individuals related to aggregate utility maximization as a social decision-making rule. A follow-up to "Measuring Marginal Utility . . . (1945)."

O–47 TX "Electronic Data Processing and Tax Policy," *National Tax Journal*, 14, Sept., 1961, pp. 271–85.

May help, but only slightly, to make cumulative assessment easier to administer.

O–48 PW "Welfare Economics," *Encyclopedia Americana*, 1961.

O–49 ST MI MA "Econometrics," *Collier's Encyclopedia*, 1961.

O–50 MA "One Economist's View of Philanthropy," *Philanthropy and Public Policy*, Frank G. Dickinson, Ed., NBER, New York, 1962, pp. 31–56.

O–51 GA "Auctions and Bidding Games," *Recent Advances in Game Theory*, The Princeton University Conference, 1962, pp. 15–27.

Further mathematical analysis of various types of auction in terms of game theory, in relation to Pareto efficiency.

O–52 GX "A Proposal for Student Loans," *Economics of Higher Education*, Selma J. Mushkin, Ed., Dept. of Health, Education and Welfare, Office of Education, 1962, pp. 268–80.

Equity investment in education, repayable on a graduated basis out of earnings attributable to education.

O–53 PW "Notes of the Macroeconomics of Disarmament," *Disarmament Journal*, March, 1962, pp. 3–7.

Disarmament, unemployment, and growth.

O–54 MA "Fiscal Strategies for Shifting $22 Billions to Civilian Economy," *A Strategy for American Security: An Alternative to the 1964 Military Budget*, Seymour Melman, Ed., New York, Lee Offset, Inc., pp. 21–5.

Various government and private uses for released resources.

O–55   EP TR   "Pricing in Urban and Suburban Transport," *American Economic Review*, 52(2), May, 1963, pp. 452–65.

Reprinted in, *Public Policy and the Modern Corporation*, Grunwald and Bass, Eds., Appleton Century Crofts, 1966, pp. 168–81.

Reprinted in, *Readings in Urban Transportation*, George M. Smerk, Ed., Indiana University Press, 1968, pp. 120–33.

Reprinted in, *The Modern City: Readings in Urban Economics*, David Rasmussen and Charles Haworth, Eds., Harper and Row, 1973, pp. 179–89.

A litany of inefficiencies related to departures of prices from short-run marginal social cost.

O–56   TX   "General and Specific Financing of Urban Services," *Public Expenditure Decisions in the Urban Community*, Howard G. Shaller, Ed., Resources for the Future, 1963, pp. 62–90.

Reprinted in part in *Readings in Welfare Economics*, Arrow and Scitovsky, Eds., Irwin, 1969, pp. 561–87.

Reprinted in, *Urban and Regulatory Economics Perspectives for Public Action*, J. E. Haring, Ed., Boston, Houghton Mifflin, 1972, pp. 234–58.

Original Draft.

Application of marginal-cost pricing and the financing of deficits. Redistribution of federal income tax revenues to jurisdictions that financed the taxpayers' education.

O–57   GX EP   "Comment on 'Civil Aviation Expenditures'" by Gary Fromm, *Measuring Benefits of Government Investments*, Robert Dorfman, Ed., The Brookings Institution, 1965, pp. 222–6.

O–58   PW   "Social Psychology and Economics," *Perspectives in Social Psychology*, Otto Klineberg and Christie, Eds., Rinehart and Winston, 1965, pp. 109–12.

O–59   EP TR   "Pricing as a Tool in the Coordination of Local Transportation," *Transportation Economics*, National Bureau of Economic Research, 1965, pp. 275–96.

Intermodal competition and substitution in terms of marginal-cost pricing.

O–60   EP TR   "Optimization of Traffic and Facilities," *Journal of Trans-*

		port Economics and Policy, 1(2), Jan., 1967, pp. 123–36. Marginal-cost pricing for control of congestion and optimal timing of construction.
O–61	MA	"Economic Criteria for Optimum Rates of Depletion," *Extractive Resources and Taxation*, Mason Gaffney, Ed., Milwaukee, University of Wisconsin Press, 1967, pp. 315–30. Implications of the perfect information model.
O–62	MA	"Comment on Dhrymes, Kurz and Anderson" (re produced durables), *Determinants of Investment Behavior*, R. Ferber, Ed., National Bureau of Economic Research, 1967, pp. 477–80.
O–63	PW	"The World Poverty Gap," *New University Thought*, 5(1,2), 1967, pp. 52–61. Some general observations.
O–64	EP TR	"Congestion Charges and Welfare: Some Answers to Sharp's Doubts," *Journal of Transportation Economics and Policy*, 2(1), Jan., 1968, pp. 107–18. A point-by-point defense of congestion charges.
O–65	PW	"Dupuit, Jules," *Encyclopedia of the Social Sciences*, 12, pp. 308–11.
O–66	EP	"Prices: Pricing Policies," *Encyclopedia of the Social Sciences*, 12, 1968, pp. 457–64.
O–67	TX	"The Problem of Progression," *University of Florida Law Review*, 20, June, 1968, pp. 437–50. Ways to measure progression and their biases. A discussion based on "Resource Distribution Patterns . . ." (1949).
O–68	TR	"Externalities in Public Utility Use: The Case of Highway Accidents," *Conference on the Economics of Public Output*, Universities-National Bureau Committee for Economic Research, April, 1968. Preliminary paper, pp. 1–19. Marginal costs in relation to insurance, traffic density, tort law, and administrative costs.
O–69	EP	"The Pricing of Tomorrow's Utility Services," *The New Economics of Regulated Industries: Rate Making in a Dynamic Economy*, Joseph E. Haring, Ed., Los Angeles Economics Research Centrer, Occidental College, 1968, mimeo, pp. 137–49. Marginal-cost pricing, again.

O–70   EP PW   "Automobile Accidents, Tort Law, Externalities, and Insurance, an Economist's Critique," *Safety: Law and Contemporary Problems*, 33(3), Summer, 1968, pp. 464–87.
Original paper, pp. 1–39.
Reviewed in, *Traffic Systems Reviews and Abstracts*, April, 1970, #T–0969 EF.
More on the inefficiencies involved in current methods of dealing with accidents.

O–71   EP TR   "Congestion Theory and Transport Investment," *American Economic Review*, 59, May, 1969, pp. 251–60.
Reprinted in, *Transportation*, pp. 119–32.
Reviewed in, *Traffic Systems Reviews and Abstracts*, August, 1970, #T–1072 EF.
Optimal investment, with and without congestion pricing.

O–72   TR EP   "Current Issues in Transportation," *Contemporary Economic Issues*, Neil Chamberlain, Ed., Irwin, 1969, pp. 185–240.
Revised edition, 1973, pp. 219–99.
A wide-ranging discussion.

O–73   PW   "Moral Issues in United States Tax Policy," with Byron L. Johnson, *Social Policy*, Nov., 1969, pp. 6–26.
Progression, equity, and incentives.

O–74   TX   "Tax Simplification Through Cumulative Averaging," *Law and Contemporary Problems: Tax Simplification and Reform*, 34 (4), Autumn, 1969, pp. 736–50.
Cumulative averaging viewed as a master stroke of simplification, in spite of being reportedly rejected out of hand as too complicated.

O–75   TX   "The Impact on Land Values of Taxing Buildings," *Proceedings of the 62nd National Tax Conference*, Boston, Sept. 29–Oct. 3, 1969, National Tax Association, Columbus, Ohio, pp. 86–89.
A concentric model in which taxing buildings lowers land values at the centre and increases them in the periphery.

O–76   PW   "Externalities in Urban Development," *Proceedings of the American Real Estate and Urban Economics Association*, 1969, pp. 3–19.
An initial foreshadowing of the thesis relating urban land rents to subsidies needed for marginal-cost pricing.

O–77   TX   "Defining Land Values for Taxation Purposes," *The Assessment of Land Value*, Daniel M. Holland, Ed., A Symposium sponsored by the Committee on Taxation, Resources and Economic Development, Madison, London, University of Wisconsin Press, 1970, pp. 25–36.

Practical and conceptual problems in assessing land values; the notion of a standard condition; problems of parcels in substantially substandard condition; effects of assembly or subdivision, internalization of externalities in large holdings.

O–78   EP   "The Possibilities of Air Pollution Control Through Various Forms of Effluent Charge," *Study of the Social and Economic Effects of Changes in Air Quality*, 1969–70, Annual Report, Air Resources Center, Oregon State University, Corvallis, June, 1970, mimeo, pp. 56–70.

Including automobile pollution charges.

O–79   EP   "Externalities in Public Utility Use," *The Analysis of Public Output*, Julius Margolis, Ed., A Conference of the Universities National Bureau Committee for Economic Research, no. 23, New York, London, Columbia University Press, 1970, pp. 317–35.

Preliminary paper, pp. 1–19.

Short-run marginal costs in terms of impacts on fellow users.

O–80   EP   "Responsive Pricing of Public Utilities Services," *Economics of the Regulated Communications Industry in the Age of Innovation*, 1970 Seminar, New England Telephone, mimeo, pp. 61–8.

Reprinted: *The Bell Journal of Economics and Management Science*, 2(1), Spring, 1971, pp. 337–46.

The original suggestion for implementing short-run marginal-cost pricing in terms of separating flexible consumer payment rates set freely by the utility from utility retention rates set by regulatory procedures, with an escrow fund to absorb differences. Also, suggestion for low-cost metering technology.

O–81   EP   "Time's Arrow and Marginal Cost Pricing: A Comment," *New Dimensions in Public Utility Pricing*, Harry M. Trebing, Ed., Michigan State University Public Utilities Studies, East Lansing, Michigan State University Graduate School of Business Administration, Division of Research, 1970, pp. 540–54.

Marginal cost is determined by impacts on the future.

O–82   EP   "Interrelations between Interest Rates and Depreciation Rates," *Utility Regulation During Inflation*, J. E. Haring and J. F. Humphrey, Eds., Glendale, California. Occidental College, 1971, pp. 59–69.
Dangers of front-end loading of costs and double counting in inflationary circumstances.

O–83   EP   "Utility Pricing During Inflation: Comment," Ibid., pp. 213–14.
Explication of the above.

O–84   MI   "Land Use in a Long Narrow City," with Robert M. Solow, *Journal of Economic Theory*, 3(4), Dec., 1971, pp. 430–47.
Allocation of land between transportation and other activities. The analysis and writing is entirely Solow's, his inclusion of my name as co-author is due merely to my having suggested the model in an offhand conversation.

O–85   EP   "Maximum Output or Maximum Welfare? More on the Off-Peak Pricing Problem," *Kyklos*, 24(2), 1971, pp. 305–29.
Critique of a naïve proposal for determining peak price differentials.

O–86   TX   "Interventions Regarding the Incidence of the Corporate Income Tax," *The Shifting Tax Burden: Implications for Capital Investment*, Tax Foundation, Inc., 1971, pp. 24, 25.

        TX   "Intervention regarding cumulative averaging," Ibid., pp. 54–6.

O–87   TX   "Cumulative Averaging After 30 Years," *Modern Fiscal Issues: Essays in Honor of Carl S. Shoup*, Richard M. Bird and John G. Head, Eds., University of Toronto Press, 1972, pp. 117–33.
Review of some of the possible causes for failure of adoption.

O–88   TX   Statement Regarding Party Planks on Federal Tax Reform, *Taxation with Representation*, 1972, pp. 439–44.
Capital gains, corporate tax, working spouses, etc.

O–89   EP   "Airline Overbooking: Some Further Solutions," *Journal of Transport Economics and Policy*, 6(3), Sept., 1972, pp. 257–70.
Pricing on the basis of a simulated futures market.

O–90   EP   "Decreasing Costs, Publicly Administered Prices and Economic Efficiency," *The Analysis and Evaluation of Public Expenditures: The PPB System*, Joint Economic Committee, 91st Congress, First Session V 1, 1972, pp. 118–48.

Marginal-cost pricing, subsidies, and the excess burden of taxation in the context of the "Program, Planning and Policy Budgeting System," In retrospect, something of a passing fad.

O–91 EP "The Use of Tolls in Controlling Urban Traffic Congestion," *Unorthodox Approaches to Urban Transportation: The Emerging Challenge to Conventional Planning*, Bureau of Business and Economic Research, Georgia State University, Atlanta, 16–17 Nov., 1972, mimeo, pp. 22–37.

O–92 EP "The Economics of Congestion Control in Urban Transportation," *The Economics of Environmental Problems*, Frank Emerson, Ed., Michigan Business Papers, no. 58. Graduate School of Business Administration, University of Michigan, pp. 55–70.

Marginal-cost pricing through electronics, again.

O–93 TR "Pricing, Metering, and Efficiently Using Urban Transportation Facilities," *Highway Research Record, No. 436. Price Subsidy Issues In Urban Transportation*, Highway Research Board, 1973, pp. 36–48.

O–94 EP PW "Measuring Social and Economic Change: Benefits and Costs of Environmental Pollution: Comments," *The Measurement of Economic and Social Performances*, Milton Moss, Ed., Conference on Research in Income and Wealth, Studies in Income and Wealth, no. 38, New York, London, Columbia University Press for the National Bureau of Economic Research, 1973, pp. 503–8.

O–95 EP TR PW Letter to *New York Times* regarding pollution and pricing of Traffic, 22 June, 1973.

O–96 EP TR "Detailed Pricing of Transportation Services," Proceedings International Symposium, "Man and Transport," Tokyo, Asahi Shimbun, 3–7 Sept., 1973, pp. 30–41.

Congestion charges, lack of burden on nondriving poor.

O–97 EP TR "Breaking the Traffic Bottleneck by Sophisticated Pricing of Roadway Use," *The Changing Challenge: General Motors Quarterly*, Spring, 1974, pp. 24–8.

A more popular exposition of marginal-cost pricing with electronics.

O–98 EP TR "Urban Transportation," *Urban and Social Economics in*

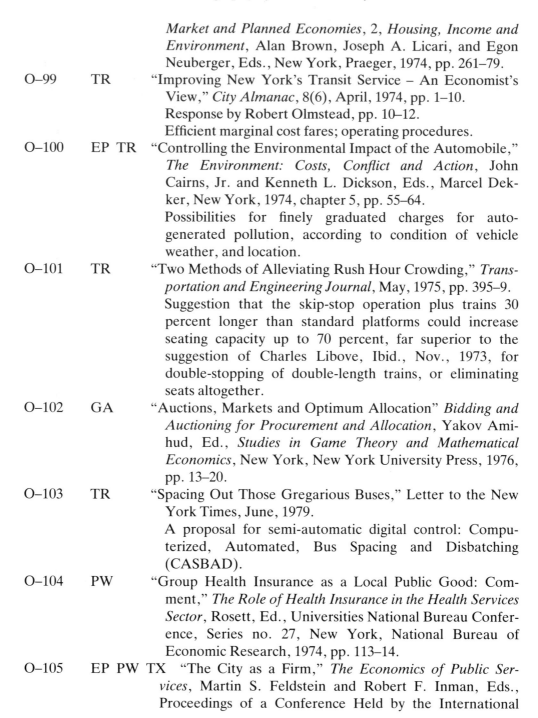

Market and Planned Economies, 2, *Housing, Income and Environment*, Alan Brown, Joseph A. Licari, and Egon Neuberger, Eds., New York, Praeger, 1974, pp. 261–79.

O–99　　TR　　"Improving New York's Transit Service – An Economist's View," *City Almanac*, 8(6), April, 1974, pp. 1–10.
Response by Robert Olmstead, pp. 10–12.
Efficient marginal cost fares; operating procedures.

O–100　　EP TR　"Controlling the Environmental Impact of the Automobile," *The Environment: Costs, Conflict and Action*, John Cairns, Jr. and Kenneth L. Dickson, Eds., Marcel Dekker, New York, 1974, chapter 5, pp. 55–64.
Possibilities for finely graduated charges for auto-generated pollution, according to condition of vehicle weather, and location.

O–101　　TR　　"Two Methods of Alleviating Rush Hour Crowding," *Transportation and Engineering Journal*, May, 1975, pp. 395–9.
Suggestion that the skip-stop operation plus trains 30 percent longer than standard platforms could increase seating capacity up to 70 percent, far superior to the suggestion of Charles Libove, Ibid., Nov., 1973, for double-stopping of double-length trains, or eliminating seats altogether.

O–102　　GA　　"Auctions, Markets and Optimum Allocation" *Bidding and Auctioning for Procurement and Allocation*, Yakov Amihud, Ed., *Studies in Game Theory and Mathematical Economics*, New York, New York University Press, 1976, pp. 13–20.

O–103　　TR　　"Spacing Out Those Gregarious Buses," Letter to the New York Times, June, 1979.
A proposal for semi-automatic digital control: Computerized, Automated, Bus Spacing and Disbatching (CASBAD).

O–104　　PW　　"Group Health Insurance as a Local Public Good: Comment," *The Role of Health Insurance in the Health Services Sector*, Rosett, Ed., Universities National Bureau Conference, Series no. 27, New York, National Bureau of Economic Research, 1974, pp. 113–14.

O–105　　EP PW TX　"The City as a Firm," *The Economics of Public Services*, Martin S. Feldstein and Robert F. Inman, Eds., Proceedings of a Conference Held by the International

Economics Association at Turin, London, MacMillan, New York, Wiley, 1977, pp. 334–43.

The original locus of the thesis that in a world of perfect competition among cities, urban land rents in each city will be just sufficient to finance the subsidies required to permit marginal-cost pricing of the goods and services produced under conditions of increasing returns to scale, the availability of which is responsible for the agglomeration of the city.

O–106   PC   "Economic Rationality and Social Choice," *Social Research*, 44(4), Winter, 1977, pp. 691–707.

O–107   TX   "Design of Taxes to Minimize Evasion," *Tax Losses in Turkey and Preventative Measures*, Istanbul, Economic and Social Studies Conference Board, 1977, English Supplement, pp. 27–37.

O–108   TX PW   "Justice, Equality, and the Economic System," *Small Comforts for Hard Times*, Michael Mooney and Florian Stuber, Eds., New York, Columbia University Press, 1977, pp. 27–37.

Rawls, Utilitarianism, Pareto efficient redistribution, and redistributive public finance.

O–109   EP   "Efficient Pricing Under Regulation: The Case of Responsive Pricing as a Substitute for Interruptible Power Contracts," *Proceedings: Marginal Costing and Pricing of Electrical Energy*, Canadian Electrical Association with Canadian Bureau of Mines and Resources, Canada, 1–4 May, 1978, pp. 38–58.

O–110   PC PW   "Application of Demand Revealing Procedures to International Disputes," *Peace Science Society*, 28, 1978, pp. 97–104.

This may be stretching things a bit, but the vital importance of the application may justify grasping at straws.

O–111   PW   "Justice, Economics and Jurisprudence," *Social Research*, 46(2), 1979, pp. 272–81.

Concepts of equity, and especially naïve concepts can be in sharp conflict with economic efficiency.

O–112   EP TR   "Pricing in the Planning of Transportation Facilities,' *Transportation Research Report, 731*, Transportation Research Board. National Academy of Sciences, Washington, 1979, pp. 37–41.

In some cases lack of pricing may cause an investment to be relatively unproductive, in other cases, inadequate pricing may make it unnecessary.

O–113   EP   "Responsive Pricing Based on Marginal Cost as a Means of Promoting Efficient Energy Use," *International Energy Strategies*, James Duesenberry, Ed., Proceedings of the 1978 International Association of Energy Economics, pp. 455–72.

O–114   TX   "Alternatives to the International Tax Credit," *US Taxation and Developing Countries*, Robert Kellawell, Ed., Columbia University Centre for Law and Economic Studies, New York, Columbia University Press, 1980, pp. 153–68.
Anomalies and distorting incentives produced by the tax credit. Solution in terms of a division of income taxes into a flat rate source-based normal tax and a graduated destination-based surtax.

O–115   EP   "Actual and Potential Pricing Policies under Public and Private Operation," *Public and Private Enterprise in a Mixed Economy*, Will J. Baumol, Ed., London, Macmillan, 1980, pp. 286–96.

O–116   TR EP   "Optimal Transit Subsidy Policy," *Transportation*, 9(4), Dec., 1980, pp. 389–409.
Ramsey pricing in terms of a marginal-social cost of public funds.

O–117   PC   "Agenda Setting and Social Choice," *Public Transfers and Some Private Alternatives During the Recession*, Martin Pfaff, Ed., Schriften des Internationalen Institute fur Empirische Sozialokonomie, Band 7(II), Berlin, Duncker & Humblot, 1983, pp. 133–40.
The power of agenda setter in social choice procedures and methods of avoiding such bias.

O–118   EP   "The Fallacy of Using Long Run Cost for Peak-Load Pricing," *Quarterly Journal of Economics*, November, 1985, pp. 1331–4.
Long-run marginal cost is not well defined for joint product situations and is irrelevant for pricing decisions that should be short run or at most medium run. Where a single price must cover outputs with differing short-run marginal costs, the relevant "average marginal cost" is obtained by weighting the component short-run marginal costs by the corresponding demand elasticities.

O–119   MA   "The Need for a Direct Anti-Inflation Program," in *Incentives Based Incomes Policies*, David C. Colander, Ed., Ballinger, 1986, pp. 27–34.
Increased product sophistication and differentiation and increasing dominance of seller-set prices lead to increased inflationary tendencies, inflation-phobia, and policies involving unsatisfactorily high unemployment levels for the sake of controlling inflation.

O–120   MA   "Design of a Market Anti-Inflation Program," Ibid., pp. 149–58.
An excess value-added tax or "excess markups" tax with inflation and allowing stimulative policies to be adopted to the point of generating a satisfactorily high level of employment without fear of accelerating inflation to an undesirable extent. The original proposal.

O–121   EP   "Commentary: Some Neglected Opportunities for User Charges," *Research in Urban Policy, Vol. 2*, pp. 127–38.
Congestion charges. Market-clearing curb parking charges.

O–122   MA   "Budget-Smudget: Why Balance What, How, and When?," *Atlantic Economic Journal*, 14(3), Sept., 1986, pp. 6–13.
The irrationality of conventional wisdom regarding deficit reduction.
Presented; Columbia University Discussion Series, pp. 1–15.

O–123   BI   "Carl S. Shoup," *The New Palgrave*, vol. IV, Macmillan, 1987, Johns Hopkins, pp. 326–7.
Original draft.

O–124   TX   "Progressive and Regressive Taxation," Ibid., vol. III, pp. 1021–5.
Original draft.

O–125   EP   "Marginal and Average Cost Pricing," Ibid., vol. III, pp. 311–18.
Original draft.

O–126   MA   "The Effect of the Tax System on the Impact of Government Debt," *Revista di Politica Economica*, July–Aug., 1990, pp. 233–9. (Also as, "Il Ruolo del sistema fiscales nell'impatto del debiot publico," *Revista di Politica Economica*, Octobre, 1991, pp. 3–9.)
In a community relying exclusively on a site value tax, Ricardian equivalence would be in full force; taxpayers

would gain from lower interest rates; with a property tax, the results of excessive debt can be disastrous.

Preliminary Copy, Revised, 20 Sept., 1990.

O–127   TX   "The Corporate Income Tax and How to Get Rid of It," *Retrospective on Public Finance*, Loraine Eden, Ed., Duke University Press, 1991, pp. 118–32.

Its baneful effects on the economy, political popularity incidence in relation to macroeconomic policy chiefly on wages, present and future, replacement with withholding tax, cumulative assessment, regression-based allocation of income by source, replacement of the foreign tax credit.

O–128   EP MA PW TR TX   "Economic Solutions and Political Hurdles: An Economist's Utopia," the P. K. Seidman Foundation, Memphis, 1992, pp. vi, 21.

Presented as The Frank Tannenbaum Lecture to the 48th Annual Meeting of *The University Seminars at Columbia University*, 22 April, 1992.

O–129   TX   "Making New York City Work," *Challenges of the Changing Economy of New York City, 1992*, Baruch College, New York City Council on Economic Education, pp. 3–11.

Market-clearing parking charges, time-of-day bridge and tunnel tolls, congestion charges, replacement of business and improvement taxes by land taxes, bringing utility rates and transit fares closer to marginal social cost, improving transit service, shifting from incarceration to strict parole conditions, strictly enforced by electronic devices and low cash loads.

O–130   EP   "Theoretical and Practical Possibilities and Limitations of a Market Mechanism Approach to Air Pollution Control," *Land Economics*, 68(1), Feb., 1992, pp. 1–6.

Presented: Originally presented at the Air Pollution Control Association Meetings, Cleveland, 11 June, 1967.

Effluent charges in general, and as a supplement to congestion charges for automobiles.

O–131   TX   "An Updated Agenda for Progressive Taxation," *Papers and Proceedings, American Economic Association*, March, 1992, pp. 257–62.

Capital gains, inflation, corporate income tax, undistributed profits tax, transnational incomes, tax-exempt bonds, home ownership, leisure.

O–132   MA   "Meaningfully Defining Deficits and Debt," Ibid., pp. 305–10.
Debt in a Georgist context; varieties of capital budgeting; deficits, unemployment, and growth.

O–133   MA   "Chock-Full Employment without Increased Inflation: A Proposal for Marketable Markup Warrants," Ibid., pp. 341–5.
Original draft.

O–134   EP   "Efficient Pricing of Electric Power Services: Some Innovative Solutions," *Resources and Energy*, 14, 1992, pp. 157–74.
Original draft.
Responsive Pricing: power factor; formulation of subsidies; pricing of hydro power; second-best considerations.

O–135   MA   "Disarmament, Unemployment, Budgets, and Inflation," *ECAAR Newsnetwork, The Newsletter of Economists Allied for Arms Reduction*, 4(2), Summer, 1992, pp. 1, 6–7.
Inhibitions against cutting defense expenditures for fear of the resulting unemployment would be mitigated by a full-employment policy implemented by vigorous fiscal policy backed by the use of markup warrants to control inflation.

O–136   MA   "The Other Side of the Coin," prepared for an address accepting the Seidman Award, 24 Sept., 1992. Revised original 30 Sept., 1992. Printed copy also.
Reaching real full employment by vigorous fiscal policy with tradable gross markup warrants as an inflation control.

O–137   MA   "Today's Task for Economists," *American Economic Review*, March, 1993, pp. 1–10. Presidential Address to the American Economic Association, as prepared for publication, 15 Oct., 1992.
Reprinted in, *Challenge*, 83(1), March–April, 1993, pp. 1–11.
A revised and expanded version.
Original draft from which address was read, 19pp.
How to raise the economy rapidly to real full employment and keep it there, using vigorous public policy and controlling inflation with marketable markup warrants.

O–138   TX EP MA   "My Innovative Failures in Economics," *Atlantic Economic Journal*, March, 1993, pp. 1–9.

Presidential Address to the Atlantic Economic Association, Plymouth, Mass., 16 October, 1992.

Tax reform, marginal-cost pricing, full employment.

O–139   MA PW "Disarmament, Unemployment, Budgets, and Inflation," *Journal of Asian Economics*, 4(1), 1993, pp. 1–4.

Adapted for a paper prepared for a meeting of the Economists Concerned Against the Arms Race, The Hague, 22 June, 1992, for the Fourth International Conference on China's Economic Development, Beijing, 10–12 Nov., 1992.

Inhibitions against cutting defense expenditures for fear that the resulting unemployment would be mitigated by a full-employment policy implemented by vigorous fiscal policy backed by the use of markup warrants to control inflation.

Unpublished Articles

U–1   EP "Observations on the Economizing of Electric Power," mimeo, Nov., 1962, pp. 1–8.

Low-cost transit controls.

U–2   TR "Some Suggestions for Open Platform Fare Collection," March, 1962, 3 pp.

Re: suburban service.

U–3   TR "Some Suggestions for Suburban Fare Collection," March, 1962, 4 pp.

U–4   TR "Further Notes on Fare Collection for Rationalized Commuter Service," 1962, 12 pp.

U–5   TR "Notes on an Interim Fare Structure for Suburban Service," 1 May, 1962, 4 pp.

U–6   EP "Suggested Fare Structure and Fare Collection Program," 10 pp.

U–7   TR "Economizing in the Use of Electrical Power by Suburban Trains," mimeo, 17 Jan., 1963, Calcutta, 5 pp.

Relieving power shortages in Calcutta by rescheduling services out of Howrah.

U–8   TR "The Cost of Using Land for Transportation." Prepared for the Second Conference on Urban Public Expenditure, February, 1964, 5 pp.

A proposal for computer modelling of urban congestion with optimization of land use for transportation with and without congestion pricing. Later attempts to carry out the program failed to produce a convergent computer program.

U–9   PW   "Investment Bias Under Regulatory Constraint." Symposium on the Economics of Public Utilities, Warrenton, Virginia, 7–10 Sept., 1965, 10 pp.

U–10   TR   "Making the Most of Urban Roadways." Sketch of remarks at Engineering Dean's Day, 25 March, 1966, 7 pp.
Rational use requires collaboration among engineers, economists, and politicians with special attention to efficient pricing of alternatives.

U–11   TR   "Information Requirements for Meaningful Evaluation of Solutions to Metropolitan Transportation Problems," 5 pp.
Questions regarding traffic patterns, costs, automation.

U–12   TR   "Continuous Automated Bus Spacing and Dispatching" (CASBAD), Nov., 1966, 6 pp.
A proposal for improving the efficiency of short-headway bus service with automatic digitalized radio signals. Also, a fragment of a more detailed treatment, pp. 5–19 (1–4 missing).

U–13   TR   "The Allocation of Land to Transportation," Oct., 1966, 11 pp. Appendix A: A One-dimensional Model of Area Optimization, 3 pp.
Various ways in which reality departs significantly from the competitive paradigm; attempts to model optimal allocation in terms of linear and polar coordinate models. Failure of market values to guide optimal allocation.

U–14   TR   "Notes on the Abstract Mode Model by Quandt and Baumol," 1966, 1 p.
Excessive abstraction hides too many essential elements.

U–15   TR   "A Flexible Change-Free Fare Collection System for Buses and Subways," 10 May, 1966, 5 pp.

U–16   PW   "Auschwitz . . . and Hiroshima." 1968?, Hecto, 6 pp.

U–17   EP   Testimony on behalf of the broadcasting companies before the Federal Communications Committee, 22 July, 1968, pp. 11, 12, 73.

U–18   TR   "Sorting in the Light of Information Theory: Some New Techniques," Hecto, July, 1969, 29 pp.
Related to the problem of processing data for congestion pricing. Now obsolete.

U–19   PW   "Redistribution of Wealth: Provision for Each Individual within the National Economy." Remarks prepared for delivery to the Institute for Religion and Social Studies, 26 October, 1969, Hecto, 5 pp.
Eliminating poverty by redistribution requires fairly drastic measures, but could be done.

U–20   TR   "Notes on Subway Finance," 22 Dec., 1971, 3 pp.
Various recommendations for sources and uses of funds.

U–21   TX   "Problems in Land Value Taxation: Equity, Expectation, and Efficiency." For the Symposium on the land tax in honor of H. G. Brown, 6 April, 1972, University of Missouri, p. 7.
The objection that a sudden shift to land taxation expropriates legitimately acquired values does not hold when this is the result of shifting from other localized taxes. Owners of land can gain from increased land taxation.

U–22   EP   "The Meaning of Marginal Cost: Some New (Empty) Boxes for Old," 12 pp.
Short- and long-run relevant product mines; immediate, ultimate, *ex ante, ex post*; queuing, travel time, and schedule delay; relevance to direct controls.

U–23   TR   "Transportation and Your Wallet," in the *Connecticut Conference on Transportation*, pp. 36–42. Hartford, The Connecticut Air Conservation Committee, 16 May, 1973, mimeo.
Congestion pricing.

U–24   TX   "Some Preliminary Thoughts on Basic Principles of the Taxation of Multinational Activity," 1974 (?), 24 pp.
Difficulties with the foreign tax credit; separation of flat rate source-based from progressive destination-based taxation. Determination of source. Dealing with fluctuating exchange rates and price levels.

U–25   TR   "New Systems Versus Better Use of Old Systems." For Econometric Society; Association for the Study of Grants Economy, San Francisco, 29 Dec., 1974, 18 pp.
Appendix A: "A Suggested Automated Scheme for High Frequency Transit Service," 6 pp.
Appendix B: "Calculation of Maximum Train Frequencies Under Various Modes of Operation," 10 pp.
A litany of inefficiencies: Monumetalism and other biases in favor of large-scale capital outlays; over-generous pen-

sions and other forms of political time-bomb planting; transit service with small cross-section, shorter station platforms, low train weight per unit length, and high frequency under continuous control and skip-stop scheduling through bottlenecks; fares simulating futures markets for car ferries and airline seats; schedule coordination; transit fares on a marginal social cost basis.

U–26   TR   "Revising the Taxi Fare Structure." Presentation to the Taxi and Limousine Commission of the City of New York, 22 May, 1974, 6 pp.

A meter drop tends to concentrate cruising unduly in high demand areas; fares fail to reflect adequately the time and congestion elements in the social cost of operation; time and mileage costs are additive, so fares should also be additive, not ratcheted in terms of time or distance; the square root rule of optimum cruising deployment.

U–27   EP TX   "Returns to Scale in Transit: a Comment," 4 pp.

Various methodological and definitional difficulties with the analysis by Paul McDevitt in *The Logistics and Transportation Review*, 1976, pp. 233–49.

U–28   PC   "Demand Revealing Procedures, Collusion, and Lump Sum Payments," Columbia University, The Economics Workshops, Discussion Paper 76–7701, 16 pp.

Ways of dealing with problems that arise in various contexts, with bibliography.

U–29   PW   "Adam and Eve and the Coal Mine." Comments on Harold J. Barnett, "Measurement of Natural Resource Scarcity."

U–30   EP   Letter to William J. Ronan, Director, Port of New York and New Jersey, 23 May, 1977, 5 pp.

Smoothly varying time-of-day tolls.

U–31   EP   "Marginal Cost Pricing: Using the Short Run for the Long Run." Presented at the Eastern Economic Association Meeting, Boston, 1983, 18 pp.

U–32   EP   "Marginal Cost as a Basis for Pricing Utility Services." For Michigan State University Conference on Public Utilities, Williamsburg, 1985.

U–33   MA   "How Successful as Innovators have Economists Been?" 9 August, 1987, 12 pp.

U–34   TR   "Observations on Modern Transit." Discussion Paper Series, Columbia University, August, 1987, 66 pp.

Fares, fare systems, and subsidies; economic infrastructure design; cost–benefit analysis of operating methods; automatic control and signalling for higher frequencies and regularity, energy saving traction.

U–35   TR   "New York's Inefficient Fare Structure and How to Fix It." Columbia Univ., Dept. of Economics, Discussion Paper, Series no. 355, August, 1987, 17 pp.

U–36   EP TR   "Traffic Measures to Reduce Air Pollution." Revised 14 Feb., 1987.
An outline, with details.

U–37   MA   "Why Balance What Government Budgets, Anyhow?," 13 pp.

U–38   EP   "The Backward Art of Utility Pricing." Discussion Paper Series 104, Columbia University, August, 1988, 13 pp.
Responsive pricing, power factor charges, lifeline rates, subsidy from land taxation.

U–39   EP   "New Approaches to Marginal Cost Pricing of Electricity," 17 Feb., 1990, 1 p. Notes for a talk at Lehigh University.

U–40   TX EP   "Site Value Taxes and Public Services." Notes for a talk at St. John's University, 17 October, 1991, 4 pp.
Owners of land could gain by agreeing to a land tax increment to be applied to bringing transit and utility service charges closer to marginal cost so as to increase rental values.

U–41   EP   "Efficient Pricing versus Privatization of Utility Services," 10 pp.
Notes for a meeting on Argentina, Waldorf Astoria Hotel, New York, 18–19 Nov., 1991.

U–42   PW   "America's Capability for Tooling up World Development."

U–43   TR   "Pitfalls in the Financing and Planning of Transport Investment." Presented at the International Symposium of Transportation Pricing, American University, Washington, DC, 17 June, 1969.

U–44   EP   "Efficient Pricing of Electric Power Service: Some Innovative Solutions," 1 Dec., 1990.

U–45   TX   "A Modern Theory of Land Value Taxation." Paper for a Session on "New Concepts of Taxation," Cope Conference, Rio de Janeiro, 8–12 Jan., 1992.
Problems in use- and state-neutral assessment.

U–46   TX   "The Corporate Income Tax in the US Tax System." For presentation at the Manhattan Institute, April, 1992, 18 pp.

Leveling the playing field for capital gains; methods of eliminating the baneful effects of the corporate income tax; rationalization of formulas for allocation of income among jurisdictions; replacing the foreign tax credit with a separation of the income tax into a normal source-based tax and a destination-based surtax.

U–47   MA   "Capital Budgeting, Unemployment and Inflation." Paper for Levy Institute Meeting, Bard College, 25 June, 1992, 12 pp.

Alternative criteria for defining a capital budget. The need for marketable markup warrants. Appendix on the detailed operation of the markup warrant proposal.

U–48   MA   "Averting Unemployment and Inflation in Transition to (a) Market Economy." Paper for a meeting at IFO Institut, Munich, June, 1992.

Use of markup warrants.

U–49   MA   "Chock-Full Employment Without Inflation." Paper presented at Prague/Bratislava meetings, 28 June–3 July, 1992.

Includes detailed discussion of the operation of a market in gross markup sales.

U–50   MA   "Fallacies of the Conventional Wisdom." Notes for a talk at Marymount, 26 Oct., 1992, 12 pp.

The paradox of savings; the crowding-out fallacy; getting to real full employment with fiscal policy and new inflation controls.

U–51   MA   Letter to *New York Times*, 30 Oct., 1992.

Regarding the need to recognize the function of the deficit in recycling savings in excess of private investment back into purchasing power.

U–52   MA   "A Macroeconomic Program for the Clinton Era." For the Annual Meeting of the Southern Economic Association, Washington, 23 Nov., 1992, 13 pp.

Rapid growth to genuine full employment, then maintenance of full employment by strong fiscal measures under control of an anti-inflation program such as markup warrants. Can this be reconciled with practical politics and keeping faith with the electorate?

U–53   TR TX   "Efficient Pricing of City Facilities and Services." Notes for testimony for NYC Controller's Office, 2 Dec., 1992, 5 pp.

Congestion pricing, subway fares and service, utility rates, and site value taxation.

U–54	EP	"Pricing for Tomorrow; The Welfare Economics of Price Structures Adapted to an Electronic Age," 81 pp. Incomplete Mss. of a book in years of gestation.
U–55	EP	"Notes Regarding Marginal Cost Pricing," 22 pp.
U–56	EP TR	"Computers, Pricing Mechanisms, and Optimum Traffic and Transit Patterns," 2 pp.
U–57	MA	Press release concerning the Presidential Address, 6 Jan., 1993, 4 pp.

Notes

N–1	TX	"Tax Reform or Tax Shuffle: Some Missed Opportunities," 10 Sept., 1986, 2 pp.
N–2	MA	"Why Worry About What Governments Budget".
N–3	EP	"Notes on the Bell-System Break-up," 2 pp.
N–4	TX	"Notes on the Land Tax,' 1 p.